Padre Pio
The True Story

REVISED AND EXPANDED, 3RD EDITION

C. BERNARD RUFFIN

Our Sunday Visitor

www.osv.com
Our Sunday Visitor Publishing Division
Our Sunday Visitor, Inc.
Huntington, Indiana 46750

This book is dedicated to the memory of my mother,
Lillian Rebecca Jones Ruffin

———

Our Sunday Visitor Publishing Division
Our Sunday Visitor, Inc.
200 Noll Plaza
Huntington, IN 46750
1-800-348-2440

ISBN: 978-1-61278-882-1 (Inventory No. T1677)
eISBN: 978-1-61278-886-9
LCCN: 81-81525

Cover design: Tyler Ottinger
Cover art: Elio Stelluto, San Giovanni Rotondo. All rights reserved.
Photo-section design: Chelsea Alt
Interior design: Sherri L. Hoffman
Interior art: See the credits in the photo section

PRINTED IN THE UNITED STATES OF AMERICA

TABLE OF CONTENTS

Preface

Padre Pio: The True Story was first published by Our Sunday Visitor in 1982 and was revised in 1991. Now, after Padre Pio's beatification and canonization and the availability of a vast amount of information that was not available before, it seems clear that a new book is necessary, in which the life of this remarkable man is put into sharper perspective by the newly available materials, and certain errors in the original work can be corrected. The documents from the Vatican Archives from the 1920s and 1930s that were made accessible for study in recent years help to clarify the events in the life of Saint Pio at a time when he was bitterly attacked by certain Church officials and his ministry severely curtailed. Although the official report of Monsignor Carlo Maccari, who made a controversial and notorious investigation in 1960, is still kept secret, several Italian researchers have had access to his notes, which have been revealed in several books in their language, but, to my knowledge, never in English. The memoirs of Padre Eusebio Notte, who was Padre Pio's assistant and confidant in the early 1960s, and those of Cleonice Morcaldi, a disciple who wrote down Pio's answers to her questions in several notebooks, also help shed a clearer light on the life and work of the stigmatized priest, as do the testimonies and recollections of others that have been made available only in recent years.

———

My parents did not attend church during my formative years, but I was sent to catechetical class at a Catholic church near our home for a year, and then to Sunday school at a Presbyterian church, which my mother later joined and in which I was confirmed. Although I had no siblings, I had numerous aunts and uncles on my mother's side, and they and their spouses were of many different religious persuasions, or none at all: Catholic, Presbyterian, Methodist, atheist, agnostic. I remember gazing into the black sky one night and wondering if there was anyone up there or whether the universe (as my father believed) was cold, dark, empty, indifferent. Sitting in my swing in the backyard, I would gaze at the eastern skies, trying to picture Christ, dressed in a red robe, returning, as the sister told us he would. One day my aunt, who was working on her Ph.D. at Catholic University (but was and remained a Presbyterian), announced that the pope had had a vision. This suggested to me that the other world, the world of God and the angels and heaven, was real and that Pope Pius XII was in contact with it and had a sort of "phone line" to God.

I first became aware of Padre Pio's existence in the fall of 1966, when I was a sophomore at Bowdoin College. Returning to school from my home in Chevy Chase, Maryland, after a holiday, I was browsing the offerings in the bookstore of the North Terminal of what is now Reagan Airport when I saw a small paperback entitled *The Priest Who Bears the Wounds of Christ*. I began to read it on the plane. That is how I learned of Padre Pio.

I was fascinated by what I read about Padre Pio. He was still alive at the time, so I wrote to him. I think I mentioned that I wanted to enter the Christian ministry. I knew I did not want to be a Presbyterian, and a friend of mine at school was a devout Catholic and pressing me to convert to his faith. I think I told Padre Pio that I was then attending a Lutheran church and that I wanted to know which Christian persuasion was best. In March, I got a little envelope from Italy in which there was a typed, unsigned note reading: "Padre Pio sends you his blessing and will pray for your intentions. He urges you to have complete trust in the goodness of God, and to pray always according to His Divine Will. FATHER SUPERIOR." That proved to be my only contact with Padre Pio, if the form letter could be considered contact at all. For many years, I believed the note to be lost, until I suddenly found it in 2000. I realized then that the handwriting on the envelope was that of Father Joseph Pius, an American Capuchin in San Giovanni Rotondo, who lived for three years with Padre Pio and whom I met several times. I would have liked to have asked him if he had actually brought my letter to the attention of Padre Pio, but, alas, Father Joseph Pius had gone to his reward just months before. Although it was clearly a form letter, the exhortation to "have complete trust in the goodness of God" addressed what was then and is now one of my greatest difficulties — but, of course, maybe it is for most others as well.

After learning of his existence, I wanted to go to Italy to see Padre Pio. My father, who identified himself as a "secular humanist," wanted me to become a doctor or lawyer and considered my interest in religion unhealthy. Still, he promised to give me the money to go to Italy (or anywhere else in Europe) when I was graduated. However, Padre Pio died the next year (nine months before I was to graduate).

Eventually, I became a Lutheran, not a Catholic, and a pastor in what is now the Evangelical Lutheran Church of America. I served as an "intern pastor" in Sugar Valley, Pennsylvania, from 1972 to 1973. It was then that I met Dorothy Gaudiose, who had made many trips to San Giovanni Rotondo to see Padre Pio, and, through Dorothy, Vera Calandra, the director of the Padre Pio Centre, then located in Norristown, Pennsylvania. In 1976, two years after I was graduated from

Yale Divinity School, I published a biography of the American hymnwriter Fanny Crosby. Afterward, the editor asked if I was interested in doing another biography. I said that I was and proposed a book on Padre Pio. Although his publishing company was associated with the United Church of Christ, the editor was interested. His editorial board, however, was not. Then my friend Father John Schug, of happy memory, suggested that I submit my proposal to Our Sunday Visitor, which had recently published his own biography of Padre Pio — even though he knew that if my work were accepted, it would cut the sales of his own book! (And for this act of self-sacrificing generosity, I am eternally grateful to him.)

And that, in short, is how the first edition of my biography of Padre Pio came about.

That was more than three decades ago, and the study of Padre Pio's life has become the work of a lifetime. Although I am not a Catholic, Padre Pio has influenced my spiritual life probably more than anyone else (with the possible exception of C. S. Lewis). It is my hope that, through an accurate and objective account of Padre Pio's life, there will be some who see evidence that the idea of a loving God who has broken into time and space is worth intelligent consideration. For those who do not, it should nevertheless prove a fascinating story and food for reflection.

I think it important to avoid the role of the "hagiographer," whose chief objective is to show how holy the subject was and to foster the image of Padre Pio as a fantastical "miracle man." (There are some who insist that biographers "say only nice things" — not just about the subject, but about anyone.) It is important to reveal Padre Pio as a normal human being (although one who was exceptionally God-fearing and endowed with unusual gifts and abilities and attributes), who had hopes, fears, temptations, affections, peculiarities, and made mistakes, just like other people. My belief is that God is best served by revealing, to the best of one's abilities, the truth. In doing so, it is necessary to recount, as fully and fairly as possible, the positions of Padre Pio's detractors.

Although this work is published by a Catholic company, it is my hope that it may reach an audience of readers of all religious persuasions and none at all, because, whatever one ultimately thinks about him, Padre Pio's life had an impact — and an overwhelmingly positive one — on millions of people, both during his lifetime and afterward.

C. Bernard Ruffin III
Reston, Virginia
February 2018

Acknowledgments

This book could never have come to be without the gracious assistance of the following persons, most of whom have since gone to be with the Lord, who aided me in my research for my original work:

- Roberta Accousti
- William Accousti
- Mario Avignone
- Vera M. Calandra
- Padre Emidio Cappabianca
- Albert Cardone
- William Carrigan
- Pastor Richard L. Cosnotti
- Sister Carolyn Cossack
- Pietro Cugino
- John L. Curry
- David Curfman
- Anne Pyle Dennis
- Riparta De Prospero
- Rosa Di Cosimo in Savino
- Padre Eusebio Di Flumeri
- Paul Dominic
- John Duggan
- Father Leo Fanning
- Pia Forgione in Pennelli
- Liliana Gagliardi
- Concetta Gambello
- Dorothy M. Gaudiose
- Emilio Ghidotti
- Giuseppe Gusso
- Monika Hellwig
- Robert H. Hopcke
- Louise Jones Hubbard
- Alice Jones
- Therese Lanna
- Tony Lilley
- Andre Mandato
- Grace Mandato
- Father Pio Mandato
- Carmela Marocchino
- Father Joseph Pius Martin
- Padre Eusebio Notte
- Giuseppe Pagnossin
- Padre Alessio Parente
- Joseph Peterson
- Monsignor George Pogany
- James T. Pyle
- Diana Pyle Rowan
- Father Robert Sarno
- Julie A. Satzik
- Father John Schug
- Hilary Smart
- Montserrat Sola-Solé
- Father John D. St. John
- Father Joachim M. Strupp
- Elizabeth Kindregan Walsh
- Paul Walsh
- Barbara Ward

To the acknowledgments that were written for the 1991 edition, I would like to include many thanks to members of the staff of Our Sunday Visitor, among whom are Jacqueline Lindsey, Bert Ghezzi, and Mary Beth Baker.

In addition:

- Charles Abercrombie and Julie Cifaldi of San Giovanni Rotondo, who graciously acted as intermediaries with the friary, obtaining books, information, and photographs.
- Father Matteo Lecce, secretary of the Provincial Library of San Severo (Italy), who made available to me excerpts from the Chronicle of the Friary at San Giovanni Rotondo.
- Elia Stelluto, of San Giovanni Rotondo, who granted permission to use his photographs.
- Marsha Daigle-Williamson, who translated a substantial amount of material for me from the Italian.
- Silvia Porcelli, who contacted several people in Italy for me and translated their responses.
- The Calandra family of the Padre Pio Centre of Barto, Pennsylvania, for their continued assistance.

The Wise Man of the Gargano

A survey taken in Italy in November 2005 concerning Italy's most beloved saints concluded:

> Padre Pio has no rivals. He is the saint most frequently invoked and most frequently stuck on the windshields of cars and trucks. And for some he is also [the unofficial] patron saint of Italy.

According to the survey, 70 percent of Italians invoke saints: 31 percent invoke Padre Pio, as opposed to 9 percent who call upon the Virgin Mary and 2 percent who call upon Christ![1] Even at the time of his death in 1968, *National Review* described him as "one of the chief religious forces in Italy."[2]

By the end of his life, five thousand letters a day were arriving for Pio of Pietrelcina, a priest in the Order of Friars Minor Capuchins. This priest lived for more than half a century in the friary of Our Lady of Grace, on the outskirts of San Giovanni Rotondo, a town of some twenty thousand in the Gargano hills in southeastern Italy near the Adriatic Sea in Foggia, the northernmost province of the region of Apulia (Puglia), which is the spur of the heel of the Italian boot. For years, throngs of people waited in pre-dawn darkness for the opportunity to attend Mass with the priest who for fifty years had displayed the wounds of Christ's crucifixion on his hands, feet, and side. Some people waited for days — even weeks — for the opportunity to make their confession to him.

Most of Padre Pio's visitors were Italian, but, especially after the Second World War, pilgrims increasingly came to San Giovanni Rotondo from all over the world. Many knew not a single word of Italian — the only language, other than his regional dialect, in which Pio was fluent. Despite the language barrier, many of them claimed that they were somehow able to communicate effectively with the holy man on the mountain. Although the overwhelming majority of his visitors were Catholics, a number of Protestants and Orthodox, as well as Jews and other non-Christians — even atheists — joined in seeking out the priest with the wounds of Christ who declared, "I am for everyone!"

Those who sought out "The Wise Man of the Gargano" included both the uneducated peasant as well as the intellectual, artists, singers, actors, politicians, and priests and religious. During the Second Vatican Council (1962–1965), someone remarked, with some exaggeration, that so many bishops were consulting Padre Pio, it seemed as if the council was being held at San Giovanni. One of his visitors was a cardinal allegedly sent by the pope to explore Padre Pio's reaction to some of the reforms.[3]

During his lifetime, at least two popes said privately that Padre Pio was a saint. On March 9, 1952, Archbishop Giovanni Battista Montini, later Pope Paul VI, remarked to a major general of the Italian national police (*carabinieri*), "Padre Pio is a saint." Overhearing the remark, a few minutes later the reigning pontiff, Pius XII, concurred, "We all know that Padre Pio is a saint."[4] During the early part of Padre Pio's ministry, when a number of high-ranking Church officials regarded the Capuchin friar with hostility, Pope Benedict XV characterized him as "a man of God."[5]

Not only churchmen, but notables from the world of politics and entertainment, made their way to Padre Pio's friary door. Aldo Moro, longtime prime minister of Italy, made frequent trips to see "The Light of the Gargano," as did many other Italian politicians. King Alfonso XIII of Spain, Queen Maria José of Italy, and Francisco Franco ("Caudillo" of Spain) were among those known to have sought his advice. Beniamino Gigli, the celebrated operatic tenor, made several trips to see Padre Pio, and Irving Berlin, the American songwriter, made at least one, as did composer Gian Carlo Menotti. Even members of the scientific community, such as American cardiologist Paul Dudley White, visited Padre Pio and professed to be "deeply impressed" with him and his work.

The gray-bearded friar, to whom the fictional character Obi-Wan Kenobi would bear a striking resemblance, who was described by *National Review* as having "the greatest moral prestige of any priest in Italy," was widely credited with transforming the life of a region of Italy that had been cruelly impoverished for centuries by bringing — chiefly through the establishment of his famous hospital, the *Casa Sollievo della Sofferenza* — prosperity, employment, education, and first-class health care.

There are innumerable testimonies to the dramatic effect the Padre had in people's lives. "I was drawn to him like a magnet!" an elderly lady from the Italian city of Taranto told the author in San Giovanni Rotondo in 1978. From the time of her first visit in 1948, she and her family traveled several times a year to see him and ask his counsel. Long after his death, she and her husband, children, and grandchildren continued to make the four-hour trip from their home at least twice a year to "visit" with Padre Pio at his tomb.

Andre Mandato (1928–2014), a native of Padre Pio's hometown of Pietrelcina who became a custom tailor in North Plainfield, New Jersey, related how "Padre Pio changed my life." He went with a friend to see the Padre in 1945 — out of curiosity. He left the confessional awestruck. Padre Pio knew — without ever having met Mandato before — that he had been debating in his mind whether or not to make his confession to him before returning home. Moreover, Padre Pio recited, correctly and in detail, all the sins of which the young man was guilty. "He knew everything that I had done," Mandato declared. "Padre Pio asked, 'Have you done this? … Have you done that?'" In every instance, the answer was yes. Padre Pio referred not merely to general categories of sin, but to specific acts which he could scarcely have guessed, even through a shrewd knowledge of human nature. After Mandato left the confessional, he said, "All I could do was cry, cry, cry." His experience had a profound and lasting effect on him. "Many times, we ask God to forgive us," Mandato said, "but with the mind and not the heart. Padre Pio made it possible for me to ask forgiveness of God with all my heart and soul, not just with my mind and lips. From that moment I have really *felt* what I prayed. He made my religion real!"[6]

Monika Hellwig (1929–2005), professor of theology at Georgetown University, spent three years in Italy during the time of the Second Vatican Council and visited San Giovanni Rotondo. She said she never met anyone in Italy who was skeptical of Padre Pio. Even radicals and anti-clericals regarded the venerable friar with "respect and reverence." Moreover, she could testify that the stigmatized Capuchin led people to "deep conversions." "What struck me most," Hellwig stated, "is how much Padre Pio mediated the presence of the Divine to all who came to him. People came away from him invariably inspired and assured of God's presence and care for them. In him they experienced a most immediate revelation of God's love and concern for them."[7]

Padre Pio was almost an exact contemporary of Rudolf Bultmann (1884–1976), the German Lutheran theologian who, in an attempt to reconcile the traditional teachings of Christianity with contemporary perceptions, devised a theology that "demythologized" the Gospels, stripping away such uncomfortable baggage as miracles and other vestiges of a "first-century worldview" in order to get at what he believed was the essential kernel of truth underlying all the "mythological" paraphernalia. Bultmann's approach and those of religious writers with a similar point of view strongly colored much of the theological thinking of the twentieth century. Bultmann wrote in *Kerygma and Myth*: "It is impossible to use electric light and the wireless [radio] and to avail ourselves of modern medical and surgical discoveries and at the same time to believe in the New Testament world of demons and spirits."[8] Meanwhile, Padre Pio convinced many reasonable and intelligent people that he regularly saw and conversed with the Virgin Mary, that he could see their guardian angels just like he saw them, that he cast out demons, and, on occasion, was bodily attacked by them.

Without publishing a book or delivering a lecture, Padre Pio convinced thousands that miracles are not mythology but reality. Through his life and ministry, thousands came to accept the Sacred Scriptures and all the historical doctrines of Christianity. Indeed, Padre Pio, whom some ecclesiastical authorities dismissed as an undereducated "peasant," is attested to have communicated the existential presence of Christ more directly, more immediately, and more satisfactorily than any of his immensely erudite contemporaries in their university chairs.

Here was a man who lived in the time of radio, television, movies, automobiles, air travel, and space exploration; who, though he did not live to see (and probably lament) personal computers and the internet, died at the beginning of the computer age; who worked miracles similar to those performed by the prophets of the Old Testament and the apostles of the New Testament. Here was a man in whom the words of Christ seem to have been fulfilled in a very obvious way: "Who believes in me will also do the works that I do" (Jn 14:12). Many sane, well-educated, and reasonably objective people have affirmed of Padre Pio that, like Moses, "The LORD used to speak to Moses face to face, as a man speaks to his friend" (Ex 33:11).

There is overwhelming testimony also that Padre Pio was gifted with the "aroma of paradise," that frequently he displayed intimate knowledge of the inner lives and thoughts of those who came to him. Without leaving his friary at San Giovanni Rotondo, many insist, Padre Pio was often seen and addressed in other parts of Italy and the world; while his colleagues observed him deep in prayer or even dozing, people hundreds, even thousands, of miles away saw and heard him.

The archives of the Our Lady of Grace friary contain, according to a friar familiar with them, more than a thousand testimonies of people inexplicably delivered from incurable maladies and the effects of crippling injuries. Even more remarkable, great numbers of people swear that when the stigmatized friar celebrated Mass, he communicated to them the reality of Christ on Calvary, and that, during his Mass, Padre Pio's face and form underwent a visible change — almost a metamorphosis. One of the friars who assisted Padre Pio in the saint's later years declared that more people were deeply touched by Padre Pio through his Mass than through his healings, bilocations, and prophecies.

Perhaps most important, thousands testify that through Padre Pio's ministry, they learned to walk in holiness and to resign themselves to God's will, offering their suffering and heartache as a sacrifice to the Almighty for the conversion of souls.

Padre Pio's disciples cherish his words, "I shall be able to do much more for you when I am in heaven than I can now while I am on earth." Many report great favors received through his intercession. Some, even decades after his death, smell the "aroma of paradise," which is believed to be a sign of his presence. Some, like

Padre Pio's old friend Andrea Cardone, a doctor of medicine, profess to have seen and talked to Padre Pio "*in his mortal flesh*," even while his wax-masked corpse reposes in his tomb.

Not everyone was impressed by Padre Pio. The local archbishop, Pasquale Gagliardi (1859–1941), insisted that the stigmata were merely "pimples" and that Pio soaked himself in perfume to produce the "aroma of paradise." Eventually, he swore on his pectoral cross that the Capuchin was demon-possessed. Agostino Gemelli (1878–1959), a prominent psychologist, Franciscan priest, and theologian, characterized Pio as an ignorant southern Italian peasant of limited intelligence, manipulated by his unscrupulous directors, whose wounds were the result of hysteria. Dr. Amico Bignami (1862–1929), professor of pathology at the University of Rome, confirmed the existence of the stigmata, but implied that the wounds were the result of autosuggestion. Monsignor Carlo Maccari (1913–1997), who conducted an investigation in 1960, dismissed Padre Pio as a "small and petty person"[9] and wrote, "How is it that a man who has no exceptional natural qualities and who is anything but free of shadows and defects has been able to build a popularity that has few equals in the religious history of our times?"[10]

To many, Padre Pio remains a curious and unbelievable figure, subject matter for supermarket tabloids, his alleged appearances after death compared to those of Elvis Presley. Many, at least in the "developed" world, cannot relate to mysterious fragrances, miraculous healings, and communication with Mary, angels, and devils.

Some might be inclined to write off Padre Pio as a curious footnote to religious history, dismissing him as the creation of the credulous piety of a backward society. Nonetheless, it is hard to deny that, for thousands of people from all walks of life — physicians, scientists, lawyers, journalists, as well as peasants and unskilled laborers — Padre Pio made Christianity real. Through his ministry, many were led to deep and permanent conversion experiences and lives changed for the better.

It also cannot be denied that many individuals — perhaps thousands — have testified to Padre Pio's mystical *charismata*. Some accounts are vague and far-fetched, the half-remembered ramblings of aged persons recalling events many years distant. However, there are other accounts contemporary to the events in question, written down in detail by educated, intelligent, reliable, and well-balanced witnesses.

One thing is certain: Padre Pio cannot be dismissed lightly. It seems plain that several hypotheses can be made about the Capuchin priest and his ministry, though only one of them can ultimately be true:

- First, that Padre Pio was one of the greatest frauds in history, a showman, perhaps in league with Satan (if one believes in the devil), a magician capable of humbugging the public to a degree unimagined even by P. T. Barnum.

- Second, that Padre Pio was the product, in large measure, of the superstitious imaginings of an ignorant and gullible peasantry who read into the life of a simple, holy priest what they wanted to see, building a cult based on their own fantasies.

- Third, that Padre Pio was delusional, perhaps even schizophrenic, who was possessed of a clever ability to convince thousands of people that his delusions were reality.

- Fourth, if none of these three scenarios is true, then it is reasonable to conclude that Padre Pio of Pietrelcina was what he appeared to be: namely, one of the most significant figures in Christian history, a man of prophetic and apostolic stature, who, through great personal holiness, enlightened wisdom, and spiritual gifts inexplicable by science, tended to confirm the truth of the Gospels and the veracity of historical Christianity to an indifferent and unbelieving age; a man capable of conveying to an extraordinary extent a sense of God's love and care; an evangelist who never conducted a crusade, and who, without traveling more than a few miles from his friary in a half-century, seemed capable of transforming lives to a degree unimagined by the most successful of preachers.

Padre Pio's life is remarkably well-supported by good primary evidence. Admittedly, there are difficulties in proving certain aspects with documentary evidence. Padre Alessio Parente (1933–2000), who was one of Padre Pio's companions and assistants in the last years of his life, recalled: "We didn't have time to write things down. At night we were so stressed and so tired that we didn't have five minutes to put a pen in our hands. We went straight to bed. That's why I never put any notes down. I'm sorry now, for being at Padre Pio's side, I could have noticed every movement, every word he said. I tried to tape him, but he knew [and would not cooperate]." Yet Alessio and other friars did, on occasion, succeed in taking down his conversations.

Father Dominic Meyer, who served as Padre Pio's English- and German-language secretary for more than a decade, wrote in one of his circular letters to family and friends in America: "As to newspaper accounts: how often have not the superiors of Padre Pio been asked to clarify statements by journalists that were positively false, exaggerated misrepresentations of the truth. [Alberto] Del Fante [an Italian writer] collected many such newspaper accounts, sometimes several of the same event. Comparing these — on the same event — one sees how unreliable they are.... There were not only misrepresentations of the truth, there were lies, calumnies. Newspaper reports taken alone are not a source of history. They must be checked and double-checked."

Father Dominic was also skeptical about the testimony of some of Padre Pio's friends. "We have plenty experience with such testimony," he wrote. "Not all who speak about Padre Pio and their experience are trustworthy. Some, wishing to pose as special friends of the Padre, have told the most incredible stories about him. Others, giving free vent to their imagination, have exaggerated, added, misunderstood, and misconstrued events. They probably did not want to lie. But they were such who could not think straight and mixed too much of their own into the story."

While many newspaper accounts and much oral history must be taken with a grain of salt, there are solid and substantial sources. Chief of these are Padre Pio's own letters, in four volumes, written to his spiritual advisers, spiritual children, and friends and colleagues. To corroborate these are the diaries and memoranda of several of Padre Pio's confreres, notably Padre Agostino Daniele of San Marco in Lamis, who kept a journal, off and on, for fifty years. Of special value are the letters that Father Dominic, who was generally regarded as a somewhat skeptical man, wrote to his family between 1948 and 1958 — notably to his cousin Albert Meyer, who became cardinal-archbishop of Chicago. Also oral and written testimony by priests, physicians, and other educated persons, which corroborate accounts by persons whose humble background and lack of education would naturally render them suspect by the sophisticated. Father Dominic, after dismissing as rubbish much of the material written about Padre Pio, nevertheless concluded that when one looked at the actual events of his life, "Truth is stranger than fiction." Moreover, in recent years the Vatican archives have made accessible documents from the pontificates of Benedict XV and Pius XI, among which are the records of a thorough investigation in the early 1920s by Monsignor Carlo Rossi from the Holy Office (or Inquisition).

The life of Padre Pio is, to be sure, replete with events that seem strange, even incredible to the average reader, but it is also a life of a real human being with real emotions, real joys, real sorrows, and real defects as well, who strove in his day to serve his fellow human beings by addressing their spiritual as well as physical needs.

Chapter One

The Roots of a Saint

Pietrelcina

A little town of about four thousand souls, Pietrelcina — the birthplace of Padre Pio — lies some six miles northeast of the city of Benevento, the capital of the province of the same name. It is about forty miles northeast of the city of Naples in a region of southern Italy known as Campania. Over the years, the town, which grew up around an ancient castle, has been called Petrapolcina, Petrapolicina, Pretapucina, and, only since the eighteenth century, Pietra Elcina or Pietrelcina. Although most people think the word means "Little Rock" or "Little Oak," no one seems to know for sure.

In 1860, the province of Benevento, until then part of the Kingdom of the Two Sicilies, was annexed by the Kingdom of Sardinia, whose prime minister, Camillo Benso, Count Cavour, created a united Kingdom of Italy the following year. A quarter-century later, Italy, a nation of twenty-eight million, was really two separate countries. While northern Italy (the area from Rome north to the Alps) was rapidly urbanizing and industrializing, the south, called the *Mezzogiorno*, remained socially, agriculturally, and economically depressed. In Pietrelcina, as in most parts of the south, the vast majority of the populace was illiterate and so isolated that many peasants still did not know that they were citizens of a united Italy.[1]

The census returns of 1881 revealed that only forty-six of every one thousand inhabitants in southern Italy were sharecroppers, and only fifty-nine were peasant proprietors. Most of the people were landless, employed seasonally as farm laborers, who lived from hand to mouth. They subsisted largely on a diet of rice, bread, pasta, and cornmeal, with almost no meat, and they were generally so unhealthy that few of their young men were found fit for military service. Malaria, pellagra, and tuberculosis were widespread, child mortality was astronomical, and every few years cholera epidemics claimed thousands of lives.[2]

Although nearly everyone in southern Italy was Catholic, Christianity there was badly vitiated by superstition, comprising, for many people, a mixture of Christian and pagan elements. A popular prayer, whether to God, Mary, or the saints, was: "You give me something, and I'll give you something in return."[3] Many approached God, Mary, and the saints only when they were in need, and sometimes blasphemed them when they failed to obtain what they wanted. One historian has characterized southern Italian men at the time as typically skeptical and anti-clerical, while their wives were wont to attend Mass daily, "rosaries in hand, fervently praying and supplicating priests, seeking out holy people who seemed closer to God." They were often completely lacking in theological understanding and ignorant even of the words they prayed in Latin.

Pietrelcina was two miles from the nearest railroad station, its only communication with the outside world, as there were no roads, not even to Benevento. The social hierarchy of the town was similar to that of others of the *Mezzogiorno*. Except for a few artisans, nearly everyone was tied to the land and belonged to one of two classes: the *possedenti*, who were the landowners, and the *braccianti*, who were landless laborers. All were considered "peasants" except four or five wealthy families who lived on big estates near Benevento and owned much of the land worked by the *braccianti*.[4] Most of the *possedenti* of Pietrelcina were the proprietors of very small farms, which they worked themselves with the help of hired *braccianti* during the busiest times of the year. While many *braccianti* lived in miserable dwellings in the country, most of the *possedenti* had houses in town and went out every day to work in their fields, remaining in the summer in cottages in the country.[5]

At Pietrelcina, the day was punctuated by the striking of the church bell, marking the various periods of prayer specified by local devotion. The year was highlighted by numerous saints' days. Few towns in the region observed so many religious feasts as Pietrelcina. One writer noted, "The year was a veritable succession of feasts, novenas, High Masses, processions, with the inevitable accompaniment of fireworks [and] music."[6]

Devotion to Mary was especially strong in Pietrelcina. Aside from Christmas and Easter, the chief feast of the year celebrated the town's local patroness, *La Madonna della Libera* (Our Lady of Deliverance), in August. During her three-day festival, the faithful went to the church, offering the firstfruits of their harvest of grain. Some of those who were better off left candles with banknotes pinned to them. The bejeweled wooden statue of *La Libera* was carried through the streets, accompanied by the town band. Padre Pio later wrote, "The main street was splendidly illuminated and in the evening there was an artistic fireworks display. There were games, horse-racing, tight-rope walking, and theatrical performances."[7]

The *Pucinari* hailed *La Libera* as their personal protectress. They were familiar with the account of how Our Lady delivered their ancestors from the wrath of the

Byzantine Greek armies, who rampaged Italy in the seventh century. When the area escaped the wrath of these invaders, the bishop of Benevento, venerated as San Barbato ("The Holy Bearded Man") taught his flock to pray to Mary under the title Our Lady of Deliverance. As late as 1854, *La Libera* was credited with rescuing the town from an epidemic of cholera that claimed 153 lives.[8] Records indicate that after the town gathered to pray for *La Libera*'s intercession, many were healed, and new cases of sickness rapidly declined.[9]

The supernatural was near at hand for the *Pucinari*. Many people believed at the time that a special prayer or combination of prayers, if repeated in a certain way, would enable one to predict the day of his death. They spoke of a formula, supposedly in Aramaic, by which a person could commit himself to Satan in return for worldly gain. The "old people" of the town made prophecies and predictions about the future, even "predicting," in the 1800s, the advent of automobiles, airplanes, and space travel.[10]

A native of Pietrelcina, who was a slightly younger contemporary of Padre Pio, described her town: "It was all farms in Pietrelcina. For us, Benevento was the big city. That's all we knew. We dressed like people did in America. We didn't have arranged marriages. We didn't wear local costumes [except on special occasions], but all our clothing was handmade. We never closed our doors. We had no running water or plumbing."[11] Another near contemporary of Padre Pio had a less rosy recollection of Pietrelcina at the turn of the twentieth century: "So uncivilized you couldn't even leave your doors [unlocked] at night because everyone was robbing each other."[12]

A God-Fearing Family

The paternal family of Padre Pio, the Forgiones, were *possedenti* — small landowners. According to local tradition, the family came originally from the Abruzzi, a region to the northeast. The earliest ancestor of record was Antonio Forgione, who died in Pietrelcina in 1837 at the age of about eighty. Little is known of him or his son Donato (1786–1841) except the vital statistics noted in the fragmentary records of the parish church. Donato had a son Michele, who was born in 1819 and died forty-eight years later, leaving behind his second wife, the young widow Felicita D'Andrea (1839–1887) and his two little children by her: seven-year-old Orazio Maria (Padre Pio's father) and two-year-old Orsola.

Orazio was born October 22, 1860. He was baptized Grazio Maria, but, although his wife usually called him "Gra," throughout his life he was almost always known as "Orazio" — the name that appeared on his death certificate and on his tombstone. He spent most of his childhood in the household of his stepfather, Celestino Orlando, who married his mother shortly after the death of his father, Michele.

Young Orazio spent his childhood in relative poverty, minding the family sheep.

While still a teenager, Orazio was named a "Master of the Feast," a member of the committee that planned the annual festivities in August. That was a great honor and a sign of the respect in which the devout young man was held among the townsfolk.

On June 8, 1881, Orazio, now twenty years old, donned the local costume — a doublet trimmed with gold buttons, knee-stockings adorned with white ribbons, and white shoes — and was escorted by his stepfather to the home of Maria Giuseppa De Nunzio, who was to be his bride. Giuseppa was dressed in a red satin gown, an azure-blue apron, and a red bodice covered with gold brocade. A white scarf adorned her head, and, to ensure fertility, around her neck she wore a cloth imprinted with the image of thirteen male saints. In her pocket she carried a pair of miniature scissors, which were said to ward off the "evil eye." Orazio's stepfather gave a perfunctory speech of advice to Giuseppa, and she kissed the hands of her future parents-in-law and left with her female companions, resplendent in red silk dresses nearly as lovely as her own. The little company went first to the town hall for the civil ceremony, and then to the church to celebrate the Sacrament of Matrimony. During the ceremony, Giuseppa tucked the hem of her skirt between Orazio's knees "to keep away evil things." The nuptials concluded, and a band accompanied the couple back to the De Nunzio house, where they were to live.[13] Thus Orazio Forgione and Giuseppa De Nunzio commenced forty-eight years of married life. (As was customary, the bride retained her family name.)

"Gra" and "Beppa," as they called each other, were remarkable people. Orazio has been described as "a little runt of a man," supple and wiry, with fair skin, dark eyes, and chestnut hair that remained full and thick to the end of his days. He exemplified what his granddaughter Pia Forgione called "the Forgione character." "Whenever there was a difficulty, Grandfather, like my father and Uncle Pio, wouldn't let it weigh on him. He would get through it. He'd sit down, discuss what was to be done, straighten it out, and go on." Trusting the Lord to give him the wisdom to solve all his problems, he never worried and tried to instill this characteristic in his children.[14] Adjectives frequently used with regard to Orazio Forgione are "simple" and "lovely." A neighbor, questioned about his character, described him as "holy." In a society in which men typically went to Mass only at Easter and possibly at Christmas, and at other times stood outside the church chatting with each other while their wives worshiped, Forgione not only went to Mass every Sunday, but, with his wife, stopped at the church to pray every day after working in the fields. He was constantly praying his rosary, a habit he instilled in his saintly son. Not an oath or a foul word ever escaped his lips, and so great a reverence for life did he have that even in the fields he would step out of the way of an ant rather than step on it. "Poor little creature, why should it die?" he would say.[15] Orazio Forgione's most characteristic trait, however, was joy. He loved to sing in a booming, resonant voice and was hailed as a wonderful storyteller. Seeing the hand of God all about him, he rejoiced in everything, radiating "a contagious joy about him which communicated itself to others."[16]

Maria Giuseppa De Nunzio, the only child of Fortunato De Nunzio (c. 1821–1896) and Maria Giovanna Gagliardi (1831–1908), was a year and a half her husband's senior, born March 28, 1859. She was evidently from a more socially prominent family than Orazio, and some of her relatives initially disapproved of her marriage to him. She had light blue eyes and was as tall as her husband. Even in her sixties, according to Mary Pyle, in whose home Giuseppa spent her last days, she had "a slim body like a teenager and very small feet." Like her husband, she was extremely devout. As an act of mortification, she abstained from eating meat, not just on the obligatory Fridays, but also on Wednesdays and Saturdays. (That such was an option for her is indicative of the family's comparatively high social standing, as most peasant families seldom had access to much meat.) Nearly everyone remarked about the grace and elegance of the woman sometimes called "The Little Princess," who was always clad, from head to toe, in spotless white. She conversed in the local Neapolitan dialect — rather than in standard Italian — as most people of her age and class did, but Pyle, an aristocratic American, marveled how she "spoke her hard vernacular with marvelous grace."[17] Beppa prefaced all her plans with, "If God is willing." Unlike many residents of small towns, she refused to gossip or criticize people behind their backs. Those who knew her were usually struck by her intelligence and sense of hospitality: "She was happier when she could give than when she could receive."[18]

"Otto Bambini"

The Forgiones lived in a modest stone house at 27-28 Vico Storte Valle (Crooked Valley Lane) in the Castle District, the oldest part of Pietrelcina, which had grown up around the site of the old castle, which had long since fallen into ruins. The Forgione domicile seems originally to have been two small houses, since one had to exit the door of Number 27 to get to Number 28. Number 27 consisted of a single room with a single window. This was used as the parents' bedroom. Number 28 consisted of a kitchen, where cooking was done at a large open hearth, and another, smaller room, which served as the girls' bedroom. The Forgiones owned another dwelling a few doors away, a single room called "The Tower," because it was accessed by steep treacherous steps and afforded a wonderful view of the rolling farmland beyond it. This served as the boys' bedroom.

The home of the Forgiones was simply furnished with the bare necessities for health and comfort. The lime-painted walls were adorned with crucifixes and lithographs of the Madonna and various saints. After the children were born, visitors were amazed at the great number of books heaped onto a square table in the parents' bedroom.[19] Although neither parent could read, they wanted their children to have an education and provided for them accordingly.

A year after Orazio and Giuseppa were married, on June 25, 1882, a son, Michele, was born, named after Gra's father. Two years later a second boy was born, who was given the name Francesco. Some say that he was named for Saint Francis, to whom Orazio had a great devotion. Others believe that, like most of the other children, he was named for a relative, in this case one of Orazio's uncles. This child lived only twenty days. A third child, Amalia, also died in infancy. Then on May 25, 1887, at 5:30 p.m. according to the parish register, but at 10 p.m. according to the records of the town clerk, a fourth child came into the world and was given the name of his dead brother Francesco. This was the child who would later be known as Padre Pio.[20]

According to family tradition, when he was baptized the next day at the parish church of Saint Anna by Padre Nicolantonio Orlando, his mother dedicated him to the Virgin Mary. It is not known whether she did this with the other children, but one might assume that she did.

Francesco II — called "Franci" (Frankie) — was followed on September 15, 1889, by a sister named for her grandmother Felicita D'Andrea, who had died two years before. The sixth child, born March 15, 1892, was named for Orazio's maternal grandmother, Pellegrina Cardone. A seventh child, born the day after Christmas in 1894, was named Grazia and called Graziella (Gracie). Most sources state that she was the youngest child.

There are some who insist that there was an eighth child, Mario, who was supposedly born March 24, 1899, and lived for eleven months. Padre Pio's niece Pia (born in the 1920s) told the author that Mario did in fact exist. However, there are no civil or church records of his birth or death, and many doubt that there was a fourth brother, however short-lived. In later years, when Padre Pio performed weddings, he often wished the couple *otto bambini* — eight babies — and some assume that this was because he was one of eight siblings.

"The God-Is-Everything People"

When the church bell rang at daybreak, the Forgione family rose for morning prayers. Then Orazio saddled his donkey and started for the family plots in the area outside town known as the Piana Romana. During the summer, he would stop either at the parish church or at the town hall to hire several *braccianti* who congregated there, hoping to be hired for the day by one of the landowners. Beppa and the children would follow Orazio on foot, making the one-hour trek to the farm.

The Forgione farm was very small, by American standards — only five acres, according to some accounts, three by others. It yielded grapes, wheat, Indian corn, olives, figs, and plums. Orazio and Giuseppa also raised sheep, goats, chickens, ducks, rabbits, and occasionally kept a milk cow or two and some hogs. On a lane near their plot, they had a cottage with a dirt floor, which stood in a row of similar dwellings, owned by neighboring families. There they stored their equipment, kept their animals, and, in summer, cooked, ate, and slept. There were only two beds: one for the parents and one for some of the children. When the entire family stayed at the Piana Romana, some of the children had to stay next door with the Scocca family, who owned the adjoining farm and, like almost everybody else in Pietrelcina, were distant relatives. Around the cottage, Beppa kept a garden, where she grew roses, wallflowers, and carnations. When water was needed, she fetched it from a nearby well in a huge jug and balanced it on her head.

Padre Pio had pleasant memories of summers on the farm. He and his siblings played with the Scocca children, one of whom, Mercurio, shared with him the same year of birth and, later, of death. Summer evenings, when the work was done, Franci would go with his family and the Scoccas to visit neighbors on adjoining farms. There, in the moonlight, they would eat macaroni and sing. As an old man, Padre Pio spoke with deep affection of the green fields, dotted with leafy elms and cooled by fresh spring water, through which he and his siblings "roamed as little kings in a kingdom without confines, whose only law was that of the Good Creation."[21] With great nostalgia he spoke of the circle of friends with whom he and his family spent so many happy times, doubting if the world would ever again see the like of the stolid, happy, pious yeomen farmers around whom he spent his youth.

Winters, the children amused themselves playing in front of the parish church of St. Anna, sometimes called the Castle Church. Nights were enlivened by storytelling, both by their father and by their maternal grandmother, Giovanna Gagliardi.

Christ was at the center of the Forgione family, whom neighbors sometimes called the "God-Is-Everything Family."[22] The Forgiones were seen in church every day, and evenings they knelt together to pray the Rosary. The baby sister, Graziella, who became a nun, in later years recalled that in her childhood home, prayer came before anything else. Whatever evening chores or diversions were planned took place only after prayer. Most of the stories that the children were told came from Scripture. Although Orazio could not read, somehow he memorized much of Sacred Scripture and transmitted his knowledge to his children in the form of entertaining stories.

Of utmost importance to the Forgione family were the Madonna and the saints, who were seen almost as members of the family. They were so close at hand that it was unthinkable for the Forgiones not to try to enlist their help, just as they might enlist the help of their neighbors. They felt that they were not alone before the awesome throne of God. They gave homage and made supplication to God *in company* with the kindly array of helpers that the Lord himself sent as guides on their way to the celestial city. Foremost of these was, of course, the Madonna. The Forgiones could not imagine any Christian failing to love and honor the Blessed Virgin. It was doubtless from his childhood training that Padre Pio derived his love of the Madonna, whom he described as "more beautiful and more resplendent than the sun … a most pure crystal that can only reflect God."[23]

Chapter Two

A Boy Who Talked to the Angels

The "Beautiful Francesco"

Unfortunately, there is little contemporary documentation about Padre Pio's childhood, except some essays he wrote in school, but these are limited help in providing a picture of the boy and his life. He kept no diary, and neither did those around him — most of whom were illiterate. Although his father worked most of the year out of the country, only a couple letters between father and son have survived the ravages of time. Pio's father, however, when he was in his eighties and living with Mary Pyle at San Giovanni Rotondo, provided numerous anecdotes from the childhood of his famous son, which she recorded. But, of course, the doting father who practically worshiped his son was not a totally unbiased witness.

The most extensive work in reconstructing Padre Pio's childhood was done immediately after his death, when Padre Alessandro of Ripabottoni and Padre Lino of Prata undertook to interview elderly persons who had known Padre Pio as a boy, taking down their oral histories. There is always the possibility that the good fathers were told what they wanted to hear. The only one of Pio's siblings who survived him was his baby sister Graziella, who outlived her brother by only seven months. Nobody seems to have interviewed her.

According to those who were interviewed, the child Franci Forgione, with his blond hair and brown eyes, "was so beautiful he looked like an angel."[1] Neighbors referred to him as "*il bello Francesco*" ("beautiful Francis"), as much for his temperament as for his appearance.

A Shaken Baby!

Like most children, Franci could be exasperating at times. His father told Miss Pyle that Franci passed through a spell when he kept the whole house awake by crying all night long. One night *Tata*, as the children called their father, was so upset by the baby's continuous crying that he leaped from his bed, grabbed the baby, and shook him, screaming, "The good Lord must have sent a little devil into my house instead of a baby!"[2] To make things worse, Orazio lost his grip and the baby fell to the brick floor. His hysterical mother gathered the shrieking child into her arms and screamed at her husband, "What are you trying to do, kill my child!"[3]

As an adult, Padre Pio recalled having terrible nightmares as a little boy. He told a friend that when his mother put him to bed when he was a toddler and turned off the oil lamp, he would start crying, and his mother would turn on the light to quiet him. "I was surrounded by frightening monsters!"[4] Although his experience was not unusual for a little child, Padre Pio reportedly concluded, "The devil was tormenting me."[5] It was reported that he claimed, as an adult, that as early as he could remember, he could communicate with his guardian angel and had visions of Christ and Mary. The supernatural world was close at hand for the farm folk of the *Mezzogiorno*, but extraordinarily so for young Franci Forgione.

The Dog That Ate the Peppers

Franci was a sickly child. "I've suffered since I was at my mother's breast," he remarked to a friend in later life.[6] When he was two, suffering from stomach problems, he was taken by his mother to a local witch. Beppa feared that someone had put the "evil eye" on the child. According to Padre Pio, the witch "took me by the legs and held me upside down [as if] I were a lamb," making nine crosses over his stomach, massaging it, and chanting eerie incantations.[7] The treatment seemed to work.

When he was about ten, Franci became seriously ill with an illness usually described as typhoid fever, a bacterial infection usually caused by poor sanitation or contaminated food. A local physician, Don Giacinto Gudagna, told the boy's parents that he had only days to live. Bluntly, the parents told Franci that he was dying. The sick child answered calmly, "If I'm dying, I want to see my beloved Piana Romana once more." Gra and Beppa agreed, and his brother Michele, then fifteen, put his little brother on a donkey and took him to the cottage on the farm. Now it was harvest time, and Beppa had prepared fried peppers as a treat for her farmhands. The peppers were so hot that the workers had eaten comparatively few, and a large pot remained on the table. Alone with Michele, Franci asked for some peppers. Michele refused. Later Beppa arrived at the cottage, and Franci said to her: "Close the door, *Mammella*. The light is bothering me. Now please leave me. I want to be alone for a little bit." So she left him alone in the house. Thereupon Franci jumped out of bed, devoured every single pepper, and downed a half a bottle of milk. When Beppa returned Franci was in a deep sleep and the pot was empty. She upbraided Michele for letting the dog get to the peppers. Next morning Franci awoke perfectly well and confessed that he had been the "dog" that ate the peppers.[8] Both Padre Pio and his brother recounted this story in later years.

Dedicated to Christ and Mary

Only three years of public school were available in Pietrelcina in the 1890s. Classes were held at night so that the children could work during the day. Michele continually played hooky and remained completely illiterate. His draft registration card in September 1918, when living in Flushing, Queens, New York, reveals that he signed his name with an "X." Franci, however, was an eager student. His first teacher was Cosimo Scocca, a fourteen-year-old boy from the adjacent farm. The next two years Franci was instructed by Mandato Saginario, who worked by day as a rope maker.

Franci's spiritual precocity manifested itself very early in life, which is not surprising, since both of his parents were extremely devout and reared their children to be saints. Of Franci's siblings, only Pellegrina rejected the faith in which she was reared. The other children enthusiastically embraced Gra and Beppa's piety.

At baptism, Beppa dedicated Franci (as she must have done with the other children) to Christ and the Virgin Mary. When Franci was five, Beppa encouraged him to dedicate himself to Christ, Mary, and his patron, Francis of Assisi.[9] From the time he could talk, Franci was always asking to be taken to church. He liked to hear stories about Jesus, Mary, and the saints, and, rather precociously, he was aware of sin. One day, when he was a very little boy, he was walking with his mother past a field of turnips. When *Mammella* remarked, "Look at those beautiful turnips. I'd sure like to eat some," Franci, with grave and solemn demeanor, looked up at her and said sternly, "That's a sin." A few days later, however, when mother and son were walking past a stand of fig trees, Franci begged his mother to pluck some figs. "Wait a minute now," she said. "It was a sin to eat the turnips, and now it's not a sin to eat the figs!"[10]

An "Unsalted Piece of Macaroni"

As a little boy, Franci was given the chore of minding the family sheep — all four or five of them. The families on the neighboring farms combined their flocks, with the result that their children played together. When interviewed in later years, Franci's surviving childhood playmates had varying recollections. Luigi Orlando recalled: "When he was with us, he never prayed. There was nothing particularly outstanding about him. With us he was a boy just like any other, [though] well-mannered and reserved."[11] Ubaldo Vecchariano characterized him as somewhat of a "nerd" — "submissive and reserved," an "unsalted piece of macaroni."[12] Antonio Bonavita recounted, "The rest of us children were wicked, but he was always good."[13] Mercurio Scocca recalled that Franci loved to play Mass and sculpt clay figures of Christ and the saints for the various religious festivals. Riparta Masone, a playmate of Franci's youngest sister, remembered that her older brother Vincenzo, who played with Franci, complained that he was "always preaching" to the other boys.[14]

Some of Franci's playmates recalled how it was customary for mothers to give their children a chunk of bread to carry to the fields to eat for breakfast. While most of them shoved it into a pocket and gulped it down unceremoniously, Franci's mother gave him bread in a white linen napkin. Kneeling down, he would pray before he ate, and if a morsel fell to the ground, he would pick it up and kiss it before consuming it. Whenever another boy cursed or swore, Franci would run away. The same Luigi Orlando who described him as "a boy like any other," recalled that once, when the two were wrestling, Luigi let escape from his lips "a strong expression," whereupon Franci, who had pinned him to the ground, jumped up, and fled.[15] Riparta Masone recalled that Graziella Forgione would, like her brother, leave the company of any child who cursed or misbehaved. This is what their mother trained them to do. Beppa forbade her children to associate with others who used vulgar or blasphemous language. In fact, whenever she heard anyone curse, she would "repair" it with the expression, "Blessed be God!" — a practice she tried to instill in all her children.[16]

Franci was exceptionally devout as a child, but his piety was not unique in his family. His sisters Felicita and Graziella were said to have been just as pious. Riparta Masone recalled that Graziella never wanted to play with the other girls. "She'd carry her jug to the well to get water and never look to the left or to the right or say anything to the other children. She spent all her time praying."[17] Franci, too, at times, would go off by himself and sit under the shade of an elm tree to pray and study. In school, it was said that he was the only boy among his companions who consistently completed all his homework. But he also liked to play and tease (even as an old man). The boy loved to sneak up quietly behind his sister Felicita while she was taking her bath in the portable tub on the kitchen floor and dunk her head in the water. Felicita, a gentle, sweet-natured girl whom Padre Pio would later characterize as "a saint" and "the best of all the family," never complained, but merely looked at him, smiled, and said, "Hey, Franci, you never stop playing, do you?"[18]

One day when Franci was taking his siesta under an elm tree, Mercurio Scocca decided to bury him in corn shocks. When Franci awoke in darkness, screaming for his mother, Mercurio burst out laughing. The next day at siesta time it was Franci who found Mercurio sound asleep on top of a small farm wagon. Pulling the wagon to the crest of a nearby hill, Franci pushed it over the brink with Mercurio still in it. The wagon crashed into a nearby tree; fortunately, Mercurio was unhurt.[19]

Franci also tried smoking — once. A neighbor gave him money to go to town to fetch a cigar. On his way back, Franci lit the cigar and took a puff. He became so ill that he never smoked again (although as an adult he used snuff).

Franci developed early a deep concern for the poor and the sick. Although he later remembered never lacking for anything as a child, he was deeply moved and troubled when he accompanied his mother on one of her frequent errands of charity and saw poor peasants without adequate food, clothing, and shelter. His school compositions reveal compassion for persons like "little Silvio," an orphan, shivering with cold, whom he described as kneeling with his grandfather at the tomb of his parents, weeping bitterly.[20] In another composition he described "little Anselm" who, at twelve, had neither mother nor father nor sisters nor brothers, who lived alone at home, and, "in order to eke out a living," was forced "to go from door to door, to beg for charity."[21]

Franci Witnesses a Miracle

When Franci was eight, he witnessed an event that remained indelibly imprinted in his mind for the rest of his life. For vacations, the Forgiones went to nearby shrines, such as that of Our Lady of Grace in Benevento and Our Lady of Pompeii near Naples (thirtysome miles away). On August 25, 1895, Orazio took his younger son to the town of Altavilla Irpina, about twenty miles south of Pietrelcina, to the church of Santa Maria Assunta in Cielo, which contained the relics of Saint Pellegrino, an early Christian martyr. The church was frequently the site of flamboyant displays of excessive piety. Padre Alessio Parente, Padre Pio's assistant in his old age, recalled seeing in that very church in the 1940s or 1950s a young man crawling around, licking the floor with his tongue!

On that summer day, Franci and his father were in a crowd of worshipers, amidst the smells of incense, garlic, and wine, when a "raging, disheveled woman" forced herself up to the altar area, where stood a statue of Saint Pellegrino. In her arms she carried a deformed, mentally disabled child. According to some versions, the boy had a grossly enlarged head; according to another he had only stumps for limbs. He ceaselessly vocalized a horrible, raucous *graak! graak! graak!* like a crow. Hysterically, the disheveled mother implored Saint Pellegrino to heal the child. Nothing happened. The child continued his obscene and pathetic litany: *Graak! Graak! Graak!*

The worshipers watched in horror as the frantic mother, with a bloodcurdling shriek and gruesome oaths, began to curse the saint. Finally, she screamed, "Why don't you cure him? Well … keep him! He's yours!" Thereupon, she threw the child at the statue. He hit the image, bounced off, and crashed to the floor. Then, to the stupefaction of everyone, the child, who had never walked or talked, got up and ran to his mother (on his stumps?), crying, in a clear and normal voice: "Mother! Mother!"

Cries of "*Miracolo! Miracolo!*" filled the church. Men, women, boys, and girls surged forward to behold what Saint Pellegrino had wrought. Franci and his father were nearly trampled in the pandemonium, but they were both so moved that they exchanged scarcely a word on the way home. As long as he lived, Padre

Pio would remember that episode at Altavilla Irpina as a demonstration of God's
mercy and love.[22]

"Don't You See the Madonna?"

The miracle of Saint Pellegrino was not the first time that Franci saw the hand of
God break into the physical world. As Fra Pio he once told his friend Padre Agostino
of San Marco in Lamis that from early childhood he had seen and spoken to Jesus,
the Virgin Mary, and his guardian angel. He said this as if he did not realize it was
unusual. "Don't you see the Madonna?" he asked. When Agostino replied that he
did not, Fra Pio replied, "Surely, you're saying that out of humility."[23]

Franci also saw and communicated with his guardian angel. In letters, he sometimes referred to his celestial protector as "the companion of my infancy." The boy
claimed that Jesus also visited him and guided him.

Margherita DeCianni, a childhood friend, recounted in later years how one day
Franci was with his father, who was attempting to dig a well at Piana Romana. After
the elder Forgione had dug forty feet without finding water, Franci announced,
"You won't find any water down there." When Orazio asked him how he knew,
the child said bluntly, "Jesus told me, if you want to find water, you must dig over
there." The boy pointed to a precise spot in another part of the field. "All right,"
said his father. "I'll dig where you tell me, but, if there's no water there, I'll throw
you in the hole!" Orazio dug three feet … four feet … five … six … seven — and
then there burst forth an abundant spring of water![24]

Today, a boy such as Franci probably would be taken to a psychiatrist, diagnosed
with some sort of mental illness, and drugged. Or perhaps he would simply be
accused of lying. Orazio and Giuseppa and their relatives and neighbors recognized
that some people who claimed to have visions were liars or crazy. But, as in the case
of the spring, Franci's paranormal experiences corresponded to a concrete reality.
Moreover, other members of Franci's family seem to have had some sort of mystical
experiences, albeit less spectacular than his. Padre Pio's niece Pia Forgione affirmed
that, although her father, Michele, never had any supersensible experiences, she
was of the firm belief that her aunt Graziella was characterized by an "enhanced
spirituality." There are also reports from several sources that once when Orazio
was visiting his son Padre Pio, he claimed to see the soul of a dead person there in
front of the door to his room.

As far as we know, it was in his tenth year that Franci had his first experience
of the death of a close relative. On August 22, 1896, his grandfather, Fortunato De
Nunzio, died in Pietrelcina at the age of seventy-five. We know nothing of Franci's
relationship with him or whether he was present at the old man's deathbed, but,
from one of his school essays, we do know that a few months earlier he had seen
a man die.

He and his mother had gone to the hospital at Benevento to visit a relative. It seems to have been the custom of Giuseppa De Nunzio to circulate through the wards, providing a word of cheer and comfort and a prayer for the various patients. Mother and son stopped to visit with a young soldier, wounded in the battle of Adowa (in which Italy, desperately seeking colonies, experienced the abject humiliation of having its armies crushed by the military forces of Ethiopia in March 1896). The soldier was being attended by a priest and a nursing nun, who were trying to cheer him. But the wounded man kept calling his absent mother, moaning, "I'll never see her again. I feel I'm dying and I'd like to see my family, especially my mother, who loves me so much, for the last time."

Many mothers would have spared a nine-year-old boy such a scene, but Beppa kept Franci with her. Just as the nun told the soldier, "Oh, come on now, don't upset yourself so. You must live, and be the joy of your parents," he "suddenly bowed his head; he remained stock-still; and after a few minutes, he died." For two days, Franci was so upset that he could not eat.[25]

"I Want to Be a Friar with a Beard"

In later years, Padre Pio insisted, "I always wanted to be a friar." His parents were first aware of this when he told them, after hearing a particularly inspiring sermon, that he wanted to be a priest.

When Franci was ten, he encountered twenty-six-year-old Fra Camillo of Sant'Elia a Pianisi, *cercatore di campagna* for the Capuchin friary at Morcone, about thirteen miles from Pietrelcina. The job of the *cercatore* was to go through the countryside, soliciting provisions, in the spirit of Saint Francis of Assisi, the founder of the order. Camillo carried with him a large sack for donations of wheat, grain, flour, eggs, and similar goods, as well as a coffer for cash donations. Fra Cami', as he was called, was a merry little man, a favorite with the children, to whom he handed out pictures, medals, chestnuts, and walnuts. Franci was attracted to this happy and genial friar and was especially fascinated by his beard. When Fra Cami' told him that all Capuchins wore beards, Francesco was determined to become a Capuchin, because, as he said, he wanted one day to have a beard like Fra Cami'.

When he discussed his desire to become a Capuchin with his parents, they told him that they would prefer that he become a parish priest, promising to finance his studies to that end.

"No, no," insisted the boy, "I want to be a friar with a beard!"

"With a beard!" his mother laughed. "Why, you're still a little kid. You don't know anything about having a beard or not having a beard."[26]

The next time she saw Fra Camillo, Beppa told him, "Fra Cami', we've got to make this boy a monk."

"May St. Francis bless him," the Capuchin said, "and help him to be a good

Capuchin." He invited her to visit the friary and talk to the authorities there. So she and Orazio went to Morcone to speak to the superior there and inspect the place. When they returned, Franci asked, "Do they want me?" When his parents nodded, the ten-year-old jumped up and down in joy, crying, "They want me! They want me! They want me!"[27]

There was a problem. If Franci was to become a priest, he needed more formal education than the three years available in Pietrelcina. This meant that the boy would have to go to private school. His parents could pay the doctor and the shoemaker in goods such as grain and eggs, but they would have to pay for Francesco's education in cash, and they had little. Orazio, once he became convinced that Franci was serious, decided to go to America to earn money sufficient to pay for his son's education.

Orazio Goes to America

By the late nineteenth century, huge numbers of southern Italian men were crossing the Atlantic to work in North and South America, as there were no jobs to be found in their region, except as farm laborers. It was said that at one time 30 percent of the males in Pietrelcina were working in other countries. Most of these men had no intention of remaining in the Americas permanently, but engaged in a sort of commute across the ocean to provide for their wives and children in Italy. It was probably in late 1897 or early 1898 that Orazio, leaving Giuseppa to run the farm, sailed from Naples to Brazil or Argentina (no one seems clear on which), but shortly he was back, without money. According to some accounts, he had become ill; according to others, he had been unable to find employment. (It would have been shortly after his return that he fathered his eighth child — if in fact there was an eighth child.) It was probably in 1899 that he sailed away again, this time to the United States.

Immigrant passenger lists show that dozens of Forgiones arrived in America from Pietrelcina, mostly at Ellis Island, but none of them was named Grazio or Orazio or anything similar. He may have arrived at another port; he may have been illegal. In 1901, he was writing to his family from Mahoningtown, Pennsylvania, where he shared a frame house on Montgomery Avenue with some fellow Pietrelcinese immigrants and worked as foreman of the hands on a farm,[28] sending home nine American dollars a week at a time when the average worker earned about eleven.[29] In this way Orazio provided Francesco the equivalent of a high school education, purchased two more tracts of land, and acquired more livestock. On November 12, 1902, he dictated a letter to his wife, telling her, "Dear wife ... put aside a good demijohn of wine for, when the feast of the Most Holy Mary comes (the one in August) next year, I return to Italy."[30] His stay at home was brief. On his return to the United States, he worked in Queens, New York. In later years, he lamented he never got to know his younger daughters well. On his brief trips home, it is said they never seemed comfortable in his arms.

School Days

Franci was enrolled first in a private school run by Domenico Tizzani on Via Caracciolo, where he studied reading, writing, and elementary Latin. Don Domenico,[31] a quiet, melancholy man in his fifties, was a married former priest. After a while, Franci's mother was not satisfied with his progress, and her husband concluded that it was not a good idea to have a boy who wanted to be a priest instructed by a man who had left the priesthood. In later years, Padre Pio said that Don Domenico never talked about his personal life and was a good teacher.

Giuseppa then enrolled Franci in a private school run by Don Angelo Caccavo. He was not a particularly religious man (in later years, Padre Pio wrote him, telling him that he prayed every day for his conversion), but he was an excellent teacher. He brooked no nonsense, however. Whenever a student got a lesson wrong, he had to take it home and copy it over several times by the next morning. Unruly children were made to hold out their hands to receive the whack of a short ruler on the open palm. If that didn't work, Caccavo would put the child "in jail" — making him kneel in front of the class, facing the blackboard. He was not averse to cracking a recalcitrant child on the head. Most Pietrelcinese respected Don Angelo and accepted his methods of discipline.[32]

Franci was once the undeserving object of Don Angelo's wrath. Several of the boys drafted a passionate love letter, signed Francesco's name, and delivered it to one of the girls, who, indignant, handed it to Caccavo. In fury, he ordered Franci to the front of the room, and, in front of the class, began to beat the boy with his fists, until his victim crawled under the desk to take cover from the blows. Hearing the commotion and knowing her husband's violent temper, the teacher's wife interposed herself between her husband and the boy, saving him from serious injury. When Don Angelo learned that the note was a forgery, he was horrified. For the rest of his life — he died in 1944 at the age of seventy-five — he said he regretted beating the future Padre Pio, who later declared, "All his remorse could not take away the black and blue marks that I carried about for days!"[33]

At fourteen, Francesco wrote to his father in Pennsylvania: "Now I am under the guidance of a new teacher [Caccavo]. I see that I am progressing day by day, for which I am happy, as is Mama." He continued, "We, too, are well, thanks be to the Lord, and I, in a special way, send continual prayers to our gracious Virgin, in order that she may protect you from every evil and restore you to our love, safe and sound." He promised to study, reported a lack of rain and poor wheat crops, and said his mother and siblings were doing well. Some time earlier he and several school friends had made a pilgrimage to the shrine of Our Lady of Pompeii —

without asking permission of his mother, who, understandably, was furious and had reported the incident in a letter that she had dictated to his father. Francesco admitted that his father was right to reprove him, but, "You should think about next year when, God willing, all festivities and amusements will be over, for I shall abandon this life to embrace a better one [in the religious life]."[34]

Francesco was remembered as a handsome teenager, with fair, rosy skin and auburn hair, and a winning smile. Steadfastly he ignored the flirtations of his female classmates, lowering his eyes when they spoke to him. He was also very fond of reading. To a spiritual daughter, he wrote: "I never felt the least attraction for the type of reading that might sully moral innocence and purity, for I held quite naturally in greatest abhorrence even the slightest obscenity. In my readings, which were not improper, but were invariably worldly, I sought merely scientific satisfaction and the pastime of honest mental recreation." He regretted, however, that such reading never helped him "acquire a single virtue" and, on the contrary, according to him, diminished his love for God.[35]

A note Franci wrote to his childhood friend Luigi Orlando on March 9, 1902, when he was two months shy of his fifteenth birthday, reveals a sensitive, affectionate boy who wanted to be loved. "Luigino" evidently had been snubbing him.

My good dear Luigino,

If you find any fault in me, I beg you explain it to me.

I know that you were angry with me yesterday evening, and I can't understand the reason. I don't think I've done anything bad to you; therefore I'm writing this letter, lovingly asking you for the reason for your new attitude towards me.

I'm sure that you'll give me an explanation for acting this way because I want to be friends with everybody.

Goodbye, today, seeing you in school or church, I hope that you don't act in the same way towards me. If you're angry with me concerning what happened yesterday evening, it wasn't I, but you should know that it was your friend Bonavita who told Sagginario to push you down.

Many regards and a hearty embrace from your most affectionate friend,

Francesco Forgione[36]

Already Francesco was beginning to adopt some of the self-denying practices for which he was later famous. While one school composition reveals that he liked to sleep late on days when he did not have to go to school, he already practiced mortification in eating. It seems as if, during certain times of the year, Francesco stayed in town while his mother lived at Piana Romana, where she supervised the farmwork. She returned to Pietrelcina, however, once a day, to prepare

Francesco's meals. (It isn't clear if the other children were there with him or elsewhere.) Sometimes she left him food to cook. When she noticed that he was leaving uneaten much of what she left him, she was deeply hurt. She was especially upset when he failed to touch "a magnificent and perfumed dish of *zucchini alla parmigiana.*" In fact, she burst into tears. Francesco was deeply contrite. In later years he remarked, "If I had realized that Mother would have been hurt, I would have eaten all the zucchini." After that he tried to eat whatever his mother left for him, for her sake.[37]

Pati

As Francesco neared the time of his entrance into the Capuchin order, he nearly got cold feet. The decision to abandon home and family for a life of prayer, obedience, and rigid self-discipline was not an easy one for the sensitive boy. Later in life, Padre Pio said that at that time he had drunk "great draughts of the world's vanity." He was unsure how he would face the prospect of having to forgo the innocent pleasures of secular life in the harsh austerity of the friary.

At this point in his life, Francesco found a friend and confidant who was to assume great importance in his life during the next few years. Salvatore Maria Pannullo, a fifty-two-year-old former college and seminary professor, became head pastor of the parish of Pietrelcina in 1901. Lively, cultured, and learned, "Zi' Tore," as he was known to his parishioners, had a photographic memory and could recite the Gospels by heart in their entirety. With Orazio in Pennsylvania, Pannullo became like a second father to Francesco, who called him "*Pati*" or "Little Father."

By the fall of 1902, Francesco's plans to become a Capuchin were nearly derailed.

Pannullo received an anonymous letter accusing Francesco of having a sexual relationship with the daughter of the stationmaster. He called his staff together, and they decided to suspend Francesco from his duties as an altar boy. Francesco, for his part, had not the slightest idea what was going on and thought this must be normal practice. Pannullo conducted a thorough investigation and discovered that some schoolmates of Francesco's had written the letter. The boys admitted they made everything up. Only after he was allowed to resume his duties as altar boy was Francesco told what had transpired. Many years later, Padre Pio's friend Padre Agostino asked him if he ever thought of taking revenge. "On the contrary," said Pio, "I prayed for them and I am still praying for them." Yet, he conceded, "At times I did mention to God, 'My Lord, if it is necessary to give them a whipping or two to convert them, please do it, as long as their souls are saved in the end.'"[38]

When he was a middle-aged man, Padre Pio told George Pogany, a Hungarian priest, "When I was a teenager, I didn't even know how human beings came about. None of the teenagers in Pietrelcina knew anything about sex in those days."[39] Around the same time, Padre Agostino, who often heard Padre

Pio's confessions, wrote, "I can swear that [Padre Pio] has conserved his virginity up to the present and that he has never sinned, even venially, against this angelic virtue."[40]

"You Must Fight a Formidable Warrior"

On New Year's Day 1903, Francesco was meditating on his vocation, wondering how he could find the strength to bid farewell to his family and the world to devote himself entirely to God in the cloister. Suddenly, he experienced what is known as an "intellectual vision," in which the physical senses are not involved. He was made "to gaze with the eye of his intellect on [things] quite different from those seen with bodily eyes."

Describing the vision, he speaks of himself in the third person:

At his side he beheld a majestic man of rare beauty, resplendent as the sun. This man took him by the hand and said, "Come with me, for you must fight a formidable warrior." He then led him to a vast field where there was a great multitude. The multitude was divided into two groups. On the one side he saw men of the most beautiful countenance, clad in snow-white garments. On the other … he saw men of hideous aspect, dressed in black raiment like so many dark shadows.

Between these large groups of people was a great space in which that soul was placed by his guide. As he gazed intently and with wonder … in the midst of the space that divided the two groups, a man appeared, advancing, so tall that his very forehead seemed to touch the heavens, while his face seemed to be that of an Ethiopian, so black and horrible it was. [Francesco had no doubt seen unflattering depictions of Ethiopians in connection with Italy's abortive campaign to set up a colony in East Africa.]

At this point the poor soul was completely disconcerted that he felt that his life was suspended. This strange personage approached nearer and nearer, and the guide who was beside the soul informed him that he would have to fight with that creature. At these words the poor little soul turned pale, trembled all over and was about to fall to the ground in a faint, so great was his terror.

The guide supported him with one arm until he recovered somewhat from his fright. The soul then turned to his guide and begged him to spare him from the fury of that sinister being, because [the guide] said [the creature] was so strong that the strength of all men combined would not be sufficient to bring him down.

"Your every resistance is vain. You must fight with this man. Take heart. Enter the combat with confidence. Go forth with courage. I shall be with you. In reward for your victory over him I will give you a shining crown to adorn your brow."

The poor little soul took heart. He entered into combat with the formidable and mysterious creature. The assault [of the creature] was ferocious, but with the help of his guide, who never left his side, [the soul] finally overcame his adversary, threw him to the ground, and forced him to flee.

Then his guide, faithful to his promise, took from beneath his robes a crown of rarest beauty, a beauty that words cannot describe, and placed it on his head. But then he withdrew it again, saying, "I will reserve for you a crown even more beautiful if you fight the good fight with the creature you have just fought. He will continually renew the assault to regain his lost honor. Fight valiantly and do not doubt my aid. Keep your eyes wide open, for that mysterious personage will try to take you by surprise. Do not fear his ... formidable might, but remember what I have promised you: that I will always succeed in conquering him."

When that mysterious man had been vanquished, all the multitude of men of horrible countenance took to flight with shrieks, curses, and deafening cries, while from the other multitude of men came the sound of applause and praise for the splendid man, more radiant than the sun, who had assisted the poor soul so splendidly in the fierce battle. And so the vision ended.[41]

On January 3, 1903, Francesco had just received the Eucharist and was engaged "in intimate conversation with the Lord," when his soul was "suddenly flooded with supernatural light," and he understood in an instant that his entry into religion in the service of the heavenly king was to be a prolonged battle against the mysterious man of hell with whom he had done combat in the previous vision. Then he understood — and this was sufficient to sustain him — that although the demons would be present at his battles to ridicule his failures, the angels would also be there to applaud his victories. He understood his heavenly guide was Jesus Christ, who would sustain him in his battles and "reward him in paradise for the victories he would win, so long as he trusted in Him alone and fought gallantly."[42]

Two days later, the evening before he was to depart from Pietrelcina to Morcone, Francesco felt his "very bones crushed" by the impending separation from his mother and siblings, to the point that he nearly collapsed. Then he experienced his third vision in five days. "The Lord came to comfort him," he wrote, and he "beheld in all their majesty Jesus and His Blessed Mother. They encouraged him and assured him of their love. Jesus, at length, placed a hand on his head. This was sufficient to make him strong in the higher part of his soul, so that he shed not a single tear at his painful parting, although at the moment he was suffering agonies in soul and body."[43]

On January 6, 1903, Francesco bade farewell to his mother and siblings. Giuseppa, in tears, blessed him and told him that henceforth he belonged, not to her, but to Saint Francis. Then, accompanied by his teacher Don Angelo Caccavo, along with two friends, Vincenzo Masone and Antonio Bonavito, who also aspired to the priesthood, Francesco boarded the train. An hour later, they arrived at the station at Morcone, a town nestled on the slopes of Mount Mucre in the Matese Mountains, overlooking the Tammaro River Valley. Don Angelo and the three boys alighted and walked the unpaved, rocky path that led to the friary of Saints Philip and James of the Capuchin province of Sant'Angelo. Fra Cami' answered the door and instantly remembered the boy who had wanted to be a Capuchin so he could have a beard. "Ah, Franci! Bravo! Bravo! You've been faithful to your promise and to the calling of St. Francis!"[44]

Chapter Three

Fra Pio

The Capuchins

The Order of Friars Minor Capuchin traces its origin to Saint Francis of Assisi (c. 1181–1226), who, in 1206, organized a community of men "to observe the Holy Gospel of Our Lord Jesus Christ by living in obedience, without property, and in chastity."[1] Padre Pio was not a "monk," but a "friar" (the word means "brother") — a member of a mendicant, not a monastic, order.

The mendicant orders forbade their members from owning any property, even in common. They were to support themselves through their own labor and the charity of the faithful. In fact, "mendicant" comes from the Latin word meaning "to beg," and mendicant brothers solicit material sustenance through begging. In addition to lives of contemplation and spiritual exercises, members of mendicant orders engage in active service to the community. Unlike a monk, who remains in one place, a mendicant friar may be assigned to any number of residences, called friaries or convents. Padre Pio remained in one convent for more than fifty years, but this was unusual. (The terms "friary," "convent," and "monastery" were used interchangeably.) The distinction, however, between a monk and a friar is appreciated by few outside the religious orders, and for most people, Padre Pio was a "monk."

Most of the friars in the monastery Francesco Forgione entered in 1903 were comparatively young men. The Capuchin order in Italy was just then recovering from more than two decades of suppression by the Italian government. The middle of the nineteenth century had seen a tide of anticlerical sentiment swamp much of Europe. This was a time of rampant nationalism that eventually would explode into World War I. Since the Church had great temporal power and exerted political control over much of central Italy, it found itself the scapegoat for many nationalistic politicians who insisted that the Church was the enemy of the state. Since

Catholics were bound in allegiance to the pope, who in those days was the head of the Papal States (a sovereign state), many European leaders, especially in the newly independent countries of Germany and Italy, considered the Catholic Church and its institutions subversive. During the 1860s and 1870s, both countries tried to weaken the Church's power, and one of the ways they did this was by suppressing the religious orders.

The problem was especially bad in Italy, where the central part of the peninsula had been torn from the political control of the papacy in spite of the vehement opposition by Pope Pius IX, who reigned from 1846 to 1878 and did not hesitate to use excommunication as a weapon against politicians who trod roughshod over the ancient privileges and prerogatives of the Church. Count Cavour, who became Italy's first prime minister in 1861, considered all religious orders "useless and harmful,"[2] and Giuseppe Garibaldi, liberator of southern Italy from the control of the Bourbon monarchy, called priests "wolves" and "assassins" and characterized the pope as "not a true Christian."[3] Some Italian politicians, in fact, called for the army to storm the Vatican and throw members of the College of Cardinals into the Tiber.[4]

Faced with such violent sentiment, in 1864 Pius IX criticized "Liberalism" in his "Syllabus of Errors," arguing against religious toleration, freedom of conscience, and freedom of the press, and denying that the pontiff had any need to accommodate himself to "progress," "Liberalism," or even "modern civilization."[5]

Partly in retaliation, but mostly as a means of raising money, the Italian government legislated in 1866 the dissolution of all religious orders and the confiscation of all their lands and goods. The Capuchin order maintained many of the 38,000 religious institutions that were closed down, with their assets sold to raise money for the Italian government. The friars were forced to become secular clergy, go abroad, or operate in secret.

The policy of selling Church property proved a failure, as most peasants were too poor to buy the parcels of land offered for sale, and the use for confiscated churches, monasteries, and convents was extremely limited. After some twenty years, the state relented, and the Capuchins and other religious orders were once again allowed to wear their habits, live by their Rule, and eventually reclaim most of their churches and convents.

The task of reorganizing the more than a dozen friaries in the Capuchin province of Sant'Angelo, in the "heel" of Italy's boot, fell to the learned and devout Padre Pio Nardone of Benevento (1842–1908), who had ministered in England and India during the time of suppression. Assuming the position of minister provincial (administrator) of the province, he actively recruited young men to restore the death-depleted ranks of the order. He saw to it that the province maintained its ascetical rigor, which prior to the suppression had been among the strictest in all of Italy. Before its dissolution, it was said that many of the friars had "died in the odor of sanctity."

The Novice

For Francesco, as for all religious who were preparing for the priesthood, there was a double formation program: the "religious," which prepared him for community life, and the "ecclesiastical," which prepared him for the priesthood. The ecclesiastical program of studies at that time was usually determined by the student's previous education.

When Francesco arrived at the convent at Morcone, he was shown to a tiny cell in which there was a mattress filled with corn husks and supported by four wooden planks; a little table; a chair; a washstand; a jug for water; and, on the wall, a wooden cross. This first stage of religious life, known as the novitiate, has been compared to "boot camp" in the life of a soldier. Like other novices, Francesco was directed to spend several days in solitary meditation.

On January 22, 1903, sixteen days after his arrival, Francesco was "invested" as a religious, kneeling at the foot of the altar before the master of novices, the formidable Padre Tommaso of Monte Sant'Angelo (1872–1932). His outer clothing was removed as the master declared, "May the Lord strip from you the old man and all his actions." As Francesco put on his Franciscan tunic, Padre Tommaso prayed, "May the Lord reclothe you in the new man who is created according to God, in justice, holiness, and truth." As he put on the hood with its *caperon*, or small scapular, the novice master said, "May the Lord put the hood of salvation upon your head to defeat the wiles of the devil." And when Francesco wrapped the cord around his waist, the novice master prayed, "May the Lord gird you with the cordon of purity and extinguish within your loins the fire of lust so that the virtues of continence and chastity might abide in you." Then the master gave the novice a candle, enjoining him, "Take the light of Christ as a sign of your immortality so that, dead to the world, you might live in God. Rise from the dead, and Christ will give you light!"[6]

The crown of Francesco's head was shaved, as well as the bottom of his hairline, leaving a circlet of hair around the skull. This was the "tonsure," worn by most religious in many parts of Europe until the early 1970s, although photographs show that religious frequently allowed their hair to grow out for long periods of time. The custom supposedly dated from Roman times, when the heads of slaves were routinely shaved. Religious wore the tonsure in token of the fact that they were slaves of Christ.

Francesco received a religious name, apparently completely the choice of the superiors. From now on Francesco would be Fra (or Brother) Pio. Many believe that he was named in honor of the father provincial, Pio of Benevento.

By the end of Padre Pio's life, most Capuchins were known by their family names. Father Solanus Casey, an American Capuchin, renowned as a mystic and servant of the poor (who was beatified in 2017), was nearly two decades Pio's senior, but was always known by his family name, as Capuchins typically were in the United States. So was the famous Irish Capuchin and temperance advocate Father Theobald Mathew, who died in 1856. In Italy, however, well into the twentieth century, Capuchins were known by their place of birth rather than their surname. And so, Francesco Forgione became Pio of Pietrelcina for everyone — except the Italian government, which did not recognize religious names. When he had to sign a legal document, he wrote, "Padre Pio da Pietrelcina, al secolo Francesco Forgione." When he was drafted into the army during World War I, Padre Pio came close to being arrested for desertion when he was home in Pietrelcina on sick leave and orders came for "Francesco Forgione" to report for duty. By that time, everybody knew him as Padre Pio and the message did not get to him.

Since the sixteenth century, the friary at Morcone was the place where Padre Pio's province of Foggia trained its novices. The friary there in 1903 was the home of about fifty religious. It had no central heating, but on the coldest winter nights, after Compline, the religious could gather before the fireplace to warm themselves before returning to their freezing rooms.

The Capuchin Constitutions specified that the senior members of the community, with the exception of the father guardian (the local superior) and the novice master, were to avoid unnecessary communication with the novices. While the other friars wore sandals, novices were required to go barefoot. Every night, except on Sundays, a bell awakened the friars a half hour after midnight. The sleepy men made their way through the corridors of the convent to the chapel, there to prepare for the Divine Office — the prayers and psalms, offered seven times daily, that characterized the life of nearly all religious communities at that time. In "devotion, recollection, mortification, quiet, and silence," as the Constitutions specified, they strove to "remember that they [were] in the presence of God and employ themselves in the angelic exercise of singing the divine praises." After praying the first two hours of the Office, Matins and Lauds, the friars went back to bed.

This repose did not last long, for they had to rise again at 5:00 a.m. Each made his bed and placed a crucifix on it to make it look like a coffin. Then they went to the choir to pray the Angelus, a prayer which begins with the words, "The angel of the Lord declared unto Mary ..." commemorating the Incarnation of Christ. This was followed by the Litany of the Saints. Then the community meditated for half an hour, spending time in mental prayer for the pope, the salvation of souls, the conversion of unbelievers, and the impartation of wisdom to cardinals, bishops, prelates, kings, princes, and superiors. Then followed the Mass known as the *Orazione*, after which the friars prayed the canonical hours of Prime and Terce. This was followed by the community Mass known as the *Messa Conventuale*. At last it was time for the friars to be rewarded with a breakfast of boiled bread and oil, after which they went back to the choir to pray the Divine Office of Our Lady.

Then the novices went to confer with Padre Tommaso of Monte Sant'Angelo, the novice master. According to the Constitutions, the master of novices was to teach his charges to subdue their passions and acquire such virtues as humility, obedience, "angelic purity," self-denial, sacrifice, love of poverty, and the spirit of mortification. He was to instruct them in the Capuchin Rule and the Breviary, which is the book that contains the Divine Office. He instructed them on the lives of the saints, especially those of the Capuchin order, and he supervised their memorization of the Rule. After their time with the master, it was time for the novices to study until they returned to the choir to recite the canonical hours of Sext and None.

At noon, the community, still in the choir, prayed the Angelus again before going to dinner. Both dinner and supper were frugal meals consisting chiefly of bread and stew. The novices frequently suffered from terrible hunger pangs during their first weeks in the community. During most meals, talking was forbidden. While the friars ate, a lesson from the Gospels was read, followed by the reading of the Rule of Saint Francis and then by another from some "pious book."

From November 2 (All Souls' Day) to Holy Saturday, except for the Christmas season, the friars fasted — that is, they were allowed one full meal (such as it was) daily, and two smaller ones that together were not to add up to a full meal. No meat was served apart from the main meal. In lax provinces, the friars made their full meal a huge feast of many courses; but in the province of Sant'Angelo in the early twentieth century, traditions were observed in all their ancient rigor. During weekdays in Lent, no meat was served at all, and on Lenten Fridays the friars were obliged to subsist on bread and water only. This was in accord with the teaching of Saint Francis that "it is difficult to satisfy necessity without yielding to sensuality." Everything was calculated to draw the religious away from an attachment to earthly things — even necessities — and focus his mind on the things of the spirit.

After the midday meal, the community took a brief siesta. At 2:30 p.m. they recited Vespers in the choir and then spent some time doing chores, including manual labor. Even while scrubbing the latrine in the basement, the friars were to recite the Rosary aloud or sing hymns. When chores were over, the community recited the Vespers of Our Lady, after which the novices had another conference with Padre Tommaso. Then they were allowed to take "recreation" in the garden, which meant that they were somewhat free to converse about spiritual things. At 7:00 p.m. they prayed the Rosary in the choir. Then there was another half hour of meditation, more prayers, and Compline, the final canonical "hour" of the Divine Office. After Compline came supper, during which there were readings from the Old and New Testaments. Following the meal, while the rest of the community enjoyed a brief period of recreation, the novices met once more with Padre Tommaso for spiritual counsel. Finally, at 9:00 p.m., after a thirty-minute visit to the Blessed Sacrament in the church, the friars retired for the night. Before going to bed, each friar was expected to pray and examine his conscience. Novices were instructed to sleep on their back in their habit with their arms folded over their chest, in the form of a cross, the better to repel any assaults of the devil.

Throughout the day, the "Evangelical Silence" prevailed, which meant that even during periods of "recreation," which consisted of two periods of one hour in the course of the day when conversation was permitted, the friars were forbidden to talk about worldly matters. The Great Silence, a total ban on all conversation whatsoever, except in cases of dire necessity, was strictly observed between 9:00 p.m. and 5:00 a.m. Anyone who willfully broke either the Evangelical or the Great Silence was required to pray five Our Fathers and five Hail Marys while lying on the floor with his arms extended in the form of a cross.

Great emphasis was placed on the practice of meditation, withdrawing attention from the material world and focusing mind and soul on God. The novices were taught to concentrate their psychic energies on one aspect of Divine Reality, such as one of the names or attributes of God, a passage of Scripture, or an event in the life of Christ. Not all the novices or even the older friars felt divine light break upon them as a result of this activity, but everyone was supposed to meditate the best one could.

Strict obedience to superiors was considered essential for anyone aspiring to the highest state of spirituality. It was part of giving up one's will, dying to oneself. The Capuchin was at all times expected to learn and carry out as diligently as possible the will and desire of his superiors. "Obedience is everything for me," Padre Pio wrote later in life. "God forbid that I should knowingly go against [a superior] who has been designated as my interior and exterior judge, even in the slightest way."[7] Padre Bernardino of Siena recalled that even as a very old man Padre Pio would ask his superiors for permission to do the most trivial things, such as getting his hair cut, changing his habit, and putting on his mantle in cold weather. What many would consider a pathetic lack of initiative and a disturbing dependency is in fact a virtue for those concerned with humility, selflessness, and surrender to the will of God. When, at one period in his life, he was accused of disobedience, Padre Pio cried, "If my superior ordered me to jump out of the window, I would not argue. I would jump!"[8]

Fra Pio and his fellow novices got plenty of opportunities to practice the virtues of humility and obedience under the not-so-tender care of the thirty-one-year-old novice master, Tommaso of Monte Sant'Angelo. A photograph of him taken around this time shows a scowling man with sunken eyes; a short, dark, neatly trimmed beard and moustache; and a grim downturned mouth. After his death at sixty, Padre Tommaso was characterized as a man "with a heart of gold, understanding, and full of charity to his novices."[9] His actions when Pio was a novice, however, are more reminiscent of a character straight out of a Dickens novel. Padre Tommaso felt that he had to carry out the rules of the Capuchin Constitutions to the letter, which prescribed that novices, along with all members of the community, "take the discipline" on Mondays, Wednesdays, and Fridays. This meant going to the choir, pulling up their habits, and striking themselves across the shoulders with a corded whip. The purpose was to subdue the sinful desires of the flesh, especially sexual passions, laziness, and inconstancy. During this exercise, the Constitutions directed the friars to meditate on the Passion of Christ.

Padre Tommaso, however, went a step further. He reportedly ordered the novices to whip themselves until their blood ran onto the floor. Moreover, without warning or apparent provocation, he would order the young novices to administer the discipline at any time or place. During meals, often he would order a hapless novice to go into a corner, strip, and flagellate himself until his back was a mass of bleeding flesh. The slightest infraction of the Rule was an occasion for harsh reproofs, mortifications, and heavy punishments. Sometimes Padre Tommaso would put a wooden collar around a novice's neck, sometimes he would blindfold him, and sometimes he would make him eat off the ground. In the refectory, before eating his meager repast, each novice had to kneel at Padre Tommaso's feet and beseech him, "Father, bless me." If the master answered, "I bless you," the novice could rise and take his place in the dining hall. But if the master remained silent, the boy had to stay there, kneeling on the cold floor until it was Padre Tommaso's pleasure to dispose otherwise. Sometimes novices were forced to remain on their knees for the duration of the meal. For breaking just one of the rules, the master made novices eat bread and water from a plate on the ground, like a dog.[10] Padre Tommaso never gave any explanations.[11] Fifty years later, Padre Pio tearfully recalled to a younger confrere, "One day the Master of the Novices declared [without any explanation], 'Tomorrow there will be no Communion for you.'"[12]

Vincenzo Masone, one of Fra Pio's two friends who entered the novitiate with him, was able to take the stifling regime only two months before he returned home. (The other boy, Bonavita, had been sent home almost immediately because he was judged to be too young.) Then there was a novice from Naples, whose name has not been recorded, who was made to kneel hungry, all through dinner, and muttered, "Back home in Naples we pay a dime to see madmen. Here we see them for free." Padre Tommaso overheard this remark and ordered the boy to strip and take the discipline there and then. The boy refused, got up, and walked out of the convent, never to return.[13]

Fra Pio never complained. When another novice urged him to leave with him, insisting that the master was insane, even diabolical, Pio answered:

> I could never agree to this. You'll see, with Our Lady's and St. Francis' help, we too, little by little, will get used to this new life just as others before us

did. Do you believe the friars here and elsewhere were not once like us? No one is born a friar.[14]

One of his confreres at the time recalled that Pio

… kept to the genuine spirit of his novitiate.… Quite often, when I went to his cell to call him, I found him on his knees at the end of his bed, or with his face buried in his hands over books. Sometimes he failed to appear in the choir for night office, and when I went to call him, I found him on his knees, deeply immersed in prayer. I never heard him complain of the poor food, although the friary could have given us something better. He never criticized the actions of his superiors, and when others did, he either rebuked them or else left their company. He never grumbled about the cold, which was really severe, or about the few blankets we were given. However, what struck me most about Fra Pio was his love of prayer.[15]

Another religious who knew him as a novice recalled that when Pio prayed, "he would weep many tears, so much so that very often the floor would be stained."[16]

Fra Pio appreciated the need to mortify the flesh. A few years later, when writing to a spiritual daughter, he quoted Galatians 5:24, in which Saint Paul declares, "Those who belong to Christ Jesus have crucified the flesh with its passions and desires." Pio wrote:

From this it is apparent that anyone who wants to be a true Christian … must fortify his flesh for no other reason than devotion to Jesus, who, for love of us, mortified his entire body on the cross. The mortification must be constant and steady, not intermittent, and it must last for one's whole life. Moreover, the perfect Christian must not be satisfied with a kind of mortification which merely *appears* to be severe. He must make sure that it hurts … for … all the evils which hurt your soul can be traced to the failure to practice due mortification of the flesh, either through ignorance or lack of the will to do so. If you want to [achieve holiness] you must master your flesh and crucify it, for it is the source of all evil.[17]

As time went on, Pio would modify this position somewhat, as he realized that few people were capable of the degree of ascetical rigor that he imposed on himself.

Novices, in addition to showing detachment from all material pleasures, were supposed to distance themselves from family and friends. Too strong a desire on the part of a novice to see his family was taken as a sign that he lacked a genuine call from God to the order. Unfortunately, no one bothered to explain this practice to Fra Pio's mother when she came one day to visit her son. Giuseppa was escorted into the guest room, and Fra Pio came down to meet her in the company of another friar, who sat a few feet away, immobile, with his head down and eyes lowered. Giuseppa was horrified that her son, instead of embracing her, sat with his hands in his sleeves, looking at the floor. When she gave him a number of presents, he showed no enthusiasm. "Thank you," he said, coldly and quietly, "I will take them to my superior."

Frustrated at her inability to draw her son into any kind of conversation, she cried, "Son, what's the matter? Why have you become mute?" Giuseppa returned in tears to Pietrelcina without either Pio or any of his superiors making any explanation for his behavior. In later years, Padre Pio recalled, "As soon as I saw my mother, my impulse was to throw myself into her arms, but the discipline of the novitiate did not permit this."[18]

It was around this time that Orazio returned home on a visit, and he was horrified at what his wife told him about their son. Hurrying to Morcone, he demanded and received an explanation from Padre Tommaso. He was mollified somewhat but still disturbed by what he thought was unduly harsh treatment of his son and others.

"An Example to All"

As a novice, Fra Pio attracted the favorable attention of his confreres and superiors because of his submissiveness and spiritual fervor. Even Padre Tommaso described him as "an exemplary novice … an example to all."[19] Fra Pio astounded Padre Tommaso by begging permission to be excused from recreation and even from meals in order to pray. So abstemious was Fra Pio that Padre Tommaso often had to command him to eat more. And when he was not praying, Fra Pio seemed to be reading the Bible, often on his knees.

Yet, despite his penances, Fra Pio was always cheerful, and people loved to be with him. When he was permitted to talk enough to display it, he revealed a vivid sense of humor. He loved to tell jokes. Nor was he averse to playing pranks.

One midnight, after the bell had awakened the community for Matins, Fra Pio was returning from the lavatory with a towel draped over his arm when he caught sight of another novice who was a nervous fellow, seemingly frightened of anything. Between them was a large, unlighted room. On a table in the room rested a pair of tall candlesticks that jingled whenever anyone walked by. Between the candlesticks was a hideous, terrifying skull, such as friaries and monasteries kept in those days to remind their residents of the transitory nature of life. Knowing the other novice was deathly afraid of the skull, Fra Pio hid behind the table in the dark, without the other boy noticing. When the boy passed, Fra Pio waved the towel in a ghostly manner and groaned a "mysterious lament." The nervous novice took off down the corridor, screaming, while Fra Pio, afraid that they would be discovered by Padre Tommaso, ran after him, trying to calm him down. The terror-struck lad became hysterical when he heard footsteps behind him. When Fra Pio called his name, the fearful novice, absolutely beside himself, stumbled and fell, and his pursuer, unable to stop, fell right on top of him. "Quiet! Don't be afraid! It's just me," Fra Pio said. The victim was so terrorized, "he didn't even know where he was," the prankster recounted years later.[20]

In the next few years, whenever, for reasons of health that will be described later, Fra Pio was forced to return home, everyone in the friary where he lived was downcast. Even Padre Tommaso missed him. One friar recalled that his absence left "a great void in our friary and in our hearts, and we lived in hope that these absences would not be long."[21]

At the end of the yearlong novitiate, the community held a Chapter to decide which novices should be invited to make their temporary vows and which should be dismissed. For nearly two weeks before the ceremony, Fra Pio's anxiety was obvious to everyone, as he spent his time in prayer and tears.[22] Finally, on January 22, 1904, Fra Pio went to the altar and knelt before minister provincial Padre Pio of Benevento. He folded his hands between those of the older man and declared, "I, Fra Pio of Pietrelcina, vow and promise to the Omnipotent God, to the Blessed Virgin Mary, to St. Francis, and to all the saints, and to you, Father, to observe for three years the Rule of the Friars Minor, confirmed by Pope Honorius, living in obedience, without property, and in chastity."

Pio of Benevento answered, "And I, on the part of God, if you observe these things, promise you eternal life."[23]

Three days later, the boy whom his superiors described as one of "impeccable deportment" and notable for "the attraction he exerts on everyone with whom he has contact" left Morcone with the minister provincial and another young friar and journeyed twenty miles north to the town of Sant'Elia a Pianisi, to the friary of St. Francis of Assisi. Here Fra Pio was to commence six years of intensive study for the priesthood and prepare for his profession of solemn vows.

At that time and place, an aspirant to the priesthood in the Capuchin order was not required to earn a college degree (although a few did). He simply took required courses that were offered at the particular friary where the father lector qualified to teach that course happened to be residing. Therefore, during his course of study, a candidate for the priesthood could expect to be transferred to several friaries within the province, to be instructed in logic, philosophy, Sacred Scripture, dogmatic and moral theology, pastoral theology, Church history, patrology, canon law, and the Rule. After ordination, a priest was expected to study "sacred eloquence" for a year. If he wanted permission to preach (and not all priests had this), he had to take further course work and then submit to an examination for a preaching license. Students were generally not issued books, which the province could not afford, but were allowed to share the text from which the teacher lectured. The students were expected to take notes in preparation for an oral exam and a written paper.[24]

In 1905, Fra Pio was sent to the friary at San Marco la Catola, a little town built around a ruined castle, some ten miles southeast of Sant'Elia, to study philosophy. In 1906, he was back at Sant'Elia for further studies in logic and philosophy. It was there, the following year, that he pronounced his solemn, or permanent vows, ratifying the promise of three years previous to live the rest of his life in poverty, chastity, and obedience in accordance with the Rule of the Friars Minor. After that, he was sent to Serracapriola, about twenty miles northeast of Sant'Elia, to study Church history and patrology under Padre Agostino of San Marco in Lamis, and fundamental theology and biblical hermeneutics with Padre Bonaventura of San Giovanni Rotondo. The following year he traveled some seventy miles to Montefusco, near the west coast of Italy, to study Sacred Scripture, Church history, and patrology under Padre Agostino and dogmatic theology under Padre Bernadino of San Giovanni Rotondo. The latter later described him as an "ordinary student," though he was impressed by the young man's conduct: "Amidst the lively, noisy students, he was quiet and calm, even during recreation. He was always humble, meek, and obedient."[25] In 1909, Pio went to Gesualdo to study canon law with Padre Bonaventura.[26]

"Let Me Know Who in the House Has Satisfied the Easter Duty"

It is not clear how often Fra Pio saw his parents, but it probably was not often. He wrote them letters like the following undated one, which seems formal, distant, formulaic, and preachy:

> Meanwhile I wish you a very long life, adorned with every prosperity, and full of blessings, celestial and terrestrial. This and nothing else is my prayer that I lift up to Jesus these days, and I will be happy if it is pleasing to the Lord, that you carry out, with all his blessings, these requests of mine.
>
> Therefore I hope that you will not be among those Christians spending all Easter in purely sensual pleasure, because this is completely contrary to the spirit and law of Jesus Christ; but instead, I exhort you to walk always more on the road of God, remembering that sooner or later we must present ourselves at the tribunal of God.
>
> To this end, therefore, I exhort you not to neglect your Easter duty, the only means of our health. Therefore let me know who in the house has satisfied the Easter duty.[27]

Early in 1908, Pio received a letter from his father, who was back in Pietrelcina for the wedding of Pio's brother Michele to Giuseppa Cardone, but he answered that he was too busy to attend:

Dearest Father,

I respond at once to your dear letter, rejoicing with you that everybody there is in good health.

I'm very pleased about my brother's upcoming wedding, and therefore I wish for a good celebration. Also, I would like to assist at the wedding celebration, if it were possible; unfortunately, because, as you have to know, these days I'm a bit busy with my exams, that will take place in days, so that I can stand, therefore, before the bishop to receive minor orders. Now you understand very well that it will be impossible for me [to come]. Perhaps [if it weren't] for this circumstance, it would be easy for me to satisfy you. Anyway, don't be upset that I'm not there; think instead that if God assists me, the day will come [when] I promise to give you a consolation greater than that I would be able to give you if [I were] present at the celebration of this wedding.[28]

A year after his wedding, Michele Forgione sailed to New York from Naples on the ship *Madonna*, reaching Ellis Island on May 12, 1909.[29] Orazio also returned to the United States, although, as before, there is no record of him.

Pio and the Bible

By the time Fra Pio was beginning his studies for the priesthood, nontraditional religious thinking was making inroads in nearly all Christian denominations. Biblical scholars of the Modernist movement were seeking to reinterpret Catholic doctrine in light of modern science and philosophy. Questioning the inerrancy of Scripture, they contended that the writers of both Old and New Testaments were conditioned by the times in which they lived and that, therefore, religious truth was subject to a constant evolutionary process. Rather than spirituality and the inner life emphasized by many traditional religious leaders, both Catholic and Protestant, they tended to stress social reform. Pope Pius X clamped down severely on liberalism in the Catholic Church and condemned Modernism as "the synthesis of all heresies." Eventually, the most intractable of the modernizers were forced from the priesthood or left voluntarily.

What effect the Modernist movement had on Padre Pio's intellectual or spiritual growth is conjectural. Most likely it had none at all. The Capuchin order appears to have been extremely conservative at the time and a bastion of historical Christianity and traditional Catholicism. Fra Pio's theological training centered on the Bible, the Church Fathers, and a handful of mystical theologians.

Knowledge of Sacred Scripture was considered essential. The numerous letters that Padre Pio wrote over the years to his spiritual directors and spiritual children make it clear he knew the Bible thoroughly — although he never quotes chapter and verse, and sometimes his quotations are slightly inaccurate, as if he was writing from memory. His letters are often a series of Bible quotations or paraphrases. He seems to have been as thoroughly familiar with the minor prophets as he was with the Gospels. Frequently, Padre Pio would tell a spiritual child that what he was advising was not his own opinion but God's word, because it was from the Bible. If the Bible said something, that was the end of all argument. A statement from Scripture was, he insisted, "a sure and infallible argument."[30] At a time when few lay people, at least in southern Italy, had Bibles, he would insist that his spiritual children study Scripture. "As regards your reading matter," he would write to one of his disciples, "there is little [contemporary literature] that is admirable and nearly nothing that is edifying. It is absolutely necessary for you to add to such reading that of the Scriptures, so recommended by all the Fathers of the Church."[31]

A Victim of Divine Love

Besides the Scriptures and the early Church Fathers, Fra Pio studied thoroughly the teachings of the Dominican Saint Thomas Aquinas (c. 1225–1274) and the Franciscan Saint Bonaventure (1221–1274). Fra Pio was probably influenced most by the Spanish Carmelite mystical theologians Saint Teresa of Ávila (1515–1582) and Saint John of the Cross (1542–1591). Their teachings about prayer, contemplation, self-detachment, and the inner life embodied the spirit of the Capuchin order at the time.

Through his study of Saint Teresa and Saint John of the Cross, two principles were reinforced for Fra Pio: total commitment to Christ and the embrace of suffering. So total must a Christian's commitment be to God that he should be able cheerfully to renounce everything else in life, even innocent pleasures. Identification with Christ means identification with his cross. Suffering is beneficial, when joined to that of Christ. Saint Paul writes, "Now I rejoice in my sufferings for your sake, and in my flesh I complete what is lacking in Christ's afflictions for the sake of his body, that is, the Church" (Col 1:24). Saint Paul does not mean that Christ's saving work is insufficient or that he really needs man's help, but rather that when Christ offered himself for the sins of humanity, his oblation included the sufferings offered to God by his followers throughout the ages; that when Christians offer their sufferings to him, Christ, in eternity, joins them to his own. The more a Christian fully gives himself up to Christ, the closer he is drawn into the Savior's love as well as into his sufferings.

Fra Pio was taught that suffering, therefore, might even be courted by some souls. Christ grants to his beloved the *privilege* of sharing his mission. For this reason, and not for any masochistic motive, suffering can be seen as desirable, because it brings about the salvation of souls. Saint John of the Cross encourages the Christian to "strive always to choose, not that which is easiest, but that which is most difficult; not what is most delightful, but what is most unpleasing; not that which gives the most pleasure, but what gives no pleasure."[32] Padre Pio no doubt had this counsel in mind when, in his fifties, he spoke of a deceased member of his religious community:

> That blessed priest, when he was here in our family, almost every day, after dinner, when I was trying to get some rest, would come to talk about his troubles to me. It took a great deal of sacrifice to listen to him. Now, every day, at the same hour, as a reward for the sacrifices he forced me to make, I say a holy Rosary for his soul, even if I feel tired and exhausted.[33]

Fra Pio was drawn to offer himself as a "victim of divine love," to suffer with Christ in order to win souls. In the tradition in which Fra Pio grew to spiritual maturity, more souls were thought to be won to Christ through the suffering of devoted men and women than through preaching, writing, or personal persuasion. The idea of offering oneself as "a victim of divine love" is implied in much of what Saint Teresa and Saint John wrote, but it seems to have been only in Fra Pio's time and shortly before that certain devout people came to make specific acts of oblation of themselves as "victims."

One such victim soul was the then recently deceased French Carmelite nun Sister Thérèse of the Child Jesus (1873–1897), who would be canonized in 1925. Her autobiography was published about the time that Fra Pio first decided that he wanted to be a Capuchin. He read *The Story of a Soul* when he was a student and learned that Thérèse, who died prematurely of painful tuberculosis, had made a special offering of herself as "a burnt sacrifice to the merciful love of Our God." Another relatively recent "victim of divine love" was Gemma Galgani (1878–1903), known as "The Virgin of Lucca," who, like Thérèse, died of consumption in her twenties. Fra Pio pored over her letters, committing many of them to memory, to the point that, in writing to his spiritual directors, he would express himself in her words.[34] Gemma, who was canonized in 1940, had many visions and ecstasies, in one of which she claimed that Jesus told her, "My child, I have need of victims, and strong victims, who by their sufferings, tribulations, and difficulties, make amends for sinners and for their ingratitude." Galgani responded, "I am the victim and Jesus the sacrificing priest. Act quickly. All that Jesus wills I desire. Everything that Jesus sends me is a gift."[35] As in the case of Saint Thérèse, Saint Gemma's act of offering was followed by increased physical, mental, and spiritual suffering, which, in the last two years of her life, included the stigmata — bleeding wounds in the hands, feet, and breast, corresponding to those of Christ's Passion.

Padre Pio several times quoted from a recently published book of Gemma's letters in his writings to his spiritual directors. For instance, he wrote to Padre Agostino in March 1912: "My heart, hands, and feet seem to have been pierced with a sword, the suffering is so great.... And meanwhile the devil never ceased to appear before me in his hideous guises and to beat me in a terribly frightening way."[36]

One biographer judged Pio's quotations, virtually word for word, from Gemma's work, as evidence of dishonesty on his part, especially since, in one of his letters, he expressed the desire to own a copy of Gemma's *Letters and Ecstasies*. Padre Pio had a tendency, in his letters, to quote from other writers without any citation. He sometimes quoted passages from the letters of his spiritual directors when writing to people who asked for counseling. In some of them, making reference to medical procedures of an earlier time, he seems to be quoting from some earlier devotional work. He was, however, not preparing a thesis, nor was he writing for publication. In quoting others, he was simply trying to express how he felt or give counsel to others. Sometimes, especially when he was quoting the Bible, Padre Pio identified his source, at least generally; other times he did not. He evidently saw no reason to quote his sources all the time. Gemma Galgani's writings obviously moved him tremendously, and he identified intensely with her sentiments. He may have had access only to excerpts from Gemma's book, and it was likely for this reason, and not to deceive, that he expressed a desire to read the entire work.

Despite the talk of "appeasing" God and "making reparation" for sins, none of these victim souls ever thought they were doing Jesus a favor or manipulating God, as these words of Padre Pio, spoken to Christ in ecstasy a few years later, indicate:

> I want to help you.... Can't you make me strong? ... I have to tell you that it grieves me to see you in this way. Have they committed many offenses against you lately? ... They have burdened you still again! ... I too can help you.... Make it possible for me to help you with that heavy, heavy cross.... Can't they make it any smaller? ... Ah, Jesus, you're right ... I am weak ... but, my Jesus, what can I do? ... Can't you help me? ... I'm aware of the impossibility ... but to support you if nothing else ... May I help you this evening? ... You don't need me.... Shall I keep myself ready? ... You are there ... what is there to fear?[37]

Chapter Four

Encounters with the Invisible World

"Manifestations and Divine Locutions"

From the beginning of his seminary studies, Fra Pio heard heavenly voices and experienced visions, a matter which is sure to make many modern people uncomfortable, and tempt many to dismiss the Capuchin as a madman or liar — or, at the very least, badly deluded. Yet, without seriously considering these manifestations, one cannot hope to understand Padre Pio, whose very existence was intertwined with the invisible world.

It would seem that from his study of Saint Teresa, Saint John of the Cross, and other mystical writers, Fra Pio learned to distinguish between three types of visions: the bodily, the imaginative, and the intellectual. A bodily vision is what most people usually have in mind when they talk about a vision. If, wide awake, I walked into my living room and, with the same organs of sight with which I perceive my furniture and my books, saw Padre Pio, I would be (assuming that I am not hallucinating) having a bodily vision. Actually, this type of vision was distrusted by both Saint Teresa of Ávila and Saint John of the Cross, partly because of the great difficulty involved in distinguishing a true vision from a hallucination. The only time bodily visions were to be taken seriously was when they were totally unsought.

Padre Pio had numerous bodily visions of celestial as well as infernal beings who were as vividly present to him as were his flesh-and-blood colleagues. As we will see, he claimed that he was beaten and bloodied by demons and that he actually kissed the hands of Christ. He told another priest, "I see my guardian angel just like I see you."[1]

The imaginative vision is hard to describe. To say that a vision is "imaginative" by no means implies that it is not real — that it is a figment of the visionary's imagination. In an imaginative vision, supersensible wisdom is infused into the soul by means of images already in the subject's imagination. It is like an allegory.

Although at the time he used the word "intellectual" to describe it, Fra Pio's vision of the black giant (described in chapter 2) really corresponds to what is classically known as an imaginative vision — a vision in which, as Pio recounts, the bodily senses are suspended and the subject "sees" reality symbolically. God wished to infuse in him some knowledge of his future work and did so by using pictures and images already in his mind.

The intellectual vision has been described as pure understanding, without any impression of images on the senses. This is a "vision," Teresa of Ávila says, which is "not seen at all." Angela of Foligno (1248–1309), an Italian mystic, describes such visions:

> At times God comes into the soul without being called; and he instills into [the soul] fire, love, and sometimes sweetness; and the soul believes this comes from God, and delights therein. But [the soul] does not yet know or see that he dwells in her; she perceives his graces, in which she delights…. Beyond that the soul receives the gift of seeing God. God says to her, "Behold me!", and the soul sees him dwelling within her. She sees him more clearly than one man sees another. For the eyes of the soul behold a [wealth] of which I cannot speak; a [wealth] which is not bodily, but spiritual, of which I can say nothing.[2]

Fifteen-year-old Francesco's "purely intellectual" revelation of January 3, 1903, when he was "suddenly flooded with supernatural light" (also described in chapter 2), providing the meaning of his imaginative vision of two days previous, was probably an example of this third type of vision.

Padre Pio actually understood his supersensible experiences as belonging to two categories: "manifestations and apparitions which are purely supernatural and without form" and those "under human form." Those manifestations that are "purely supernatural," he claimed, all "concern God, his perfections and his attributes." He drew this analogy:

> Let's stand before a mirror. What do we see? Nothing but a human image. Our intellect, if it is not deranged, will have no doubt that this image is our own.
>
> Now, let us suppose that everybody wants to prove that we are deceived in wishing to believe that the image which we see in the mirror is ours. Could they possibly succeed in dissuading us from our conviction or even causing the slightest doubt to rise within us? No, certainly not.
>
> Well, the same thing happens to me in these manifestations and divine locutions. The soul beholds these heavenly secrets, these divine perfections, and these godly attributes much better than we see our image in a mirror. My efforts to doubt their reality succeed in nothing other than making my soul stronger in its conviction. I do not know whether you have ever seen a great

fire come in contact with a drop of water. This small amount of water fails to quench the flames, but, on the contrary, we see that it serves to stir them up even more. This happens to me when I try, with all my strength, to doubt that these things have their origin in God.

He went on to say that one can neither separate the image from the mirror, nor touch it physically:

> And yet the same image exists outside of us if not apart from us…. The same thing happens to me. My soul remains fundamentally convinced that these heavenly manifestations cannot come except from God, even though with my reason I attempt to question this. But just as it is impossible to separate one's image from a mirror and touch it at the same time, it is still more difficult to succeed in committing these heavenly secrets to writing, simply because of the inadequacy of the human language. The soul, without deceiving itself, can affirm only what these are not.[3]

Referring to the bodily, or "human" manifestations, Pio wrote that they are usually visions of the Lord in human form — at the Last Supper; in the Garden of Gethsemane; scourged, bound to a column; or glorious and resplendent in the Resurrection and Ascension. There were visions of the Virgin Mary and "other exalted heavenly beings." Although these were "in human form and appearance," and he could describe them more accurately than the visions without form, he preferred to remain "in perfect reticence, because we do wrong when, in expressing ourselves, we do not see the great distance between the thing that is perceived within our consciousness and that which we are able to express in words."[4]

Pio wrote of these supernatural manifestations:

> I always emerge from them more steeped in a sense of my own unworthiness. In this light I realize that I am the most miserable of the creatures that have ever seen the light. I feel greatly detached from this wretched world. I feel that I'm in a land of exile … and I suffer immensely in seeing how few among my companions in misery aspire as I do to the Promised Land. I always feel ever more filled full of the goodness of God, and I groan that there might be at least a few who love him wholeheartedly. I suffer in seeing myself so poor, for no other reason than that of not being able to offer anything as a sign of gratitude to so excellent a Benefactor.[5]

Another result of these "manifestations" was a great continuous peace. "I feel myself strongly consumed by an exceedingly powerful desire to please God," Pio wrote. "The Lord who favored me with this grace causes me to look with immense revulsion on that which does not help me draw near to God."[6]

Padre Benedetto

Fra Pio exceedingly was reluctant to discuss his "heavenly secrets" with anybody, but through "Holy Obedience" he was bound to do so with his superiors, who decided that it was advisable to assign him a spiritual director. Under this arrangement, the disciple would make a commitment of obedience to his spiritual director. Unless the director counseled an obviously sinful act, the disciple would be bound to obey him exactly, as the "internal and external judge" of his soul. If the director should lead the disciple into sin, he and not the "spiritual child" would have to answer before God.

A spiritual director is supposed to be both learned and holy, and Fra Pio's superiors settled on a man who was considered to be one of the holiest and most learned in the province. Padre Benedetto Nardella of San Marco in Lamis, then in his mid-thirties, was a professor of philosophy and physics. Fra Pio had studied under him from 1905 to 1906, and Benedetto had been very much impressed by the young man's spiritual precocity. It was said that he himself was a mystic, at times the recipient of visions and locutions.

Benedetto was born in 1872 in the town of San Marco in Lamis, five miles west of San Giovanni Rotondo, where Pio would live most of his adult life. He entered the Capuchin order at eighteen and was ordained at twenty-six. By his thirties, he was a respected theologian and considered an authority on mysticism. He published nine books, most of which dealt with mysticism and the inner life. A celebrated preacher, Padre Benedetto was greatly in demand in southern Italy. When Padre Pio of Benevento died in 1908, Benedetto was elected to replace him as minister provincial.

Photographs of Padre Benedetto show an impressive-looking man of stout build with light eyes, and a full head of hair, whose strong, regular features were almost obscured by a gigantic beard. From his letters to Fra Pio, Padre Benedetto appears to have been somewhat distant and not a little authoritative. At times, he seemed almost tyrannical and was characterized by Fra Pio as stubborn. Even so, Fra Pio always held the man he addressed in his letters as "Daddy" in utmost reverence and respect. As his spiritual director, Padre Benedetto insisted that Fra Pio describe to him in detail all his mystical experiences; they were to be submitted "to the judgment of the one who directs you." Padre Benedetto warned that revelations that seemed certain and thoroughly reliable could come from nature, the devil, or "the very propensity or fondness we have for believing what we consider to be revealed." When the younger man was uncertain as to whether or not he was pleasing God, Padre Benedetto urged him to trust in his director's judgment as totally as a blind man trusts the person or dog who leads him. Padre Pio was later to write that in his various spiritual trials he could find calm only in the counsels of Padre Benedetto of San Marco in Lamis.

Padre Agostino

As a student, Fra Pio formed a deep and lasting relationship with another teacher, Padre Agostino of San Marco in Lamis, under whom he studied sacred theology at Serracapriola in 1907. Padre Agostino came from the same town as Benedetto. Born Michele Daniele in 1880, he entered the Capuchin order after graduation from a public high school. In March 1903, two months after Fra Pio entered the novitiate, he was ordained a priest. Renowned as a preacher, Padre Agostino studied French and Greek in university and earned a degree in philosophy.

Padre Agostino was a large, heavy man, whom some called, behind his back, "Big Daddy." His enormous forked beard was then brown, and he had rosy cheeks and a booming bass voice. He seems to have been more warm and approachable than Padre Benedetto. In fact, since Padre Agostino was only slightly older than Fra Pio, the "Dear Professor" became his lifelong confidant and probably his best friend. When they lived at the same convent, Padre Agostino was Fra Pio's confessor. Fra Pio often poured out his heart on paper to Padre Agostino, instructing him to forward the letter to Padre Benedetto, who would, upon receiving it, offer his advice. In this sense, Padre Benedetto and Padre Agostino formed a team in their direction of Pio.

Padre Agostino was not a mystic, however, and there were certain things he could not understand as clearly as Padre Benedetto did. In 1946, Padre Pio told one of his confreres, who asked about the advisability of having a spiritual director, "It is usually sufficient to have a confessor. If the confessor is incapable of understanding spiritual matters, you should simply trust in the goodness of God."

"Don't you have a spiritual director?" the man asked Pio.

"I had one," Pio answered, "and he was Padre Benedetto. But since they took him from me, I have been without one."

When asked, "Don't you have Padre Agostino for your confessor?" Pio answered, "Yes, but he doesn't understand me and I have to carry on putting my trust in God."[7]

Nonetheless, the mutual affection between Padre Pio and Padre Agostino was very deep. Their letters abound with expressions of affection. Pio sometimes called Padre Agostino, "The most beloved person in the world." Agostino, in 1912 wrote, "My dear son, I love you very much, as God wishes me to, and I desire nothing other than to embrace you here below again and then to be together with you forever in heaven with our most merciful Lord."[8]

During his Capuchin student years, knowledge of the supernatural events in Fra Pio's life was limited to Padre Benedetto. Even Padre Agostino knew nothing about these things until 1911. Although impressed by the young man's goodness, obedience, and diligence, Padre Agostino was, at that time, "unaware of anything extraordinary or supernatural." Even so, some remarkable events were taking place.

"The Madonna Carried Me Away … to Your Mansion"

One of the most remarkable — and best documented — of these events took place two years after Fra Pio's entry into religious life. He was then studying at Sant'Elia a Pianisi. He described his experience in writing within three weeks of its occurrence and consigned it to his superiors. The archives of the friary of Santa Maria delle Grazie at San Giovanni Rotondo have preserved Fra Pio's deposition, dated February 1905:

> Several days ago, I had an extraordinary experience. Around 11:00 p.m. on January 18, 1905, Fra Anastasio and I were in the choir when suddenly I found myself far away in a wealthy home where the father was dying while a child was being born. Then the Most Blessed Virgin Mary appeared to me and said to me: "I am entrusting this child to you. Now she is a diamond in the rough, but I want you to work with her, polish her, and make her as shining as possible, because one day I wish to adorn myself with her."
>
> I answered, "How is this possible, since I am still a mere seminarian and do not yet know whether I will one day have the fortune and joy of being a priest? And even if I become a priest, how can I take care of this child, since I am so far away?"
>
> The Madonna said, "Do not doubt. She will come to you, but first you will meet her at St. Peter's in Rome." After that I found myself again in the choir.[9]

That very night, January 18, 1905, some three hundred fifty miles to the north, in the city of Udine, a wealthy man in his early forties named Giovanni Battista Rizzani was dying. He had been taken ill shortly after his wife, Leonilde, had become pregnant with their sixth child. Rizzani was a fervent Mason and would have nothing to do with the Church or religion. As his illness progressed, he grew even more hardened and strictly forbade his wife to summon a priest. When it was apparent that the end was near, his Masonic friends surrounded the house day and night to frustrate the efforts of any priest to see the dying man.

Leonilde, a devout Christian, prayed fervently to God that her husband might put his trust in the Lord before he died. About the same time that Fra Pio had his experience in the choir at Sant'Elia a Pianisi, Leonilde was kneeling in prayer by the bedside of her husband, who was now in a coma. Suddenly she looked up and saw a young man. She recognized his Capuchin habit but did not get a good look at his face. As soon as she saw him, he left the room. Leonilde got up to follow him, but he seemed to vanish into thin air!

She had no time to try to figure out an explanation for the appearance and disappearance of this strange young man, for the family dog immediately began to howl — a harbinger, it was believed, of imminent death. Unable to stand the baying, Leonilde decided to go into the yard and untie the dog. Before she reached the doorway, however, the distraught woman, then in her eighth month, was seized with labor pains. She called the family business manager, who lived on the premises, and he successfully helped her deliver her baby girl.

Within moments, the mother gathered the child in her arms, laid the baby on a bed, and returned to her husband's side. The business manager went outside and demanded that the Masons admit the priest, who was trying to enter. Even if they were carrying out the wishes of their friend who refused to see a priest, he said, they had no right to bar him from entering to baptize a premature baby. They relented, and the priest went into the house. Just as he entered the sickroom, the dying man opened his eyes, regained consciousness for a short time, looked at the priest, and said distinctly: "My God! My God! Forgive me!" The priest was able to administer the last rites, and the sick man died the next morning.

In order to comprehend fully what took place in 1905, we have to advance in time to the year 1922. After her husband's death, Leonilde moved to Rome with her children. In the summer of 1922, Giovanna, the girl born the night of her father's death, was in St. Peter's Basilica with a friend. She was about to enter college and was troubled. Her high school teachers had instilled serious doubts in her mind about the doctrine of the Trinity. She wanted to make her confession as well as talk to a priest about her dilemma. A guard told Giovanna and her friend that all the priests who were hearing confessions had already left, as it was almost time for the basilica to close for the day. Before they could exit the church, however, the girls encountered a young Capuchin priest who said that he would gladly hear Giovanna's confession.

When Giovanna told the priest about her theological problem, he explained the doctrine of the Holy Trinity in such a way as to dispel all her doubts. Giovanna emerged from the confessional and stood, waiting with her friend for the priest to emerge from his side of the booth. The only person to appear was an irate guard who demanded: "What are you doing here? We're closed. You have to leave the basilica. Come tomorrow morning and you'll be able to make your confession."

"But I already made my confession," Giovanna explained to him. "We're waiting for the priest to come out of the confessional so that we can kiss his hand. He's a Capuchin Father."

The guard went up to the confessional and opened the door to the priest's compartment. "You see, young ladies, there's no one here!"

"But where did he go?" Giovanna exclaimed. "We've been standing here, watching, and we haven't seen him leave!" The girls agreed that there was no way the priest could have left the confessional without being seen by them.

That fall, Giovanna entered college. Sometime the following year, she was shown a picture of Padre Pio, who was by then becoming well-known in Italy, although she had never heard of him. She thought he resembled the Capuchin priest whom she had encountered at St. Peter's and wondered whether it might in fact have been he. She dismissed the idea and thought no more of it until the following summer when she decided to go to see Padre Pio, along with an aunt and several friends. It was late afternoon when, standing in a crowd of people in the sacristy of the church, Giovanna caught her first glimpse of Padre Pio. To her amazement, he came up to her and extended his hand for her to kiss (as was the custom with priests in southern Italy), exclaiming, "Why, Giovanna! I know you! You were born the day your father died."

Giovanna was nonplussed. How could this man have known such a thing? The next day, Giovanna made her confession to Padre Pio, after which he said to her, "At last you have come to me, my dear child. I've been waiting for you for so many years!"

"Father, what do you want of me?" the young woman asked. "I don't know you." She had come to San Giovanni Rotondo the previous day with her aunt and had never been there before. "Perhaps you're mistaken and have confused me with some other girl."

"No," said Padre Pio. "I am not mistaken. I knew you before."

"No, Father," Giovanna objected. "I don't know you. I never saw you before."

"Last year," Pio continued, "one summer afternoon, you went with a friend to St. Peter's Basilica and you made your confession before a Capuchin priest. Do you remember?"

"Yes, Father, I do."

"Well, I was that Capuchin."

The student listened in absolute amazement as the priest continued: "Dear child, listen to me. When you were about to come into the world, the Madonna carried me away to Udine, to your mansion. She had me assist at the death of your father and she told me, 'See, in this very room a man is dying. He is the head of a family. He is saved through the tears and prayers of his wife and through my intercession. The wife of the dying man is about to give birth to a child. I entrust this child to you. But first you will meet her at St. Peter's.' Last year I met you at St. Peter's, and now you have come here to San Giovanni Rotondo on your own accord, without my sending for you. And now let me take care of your soul, as the Heavenly Lady desires."

Giovanna burst into tears. "Father, since I'm your responsibility, take care of me," she answered. "Tell me what I must do. Shall I become a nun?"

The Padre responded, "By no means! You will come often to San Giovanni Rotondo. I will take charge of your soul, and you will know the will of God."

Giovanna told her mother what had happened, and so she went to see Padre

Pio herself. He told her: "Madame, that little monk whom you saw walking towards the gallery of your mansion in Udine when your husband was dying — was me. I can assure you that your husband is saved. The Madonna, who appeared to me in the mansion and bade me pray for your dying husband, told me that Jesus had pardoned all his sins and that he was saved through her maternal intercession."[10] Both Giovanna and her mother utterly were convinced.

Giovanna Rizzani, who became the Marchioness Boschi of Cesena, remained a devoted disciple of Padre Pio and later gave a detailed deposition before the Archepiscopal Curia of Manfredonia. The curia noted that her account of what Padre Pio had told her about her birth and her father's death when she first talked to him at length in 1923 was in exact agreement with the account Padre Pio had written in 1905 — a document which the marchioness had not yet read. Padre Pio's account of his bilocation had been given to his superiors, and they had not shared it with anyone.

"Something That Distinguished Him from the Other Students"

During his years of study, except for Padre Benedetto and a handful of his superiors, Fra Pio's confreres — including his fellow students — knew nothing about his mystical or supernatural experiences, about which he never spoke. They were, however, aware that he was different. Padre Guglielmo of San Giovanni Rotondo, who was just a year Pio's senior, wrote of the "purity that was revealed by the great modesty in his eyes ... the penances he asked with insistence to perform ... the change in his countenance that could be observed when he unexpectedly encountered an immodest picture ... his betrayal of distress when he observed in others an action of a dubious nature — all of these proof of his love and angelic virtue."[11]

Padre Raffaele D'Addario of Sant'Elia a Pianisi (1890–1974), who studied with Pio and became a close friend, recalled, "In particular, he aroused in me a sense of great admiration for his exemplary conduct." Whenever Padre Raffaele encountered Pio, whether in the hallway, the choir, in the sacristy, or in the garden, the latter always seemed to be in a state of recollection — that is, an awareness of God's presence. "There was never the danger that he would say a single word that was not necessary," Padre Raffaele recalled. "Though I was still very young and no expert on virtue, I noticed something in him that distinguished him from the other students."[12]

Padre Damaso of Sant'Elia a Pianisi (1889–1970) had a similar observation. He found Pio "a little different from the others.... He was more lovable, and he knew how to say just the right thing to [the younger] boys. He would suggest something in the way of advice in a very sweet manner, and we used to listen to him of our own accord."[13]

There was something other than his sterling character that drew the attention and solicitude of others — Fra Pio's precarious health.

Chapter Five

"A Holy Priest, a Perfect Victim"

A Mysterious Illness

Fra Pio was plagued by a variety of ill-defined physical problems from the very beginning of his novitiate. He suffered from intestinal irritability and attacks of vomiting so intense that he was sometimes unable to retain food for weeks on end. Once, for a space of six months, he was forced to subsist largely on milk. He suffered from spasms of violent coughing, was tormented by headaches, and frequently ran high temperatures. Several times he was sent home to try to regain his health. Repeatedly, Fra Pio seemed to be reduced almost to the point of death, only to recover just as suddenly. His superiors, with the help of medical consultation, tried unsuccessfully to pinpoint the cause of his physical afflictions.

In 1908, while Fra Pio was studying at the friary of St. Egidio at Montefusco, physicians made a devastating diagnosis. Noting the weakness of the twenty-one-year-old patient, coupled with his severe respiratory symptoms and his fevers, which were most severe at night, they diagnosed him with an active case of tuberculosis of the lungs, a disease that exacted a tremendous toll among the overworked and undernourished peasantry of southern Italy at the time. The diagnosis of this contagious, life-threatening disease indicated that Fra Pio would have to remain outside the friary indefinitely.

Orazio (who was home at the time) and Giuseppa were not satisfied with their son's diagnosis and took him to Andrea Cardone, a young doctor in Pietrelcina. Cardone, who boasted of a doctorate in medicine (as many practitioners in southern Italy at the time could not), was said to have been a brilliant physician who, even in his nineties, kept abreast of the latest medical advances. Cardone took issue with the diagnosis of tuberculosis, but, just to be sure, he convinced Pio's parents to send him to specialists some sixty miles away in Naples, who confirmed that the friar was not suffering from any form of tuberculosis.

However, the doctors in Naples were not able to say what was wrong with Fra Pio. Cardone was convinced that his illness was a case of chronic bronchitis aggravated by his ascetic lifestyle. He recommended a period of rest and "abundant nourishment" in Pietrelcina. After a short time, Fra Pio seemed cured and was able to return to community life, assigned to the convent at Montefusco, eighteen miles south of home. His mysterious illness, however, was to plague him off and on for the next decade, and it very nearly derailed his vocation.

Until 1909, his health did not prevent his progress toward ordination. Fra Pio received minor orders on December 19, 1908, and two days later was ordained to the subdiaconate. The next month, he was ordained a deacon. But now Fra Pio was in a state of near-total collapse. His stomach could retain nothing, and, judged by his superiors as too ill to remain in a community, he was sent home to complete his studies in moral theology under Don Giuseppe Maria Orlando, a professor in the seminary at Benevento.[1] Orlando, seventy-eight years old, was said to be subject to periods of "mental derangement," but very intelligent and very pious. In this way, Fra Pio completed the studies necessary for ordination.

During this period, Fra Pio kept in constant touch with Padre Benedetto, and his letters from this period suggest that he was in very low spirits, depressed by his poor health and inability to live in a friary. He seemed to have cherished a desire to be ordained a priest and then die. Even in Pietrelcina, he seems to have been constantly ill. In March 1910, he complained to Padre Benedetto of continuous fever, especially at night; a cough; pains in his chest and back; and profuse sweating. In April, he was confined to bed. In May, he was suffering from chest pains. In July, he insisted that these pains were so bad as to render him speechless at times.

"If Almighty God in His mercy desires to free me from the sufferings of this body of mine, as I hope he does, through shortening my exile here on earth," he wrote Padre Benedetto, "I shall die very happy."[2] In another letter, he confided: "The notion of being healed, after all the tempests that the Most High has sent me, seems to me as only a dream, even madness. On the contrary, the idea is very attractive to me."[3]

Fra Pio was afraid, however, that his illness might be a punishment from God on account of unconfessed sin. He told Padre Benedetto:

For several days my conscience has been continually troubled over my past life, which I spent so wickedly. But what particularly tortures my heart and afflicts me exceedingly is the worry about my uncertainty as to whether I confessed all the sins of my past life, and, more than that, whether I have confessed them well.… Dear Father, I need your help to still the disquietude of my spirit because — and you must believe me — this is a thought that is destroying me … I should like to make a general confession, but I don't know whether that would be good or bad. Please help me, O Father, for the love of our dear Jesus.[4]

Troubled that these conflicts and doubts could exist in a heart "that prefers death a thousand times to committing one sin," Pio declared, "I would like to make a bundle of all my bad inclinations and give them to Jesus so that he might condescend to consume them all in the fire of his divine love!"[5] Yet, through it all, Fra Pio was resigned to the will of God: "I do not know the reason for this, but in silence I adore and kiss the hand of the One who smites me, knowing truly that it is [God] himself who, on the one hand, afflicts me, and, on the other, consoles me."[6]

Meanwhile, Padre Benedetto was working to make it possible for Fra Pio to be ordained. On July 6, he informed Fra Pio that all the necessary dispensations had been obtained and that the day of his ordination had been tentatively set for August 12. It would be necessary, however, for Fra Pio to journey to Morcone in mid-July to learn the ceremonies involved in exercising priestly ministry. He would also have to go to go to Benevento for his final examination.

And so, on July 21, Fra Pio, along with one Padre Eugenio of Pignataro Maggiore (Capuchins were supposed to travel in pairs), journeyed from Pietrelcina to Morcone. As soon as he arrived at the friary, Fra Pio was seized with cramps and started to vomit, and the next day, Padre Tommaso, the old novice master, wrote to Padre Benedetto to tell him that he was sending Fra Pio home. A sympathetic Padre Benedetto wrote Fra Pio immediately after his return to Pietrelcina, saying that he would authorize Don Salvatore Pannullo to instruct him on the rubrics of the Mass. "Your sufferings," he added reassuringly, "are not punishment, but rather ways of earning merit that the Lord is giving you, and the shadows that weigh on your soul are generated by the devil, who wants to harm you." He exhorted Fra Pio to remember that "the closer God draws to a soul, the more the enemy troubles him."[7]

"That Beautiful Day of My Ordination"

The day of Fra Pio's ordination was set for August 10, 1910. His father and brother, both living and working in Jamaica, Long Island, New York, were unable to come, but twenty-three-year-old Fra Pio boarded a horse-drawn cab, along with his mother and "Pati," and bounced over what passed for a road to Benevento, where, in the cathedral, he was ordained a priest by eighty-three-year-old Archbishop Paolo Schinosi. After a light lunch, which Pio — now and forevermore to be known as Padre Pio — presumably was able to hold down, the little party returned to Pietrelcina, arriving home at 5:00 p.m. They were met on the edge of town by the local band, which had been hired by Giuseppa Cardone, Michele's wife. The band accompanied Padre Pio to his home while, along the way, cheering townspeople showered him with coins and candy. At the house, his mother put on a great feast. Through it all, Padre Pio sat with his head bowed, blushing with emotion. "That beautiful day of my ordination" he would always recall as a day on which he felt as if he were in heaven.

As a souvenir of his ordination, Padre Pio passed out holy cards on which were printed words he intended as the theme of his ministry:

> Jesus, my life and my breath, today I timorously raise thee in a mystery of love. With thee may I be for the world the way, the truth, and the life, and, through thee, a holy priest, a perfect victim.[8]

Four days later, at the parish church of Our Lady of the Angels in Pietrelcina, Padre Pio celebrated his first public Mass. The sermon was preached by Padre Agostino, who described the triple mission of a priest as the altar, the pulpit, and the confessional. Actually, at that stage, Padre Pio was authorized to perform only one of those functions: celebrating the Eucharist. He had not taken — and never would take — the courses required to obtain a license to preach, and so far Padre Benedetto, the minister provincial, was unwilling to grant him the faculty to hear confessions, partly because of Padre Pio's health and partly because he did not think the young priest had the proper theological preparation because his studies had been interrupted so frequently by sickness.

"I Tremble from Head to Toe with Fear of Offending God"

Although he was allowed to wear the Capuchin habit, because of his physical inability to remain in any of the friaries, Padre Pio was allowed by his superiors to function temporarily as a secular priest on the staff of the archpriest Pannullo. Even at Pietrelcina, however, his health continued to be unsatisfactory. Over the next few months, he suffered severe attacks of asthma accompanied by pains so severe that he felt as if his back and chest were about to explode.

The young priest spent much of his time at Piana Romana, where his father, home on vacation from America, constructed a little cabin for him, and, as Padre Pio recalled years later, "There ... I would remain night and day, breathing the pure fresh air. It truly became a small chapel for me where I performed all the practices of piety and said my prayers."[9] Often Padre Pio would sit beneath an elm tree to pray his Office and commune with God. Gradually, his health began to show some improvement, but not enough for him to return to community life.

There, in his rural retreat, Padre Pio reported to Padre Benedetto that he was frequently the subject of assaults by the devil. These attacks seem to have taken three forms: temptations against purity, fear of unconfessed sin, and a conviction that he was wicked. During the Easter season of 1911, he wrote: "Even in these holy days the enemy tries with all his might to induce me to acquiesce to his wicked designs, and, in particular, this malignant spirit tries with every sort of fantasy to tempt me into thoughts of uncleanness and despair." Far from being titillated, Padre Pio was horrified, reporting, "I tremble from head to toe with fear of offending God."[10]

Padre Pio's longtime friend Mercurio Scocca suggested that this mysterious illness was due to sexual frustration. When, however, Scocca proposed that his friend could cure himself by marrying or just giving in to sexual desire, Padre Pio picked up a pitchfork, swung it at his friend, and chased him out of the barn.

Padre Pio was so determined to avoid occasions of sin that, like many religious of the time, he avoided even innocent, perfunctory physical contact with women — even his relatives. One night he was sitting by the fire alone with his sister-in-law Giuseppa Cardone, who was nursing her infant son. When she fell asleep with the baby at her breast, Padre Pio, concerned that the infant would fall, called out to her, but could not wake her up. So as not to have to touch her with his hands, he took his breviary and clobbered her on the head with it. "My God, it's a good thing you became a monk!" Giuseppa exclaimed.[11]

Padre Pio said that Satan was "constantly representing the picture of my life in the grimmest possible way." He wrote, "Our common foe ... wants me to be damned at all costs and is constantly putting before my mind a horrible picture of my life and, what's worse, he craftily sows thoughts of despair in me."[12] In June 1911, he described himself as in such terror over his sins and his helplessness to save his soul that he was on the point of being "reduced to ashes." He was terrified by the thought of being punished by God for sins unknown to him, of being condemned for his sins before he entered religious life. This anguish contributed, to a great extent, to his physical illnesses. In fact, in 1939, Padre Pio would tell Padre Agostino, "My illnesses [in my youth] stemmed from this spiritual oppression."[13]

Padre Benedetto frequently had to remind Padre Pio that God is gracious. "The fear of the sins that you have committed is illusory and a torment caused by the devil," he counseled. "Let go, once and for all, and believe that Jesus is not the cruel taskmaster that you describe, but, instead, the Lamb who takes away the sins of the world and intercedes for our good with ineffable groans."[14] He assured the younger priest that his trials, both bodily and spiritual, were prompted by the devil but permitted by God so as to cause him to grow in holiness. Padre Benedetto wrote: "I see clearly that [the Lord] has chosen you to make you close to him, even without merit on your part. Now you can be sure that he wants to take perfect possession of your heart ... to transfix it with pain and love like his own."[15]

In other words, to be close to Christ, one must suffer with Christ. Padre Benedetto elaborated in another letter:

You want to know what Jesus wants of you? The answer is simple. He wants to toss you, shake you, pound you, sift you like grain until your spirit arrives at that purity and cleanness that he desires.... Nonetheless, do good and desire that the Lord free you from these temptations, and also pray to this end.... You must not fear that the Lord will leave you at the mercy of the enemy. He will permit him to molest you only in such a way as serves his paternal designs for the sanctification of your soul. Therefore, be strong and cheerful in heart.[16]

In still another letter, Padre Benedetto counseled:

Hearing that the storms are raging more fiercely consoles me because it is a sign that God is establishing his reign in your life. The temptations are a sure sign of divine predilection, and fearing them is the most certain proof that you do not consent to them. Be of good cheer and do not be discouraged. The more the foe increases his violence, the more you must abandon yourself in the faithful Lord, who will never permit you to be overcome. As it is written, "God is faithful and will not permit you to be tempted beyond your strength...." Is not Our Lord good beyond our every thought? Is he not more interested in our well-being than we are ourselves? When we think of the love that he bears us and of his zeal for our benefit, we must be tranquil and not doubt that he will always assist us with paternal care against all our enemies.[17]

Continually, as Padre Pio poured out his soul in anguish Padre Benedetto consoled him with verses from Scripture and with reminders that physical and moral sufferings are God's way of making him pure and holy, more like himself. "I exult," wrote Benedetto, "in knowing with certainty that the fury is permitted by ... the Celestial Father to make you like his dear Son, persecuted and beaten to death on the cross! The greater the pains, the greater the love God bears you!"[18]

"I Feel My Heart Throb in Unison with the Heart of Jesus"

Padre Pio also had his consolations. He realized that the only way to overcome his temptations was to place them in the hands of Jesus. "All ugly fantasies," he wrote, "that the devil introduces to my mind vanish when I abandon myself to the arms of Jesus. Therefore, when I am with Jesus crucified — that is, when I meditate on his afflictions — I suffer immensely, but it is a grief which does me good. I enjoy a peace and tranquility which are impossible to explain."[19]

Although he was suffering, nevertheless he often experienced periods of intense holy joy. He wrote to his spiritual director:

From time to time Jesus alleviates my sufferings when he speaks to my heart. Oh, yes, my father, the good Jesus is very much with me! Oh, what precious moments I have with him! It is a joy which I can liken to nothing else. It is a happiness that the Lord gives me to enjoy almost only in suffering. In such moments, more than ever, everything in the world pains and annoys me and I desire nothing except to love and to suffer. Yes, my dear father, in the midst of all these sufferings, I am happy because I feel my heart throb in unison with the heart of Jesus. Now, imagine what consolation is infused in my heart by the knowledge of possessing Jesus with certainty.

It seems clear that, while there were times when Padre Pio felt forsaken and rejected and even doubted his salvation, at other times he possessed the certainty of God's love for him. He continued in his letter to Benedetto: "It is true that the temptations to which I am subjected are very great, but I trust in divine providence so as not to fall into the snares of the tempter. And, although it is true that Jesus very often hides himself, what is important is that I try, with your help, always to stay in him, since I have your assurance that I am not abandoned, but toyed with by Love."[20]

Truly, God seemed to be playing a game of hide-and-seek. The oscillation between extreme exaltation and violent desolation is a common experience among mystics. Both Saint Catherine of Siena and Saint Teresa of Ávila spoke of a "game of love," in which God seems, by turns, to hide and then return to the soul. At times, Padre Pio was "almost in paradise"; at other times, he felt as if Satan was about to snatch him out of the hands of God. Padre Benedetto assured him continually that this was a normal part of spiritual growth, at least for someone so mystically precocious.

As Padre Pio grew in faith, gradually he was able to rise above the temptation to worry that he would give in to the devil and lose his salvation — at least most of the time. To the very end of his life, he never felt that his salvation was entirely secure. Far from being of the "once saved, always saved" school, he felt that the possibility of being lost remained as long as he lived. Toward the end of his life, when they were walking together, Padre Pio horrified his friend Pietro Cugino by asking him, "Tell me seriously, do you think I'll be saved?"[21]

Realizing, therefore, his helplessness and inability to save himself, in moments of spiritual desolation, Padre Pio learned to cast himself into the arms of Jesus. His letters to Padre Benedetto in the summer of 1911 reveal a growing confidence in resisting the temptations of the evil one. That August he wrote:

The attacks of the devil continue, as always, to afflict my soul. Yet, meanwhile I have observed for some days a certain spiritual joy that I am unable to explain … I no longer have the difficulty I once felt in resigning myself to the will of

God. I even repel the slanderous assaults of the tempter with such ease that I feel neither weariness nor fatigue.[22]

In September, he wrote Padre Benedetto:

Jesus continues to be with me, and ability to repel temptations and resign myself to God has not left me.... Doing this is growing easier. Marvel, then, at such a token of the sweetness and goodness of Jesus, that comes to such an evil wretch as me. And meanwhile, to what can I liken such amazing grace? What can I render to him for such benefits? How many times in the past, if only you knew, I exchanged Jesus for some vile thing of this world![23]

"A Victim for Poor Sinners and for Souls in Purgatory"

Padre Pio's spiritual commitment went further than merely accepting suffering for his own good. During this period, he offered himself to God as a victim for the salvation of souls. As we have seen, he was familiar with the concept of the "victim of divine love," and in the prayer card from his ordination, he had expressed the desire to be a "perfect victim." A few months after his ordination, on November 29, 1910, he wrote to Padre Benedetto:

For some time I have felt the need to offer myself to the Lord as a victim for poor sinners and for souls in purgatory. This desire has grown continuously in my heart until now it has become a powerful passion. I made this offering to the Lord on other occasions, imploring him to inflict me with the punishments that are prepared for sinners and for souls in purgatory, even multiplying them upon me a hundredfold, so long as he converts and saves sinners and quickly releases the souls in purgatory.... Now, however, I wish to make this offering to the Lord with your authorization. It seems to me that this is what Jesus wants. I'm sure that you will not find it difficult to grant me this permission.[24]

Padre Benedetto's response was an unqualified and enthusiastic assent. "Make the offering!" he advised. "Extend your arms on the cross and offer yourself to the Father as a sacrifice in union with the loving Savior. Suffer, groan, and pray for the sins of the world and the miserable ones of the other world [that is, the souls in purgatory]."[25]

Two years later, in a letter to Padre Agostino, Padre Pio further defined what it meant to be a "victim of divine love," writing:

[The Lord] chose certain souls, and among them, despite my unworthiness, he also chose me, to assist in the great work of the salvation of mankind. The more these souls suffer without any consolation, to that extent are the pains of our good Jesus made lighter. This is why I want to suffer increasingly and without comfort. And this is all my joy. It is only too true that I need courage, but Jesus will deny me nothing.[26]

Some years later, again writing to Padre Agostino, Padre Pio further elaborated on his mission: "With your prayers assist this Cyrenean who carries the cross of many people, so that there might be accomplished in him the words of the Apostle, 'I make good and complete what is still lacking in the Passion of Christ.'"[27] Padre Pio identified himself with Simon of Cyrene, the man who was forced to carry the cross to Calvary after Jesus collapsed under its weight. Like Simon, Padre Pio did not imagine that he had chosen this mission himself. He was certain that he had been chosen by God to be a victim, to help Jesus bear the cross.

Even by the time Padre Pio asked Padre Benedetto's authorization for his self-oblation as a "victim of divine love," he had received signs in his body which led him to believe that the Lord had accepted his offering.

"Fiery Red Spots"

On the afternoon of September 7, 1910, Padre Pio appeared at Pannullo's office and showed the archpriest what appeared to be puncture wounds in the middle of his hands. When questioned about them, Padre Pio told him that he had been praying in Piana Romana when Jesus and Mary appeared to him and gave him the wounds. Pannullo examined the hands of his protégé and insisted that he see a doctor. The first physician he consulted diagnosed the phenomenon as tuberculosis of the skin. Padre Pio then went to Andrea Cardone, who vehemently rejected his colleague's diagnosis. He observed on Pio's hands, both on the palms and back, wounds about a half-inch in diameter. Although they apparently did not bleed, the wounds seemed to extend all the way through the hands. Apart from the fact that they were definitely not of tubercular origin, Cardone could not explain them.

The wounds, which Pio tried to conceal, were a source of great embarrassment. Besides the doctors and Archpriest Pannullo, the only person to whom he showed them was Mercurio Scocca. He concealed them even from his mother, who noticed that something was wrong and remarked that he was moving his hands as if he were playing the guitar. But Padre Pio successfully evaded her questions and hid the lesions under the long sleeves of his habit.

A few days after seeing Dr. Cardone, Padre Pio went to Pannullo and said: "Pati, do me a favor. Let's pray together and ask Jesus to take this annoyance away. Yet, if it is God's will, [I] must yield [myself] to do his will in all and over all. And, remember, since this is for the salvation of souls and for the good of the entire world, [we] must say to Jesus, 'Do with me as you please.'"[28] The two men prayed, and the wounds went away — for a season.

Padre Pio said nothing to Padre Benedetto about his stigmata at this time. However, a year to the day after their first appearance, the wounds reappeared, and only then did Padre Pio feel comfortable in telling his superior about the wounds:

> Yesterday something happened, something I cannot explain or understand. In the middle of the palms of my hands there appeared a small red spot the size of a small coin, accompanied by a strong, sharp pain in the middle of the red spots. The pain was most intense in the middle of the left hand, so much so that I still feel it. Also I feel some pain in the soles of my feet.
>
> This phenomenon has been going on for almost a year, yet recently there has been a brief period of time in which it has not occurred. Please do not be upset that I have not mentioned it to you before. The reason is that I was too darned embarrassed to tell you about it. If you only knew the great effort I had to make to tell you about it![29]

In later years, Padre Pio downplayed these early manifestations of the stigmata. When Padre Raffaele D'Addario conducted a series of interviews with Padre Pio in 1966 and 1967, Pio — who was then in his eightieth year and in decline — had at first forgotten all about the earlier phenomenon, declaring that the stories about an earlier stigmatization were false and that "everything happened at San Giovanni Rotondo." When shown his own letters of fifty years before, the old man's memory was refreshed, and he recalled that, while praying in his cabin in Piana Romana, "in profound meditation and ecstasy, more than once I noticed fiery red spots in the palms of my hands, accompanied by extremely sharp pains that lasted several days. [I noticed] puncture wounds in my side as well. But it was only at San Giovanni Rotondo that they appeared in permanent form and with an issue of blood."[30]

From the moment he received the letter describing the marks in Padre Pio's hands, Padre Benedetto was determined to have him return to community life, at all costs.

Chapter Six

Illness and Ecstasies

"Your Living Outside the Friary Is Serving No Useful Purpose"

Padre Benedetto, still minister provincial, wrote to the minister general of the Capuchin order, Padre Pacifico of Seggiano, telling him about the young friar's holiness and asking about the advisability of sending him once more to live in a religious community.

Describing Padre Pio as "a young priest of angelic character," the provincial mentioned his oblation as a victim of divine love as well as his mysterious illnesses, linking the two together:

> He had also asked to participate in the pains of the Savior, and has been granted this in an ineffable way. Migraine headaches, resistant to any remedy, and an illness inexplicable to any doctor, however renowned in the healing art, have come to torment him along with great spiritual suffering. It was suspected that he had been stricken with tuberculosis, and doctors ordered him to breathe the air of his native town, especially when uncontrollable vomiting prevented him from holding even a spoonful of broth for days and days."[1]

He also told Padre Pacifico about the stigmata, which he judged to be "the seal of his special calling."

Padre Benedetto asked for advice. Several times in recent years, he said, Padre Pio had been sent to various friaries, only to suffer relapses which forced his superiors to send him home. "Well aware that until now this has been the will of God," Padre Benedetto wrote, "I want to summon him at this time to return to the cloister in any way possible. I am concerned, however [if anything should go amiss], it would be my fault. What do you say about this?"[2]

Padre Pacifico must have encouraged Padre Benedetto to reassign the "angelic" young priest to a friary, because in the fall of 1911 the minister provincial began to urge Padre Pio to return to community life. He did not command him to do so, however. Rather, he tried to persuade him to consent.

But Padre Pio was extremely reluctant. "You know that I want to return to the friary," he wrote Padre Benedetto. "The greatest sacrifice that I have made to the Lord is precisely my inability to live in community." He added, though, that he could not bring himself to believe that God wanted to kill him, as he would surely die of vomiting and inanition were he to return to the cloister. Moreover, at Pietrelcina he was able to celebrate Mass, whereas, if past experience was any guide to the future, he would be physically unable to do so in a convent. "If I must suffer alone," Padre Pio wrote, "that is well, but to be a cause of pain and anxiety without any result other than my death, to that I do not know how to respond." Despite his misgivings, Padre Pio indicated that he was willing to obey the command of his superiors. "It seems to me that I have the right and duty of not depriving myself of life at the age of twenty-four! It seems to me that God does not want this to happen. Consider that I am more dead than alive, and then do as you believe best, for I am disposed to make any sacrifice if it is a case of obedience."[3]

Under his vow of obedience, Padre Pio, as a good religious, was prepared to obey the command of his superior, even if it should result in his death; but Padre Benedetto worried that God would hold him responsible if Padre Pio died, so he was unwilling to order him under obedience to report to a friary. He tried again to convince the sickly priest that such course of action would be best, writing on September 29:

> I tell you that your staying with your family troubles me very much, since I would not only want to see you at one of our friaries, but also at my side, so that I could watch over you, for you know that I love you like a son. I therefore believe that your living outside the friary is serving no useful purpose.... If your illness is the express will of God and not a natural phenomenon, it is better for you to return to the shadow of community life. Native air cannot cure a man visited by the Most High.... Either at home or in community, your health will always be what God wills."[4]

Padre Pio's reply to Padre Benedetto has not been preserved, but whatever he said, it caused Padre Benedetto to explode in anger. On October 4, the minister provincial wrote: "When one writes as superior and spiritual director, you ought to listen to what he tells you with reverence and inward submission and not argue with him with a kind of resentment! As your superior and director, I declare to you that your illness has no need of doctors, since it is a *special dispensation* from

God, and for this reason I am not of a mind to arrange an examination by another specialist." He went on to recount the enormous expenditures made for Padre Pio of Benevento in his last illness and for other friars who had recently suffered serious health problems:

> You see, then, how unfounded your accusation is and how wrong you are in obstinately believing in your own way. But you do not want to submit humbly to my judgments, and you are acting wickedly! I hope that this will be the last time that you refuse to submit to my instruction. Otherwise, I will not write to you anymore. Moreover, you really hurt me by saying that I do not love you [and] that I want to kill you.[5]

In response to the minister provincial's letter, Padre Pio wrote in abject contrition:

> With reddened eyes and trembling hand I write you this letter to beg your forgiveness on bended knee … I repent of this matter as one who loves God is able to repent of his sins. Please pardon me, Father. I know I do not deserve pardon, but your goodness towards me gives me hope. Do not be upset. Didn't you know that I am full of pride? Let us pray together to the Lord that he strike me down before I fall again into such excesses.[6]

The Friary at Venafro

After receiving Padre Pio's submissive reply, Padre Benedetto acceded to his request for another medical examination. He was sent to Naples, where the specialists concluded that Padre Pio was hopelessly ill (with what disease is unclear) and maintained that it would make no difference whether he spent his last days at home or in a convent. Padre Benedetto decided, therefore, that if Padre Pio was destined soon to die, he might as well depart the world from a friary. He ordered Padre Pio to report to the convent of San Nicandro in Venafro, a town about fifty miles north of Pietrelcina, famous for its pure air, which Padre Benedetto hoped might prolong the young priest's days. While awaiting his appointment with "Sister Death," Padre Pio would take a course on sacred eloquence.

It was at Venafro that the supernatural aspect of Padre Pio's life became apparent to many of his confreres.

Built in 1573, the friary at Venafro was named after the Roman martyr San Nicandro and was adjacent to the tomb and thirteenth-century basilica erected in his honor. The Capuchin community consisted of thirteen men: nine priests and four brothers. The father guardian, or local superior, was thirty-three-year-old Padre Evangelista of San Marco in Lamis. Padre Agostino was vicar as well as lector of sacred eloquence. Among the community were Padre Anastasio of Roio, who had been with him during his January 1905 bilocation with the Rizzani family, as well as Padre Guglielmo of San Giovanni Rotondo (who later wrote an account of the early years of Padre Pio's ministry), and the learned, ascetical sixty-eight-year-old Padre Francesco Maria of Gambatesa.

Padre Pio arrived on October 28, and for the first few days everything proceeded smoothly. Each member of the religious family had a job to perform, and Padre Pio, besides his studies, was assigned the task of instructing local children in Christian doctrine and teaching them hymns. By mid-November, however, he was sick again, unable to hold anything in his stomach. Soon he was able to leave his bed only to celebrate Mass, having to give up his studies and teaching.

Mysterious Noises

Padre Evangelista decided to take Padre Pio to Naples once more for medical consultation. As usual, the doctors were unable to diagnose his illness, and the two friars left the clinic knowing no more than before.

That evening the priests took a room in a hotel. During the night, Padre Evangelista was awakened by loud noises that rendered him petrified with terror. When the noises ceased, Padre Pio asked whether he had heard them, and then told him not to worry. He gave no explanation for the noises, although he seemed to be familiar with them. Although Padre Evangelista continued nervous and troubled, Padre Pio awoke bright and cheerful.

The digestive ailment persisted. Before the friars left Naples to return to Venafro, Padre Pio suggested that they stop for dinner at a restaurant. "Do you want to throw up in front of all those people?" Padre Evangelista asked. "Do you want to make a spectacle of yourself?" Padre Pio was feeling well and assured him that nothing would happen. He downed two courses — then had to run to the window and vomit into the flower beds outside.

At Venafro, the vomiting persisted. The only nourishment that Pio was able to retain was the sacred Host, which was brought to him in his room. He became too weak even to celebrate Mass.

Up to this point, Padre Pio had been regarded by his confreres simply as a good religious suffering from an undiagnosable and probably fatal illness. The stigmata had disappeared, and no one at Venafro — not even Padre Agostino — was aware that the marks had ever existed. The only people privy to this secret — Pannullo, Benedetto, Cardone, Scocca, and the doctor who thought the wounds were the result of tuberculosis — kept it well.

Between Heaven and Hell

One day Padre Agostino, advised that Padre Pio was doing very poorly, entered his room to find the young man raving about a huge black cat he said was about to pounce on him. Padre Agostino was convinced that Padre Pio was hallucinating and about to die, so he withdrew to the choir to pray for him. During his prayers, his mind wandered, and, thinking that he would be asked to preach at Padre Pio's funeral, he began to plan what he would say.

When he returned to Padre Pio's room, he was amazed to find his friend lucid and cheerful. "You went to the choir to pray," he said, "and that was fine, but you also thought about my funeral eulogy. ... There's time, Lector, there's plenty of time!"[7] Needless to say, Padre Agostino was astounded.

On another occasion, Padre Pio asked Padre Agostino to remember him in prayer when he was saying Mass, and Padre Agostino agreed. He remembered his promise while going downstairs to the church, but forgot all about Padre Pio while he was celebrating Mass. When Padre Pio asked him if he had remembered to pray for him, Padre Agostino, embarrassed, lied and said, "Surely, I remembered." Padre Agostino was dumbfounded at Padre Pio's reply: "Well, at least Jesus accepted the intention that you made while you were going down the stairs."[8]

Padre Agostino was not the only other resident at the friary who observed extraordinary things. One day Padre Guglielmo and the sixty-seven-year-old doorkeeper, Fra Cherubino of Morcone, were keeping Padre Pio company. The vestments used by the priests were regularly laundered in town. Fra Cherubino looked at his watch and excused himself, because he had to go to the door to meet the lady who was bringing the vestments at any moment. "You don't have to go to the door now," Padre Pio told the doorkeeper. "Save your energy. Wait here. She's going to be one hour late." Fra Cherubino remained. One hour later, Padre Pio told him to go to the door. Fra Cherubino did so, and found the laundry lady, who had just arrived and hadn't even had time to knock.[9]

Padre Agostino spent a great deal of time in Padre Pio's room and became convinced that he was neither delirious nor insane. Sometimes, rather crassly, he brought his students to observe him, because he and Padre Evangelista were in agreement that some of Padre Pio's experiences were true cases of ecstasy, and they wanted the students to have the opportunity to observe such phenomena firsthand.

Padre Agostino observed that Padre Pio went into ecstasy two or three times a day. He transcribed everything that Padre Pio said while in ecstasy on seven occasions, although many others he did not record. These celestial encounters, in which Padre Pio seemed to converse with Jesus, Mary, and his guardian angel, were preceded or followed usually by diabolical vexations. The heavenly colloquies, Padre Agostino observed, usually lasted between thirty and forty-five minutes, while the demonic encounters usually lasted less than fifteen minutes.

Padre Agostino observed ten "diabolical apparitions." In one of them, Padre Pio was terrified by a black cat that no one else could see. In another, he had a vision of a naked woman who "danced lasciviously" in his room. Another time, the devil invisibly spat in his face. On yet another occasion, Padre Pio complained of hideous noises which nobody else could hear.

One day Padres Evangelista and Agostino were horrified to discover Padre Pio writhing as if he were being repeatedly struck. Alarmed, they fell to their knees and began to pray and sprinkle him and the room with holy water. After a quarter of an hour, Padre Pio came to himself and said that he had been flogged by horrible men who looked like executioners. Other times he said demons appeared in the form of various friends, colleagues, and superiors, even in the forms of Pius X (the current pope) and Jesus, Mary, Saint Francis, and his guardian angel. He recognized the diabolical ruse through a certain feeling of disgust and by insisting that his visitors praise Jesus. When they refused to do so, he knew that they were from the devil.

Padre Pio made his confessions to Padre Agostino, but one morning Padre Agostino did not have the time and told the sick priest to go ahead and partake of the Eucharist, and he would hear his confession that evening. When he appeared in Padre Pio's room that evening as he had promised, Padre Agostino was puzzled when the ailing friar gazed at him with an expression of fear and distrust.

"Are you my lector?" Padre Pio asked.

"Of course I am! Why do you ask such a peculiar question?" replied Padre Agostino.

Looking intently into his eyes, Padre Pio demanded, "Say: 'Praise Jesus!'"

"Praise Jesus a thousand times!" Padre Agostino replied. "Now, tell me what happened."

Padre Pio then related how, shortly after Padre Agostino had left him in the morning, there was a knock on his door, and there was Padre Agostino back again — or what appeared to be Padre Agostino. The lector said that he was now ready to hear Pio's confession. Padre Pio, however, felt an unaccountable disgust. Moreover, although "Agostino" looked as he always did, he had a wound on his forehead that hadn't been there a few minutes before. When Padre Pio asked what had happened, "Agostino" replied, "Oh, I fell while I was going downstairs. Now, son, I'm here to hear your confession."

"Say, 'Praise Jesus,'" Padre Pio demanded.

"No!" shouted the demon who had taken Padre Agostino's form — and vanished into thin air.[10]

When he went into ecstasy, Padre Pio spoke, quite coherently, to various unseen visitors. Agostino wrote down what Padre Pio said, seeing and hearing nothing of those to whom the young priest was speaking. From Padre Pio's words, however, it is possible to capture the general sense of the dialogue.

The first ecstasy that Padre Agostino transcribed took place on November 28, 1911, between 9:45 and 11:00 a.m. When it began, Padre Pio seemed to be talking with the Virgin Mary. Then he began to pray for various souls, addressing Jesus as he would a friend:

> O Jesus, I commend that soul to you ... You *must* convert her! You can do it! ... Convert her, save her! ... Don't only convert her, for then it might be possible for her to lose your grace, but sanctify her. Yes, sanctify her.... Oh, didn't you shed your blood for her, too? ... O Jesus, convert that man.... You can do it. Yes, you can! ... I offer all myself for him.

The desire to offer himself as a victim for the conversion of sinners was a theme that ran powerfully throughout the ecstasies that Padre Agostino recorded.

After pleading with the Lord to "stay a little longer," Padre Pio reproached him for leaving him at the mercy of the devil the previous morning: "Ah, how he frightened me! ... Jesus, don't let him come anymore! ... I'd rather forfeit the sweetness of your presence than have that fiend come back again!" Then Pio exclaimed in rapture:

> O Jesus, another thing — I love you ... very much. I want to be all yours. ... Don't you see that I am burning for you? ... You ask love from me — love, love, love. See, I love you.... Come into my being every morning [through the Eucharist]. Let us tarry together, let us tarry alone — I alone with you, you alone with me. ... O Jesus, give me your love! ... When you come into my heart, if you see anything that is not worthy of your love, destroy it! ... I love you! ... I will hold you tightly, so tightly! ... I will never let you go! ... You are free, it is true, but I ... I will hold you close, so very close ... I will almost take your freedom away![11]

The ecstasy ended with Padre Pio urging his angel to "praise Jesus for me.... My lips are unworthy and foul, but yours are pure." The angel seems to have said something, to which Padre Pio responded: "Are you an angel of the darkness? ... You are an angel without sin! ... Then praise Jesus for me.... Dear Guardian Angel, drive that fiend away." And then he whispered: "O Jesus ... Sacred Host ... Beauty ... Love ... Jesus." After a few moments, he became once more aware of his physical surroundings.

The next day Padre Pio expressed concern to Jesus that he had been observed. He didn't mind Padre Agostino watching, but he was particularly concerned that the physician, Nicola Lombardi — a layman — had observed and overheard the ecstasy: "To friars, that's one thing ... but to a layman! ... I know that he's a good man, but he's still a *layman!*"

Padre Pio began once again to pray for conversion: "O Jesus, you can't refuse me! Remember that you shed your blood for everybody ... and what does it matter if he is a hardened sinner?" He prayed for the confreres who ministered to him in his sickness: "Jesus, I commend these friars to you. They get up at night. You know that.... After all, who am I? ... Help them ... I am not good enough even to celebrate Mass, but they exercise their ministry."[12]

Pio's conversations with his guardian angel were a good deal less reverent:

Angel of God, my angel — aren't you my guardian? God gave you to me.... Are you a creature or are you a creator? ... You're a creator? No! Then you're a creature and you have a law and you have to obey.... You must stay close to me whether you want to or not.... You're laughing! ... What is there to laugh about? ... Tell me one thing — you *have* to tell me. Who was it? Who was here yesterday morning? ... You're laughing! ... You have to tell me! ... Who was it? ... Either the lector or the guardian — tell me! Come on now, answer me! ... You're laughing! An angel laughing! ... I won't let you go until you tell me! ... If you won't tell me, I will ask Jesus ... and then you will listen! ... Well, my boy, tell me who it was! ... You're not answering! ... All right, just stand there — just like a block of wood! ... I want to know ... I asked you just one thing, and after such a long time, here we still are. Jesus, you tell me![13]

Jesus apparently made the angel tell Padre Pio that only Padre Agostino had been watching the ecstasy of the previous day.

Toward the end of the ecstasy, Padre Pio spoke of a mysterious thirst that he experienced prior to receiving Holy Communion. (It is common for mystics to feel a real hunger and thirst for the living God.) The ecstasy closed with the enraptured priest kissing the Savior's bleeding wounds.

The next day Padre Pio expressed a desire to help Jesus bear his cross. Jesus told him that he really did not need man's works, but Padre Pio begged for the grace to participate in his redemptive suffering. From Padre Pio's responses, it would seem that Jesus conceded him this privilege.

Padre Pio remained depressed over the fact that he was able to exercise his priestly duty of celebrating Mass only in his hometown. "Why there and not here?" he asked his celestial visitors. "Am I a priest only at Pietrelcina?" He was distressed about Padre Benedetto's refusal to permit him to hear confessions. From Padre Pio's responses, it appears that Jesus, too, was unhappy about this and actually accused the minister provincial of having a "hard head." Even so, Padre Pio prayed that the punishment deserved by Padre Benedetto might fall upon himself. Furthermore, Padre Pio accused himself of being worthy of damnation. "You want to glorify yourself in *me*?" Pio asked in amazement. "Who am I? ... I am a priest, true, but a useless one. I don't even say Mass anymore, or hear confessions."[14] The ecstasy ended with Padre Pio praying for Padres Benedetto, Agostino, Pannullo, and for all priests, good and evil.

The next day, Friday, December 1, Padre Pio apparently saw Jesus crucified, bleeding, and suffering. "Jesus, I love you," he exclaimed, "but don't appear like this to me anymore.... You tear my heart to pieces.... It's true, then, that you bore the cross all the time of your life ... and therefore it's wrong when wicked men say that your suffering was only a matter of a night and a day.... Your suffering was continuous."[15]

Once again Padre Pio offered himself as a victim and prayed for the stigmata to return: "If you give me the strength, permit that those nails ... permit it, yes, in my hands ... if it be your will ... but invisibly, because people despise your gifts."[16]

Although Padre Pio suffered distress and anguish, there were moments of sublime rapture as well. "Tell me," he asked Jesus, "if on earth it can be so lovely, what will heaven be like? ... There we will die of love! ... Jesus, all the things of this world are but as a shadow."[17]

Touched when told how fervently Padre Evangelista and the rest of the community were praying for him, Padre Pio told Jesus: "Try to console him. Maybe he doesn't even pray for himself.... Give him the grace [he is seeking].... You can do anything!"[18]

On Sunday, December 3, as he talked with Jesus, Padre Pio was troubled about the sins of unworthy priests. Again, he offered himself as a victim, specifically on their behalf:

> My Jesus, why are you so bloody this morning? ... They did wicked things to you today? ... Alas, even on Sunday you must suffer the offenses of ungrateful men! ... How many abominations took place within your sanctuary! ... My Jesus, pardon! Lower that sword! ... If it must fall, may it find its place on my head alone.... Yes, I want to be the victim! ... Here is the usual excuse: "You are too weak." ... Yes, I'm weak ... but, my Jesus, you are able to strengthen me.... Then punish me and not others.... Even send me to hell, provided that I can still love you and everyone is saved. Yes, everyone![19]

It was in this ecstasy that the Lord apparently explained to Padre Pio that he would have to return to Pietrelcina. In previous ecstasies, he had expressed his alarm at his inability to remain in any friary. He had been terrified on learning that the minister general was thinking of dismissing him from the Capuchin order because of his poor health, and that it might be necessary for him to journey to Rome to plead his cause. "O my Jesus," Padre Pio lamented, "you want to send me to that land of exile! ... Aren't I a priest here? ... What do I have to do?" Jesus evidently told him that his return to Pietrelcina was part of his plan to glorify himself in the friar. "You want to glorify yourself in me?" Pio exclaimed. "And who am I? ... If only people could know my sins! ... Daddy is proud of me and goes around boasting about me.... Oh, if he only knew, if he only knew."[20]

Saint Francis of Assisi also appeared to him. "Seraphic Father," Padre Pio complained, "are you expelling me from your order? … Aren't I your son anymore?" Padre Pio seemed to be assured by Saint Francis that he would not be expelled from the Capuchin order and that it was God's will for him to remain in Pietrelcina for a time.

A Cataleptic Trance?

Two of Padre Pio's ecstasies were observed by Dr. Nicola Lombardi. On November 28, 1911, Lombardi found Pio lying in bed and apparently staring at the ceiling. The Capuchin was talking to the Lord. Lombardi lit a candle and held it in front of Pio's eyes. "He's in a cataleptic trance," Lombardi explained to Padre Agostino. "When he comes to himself, you'll see that he remembers nothing of what happened." Lombardi was wrong. Without being told of the doctor's visit, Padre Pio complained bitterly the next day about being observed by a layman.

Lombardi was called back on December 3. Padre Pio was again talking to unseen visitors. "Take my heart and fill it with your love," he murmured. Lombardi measured the heartbeat with his stethoscope and took the pulse under the wrist, marveling that the two were not synchronous: the pulse in the wrist was strong and rapid, but the actual heartbeat was significantly stronger and faster. Lombardi called the priest's name in an attempt to bring him out of the trance. "Ah, what called me?" Padre Pio said. "My angel, let me stay with Jesus." And he remained in the ecstatic trance.

"Let me show you something, Doctor," Padre Evangelista said a few moments later. Instructing the doctor to remain in the room, the father guardian went outside. Within moments, Padre Pio awoke, alert and cheerful. Padre Evangelista, returning to the room, explained to the physician that, while standing in the corridor, he had called to Padre Pio in obedience, but in such a low voice that his command could be heard by no one in Padre Pio's room. Even so, Padre Pio awoke. Evidently, he was unaware through his physical senses of anything going on in the room, much less in the hallway, but his guardian angel let him know when anything of importance was happening. When Evangelista called him through "holy obedience," even though Padre Pio might be talking to the Lord, the Lord directed him to break off his conversation and obey the command of his earthly superior.

During late November and early December, Padre Agostino brought Holy Communion to Padre Pio several times while he was in ecstasy, but the ailing friar apparently was unaware of it because several times he asked Jesus, "Did I receive Communion this morning?" Padre Agostino could deduce from Padre Pio's surprised response that Jesus had told him that he had indeed partaken of the sacred host. Padre Pio, apparently echoing Jesus' words to him, repeated, "Pio, see Jesus! I command you to partake, in the Name of Jesus, whom I hold in my hands." Padre Agostino recognized these as the exact words he used when he gave

Padre Pio Communion. Padre Pio also repeated the French phrase *"petit enfant"* (little child), which he had also used. It did not seem as if Padre Pio was repeating words he remembered hearing; it seemed as if someone — evidently Jesus — was telling him something that he had not known until that moment.[21]

As mentioned earlier, Padre Agostino did not record all of Padre Pio's ecstasies, especially those that concerned Padre Pio's personal life. He did note that Padre Pio prayed several times that Padre Agostino might be freed from the assaults of the devil, and it seems that Padre Pio went into more detail than Padre Agostino cared to record. Later Padre Agostino recounted:

One day he prayed in ecstasy for a soul whom I knew as well as myself. The soul was troubled for more than a year by terrible temptations, which were known only to God and to his confessor. Of these, Padre Pio was able to know absolutely nothing. And then one day he prayed for this soul, that the Lord might free him from those terrifying temptations. He was in ecstasy and only through divine revelation could he know the interior of that soul. Jesus answered Padre Pio that he would help that soul, but that the soul would have to be tried and tested. From that day on this soul felt strengthened, and thank God, the temptations … were not so violent as before.[22]

In his ecstasies, Padre Pio seemed to be told to pray for certain individuals. Padre Agostino could not identify three of them. When asked, Padre Pio told him that he had never met these people or heard of them. Padre Pio would later write to Padre Benedetto: "At times I feel moved, when I am praying, to intercede for those for whom I never intended to pray, and, what is more wonderful, at times for those whom I have never known, nor seen, nor heard, nor had recommended to me by others. And, sooner or later, the Lord always grants these prayers."[23]

Dr. Lombardi at first diagnosed Padre Pio as suffering from catalepsy, a condition sometimes associated with schizophrenia in which the body becomes rigid and frozen and often impervious to external stimuli. After observing him more extensively, Lombardi ruled out catalepsy and expressed the opinion that the trances had no natural explanation. Noting that in these episodes Padre Pio's face assumed an unearthly beauty and that everything he said was totally coherent, Lombardi expressed his conviction that the young Capuchin was experiencing "true ecstasy" — a purely religious experience.[24]

As for Padre Pio's physical condition, Lombardi noted abnormal sounds in his respiration, but thought this had more to do with the larynx than the lungs. He found that his patient did not suffer from evening sweats or fever, characteristic of tuberculosis. Even though he vomited almost everything he ate, he showed no signs of emaciation or malnutrition. He found it significant that these symptoms occurred in every friary to which he had been sent, but much less when he was at home in Pietrelcina. Lombardi wrote, "From these facts I excluded a specific affection of the lungs, and I judged that this was a case of a nervous disturbance."[25]

Mystics and visionaries very often suffer from ill health and undiagnosable illnesses. Some have posited that this is because of the great duress the body is put under in such experiences.

Back to "Breathe His Native Air"

However Padre Pio's superiors were inclined to interpret his illness, it was both real and distressing. Padre Evangelista — concerned because Padre Pio had been unable to retain any food for weeks — wrote to Padre Benedetto, begging him to permit the young priest to return once more to Pietrelcina. When he received no answer, he risked offending Padre Benedetto by going over his head and writing directly to the minister general, Padre Pacifico. Padre Evangelista told the minister general that he had written several letters to the provincial without receiving a reply, declaring on December 3, 1911:

> Along with all my friars here and even all the friars of the province, I am able sincerely to attest to the fact that Padre Pio of Pietrelcina, sick now for three years, is unable to retain any food in his stomach except in his native town. For nearly two years he breathed the air of his hometown, and there he never suffered from vomiting, while, each time he has gone to a friary, even for a single day, he has been seized with agonizing pains and, especially, by vomiting. He has been here a month and a half and I can sincerely attest that he has never held his food for a quarter of an hour. For sixteen or seventeen days he has been bedfast and has not been able to retain even a spoonful of water.... Scarcely had he arrived in this friary than he began to vomit, and this has persisted to the present time. As soon as he sets foot on his native soil, however, his stomach recovers. Could this be the will of God that his poor priest must always remain at home?

In order not to give the minister general the impression that Padre Pio was malingering because he did not enjoy life in the friary, and so as not to put him in danger of being dismissed by the order, Padre Evangelista added: "Everyone can attest to the fact that he is the best kind of priest. Therefore he has not the slightest wish to stay at home, nor do we, his brethren, wish to deprive ourselves of his treasured presence."[26]

Padre Pacifico thereupon instructed Padre Benedetto to send Padre Pio home. Benedetto was furious and wrote to Padre Agostino, fuming: "I don't know what to make of this concern to run to Rome for a provision that is supposed to be left to my wisdom. I'm troubled because it's a sign of a lack of respect and reverence toward one's immediate superiors."[27]

Padre Benedetto nevertheless granted his consent for Padre Pio to return to Pietrelcina and authorized Padre Agostino to accompany him. On the morning of December 7, 1911, the two priests set out for Pietrelcina. The next day Padre Pio was able to celebrate Mass in his hometown — "as if he had suffered nothing."[28]

Chapter Seven

The Double Exile

Back in Pietrelcina

Padre Pio called the five years between 1911 and 1916 his "double exile" because he was separated from his religious community as well as from heaven. It was, however, during these years that his reputation for sanctity spread from his religious community to his hometown.

Since the Capuchin Constitutions specified that a friar forced by some exigency to live apart from his community was not to live at home with his family (as many secular priests did), Padre Pio lived during the summer in the cabin his father had built him in the Piana Romana, and during the winter he dwelt in "The Tower," the one-room structure owned by his parents near the family home.

This was not a time of placid retreat. Padre Pio's health, although better than it was when he was living in community, continued precarious; there were difficulties with his family; there was, at first, misunderstanding on the part of the townsfolk. There was trouble with his superiors. And there were also great spiritual trials, including terrifying diabolical assaults.

In addition to his usual disorders, Padre Pio began to suffer from unspecified eye troubles. During much of 1912, he had difficulty reading and writing, and saying Mass posed a great problem because, in addition to the text that is the same every day, there are different propers — that is, prayers and readings that are intended specifically for each day's liturgy, too many to memorize. He had to struggle through the Mass holding a lamp in front of his missal. To save Padre Pio from straining his weak vision, his superiors gave him permission to use one of two Masses each day: the Mass of Our Lady and the Mass of the Dead. He was thus able to memorize the propers for these two Masses and not worry about using any others. He was also excused from reading the Divine Office and was permitted to pray the Rosary in its place.

Family Troubles

In the letters he wrote to his superiors, Padre Pio almost never made any direct references to his relatives. Orazio was living in Queens, New York, doing "pick and shovel work" for the Erie Railroad.[1] Michele was also working in New York, while his wife and little son, Francesco, remained in Pietrelcina. "Franceschino" (Little Francis) was adored by his namesake, Padre Pio.

Padre Pio's mother, Giuseppa, had been managing the farm virtually alone for more than a decade. Felicita, who was closest in age to Padre Pio and who was his favorite sibling, married Vincenzo Masone (perhaps the same person who entered the Capuchin order with Padre Pio, but quickly left). Masone was an administrator in the town hall. Their daughter, Giuseppina, was born in 1912, followed by sons Pellegrino and Ettore. Padre Pio's sister Pellegrina, at the age of twenty, gave birth out of wedlock to a son named Angelo Michele in July 1912. A year later, pregnant again, she married a tailor named Antonio Masone and moved with him into his parents' house, where she gave birth to a daughter whom she named Maria Giuseppa, after her mother. Her husband acknowledged paternity of both children. Sadly, both died as toddlers. Then Pellegrina's husband deserted her and left for America, never to return to her. Baby sister Graziella evidently still lived at home. A "pale, fragile" girl, she aspired to become a nun, but to enter most women's religious orders at the time required a university degree, or else a substantial financial payment called a "dowry." She hadn't the means to obtain either.

There were clearly some family troubles at this time. In later years, Padre Pio told his niece Pia (Michele's daughter, who was born several years later in 1924), "I had to go to Pietrelcina to straighten things out at home."[2] Just what things needed to be straightened out he did not say.

In a letter to Padre Agostino on May 1, 1912, Padre Pio made a brief comment that may be an allusion to some tension with his mother: "In my greatest sufferings it seems to me that I no longer have a mother on this earth, but a very compassionate one in heaven [Mary]."[3] It seems Giuseppa blamed her son's poor health on the ascetical life of the Capuchins and evidently opposed his return to community life. She and the archpriest Pannullo were pressuring him to leave the order and become a secular priest. Giuseppa frequently told Padre Pio, "Dear boy, with your poor health, how can you get along in a monastery with monks? I weep for you, my dear."[4]

Comments like this caused Padre Pio grief and frustration, but his relationship with his mother was not the family crisis that seems to have been part of the reason why he believed the Lord wanted him in Pietrelcina. If not always in agreement with his goals, "Mammella" was entirely supportive. Referring to the fact that his order expected his parents to pay his medical bills, Padre Pio insisted, "They give their very blood for me without the slightest regret."[5]

The greatest problem seems to have been Padre Pio's sister Pellegrina. In May

1913, surmising his unmarried sister was pregnant for a second time, he wrote to Padre Agostino: "How I suffer … because of certain obstinate souls, and how I would even give my life that they might come to their senses and give themselves entirely to God. What devastates me most is that among these are souls united to me by ties of kinship."[6] The subject of Pellegrina seems to have been a forbidden topic for most who knew the family. Pellegrina was remembered by her niece Pia as lively and very beautiful — the prettiest of the three Forgione sisters — with long auburn hair. But she would say no more. Other people, willing to speak only anonymously, characterized her as "evil" and "a devil." One Italian author described her as a "prostitute," by which he probably did not mean that she exchanged her favors for money, but that she was "sexually liberated." A man who knew her well said that she was perhaps the greatest source of grief and pain in Padre Pio's life, but refused to elaborate, saying it was too painful. Apparently rebelling against everything the rest of her family believed and practiced, Pellegrina evidently led a life that scandalized not only her family but her neighbors too. The prayers and counsel of her family seemed all in vain. With her father and older brother in America, one wonders whether she displayed violent conduct toward her mother, which might be why, as the only adult male in the family, Padre Pio felt he had to be nearby to protect his mother and his youngest sister.

Assisting the Archpriest

Pannullo, the archpriest, loved Padre Pio like a son. Once, as the two of them took their evening walk, he confided his hopes that the younger man would leave the Capuchins so that he could succeed him as archpriest at Pietrelcina. "Pati," answered Padre Pio, "I'd die before I'd abandon the habit of St. Francis!"[7]

During his "exile" in Pietrelcina, Padre Pio celebrated Mass nearly every day, often in rural churches that were part of the parish. He also taught school. One of his students, Celestino Orlando, recalled in his seventies how diligently Padre Pio had worked to help him, a slow student, learn mathematics. Once, as a reward for mastering a particularly hard problem, Padre Pio invited the boy to his home to enjoy a dinner of fried fish. Orlando remembered Padre Pio as a strict disciplinarian who always prayed before he taught. If two boys fought and swore, Padre Pio would not hesitate to take off one of his sandals and swat at them with it.

Padre Pio also organized adult education classes and held school in the fields, successfully teaching farmers and laborers to read and write. Moreover, he got together a choir of fifteen boys and taught them how to sing various hymns. He led them without accompaniment, singing along in what has been described as a robust, fervent, but unmusical baritone voice.

Padre Pio was not welcomed at first at the archpriest's domicile. Pannullo lived with a brother and his three daughters: Antonietta, Rosina, and Grazia. Antonietta, the oldest, was married and had children who lived there at the house. She was afraid that Padre Pio had tuberculosis and would infect her children, and whenever the young priest came to see her uncle, she and her sisters refused to talk, for fear of being infected if they opened their mouths. They made Padre Pio sit on the same chair every time he came and drink out of the same cup, which they set apart for his exclusive use. One evening Antonietta humiliated Padre Pio terribly when Archbishop Schinosi of Benevento came to visit Pannullo and insisted that Padre Pio join them at the dinner table. Antonietta flew into a terrible rage, berating her uncle for allowing a tubercular priest to eat at the same table with her children, and she forced him to tell Padre Pio to leave.

Antonietta's sister Rosina was horrified that Padre Pio was using the same vestments, chalice, and paten as the other priests in the parish, and she demanded that her uncle provide a separate set for Padre Pio's exclusive use. The henpecked archpriest yielded to the demands of his niece.

One day the sacristan, Michele Pilla, got drunk and forgot to change the chalice. While Padre Pio was celebrating Mass, Rosina noticed he was not using his special chalice. She called the sacristan and demanded that he switch the chalice on the spot. In front of the entire congregation, the sacristan interrupted Padre Pio's Mass to exchange chalices.

This was too much for Padre Pio. That evening, as they took their walk, he complained to Pannullo: "I must tell you that I'm angry about two things. First, your niece Antonietta doesn't want me in the house, lest I give my disease to her children. Second, your other niece, this very morning, while I was celebrating, told the sacristan to change the chalices. Well, today the Lord gave me the grace of knowing that my disease is not contagious." This motivated Pannullo to put his foot down. He had a conference with his nieces, and, after he laid down the law to them, they ever afterward welcomed Padre Pio into the house, without insisting on demeaning restrictions.[8]

The "Mad Monk"

The people of Pietrelcina sensed that there was something extraordinary about Padre Pio. The curious would peer into his cabin to watch the "mad monk" take "the discipline" on Mondays, Wednesdays, and Fridays in accordance with the practice of the Capuchins — thrashing himself with a whip in order to subdue his bodily passions. Even though his mother insisted on making his bed, Padre Pio would usually sleep on the ground with a rock for a pillow. Giuseppa complained to a relative who was a priest and lived nearby, and he called on Padre Pio, explaining that his refusal to sleep on the bed his mother prepared for him was a breach of the obedience he owed to her as a son. Thereafter, he slept on the bed.

During Mass, Padre Pio tended to take interminably long pauses, seemingly oblivious to his external surroundings, conversing with God and celestial beings. During the prayers for the living and the dead, he paused for an unconscionably long time, interceding for various souls. He seemed to perceive the spiritual state of certain people when he was in this state. Moreover, during the consecration, he seemed to identify so closely with Christ's sufferings that at times he was barely able to speak the words of the liturgy. Masses that were supposed to last about half an hour were prolonged to more than two hours, leading many men to complain that Padre Pio was making them late to work. After a while, only old ladies were attending his Mass. Pannullo had to explain to Padre Pio that, although it was wonderful that he was having supernatural raptures during the Mass, he had to be considerate of the congregation, many of whom had other obligations.

After Mass, while making his prayer of thanksgiving, Padre Pio frequently went into ecstasy, just as he did at Venafro. Other priests were horrified when they found him in a state resembling death. In fact, one day the sacristan went to Pannullo to say he found Padre Pio dead in church. "No, he's not dead," said the archpriest. "Let him be. Ring the midday bell and go home." Returning later that afternoon, the sacristan found Padre Pio still without signs of life. "Uncle Torey," he told Pannullo, "this time the monk is dead. He's *really* dead." Still the archpriest was unconcerned: "I told you, don't worry. He'll revive." Thereupon Pannullo went into the church and commanded Pio on his vow of obedience to revive — and he did.[9] Padre Pio described his experience that day in a letter to Padre Agostino:

> It seemed as if an invisible force was immersing my whole being into fire.… My God, what fire! What sweetness! I felt many of those transports of love, and for some time I remained as if out of this world.… Had this lasted a moment, nay, a second, longer, my soul would have been separated from my body and I would have gone to be with Jesus![10]

At first, there were some who wondered if Padre Pio was insane. Gradually, however, they came to respect and revere him — not so much because of any miraculous occurrences, but because of his exemplary conduct and his love and concern for others.

Whenever Padre Pio passed the home of his old tutor, Don Domenico Tizzani, he would ask his wife and daughter, whom he frequently saw outside, to give his greetings to him. Tizzani, who had left the priesthood to marry, had become an unhappy recluse and refused to have anything to do with the clergy. When the archbishop of Benevento came to call on him, Tizzani refused to see him. One day, when Padre Pio asked Tizzani's daughter about him, she said that her sixty-nine-year-old father was sick and close to death. When Padre Pio asked if he could visit, the daughter told him, "Certainly you can!" and led him into the house, calling out,

"Daddy, Padre Pio is here!" Tizzani began to weep when he saw his old student. And, even though for years he had seemed to be hopelessly hardened, impenitent, and irreligious, he asked Padre Pio to hear his confession. He wept bitterly over his sins and committed himself to the mercy of Jesus. When Padre Pio told Pannullo what had happened, the archpriest was so overcome with joy that he fell to his knees, thanking the Lord. One day later, Tizzani died.

When walking back to town after celebrating Mass in neighboring villages, Padre Pio would always stop to talk to farmers in the field. Everyone found him friendly, concerned, and approachable, yet he wrote to Padre Benedetto:

> Most of the time it gives me great pain to talk to anyone except those of whom God speaks to me.... Because of this, I am a great lover of solitude.... When I am passing the time of day and conversations are prolonged ... and I cannot decently get away, I force myself to remain with the greatest of effort, since these conversations give me great pain.[11]

As a priest, Padre Pio was friendly, cheerful, polite, and witty — but basically serious. He would mince no words if he had reason to believe a parishioner was violating any of God's commandments. But so effective was he at reaching people's hearts that the townsfolk accepted rebukes they would often refuse to tolerate from other clergy.

For instance, Padre Pio was totally opposed to any labor whatsoever on the Sabbath, although he was not against wholesome play. He organized Sunday games for the townspeople so that they could have recreation and not think about breaking the Sabbath by doing work. His father, who returned to oversee the harvest, insisted that at harvesttime it was necessary to gather ripe wheat as quickly as possible, lest it be scorched by hot sun or beaten down in rainstorms. Surely, Orazio reasoned, God would not fault a man for working on Sunday to provide the necessities of life. Padre Pio disagreed. The Scriptures say: "Remember the sabbath day, to keep it holy. Six days you shall labor, and do all your work; but the seventh day is a sabbath to the LORD your God: in it you shall not do any work" (Ex 20:8–10). Was this not God's word? Could there be any excuse for breaking it? Conceding that his son was right, Orazio skipped his Sunday labors and found that his crops were none the worse for it.

In town, near "The Tower" where Padre Pio stayed during the winter months, lived a woman by the name of Mariandreana Montella. One Sunday, coming from Mass at the new parish church, Padre Pio saw her sitting on her front steps, sewing a ribbon onto a dress. "'Ndrianella," he said sternly, "today is Sunday. Today no one must work." 'Ndrianella made it clear that she did not want to be bothered. Padre Pio, in a huff, went home and reappeared a few minutes later, armed with a pair of scissors. He seized the ribbon and cut it to pieces. The woman was so furious that, according to some accounts, she chased the priest down the street, but later she admitted doing wrong in laboring on the Sabbath.[12]

"Our Saint"

The people grew to love this strange, zealous priest, and soon some were calling him "our saint." More and more people were attracted to his Masses, which, though he was trying to shorten them, still lasted far longer than customary. During Padre Pio's Masses, they came to feel the presence of God in an uncanny way. They seemed to comprehend the mystery of the Cross as never before. Early on, it was agreed that if anyone had a special intention "the little friar who lives in the Castle and whom everybody considers a saint"[13] should be sought out.

In April of 1912 or 1913, all the trees in the area were infested with lice and the fruit crop was threatened with ruin. One day "a simple peasant" approached Padre Pio and asked him to come with him to his field to bless the trees and curse the lice, and he consented. The peasant was amazed that within a short time all the lice fell to the ground. When they heard about this, farmers miles around begged Padre Pio to go through their fields, cursing the lice on their trees. It was claimed that the lice on all the trees died and that an excellent harvest ensued. Whatever natural explanations a scientist might offer, the Pietrelcinese were certain that a calamity had been avoided solely through the intercessions of their "little saint."

In September 1912, Padre Agostino gained impressive evidence of the presence and activity of Padre Pio's guardian angel. Agostino wrote Padre Pio a letter in Greek in order to keep its contents hidden from various local busybodies eager to read Padre Pio's mail. Although Padre Pio had taken a course in Greek, the little he learned he had forgotten. Padre Agostino wrote, "What will your angel say about this? God willing, your angel will be able to make you understand it. If not, write me."

Padre Pio took the letter to Pannullo, who understood Greek well. The archpriest later recounted, "Padre Pio … explained the contents to me, word for word." When he asked Padre Pio how he could read and understand the letter, Padre Pio replied, "You know, Pati, my guardian angel has explained everything to me!"[14]

For several years, Padre Agostino sent some letters to Padre Pio in French, another language his friend did not know. Even so, Padre Pio had no trouble reading his friend's letters and even once sent him a postcard entirely in French. He said that his "little angel" had told him what to write. The angel, however, must have been a poor student because a professor of French (the author's aunt) who read the text of the post-card declared Padre Pio's French abominable — even worse than Padre Agostino's.

"Those Foul Creatures"

In November 1912, when Padre Agostino's letters began arriving smeared with ink, Padre Pio suspected the handiwork of devils. At the suggestion of Pannullo, Padre Pio began placing a crucifix on the smudged letters. At once, "they became a little lighter, at least so that we could read them, even if with difficulty," the archpriest noted.[15]

There are numerous stories concerning Padre Pio's encounters at Piana Romana and in "The Tower" with demons in physical form. Several former neighbors swore that a demon (or demons) used to interfere with Padre Pio's prayer and meditation at the Piana Romana by appearing in the form of a snake with an enormous head.

One night, neighbors heard terrible noises — crashes, bangs, and shouts — coming from Padre Pio's apartment, and they complained to his parents. (Orazio seems to have returned home for good around 1912.) At first, they thought people were fighting. When they reached their son's apartment to investigate, Orazio and Giuseppa found things strewn about the room and Padre Pio lying in a state of collapse. Seeing the disorder, they asked him with whom he had been fighting. "With those foul fiends," Padre Pio replied.[16]

Many of the accounts of supernatural activity in Pietrelcina are from the testimony of people many years after the events. However, a letter that Padre Pio wrote to Padre Agostino on January 18, 1913, seems to corroborate the accounts of demonic activity in Padre Pio's abode. He wrote that he heard a "diabolic noise" but "saw nothing at first." Then a number of demons appeared "in the most abominable form" and "hurled themselves upon me and threw me on the floor, struck me violently, and threw pillows, books, and chairs through the air and cursed me with exceedingly filthy words. It is fortunate that the apartments beside me and below me are vacant."[17]

It is obvious that Padre Pio was not using a metaphor for an inward temptation or a state of mind. He saw, heard, and apparently felt specific phenomena which, despite the vacancy of the adjoining apartments, were heard by neighbors several doors away.

A few days later, on February 13, 1913, he wrote to Padre Agostino, "My body is all bruised because of the many blows that our enemies have rained on me." More than once, in the same month, he added, the demons snatched away his nightshirt and beat him while he shivered, stark naked, in the cold: "Even after they left me, I remained nude for a long time, for I was powerless to move because of the cold. Those evil creatures would have thrown themselves all over me if sweet Jesus hadn't helped me."[18]

Even after Padre Pio left Pietrelcina, "The Tower" was allegedly the site of apparent demonic activity. People claimed that in his room horrible noises could be heard from time to time, earthen pots spontaneously shattered, and chairs were thrown about by unseen forces. Michele (who did not return to Pietrelcina, at least for good, until 1919) reported these disturbing phenomena to his brother, now living in San Giovanni Rotondo, who told him that the apartment was still haunted by "those foul creatures" and directed him to summon a priest to perform an exorcism on the place. When this was done, there was no more trouble.

It is indisputable that there were phenomena associated with Padre Pio that cannot be readily explained. Many stories can be ascribed to hearsay, but for some there is good documentation. It would be a mistake to dismiss them all out of hand as legends and the figments of superstitious imaginations.

There is much about Padre Pio, especially concerning the supernatural aspect of his life, that will probably never be completely understood — especially if one wishes to exclude the possibility of it.

Chapter Eight

"Supernatural Graces"

"Totally Lost in God"

Padre Pio's interior life — his prayer, meditation, and communication with God and the invisible world — was the most important aspect of his existence.

For most people, as far as conscious experience is concerned, prayer is a one-way conversation. They trust that God hears their petitions, accepts their praise and thanksgiving, and pardons their sins, but their senses do not perceive his response. For Padre Pio, prayer was often an emphatically different kind of experience. He was certain that God spoke to him literally and directly, sometimes through a word perceived through his organs of hearing, sometimes through vision perceived through his organs of sight, but more often through "the vision that is not seen" and "the voice that is not heard," through which the spiritual realm was just as real and accessible as the beings of flesh and blood around him.

During his exile in Pietrelcina, Padre Pio wrote to Padre Benedetto:

My ordinary way of praying is this: as soon as I begin to pray I feel my soul begin to recollect itself in a peace and tranquillity (*sic*) that I cannot express in words.... The senses remain suspended, with the exception of my hearing, which sometimes is not suspended; yet usually this sense does not cause me trouble, and ... even if a great deal of noise were made around me, this would not bother me in the slightest.[1]

Padre Pio wrote of a "continuous thought of God." Sometimes he felt "touched by the Lord ... in a way that is so vivid and so sweet that most of the time I am impelled to shed tears of sorrow for my infidelity and for the tender mercy of having a Father so loving and so good as to summon me to his presence in this way." "Enriched by supernatural graces," he felt a "spiritual devotion" so intense that his soul was "totally lost in God." Other times he experienced "an impulse so powerful" that he found himself "languishing for God, almost ready to die." He emphasized that "all this arises, not from my own mental efforts or preparation, but from an internal flame and from a love" poured into his soul from God, "so powerful that if God did not quickly come to my aid, I would be consumed!"[2]

In another letter to Padre Benedetto, he described "the internal flame":

Hardly do I apply myself to pray than all at once I feel as if my heart is possessed by a flame of living love … unlike any flame of this poor world. It … consumes, but gives no pain. It is so sweet and delicious that the spirit finds great pleasure in it, and remains satiated in it in such a way that it does not lose its desire. Oh, God! This is a thing of supreme wonder to me. Perhaps I will never come to understand it until I reach the heavenly country.[3]

Within this mystical state, Padre Pio frequently received heavenly visitors. Writing to Padre Agostino in 1912, he declared, "Heavenly beings do not cease to visit me and make me anticipate the delight of the blessed."[4] On another occasion, Padre Pio wrote to him: "At night, as my eyes close, I see a veil come down and paradise opens to me, and, rejoicing in this vision, I sleep with a happy smile and with complete calm, expecting the little companion of my infancy [his guardian angel] to come to wake me and sing praises each morning with me to the delight of our hearts."[5] He could be referring simply to dreams in this case, but on many other occasions he made it clear that his experience of the supernatural world and its inhabitants was as real to him as the material world.

This, however, was not always true for him. Sometimes, Padre Pio found himself in a "great aridity of spirit," in which it was impossible for him to become recollected and pray, no matter how strongly he desired to do so. Sometimes he wondered whether his visions were mere hallucinations, whether his experiences truly corresponded to reality. In 1913, he confided to Padre Benedetto: "An atrocious thought crosses my mind: namely, that all this could be an illusion without my recognizing it."[6]

Most of the time, however, Padre Pio was absolutely convinced of the reality of his supersensible experiences, but he realized that it was very difficult for him to communicate effectively to others what he was experiencing. He explained to Padre Benedetto:

What happens to my soul is like what would happen if a poor little shepherd were led into the drawing room of a king, where an infinite world of precious objects were displayed that he has never seen before. The shepherd, when he leaves the palace of the king, will surely carry all those different objects in the eye of his mind, but he certainly will not know their number, nor will he be able to assign proper names to them. He might want to speak with others about all that he has seen. He might gather all his intellectual and scientific powers to make a good try, but seeing that all his powers would not succeed in making known what he intends, he prefers to keep silence.[7]

"A Surfeit of Sweet Joy"

On March 16, 1912, Padre Pio wrote to Padre Agostino, "Sometimes I seem to be on the point of dying of a surfeit of sweet joy!" Five days later he wrote:

Only God knows what sweetness I experienced yesterday … especially after Mass.… If only now, when I still feel almost all of his sweetness, I could bury these consolations within my heart, I would certainly be in paradise! How happy Jesus makes me! How sweet his spirit is! … He continues to love me and draw me closer to himself. He has forgotten my sins, and … remembers only his own mercy. Morning by morning he comes into my poor heart and pours out all the effusions of his goodness![8]

On April 18, he wrote: "Oh, how delightful the conversation was that I held this morning with Paradise! … Things impossible to translate into human language.… The heart of Jesus and my heart were — allow me to use this expression — fused. The joy in me was so intense and so profound that I was no longer able to contain myself, and my face was bathed in the most delightful tears!"[9] On July 7, 1913, he said that Christ had appeared to him and "immersed my soul in such peace and contentment that all the sweetest delights of this world, even if they were doubled, pale in comparison to even a drop of this blessedness!"[10]

These spiritual "sweetnesses," as Padre Pio called them, only increased his desire for God, a desire that he knew could never be consummated in this world. Because of this, he longed for death. Writing to Padre Agostino on August 9, 1912, Padre Pio declared: "My spirit runs the risk of separating itself from my body because I cannot love Jesus on earth. Yes, my soul is wounded with love for Jesus. I am sick with love. I continuously experience the bitter pain of the fire that burns but does not consume."[11] On December 29, 1912, reflecting on how many souls in the past year had "entered into the house of Jesus, there to remain forever," he exclaimed: "Life here below is a bitter grief to me, a life of exile that is a torment so bitter to me that I can scarcely bear it. The thought that any moment I could lose Jesus distresses me in an unspeakable way."[12]

In one of his most sublime descriptions, in which he seemingly describes a "near-death experience," Padre Pio wrote eloquently to Padre Agostino:

After my poor little soul has sighed for the moment of departure, after it has come several times to the limit of life, after it has relished the sweetness of death and has suffered all the struggle and torment that come from nature reclaiming its rights, after my soul has left my body, even to the extent of losing sight of this world below, and after I have almost touched the portals of the heavenly Jerusalem with my hand, I reawaken in this place of exile, becoming once more a pilgrim, always capable of being lost, and a new kind of agony seizes me that is worse than death itself and worse than any kind of martyrdom.... Alas, dear Father, how terribly hard this mortal life is! As long as it lasts, eternal life is uncertain. O cruel life, enemy of the Love that loves us infinitely more than we can possibly love or understand him … why do you not come to an end?

He longed to enter at once into "that eternal rest, where I shall live forever, lost in that immense ocean of good … and enjoying that by which He Himself is blessed! … Ah, dear Father, when will that long-awaited day come when my poor little soul will break up like a foundering ship in that immense ocean of eternal truth, where we will no longer be able to sin, or be aware that creatures are endowed with free will, because there all miseries are ended and we will no longer be able to withdraw our eyes from the limitless beauty nor cease to delight in God in one perpetual ecstasy of sweetest love!"[13]

The Dark Night

Not only was Padre Pio in agony at being separated from God, but he was also devastated by his own sinfulness, as he perceived it. His letters to Padre Agostino and Padre Benedetto abound with references to his own worthlessness. This seems to be the essence of the dark night that he experienced all his life, which alternated or even perhaps coexisted with his experiences of divine sweetness.

In May 1914, speaking of the "deep darkness … thickening on the horizon of my spirit," Padre Pio confessed:

I know that no one is spotless in the sight of the Lord, but my impurity is without bounds before him. In the present state in which the merciful Lord, in his infinite wisdom and justice, condescends to raise the veil and reveal my secret short-comings to me in all their malignity and hideousness, I see myself so deformed that it seems as if my very clothing shrinks in horror of my defilement![14]

Not only was Padre Pio horrified by his actual sins, he was filled with terror at his potential to sin. In September 1915, he wrote to Padre Agostino that "the thought of going astray and … offending God fills me with terror. It paralyzes my limbs, and both body and soul feel as if they are being squeezed in a powerful vise.

My bones feel as if they were being dislocated ... crushed and ground up."[15] All this at the mere *thought* of sinning!

Padre Pio said the agony his soul experienced in this "dark night" was so great that he could not conceive of it being much less than "the atrocious pains that the damned suffer in hell." Of these experiences, which occurred frequently throughout his life, Padre Pio said, "Such torture does not last long, nor could it do so, because, if I remain alive at all while it lasts, it is through a special favor from God!"[16] In various letters, he speaks of being "mad with anguish" and not knowing whether he is in hell, purgatory, or earth, and of being in "an endless desert of darkness, despondency, and insensibility, a land of death, a night of abandonment, a cavern of desolation, in which my poor soul finds itself far from God and alone with itself."[17]

Sometime later, writing to a woman who was suffering similar trials, Padre Pio declared that her sufferings were a grace ordained by God "to exalt your soul to the perfect union of love." Before attaining to this union, a Christian needs to be purged of her defects and her attachments to things both natural and supernatural. This is necessary because every "natural inclination and mode of behavior" must be surrendered to God so as to be transformed to "work in another way more divine than human."[18] He went on to describe how God purges the soul, totally emptying it of itself. All self-centeredness must be replaced by "a new way of thinking and wishing that is simply and purely supernatural and celestial." In order to arrive at this state, the soul must be subjected to this painful trial whereby it is purged by an intense light that reveals faults hitherto unseen, showing God not as a loving Father but as a terrifying Judge. The soul feels as if God were casting it out. It is through this passive purgation that God unites the soul to himself "with a chain of love." Yet this process "produces a darkness thicker than that which enshrouded the Egyptians at the time of the Exodus." This is because the intellect is incapable of receiving the light and is indisposed by many imperfections and weaknesses. The "dark night" affects the intellect, the higher powers of the soul, and even the physical appetites.[19]

This "purgative light" reveals to the soul its own "nothingness, its sins, its defects, its wretchedness." It "eradicates every bit of esteem and conceit and complacency, to the very roots of the soul."[20] It also prepares the will for the joy of mystical union with God. Moreover, the purgative light shows the soul its absolute dependency upon God for its salvation and its inability to do anything to save itself. Through this light, Padre Pio maintained, the Christian realizes that he cannot repay God's love for him, that there is nothing naturally within him except falseness and deformity, and that God is the only fountain of truth and grace and love, the only source of salvation.

Even though Padre Pio could explain and analyze his trial in detail, this made it no less painful, nor was his anguish less acute in those moments when he felt abandoned by God, when he saw everything as darkness and desolation. All he could do was throw himself into the arms of Jesus.

Padre Pio at times felt as if he were sinking through quicksand into hell, yet he continued to wait for God. Constantly he repeated, as an act of faith, the words of Job, "Though he slay me, yet will I trust him" (Jb 13:15, KJV). He continued diligently to search the Scriptures, deriving comfort from the fact that Jonah, Jeremiah, David, and Paul, like him, passed through the same deep waters of desolation. He was also comforted by Padre Benedetto, whom he accepted as the "internal and external judge" of his soul. Padre Benedetto wrote to Padre Pio, "You must calm yourself by means of my assurances and hold them as if sworn by oath." In other words, Padre Pio was to have confidence and not despair of God's mercy, if for no other reason than he was ordered to do so through "holy obedience." The "Night," Padre Benedetto explained, was sent by God "to extinguish human understanding so that divine understanding can take its place, and you, having been stripped of the ... usual way of using your mental faculties, might be able to rise to that supernatural and heavenly purification."[21] Pannullo, however, was not as helpful as Padre Benedetto, for Padre Pio wrote, "He scolds me and I find no consolation in his sermons to me."[22]

A Conversation with an Angel

Padre Pio continued to be subject to attacks by demonic forces. In August 1912, for a space of several days, whenever he decided to write to his superiors, he was seized with violent migraine headaches and spasms in his writing arm. Recognizing devilish interference, he prayed and then was able to write. The devil continued to visit him with temptations against purity, which Padre Pio in his modesty did not detail. In addition, he continued to be subject to physical attacks by infernal forces, accompanied by terrifying noises clearly audible to neighbors. But he also continued to receive visits from his guardian angel, as well as from Jesus and Mary. It was his angel who frequently rescued him from physical assaults by demonic powers. This is the topic of a beautiful but rather strange letter that Pio wrote in November 1912 to Padre Agostino:

> I cannot describe to you how those wretched creatures beat me. Sometimes I feel as if I were near death. Saturday it seemed as if they really wanted to finish me, and I didn't know which way to turn, so I turned to my angel, who, after keeping me waiting for a time, appeared and flew all around me and, with his angelic voice, sang hymns to the Divine Majesty.
>
> There followed one of those usual discussions. I scolded him harshly for making me wait so long while I was continually calling for him to help me. In order to punish him, I did not want to look him in the face. I wanted to withdraw and get away from him. But the poor fellow overtook me, almost weeping, and caught hold of me, trying to make me look at him. And then I glanced into his face and found him full of regret.

"My dear boy, [the angel said], I am always near you. I always hover ‸ut you with the love aroused by your gratitude to the Beloved of your ‸t. My love for you will not pass away, even with your earthly life. I ‸hat your generous heart always palpitates with yearning for him ‸e both love. You would climb every mountain and traverse every ‸rt in search of him, to see him again, to embrace him again … and ask ‸im to break immediately the chain which unites you to the body…. You would tell him that, separated here from him in this world, you have more sadness than joy…. As for now, he is able to give you only the ray of a star, the perfume of a flower, the note of a harp, the caress of a breeze. But do not cease to ask him insistently for [what you desire], because his supreme delight is to have you with him. And although he cannot yet satisfy you, since Providence wills that you remain in exile a little longer, in the end he will fulfill your desire."[23]

It is clear that even when Padre Pio cried out that God had forsaken him, this situation was often followed by encounters with Jesus, Mary, and his guardian angel, who, at times, responded to questions that his superiors put to him. To the end of his life, it caused him great anguish that, although heaven often showed him the state of others' souls, he remained in the dark about his own.

"I Want to Bring Everyone to God!"

Most of Padre Pio's visions related to his ministry to others. For instance, in March 1913, he described a vision in which Jesus deplored the lack of spirituality among contemporary Christians and a lack of dedication among the clergy. In this bodily vision, Jesus appeared in human form and spoke words perceptible to Padre Pio's physical ears. At times, the Lord was silent; at other times, his throat was choked with sobs as he lamented that people

> … make no effort to control themselves amidst their temptations and … even delight in their iniquity. The souls in whom I most delight lose their faith when they are put to the test. They ignore me, day and night, in the churches. They no longer care about the Sacrament of the Altar…. No one cares any more about the love that I bear them. I am continually saddened. My house has become for many a theater of amusements…. My ministers … whom I have loved as the apple of my eye … ought to have comforted my heart, which is now filled with sorrow. They ought to have aided me in the redemption of souls, but instead … I receive ingratitude and thanklessness from them. Son, I see many of them who … betray me with hypocritical faces and … sacrilegious Communions.[24]

Jesus seems almost humanly petulant in this vision, and it further kindled Padre Pio's zeal to win souls for Christ and to renew his self-offering as a victim. In other visions, Jesus presented souls to Padre Pio whom he never met before. Through his revelations, Padre Pio learned about the interior state of these souls so that he could help them when God gave him the opportunity to meet them.

Those inclined to dismiss Padre Pio as a madman (or at least a sane man with a very vivid imagination) must understand that his revelations and locutions usually corresponded to some generally observable reality. The supersensible communications almost always resulted in some act of kindness or concern, and all his supernatural experiences centered on love for God and man. Moreover, the hellish noises that Padre Pio reported could sometimes be heard by others.

The more Padre Pio's spiritual life intensified, the more his love and concern grew for other people. In a letter to Padre Agostino written in the fall of 1915, Padre Pio prayed that God would give life to souls dead in sin:

I have always implored you, trembling as I beg you now, in your mercy, to withdraw the thunderbolt of thy glance from my unhappy brethren. You have said, O my sweet Lord, that "Love is as strong as death and lasts as long as hell"; therefore, look with an eye of ineffable sweetness upon these dead brethren. Chain them to yourself with a strong bond.

May all these dead souls arise, O Lord! O Jesus, Lazarus [whom Jesus raised four days after death] made no request at all that you should raise him. The prayers of a sinful woman sufficed for him. Ah, behold, my Divine Lord, another soul, also sinful and guilty beyond all measure, who beseeches you in behalf of a multitude of dead souls who have no interest in praying to you. I beg you to raise them. You know, my Lord and King, the cruel martyrdom that these Lazaruses cause me. Call them with a cry so powerful as to give them life, and at thy command, let them come forth from the sepulchre of their obscene pleasures![25]

Much of Padre Pio's spiritual life was directed at the raising of modern-day Lazaruses. All of it fed into his ministry for the salvation of souls. Frequently he prayed, echoing Moses: "Either save this people or blot me out of thy book of life!" Once someone told him of a prophecy that a member of the Franciscan order would lead a third of the world to Christ, implying that it referred to him. Padre Pio retorted, "What do I want with a third? More! More! I want to bring everyone to God!"[26]

Chapter Nine

Return to the Friary

"The Saint at Mecca"

Although Padre Benedetto continued to function as Padre Pio's spiritual director and Padre Agostino continued to give him advice and counsel, both men increasingly came to look to their protégé for wisdom in their own difficulties. It is interesting to read through the letters the three priests sent to one another during this period. Padre Pio would agonize about his spiritual state and other problems. Padres Benedetto and Agostino would, in turn, give him counsel, chide him for not surrendering himself sufficiently to the "word of obedience," and then pour out their own troubles to him, begging him for a word of comfort or direction. They would travel to Pietrelcina to consult him on matters concerning their Capuchin province. This was so often that, when learning that the two priests had gone once more to see Padre Pio, various other priests and brothers would grumble, "They went to consult the saint at Mecca."[1]

Padre Agostino, in particular, was forever asking questions that he expected Padre Pio to answer on the basis of supersensible wisdom. On May 13, 1914, for example, Padre Agostino asked Padre Pio about the upcoming elections in the province. Mentioning that he had spoken to Padre Benedetto about him, Padre Agostino suggested, "Perhaps the Lord will reveal the content of our conversation."[2] When Padre Pio failed to mention the subject in his next letter, Padre Agostino again urged him to tell him what had happened during his conference with Padre Benedetto. This time Padre Pio responded that he had no idea. In August of the same year, Padre Agostino wrote on behalf of another priest who wanted Padre Pio to ask the Lord to reveal something about his future. Padre Pio replied that Jesus did not want the priest to know more than he already knew through natural means. Moreover, this time he warned Padre Agostino that he was going a bit too far and was coming close to putting the Lord to the test.

Despite the fact that Padre Pio was in the dark as to his own relationship with God, he was able to discern the divine will for certain people whom God evidently entrusted to him. Replying to a letter from Padre Agostino early in 1916, for example, Padre Pio commented on a soul about whom he was enlightened: "Jesus wants to test her some more, and for the moment he will not grant her request. Let this blessed soul have a little patience, because, in the end, he will satisfy her."[3] Padre Benedetto wrote to Padre Pio concerning a woman who had tragically backslid in her Christian life. He asked how this could have happened, and Padre Pio gave a detailed reply:

This is how that soul was snared in the devil's net: When she saw that she was so favored by God … she was amazed at all the good that God sent her and she clearly discerned the difference between the goods of heaven and those of earth. At this point she was proceeding well.

But the Enemy, who is always alert, seeing such affection, convinced her that such great confidence and certainty could never diminish.… Furthermore, he put into her heart a clear vision of the heavenly prize, so that it seemed impossible for her to renounce so great a happiness for things so base and vile as earthly pleasures.

The devil used this immoderate confidence to make her lose that holy distrust in herself, a diffidence that must never leave the soul, no matter how privileged it is by God.

Meanwhile, having lost, little by little, this distrust of herself, she was cast severely into temptation, still persuaded that she had nothing to fear.… This then was the origin and cause of her final ruin. What remains for us to do? Let's pray to the Lord that he might put her back on the right path.[4]

God enlightened Padre Pio about some people; but about many others, especially if he had never met them, he could say nothing. Padre Eusebio Notte, Padre Pio's assistant in the 1960s, recalled how Padre Pio responded to a request for advice by his current father superior with a promise to pray. A few days later the superior asked again, only to have Padre Pio assure him, "I'm praying." When the superior expressed his surprise that the man by then venerated as a prophet had no answer, Padre Pio told him, "My son, if the answer doesn't come from above, what can I myself say? … If nobody up there says something, what answers can I give?"[5] This was true throughout his ministry.

The Sisters Cerase

Padres Benedetto and Agostino were eager for Padre Pio to be a spiritual director to others, and they recommended several women to be his "spiritual daughters."

These included Margherita Tresca, from Barletta, and Annitta Rodote, from Foggia, both of whom eventually became nuns. By 1915, Padre Pio was also advising two sickly spinster sisters, Giovina and Raffaella Cerase of Foggia. They were considered "saintly," and, although Giovina was fifty-three and Raffaella forty-six, the twenty-eight-year-old friar considered them "elderly." The Cerases came from a wealthy family but were involved in an ongoing quarrel over their inheritance with their brother and his wife. Giovina suffered from what her sister described as "a sick stomach brought about by constant worry" and was emaciated and "worn out, physically and mentally," from a life that had been "one long series of conflicts, contradictions, sighs, and tears."[6] Although she had "a heart of gold and great ideals," she was irritable and "bored by everything and everyone,"[7] constantly muttering, "A sad youth, a sadder old age."[8] Raffaella (or Raffaelina), the more cheerful and outgoing of the sisters — who, by her own admission, lived like "cloistered nuns" — was also nervous, frail, and constantly ill, complaining of her "forty-six years of useless, empty, and sinful life."[9] She admitted that she was "afraid of life,"[10] wracked with "hellish interior martyrdoms,"[11] and "drowning in a sea of sorrows."[12] She thought of herself as "a handful of filth,"[13] "a mass of sin,"[14] and "empty, wretched, and useless."[15]

For the better part of two years, Padre Pio maintained an extensive correspondence with Raffaelina Cerase. Although he was almost two decades her junior, he did not hesitate to adopt a paternal tone in his letters to her, and she one of childlike submission. In his letters, the Capuchin stressed that Raffaelina's temptations were "proof of the soul's union" with God and that the storms that raged around her were proof of God's presence and love:

> The fact of being harassed, therefore, means that you are in the Lord's service, and the more fully you become the friend and intimate of God, the more you will have to endure temptation. Temptation is a most convincing proof that God is united with a soul.... All the disheartening thoughts that are running around in your mind, such as the idea that God may be punishing you for Communions and Confessions badly made and for all the other devotional practices carelessly performed, believe me, are nothing but temptations which you must drive far from you, for it is by no means true that in all these things you have offended God, since Jesus, by his watchful grace, has guarded you very well against all such offenses.[16]

Padre Pio assured Raffaelina that God was with her and that a soul who is afraid of offending God is not far from him; rather, her fears and worries had their origins in Satan, whose attacks were permitted by a merciful heaven "because [God's] mercy makes you dear to him and he wants to make you similar to his

Only Begotten Son, who took upon himself all the iniquities of men and was subjected to terrible and unspeakable torture."[17] Therefore he urged Raffaelina to praise God, who was treating her as "one chosen to follow closely in the steps of Jesus up the hill of Calvary."[18]

Padre Pio points out that suffering is a sign of God's favor, and the Christian, instead of complaining of trials and temptations, should "follow the Divine Master up the steep slope of Calvary, loaded with our cross, and when it pleases him to place us on the cross by confining us to a bed of sickness, let us thank him and consider ourselves lucky to be honored in this way, aware that to be on the cross with Jesus is infinitely more perfect than merely contemplating [him] on the cross."[19]

Likewise, Padre Pio stressed that joy is an integral part of the Christian life. He exhorted Raffaelina to "rejoice at all times, for the Lord's yoke is an agreeable one. You are glorifying the Lord by your life and he is pleased with you. Never leave any room for sadness in your heart, for this would be in conflict with the Holy Spirit poured out into your soul."[20] If she found herself oppressed by melancholy, she should think about Jesus, read a good book, then give herself "to some manual work or something which distracts ... even ... singing some cheerful song, and ... [inviting] others to sing with you."[21] Moreover, she should keep her thoughts on heaven, and "the fact that here on earth we are on a battleground and that in paradise we shall receive the crown of victory; that this is a testing-ground and the prize will be awarded up above; that we are now in a land of exile, while our true homeland is heaven, to which we must continuously aspire."[22]

Padre Pio told Raffaelina that she was undergoing the "purgation of the senses," characterized by the impossibility of fixing the "imagination on any truth whatsoever in order to meditate on it." God permitted her to encounter difficulty concentrating in prayer so that he might "infuse" into her mind "a more perfect light, a much more spiritual and purer light" through which she could focus on God "without any words," simply "contemplating him with a simple gaze, a pure, delightful, delicate, and divine gaze."[23]

After the "purgation of the senses," Raffaelina could expect "a much more severe purification which is known as the purgation of the spirit," which would lift her soul to an even higher degree of perfection. "The trial will most certainly be a very severe one, but do not be frightened. The Lord, as always, will be with you and will console you. This new purification will consist entirely in detaching you from what is called accidental spiritual devotion and love of God" — in other words, from a love of God that is based on his gifts rather than on him, for his own sake. This would happen through a "spiritual aridity" that consisted of "absolute privation of all comfort of a purely spiritual nature." This was to enable her to love God for himself alone and not for any pleasure or enjoyment. In this state, Padre Pio warned

Raffaelina that she could expect to be "enveloped in deep darkness," with all spiritual activity "difficult and repugnant."[24]

"Did You Enter the Seraphic Order Only to Live and Stay Well?"

Even though pleased with Padre Pio's work as a spiritual director, his superiors were not happy about his remaining away from the cloister for so long. In December 1913, Padre Benedetto, as minister provincial, began to insist once more that Padre Pio return to the friary. It had been two years since he had been forced to leave Venafro, and, at Pietrelcina, "breathing [his] native air," his health had shown minimal improvement. "Return to community life, even though you are convinced that in doing so, you will grow worse," Padre Benedetto insisted. "It seems to be contrary to God's will … for you to stay outside the community so long for reasons of health. Did you enter the Seraphic Order to live and stay well and vow to remain in it only if you did not have to be ill and die?" He urged Padre Pio to accept an appointment as vice-master of novices at Morcone. This would involve very little work, just setting an example. "And if death comes, welcome it. It will mean that the fetters of the body will be broken all the sooner!" Padre Benedetto exhorted him.[25]

Padre Pio balked, saying that he would be only an encumbrance to any community where he might be sent. Instead, he requested that Padre Benedetto seek permission from the Vatican for him to remain in the Capuchin order while continuing to reside in Pietrelcina. In doing this, perhaps he was seeking a compromise between the demands of Padre Benedetto, who wanted him to return to community life immediately, and those of his mother and Archpriest Pannullo, who wanted him to leave the Capuchin order to become a secular priest.

When both Padres Benedetto and Agostino asked Padre Pio to inquire of Jesus why the divine will was for him to remain outside the friary, Pio reported that Jesus said to tell them that they should not ask. This did not satisfy Padre Benedetto, who, in June 1914, ordered Padre Pio to report to Morcone. "Have fear of nothing," wrote Padre Agostino, who was to accompany him there. "Everything will result in God's glory and your good. If you die, I am sure you will go to enjoy the beauty of our Divine Bridegroom.… If he asked your life, wouldn't you content him? Then, let the Lord's will be done."[26]

Padre Pio obeyed his superiors and reported to Morcone, only to become so ill that he had to leave after five days. When he returned to Pietrelcina, he wrote Raffaelina, "I had hardly entered the town when they all came out to greet me, adding to their thanks to the Lord the cries, 'Long life!' and 'Welcome back!' I was moved to the point of tears."[27] To Padre Benedetto, describing his terrible asthma attacks, Padre Pio begged, "Good Father, don't be angry with me. I just don't know which way to turn. I would like to have spared you this new pain, to shoulder the weight of this cross by myself, but this I was not allowed to do."[28] Padre Benedetto was so enraged that he would not write to Padre Pio for six months. When Padre Pio once again sought dispensation from Rome to remain at Pietrelcina as a Capuchin, Padre Benedetto wrote Padre Agostino, "I will obtain the brief, but I will not believe in his sanctity anymore!"[29]

Padre Agostino tried to explain the provincial's position to Pio:

> Like me, he is convinced that God is at work in your spirit, but he … does not believe that the Lord wants you there, out of the cloister … [Padre Benedetto asks:] "How could God, for the purpose of greater perfection, take a soul out of the cloister and place him forever in the secular world?" … [Padre Benedetto desires] that you might have the strength to come to the cloister to die, like every true son of St. Francis."[30]

Padre Agostino took it upon himself to plead Padre Pio's case with the minister general of the Capuchin order, Venantius Dodo (1862–1926) of Lisle-en-Rigault. Venantius was sympathetic and agreed to obtain the "brief" from Rome that would give Padre Pio permission to remain in Pietrelcina while retaining his Capuchin habit for as long as he remained ill. Permission was granted in March 1915.

Although he had requested the brief, Padre Pio was nevertheless upset. He wrote Padre Agostino: "What humiliation for me, my father, at seeing myself practically cut off from the Seraphic Order!" Padre Agostino wrote back, comforting him, "The minister general has seen God's will and grants you the brief, but only on a temporary basis. Therefore you belong to us and even more to the Seraphic Father [Saint Francis]."[31]

War

As early as May 1914, Padre Pio had been sought for supernatural illumination on the deteriorating international situation. In response to a question from Padre Benedetto, Padre Pio related that Jesus didn't want him to disclose the ultimate outcome of the world situation, and urged: "Let's pray with true faith to our heavenly Father for a favorable outcome, because the situation is getting rather grave, and, if God does not bring about a solution, the outcome will be very grim. We do not deserve divine assistance, since we have willingly banished the most lovable Jesus from our hearts…. However, may we at least be permitted to hope in God's infinite Providence."[32]

On June 28, a Serbian terrorist assassinated Archduke Franz Ferdinand, the heir to the Austro-Hungarian Empire, and by early August most of the world's major powers were at war, although Italy and the United States held back initially. Padre Pio saw the terrifying conflict as God's punishment for man's unbelief, and he feared that the wrath of God would soon break out upon his country, which, like its neighbors, had apostatized from God. He also was grieved deeply by the passing of Pope Pius X, who succumbed to a heart attack on August 20. Padre Pio characterized the pontiff as "a truly noble and holy soul whose equal has never been seen by Rome."[33]

On September 7, Padre Pio wrote Padre Agostino, begging him to pray to "disarm the hand of divine justice, rightly inflamed against the nations who do not want to know the law of love. Above all, let us pray to disarm God's wrath towards our country. She, too, has many accounts to settle with God. May she at least learn from the misfortune of others, especially from her sister France, how harmful it is for a nation to distance itself from God."

When Italy entered the war on the side of the Allies in the spring of 1915, Padre Pio said: "Italy did not want to listen to the voice of love." Writing to Raffaelina Cerase, he lamented:

Up to the present, nothing has worked to make our country repent and come back to God. Alas, because of our nation's sin, since it has become abominable and detestable in God's sight, I fear that the Lord in his furious anger will punish us according to strict justice. May it please this God of goodness, who is rightly enraged with our country, to behave as a loving father and not as a righteous judge, as we deserve only too well. In the excess of his love for his creatures, may he change the punishment itself into a wholesome cleansing for all of us."[34]

Later he wrote Cerase:

The solemn moment through which our country is passing … does not mean that heaven has abandoned us. While heaven speaks, we are still loved. How wretched those countries are to whom the Lord doesn't speak anymore, not even in quiet indignation, for this is a sign that he has cast them off, that they are abandoned and left alone in their blindness and obduracy. In you, wretched nations, there has been fulfilled what God said through the prophet Ezekiel: "My jealousy shall depart from you; I will be calm and will be no more angry." Tremble, all nations who no longer hear even the angry voice of God, for this silence is the greater punishment which heaven has dealt out to you.… Let us be comforted, then, and trust in the Lord, for he still loves our own Italy … He is waiting for the voice of our repentance to silence his thundering. He is waiting for our tears to extinguish his lightning. Well then, let our tears of true contrition never fail us. Let us lift up our hands to heaven and implore tears of this kind for all our fellow-travelers.[35]

Padre Pio wrote Padre Agostino, "The horrors of the war … keep me in a constant mortal agony. I would rather die than witness such slaughter!"[36] A few weeks later he complained, "The horrors of war are driving me nearly mad. My soul is plunged into extreme desolation. I had prepared myself for this, but it still has not prevented the terror and anguish that are gripping my soul!"[37]

Padre Agostino wrote back: "My God, what a slaughter! What a bloodbath! What is going to happen to the world?"[38]

Even so, Padre Pio had hopes that the war would prove to be a "health-giving purge" for the world, for Italy, and for the Church. He hoped that it would turn people back to God. It was his fervent prayer that, after passing through a night "shrouded in thickest darkness," mankind would emerge into a "new day." Just as Woodrow Wilson, who would take America into the "Great War" two years later, hoped that the result of the conflict would be a "world safe for democracy," Padre Pio prayed for a world of reawakened faith, peace, love, and justice:

> Ah, may all the nations afflicted by this war understand the mystery of the pacific wrath of the Lord! … If he turns their poisonous joys into bitterness, if he corrupts their pleasures, and if he scatters thorns along the paths of their riot, paths hitherto strewn with the roses of slaughter, the reason is that he loves them still. And this is the holy cruelty of the physician, who, in extreme cases of sickness, makes us take most bitter and most horrible medicines.… The greatest mercy of God is not to let those nations remain in peace with each other who are not in peace with God."[39]

Private Forgione

The clergy in Italy were not exempt from conscription, and by the end of May 1915 thirteen priests and eight seminarians from the Capuchin province of Sant'Angelo had been drafted. "My God, what a terrible situation!" Padre Agostino lamented, terrified at the prospect of conscription. He assured Padre Pio that, with his poor health, he would surely be rejected for military service. However, Padre Pio was not so sure, as it was common knowledge that the medical officer for the Benevento district (under whose jurisdiction he was) was notoriously unwilling to grant exemptions for physical disability.

In November, Padre Pio was drafted. However, the "ferocious medical captain" who examined him at Benevento diagnosed tuberculosis and sent him to Caserta for further examinations. There, to the dismay of the sickly priest, "the stupid colonel" pronounced him physically fit and roared, "Go to your regiment and meet your new superiors!"

Private Francesco Forgione was assigned to the Tenth Company of the Army Medical Corps in Naples, where some nine hundred priests and religious served in uniform.[40] Padre Pio was given janitorial duties. Almost immediately, he began to vomit everything he ate. His company commander ordered further examinations. He was removed from the barracks and lodged in a hotel in Naples — and required to pay for his bill out of pocket. Not having any money, he had to wire his father, who came at once with money and provisions. Finally, just before Christmas, he was diagnosed with chronic bronchitis and given a year's leave.

"Dead or Alive, You're Staying Here at Foggia!"

Since Padre Pio had weathered several weeks in the army without dying, Padre Benedetto was determined to make him return to community life, especially now that so many friars were in the service that most of the convents were nearly empty. (Because the Capuchin order had only recently been reestablished, most of the friars were younger men.) On December 20, Padre Agostino wrote Padre Pio to inform him that Padre Benedetto wanted him back at the friary, telling him, "It's being repeated all over the province that you are being deceived by the devil, who is taking advantage of your affection for your native soil."[41] On Christmas Eve, Padre Benedetto wrote, "Foggia awaits you." Still Padre Pio balked. He accused Padre Agostino of being like one of Job's comforters in insisting that it would be good for him to return to the cloister. He argued that since Padre Benedetto did not order him under obedience to return to community life, he did not have to go. Padre Agostino wrote back:

> It is an unshakable principle in the economy of our salvation that obedience must prevail over all worldly reasoning. Well, authority has spoken clearly concerning your return to the cloister. Therefore, no other advice and no other person can make an exception. The authority can be mistaken, but obedience is never mistaken. God himself has never dispensed any saint from obedience to authority.[42]

Ultimately, it was Raffaelina Cerase who was the direct cause of Padre Pio's return to community life. The previous summer her sister Giovina had been hospitalized in a nearly skeletal state with a life-threatening liver disease. Raffaelina thereupon offered herself as a victim to God for her sister's recovery. The next month she wrote to Padre Pio about "a fresh gift Jesus has given me" — a painful tumor rapidly developing in a breast.[43] Nevertheless she refused to see a physician for fear of exposing her naked body to the gaze of a male doctor.[44]

"Do you mean to say that you don't know that anyone who refuses human remedies exposes himself to the danger of offending the Lord?" Padre Pio wrote back. "And don't you know that God tells us through the Sacred Scriptures to love the physician for love of himself?" He ordered her to seek immediate medical help, to pray for a cure, but to "be resigned all the time to do whatever God wants."[45]

The physician she consulted promised Raffaelina that a mastectomy would result in her being "perfectly cured," but she wrote to Padre Pio that she had "no illusions."[46] He wrote back that the cancer was "precisely God's will," proof that he "wants to bring you by this path to greater conformity to the divine prototype, Jesus Christ" — that is, to unite her with his suffering. He urged her to look to the future, when "Jesus will reward your faithfulness and resignation [in heaven]."[47]

Three months after Raffaelina's mastectomy, it was apparent that it had been unsuccessful and that her sickness was spreading throughout her body. However, Giovina was now perfectly well. The doctors could find no trace of her illness. Raffaelina confided to Padre Pio: "I asked Jesus for an exchange. Has he granted it to me?"[48] (Giovina wouldn't die for another fifteen years, when she was seventy.) To Padre Agostino, who visited her at her home in Foggia, Raffaelina confided that she had also offered herself as a victim for Padre Pio's return to the cloister.

Meanwhile, Padre Agostino was concerned by the attitude of the people in Pietrelcina — and in particular Padre Pio's mother, who did not want him to leave. "You must understand that Padre Pio belongs to us," he insisted to Giuseppa. "You've got to give him up." She seemed mollified, but Pannullo was concerned about mob violence. In fact, someone had told Agostino, "If you run off with our little saint, we'll cut your head off!" When he told Raffaelina about this, she told him: "Father, don't be afraid. Make arrangements with Padre Benedetto. Padre Pio will come here [to Foggia]. He will hear my confession and he will assist me at my death. Make the superiors give Padre Pio the faculties to hear confessions. He will save many souls."[49]

Padre Agostino then pleaded with Padre Pio to come to Foggia, if only for a few days. "Don't you want to console this poor soul? Do you want to let her leave the world with this disappointment? ... Don't you feel any obligation to this soul who has prayed so much, and, indeed, is still praying for you?"[50]

On February 17, 1916, telling his parents and relatives and neighbors that he was going to Foggia for a few days to assist a dying woman, Padre Pio went to the railroad station at Benevento to meet Padre Agostino. The two set out to the city of Foggia, a train ride of about two hours to the northeast. The moment Padre Pio set foot in the friary of St. Anna in Foggia, Padre Benedetto, who was there to greet him, growled, "Here's a pen and paper. Write your Mama and tell her to send your belongings, because, dead or alive, you're staying here at Foggia!"[51]

Chapter Ten

San Giovanni Rotondo

Refused Permission to Die

Shortly after Padre Pio arrived in Foggia, Padre Agostino took him to the Cerase home, to meet in person for the first time the lady with whom he had been corresponding for two years. Agostino wrote: "The meeting of Padre Pio and Donna Raffaelina was that of two souls who had known each other before the Lord for a long time.... The way they looked at each other — it was angelic — more eloquent than words can tell."[1]

For the next couple of months, Padre Pio paid regular visits to the sick woman as her physical condition continued to deteriorate. On March 17, Padre Pio wrote to Padre Agostino, who was at the friary at San Marco la Catola, "For several days now Raffaelina has been on the cross of the Beloved. She is suffering with unconquerable resignation. It breaks my heart to see her in such a state."[2] The same day he wrote to Padre Benedetto, "She is already in the antechamber of the King. Before long she will be led in to the nuptial banquet."[3]

Giovina, eavesdropping, heard the friar say to her sister, "My dear daughter, let's tell Jesus to take me in your place."

"No, Father," answered Raffaelina, "I want to go first to Jesus myself. Then I will tell him to send me to take you."[4]

On March 25, Padre Pio wrote Padre Agostino: "At 4:00 this morning we gained another intercessor at the throne of the Most High. Raffaelina has finished the course; she has celebrated the nuptials with her Divine Spouse. She fell asleep, happy soul, with a smile of disdain for this world."[5] Agostino praised the "lovely soul," the "veritable treasure of goodness and piety," who had "immolated herself" in exchange for the permanent return of Padre Pio to the cloister.

Padre Pio now passionately yearned for death. He begged Padre Agostino to give him permission to die. Shortly afterward, he had a vision of Raffaelina in her heavenly glory, who conveyed to him a message that he was not eager to hear. To

Padre Agostino, who had refused him permission to die, Padre Pio lamented, "The whole lot of you are cruel! Padre Benedetto, the provincial, says no, you say no. And now that other spirit … comes to tell me that she can't do anything because Jesus doesn't want it! If I had known that, I would never have given her permission to go to heaven before me! All of you are cruel!"[6]

More Extraordinary Phenomena

For about six months, Padre Pio remained at St. Anna's, during which time he was constantly ill and spent much of his time in bed. His confreres found it unusual that, even though he was able to retain hardly any of the food he ate, he showed no signs of starvation. What concerned them most, however, were the horrific noises that issued from his room early every evening.

Padre Paolino di Tommaso of Casacalenda (1886–1964), who was assigned to the friary of Our Lady of Grace in San Giovanni Rotondo, twenty-five miles away, found the friars there worried about the terrifying noises that came from Pio's room. He passed through Foggia in May on his way to a medical examination for military service (which, to his relief, he failed).

Padre Paolino was skeptical, until the dinner hour came and the community sat down to eat. Padre Pio, who seldom, if ever, partook of the evening meal, remained upstairs in his room. During the course of the meal, everyone heard a terrific crash, just as if, as Padre Paolino put it, a huge drum of oil or gasoline had been dropped and crashed to the floor. Immediately Padre Paolino ran upstairs to find Padre Pio pale and drenched in sweat, as if he had gone swimming in his nightshirt. The same thing happened for several successive nights.

Word of this reached Padre Benedetto, who hurried to the friary. The minister provincial conferred with Padre Pio and asked Padre Paolino to be present as a witness. Padre Benedetto ordered Padre Pio to have the noises stopped.

Padre Pio humbly responded, "Your Paternity knows very well that I am not to blame and that I have nothing at all to do with what is happening.… It is God's will that is permitting this!"

"Well, you tell the Lord," commanded Padre Benedetto, "that I, as superior, for the greater good of this community, want to be pleased … in having these noises stop!"[7]

The noises stopped. Padre Pio told Padre Paolino that the noises were of demonic origin and were associated with temptations so frightening that they made him break out in a cold sweat. He did not describe the nature of the temptations, and Padre Paolino did not ask. Padre Pio later affirmed that the temptations continued — but silently. Word of the ghastly noises, however, spread among the Capuchin community and the lay people of the area. Soon several local women, convinced that this was evidence of Padre Pio's divine predilection, were seeking out the "holy monk" for spiritual direction.

One of these "spiritual daughters" was Annitta Rodote. One day, when Padre Paolino was in Foggia, Annitta told him, "Father, yesterday something happened that never happened before in my life!" She went on to recount that one afternoon, around two, she was in her kitchen when she heard "a clear and intelligible voice" calling her by her nickname: "Annina! Annina!" At first, she thought she was dreaming, but as the voice continued to call her, she realized that she was wide awake. After calling "Annina!" twice more, the voice directed her, "Kneel down and pray for me, for I am at present very much tormented by the devil." Rodote was terrified and confused. Then the voice spoke again: "Quickly, quickly, Annina! Don't doubt, because this is Padre Pio who is asking you to pray! Kneel and let's pray the litanies of the Madonna together." When Rodote fell to her knees, Padre Pio's disembodied voice began the *Kyrie Eleison* ("Lord, have mercy"), the beginning of the responsive prayer. They continued to the end, when the voice said, "Thank you. I am calm now."

Padre Paolino wondered if this experience was a diabolical trick, but he dismissed the possibility because it would have meant that hell was invoking people's prayers against itself. He told Annitta: "If you receive any other signs of this nature, tell the voice that you always pray for Padre Pio, but that you do not like this method of requesting prayer because you do not want to encounter illusions. You can also say that this was the counsel of your confessor."

The next day Rodote told Padre Paolino that the same thing had happened again. When she had spoken of the danger of "illusion," the voice had said: "But this is no illusion! I have need of souls to join with me in prayer, especially now, when I am tempted by the devil and feel the need acutely. So don't deny me the charity of praying with me!"

Padre Paolino told Rodote that if Padre Pio should call her in the same manner the next day, to say to him, "Tell me where you are." So, the next day Padre Paolino carefully monitored Padre Pio's movements, especially around 2:00 p.m., the time that Annitta had been hearing the voice. When she reported a recurrence of the phenomenon, Paolino asked, "Did Padre Pio tell you where he was?" The place Annitta indicated was the very spot where Padre Paolino had observed Padre Pio at that very hour. Satisfied, Paolino left Rodote in full liberty to pray with Padre Pio every time he called her invisibly. He never questioned Padre Pio about the phenomenon, however.[8]

"Finding a Most Edifying Religious Community"

The summer of 1916 was very hot, and Padre Pio, who always suffered greatly from the heat, was so uncomfortable at night that he couldn't sleep. Padre Paolino invited his friend to come and spend a few days at the friary of Our Lady of Grace outside of San Giovanni Rotondo, where he was the superior. Situated in the mountains, it tended to be significantly cooler than Foggia. A similar suggestion was made by Rachelina Russo, who ran a clothing store in that town. She had befriended the friars when they reestablished their friary in San Giovanni a few years before, giving them financial and material assistance. She had been going to the "holy monk" in Foggia for counsel. "You must come to San Giovanni Rotondo," she told Padre Pio. "There the air is fresh."

Padre Pio was reluctant to make the visit without the consent of Padre Benedetto. Padre Paolino pointed out that for a visit of just a few days he needed only the consent of his local superior, Padre Nazareno of Arpaise, father guardian of St. Anna. Russo appealed to him, pleading, "Let him come, let that boy come to San Giovanni. The air is good there."

"Will you pay for the journey?" asked Padre Nazareno. "We don't have money for the bus fare."[9]

Russo paid the fare, and on July 28, 1916, Padre Paolino returned to his friary at San Giovanni Rotondo with Padre Pio.

Padre Pio returned after about a week and wrote to Padre Benedetto, asking for permission to spend a more extended period of time there. Though touchy about the breach of protocol in which Padre Pio had showed "willingness to please an ordinary priest, but not your superior," the minister provincial conceded, "I am nonetheless happy that you went to San Giovanni Rotondo and hope that this has brought an improvement in your health." In fact, he granted permission for Padre Pio to live there permanently, if he so desired.[10]

After Padre Pio begged Padre Benedetto's pardon, accepted his forgiveness, and secured his permission to transfer to Our Lady of Grace, he arrived at his new home on September 4, 1916. A week later he wrote to Padre Benedetto, saying that he gave "fervent thanks to the Most High for making me worthy of finding a most edifying religious community."[11] The same day Padre Paolino wrote Padre Agostino: "You can imagine the benefit we experience in the presence of Padre Pio! He is likewise pleased with us, with the air, the living arrangements, the quiet, the solitude, and everything else, and, except for the interior pains with which it pleases the Lord to test him, he might be said to be truly happy. What is most important is that we are happy with him."[12]

Some had a different explanation for the reason for Padre Pio's transfer to San Giovanni Rotondo. Raffaello Carlo Rossi (1876–1948), who a few years later would be sent as an inquisitor by the Holy Office to investigate Padre Pio, wrote:

> At that time [1916], the superior of the Capuchins at San Giovanni Rotondo was a Father Paolino, a rather intrusive religious. During [the time when the office of archpriest of San Giovanni was vacant], he had started hearing confessions in the town's churches, without asking for the appropriate faculties,

as if he were in his own church, so much so that the new archpriest ... once in office, was forced to have recourse to the ordinary [the archbishop of Manfredonia]. Obviously, the superior was looking for "people." His church, far from town, was isolated; it needed to be enlivened. He started talking about a holy monk living in Foggia [rumors about the extraordinary things happening around Padre Pio already existed]; in turn, some devout women lobbied, it seems, to have Padre Pio definitely transferred to San Giovanni Rotondo, the wish was granted, and Padre Pio settled in the town where he is now.[13]

The source of this interpretation, however, appears to have been the new archpriest of San Giovanni Rotondo, Don Giuseppe Prencipe, who, as we shall see, was no friend of Padre Pio or the Capuchins.

San Giovanni Rotondo

San Giovanni Rotondo (Saint John-in-the-Round), a town with approximately ten thousand inhabitants in 1916, derives its name from an ancient circular temple dedicated in Roman times to the god Janus, but, with the coming of Christianity, consecrated to Saint John the Baptist. A "commune" in the province of Foggia and the region of Apulia, San Giovanni lies about 1,800 feet above sea level in the Gargano Mountains, on the spur of the Italian "boot," within sight, on clear days, of the Adriatic Sea. A native has written: "To the north, the mountains, verdant with trees, bushes, and aromatic herbs, form a marvelous background for the town, which rests on a gentle shell. The horizon is bounded by the nearby mountains to the east and west; to the south, by the almost uniform prominence of the lower hills."[14]

In 1916, the town, which was circular in shape, like the old temple, was a "conglomerate of old houses, one on top of another," on either side of narrow, curving lanes. Most of the land near the town was in the hands of a few wealthy landowners, and most of the inhabitants eked out an existence working for them, either on the mountains as shepherds or in the plain as farm laborers, with both men and women toiling in the fields. There were only a few poorly stocked stores in town. To buy staples, people had to go to the cities of Foggia and San Severo, both more than twenty miles away. Although there were a few primitive motorized buses, people still traveled mostly by stagecoach. Most people subsisted on a diet of cereal, vegetables, and potatoes. Spaghetti was a feast-day meal, and meat was a luxury, eaten only on Sundays.[15] Lives were weakened and shortened by malaria, vitamin-deficiency anemia, and tuberculosis. A visitor around that time described streets that were narrow alleys, "almost unbelievably filthy and muddy, flanked by a row of poor, squat, miserable huts out of which burst gangs of runny-nosed children and pigs, wallowing and snorting in the mud; houses with primitive furnishings, men and women who stare at you with sorrowful, unsmiling, suspicious faces, and nowhere a flower."[16]

Most of the houses had one room on the upper story, where the inhabitants lived and slept, which was accessed by means of wooden stairs. The lower level was occupied by chickens and donkeys.[17] A scholarly visitor, while noting the cheerful appearance of the friary in the midst of a green garden, found the townspeople "monumental and savage," showing signs of malaria and trachoma (a contagious eye disease that often leads to blindness). The streets were full of women "with red stockings and noisy little clogs, sheathed in long severe shawls" and "huge, somber men," dressed in black cloaks and leather collars, congregating in little groups.[18] Most of them seemed old, as many of the younger men had left for northern Italy or the Americas in search of work.

The Convent of Our Lady of Grace

The Convent of Our Lady of Grace was about a mile and a half from town, on a branch of a five-mile, zigzagging mule track that passed for a road, which ran to the town of San Marco in Lamis. The track was full of stones and potholes, covered with mud in winter and infested with snakes in summer. Our Lady of Grace (*La Madonna delle Grazie*) was one of the oldest and poorest friaries in the province of Sant'Angelo. The terrain between the town and the friary was desolate, rocky, and all but devoid of verdure, with the exception of an occasional olive, pine, or cypress tree, and was dominated by a mountainside "squalid, parched, fissured, with green patches of oak groves and the rest bare rock."[19] At the time of Padre Pio's arrival, according to a resident of the town, the path to the friary was

> bordered by hedges and a few trees along the way. In front of the convent and church the path widened, creating a small square, where two elm trees stood, facing one another, on the left and on the right-hand side of the façade. When it rained, the water descended from the side of the ... mountain like a waterfall that widened the rural churchyard. The friars changed what could have been a source of damage into a benefit: they made a hole at the bottom of the boundary wall to let the water flow through a duct into a tank built in the vegetable garden. Around the friary there were small plots of land dug out of the rocks and preserved by dry stone walls, a few poor houses and a few barns.[20]

The little friary had been built around 1540, "at the request and expense of the people," with the consent of the archbishop of Siponto, Giovanni Maria Cardinal Ciocchi del Monte, who later became Pope Julius III.[21] After a severe earthquake in 1624, the friary had to be rebuilt. In 1676, a church was built adjacent to the friary. The Capuchins of San Giovanni Rotondo had long been revered for their holiness and austerity. The community, in fact, was reputed as one of the strictest in all

Italy, and many of the friars who lived there over the years, although not officially canonized, were regarded as saints by the local people.

When the Italian government shut down the religious orders, the friary was converted into a nursing home. It was reopened as a friary in 1909 and became the home of four religious: Padre Bernardo of Pietrelcina, Padre Luigi of Avellino, Padre Ermenegildo of San Giovanni Rotondo, and Fra Nicola of Roccabascerana. These men supported themselves through the offerings contributed at Mass and through the quests of Fra Nicola, who went begging, on foot in summer and on muleback in winter. The contributions he received, supplemented by fruit and vegetables from the friary's garden and orchard, comprised the simple and nearly vegetarian board of the community.

There was a feud that evidently went back to a time long before the closure of the monastery, between the friars on the hill, who had a reputation for asceticism and deep spirituality, and the secular clergy who ran the three parish churches in town, who had a reputation for worldliness. As stated earlier, the archpriest of San Giovanni Rotondo accused Padre Paolino of interfering in his work by hearing the confessions of his parishioners without obtaining his permission to do so. The fact seems to be that many of the people of town preferred to have the Capuchins on the hill as their confessors rather than Archpriest Don Giuseppe Prencipe and his staff. The latter were often accused of siding with the great landowners against the poor, whose material plight they allegedly ignored. To complicate matters further, both friary and the parish churches were in the archdiocese of Manfredonia, whose archbishop, Pasquale Gagliardi, openly sided with the secular clergy.

When Padre Pio arrived, the community at Our Lady of Grace numbered seven. There was, of course, the "guardian," or superior, Padre Paolino DiTomasso of Casacalenda, a short, rotund, bespectacled man of thirty, described as "everybody's stereotype of a monk" and a "kind, gentle, spiritual, and beautiful man,"[22] who was Padre Pio's lifetime friend and supporter. Twenty-eight-year-old Padre Angelico of San Marco la Catola was the principal of the "Seraphic College," the high school for boys that the Capuchins founded there in 1911. (He seems to have left the priesthood in the 1920s.) Padre Luigi of Serracapriola, age forty, taught at the "college." Forty-five-year-old Fra Nicola of Roccabascerano, as we know, was the "questor." Forty-two-year-old Fra Leone of Terre was the cook. Another lay brother, thirty-eight-year-old Fra Costantino of San Marco la Catola, provided assistance in manual labor. Within a few months, four of the seven (Angelico, Luigi, Leone, and Costantino) would be drafted into the army.

Padre Pio, in fact, was called to report for another physical in Naples in December, but after an examination at Trinity Hospital revealed that he still suffered from chronic bronchitis, he was given another six-month leave to recuperate. Padre Paolino was excused because of a double hernia, and Fra Nicola was too old. By now, sixty friars in the province were in military uniform, including Padre Agostino, who was operating a military hospital for the Red Cross in northern Italy, but who still wrote frequently to Padre Pio, to ask for prayers and guidance.

"He Cast a Spell Over People"

Padre Pio's chief duties during his early years at Our Lady of Grace were teaching in the "Seraphic College" and serving as spiritual director to the twenty or so students. He became a great favorite of the boys, who seemed unaware of his mystical interior life. To them, he was simply a kind teacher and an exceptionally warm human being. He taught the boys how to prepare for reception of Holy Communion and how to make a proper thanksgiving. He heard their confessions and prayed with them, accompanied them on walks, supervised their chores, and took part in their recreation.[23]

Padre Aurelio DiIorio of Sant'Elia a Pianisi (1904–1978) studied under Padre Pio from 1916 to 1918, between the ages of twelve and fourteen. Later in life, he recalled that Padre Pio was not the world's greatest teacher: "He had a superficial way of teaching. He taught history and grammar, but he knew little of the former and none of the latter. His lectures were never more than twenty minutes long, and they were unprepared. He was not strict, even when he administered examinations. He let the kids do pretty much what they wanted."[24] Padre Aurelio nonetheless recalled that there was something special about the friar with the dreamy eyes and beautiful smile: "He cast a spell over people. There was just something about him — a charm, a spell. It was only later that people considered him a saint. We boys were attracted to him in those days because he was very human, because he could understand us. He was very good with everybody. The key to his charm was his humanity. His sanctity was his humanity."

The former student recalled how he and his fellow students, overcome with hunger, would raid the friary kitchen at night. Padre Pio, they later discovered, knew about it but did not report them. Whenever anyone brought him fruits and candies, Padre Pio would share them with the boys. He would sometimes even violate friary rules to help them. "One time in my life, I was desperate," recalled Padre Aurelio. "Padre Pio would come into my room and sit on my bed and talk to me until 2:00 a.m. This was against the rules, but he did it."

Padre Aurelio was aware of at least one supernatural occurrence. One day he scolded one of the younger boys harshly, even going so far as to call his faith into question. That night he awoke to see in his room a terrifying shadowy form breathing on him with fetid breath. Objects in the room began to crash to the floor. In terror, Fra Aurelio ran into Padre Pio's room, which was next to the boys' dormitory, shouting: "I don't want to go back there! There's a devil in my room!"

Padre Pio did not seem at all alarmed, but smiled and said: "Go back to your room. This is a proof that God wanted to give you so that you'll be better.... You did wrong in judging your fellow student so harshly. Yes, that was a devil — and, thank God, you didn't see his face."

Padre Pio soon had an active circle of disciples in San Giovanni. Even before Padre Pio arrived, Rachelina Russo and Lucia Fiorentino had been informing their friends about him. Pietro Cugino, who was then a little boy, remembered Russo telling his parents about the wonderful priest from Foggia who went into ecstasy and was considered a "holy man." Lucia Fiorentino, while ill with tuberculosis in 1906, had a vision in which she saw a gigantic tree take root in the friary at San Giovanni Rotondo. In 1923, she would write in her diary about this experience of seventeen years previous in which she had seen "a tree so huge and well-rooted that it would cover the whole world with its shade. Whoever, having faith, takes refuge under this tree, so beautiful and rich with leaves, will receive true salvation, and whoever will despise and ridicule this tree, Jesus threatens with punishment." Fiorentino now believed that the tree in her vision was Padre Pio, who, "coming from afar, by the will of God, planted his roots in the friary."[25]

Within weeks of Padre Pio's arrival, a group of devout "spiritual daughters" was meeting and praying with him twice weekly in the *parlatorium*, or guest room, of the friary. The group included Russo and Fiorentino; Giovanna Fiorentino (Lucia's sister); Vittoria, Elena, and Filomena Ventrella; Maria and Lucia Campanile; Eva and Antonietta Pompilio; Maddalena Cascavilla; and Filomena Fini. Several of them were elementary-school teachers.

Padre Pio spent his spare time reading the Bible and answering a growing correspondence from spiritual children in other towns. His superiors encouraged him in this ministry of correspondence, and he spent several hours a day painstakingly composing letters of spiritual counsel and enlightenment.

In early 1917, after Padre Angelico was called into the military, Padre Pio was made principal of the college. In addition to administrative work, he continued to teach, dividing classroom duties with Padre Paolino, who, with most of his community gone, was forced to act as a jack-of-all-trades.

A Temperature That Broke the Thermometer

Padre Pio's bronchial and digestive problems persisted. He ate the midday meal in the dining room but was still subject to fits of vomiting and had to keep a little box beside his seat — just in case. Then there was the matter of the fevers. On January 27 or 28, 1917, he took to his bed. Padre Paolino was concerned when he saw that his friend's face was flushed and that he had trouble breathing. Padre Pio seemed to lack the energy to speak or even move his limbs. The superior was even more horrified when he tried to take his temperature. The mercury climbed to 108 degrees Fahrenheit, then broke the bulb of the thermometer. Padre

Paolino hurried to the bathroom and fetched a bath thermometer, freeing it from its wooden sheath, and placed it under Padre Pio's armpit. The temperature registered at 125.5 degrees! When Padre Paolino fed the sick man some custard, it was vomited "coagulated" and "almost baked." When Padre Paolino put his hand on Pio's forehead, it was, strangely, not hot at all. When the physician arrived, he noted the abnormally high fever, but, in the absence of other specific symptoms, he prescribed the usual remedies for a bad case of the flu. To Padre Paolino's amazement, within days the fever vanished, and Padre Pio seemed completely recovered. On February 12, Padre Pio wrote to a spiritual daughter named Maria Gargani of the "extreme fever which the thermometer was inadequate to measure because its heat was so great as to explode it."[26] On February 23, he wrote to Padre Agostino of his "miraculous recovery."

In Rome

Around the time of his thirtieth birthday, in May 1917, Padre Pio took the longest trip of his life when he and Padre Benedetto accompanied his sister Graziella to Rome, which was about 230 miles away from San Giovanni. There she would take the veil as Suor Pia of Our Lady of Sorrows, in the Order of St. Bridget, a semi-cloistered community founded in the fourteenth century by a Swedish mystic and which was reorganized in 1911. Graziella was twenty-two, her vocation made possible by the generosity of her brother Michele's wife, Giuseppa Cardone. An only child, Giuseppa sacrificed her inheritance from her family to provide the "dowry," then required, in lieu of a university degree, for admission to the order.[27] Padre Pio's only recorded comments on this trip were made in a letter to Padre Agostino: "I leave it to you to imagine my impressions of the visit to the city."[28] In later years, he is alleged to have remarked that he was disgusted by the city, without giving any particulars.

The "Deserter"

Padre Pio had received a six-month leave of absence from the army on January 2, 1917, and was told he would be notified when to report for duty. After six months, he heard nothing and did nothing. In mid-August, however, he received a telegram ordering him to report for duty in Naples the very next day. When he arrived, he learned that he had come close to being arrested for desertion. His orders had in fact been sent to the post office in San Giovanni Rotondo, addressed to Francesco Forgione. The postmaster could not locate anyone by that name, so the orders failed to reach Padre Pio. The military authorities, who knew that the man they were seeking came from Pietrelcina, dispatched the military police to the Forgione home to arrest the deserter. Fortunately, one of Padre Pio's sisters was able to explain that her brother was not a deserter and that, at San Giovanni Rotondo, Francesco Forgione was known only as "Padre Pio."

Private Forgione was placed in a hospital in Naples for observation. Two doctors diagnosed "infiltration" of the upper part of his lungs, but judged him fit for noncombat duty within Italy, so he was assigned to the Fourth Platoon of the Tenth Company of the Italian Medical Corps. There he was miserably unhappy. He now had to wear an army uniform, which he despised. Complaining to Padre Benedetto, he wrote, "Just thinking about these rags makes me shudder and throws me into a deathly depression." He characterized his officers as "executioners." His lieutenant, whose name was Gargani, was a "gentleman," but his captain, named Giannatasio, was "a neurotic of the first order" and "the terror of poor soldiers." Soon his stomach was refusing all food, and by mid-October he was back in Trinity Hospital with a high fever. Padre Benedetto could not understand why Padre Pio was not discharged. "How can you be a soldier in bed?" he asked. By October 20, Private Forgione could not eat at all and complained that he was reduced almost to a skeleton. Finally, on November 6, he was given a third leave of absence, this time for a period of four months.

An army certificate from this time provides a description of Padre Pio at the age of thirty. He stood just a shade over five feet five inches tall. His weight was not given, but it must have been somewhat less than the one hundred seventy pounds that was normal later in life. His hair was described as "chestnut" (light reddish brown), as were his eyes. His complexion was characterized as "rosy," and his teeth were in good condition, with none missing.[29]

Just before Christmas, Padre Pio wrote to Padre Benedetto: "In one of the visits that I received from Jesus in recent days, I asked him insistently to have compassion on the poor nations, so tried by the misfortune of war, and to cause his justice to give way at last to mercy. It was strange: he answered only by means of a gesture that seemed to say, 'Slowly, slowly.' But when? I asked. And he, with a serious expression, but with a half-smile on his lips, gazed at me briefly, and, without another word, dismissed me."

He had never remembered Jesus making such a gesture before when he questioned him about the war; he had "always observed a profound silence."[30] Therefore he felt this vision seemed to signal the approach of peace. Padre Benedetto confided that he, too, had experienced a similar vision, in which Christ had made the same gestures but, in addition, had shown his wounds, saying, "Now they are covered, but they are not healed."[31]

When his leave of absence expired, Padre Pio had to submit to another military medical exam, entering Trinity Hospital once again on March 6, 1918, expressing the hope that the Lord "will quickly free me from this humiliation." His prayer was answered on March 16, when he was discharged permanently, with a diagnosis of "double broncho-alveolitis" (an inflammation of the air tubes of the lung).

A Last Trip Home

Before returning to San Giovanni Rotondo, Padre Pio stopped at Pietrelcina to visit his parents.

Michele was still in New York, unable to come home because of the war. Although he was never an American citizen, he nevertheless had to register for the draft. His registration, made later that year, shows that he was working as a "boiler fireman" for the Kleiner Rubber Company in College Point, New York, residing at 143 Farrington Street in Flushing, Queens, New York. He is described to be of "medium" height and build, with brown eyes and black hair. Unable to write, he signed his name with an "X." Michele's wife, Giuseppa, who never accompanied her husband to America, lived in Pietrelcina with their nine-year-old son, Francesco.

Felicita, Padre Pio's oldest sister, was living in town with her husband, Vincenzo Masone, and they had three children: six-year-old Giuseppa, three-year-old Pellegrino, and one-year-old Ettore.

Pellegrina, the middle sister, was evidently now living in Benevento, working as a seamstress. The previous July, after the death of her first child and considerably more than nine months after her husband had left her to go to America, she had given birth to son named Alfredo. It was understood that the baby's father was Vincenzo Masone — her sister's husband. According to a friend of the family, the saintly and long-suffering Felicita forgave her erring spouse and sister. Michele, however, when he learned what Pellegrina had done, vowed never to speak to her again. When he returned to Pietrelcina the following year, he maintained his resolve. According to the family friend, Padre Pio told Michele, "If you don't forgive your sister, you'll never see my face again. It was foreordained that her life was to go this way. It's her destiny. It's God's will. I can do nothing."[32] (The friend remembered the exchange this way, but it seems highly unlikely that Padre Pio actually insisted that it was *God's will* that his sister maintain an immoral lifestyle.) It is not known how Orazio and Giuseppa felt about their wayward daughter, nor do we know what Padre Pio did or said during his visit to his home. A few days later, he returned to San Giovanni Rotondo. Nobody foresaw that he would never return to Pietrelcina again.

Chapter Eleven

The Stigmata

More Paranormal Occurrences

Finally freed from military service, during the spring and summer of 1918 Padre Pio continued his work as a teacher at the "Seraphic College" and spiritual director to the boys there. As his reputation as a holy man grew, so did his renown as a miracle worker. Often, he complained that people were reporting that he had said what he never said and done what he never did.

In the fall of 1917, an Italian army suffered a humiliating defeat at the hands of the Austrians and Germans at Caporetto, in Italy, near its border with the Austro-Hungarian Empire. General Luigi Cadorna was relieved of command after the debacle — called by many the worst military defeat in Italian history — in which 10,000 of his troops were killed, 30,000 wounded, and over 250,000 captured, as his army was forced to retreat south almost to Venice. The story goes that the disgraced Cadorna — a sour-faced man in his late sixties, with a droopy walrus mustache, who was widely disliked and characterized as a cruel martinet — was in his quarters, about to kill himself, when he smelled the fragrance of roses and violets and saw a "friar with bleeding hands" who told him to remain calm. When he told his friends about this experience, he was informed that "this could be none other than the stigmatic of San Giovanni Rotondo." Visiting Our Lady of Grace, in 1920, he promptly recognized Padre Pio as "the friar who came to see me." Padre Pio is supposed to have told him, "General, we went through a bad time that night."[1]

This story was published as early as the 1950s, but there are problems with its veracity. Padre Pio, who, at the time of the Caporetto disaster, was in the military in Naples, was getting to be well-known in and around Pietrelcina and San Giovanni Rotondo, but nowhere else. He most certainly did not have the reputation as "the friar with the bleeding hands," because the visible stigmata for which he would be renowned did not yet exist. It is true that he suffered the pains of the "invisible stigmata" and that from time to time marks had appeared temporarily on his hands. But few people knew about this. (According to some versions, Cadorna merely smelled the fragrance, and some have speculated that the incident may have occurred as late as 1919, after the visible stigmata appeared on Padre Pio's hands.)

Other reports of supernatural occurrences are somewhat better documented. Padre Alberto D'Apolito wrote that in May 1922 Padre Pio spoke of a visitor from another world. According to D'Apolito, Bishop Alberto Costa of Melfi and Padre Lorenzo of San Marco in Lamis were present, as well as four other friars. Padre Pio recounted that "in the middle of the war," on a winter evening, after a heavy snowfall, he was seated by the fireplace in the guest room, absorbed in prayer, when an old man, wearing an old-fashioned cloak once common among peasants of that region, sat down beside him. "I could not imagine how he could have entered the friary at this time of night," Padre Pio said. "I questioned him: 'Who are you? What do you want?'"

The old man told him, "Padre Pio, I am Pietro Di Mauro, son of Nicola, nicknamed Precoco." He went on to explain, "I died in this friary on the 18th of September, 1908, in cell number 4, when it was still [a home for the aged]." He fell asleep smoking in bed, and his cigar ignited the mattress; he died of burns and smoke inhalation. "I am still in purgatory. I need a holy Mass in order to be freed. God permitted me to come and ask you for help."

According to Padre Pio:

After listening to him I replied, "Rest assured that tomorrow I will celebrate Mass for your liberation." I arose and accompanied him to the door of the friary, so that he could leave. I did not realize at that moment that the door was closed and locked. I opened it and bade him farewell. The moon lit up the square, covered with snow. When I no longer saw him in front of me, I was taken by a sense of fear, and I closed the door, reentered the guest room, and felt faint.[2]

A few days later Padre Pio told the story to Padre Paolino, and the two decided to go to the town hall, where they looked at the vital statistics for the year 1908. There they found that on September 18 of that year, there had been a fire in Room 4 of the home for the indigent poor, which was housed in the former friary. The sole fatality had been one Pietro Di Mauro![3] Padre Pio, of course, was the only source of the story about Precoco, but both Padre Alberto and Padre Paolino attested that he had recounted it, and Paolino affirmed that he had gone to town hall to confirm the death.[4]

Padre Pio told Padre Alberto of another apparition that appeared around the same time as the visit by Precoco:

One evening, when I was absorbed in prayer in the choir of the little church ... I was shaken and disturbed by the sound of footsteps, and candles and flower vases being moved on the main altar. Thinking that someone must be there, I called out, "Who is it?" No one answered. Returning to pray I was again disturbed by the same noises. In fact, this time I had the impression that one of the candles, which was in front of the statue of Our Lady of Grace, had fallen. Wanting to see what was happening on the altar, I stood up, went close to the grate and saw, in the shadow of the light of the tabernacle lamp, a young confrere doing some cleaning. I yelled out, "What are you doing in the dark?"

The little friar answered, "I am cleaning."

"You clean in the dark?" I asked. "Who are you?"

The little friar said, "I am a Capuchin novice, who spends his time of purgatory here. I am in need of prayers," before disappearing.[5]

Before the religious orders were suppressed, the friary at San Giovanni Rotondo was the place where novices were trained. Since "the little friar" did not give his name, it was impossible to verify his existence. Padre Pio said a Mass for him and never saw him again.

Padre Paolino recorded another extraordinary incident. He was sitting in Padre Pio's room, talking to him, when both of them fell asleep. Around midnight, Padre Paolino awoke to find Padre Pio "half lying on the bed with his right elbow raised up on the pillow, his head propped up in the palm of his hand, his usual position for meditation. He was panting ... loudly." By the dim light of the oil lamp, Padre Paolino noted that Padre Pio's face, normally florid, was pale, and his eyes seemed to be fixed on something, although Padre Paolino could see nothing unusual in the room. At the same time, Padre Pio spoke in the way Padre Agostino had observed in Venafro, imploring, "Yes, Jesus ... give me this grace ... I can't remain on earth any longer without obtaining it from you." A deep silence followed. Then Padre Pio's face brightened as he exclaimed, "Why, Mary, it's you!" Silence again. Then the visionary smiled and protested, "It seems as if you are both mocking me!" A few more moments of silence were broken when Padre Pio exclaimed: "Thank you, Jesus! Thank you, Mary!" Then he came to himself.

Curious as to how he could ascertain whether Padre Pio was truly in ecstasy, Padre Paolino, who made no comment when Padre Pio emerged from this ecstasy, decided to conduct a test. Three or four days later, he found Padre Pio again caught up in mystic reverie. Noiselessly, he closed the door, and, going to the part of the friary that was farthest from Padre Pio's cell, he mentally spoke the words, "Padre Pio, I command you through holy obedience to come out of your ecstasy." Immediately, he heard Padre Pio calling him.

"What do you want?" asked Padre Paolino.

"What do *I* want? *You* tell me what *you* want."

Still testing him, Padre Paolino shrugged and said: "Me? I don't want anything. I came here because you called me."

Smiling, Padre Pio looked Padre Paolino straight in the face and insisted, "Father Guardian, you know only too well!"

The fact that Padre Pio responded to a command of obedience that was given mentally convinced Padre Paolino that his confrere was neither dreaming nor hallucinating, but in true ecstasy.[6]

Padre Paolino was also convinced that Padre Pio could, on occasion, read minds. One time Pio said or did something that annoyed Padre Paolino to the point that he avoided him for three days. One night Padre Pio went to Padre Paolino's room and pleaded, "Paolino, let me know what I did so that you won't treat me like this anymore. If I've done something to offend you, tell me what it is and I won't do it anymore."

Still upset, Padre Paolino declared, "I'll never tell you the reason for my resentment. If the Lord in his goodness wants to reveal it to you, so much the better."

When, after further pleas, Padre Paolino still refused to tell Padre Pio what was wrong, Padre Pio put his elbow on the table, and, supporting his head in the palm of his hand, he assumed his usual meditation position and began to gaze intently into Padre Paolino's eyes. "All at once I felt as if something was being turned upside down in the inmost part of my being," Padre Paolino wrote. "It was not a physical sensation, but I do not know how to express myself otherwise." At the same time, Padre Pio cried: "So this is the cause of your resentment towards me! I didn't think you would be upset over something so trivial and so beyond my control!" Padre Pio then proceeded to reveal in minute detail the precise nature of Padre Paolino's grievance.[7]

When Padre Pio refused to answer Padre Paolino's questions about the former's guardian angel, the latter decided to conduct an experiment. One day Padre Pio was sick in bed and told Padre Paolino that he had called him several times the previous night, all in vain. Padre Paolino, whose room was a good distance from Padre Pio's, told his confrere that he was such a heavy sleeper that "if you want me to wake up, you'd better send your guardian angel to rouse me."

That following night, at midnight, Padre Paolino was roughly shaken awake. "I thought of Padre Pio and intended to go to him, but, unfortunately, dawn found me still in bed. My fatigue was so great that I couldn't bring myself to get up and go to the Padre," he wrote.

Next morning, Padre Paolino asked Padre Pio: "Why did your guardian angel come to wake me, only to let me fall back asleep? That was a useless effort. If he comes tonight, he must wake me in such a way that I get up."

That night, Padre Paolino was again convinced that someone had roused him, but once more he fell asleep again. The next morning he told Padre Pio, who was still sick, not to let his angel leave him in peace until he got out of bed. At 1:30 a.m. of the third night, Padre Paolino reported, "I felt myself being shaken so that I awoke so thoroughly that I immediately jumped out of bed and went to Padre Pio," who was drenched in sweat and asked for help in changing his clothing.

"Lost in Thickest Darkness"

Generally, Padre Pio's physical health was better than it had been at Foggia, but spiritually he continued in the dark night. Periods of "celestial inebriation" became less frequent, leaving him in "a prison darker than before, where eternal horror reigns." He wrote:

> I keep my eyes fixed on the east in the night which surrounds me, to discover that miraculous star which guided [the Wise Men] to the Grotto of Bethlehem. But I strain my eyes in vain to see that light rise in the heavens. The more I fix my gaze, the dimmer my sight becomes. The greater my effort, the more ardent my search, the deeper the darkness which envelopes me. I am alone by day and by night and no ray of light comes through to enlighten me. Not a cooling drop comes to mitigate the flame which devours me continually without consuming me.[8]

Not only did his experience fail to satisfy his almost violent longing for God, but Padre Pio also worried constantly about whether he was acceptable to God. He frequently confided in his letters to Padre Benedetto his fears of damnation, leading his spiritual director to urge him to calm himself "through my assurances and hold to them as if sworn by oath." Padre Agostino, still with the Red Cross, likewise urged him to trust blindly in the assurances of his director.

During 1917 and 1918, Padre Pio frequently wrote that God was hidden from him by what he likened to "those mists which tend to rise certain mornings around a river." He confided to Padre Benedetto that, while the mists hindered his soul from "fixing its gaze" on Christ, his desire to gaze upon the Lord grew in proportion to his yearning.

Padre Benedetto wrote back:

> The mists are an indication of the nearness of God. Moses found the Lord in the mists of Sinai. The Hebrew people saw him in the form of a cloud, and as a cloud he appeared in the Temple. Christ, in the Transfiguration, was at first visible and then became invisible because he was immersed in a luminous cloud. God's hiding in a mist signifies that he is growing greater in your gaze and transfiguring himself from the visible and intelligible into the pure divine.[9]

Despite his spiritual darkness, Padre Pio had not in the least lost faith in God, and he realized that his inability to feel God's presence was a result of his oblation of himself as a victim of divine love.

In fact, Padre Pio frequently renewed his offering of himself as a victim for various intentions. When Pope Benedict XV urged all Christians to pray for an end to the war, Padre Pio offered himself as a victim to end the bloodshed. "No sooner had I made this offering," he wrote, "than I felt myself plunged into a terrible prison and heard the crash of the gate behind me." From that moment on, for days, he felt as if he were in hell, telling Padre Benedetto, "I no longer know the way, I no longer have a single ray of light, not one torch, not one single guideline, no life and no more truth to understand how I can nurture or refresh myself." Willing to be swallowed by the tempest, he confided to his director his fear that "at the bottom of the sea … I will find nothing but everlasting death."[10]

Padre Benedetto assured Padre Pio that his bitter anguish was part of a participation in the Passion of Christ to save mankind. "The Omnipotent wants to make a holocaust [burnt offering] of you," he told Padre Pio. Padre Agostino felt that God was causing this trial to keep Padre Pio humble. If he knew how successful he was in fulfilling the divine will, this would prove too great a temptation to spiritual pride.

Padre Pio turned to others for help. On March 30, 1918, he wrote to Don Pietro Ricci, a seventy-one-year-old priest from Rignano Garganico, a few miles away from San Giovanni, whom he loved and respected:

Don't stop putting in a good word for me to the Lord … that he might free me from myself and, subsequently, the fear about my salvation that keeps me in turmoil. Oh, what a burden this is for me and how it grows when I consider how little strength I have to become better, despite the violent effort I make to do so! Meanwhile, it seems that the Lord is more and more taking away his favor as a just penalty for my infidelity and condemning me to live amidst deepest darkness. What can you tell me? The assurances that my director [Benedetto] makes don't succeed in calming me, because I suspect that my life has been one of continually offending the Lord, and, as a just punishment, all the confessors are deceived, even my own guide. Ask, I beg you, light from the Lord, and answer me clearly at your leisure, as to whether my fears are justified.

Padre Pio revealed to Ricci something else that was bothering him:

I don't know how to counsel the souls whom the Lord sends me. For some there is truly the need for supernatural light and I don't know whether I have a sufficient abundance and I proceed gropingly, giving counsel with a little cold and insipid doctrine learned from books and with that little bit of light that comes to me from the Most High. Who knows what these poor souls won't have to suffer through my fault! ... I beg you ... by means of the love that binds us together, to assault the Divine Heart and tell me what you are able to think about this.[11]

Many years later Padre Amedeo Fabrocini of San Giovanni Rotondo, who was then Padre Pio's superior, recalled that when Padre Pio first came to San Giovanni, he was in anguish as to whether he was properly directing those who came to him for counsel. "Sometimes he went ... to his spiritual director Padre Benedetto of San Marco in Lamis to get light and possible approval, and would return in more anguish than before, because, according to the judgment of the said Padre Benedetto, he wasn't assured that this method was good." In fact, at one point, Padre Pio went to one of his "spiritual daughters," the young schoolteacher Maria "Nina" Campanile (1893–1988) and cried, "Nina, I beseech you in the name of God to tell me if I'm directing souls well nor not." When she responded, "Father, be calm, because ... you direct souls well," he seemed to calm down.[12]

The "Transverberation"

On August 5, 1918, Padre Pio wrote Padre Benedetto:

I was hearing the confessions of our boys ... when suddenly I was filled with extreme terror at the sight of a heavenly Being who presented himself to the eye of my intellect. He held some kind of weapon in his hand, something like a long, sharp-pointed steel blade, which seemed to spew out fire. At the very instant that I saw all this, I saw that Mighty Being hurl the weapon into my soul with all his might. It was only with difficulty that I did not cry out. I thought I was dying. I told the boy to leave because I felt ill and did not feel that I could continue. ... This agony lasted uninterruptedly until the morning of the seventh. I cannot tell you how much I suffered during this period of anguish. Even my internal organs were torn and ruptured by that weapon.... From that day on I have been mortally wounded. I feel in the depths of my soul a wound that is always open and causes me continual agony.[13]

Pio's experience, known as a "transverberation of the heart," was similar to that of several other mystics, most famously Teresa of Ávila. It is unclear from Padre Pio's letter to Padre Benedetto whether a physical wound was involved, but in a deposition made in February 1967, Padre Pio stated unambiguously that a visible, physical wound in his side resulted from the experience. For a time, he was able to conceal it from everyone.

Padre Pio asked his mentors whether his experience was a new punishment for his sins and whether he had cause to fear. Padre Agostino, who learned of the vision from Padre Benedetto, wrote to Padre Pio: "The spiritual wound from that celestial being is the token of God's love for you.... Didn't you consider how the sixth [of August] was the feast of the Transfiguration of Our Lord? Jesus wanted not only to transfigure your spirit but to pierce it with a wound that he alone can cure.... If it pleases him to keep it open until he calls you to himself, so be it."[14] Padre Benedetto wrote: "No abandonment, no vengeful justice, no unworthiness on your part deserving of rejection and condemnation — everything that is happening to you is the effect of love. It is a trial, a calling to co-redeem, and therefore it is a fountain of glory!"[15]

"I Unite You with My Passion"

In the late summer of 1918, with the Great War still raging, the terrible worldwide pandemic of Spanish influenza struck southern Italy. It is believed that more than twenty million people perished worldwide in this epidemic, which sickened an estimated one billion people. By September, everyone in San Giovanni Rotondo seemed to be ill, the schools were closed, and what little commerce there was in town was brought to a halt. In the next couple months, two hundred people from a population of ten thousand would perish.

Padre Pio's spiritual daughters came to him terrified, begging him to save them. "Never fear," he assured Nina Campanile. "Put yourself under the protection of the Virgin, do not sin, and the sickness will not overcome you." Although some of the "daughters" fell ill, none of them died.

Padre Pio had already offered himself as a victim for the cessation of the war. He also offered himself as a victim for the boys of the "Seraphic College," of which he was now serving as principal. And on September 17, he offered himself as a victim for the end of the influenza.

Almost all of the roughly two dozen boys now in the college were ill. A doctor examined them and prescribed injections and taught Padre Paolino and Padre Pio how to administer them to the patients. Since alcohol was not available, the doctor left some carbolic acid to sterilize the site of the injection. Unfortunately, the exhausted physician didn't think to tell the friars to dilute the carbolic acid before applying it to the pupils' posteriors. And so, before giving the shots, they swabbed on the acid full strength. Because they spilled some of the solution on themselves in the process of giving the injections, they were left with angry red spots on their hands. As for the boys, Paolino recounted, "You can imagine what happened to the part of the body we had disinfected for the injection!"

As they sat for his lectures on their sore bottoms around September 21, the boys wondered why Padre Pio kept his hands covered with his shawl. Padre Paolino observed that when the two men were praying together in the choir, red spots were still in evidence on Padre Pio's hands, while those on his own had already disappeared. Padre Pio, when he noticed that the superior was looking at his hands, reacted by covering them with the sleeves of his habit.

During the last week of September, Nina Campanile went to Padre Paolino and asked to speak with him alone. "Do you know that Padre Pio has the stigmata?" she asked. The superior, laughing at the credulity of the country schoolmarm, explained that the marks she saw were the result of contact with carbolic acid. She disagreed, insisting that the marks on Padre Pio's hands were of supernatural origin.[16]

Fifty years later, at the age of seventy-five, Campanile recalled: "On September 18 I was at the friary, and I spoke with the Padre, kissed his hand when I came and when he dismissed me, but there was no mark on his hands." Saturday afternoon she returned to ask for prayers for a sister who was six months pregnant and gravely ill with the flu (which was especially dangerous for expectant mothers). Padre Pio assured Campanile that her sister would recover. When she handed him a Mass offering, she noticed a mark on his right hand and commented, "Oh, Father, you've burned your hand!" He turned pale and hid the hand in his habit. When she was about to leave and, in keeping with southern Italian custom, tried to kiss his hand, Padre Pio exclaimed, "If you only knew the humiliation this causes me.... Pray very hard to the Lord that he causes everything to disappear."[17]

Padre Paolino was still skeptical; then Filomena Ventrella informed him that Padre Pio had the stigmata "like Saint Francis." So the superior went to Padre Pio's room, entered without knocking, and found him at his desk. "Go on writing," he directed. "This morning I don't have anything to talk to you about." As Padre Pio wrote, Padre Paolino was able to get a good look at his hands. The marks on them were definitely not those left by the carbolic acid. "Drawing closer to him, I was first able to see the wound on the back and in the palm of the right hand. Then I saw the wound on the back of the left hand. I could not see the palm of the left hand because he was resting it on the table to steady his paper."[18]

Padre Paolino left the room without saying anything. He immediately wrote Padre Benedetto, urging him to come at once, because Padre Pio had the stigmata. Padre Benedetto did not come and warned Padre Paolino to observe the strictest silence about the matter.

Padre Benedetto evidently did not get along well with Padre Paolino and perhaps took his report "with a grain of salt." Moreover, he was aware that Padre Pio had displayed the stigmata before and that the marks proved transitory. His attitude changed when Padre Pio wrote to him about the "Mighty Being" who had wounded his entire being. "Ah, help me, dear Father, for pity's sake," Padre Pio wrote. "I am bleeding profusely within and many times I must resign myself to seeing the blood flow externally as well."[19]

"Dear son, tell me everything quite frankly," Padre Benedetto wrote. "What is this Mighty Being [*personaggio*] doing? Where is the blood coming from and how many times a day or week? What has happened to your hands and feet and how did it happen? I want to know everything in detail, under holy obedience."[20]

On September 20, Padre Pio was the only member of the community in the friary, as Padre Paolino was out of town and Nicola was on his quest. The boys were in the garden when Padre Pio went to the choir between nine and ten in the morning and sat on the "vicar's bench" to make his thanksgiving after celebrating Mass. It was then, he told Padre Benedetto: "I was overtaken by a repose, similar to deep sleep. All my internal and external senses and even the very faculties of my soul were steeped in indescribable quiet. In this state absolute silence reigned within me.... I was filled with great peace and abandonment that blotted out every other worry or preoccupation. All this happened in a twinkling."[21] It was then that he saw the same "Great Mysterious Being" [*misterioso personaggio*] who had wounded him in August. He did not identify the Being as Christ but said that the hands, feet, and side were dripping blood (like the crucifix that hung in the choir). The countenance of the heavenly visitor frightened him. "I thought I was going to die and really would have died if the Lord hadn't intervened to strengthen my heart, which was ready to burst out of my chest."[22]

Who was this "Mysterious Being"? Three years later, when questioned by the inquisitor, Cardinal Raffaello Carlo Rossi, Padre Pio stated that his encounter was with Christ and gave a more detailed account to him than he had to Padre Benedetto:

After celebrating Mass, I stayed in the choir for the due thanksgiving prayer, when suddenly I was overtaken by a powerful trembling, then calm followed, and I saw our Lord in the posture of someone who is on a cross (but it didn't strike me whether he had the cross), lamenting the ingratitude of men, especially those consecrated to him and by him most favored. This revealed his suffering and his desire to unite souls with his Passion. He invited me to partake of his sorrows and to meditate on them. At the same time he urged me to work for my brothers' salvation. I felt then full of compassion for the Lord's sorrows, and I asked him what I could do. I heard this voice, "I unite you with my Passion." Once the vision disappeared, I came to, I returned to my senses, and I saw these signs here, which were dripping blood.[23]

In March 1966, when questioned by a confrere, Padre Pio said: "All of a sudden, a great light shone around about my eyes. In the midst of this light there appeared the wounded Christ." In direct contradiction to what he had told the inquisitor forty-five years earlier, he insisted, "He said nothing to me before he disappeared."[24]

By this time, however, Padre Pio was seventy-nine and in decline. When questioned again on February 6, 1967, he said that the crucifix in the choir transformed itself "into a great Exalted Being, all blood, from whom there came forth beams of light with shafts of flame that wounded me in the hands and feet. My side had already been wounded on the fifth of August of the same year."[25]

Later, Padre Pio told his friend Padre Giuseppe Orlando that after the vision he was in such great pain that he could not stand up and had to drag himself down the corridor to his cell. Once there, he cleaned the oozing wounds and went to bed, weeping and singing hymns of thanksgiving.[26] He was glad for this opportunity to unite himself with the sufferings of Christ.

He was not giving thanks for the *visible* wounds, however. These he did not want people to see. To Padre Benedetto he wrote that he would not cease to implore God "until, in his mercy, he removes, not the wounds nor the pain (this is impossible, inasmuch as I want to be inebriated with pain), but these visible signs that are an embarrassment and an indescribable humiliation."[27]

When the inquisitor Rossi asked whether others noticed, Padre Pio answered, "Nobody asked anything directly, except for the director, Father Benedetto.... He was not here — perhaps he had heard of it; he wrote to me and later came here."[28]

Actually, as we have seen, Padre Paolino and Nina Campanile were aware of the stigmata within a couple of days. Padre Agostino was not, apparently. He came to see Padre Pio at the end of September and observed a red mark on the back of one of his hands but didn't ask him about it.[29] The boys of "Seraphic College" knew, however. Years later, Padre Emilio D'Amato of Matrice, who was a boy of fifteen when Padre Pio received the visible stigmata, recalled:

> The morning of September 21, 1918, as soon as we approached dear Padre Pio, we were aware that he had a wound in the palms of his hands, that he walked with a certain difficulty and his face was redder than usual. We began to investigate the reason for all this, but only from Padre Paolino did we learn, a few days later, that our Padre Pio had received the wounds of our Lord ... in the heart, the hands, and the feet, from the Crucifix in the choir. Padre Paolino finally recommended that we stay quiet and not talk with anyone and to be really good to the Padre who suffered so much. Padre Pio, although he didn't talk about his wounds, after a few days permitted us to kiss the wounded palms of his hands with reverence. We students were quiet — I don't know how.[30]

Actually, Padre Benedetto did not go to see Padre Pio for another six months. After he did, he wrote to the minister general on April 24, 1919: "Early in March I personally went to see with my eyes what was going on. It was Friday, and shortly after I arrived in the evening I easily observed the hands: they were perforated and bloody. In the side I saw a gash of several centimeters, wet with blood, and the bandage that was applied, which I held, was soaked with water and blood."[31]

"God Gave Me My Poor Sister, and God Has Taken Her!"

One reason why word of Padre Pio's stigmata did not spread immediately was that the war was still raging and, even more so, because most people that autumn were too sick to travel. In most places, half of the population was stricken, and one out of five of those died.

Not only did Padre Pio himself come down with the flu, he was devastated by news from Pietrelcina. His mother was gravely ill for weeks. Pellegrina's baby Alfredo died. Franceschino, the only child of Padre Pio's brother, was taken ill and, it seems, never fully recovered. All of Felicita's family were sick. Six-year-old Giuseppina and two-year-old Ettore recovered, but the girl developed tuberculosis, and the boy became subject, for the rest of his life, to grand mal epileptic seizures. Felicita was pregnant at the time, and the influenza was particularly deadly for women in her condition. She lost her baby and told her husband, Vincenzo, that she was dying. Reportedly, she urged him to marry her sister Pellegrina — with whom he had been carrying on an affair. (He could not do this with the blessing of the Church, since Pellegrina's husband, who had left her, was still alive in the United States.) Then, on September 22, Felicita's four-year-old son, Pellegrino, went to his father and complained, "Papa, my head hurts!" He collapsed and died within hours.[32]

For the next three days, Felicita kept asking for Pellegrino. Not having the heart to tell her that the child was dead, Vincenzo assured her, "Oh, he's over at the neighbor's, playing." Then, on September 25, the sick woman raised herself on her pillow and shouted at her husband, "You deceived me! You deceived me! You said Pellegrino is playing outside. But he's dead!"

"What's making you talk like this?" exclaimed the husband. "What's going through your mind?"

"Oh, no, it's true. He's dead," insisted Felicita. "Look, Pellegrino is coming with all the angels, with all the little angels around him. He's coming to fetch me, and behind him I see the face of Padre Pio!" She never spoke again and breathed her last a half hour later. She was twenty-nine.

When Padre Pio received the telegram announcing his sister's death, completely unprepared for the horrible news, he screamed and collapsed (a fact which would make it difficult to interpret Felicita's deathbed vision as an instance of his bilocation). For days, he was almost wild with grief. He always regarded Felicita as the family's saint. Later he would say of her: "She was a saint ... I never saw her upset. Even with all the woes that befell her, she was always smiling. From childhood on,

God kept her good and simple.... Everyone else in the family she surpassed in goodness and loveliness."[33]

The next day Pio wrote to his parents:

What can I tell you, when every word is strangled in my throat by the bitterness of grief? My dear ones, in the harshness and bitterness of grief I haven't the strength to do other than exclaim, "Just thou art, O Lord, and righteous your judgments." God gave me my poor sister and God has taken her and blessed be his holy Name. In this exclamation and in this resignation I find sufficient strength not to succumb to the weight of grief.

In November, Padre Pio wrote Padre Benedetto: "Unhappy man that I am, who will free me from this mortal body!" He reported that all the assurances from his spiritual director vanished from his mind as soon as he received them. He felt quite alone, his heart "turned to stone with pain," his frame "frozen rigid from the agony that, experienced in the soul, spills over into the body."[34] However, in January, he reported, "I feel as if I were drowned in an immense sea of the love of my Beloved.... The bitterness of this love is sweet and the burden is [also] sweet."[35]

World War I's armistice was declared on November 11, just as the epidemic was beginning to subside. The local women began to spread word of the stigmatized priest in their midst. Although Nina Campanile had been sworn to secrecy, as she later admitted, she informed her mother and sisters. Padre Paolino commented: "Women ... are not made to keep secrets. And even when they have good intentions ... they still have to reveal that secret to an intimate friend. And then it happens that from the intimate friend, the secret passes to another intimate friend until, at length, the secret becomes public knowledge."[36] By the spring of 1919, news of the stigmata was beginning to trickle out beyond San Giovanni Rotondo.

Chapter Twelve

"Holy Man"

A Rumor of Sanctity

In 1919, in Italy and elsewhere, men and women were emerging from the carnage of war disillusioned and broken. Many philosophers of the eighteenth and nineteenth century had imagined that the world was getting better and better and that mankind would ultimately create an earthly utopia of peace and justice. Now this utopian vision was shattered. While many gave themselves over to bitterness and despair, and others tried to assuage the pain of their loss through the indulgence of the senses, still others, deeply affected by humanity's helplessness, turned to the supernatural in their search for meaning.

The news of Padre Pio's stigmata found especially fertile soil at this time. Large numbers of people were seeking someone who was truly close to God, someone who had answers for life's problems. Dissatisfied by the vague, relativistic teachings of secular philosophers and the abstruse and tentative doctrines of scholarly theologians, they sought someone to speak to them clearly, to tell them how to live, how to know God. They wanted someone to show them that there was a God, that life had meaning, and that there was something beyond this life. Now there were rumors of a priest who bore the wounds of Christ on his body. In the minds of many Italians, the stigmata were a sure sign of divine intimacy. Such a person was one to whom they might turn for answers.

When Padre Benedetto visited in March, he wrote to Padre Agostino that the marks on Padre Pio were "not spots or blemishes, but real wounds, perforating the hands and feet.... The wound in the side is a real gash that issues either blood or bloody fluid. Friday it issued blood."[1] He ordered Padre Paolino, the superior, to observe "the most profound silence" about Padre Pio, but the news spread. Padre Paolino (who complained that women couldn't keep secrets) confided the secret to his sister Assunta Di Tommaso, who lived in Foggia. She, in turn, told her friend, who appeared at the friary in May with her two daughters, asking to see Padre Pio. The very next day a large group of people from nearby villages and towns came, asking for Padre Pio. In the following days, more people came, including a man who claimed to be healed of blindness when Padre Pio blessed him. The alleged miracle was reported to the press.

On May 25, a newspaper from Lucera — a city about thirty-five miles to the southwest — reported that San Giovanni Rotondo was on the verge of becoming famous throughout Italy because "of the existence of a humble friar with a reputation for sanctity."[2] Soon other newspapers were running articles about Padre Pio, and, in Padre Paolino's words: "There began a vast influx of crowds who besieged our friary and deprived us of the peace which until then we had enjoyed.... We were completely ignorant of what certain journals had said ... because the Catholic papers we read in the friary, in their prudence, said nothing," and so "we were amazed at the growing number of people who were coming."[3]

Padre Benedetto invited Professor Luigi Romanelli (1883–1951), a friend of his and a physician in the city of Barletta, to examine Padre Pio's wounds, which he did on May 15 and 16. Romanelli wrote a report suggesting that the lesions were incapable of medical explanation, and one of the friars leaked it to the Naples *Mattino*, which then ran a sensational article on the stigmatized priest of San Giovanni Rotondo. When he read the article, Padre Benedetto was furious at Padre Paolino, whom he blamed for the disclosure and, threatening to transfer the priest who actually handed over the doctor's report, warned the superior that he was risking the fury of the Holy See by allowing the release of confidential information to the press. "Under pain of mortal sin," he forbade any member of the community to disclose any information about Padre Pio. "To do so would be detrimental to the decorum of our Order as well as the cause of Padre Pio."[4]

On June 1, another newspaper, *Il Tempo*, reported that Padre Pio had healed a veteran with a gangrenous foot, with statements not only from the man but "many others" who witnessed it. The *Mattino*, on June 21 and 22, ran articles under the title "The Miracle-Worker." At the same time, an article by Ferdinand Tuohy appeared in the British *Daily Mail*, under the title "The Friar of Foggia," which reported, "Extraordinary scenes are being witnessed in Foggia from day to day ... long queues besiege the young Franciscan and gaze in wonder at the markings on his hands, sandaled feet, and head [*sic*]."[5]

"I Haven't a Moment Free"

The community at San Giovanni Rotondo was now augmented by five friars, all in their thirties, who had just been discharged from the service. Immediately, they were swamped with work as, suddenly, the life of the friary and church of Our Lady of Grace now revolved around Padre Pio and his ministry. Padre Paolino recounted that it was "raining letters." A room in the friary was set aside for the handling of correspondence, and Padre Raffaele of San Giovanni Rotondo — the one who leaked the medical report — was put in charge of it. The other priests spent much of their day hearing confessions. Padre Pio, who had been granted permission to hear confessions two years before by Archbishop Gagliardi, administered the Sacrament of Penance to men in the sacristy (the room where the vestments were stored and where priests prepared for Mass), while women, for the time being, made their confessions to the other priests.

By late spring, men were waiting up to two weeks for an opportunity to make their confessions to Padre Pio. As there were no hotels yet in San Giovanni Rotondo, many slept outdoors, in the fields. Padre Paolino was astounded by the great number of farmers who neglected their crops to spend a fortnight in an effort to see "the man of God." The crowds increased as the numerous pilgrimages to the nearby time-honored shrines of Our Lady Crowned and St. Michael the Archangel began stopping at the friary too — to see Padre Pio.

By summer, the scene was one of near pandemonium. Padre Paolino described the little church, which accommodated two hundred people, as "invaded" by people from all walks of life — not only peasants, but physicians, lawyers, and journalists. There were sick people who came in hopes of a miraculous cure. There were many who believed that they were possessed by demons, as well as multitudes drawn simply by curiosity. Inevitably, too, there were pickpockets who plied their trade not only in the streets and courtyard, but in the very church. Even Padre Pio was not safe from them: someone walked off with his breviary.[6]

The clothing of the friars was laundered in town. Frequently, Padre Pio's underwear and night clothes were cut up into pieces and sold as relics, while new linen was sent back in return, with the expectation that the exchange wouldn't be noticed. Village entrepreneurs were even daubing pieces of cloth with chicken blood and selling them as articles of clothing stained by Padre Pio's stigmata. Zealous devotees sometimes sneaked into the sacristy to cut pieces from cassocks, chasubles, and albs that they had reason to believe had been worn by "the man of God." They even went so far as to remove the straw from chairs in which he sat. To make matters worse, fistfights were breaking out among men disputing places in line for confession. At length, policemen had to be assigned to the friary to keep order. Whenever Padre Pio appeared in public, they had to surround him to keep fanatics from cutting his clothing right off his back.

Padre Pio often put in a sixteen-hour day, mostly spent in hearing confessions. He spent his evening hours trying to keep up his correspondence with his "spiritual daughters," with various priests, lay brothers, and seminarians, and with Padres Benedetto and Agostino. He usually did not retire until one o'clock in the morning, leaving him only a few hours of sleep. He answered Padre Benedetto, who complained about his failure to write him frequently:

I haven't a moment free. All my time is spent in freeing my brethren from the bonds of Satan. I beg you, don't afflict me more by making an appeal to charity like the others do, because the greatest charity is in snatching souls bound to Satan and winning them for Christ. And this is just what I am doing … day and night.[7]

On at least one occasion, Padre Pio, in good humor, forced Padre Paolino to share the responsibility for "making miracles." One evening, answering a knock on the convent door, Padre Pio encountered a peasant who asked for "the friar who works miracles." Padre Pio cheerfully led the peasant to Padre Paolino's room and remained outside the closed door, eavesdropping.

"Friar, my horse has been stolen," the peasant told the superior. "Since I have been told you know everything, you must tell me who stole it."

Padre Paolino replied: "If I tell you who stole your horse, you will go to him and you might even come to blows. But all the same I want to help you. Listen to what I say and think it over carefully. The proverb says: 'He who knows your habits goes in and robs.'"

Eight days later the peasant returned with a present of cheese for Padre Paolino, telling him: "Friar, when I got back home, I thought a lot over what you had said and I asked myself who could have known on that day I was sure to be in the fields. I singled him out and I went to his house and said to him, 'You have stolen my horse. The friar who works miracles told me.' At these words, he owned up and gave me back my horse."

Miracles notwithstanding, the burden of work exhausted Padre Paolino. But when he groused to Padre Pio that the crowds "have completely taken away our liberty and cause us so much work that we have no time to rest," Padre Pio retorted:

You know very well that when preachers proclaim God's Word in church, they have to work hard just to get a few people there to listen to their sermon. It's worse when it comes to confessions. People stay away from the confessional except when they have to fulfill their minimum obligations. Now, instead, when the Lord, through his grace and without any effort on our part, sends us so abundant a congregation, you nevertheless complain in this way and would want to let many souls go without being reconciled to their Lord! Let's work diligently and thank the Lord who has permitted us to work for his glory and for the good of souls.[8]

Opposition

Inevitably, there was criticism. Archpriest Giuseppe Prencipe (1872–1956) and the other secular clergy took a jaundiced view of Padre Pio's celebrity, as great numbers of people began to forsake the city churches to worship at Our Lady of Grace and make their confessions to the friars.

Don Giovanni Miscio, a thirty-year-old priest who ministered in town, in early 1919 began to write letters to the newspapers, to Archbishop Gagliardi, to the Capuchin minister general, and even to the Vatican, accusing the friars of "putting Padre Pio on display for the purpose of making money," alleging that the Capuchins on the hill were running a lucrative business, hawking items supposedly worn or handled by the stigmatized priest.

One Sunday, in the city of San Severo, a priest declared that a member of the Italian parliament named Fraccacreta, a Freemason and agnostic, had been converted by Padre Pio. Actually, the convert had been a man with the same name, and the legislator, when he heard the story, was so furious that he attacked the priest, striking him in the face, and complained to the Italian minister of the interior about the "farce" being perpetrated by the Capuchins, demanding that police be dispatched to break up the "dirty business."

Miscio accused Fra Nicola of soliciting money for Padre Pio's personal use on his quests, so Padre Benedetto ordered the begging friar not to go into the countryside anymore, but to receive offerings at a special desk in the church. In addition, the provincial arranged for several men to surround Padre Pio as he proceeded between the sacristy and the church, to prevent him from being mobbed by the multitudes. He further requested the police to create a barrier between the altar and the crowd when Padre Pio was celebrating Mass. All vestments and anything else Padre Pio used were to be carefully locked away, and the friars were ordered to exercise a "prudent reserve" in talking about him.

At this time, Padre Pio was celebrating Mass at noon, after hearing confessions all morning. After Mass, he remained in the sacristy so that the women, who had no opportunity to make their confessions to him, could kiss his hand and exchange a few words with him. So that he could greet those unable to find a place either in the cramped church or tiny sacristy, Padre Pio was allowed to go, at certain times, to a window to bless the throngs who gathered in the courtyard. This drew sharp criticism from the city clergy, who held this as proof that the Capuchins were putting the stigmatist on display.

Miracles?

Despite the efforts of Padres Benedetto and Paolino, the newspapers continued to report miracles. One of them concerned a man named Francesco Santarello (or Santierello), San Giovanni's village idiot, a gaping-mouthed, grotesque-looking, cross-eyed little man, sometimes described as a dwarf or hunchback, with clubbed feet, who dragged himself about on his knees, supported by a pair of miniature crutches. Children would laugh at him and even pull away his crutches and burst into laughter as he tumbled to the pavement. One day he cried out to Padre Pio, "Give me a blessing!" According to some witnesses, Padre Pio looked at him and declared, "Throw away your crutches!" Don Giuseppe Prencipe said, "The poor man started walking as best he could, floundering, leaning right and left against the people who surrounded him, filling the air with deafening cries of 'miracle.' (He wasn't healed at all)."[9] Padre Paolino, however, claimed that Santarello, who lived for some time after that, never used his crutches again, but walked with the help of only a cane. Although his physical and mental condition remained unchanged, he was now at least ambulatory instead of crawling, and to some people, that was miracle enough.[10]

Don Prencipe was extremely skeptical of the miracle stories, which he dismissed as products of superheated imaginations, like the testimony of a potter from the nearby town of Torremaggiore, who swore that he used to curse continually until one night he swore "in a horrendous way" when his kiln wouldn't light. And then, to his amazement, Padre Pio materialized before his eyes, scolded him for his blasphemies, and then made the kiln ignite![11]

According to Padre Paolino, a priest named Carlo Naldi came in 1919 from Florence with a Jewish friend named Lello Pegna. Naldi explained to Paolino that Pegna had recently become totally blind and had come to ask Padre Pio to intercede with God for a cure. Padre Paolino did not specify the cause of the blindness, but there was no doubt in his mind or in those of other witnesses as to his condition, as someone had to help Pegna eat, putting his plate in front of him, cutting his bread and meat, and placing the glass of wine in his hand.

Padre Pio told the blind man, "The Lord will not grant you the grace of physical sight unless you first receive sight for your soul. After you are baptized, then the Lord will give you your sight."

Pegna returned to San Giovanni several months later, evidently able to see very well. He explained that, despite opposition from his family, he accepted Christ and had been baptized. He remained blind and was very discouraged. However, gradually, over a period of months, his sight returned, and the doctor who had previously told him that his blindness was incurable conceded that his sight was now perfect. Padre Paolino kept in touch with Pegna and reported that, thirty years later, the man who was once blind could still see perfectly.[12]

Padre Paolino wrote Padre Benedetto a letter describing two other occurrences that he considered miraculous. In June 1919, a young woman identified only as "the niece of the archpriest of Cagli" asked Padre Pio to pray for her to receive the grace of healing. One of her legs was so much shorter than the other that she could just barely touch the ground with the tip of the foot. According to Padre Paolino, in the presence of numerous witnesses, after the woman spoke to Padre Pio, all at once she could rest both feet squarely on the ground and walk without a limp.[13]

That same month, Maria Scotto-DiFesta, forty-nine years old, from a town near Naples, came to see Padre Pio. Her right leg had been paralyzed for eighteen years. After Padre Pio assured her of his prayers, she headed back home in a car, still paralyzed. During the ride, however, she suddenly felt the sensation returning to her affected limb. When she and her friends reached Foggia, to their amazement, she was able to get out of the car and walk normally and unaided.[14]

The "Mysterious Formula"

One of the most interesting visitors to San Giovanni Rotondo during this time was Prince Karl Klugkist, a forty-eight-year-old aristocrat, a native of Kiev, in what is now Ukraine, but at the time of his birth was in the Russian Empire. For some years, he had lived in Italy, working as a painter and a tutor to wealthy children. Although he had become a Catholic several years before, he was deeply interested in Eastern religions and the occult. After reading the report of Dr. Romanelli in the Naples *Mattino*, he decided to visit Padre Pio. He asked to see "the saint" and was escorted to the sacristy where Padre Pio was hearing confessions. The room was packed with men. From behind the door at the other end of the room, Klugkist could hear the noise of a scuffle as several farmers were trying to force their way past the guards. As he withdrew to a corner to prepare to make his confession, Klugkist was fascinated by the beauty of Padre Pio's face and his whole demeanor. The painter recounted:

> I was able to observe ... from the expression on his face that he only heard the words of the penitent.... He didn't see him with bodily eyes. His body and especially his crossed arms were strangely immobile, almost cataleptic. At the end of each confession he became quite animated and answered in a clear voice, the tone of which revealed his brotherly love for the penitent. After he had spoken, his face always changed completely. His whole attention seemed to be fixed on the heart. While there had been a radiance about his head and torso before, it was seemed to be extinguished.

While observing Padre Pio hearing confessions, Klugkist, who apparently was able to hear some of Padre Pio's words, noted: "Slowly, in guttural tones, he recited a rhythmic prayer, a mystical formula, in an oriental language unknown to me. I remember the words which recurred continually: 'Adai nanda' and 'nanda.' This unusual and mysterious invocation aroused my curiosity and I regretted being unable to ask him for an explanation." Then, raising his eyes, "his face shone, and with a solemn gesture he gave absolution." This seems to be an instance in which Padre Pio was "speaking in unknown tongues."

A half-dozen men were in line ahead of Klugkist. The last was a priest who asked to see Padre Pio's stigmata. "Thomas," chided the priest, recalling the "doubting" apostle, "have you to touch in order to believe?" He uncovered his hands and let the priest kiss the wounds.

When it was his turn, Klugkist said to Padre Pio, "I came here hoping to have a chat with you," to which the Capuchin replied: "I don't allow people to chat with me because there are too many. If you have something to tell me, say it now, during confession."

Klugkist began to relate his story, "without any sort of order, jumping from one period of my life to another, mixing up sins and adventures, study and research, in a fantastic, pell-mell story." Padre Pio listened without looking him straight in the face. As he spoke, Klugkist "studied him, feeling more and more fascinated by the sincerity of his holiness." The penitent noted that from time to time the priest blew on his hands "almost unconsciously ... as if they were burning."

After ten minutes Klugkist stopped, and then

> the holy man's reply came at once, clear and beautiful, at times vivacious and accompanied by expressive gestures. He uttered no reproof. He spoke with such certainty about my supernatural experiences that I was at once convinced of being in the presence of a true master. He could not have been a scholar in the field of occult science, but it was evident that he had studied at the school of personal experience and possessed the Truth which shines forth, unique and individual, over and above every symbol.... He ... spoke to me of the danger of mirages created by Lucifer and ended by saying what I may summarize in the words: *You are seeking the way, but you have already found it.*

"I found myself faced with the Divine Ego," Klugkist reflected. "In [Pio] alone I found no trace of the human ego." Other spiritual teachers, he was convinced, "were men more or less imbued with the divine, while he, on the other hand, is nothing but an instrument of the Divine. He has reached the goal of Union."[15]

Sometime later, Klugkist, while praying before the Blessed Sacrament in Rome, saw a vision of two hands reaching out, holding a white habit with a red and blue cross. When his confessor told him that the Trinitarian order wore such a habit, he decided that he was to serve God as a member. Ordained a priest as Father Pio of the Holy Trinity in 1924, he ministered in Halifax, Nova Scotia, in Canada, until his death at seventy-seven in 1948.

Sometimes an Angel, Sometimes a Demon

Another man met Padre Pio in the summer of 1919 who would play a major role in his life and ministry. He learned about Padre Pio through an article in the *Mattino*, describing a miracle that never happened.

Earlier that spring a war veteran had appeared on crutches in San Giovanni, claiming to be suffering the effects of a wound in his foot that refused to heal. He suddenly announced that he was cured. Padre Paolino insisted that the veteran, Antonio Colonello, submit to an examination by three doctors. When he did, the doctors told Padre Paolino that Colonello's scar was at least six months old. Paolino then wrote to the ex-soldier's doctor and learned that the wound, in fact, had been completely healed for six months or more. The veteran had, apparently, for reasons best known to himself, been hoping to make himself the center of attention. The newspapers, however, reported that he had been cured instantaneously by Padre Pio.[16] (This may have been the incident of the gangrenous foot reported by the *Tempo*.)

The articles were read by a twenty-seven-year-old ne'er-do-well named Emmanuele Brunatto. Born in Turin, on September 9, 1892, to a privileged family, Brunatto was a complex and interesting character, highly intelligent, crafty and clever, uncompromising, volatile, and intensely loyal. In the following years, he would exhibit a talent for making money aboveboard (and below), and for gaining access to some of the most influential people in Italy. Educated by the Salesian order, Brunatto, at one time, entertained thoughts of becoming a priest, but, by the time he reached adolescence, he had drifted away from the Church and found that his chief interests in life were money and sex. Wanting neither to work nor further his education, Brunatto was leading the life of a drifter and confidence man when he had a vivid dream about his dead father. In the dream, his father blessed him. "His face irradiated an indescribable spiritual light," Brunatto wrote later. "He said, 'Kneel.' I obeyed. He put his hands on my head, and I felt a warmth go out of the palms that was like a liquid that penetrated my body and soul."[17]

When Brunatto awoke, he thought about the dream for a while, then continued his frantic pursuit of pleasure. After he read the article about Colonello in the *Mattino*, he was seized by a sudden impulse to visit Padre Pio. At the time, Brunatto was living in Naples with a woman named Giulietta, in "a putrid alley infested by prostitutes of the very lowest kind." He began to wonder if he was a hopelessly ruined man. No, he answered himself, for God, "who had thrown me into the gutter to convince me of my weakness and my sins, was already preparing the way of my redemption. Like a call from afar," Brunatto wrote, "the thought of Padre Pio came incessantly to my mind. I wanted to go to him at once, but did not have the money for the trip."

Brunatto obtained temporary work and earned enough for the bus trip as far as San Severo. Then he had to walk the rest of the way to San Giovanni — ten hours — at night:

It was a moonlit night. I passed through an inhospitable and desolate valley without encountering a living soul. Volcanic rocks immersed in a cold white light suggested illusions of the ruins of dead cities. Here and there I encountered, like motionless phantoms, the tormented forms of old Indian fig trees. I seemed to be reliving the journey of my life, a long night's journey to an unknown dawn.

Day was breaking when he came in view of a barren mountain marked by the white rectangle of the Capuchin convent of Our Lady of Grace. Going in, he found a friar seated, hearing the confession of a farmer, who was on his knees. A crowd of men was standing around, waiting their turn. "Is this Padre Pio?" Brunatto asked a man nearby, who replied in the affirmative.

At that very moment, Padre Pio turned and looked at him. "Rather," wrote Brunatto, "he pierced me with his gaze, which was hard and angry." The visitor saw before him a man with coarse features, a harsh expression, and an unkempt beard. "Is this the saint?" he asked himself. "With that bandit's face? And why does he look at me with such hatred? How lovely, to spend all my money to make this trip and then to meet — *him!*" Terribly shaken, Brunatto stormed out of the friary. "I fled the sacristy like a madman and found myself in the open, alone, along the crude fence that enclosed the monastery garden, my hands grasping the loose-fitting stones. I sobbed and wailed like a wounded child, 'My Lord and my God!' It was impossible to describe the grief and the hope that tormented me as I poured out my soul."

Brunatto returned to the friary and found Padre Pio all alone. He was waiting for him. His countenance had undergone a remarkable change. It now seemed to be "of surpassing beauty, radiating indescribable joy. Even his beard no longer appeared unkempt. And in his eyes was love." Without a word, Padre Pio signaled Brunatto to kneel. "Memories of my past," Brunatto wrote afterward, "rushed from my lips like the waters of a river in flood. How many errors and infamies from my youth till today! I would never have finished confessing them had not the Padre stopped me: 'You confessed during the war and the Lord has pardoned your sins and put a great boulder over them, and you must not try to raise it. Tell me only that which you have to regret since that time.'"

Brunatto then recounted that Padre Pio helped his memory and gave advice that was "simple, clear, and compassionate," and "when he came to the absolution, he had to begin over several times, as if he were struggling against an invisible adversary who was clinging to my shoulders. The sacramental words broke and came together again … while from his mouth there came an intense perfume of roses and violets, which bathed my face. Finally, as if freed from a great weight, I arose."

When he asked Padre Pio to bless him: "He put his two hands, covered with half-gloves, lightly around my neck. It was then that I felt exactly the same warmth emanating from the palms of his hands, the same mysterious liquid I had felt three years earlier when I dreamt that I was receiving the blessing … from my father."

Several days later, back in Naples, Brunatto recounted: "All of a sudden my past life began to pass before me like the projection of a film: the dangers run, the sins committed, the griefs and the joys, the gifts and the graces, the flights and returns, all reconstructed chronologically in a wonderful experience of my life under the incessant protection of the Mother of God. For long hours I lingered, a simple spectator, moved to tears by the film of my past.... One fact, however, was clear to me: the projector of this film was Padre Pio."[18]

Shortly afterward, Brunatto returned to San Giovanni Rotondo, where he settled in a little hut by the town cemetery. There he raised rabbits and chickens and spent the rest of his time in prayer and meditation. Eventually, he was hired as a teacher at the "Seraphic College" and was given a room in the friary. He would pray in the choir beside Padre Pio during the Divine Office. He would sometimes doze off during the prayers, only to be reawakened by a gentle nudge from Padre Pio, who jokingly asked him, "Now, how do you expect to go to heaven if you keep falling asleep during the prayers?" One day Padre Paolino asked Brunatto to consider joining them in the religious life, as a friar — but before he had a chance to answer, Padre Pio threw his hands into the air and cried, "Never! Never! Never!"[19]

Emmanuele Brunatto would emerge periodically for the next forty-five years in Padre Pio's life as his fervent defender, although he often made matters worse for him by the way he fought against the Capuchin's real and imagined enemies in high places. Padre Pio would later say of Brunatto, "Sometimes he seemed an angel to me, and at other times a demon."[20]

Chapter Thirteen

Holiness or Hysteria?

Examinations of the Wounds

There are no recorded instances of the stigmata before 1224, when five wounds appeared on the hands, feet, and side of Saint Francis of Assisi, as he prayed in ecstasy on Italy's Mount Alverna. Padre Pio was the first priest of the Catholic Church known to have had the stigmata. There is no doubt that he exhibited persistent, bleeding wounds in his hands for nearly fifty years, since the wounds were seen by thousands of people over the years when he exposed his hands (as required) while saying Mass.

Before he was forbidden by the Supreme Sacred Congregation of the Holy Office (called, after 1965, the Congregation for the Doctrine of the Faith) to show his wounds, his stigmata were examined by several doctors. Apparently, the first was Angelo Maria Merla, a physician who also served for a time as San Giovanni Rotondo's mayor. Merla declared that he could affirm that the lesions were not the result of tuberculosis, but that he could not say with any certainty what caused them without extensive tests.[1] The personal physician of Pope Benedict XV, Professor Giuseppe Bastianelli (1862–1959), who was an expert on malaria, examined the wounds, but no written report of his examinations has come to light. Detailed reports exist from three physicians who examined Padre Pio in 1919 and 1920. Luigi Romanelli, physician-in-chief of the City Hospital of Barletta, examined his wounds five times between May 1919 and July 1920. Amico Bignami (1862–1929), a highly respected physician who was professor of pathology at the University of Rome, studied Padre Pio's stigmata for a period of several days in July 1919. Giorgio Festa (1860–1940), a surgeon in private practice in Rome, made three examinations of Padre Pio's stigmata, the last in 1925, when the Capuchin underwent a hernia operation. By then, the Holy Office had forbidden Padre Pio to show his wounds to anyone — even a physician — without its permission. Since Festa didn't have permission, in order to show his obedience to ecclesial authority, Padre Pio refused anesthesia! Fortunately, for Festa, Padre Pio passed out from the pain during the operation, providing the surgeon the opportunity to observe the wounds he had first examined five years before. Because of the continuing ban by the Holy Office, there were no more formal, extensive examinations of the stigmata, except by an inquisitor in 1921, although several physicians over the years were, like Festa, able to observe the wounds when treating Padre Pio for something else.

For example, Padre Alessio Parente (1933–2000), who was Padre Pio's helper when the latter was old and infirm, claims he was on one occasion able to get a good look at the stigmata. He later recalled:

> The wounds in the hands were the size and shape of a coin. They were covered with a crust of dried blood.... Once the crust would start to break, it would form sharp projections that pointed into his flesh and would be very painful. So, when the crusts dried, he would pull them away. One day when he was doing this, he fainted. He must have pulled some skin or flesh away and the pain was so bad he fainted.

It was then that Alessio was able to get a good look at the wounds: "The stigmata were very scary to look at. They were horrible to look at. I had always wished to see them, but once I saw them, I prayed, 'God, don't ever let me see them again.' His hands were like those of a leper, they were so corroded."[2]

Padre Pio was able to work fifteen hours straight without a bite to eat. When he did eat, Bignami observed, Pio consumed very little.[3] Festa noted, as had Bignami, that Padre Pio was thin and pale, with a face illuminated "by a very clear gaze." Despite the fact that he ate very little, the friar seemed full of "spiritual energy."[4] Sophisticated blood tests evidently did not exist in 1919, but when Dr. Luigi Pancaro treated Padre Pio in the 1950s for unrelated physical problems, he ran a battery of tests and found the blood work entirely normal. There was no sign of anemia nor any abnormality in the clotting factor. His blood pressure was 166 over 90, which Pancaro considered normal.[5] Dr. Giuseppe Sala, Padre Pio's physician from 1956 to 1968, also reported that none of the tests he ran on the priest's blood revealed any abnormality. "He had beautiful blood work."[6]

Lesions were clearly visible on both the upper and lower surfaces of Padre Pio's hands, in the center of the palm. All the physicians who saw them were in agreement that the wounds were circular and approximately three quarters of an inch in diameter. The wounds consisted of "a shiny viscous red membrane," slightly raised, that when not covered with a scab or with blood, resembled a tiny button.[7]

There is some disagreement as to the depth of the stigmata. Dr. Andrea Cardone, in a statement signed in November 1968 (when he was ninety-two years old), stated that he had examined Padre Pio's stigmata but did not give the date or circumstances. Cardone — a general practitioner from Pietrelcina — declared that the wounds "pierced the palms of the hands completely through, so much so that one could see light through them."[8] Dr. Romanelli wrote, "Placing one's thumb on one side of the wound in the hand and an index finger on the other side and pressing together … one has the feeling of emptiness between the fingers, divided only by a soft membrane of skin, which feels like sand, and there is no resistance of bone or flesh that should be there."[9]

On the other hand, Bignami, who examined the stigmata within days of Romanelli, described the wounds as shallow, concluding that the hand lesions involved only the epidermis and dermis (the two uppermost layers of tissue). Festa was not certain. At first, he agreed with Bignami that the wounds were shallow, but, after two more examinations, he concluded that they only appeared to be superficial when they were covered with a scab. When he looked at the lesions when they were perfectly clean, they appeared deep.[10] Yet he concluded that they could not have penetrated through the entire structure of the hand, since the location of the wounds on the back of the hands did not correspond exactly to the position of the wounds on the palms.[11] Sala, when he observed the lesions forty years after Romanelli, felt an indentation in the flesh of the palm.[12] Padre Alessio estimated that they were a half-inch deep. When Dr. Alberto Caserta of Foggia x-rayed Pio's hands and feet on October 14, 1954, he found no abnormality in the structure or position of the bones.[13] Likewise, when the radiologist Luigi Massenti did X-rays, he found "no morphological alterations concerning the skeleton."[14]

Both Bignami and Sala commented on the clean, clearly defined edges of the stigmata, something unusual in ordinary wounds of long duration. Festa wrote: "At the edges of the lesions, the skin is perfectly normal and does not show any sign of edema [that is, a collection of fluid in the tissues], of penetration, or of redness, even when examined with a good magnifying glass."[15] Romanelli likewise observed no signs of redness or inflammation.

The wounds in the feet were seen and described much less often than those in the hands. Festa wrote:

> On the backs of both feet, and corresponding exactly to the middle of the second metatarsal, I noticed a circular lesion, red-brown in color, covered by a thick, blackish scab, which had exactly the same characteristics as those described on the hands. Maybe these were a little smaller and more superficial … here also the skin which surrounds the lesions presents no traces of infiltration, nor of swelling, nor of phlogistic [inflammatory] reactions; here also there is a slight but continued oozing of bloody serum. On the soles of the feet, and at a point which more or less corresponds to those on the back

of the feet, may be seen two lesions, one in each sole, quite clear in their edges and perfectly identical to the preceding ones.[16]

Padre Eusebio Notte, who assisted Padre Pio in the 1960s, saw the foot wounds once. They were dark spots, but not holes, very defined, the size of a Euro coin, on the center of the feet.[17]

Most witnesses testify that the wound in Padre Pio's side was shaped like a cross. Padre Paolino believed that the first slash had come at the time of the "transverberation," in August 1918, and the second, along with the lesions of the hands and feet, in September. Romanelli, however, was certain that when he examined Padre Pio in June 1919, the side wound was not cruciform, but "a clean cut parallel to the ribs," about three inches long.[18] In subsequent exams, nearly everyone, including Romanelli, observed the wound, in the left side, just under the nipple, in the shape of a cross.

If there is some difficulty in ascertaining the exact depth of the wounds, it is even harder to determine the amount of blood that issued from them. Romanelli observed a profuse effusion of arterial blood from the side wound,[19] but none of the wounds bled when Bignami examined them.[20] When Festa examined the stigmata, little drops of blood oozed from the edges.[21] Father Dominic Meyer (1892–1966), the American Capuchin who served as Pio's English and German corresponding secretary for thirteen years, never examined the wounds, but he wrote Father Edmund Kramer in Detroit, "Padre Pio's wounds, as far as is known, bleed slightly, but continually."[22]

At times, especially in Lent, the wounds seem to have bled heavily. There are persistent reports that sometimes Padre Pio bled from extensive lesions on his torso, suggestive of the wounds received by Christ during the scourging. The best evidence for this is a photograph of Padre Pio's nightshirt, stained from top to bottom with blood.

Padre Pio took great care to conceal the wounds. Father Dominic Meyer wrote in 1949:

> Padre Pio wears BROWN gloves (woolen) during the day. These absorb the blood, if there should be any, and at the same time don't show. During the night he frequently wears white cloth gloves, which sometimes are all soaked with blood in the morning. Padre Pio washes these himself in his room. Padre Pio washes his feet in the kitchen, but in a corner so that his wounds are not open to anyone's gaze. As regards the wound in his side: this also bleeds continually, so that he must change the cloth over it two and three times a day. The small pieces of linen cloth are furnished by people around here.... [These] he keeps ... in place with a band around his chest.[23]

Although almost no one was able to see the stigmata up close or examine them, the hand wounds could be seen clearly when Padre Pio celebrated Mass and was required to remove his gloves. People seated toward the front of the church, and especially those assisting him at the altar, could see the lesions rather well. When Padre Bernardo of Pietrelcina asked him why he didn't clean off the dried blood crusts, Padre Pio answered: "If I removed the dried blood, the cutaneous membrane would rip off and there would be more flow of blood. Because of that the hand would be terrible to look at" — and people, he was convinced, would be horrified.[24]

In addition to the inconvenience of persistent, messy, bleeding wounds that had to be frequently cleaned and dressed, Padre Pio suffered real pain. He frequently replied to people who asked if the stigmata hurt: "Do you think the Good Lord gave them to me for decoration?" Festa noted that Padre Pio couldn't close his hand completely, and that even the gentlest pressure on the feet caused great agony. A generation later, Padre Eusebio made the same observation. When an American priest asked Padre Pio about the pain in the wounds, Pio told him, "The suffering and pain are very intense on Thursday nights and Fridays."[25]

One of the most extraordinary characteristics of Padre Pio's stigmata was the peculiarly fragrant aroma of the blood that issued from them, despite its normal chemical composition. Some witnesses, in fact, claimed that the blood was unusually "shining," and even that rays of light were to be seen emanating from it. Regarding the fragrance, Festa wrote:

> I can affirm that on my first visit I took from [Padre Pio's] side a small cloth stained with blood, which I brought back with me to Rome for a microscopic examination. I personally, being entirely deprived of the sense of smell, did not notice any special emanation. But a distinguished official and other persons with me in the automobile on our return to Rome from San Giovanni, not knowing that I had brought with me that piece of cloth enclosed in a case, despite the strong ventilation owing to the speed of the automobile, smelled the fragrance very distinctly and assured me that it precisely corresponded to the perfume that emanates from the person of Padre Pio. In Rome ... for a long time after, the same cloth conserved in a cabinet in my study filled the room with perfume — so much so that many patients who came to consult me spontaneously asked me for an explanation of its origin.[26]

Explanations

The question remains as to how Padre Pio's stigmata can be explained scientifically. When Padre Benedetto questioned Romanelli, he was told: "From all that I know and all that I can tell, these lesions cannot be classified among ordinary injuries ... I have never found a clinical indication that would authorize me to classify the injuries. I do not wish to speak of 'stigmata', because doing so would be outside the competence of a physician."[27] Festa, who was a devout Catholic, did not hesitate to describe Padre Pio's wounds as true stigmata, of supernatural origin.

Bignami, who was a skeptic on the subject of religious matters, suggested three possibilities: first, that Padre Pio "artificially and voluntarily" created his wounds; second, that they were the result of a "morbid state"; and third, that they were caused partly by a morbid state and partly by artificial means. Because of the "impression of sincerity that Padre Pio made on me," Bignami ruled out the possibility that Padre Pio caused his own wounds. He expressed a belief that the wounds had a "pathological origin, due to neurotically-caused cell deterioration," but that this could not explain the symmetry of the wounds. He then concluded, "We can in fact think that the lesions … began as a pathological condition," which was artificially maintained by the use of chemicals.[28] Padre Pio had in fact admitted to using iodine in an attempt to cure the wounds.

Bignami recommended a procedure for healing Padre Pio's wounds. First, all chemicals in Padre Pio's room were to be confiscated. The only chemical found there was iodine, and it was removed. Then, Padre Pio's hand, feet, and chest wounds were to be bandaged and securely sealed in the presence of witnesses. Each day, for eight days, the bandages would be changed and resealed. Without the application of iodine or any other substance, Bignami expected a significant reduction in the bleeding and the size of the wounds. Padre Paolino and three other priests carried out Bignami's instructions. Padre Paolino wrote:

> In the presence of the witnesses, I helped to remove the habit and undershirt, together with Padre Pio's socks. Along with the other Fathers, I was able to see quite clearly the mark on his chest and those on the feet and hands. Thus, during the space of eight days every morning we removed the bandages of the preceding day after having verified that the seal was intact, and we put new ones on, and in this way we easily observed the stigmata on Padre Pio, who however suffered immensely in the depths of his heart in exposing these wounds, which he always tried to keep hiding from the eyes of others.

Padre Placido, one of the witnesses, wrote: "Never had the wounds shed so much blood as in those days. In the morning, before [Padre Pio] ascended the altar to celebrate Mass, we unbound the hands, and in order to prevent blood from staining the vestments and altar cloths, one of us every so often dried the wounds with a cotton wad." At the end of eight days, the hand wounds were bleeding more than ever and there was no sign of healing.[29] This would seem to undermine Bignami's hypothesis.

As for the hypothesis about a "morbid state," there is no evidence that Padre

Pio suffered from "neurosis," as it was, and is, commonly understood. Everyone who knew him found him cheerful, serene, and well-balanced. While the stigmata remained for fifty years, all other wounds he sustained during the course of his days mended normally. He carried all his life a large scar on one of his fingers caused by cutting it with a knife when he was a boy.[30] It had healed normally. During the 1920s, he underwent surgery for an inguinal hernia and for a cyst on his neck. Both incisions healed and scarred normally, while the wounds on his hands, feet, and side persisted until the last days of the Capuchin's life, when they disappeared spontaneously, without leaving the slightest scar. Even Bignami, who believed the wounds to be superficial, conceded that the wounds in the hands and side involved the dermis as well as the epidermis. According to dermatologists, any wound involving more than the epidermis will leave a scar. Yet, despite the fact that there were scars on Padre Pio's body at death from various injuries and surgical procedures, the stigmata, when they vanished, left no traces at all.

Padre Pio showed no interest whatsoever in attempts to explain his stigmata. When asked why his hand wounds were in the palms rather than in the wrists (where victims of crucifixion were usually nailed), he shrugged his shoulders and said, "Oh, I guess it would be too much to have them exactly like they were in the case of Our Lord." When people suggested that the stigmata were caused by his obsession with the Passion of Christ and his continual meditation before the bloody crucifix in the friary choir, Padre Pio responded: "Go out to the fields and look for a bull. Look very closely at him. Concentrate on him with all your might — and see if you start to grow horns."[31]

Chapter Fourteen

The Spiritual Director

Spiritual Children

It was not merely to gape at the stigmata (which could be seen only during Mass and then barely) that crowds made their way to the remote Capuchin friary of Our Lady of Grace to see Padre Pio. Some came in expectation of a miracle, but most came hoping for a word of spiritual enlightenment. For many this came during the Sacrament of Penance, which, at first, he administered only to men, who were also permitted, most of the time, to talk to him in the sacristy and in his room. When he was allowed to hear the confessions of women, they came to him in such numbers that he was in the confessional twelve hours or more a day.

There were certain people whom Padre Pio designated as his spiritual sons and daughters. Many people begged to be his spiritual children, but he was reluctant to accept a person he did not "know before the Lord" — that is, about whom the Lord had not given him some "illumination." These were the people whom he believed God had entrusted to him, and it was to these people that confidently he communicated God's will, advising them on the state of their soul. Because he tended to spend much more time with them than with others, this would lead, in the coming years, to accusations of favoritism that posed a threat to his reputation.

Unless he was provided some supernatural illumination when he counseled, Padre Pio tended to be rather diffident, as he was forced to "proceed gropingly," guiding himself with "a little cold and pallid doctrine learned in books."[1] For those relatively few people for whom he had "recourse to divine light," he understood their spiritual state through "a light that Divine Goodness does not deny to ministers called to act as his proxies on earth."[2]

It seems that Padre Pio, even when he was not truly "illuminated," had at least some recourse to supersensible wisdom. He always insisted that Mary, the saints, and his guardian angel were in the confessional with him, apparently in a literal sense. "When the moment to give absolution comes," he averred, "if Our Lady wasn't in front of me, sitting down … I would never give absolution to anybody, not so much because of the unworthiness of the penitents, but because giving absolution would seem to me like a theft, a deceit."[3]

There were several people whom Padre Pio counseled by letter, and many of these writings have been preserved. Many are written to spiritual daughters (who at first did not have access to him in confession); others were written to priests, religious, seminarians.

Padre Pio did not flatter himself. To one of his spiritual daughters he wrote:

Give praise and thanksgiving to [God] alone, and not to me. You owe nothing to me. I am but an instrument in the hands of God, capable of serving a useful purpose only when handled by the Divine Craftsman. Left to myself, I know how to do nothing except sin, and sin again.[4]

His letters generally are without extravagant claims of supernatural knowledge. For example, in November 1916, he responded to the request for prayer by a priest, "I've commenced to recite the two *Ave Marias* with two *Gloria Patris* for your spiritual and bodily needs and am resolutely determined to continue forever."[5] To the same priest he wrote on another occasion: "Now we come to your worthy request concerning the case of your good nephew. I have no doubt that the Lord will come to console your hearts and it won't be long. This is what my heart told me and I would expect not to be disappointed by Divine Mercy."[6] (The nature of the problem and the outcome of the situation are unknown.)

Advice to His Students

Padre Pio wrote long letters of counsel to the students (as a group) at the "Seraphic College." He urged them to confide faithfully and conscientiously in their spiritual director:

Children, I say, with St. Ambrose, it is necessary for the one who wants to be perfected in the spirit to open his heart and reveal his own infirmities and inclinations to his own guide.… Can a doctor heal a wound … that you don't want to show him? And how can the guide who is the doctor of your soul cure us of those weaknesses into which we fall, if we do not disclose them? How can he free us from those little passions that dominate us if we hide them from him? … What a weakness it is for us, concludes St. Augustine, to be ashamed to talk about what we are not ashamed to do?[7]

He liked to use homely metaphors. In January 1918, he wrote to the students:

Remember when I was in Rome last May? There I saw a tree which was supposed to have been planted by the patriarch St. Dominic. Everybody who goes, out of devotion, to see it, hugs it out of love for the one who planted it. Having seen in you the tree of the desire of holiness, that God himself has planted in your spirits, I love it dearly and feel pleasure in thinking about it … and I therefore urge you to do the same and say together with me: "God, make me grow, O beautiful tree, planted by divine seed." I would wish for God to make you produce your fruit to maturity, and when you have produced it, that it may please God to preserve you from troublesome winds that cause all the fruit to fall for the dumb beasts to come and devour.

He told them to be like the orange trees on the coast of Genoa, which are full of fruit almost all year round. He liked to compare the Christian life to the halcyon, or kingfisher, as he did both to his students as well as his spiritual daughters:

A few days ago I was thinking about what some say about the halcyons — little birds that make their nests on the beach by the sea. They construct their nest in a form that is round and so compressed that the water of the sea is unable to penetrate it. On top of it is an opening through which they can get air. Inside they keep their young. The nests can safely roll and float on the waves without overturning or submerging, and the air that is breathed from that opening serves as a counterweight and balance so that those little round structures never overturn. Oh, my dearly beloved children, how I wish that your heart should be like that — closed securely from every side, so that if they are surprised by the agitations and storms of the world, the flesh, and the devil, they cannot penetrate you, and that there should be no other opening except on the side of heaven, through which to breathe and aspire to our Lord Jesus....

O, my good children, the sweet Jesus is pleased to make you like that: surrounded, that is, by the world and the flesh, may you live on spirit; amidst the vanity of the earth may you live in heaven; living with men, may you praise and love him with the angels, and may the foundation of your hopes always be on high and in paradise.[8]

Confidence in God

Padre Pio advised the students, in March 1918, that when things are going badly, the devil "suggests to you that God is punishing you for some sin that you're not aware of and wants to chastise you because you haven't removed it from your soul." He insisted:

This is not true at all, because when your soul groans and fears offending God, you aren't offending him and you are very far from doing so. Instead, think about what I told you: that your present state [in which you are afraid of God's wrath] is the result of your love for God, and at the same time, a trial of God's incomparable love for you. Know for sure that God can reject everything in a creature conceived in sin who carries the indelible stamp [of original sin] from Adam, but he absolutely cannot reject a sincere desire to love him. Therefore, if you can't be sure of his celestial mercy for other reasons, you must be assured at least for this one.[9]

People should not imagine that their misfortunes are sent as punishment by God. When someone asked him if a man who had been killed in an accident was punished by God, Padre Pio said, "Punishment for our actions is like our reward: We will have it only in eternity."[10]

Imperfections
To Fra Marcellino Disconsole of Foggia, who eventually left the order, Padre Pio counseled: "If you want to be perfect, be patient in bearing with your imperfections.... Divine Mercy has never cast aside those who are troubled about this, but rather gives them his grace, covering their pride and vileness with his ... glory."[11] Continuing, he said: "As long as you knowingly don't want to do what you know is evil, those evils that God permits and that you do without wanting to do them, serve to make you humble and keep you safe from pride. Don't fear them and don't torment yourself and doubt your conscience, because you know well that, after you have been diligent and done what you could, there is no reason for you to be distressed or afraid anymore."[12] To Fra Emmanuele Bozzuto of San Marco la Catola, Padre Pio wrote: "When your will is in the habit of pleasing God, every action will be acceptable to him.... Jesus knows what you want to do and that you always want to please him."

Padre Pio told Fra Emmanuele:

Be suspicious of those desires which ... cannot produce results, such as the desire for a certain Christian perfection that can be imagined but never put into practice, about which many can give a good lesson, but nobody can carry out.... Right often we are so frustrated in our desire to become angels of paradise that we neglect to be good Christians.... Our imperfections, my son, must accompany us to the grave. We can't walk without touching the ground. While it's true that we shouldn't lie down on the ground or keep our gaze fixed on it, nevertheless it is also true that we shouldn't even think of flying, because, in the life of the spirit, we are like baby birds whose wings haven't yet developed. Our mortal life is dying in us little by little.... It's necessary to let our imperfections die in us. For the devout souls who endure them these imperfections can also be sources of merit, and powerful reasons to acquire the various virtues. Through them, in fact, we come to understand ever better the abyss of misery that we are and therefore receive an incentive to exercise humility, patience, diligence, and self-denial.[13]

Furthermore, he said:

Even if we were the most perfect creatures in the world, it doesn't serve any useful purpose to know it. We must always consider ourselves imperfect, without worrying about it at all. And it's also a waste of time to examine ourselves as to whether we are imperfect, because we must always be convinced of this. Therefore we must never be surprised when we catch ourselves in imperfections. In fact, we can very well suppose that in this life such will always be the case.[14]

"Take No Thought of the Future"

Padre Pio told Padre Emmanuele: "Don't be afraid of those dangers you discern far off.... They seem like armies to you, while they are nothing more than the branches of willow trees. As long as you obsess about them, in your walk [with Christ] you'll always be in danger. My son, have a firm, basic resolve to want to serve and love God with all your heart. Aside from this, take no thought of the future. Think only about doing good in the present day. When tomorrow comes, then it will be called 'today' and worry about it then."[15]

"Don't Be Afraid of Anything"

Padre Pio urged Padre Emmanuele:

I want you to conduct yourself like little children do with their mothers. As long as they feel themselves held by the straps of their baby-clothes, little children walk confidently and run here and there, not worrying about falls caused by the weakness of their legs. So, too, with you. As long as you realize that it is God's good will to hold you steady in the intentions that he has made you have, to serve him and love him, walk boldly and don't marvel if you should slip or fall a little. You shouldn't be annoyed with yourself as long as, from time to time, you throw yourself into God's arms and kiss him with the kiss of love....

Walk cheerfully and with a sincere and open heart as much as you can. If you can't always maintain that holy joyfulness, at least never lose courage and confidence in God. Frequently say to Our Lord, along with the holy King David, "I am yours, save me," and, like Mary Magdalene, standing before him, "Rabboni. Ah, my master!" Then leave it in his hands. He will, with you, within you, around you, and even through you, make his name holy, to whom be eternal honor and glory. Don't be afraid of anything … and have no fear of anything separating you from God. Don't lose heart because of the darkness in which you find your spirit immersed most of the time. Remember that Jesus is ever so closely united to you, whatever your state of soul.[16]

Confession, Communion, and Bible Study

Padre Pio met twice a week with his "spiritual daughters" in the guest room of the friary, where he would discuss the Bible and "the means of perfection." Nina Campanile recalled his gift for explaining the Bible. "He took away our doubts and illuminated our spiritual darkness,"[17] she wrote. Padre Pio established five rules for spiritual growth: weekly confession, daily Communion, spiritual reading, meditation, and examination of conscience.

When Campanile asked Padre Pio why he insisted on such frequent confessions, he told her, "A room needs to be dusted once a week, even if nobody is there." Some of the ladies were likewise afraid that they were taking Communion too often. "Unless you are positive that you are in mortal sin," Padre Pio told them, "you ought to take Communion every day." According to Campanile, it was through Padre Pio's influence that the daily reception of Communion became a common practice at San Giovanni Rotondo.

Padre Pio loaned spiritual books from the friary library. "If the reading of holy books has the power to convert worldly men into spiritual persons, how very powerful such reading must be in leading spiritual men and women to greater perfection,"[18] he insisted. At a time when it was unusual for lay Catholics to read the Bible, Padre Pio encouraged the reading of the Scriptures. A spiritual daughter wrote that when she was able to borrow a Bible, "I was out of my mind with joy. I had in my hands a book that only the priests and the nuns possessed! … Like a thirsty deer, I drank the words of the Lord." She spent her nights copying passages from the Scripture until she had to return the Bible to its lender. When Padre Pio gave her a copy of her own, he wrote in it: "May the Holy Spirit guide your intelligence. May he cause you to uncover hidden truths, contained in the reading of this book, and may he set your will on fire to practice them."[19]

Meditation

"Meditation," Padre Pio told Campanile, "is the key to progress in the knowledge of self as well as the knowledge of God, and through it we achieve the goal of the spiritual life, which is the transformation of the soul in Christ."[20] He even suggested a physical position for meditation: "Try to put yourself in the presence of God and thus understand that, with all the celestial court, he is there within your soul. Then begin your prayer and meditation. [When you are meditating], try to close your eyes and, if possible, hold your head upright and put your forehead in the palm of your hands."[21]

As subjects for meditation, Padre Pio suggested such themes from the Bible as Jesus' passion, death, resurrection, and ascension. "Ask God," he insisted,

for the grace to make good the mental prayer that you are about to undertake, so that you can derive the fruit that God most desires. Finally, recommend yourself to the intercession of the Most Holy Virgin, as well as to all the heavenly court, so that they may help you meditate well and keep every distraction and temptation away from you.

After you have meditated thoroughly on the subject in all of its aspects, then pass on to resolutions. Make it your purpose to amend yourself with regard to that defect which most hinders your union with God and which causes many other defects and sins. Propose to exercise a particular virtue.

Then ask God for all those graces and for all those helps of which you feel the need. Recommend all people to the Lord, either in general or in particular.... Pray for the living, pray for the dead, pray for the unbelieving, pray for heretics, and pray for the conversion of sinners.

After you have done this, offer your meditation and your prayer, along with yourself and those closest to your heart. Offer them all to God, along with the merits of Jesus.[22]

Padre Pio urged two periods of meditation and self-examination daily: in the morning, "to prepare for the battle," and in the evening, "to purify your soul from every earthly affection that might have been able to attach itself to you during the day."[23] Each of these periods of reflection and recollection was to last at least a half hour.

Concerning eating, he suggested, sitting down, to "call to mind some pious thought." He recommended imagining oneself sitting with Christ at the Last Supper. Then one should make the "effort to ensure that the supper by which we satisfy the body may be a preparation for ... the Holy Eucharist." "Never rise from the table," he warned, "without having given due thanks to the Lord. If we act in this way, we need have no fear of the wretched sin of gluttony." While a Christian shouldn't leave the table hungry, he should never eat more than he really needed.[24]

On retiring, Padre Pio advised: "Never lie down to sleep without having first examined your conscience on the way you have spent the day and without first turning your thoughts to God. Then offer and consecrate your whole person and that of every Christian ... to God.... Offer, moreover, to the glory of his Divine Majesty the rest you are about to take and never forget your guardian angel, who is always close to you, who never leaves you, no matter how badly you treat him."[25]

Different Approaches for Different Souls

Padre Pio treated his spiritual children in accord with their spiritual advancement, as he understood it. He tended to spend more time with people who were at the very beginning of their walk with God and with people who had the most problems. He was often indulgent to his newer disciples. Campanile was surprised, when she first came to him, that Padre Pio gave her candy. She asked him why, since his abstemious attitude toward food and drink was notorious. "Because I don't eat them, I give them to you," he twitted.[26] Campanile wrote, "He won souls ... by first showing compassion and catering to their wishes so that they might not fall into sin."[27]

Padre Pio felt that people deeply attached to material things could not be suddenly divorced from them without the danger of falling into despair or losing their spiritual commitment. He had an earthy way of saying this: "Outside the shit the cockroach dies."[28] As a spiritual child progressed, Padre Pio tended to be more severe, and he also tended to spend less time with her. When one woman accused Padre Pio of favoritism, he told her: "Look, Jesus had three souls. The first he embraced, the second he treated so-so, and the third he treated badly. Who do you think he loved to most? ... It was the one he treated the worst."[29]

Guidelines for the Christian Life

With regard to daily living, Padre Pio's advice to those who consulted him, from his letters as well as from the recollections of others, can perhaps be condensed and summarized in the following points:

1. *Put your trust in Christ as your personal Savior.* Padre Pio believed that people can and must choose to serve God. To one correspondent he wrote, "I want you to be saved at all costs, and for this purpose you need to surrender to Jesus."[30] On another occasion, he wrote, "I want you to be saved.... When will you give me this consolation, brother?"[31] People are to abandon themselves to Jesus "like a child to his mother's arms." Padre Pio urged his disciples to pray to Christ: "Whom have I on earth besides you? Whom have I in heaven but you, my Jesus! You are the God of my heart and my inheritance, whom I desire eternally."[32]

2. *Realize that you have no righteousness of your own.* "No one can worthily love God," Padre Pio wrote to Raffaelina Cerase, to whom he also declared, "How delightful and consoling it is to know that without any merit of our own, this most tender Father has raised us to such dignity!"[33] To another spiritual daughter he wrote, "Consider yourself ... what you really are: a nothing ... the epitome of feebleness, a fountain of perversity without limit or bounds, capable of converting good to evil, of abandoning good for evil, of ascribing goodness to yourself and justifying yourself in evil, and for the love of the same evil, despising the Supreme Good."

He gave the following rules:

- Never be pleased with yourself.
- Do not complain about offenses perpetrated against you.
- Forgive everyone with Christian charity.
- Always groan as a poor wretch before your God.
- Never marvel at your weakness, but recognize yourself for what you are; blush over your inconstancy and faithlessness to God, and confide in him, tranquilly abandoning yourself to the arms of the heavenly Father like a babe in the arms of his mother.
- Never exult in any way in any virtues, but ascribe everything to God, and give him all the glory and honor.[34]

According to Padre Pio, all goodness is in God and comes from God. Men and women have no righteousness of their own or any reason for pride, but souls who put their trust in Christ have nothing to fear. "No pilgrim soul can worthily love his God, but when this soul does everything possible on his part and trusts in divine mercy, why would Jesus reject [him]? Hasn't [Jesus] commanded us to love God according to our strength? If you have given and consecrated everything to God, why fear?"[35] All of our actions, Padre Pio wrote more than once, are mixed with inclinations toward pride, vanity, self-love, and similar sins, but if our motives are God-centered and our actions consecrated to God, they are accepted; if what we do is done with a desire to please God, we should not worry.

Padre Pio explained, "The Scripture says that we of ourselves cannot say the name of Jesus except through the action of the Holy Spirit."[36] God gives us the ability to please him. People cannot do it on their own.

Moreover, "do everything for the love of God and his glory, without looking at the outcome of the undertaking," he opined. "Work is judged, not by its result, but by its intention."[37] Padre Pio told Raffaelina Cerase, "If the Lord were to judge us according to strict justice, none of us, perhaps, would be saved."[38] He also said that if the mercy of God was what many people believe it to be, "then all men would be in hell."[39]

3. *Beware of the devil and resist him.* Padre Pio told one of his spiritual daughters: "There are so many [devils] that if each one wanted to assume a body as small as a grain of sand, they would block out the sun."[40] Yet he insisted that the Christian should have no fear. "You must not marvel if our common enemy has mustered all his strength to keep you from hearing what I'm writing to you," he explained to one correspondent. "This is his job, and it is to his profit. Therefore, despise him, and arm yourself against him with all the more steadfastness in faith, because it is

written, 'Your adversary, the devil, like a roaring lion, walks about, seeking someone to devour. Resist him strongly in the faith.' Don't let the many snares of the infernal beast terrify you; Jesus, who is always with you and who fights with you and for you, will never let you be deceived or conquered."[41] Quoting Saint Augustine, he declared, "The devil is a formidable giant to those who fear him, but a cowardly child to those who scorn him."[42]

4. *Continually pray to God and say, in every circumstance, "Thy will be done."* To one of his spiritual daughters, Padre Pio wrote: "In all human affairs ... learn most of all to recognize and adore God's will in everything. Frequently repeat the divine words of our dear Master, 'Thy will be done on earth as it is in heaven.' May this beautiful exclamation always be in your heart and on your lips in all the changes of life. Repeat it in affliction. Repeat it in temptation and in the trials to which Jesus will be pleased to subject you. Repeat it still when you find yourself immersed in the ocean of Jesus' love. This will be your anchor and your salvation."[43]

Once a spiritual son asked him, "Padre Pio, when I'm praying, I very often get distracted. Does that mean I have to go back to the beginning of the prayer and start all over again?"

"No," the priest replied. "Keep on praying. You might get distracted again."[44]

Padre Pio believed that prayer changes things, even to the extent that, from a human point of view, God seems to change his mind as the result of human prayer. When Giovina Cerase recovered from a severe siege of illness, Padre Pio wrote to her sister: "She has been snatched from the jaws of death. It has been intended conditionally that she should join her parents up above, and it was only the many prayers that suspended the fulfillment of this intention."[45] During the early months of the Great War, the Cerase sisters were vacationing at Savona, in northern Italy, when Padre Pio sent them an urgent message to leave at once, and they did. Later, when they asked why he told them to leave, he answered: "A great misfortune was about to occur, especially beneath the beautiful sky of Savona. Victims and prayers succeeded, at least for the moment, in restraining God's anger." He explained, "It's true that God's power triumphs over everything, but humble and suffering prayer [so to speak] prevails over God himself."[46]

In no way did Padre Pio feel that people could manipulate God or obtain anything they wanted. He prayed constantly for the conversion of his sister Pellegrina, but no amount of prayer and suffering seem to avail. He expressed his belief that some things are decreed from eternity, but other things depend on the prayers of human beings.[47]

In keeping with the teachings of his Church, he enthusiastically recommended prayer for the departed. When Pope Pius X died, Padre Pio said, "I believe that his holy soul has no need of our intercessory prayers, but let us pray for his eternal rest just the same, since our prayers will never go to waste."[48] He advised a spiritual daughter: "Even if your parents are in heaven, we must always pray. If they no longer need prayers, they are applied to other souls."[49] He even recommended prayer for people long dead, telling a friend: "Maybe you don't know that I can pray even now for the happy death of my great-grandfather.... For the Lord, the past doesn't exist, the future doesn't exist. Everything is an eternal present. Those prayers had already been taken into account. And so, I repeat that even now I can pray for the happy death of my great-grandfather."[50]

5. *Love the cross.* According to Padre Pio, suffering can be a special sign of God's love. "Without love for the cross," he wrote, "we cannot make much profit in the Christian life." He frequently reminded people, "The heavenly Father wants to make you resemble his divine Son in his anguish in the desert and on Calvary." He declared: "Religion is a hospital for spiritually sick people who want to be healed. To be healed, they must submit themselves to suffering, namely, to bloodletting, to the lance, to the razor, to the probe, to the scalpel, to the fire, and to all the bitterness of medicine. In order to be spiritually cured, we have to submit to all the tortures of the Divine Physician."[51]

The children of God must not grumble. "Complaining is a voluntary vice that kills love [of God]," he told a spiritual daughter.[52] In his correspondence, he more than once cited the ancient Israelites, who were barred, because of their grumbling, from the Promised Land. "Keep your eyes fixed above on the one who is your guide to the heavenly country, to which he is leading you," he wrote. "Why worry whether it is through desert or meadow through which you pass, so long as God is always with you and you arrive at the possession of a blessed eternity?"[53]

Padre Pio often explained the necessity of suffering by the example of a woman who is embroidering: "Her son, seated on a low stool, sees her work, but in reverse. He sees the knots of the embroidery, the tangled threads ... [and] he says, 'Mother, what are you doing? I can't make out what you are doing!' Then the mother lowers the embroidery hoop and shows the good part of the work. Each color is in place and the various threads form a harmonious design. Thus, we see the reverse side of the embroidery because we are seated on the low stool [of this life]."[54]

He wrote to a seminarian: "I know, my dear son, that you are suffering, but resign yourself because, when suffering is endured in a Christian spirit, it will sanctify you. Suffer, but also rejoice, because your suffering will one day be transformed into joy for you. Suffer, but never be afraid, because with the prophet [he says], 'I am with you in tribulation.' Suffer, but believe that Jesus himself suffers in you and through you and with you, that Jesus has not abandoned you and will not abandon you."[55] Moreover, to the same seminarian he wrote: "What do you make of the holy cruelty of Jesus towards you? That he loves you. Yes, my dearest, and you will understand in paradise! Have no fear, then, and let him do with you as he sees fit."[56]

6. *Offer every action up to God.* Padre Pio urged his spiritual children to make short mental prayers, offering everything they did, no matter how trivial, to Christ. "Let's refer everything to God and live and move in him," he wrote. In particular, Christians were to offer their sufferings as a sacrifice to be united with Christ's sacrifice. Since Christ is God, his saving work, including his suffering, was not confined to the first century A.D., but extends outside of time, as human beings understand it. Therefore, people throughout the centuries can unite their experiences with his saving work. While not everyone was called, like Padre Pio was, to become a "victim soul," everyone should use whatever suffering that comes to good purpose, by making an offering of it to God. To Campanile, he wrote, "Physical and spiritual ills are the most worthy offering you can make to him who saved you by suffering."[57]

7. *Never worry.* "Anxiety," Padre Pio insisted, is "the mother of all imperfections."[58] The devil uses worry to befoul our good works because of our lack of confidence in God's goodness. "Our sweet Lord is deprived of giving us many graces, solely because the door to our heart is not open to him in holy confidence," he insisted. Worry "dries up Christian piety and makes it sterile."[59] "Don't worry about anything," he exhorted those who sought his counsel. "One thing should be your concern: to love Jesus, to love virtue, and to aspire to heaven. The Little Mother [Mary], to the extent that you depend on her, will always assist you and hold out her arms to you."[60] Not only is it bad to worry about future events, but anxiety about one's salvation is also detrimental. "Don't worry," Padre Pio said. "Let's do our best and Jesus will be happy all the same."[61]

8. *Aspire to the heavenly prize.* Padre Pio made it clear that life would be meaningless and unbearable were it not for the hope of heaven. He spoke continually of Christian hope. In heaven, the child of God is forever happy, united with loved ones, watching over family and friends on earth. When their father died, he told two sisters to comfort themselves "with the sweet thought that your Daddy is not dead.... He lives a life of joy that will have no end. He lives in heaven. He lives in the midst of his dearest ones."[62] To a couple who had lost a two-year-old son, he wrote: "Your child is in paradise, watching over you, assisting you, smiling on you, and preparing a place for you."[63] When someone asked him if we will know our loved ones in heaven, Padre Pio replied: "What kind of heaven would it be if we didn't have with us those whom we love?"[64] To another person, he explained: "The joy of paradise will be enough to carry us all on. Every sacrifice we make on earth will be recompensed. Heaven is total joy, continuous joy. We will be constantly

thanking God. It's useless to try to figure out exactly what heaven is like, because we can't understand it, but when the veil of this life is taken off, we will understand things in a different way."[65] "No suffering, no matter how low the motive on which it rests," he assured Raffaelina Cerase, "will go unrewarded in eternal life. Trust and hope in the merits of Jesus, and in this way even poor clay will become finest gold which will shine in the palace of the king of heaven."[66]

9. *Love the Madonna.* When a woman asked, "Teach me a shortcut to reach God quickly," Padre Pio answered: "The shortcut … is the Virgin."[67] "The Holy Virgin," he insisted, "is the perfect example of God's mercy on earth. She acts as his double."[68] He told another priest, "She is the one who brings us a ray of God's immensity and of divine powers."[69] To the same priest, he said: "I feel like a sailing ship, pushed by our heavenly Mother's breath. Even if I am lost on the high seas, I'm not worried. I can't say where I start nor where my various works will end, but I never feel uncertain because I am spiritually directed by her. … She accompanies me in the confessional, to let me aid my brothers and sisters, and she shows me, already covered by the veil of her pity, the numberless souls waiting for an absolution which will destroy all evils and be the creator of all good."[70] When it was suggested that his devotion to Mary was exaggerated, Padre Pio responded: "Heaven for you is just like a cemetery, full of dead things, finished things. For me instead it is a place of rest, that at one sign of Our Lady's wakes up and starts moving for our conversion and salvation."[71]

10. *Rejoice in the Lord.* Even though his life, his ministry, and his theology were very much connected to suffering, Padre Pio was generally a cheerful man, at times happy and jovial. He told Cerase, "Drive melancholy away. Joy, with peace, is the sister of charity.… Serve the Lord with laughter."[72] He urged people, "Be serene and don't let your imagination work too much. It's enough for us to know that Jesus loves us and will console us."[73] "Be of good cheer," he said. "He who opens wounds will also know how to close them and heal them."[74]

Padre Pio discouraged too great a curiosity about the miraculous and extraordinary. When people asked him about visions or alleged miraculous events, he often said, "That is for the ecclesiastical authority." He once told a friar, "I'm convinced that a great many people don't want to live by faith, but seek the extraordinary."[75] He always told his secretaries to answer people who wrote to him seeking miracles, "Live by faith!"[76]

Not only did Padre Pio advocate living by faith, he also advised living by love. He insisted, "God's judgment is not man's judgment." When he heard people criticizing others, he told them, "Leave justice in the hands of God!"[77] When a woman asked what she could do to become better, he replied: "Love! Love! Love!"

"In spite of our sins?" she asked.

"In spite of everything!" said he.[78]

When people told him that they did not believe in God, Padre Pio usually said, "But God believes in you!"[79] He promised his spiritual children that he would guide them all their lives and see that they found salvation. "Like a bad mother who bears a child and then deserts it, could I ever forget those whom I have regenerated to grace?"[80]

Chapter Fifteen

Skeptics and Detractors

"Full-Blown Paganism"?

In the summer of 1919, the Capuchins of the province of Foggia held a chapter meeting, during which Padre Pietro of Ischitella was elected as father provincial to replace Padre Benedetto, whose term had ended. Padre Pietro transferred Padre Paolino to the friary at Gesualdo and replaced him as father guardian at San Giovanni Rotondo with Padre Lorenzo of San Marco in Lamis. Padre Pietro evidently blamed Padre Paolino, at least partly, for the leak of Professor Romanelli's report on Padre Pio's stigmata to the press, and this left the former superior hurt and resentful. Next to Padres Benedetto and Agostino, Padre Paolino seems to have been Padre Pio's closest friend at the time. Padre Pio wrote to him in November, "May Jesus continue to comfort you and make you feel less bitter about our separation and so it will be less of a cross to me."[1]

Reports continued of occurrences that the locals considered supernatural interventions. Nina Campanile reported two occurrences in her family that she considered miraculous. Her mother was diagnosed with double pneumonia, and her doctors applied eight leeches to draw blood. Padre Pio was horrified when he learned of this primitive, backward treatment and shouted, "She mustn't be bled!" Insisting that there had been a mistake in diagnosis and that the woman was suffering not from pneumonia but malaria, he urged Campanile to find a more competent physician, which she did. The new doctor ran tests that, in fact, revealed malaria and not pneumonia. With all his illnesses and medical examinations and consultations, Padre Pio might have had a bit of medical knowledge, but Campanile considered the event "miraculous" because he never saw or examined her mother (although in her memoir she did not state whether she described the symptoms to him).[2]

A more convincing argument for a miracle could be made concerning the recovery of Campanile's sister, who complained of violent pains in the liver after a fall in her home and then lapsed into a coma. There was no hospital nearby, and the doctor who examined her declared that she had serious injuries to her liver and other internal organs and that there was nothing to be done except wait for her to die. Campanile hurried to the friary and told Padre Pio, who said not to worry, assuring her that her sister would recover. However, that evening the injured woman was still unresponsive and vomiting every fifteen minutes. Then a friend who was there in the room began to turn pale. When Campanile asked her if she were ill, she replied, "No, the Padre is here."

"What do you mean, 'The Padre is here'?"

"He's here in spirit," the friend told her.

"How is he dressed?" asked Campanile.

"Like a monk."

"If I touch him, will I feel anything?"

"Of course not. He's a spirit. See," she said, poking the air. "He has come near your sister and said, 'Poor child.'"

Ten minutes later, the friend said, "Now he has gone away."

Immediately, Campanile's sister came to herself and announced that she felt "much better." It was 8:00 p.m.

The next day, with her sister clearly on the mend, Campanile went to the friary and asked Padre Pio, "Padre, what time did you come to my house last night?"

In a matter-of-fact way he replied, "Around eight."[3]

Not everyone was convinced that Padre Pio was a holy man. A letter signed by "A group of faithful at San Giovanni Rotondo" was sent to the Holy Office in June 1919. The writers conceded that Padre Pio was a "good, obedient, patient, humble brother," but insisted that his growing reputation for holiness, spread by simple, naive people, was creating a "popular fantasy." Thousands of people, pouring into San Giovanni in search of miracles, were creating a cult. "It may seem an exaggeration if we dare to say that here we find ourselves faced with full-blown paganism" and "idolatry … on a grand scale." The writers insisted, "For these fanatical visitors, God and the Blessed Virgin no longer exist; only Padre Pio exists: 'the saint' who predicts, reads people's hearts, heals the sick, and bilocates from place to place." They went on to accuse the friars of embroidering "certain trifles" while fanatics go around "disseminating … fairy tales that the populace welcomes … while the clergy and educated public are supposed to believe them in order to save their lives. We appeal to the healthy judgment of the Holy Church."[4]

A second letter, written in July, argued that the atmosphere of fanaticism was stirred up by the friars at the monastery as well as a group of fanatical women called "the twelve disciples." The writers alleged that Padre Pio "would converse late at night with his twelve favored eldest daughters," scandalizing and alienating the women who found themselves excluded from the circle of the "chosen." If this was not bad enough, the informants declared, "the saint has alienated all the people in our church and claims that the priest [of that church] goes to render acts of veneration to him."[5]

Padre Pio's supporters believed that these and similar complaints could be traced to the local clergy, who were furious that Padre Pio was drawing people — and financial contributions — away from their churches. Archpriest Giuseppe Prencipe, although skeptical of the miracle stories, had made his confession to Padre Pio and wrote in his diary that he had found himself "in the presence of a man graced with an extraordinary gift," but he was concerned about the fanaticism of the devotees of the stigmatized Capuchin. The archpriest had warned Pio, "I'm under great pressure ... to denounce you, and you're not praying for me."

"If I didn't pray, things would be worse," was the Capuchin's response.[6]

The source of that "pressure" was becoming clear. Archbishop Gagliardi of Manfredonia, becoming more hostile by the day to Padre Pio and the Capuchins, was urging his clergy to denounce them.

The Pope's Opinion

In March 1920, Pope Benedict XV dispatched his personal physician, Giuseppe Bastianelli, to San Giovanni Rotondo, where he examined Padre Pio's stigmata in the presence of two Capuchin prelates, Anselm Edward John Kenealy (1864–1943), archbishop of Simla, India, and Giovanni Antonio Zucchiti (1843–1931), bishop of Smyrna (in what is now Turkey). No report of the examination has been found, but it is believed to have been favorable. Shortly thereafter, Benedict sent Bishop Bonaventura Cerretti (1872–1933) (later made a cardinal), secretary of the Congregation for Extraordinary Ecclesiastical Affairs, and Augusto Cardinal Silj (pronounced "Seeley") (1846–1926), prefect of the Supreme Tribunal of the Apostolic Signatura. They, too, are said to have given the pontiff a positive report. They were followed by Alberto Valbonesi (1868–1935), a Vatican official who said that talking to Padre Pio for just a few moments had "compensated me for years of pain," and Alberto Costa (1873–1950), bishop of Melfi and Rapolla, who wrote, "My impression can be boiled down to one: that of having talked with a saint." Giuseppe Angelo Poli (1878–1970), bishop of Allahabad, India, and fellow Capuchin, wrote: "I came, I saw, and I was conquered. Not the slightest doubt remains in me. The finger of God is here." Even Cardinal Pietro Gasparri (1852–1934), the Holy See's secretary of state, was said to have asked for Padre Pio's prayers.[7]

Pope Benedict seems to have been convinced of Padre Pio's holiness, remarking to a prominent attorney, "Padre Pio is truly a man of God," and describing the Capuchin to a priest from South America as "an extraordinary man, the like of whom God sends to earth from time to time for the purpose of converting people."[8] In the case of Archbishop Gagliardi, who was continually complaining about Padre Pio and the fanaticism around him, the pope warned, "You must proceed cautiously concerning Padre Pio. It's bad to be too unbelieving."[9]

"Padre Pio Is a Psychopath!"

On April 18, 1920, Padre Pio received a visit from another prominent churchman who proved to be far less laudatory. Padre Agostino Gemelli (1878–1959) was a brilliant, learned, and outspoken priest, physician, and psychologist from Milan. Raised in an agnostic family, Edoardo Gemelli had been an unbeliever until he was twenty-five when, shortly after finishing medical school, he read a biography of Saint Francis of Assisi that led to a religious conversion. Joining the Order of Friars Minor — the oldest of the Franciscan orders — he took the name Agostino. Over the years, he published a number of articles on the relationship between religious experience and psychological disorder. While he believed that certain mystical phenomena — such as the stigmata of Saint Francis — were genuine, he rejected many, if not most, as the result of neurosis.

Padre Gemelli served as a chaplain during World War I, becoming notorious for his militarism and his vituperative sermons in which — dressed in the uniform of a captain, with gloves and spurs and horsewhip — he furiously denounced and reviled the Germans.[10] His virulent militarism led to a reprimand from his minister general, who wrote him, "Could a hardened war monger write worse? Could a secularist be more vicious and less Christian in promising to ruin the enemy, whoever he may be?"[11]

Gemelli was in the process of founding the Catholic University of Milan when he arrived in San Giovanni along with his friend and cofounder, the social activist Armida Barelli, as well as Monsignor Giovanni Musmusei, vicar general of the diocese of Manfredonia; Padre Giuseppe Patané, secretary to the bishop of Foggia; Padre Filippo Gerardi, from the cathedral of Foggia; and Padre Benedetto, who was now working in Rome. Emmanuele Brunatto was also present when they met Padre Pio.

A few days later Padre Gemelli wrote to the Holy Office that he had gone to San Giovanni "attracted by [Pio's] reputation for holiness and to ask for the assistance of his prayers." He had also been asked to go by Salvatore Bella, bishop of Foggia, who had heard unfavorable reports from the archbishop of the neighboring archdiocese of Manfredonia. Padre Gemelli later wrote that Bella "expressed a desire for me to examine Padre Pio and then bring back the results of my examination. He did not hide from me what he had heard, thanks to the information he had gotten from the Archbishop of Manfredonia, and it had made him skeptical about the supernatural character of the facts present about Padre Pio."[12]

Padre Gemelli's attitude toward Padre Pio and his community, like that of other intellectuals from northern Italy, may have been tinged with ethnic prejudice. Many northern Italians in the 1920s regarded the inhabitants of southern Italy the same way many Americans from New England at the time regarded the people of their own southland — as backward hicks.

Barelli was the first of the visitors to question Padre Pio. She asked him if the Lord would bless the university they were planning, and he answered, "Yes."[13] The next day, Padre Gemelli asked to examine Padre Pio's stigmata. In July 1952, he wrote to the English Jesuit Cyril C. Martindale: "I accurately examined Padre Pio and his stigmata. During the examination of the stigmata, the provincial was present." Gemelli was, by then, claiming that he was sent by the Holy Office, and, in response to Martindale's questions about his orders, he answered, "I do not remember the exact wording of the order I had from the Holy Office because I am not in the habit of saving notes of what I do for the tribunals of the Roman Curia."[14]

On the other hand, Padre Benedetto and Brunatto were both in agreement that Gemelli was never alone with Padre Pio and that no examination of the stigmata ever took place. Because the minister general of the Capuchins had not authorized an examination, Padre Benedetto, who was evidently given authority to act as his proxy, told Padre Gemelli that he would not permit it. Barelli pleaded with him, also in vain. Padre Benedetto told them, "I can't understand the need for an observation, since there are accurate reports from other doctors about all this."[15] Padre Benedetto made it clear to Padre Gemelli and Barelli that they would have to be satisfied with a brief conversation with Padre Pio. This took place in the sacristy, according to Padre Benedetto, and lasted but a few minutes.

Padre Gemelli wrote, nonetheless, that he had undertaken a "psychiatric examination" of Padre Pio without his subject being aware of it. Padre Benedetto recalled, however, in a letter written in 1932, "I was in a far corner, but I had the impression that Padre Pio was dismissing [Gemelli] as if he were annoyed." He recalled that Padre Gemelli left "looking furious."[16] Brunatto recalled Padre Gemelli shouting, "All right, Padre Pio, we'll meet again!"[17] Padre Gemelli, however, failed to reveal any negative feelings when he wrote in the friary's visitors' log, "Every day we confirm that the Franciscan tree has new fruit, and that is the greatest comfort for those who draw sustenance and life from this marvelous tree."[18]

The next day, April 19, Padre Gemelli wrote to Monsignor Carlo Perosi of the Holy Office: "I went to San Giovanni Rotondo … to see Padre Pio.… Once I reached Foggia I became aware that opinions about him are quite contradictory … I believe the intervention of ecclesiastical authority would never be more timely here," because, "if we are dealing with a true case of sanctity it would remove the occasion for people to foment legends and superstitious practices … and if, on the other hand, it concerns [phenomena] that are attributable to other causes, it is … urgent to avoid the discrediting of religion." He went on to say that psychologists, not medical doctors, were in the best position "to distinguish between true and false mysticism. I know … that there have been medical exams, but it is clear that those exams were insufficient."[19]

Padre Gemelli went on to concede that while Padre Pio was "a man with a truly elevated religious life, an exemplary man," the Capuchin was, in fact, a man of "very limited intelligence," with signs of "a notable degree of mental deficiency which results in a restricted field of awareness." He asked, "How could a gift so extraordinary as the stigmata be accompanied by such spiritual poverty?" He theorized that there was perhaps an "incubus succubus relationship" between Padre Pio and his spiritual director Padre Benedetto, who, Padre Gemelli believed, planted ideas in Pio's weak mind. Little by little, Padre Gemelli concluded, Padre Pio likely "fell victim to the collective suggestion that was created about him. He is a good religious — tranquil, quiet, meek — more as a result of his mental deficiency than as a result of virtue; a poor man who repeats certain stereotypic phrases of a religious character, a poor sick man who has learned his lesson from Padre Benedetto, his master." Padre Gemelli's imperious conclusion: "I believe that Padre Pio is a psychopath, without being able for now to pronounce on the type and nature of this psychopathic state." He urged that Padre Pio be removed "from the artificial atmosphere he is in, and be studied by a team of experts in medicine, psychology, and theology."[20]

When asked by Monsignor Perosi how to proceed in evaluating Padre Pio, Padre Gemelli replied in July, urging that the investigation team he recommended should (1) inspect Padre Pio's cell; (2) stop the receiving or the use of medical drugs without the prior permission of the specialists; (3) plaster one of Padre Pio's arms and one of his legs; (4) conduct a psychological exam to determine the presence of hysteria or psittacism (the repeating of stereotypic phrases — like a parrot); (5) keep Padre Benedetto away from Padre Pio; (6) verify the existence of the "inner" mystical experiences of Padre Pio that parallel the "external mystical events"; (7) analyze in a laboratory the blood droplets from Padre Pio's hands; (8) examine Padre Pio's food intake; (9) note precisely when the perfume occurs; and (10) perform a thorough neurological exam.[21]

Six years later, when Cardinal Michele Lega heard a Capuchin priest in Rome praising Padre Pio, he said, "If you could only read the report Gemelli submitted, you would change your mind about Padre Pio." While the cardinal claimed he was not at liberty to share it, he assured the priest, "It was terrible! If you could read it, it would change your mind on Padre Pio!"[22]

Carbolic Acid?

The same month that Padre Gemelli wrote his second letter, Bishop Bella of Foggia received a sworn declaration by one Dr. Domenico Valentini-Vista, a Foggia pharmacist, who had gone to Padre Pio for comfort the year before, only to be dissatisfied and disappointed. Although friendly, Padre Pio did not manifest any supernatural knowledge when he heard the apothecary's confession. He did not recognize him and even asked Valentini-Vista if he were a Freemason, which offended him greatly, making him wonder about the authenticity of Padre Pio's mystical gifts. He began to ask himself, "Why does Padre Pio wear these gloves? Is it perhaps to avoid someone wanting to study his stigmata up close?"

Then, "sometime later," Valentini-Vista claimed, a cousin of his, Maria DeVito, returned from a visit with Padre Pio. "She asked me, in Padre Pio's name and in strict secrecy, for carbolic acid, saying that it was for Padre Pio, and presented me with a small bottle given to her by Padre Pio himself that could hold 100 grams." Carbolic acid — or phenol — was widely used as an antiseptic in the early twentieth century, but it can cause severe burns to the skin. Valentini-Vista gave DeVito the carbolic acid, but began to wonder if Padre Pio used it to create his stigmata.

Soon afterward, Padre Pio requested four grams of veratrine (also called veratridine), which in those days was used in ointments for arthritis, but which caused violent sneezing if inhaled. Valentini-Vista refused this request and questioned why it was "made with such secrecy." On July 27, he went to Bishop Bella and told him all that had transpired. DeVito had already made a deposition on oath about Padre Pio's request for the carbolic acid, which the friar claimed he needed to disinfect the syringes he used "for the injections he was giving the novices whom he was supervising." Bella requested and received from DeVito Padre Pio's letter about the acid as well as his request for the four grams of veratrine that he said he was awaiting "anxiously."[23]

The Holy Office Becomes Suspicious

When Bishop Bella forwarded the depositions to Rome, they aroused more concern than Padre Gemelli's report. As an official in the Holy Office wrote: "Now it is to be noted that Padre Pio made a request for these very potent poisons requiring the utmost secrecy on the part of the person entrusted with this request.... He urged as the reason (for a kind of pure carbolic acid) that it would serve for the disinfection of syringes that he was using for injections of the novices. *Now this circumstance of secrecy makes the Holy Office suspicious* ... [if] these poisons really do serve the goal that Padre Pio said they did, so then why hide its acquisition from his superiors?" If he was using the acid for other purposes, then Padre Pio would have been deliberately lying. If he were a liar, how could this be reconciled with his claim that his stigmata were of supernatural origin? "Therefore the [Holy Office] believes it to be its duty to follow through with an investigation."[24] Cardinal Rafael Merry Del Val, secretary of the Holy Office, and the minister general of the Capuchin order, Padre Giuseppe Antonio of Persiceto, both wrote to Archbishop Gagliardi (because Pio's friary was in his archdiocese), requesting more information.

Gagliardi did not directly condemn Padre Pio at this time. In fact, he characterized the Capuchin as "quiet and collected ... with keen intelligence, a penetrating
look, a pleasing demeanor and gentle manners — someone who can attract everyone to himself." The problem, the archbishop averred, was Padre Pio's confreres
and the "pious women," as well as the attention given to unconfirmed miracles.
Moreover, Padre Benedetto, as Padre Pio's spiritual director, showed too much
"credulity." Gagliardi concluded, "In the past it would have been opportune to send
Padre Pio away. Now it is too late and would make things worse."

Minister General Padre Giuseppe Antonio received a letter from Padre Pio's
provincial, Padre Pietro, enclosing the medical reports on the stigmata by doctors Bignami, Romanelli, and Festa, and emphasizing the complexity of the case.
The widespread devotion in and around San Giovanni to the stigmatized friar
was proving financially profitable for some. According to Pietro, Pio was receiving
mountains of mail per day, including up to seven hundred letters from the United
States alone, and many of the letters contained monetary offerings. Furthermore,
the loyalty of the local people bordered on fanaticism, and there was the risk of
civil disorder should the order decide to transfer him.[25]

The Holy Office, which seemed to be concerned not so much about Padre Pio
and his stigmata as the clamor and fanaticism around him and the possible mismanagement of monies, handed over its now voluminous dossier on Padre Pio to
Joseph Lémius (1860–1923), a French Dominican priest who was serving as the
general procurator of the Oblates of Mary Immaculate. Lémius, after studying the
documentation, concluded that he could not affirm "anything for sure about the
origin of the stigmata" without a direct examination. He suggested an "apostolic
visitor" who would perform an investigation of Padre Pio and his community and
surroundings.

Chapter Sixteen

The Friar and the Inquisitor

"Padre Pio Made a Rather Favorable Impression on Me"

Raffaello Carlo Rossi, the forty-five-year-old bishop of Volterra (a city in Tuscany), was the inquisitor chosen by the Holy Office to investigate Padre Pio. His photographs reveal a slightly built man with a round face; thin, taut lips; and hard, piercing eyes behind round, wire-rimmed glasses. Rossi, who would later become a cardinal, had visited and inspected seminaries in southern Italy and censored the works of modernist theologians and at least one visionary. When he arrived in San Giovanni Rotondo for a visit of eight days, in June 1921, there were widespread rumors that he was going to recommend that Padre Pio be removed from San Giovanni and transferred to a friary far away.[1]

The inquisitor conceded, in the extensive report he compiled after his visit for the Holy Office, that he had gone to San Giovanni "rather unfavorably prejudiced," but that at the conclusion of his visit, "I must admit Padre Pio made a rather favorable impression on me." The thirty-four-year-old priest, Rossi reported, had a "high serene forehead," a pale complexion, looked "somewhat sickly and suffering," and walked with a "slow and sometimes uncertain gait." However, Rossi noted that Padre Pio's eyes, "sometimes wandering, sometimes vibrant, had a lively, sweet look" and that he exuded "goodness and sincerity." He described him as "a serious religious, distinguished, dignified, but also frank and casual in the convent.... The composure of his person is grave, recollected, without exaggeration or affectation."[2] The stigmatized friar appeared "serene, jovial, even humorous," and, to the mild dismay of the very proper inquisitor, not averse to interjecting in his conversations the phrases "My God," "My Jesus!" and *Per Bacco*" ("By Bacchus") or "By George!"[3]

Examining Padre Pio's cell, Bishop Rossi found it somewhat messy, with "disordered drawers" and "sheets of paper, gloves, quinine, candies for the boys, images, everything rather muddled."[4] The inquisitor noted that Padre Pio's southern Italian speech lacked some of the grammatical niceties expected in polished conversation: he used the second-person pronouns "*tu*" (normally for friends and family) and "*voi*" (for less-intimate address) interchangeably and never used the formal "*lei*" to address those in authority.[5] Rossi observed no signs of mental illness: "Padre Pio is not hysterical at all; he is absolutely normal, from what can be seen, from what can be known."[6]

Padre Pio as Seen by Other Religious

Bishop Rossi interviewed several other friars in the convent. Padre Lorenzo, the father guardian, said Padre Pio was "a simple man, devoid of duplicity, very kind, dedicated in piety — ordinary piety. In matters of obedience, he hears the superior's voice when it manifests itself clearly, and with regard to chastity [he is] ... angelic."[7] When asked about Padre Pio's prayer life, Lorenzo responded:

> He dedicates some time to it in the morning — then he goes to hear first the men's confessions, then the women's; he celebrates Mass with devotion — he can be rather long at [the points in the Mass where prayers are offered for the living and for the dead].... After the Mass, [he offers] the thanksgiving prayer — for twenty to thirty minutes — then he has lunch. Then he rests like everyone else; afterwards he attends the Office; then he stays in the choir for fifteen to thirty minutes; then if need be, he goes to hear confessions. In the evening he attends the communal prayer and Rosary, and then he stays for a while in the choir to pray, since he doesn't come to dinner. He goes back in the choir at 10 p.m. with the other religious. As far as I know, he doesn't get up at night to pray.[8]

Padre Romolo of San Marco in Lamis told the inquisitor, "Padre Pio is like a child, quite a simple soul, because he says things as a young child would, although in serious matters he leaves you speechless."[9] Romolo related: "I have heard that during an ecstasy ... witnesses heard Padre Pio allegedly say, 'How could you, O Lord, be glorified in me, who am a good-for-nothing? In me, who am not even a preacher?' And then he would apologize to the Lord for addressing him now as *tu*, now as *voi*."[10] Padre Pio had confided in him, Romolo continued, "that if the same things he counsels others about happen to him, he can't make up his mind and needs advice." In response to another question, Romolo declared, "I noticed in Padre Pio — at least two or three times — a bit of a rush to judge the superiors (perhaps he might have had his reasons.)"[11]

Padre Luigi of Serracapriola testified concerning Padre Pio: "As for his life, I do not have anything to remark. I do not see anything extraordinary, no apparent signs of an extraordinary life. It's a simple life, common, ordinary. In the evenings he stays longer in the choir or in church while we're having dinner; he is attentive, more than the others."[12]

Padre Lodovico of San Giovanni described Padre Pio as "kind and affable with everyone, always smiling — sometimes he makes jokes, too." However, "he devotes himself greatly to prayer — he protracts it, and one tires of waiting for him, especially if he's meditating."[13]

Don Giuseppe Prencipe, the archpriest, and Don Domenico Palladino, the bursar of the archdiocese, who were less than enthusiastic about Padre Pio, were also summoned by the inquisitor. The forty-nine-year-old archpriest replied to Rossi's questioning: "Padre Pio was preceded by the fame, spread by his then-Brothers, of wondrous facts, especially about a noise of chains heard in the convent in Foggia, about the devil, appearing in the form of a woman, etc."[14] He claimed that Padre Pio had "been transferred from the convent to the guest quarters, these so-called devout women taking turns caring for him, an irregularity that the Father Provincial took care to stop. During his illness he couldn't easily keep food in his stomach; to show the degree of fetishism reached by the Brothers, I know they would show what Padre Pio had not been able to keep in his stomach."[15]

Prencipe was extremely skeptical of miracle stories:

More than once I pressed Padre Pio himself to do something extraordinary in San Giovanni, even just the miracle of a bilocation for the conversion of the incredulous — especially for the conversion of a medical doctor, a friend of mine, who had told me these precise words: "If I saw Padre Pio come into my room at night or during the day, or if I saw Santariello (a monstrous cripple) really standing straight on his legs and healed in his eyes (he's cross eyed) and in his mind (he's a halfwit), I would be the first to believe in the supernatural." Padre Pio laughed at my words, and only once did it seem to me that he believed in the miracles attributed to him when he said these words: "The San Severo one isn't enough?" He meant to allude to a young lady who received her sight: a miracle I was never able to verify despite the volume of information I received.[16]

The thirty-one-year-old Palladino told the inquisitor about a conversation he had with Padre Pio about a strike by elementary-school teachers. Padre Pio, Palladino said, went on a tirade and insisted that if he were the government, he would send the striking teachers to the poorest part of Italy. Palladino had never seen any evidence of the miracles that were claimed but reported seeing a "pious lady" apply a bandage allegedly drenched with Padre Pio's blood on a sick person, mumbling, "Saint Pio," and hearing "ignorant common people" saying "that Padre

Pio was Jesus Christ himself." Palladino conceded that he thought Padre Pio was "a prayerful person and a good priest," but insisted that "the monks around him and these women have made me and others lose some of our esteem for him."[17]

Padre Pio Responds to Questions About the Stigmata

Rossi spent some time interviewing Padre Pio himself. He questioned him extensively about his stigmata. Padre Pio told him, "The pain started around 1911–1912, during my first years of priesthood." At the time, he had red wounds "dripping a little blood."[18] In those early years, the pain was intermittent, Padre Pio said, and usually occurred from Thursday evening through Saturday morning, and occasionally on Tuesdays.[19] Only Padre Benedetto and Archpriest Pannullo knew about them. When asked his opinion as to why he had these wounds, he told the inquisitor, "I don't know." When asked how he cared for the visible wounds during the past three years, Padre Pio answered: "I've tried to keep gloves on.... Initially I would use some iodine every once in a while, but a doctor told me to stop, since it could irritate them even more. They had me use a little petroleum jelly when the sores would lose their scabs; I used it several times, but I haven't in a long time. It may be over two years that I have used nothing at all."[20] When asked if the stigmata hurt, Padre Pio answered that they did, especially on the days they bled. "Sometimes I cannot bear it."[21]

On June 16, Bishop Rossi examined the stigmata. He observed:

> On the palm of the right hand a large round spot can be observed, two inches in diameter, covered with — or formed by — small scabs made of bloody matter, with the edges turned up on the same side, attesting therefore their tendency to fall off. These small scabs are divided into sections, according to the lines formed by the movements of the hand.... All around the spot there is something like a rose of light-colored blood that adheres to the skin — blood that obviously must disappear when washed with water, as confirmed by Padre Pio. It is obvious that there is no lesion of the skin, no hole, either central or lateral. From this, it seems possible to infer that the blood that is visible on the hand and that coagulates in these scabs comes out of the skin itself through exudation.

Asked if he felt pain, Padre Pio replied, "My whole hand is aching; the pain is stronger in the middle, inside."

The inquisitor continued:

> On the back of the right hand, in the middle, there is also a round spot, smaller, about 1.4 inches in diameter, also covered with scabs.... The epidermis under

the scabs is tougher: one can see it's less tender than on the palm — it's like a scab-like sediment, bloodier, brighter, over which lay the denser scabs, drier and more black, that are about to fall off. All around this there is not the bloody rose that is observable on the palm (which is superficial and easily washable with water). Here, too, in the spot on the back of the hand, there is no lesion. In the middle the scab adheres more to the skin, as if more deeply, and is almost more concave. Using two fingers like calipers, with Padre Pio's hand in the middle, it appears that the center of the sore on the palm corresponds with the upper edge of the sore on the back, in a straight line.

The other hand was similar.

Of the wounds on the feet, Rossi observed: "Padre Pio wears socks and shoes. Once the foot is uncovered, on the upper side there is something like a rosette, of about one inch in diameter, with no trace of blood, neither recently flowed, nor long ago. To clarify, let's imagine a closed wound, fully healed, over which a more delicate and whiter skin has grown. Such is the sign that appears on the upper side of the right foot."

Concerning the foot wounds, Pio said, "Sometimes there are droplets of blood; sometimes there are very small scabs that have never even turned black."

Rossi noted: "On the sole, in the middle, a rosette is observed of a 0.6-inch diameter. Here, too, no trace of blood. Actually, it is covered with a thin layer of almost callous skin about to come off, since its edge is turned up all around.... It seems that the center of the rosette on the upper side of the foot corresponds directly to the center of the one on the sole." Padre Pio, when asked about the pain, said, "Just like in the hands." The other foot was similar. Asked if he could walk easily, Padre Pio replied, "I don't always experience the same fatigue. I cannot stand up for long because of the internal pain."

Examining Padre Pio's chest, Rossi noted "a triangular spot on the left side, 1.2 inches from the last rib, 0.8 of an inch long, the color of red wine. About 2.8 inches above it, there are other small, scattered spots, but small, the last one, on top, slightly bigger." Asked if "blood comes out of this sign," Padre Pio replied: "From time to time, not always. When the bleeding is most intense it can soak a whole handkerchief."

The lesions emitted no foul odor, but rather a pleasant perfume. Rossi noted, "Considering the absence of [open] wounds, it can be justifiably supposed that the blood comes out through exudation." Asked if he had other signs on his chest, back, or elsewhere, Padre Pio replied, "No, I never had."[22]

Rossi questioned Padre Pio about the possibility of "dermatography" — a phenomenon in which a person deliberately scratches his skin to produce a red mark. "Does Your Paternity swear on the Holy Gospel that he has never made use of dermatography on his person, that is, that he has never, on account of a sort of autosuggestion, made signs that could then appear visible depending on fixations or obsessions?" Padre Pio replied, "I swear, for goodness' sake, for goodness' sake! Quite the contrary, if the Lord relieved me of them, how grateful I would be!"[23]

When Rossi asked about reports of "signs" on his forehead, Padre Pio laughed and said: "Oh, for the love of God! What do you want me to answer! Sometimes I've found some small blisters on my forehead or my head, but I never gave them any thought, and I certainly never dreamed of telling anyone."[24]

Carbolic Acid and Veratridine

One of the chief reasons why Bishop Rossi had been sent to investigate Padre Pio was the suspicion that he had used caustic substances to create his stigmata, so, of course, the inquisitor questioned him about that. Asked if he had ever used carbolic acid, Padre Pio said he had not, except when the doctor directed him to use it to sterilize the place where a boy in the school was about to get an injection. Asked if he had ever requested carbolic acid, Padre Pio replied, "I recall requesting some for the use of the Community — actually, of the minor seminary, of which I was director, in case it wasn't available in the convent." He admitted that once, "through a young woman [presumably DeVito] whom he had urged to keep great secrecy," he had asked one of her relatives who was a pharmacist in Foggia for a bottle of pure carbolic acid. On a second occasion, he requested four grams of veratridine (also called veratrine). The only purpose of secrecy was "to prevent the people who had to carry it from knowing that it was a medicament requested without a doctor's prescription." He needed the carbolic acid to disinfect syringes needed for injections. The veratridine was "for a prank to be played during recreation." Rossi noted: "Padre Pio had experienced the effect of this powder [which induced violent sneezing] mixed, in an imperceptible dose, in the [smokeless] tobacco offered to him by a Brother. Without knowing anything about poisons, without even considering what veratridine was (and this is why he asked for *four* grams), he requested it to repeat the joke and laugh at the expense of some Brothers! That's all."

The inquisitor concluded, "I don't think there is reason to doubt the sincerity of Padre Pio, who was required to take oaths that should have struck a chord in his priestly soul and under whose sanctity he attested he had not artificially caused or completed the stigmata."

Padre Pio had used iodine, not to disinfect the wounds, but to stop the bleeding. He explained, "I didn't even know if it would work. I saw others use this medication when they happened to cut themselves to stop the bleeding." He also used petroleum jelly — "when the sores would lose their scabs." Padre Pio stopped using iodine and since 1919 used nothing on the wounds, yet the stigmata persisted.[25]

Padre Pio Questioned on His Prayer Life

Bishop Rossi questioned Padre Pio extensively on all aspects of his life. When asked if he preached, the Capuchin replied, "I have never preached." As to confessions: "From around the time of my priestly ordination, I was able to hear a few confessions in my hometown; here, I was conferred the faculty by the ordinary [i.e., archbishop] about three years ago; in Foggia I never heard confessions, since, on account of my poor health, I hadn't even requested the faculty to do so."[26]

Padre Pio's prayer life was the subject of further questioning by the bishop. He said that he set his alarm clock for 4:30 each morning so that he could pray. When asked whether he practiced mental prayer, he answered: "Usually, for a couple of hours, sometimes more, sometimes less. To prepare, I fix my mind on a subject from the life of Our Lord. I develop it, and I meditate over it. I do the petition, the resolution, etc." In addition, he meditated "usually for about an hour, an hour and half, in the morning, then in the evening" as well as with the whole community for a half hour each evening.[27] When Rossi asked whether he followed closely "the structure of the meditation, or [was] inclined to change subjects," Padre Pio responded, "Ordinarily, I do follow the order, but sometimes it happens that something, some truth, will strike me more, and I stay there, like someone who admires an object that is more striking than others."[28]

Padre Pio prayed in preparation for Mass "depending on the opportunity" and prayed the thanksgiving prayer for fifteen to thirty minutes, "depending on the circumstance." "The whole Rosary" was his habitual prayer, followed by short prayers called "ejaculations." When asked about "penitential practices," except for the ones "prescribed communally," he answered: "None. I take the ones the Lord sends. I have been forbidden penitential practices on account of my poor health."

When asked if he was devoted to study, he told Rossi, "I am always hearing confessions. For this reason I am always keeping up to date with the necessary studies." Asked about mysticism, he answered somewhat vaguely that he believed "that nobody goes along that path unless the Lord himself leads him that way, by an extraordinary manifestation of his grace."[29] When Rossi asked, "While praying, do you keep the notion of place, time, of your following duties?" Padre Pio replied, "Usually, yes — sometimes I don't have a perception of place, the time, or of what is all around me, all that could be defined as external." Asked if he had to make an effort to pray, the friar answered, "Ordinarily I don't find it too hard to concentrate on the subject … I sense the desire, a deep, spontaneous, genuine desire to stay."[30]

"Episodes of ... an Apparently Mystical Nature"

There were reports that Padre Pio conversed with supernatural beings. Padre Lodovico of San Giovanni Rotondo told the inquisitor, "Even when he speaks, it seems there might be another one whom he might be addressing — it's commonly said that he speaks with his guardian angel."[31]

"During your prayer, does anything mystical happen to you?" the bishop asked.

"Yes," was Padre Pio's forthright answer. "Visions of heavenly persons."

When the inquisitor asked whether they were physical or intellectual visions, Pio responded, "Intellectual visions, through the eyes of the intellect."

"Do these things happen often during your prayer, ordinarily, or as isolated episodes?"

"As isolated episodes," Padre Pio replied.

Asked to describe some of these supernatural encounters, the Capuchin recounted: "Since around 1912, I had heard noise that in Foggia started being heard also by others, who would come to see me — I was ill — to inquire what was going on. Also, I had malicious external visions, now under human shape, now under beastly shapes, etc. I haven't heard noises or had visions in years." Asked if there were "other episodes ... of an apparently mystical nature," Padre Pio replied, "Yes, apparitions of Our Lord, of Our Lady, of Saint Francis, while I was awake." Although Padre Pio claimed to have visions during his youth, and despite documentary evidence (in a statement he wrote at the time) of the 1905 vision of the Virgin Mary that led to the bilocation at the Rizzani mansion, he insisted that they began "around 1911–1912." These heavenly apparitions continued to the present day, "even though they are rarer."[32]

When Rossi demanded to know whether the apparitions were silent or conveyed warnings or exhortations, Padre Pio replied, "Yes, I would receive exhortations regarding myself, as well as others, and even reproaches, about the spiritual life." Concerning his alleged ability to read hearts, Padre Pio answered, "A very few times I happened to feel inside me with clarity someone's fault or sin or virtue — of people of whom I had some knowledge, at least generally."[33] Yet he said nothing about cases like that of the Rizzanis, when he was directed to people of whom he had no previous knowledge! It seems possible that, when he was interrogated by the inquisitor, Padre Pio might have considered it wise — or been advised — to play down the extent of his mystical experiences.

The Aroma of Paradise

The inquisitor confirmed that the fragrance that emanated from Padre Pio, which some called "the aroma of paradise," was real. He wrote in his report: "This very intense and pleasant fragrance, similar to the scent of the violet — as it was well described by the Bishop of Melfi — is attested by everyone and may the Most

Eminent Fathers let me attest to it, too. He kept only soap in the cell.... They say it is sensed at times in waves, inside the cell and outside, when he walks by, in his spot in the choir, even from a distance. One such case occurred to Archpriest Prencipe, who noticed it in the parish church, when giving Communion to one of the people who was closest to Padre Pio. It happened to Padre Lorenzo when the others around it didn't sense it."[34] Rossi didn't try to explain the aroma.

Extreme Temperatures

There were persistent rumors that Padre Pio, on occasion, exhibited spectacularly high body temperatures, and Bishop Rossi questioned members of the community about this. Padre Luigi recounted that when Padre Pio was living in the friary in Foggia, "he would fall ill every once in a while, and sweat in an extraordinary manner, so much that they had to change his undergarments. Father Paolino said that then the thermometer would read over 104 F. I attributed it to a natural predisposition, while Father Paolino presented it to me as a supernatural phenomenon.... It is said that several thermometers also broke, so I was told."[35]

Padre Lorenzo admitted:

> As superior I was skeptical. Once, when Padre Pio had a fever, I wanted to use a thermometer: Padre Pio advised me not to, for it would break. I yielded, but a second time I absolutely wanted to try and the thermometer went up to 109.6 F — that is, up to the last mark — but it didn't break. A third time a thermometer that would read up to 113 F was used, and the mercury went up to 113 F, but it did not break. There were Dr. D. Franco Antonio Gina and Dr. Angelo M. Merla, the house doctor, a socialist. Another time I myself wanted to measure the temperature with a thermometer brought by Dr. Festa of Rome, one that would read up to 130 F, and it went up to 118 F.[36]

The inquisitor noted that these extreme temperatures occurred in "special spiritual circumstances." Padre Pio, who called it "a moral rather than a physical illness," told him that when the fevers occurred, he experienced "internal feelings, the considerations, or some representation, of the Lord." It was as if he were in a furnace, but always conscious.[37] Yet Padre Pio was not incapacitated, the bishop concluded, "not knocked down, but gets up, moves about, and does everything." Rossi wrote, "Whether this phenomenon, besides being exceptional, is also miraculous the Lord will reveal when he thinks the time is right."[38]

The Priest Who Never Eats?

The bishop had heard many reports that Padre Pio never ate. After observing him and talking to his intimates, he concluded, "Clearly, his nutrition is not abundant, but I don't think we are at the point of making Padre Pio a 'phenomenon.'"[39] Every-one agreed that Padre Pio never ate breakfast — but, of course, many people don't. As for dinner, the main meal that was served at midday, Rossi observed that for Padre Pio it "certainly isn't lavish." Padre Romolo declared, "You might say he eats everything." He ate meat — usually pork, liver, or fish — but sparingly. He ate bread, but also in small quantities. Romolo estimated that Padre Pio drank about a half liter of beer at dinner, and throughout the day, another half-liter. In the evening, Padre Pio typically drank a cup of hot chocolate, "rather thick," and sometimes ate an apple or two. Romolo concluded that his confrere ate "rather sparingly," leaving "food in every dish; he eats some of everything, but just a little bit."[40] Padre Lorenzo told Rossi that for dinner Padre Pio usually ate "some vegetables with oil." Usually, for supper, he had nothing but a cup of hot chocolate and some beer.[41] Padre Luigi of Serracapriola said that at noon "he would eat angel hair pasta, vegetables with oil, potatoes with oil, dairy products, a few bites of sponge cake, and, especially fruit." In the evening, at supper, he sometimes ate a much smaller quantity of what he ate at dinner. Sometimes he had sardines, taken with a cup of hot chocolate and fruit. He drank beer. Many evenings he took no supper at all.[42]

Miracle Cures

Bishop Rossi acknowledged that the friary received many "letters of thanksgiving for spiritual or temporal graces that are said to have been granted on account of Padre Pio's prayers, some of which mention, for instance, true cases of sudden and unhoped for healings." One of them concerned the case of Maria Cozzi, "a patient in the main hospital in Florence, afflicted by an epithelial carcinoma of the tongue, and who was found perfectly healed the very moment she was supposed to undergo surgery (August 1919). There was, in addition, the more recent case of a Canadian young man suffering from tuberculosis with hemoptysis [the coughing up of blood], who was healed to the point that there was not even a trace of the illness in him, after two 'apparitions' of Padre Pio." Rossi wrote: "To be sure, these, shall we say, prodigious cases have been neither subjected to formal examinations, nor expounded with due documentation and in the proper legal form, but they nevertheless make us ponder, in general and since they confirm each other, whether the Lord truly is availing himself of this pious Religious in order to once again manifest his goodness and his might."[43]

Asked by Rossi if he could recall some "true, certain, complete healings," Padre Pio answered: "I have prayed, yes. They [that is, the people prayed for] know the outcome, not I." Rossi spoke of two mute girls who said that Padre Pio promised them a grace for a certain day, Holy Saturday, and when it didn't happen, claimed that Padre Pio set other dates, again without anything happening. To this, the stigmatic priest replied: "No, no, no. ... Even from a human point of view, who would want to make such a promise without any certainty? ... I only said: 'Pray.' They said, 'On such and such a day you must grant us the grace — we'll be waiting for it.' I would add: 'You can't give God deadlines.'"[44]

Bilocation

Rossi asked Padre Pio about three accounts of bilocation:

> As usual, I challenged Padre Pio on each episode. With childishly candid answers, he admitted to the first and third, explaining that they had happened. He flatly denied the veracity of the second: In fact, it was ascertained that it had been a Father Pio of Benevento. It is indispensable to concede that, until proven otherwise, these facts hold true, and we have two sources for them: those who attest they have met Padre Pio and have talked to him, and Padre Pio who confirms, protesting that he has never mentioned a word to anybody and has done so now for the first time.[45]

When questioned, Padre Pio answered: "I don't know how it is or the nature of this phenomenon — and I certainly don't give it much thought — but it did happen to me to be in the presence of this or that person, to be in this or that place. I do not know whether my mind was transported there, or what I saw was some sort of representation of the place or the person. I do not know whether I was there with my body or without it."[46] He gave an example: "One night I found myself at the bedside of a sick woman: Mrs. Massa of San Giovanni Rotondo; I was in the convent; I think I was praying. It must have been over a year ago. I spoke words of comfort; she begged me to pray for her healing. This is the substance. I didn't really know her personally. She had been recommended to me." When asked if he thought it was possible that the woman had hallucinated, Padre Pio's answer was, "I won't discuss the state of this lady. I'm only saying I was there." It will be recalled that Archpriest Prencipe had expressed skepticism about accounts of Padre Pio's appearance to a foul-mouthed potter from Torremaggiore. Padre Pio explained, "A man presented himself to me, or I presented myself to him, in Torremaggiore — I was in the convent — and I rebuked him and reproached him for his vices, urging him to convert, and then later on this man came here, too."[47]

On the other hand, when Rossi asked, "Is it true that, in a similar case, while you were in the convent, you found yourself one day in Foggia, with the lieutenant general commanding the military division?" the Capuchin replied, "Excellency, I don't think so — I don't have any memory of this."[48]

Padre Pio also recounted a rather curious occurrence:

> I was hearing confessions in the sacristy, on a raised area; the sacristy was

overcrowded with men; it was hot; we were suffocating; they screamed and squalled asking for help. I saw that the best thing to do was to leave, because once the confessor left, they, too, would come out. I finished the confession of the first one who happened to be there; I remember … that I couldn't go down the steps, because they were occupied; I had to step over those men — at least the first ones — then I found myself outside, and I turned to send them away.[49]

"They Make Me Say What I Don't Think"

Bishop Rossi observed no healings or anything extraordinary during the eight days he was at San Giovanni Rotondo. He reported that Padre Pio rejected as fabrication many of the sensational tales that had been broadcast about him. Responding to some incredible story, Padre Pio told Rossi: "Excellency, I don't know anything about this. There has been recklessness on the part of some who wanted to use my name for things I would have never dreamed of either saying or revealing. It was crazy, and I have to thank the Lord that the greatest grace I know I received concerning this matter was indeed the grace not to lose my mind and my health, so numerous were the lies that were told." He insisted that, in the case of many of the phenomena attributed to him, "the last one to know, or the one who knew the least, was myself."[50]

Likewise, Padre Pio denied predicting a specific time when graces would occur: "You don't give the Lord deadlines!" He would tell people, only "trust in the Lord. I will commend you to him." He told the inquisitor about a man who came to him and declared, "This year I came here instead of going to a spa," to which Padre Pio replied, "You made a mistake. You should have gone there."[51]

Padre Luigi told Rossi that most of the friars "gave little credence" to the "prodigious events," with the exception of Padre Benedetto and two or three others. One of the "others" may have been Padre Romolo, who told the inquisitor, "I ask [Padre Pio] many things: whether my grandmother who had died suddenly was saved — and he answered me: Her account is settled; whether I would be reunited with her in Heaven — he told me yes. But before he spoke, he would turn away, saying the words in a low voice, as if he were talking to another person." Of course, there was no way of confirming this prophecy. However, Padre Romolo mentioned, "Many times he has told me, 'Statutum est mori senex' — it is decided that I die in old age — but I do not know if he meant to joke." Padre Romolo was then in his mid-thirties. In fact, he survived Padre Pio and lived to his mid-nineties. Padre Romolo told Rossi that he wondered, "Either this man is an imposter, or otherwise, how can he know the future?" Since he could not consider him a fraud, Padre Romolo believed him to be "an extraordinary soul."[52]

Rossi observed no healings or anything extraordinary during the eight days he was at San Giovanni Rotondo.

The Disposition of Money

From supernatural matters, the inquisitor moved on to more mundane affairs, such as the letters that poured in from all over, sometimes six hundred to seven hundred a day, many of which contained monetary donations. Padre Lorenzo told Bishop Rossi: "Regarding the donations that are sent to him with the explicit purpose of helping the poor, he used to manage them himself, with the verbal assent of the provincial of that time, now he gives the money to the bursar and then, with a written permission signed by the Father Provincial, he proceeds to distribute it, either according to his own judgment or through a devout person chosen for this purpose."[53] Padre Ignazio of Jelsi, bursar of the convent at San Giovanni Rotondo and correspondence secretary, when interviewed, explained:

> Generally, [Padre Pio] doesn't read the correspondence, except for a few letters that I give to him. The lack of time prevents him. On the average, about seventy letters arrive each day — now mainly from Spain, Brazil, Argentina, etc. Essentially, the letters describe miseries, maladies, spiritual afflictions, and ask for the help of Padre Pio's prayers. Not so much from abroad, but from Italy donations also arrive for the offering of Masses, for the poor — actually, for these there is a specific administration, since Padre Pio absolutely refuses [to put donations to use for any other purpose than that designated by the benefactors]. Thank you notes also arrive almost every day. A reply is generally sent to those who write with certified mail, or send donations, or include a stamp; then, of course, a reply is sent also to those whom it is opportune to respond, for example, to communities [of religious]. In fact, many are those who write, nuns especially. The replies are vague. [For example:] Padre Pio prays and sends his blessing. We don't venture anything else. Padre Pio, on the other hand, can reply in a decisive way, and I can recall some special cases when Padre Pio did so.

Behavior with Women

Rossi's investigation also addressed Padre Pio's relations with women. Some of his own confreres had concerns about his behavior. Padre Luigi of Serracapriola, whose comments about other aspects of Padre Pio's ministry seemed less than enthusiastic, told Bishop Rossi:

> I cannot ... square these apparently prodigious occurrences with some things that are at least in themselves faults — at least objectively; subjectively, I think they may not be." He went on to declare: "I've heard that while he was ill in the guest quarters, he was tended to by some women, and that these women once showed their displeasure at the presence of another, older woman.... It

is also a known fact that he received his penitent women in the guest quarters for their spiritual direction one at a time — something we did not like, especially since a circular on this subject had come from Rome. We must certainly suppose that he did not mean to disobey; rather, the circular itself must have been benignly interpreted. Now there have been some changes in this area, and some of these women — who call themselves "Spiritual Daughters" — got upset, because they thought we had no trust in them. The imperfection of these irregularities is certainly caused by the fanaticism. Padre Pio is very simple. Until some time ago, these women stayed until late to talk, to kiss his hand, etc. So, if these irregularities could be eliminated, it would be a good thing.

Padre Luigi concluded, "I believe Padre Pio has been poorly directed,"[54] evidently placing the blame on Padre Benedetto. Other priests were likewise uncomfortable with Padre Pio's meetings with women but said that they were afraid to bring it up. In fact, Padre Pietro, the new provincial, told Rossi of a young woman who complained that Padre Pio had "caressed" her after he "gave her something like a little pat on the shoulder." After this incident, he reported, "Padre Pio was warned."[55]

When Rossi asked him about the reports that women had nursed him in the guest room or parlor of the friary, Pio explained that this happened during the war when he and Padre Paolino, the superior, were alone. Padre Paolino "had to take care of the church, to teach in school — everything" and could not attend to his sick confrere. Asked who it was who looked after him, Pio mentioned Assunta DiTomassi, Padre Paolino's sister, as well as "other women." He admitted that they attended to him, both day and night. When the inquisitor pointed out that this was contrary to the Rule of the order, Padre Pio said, "Surely, it is not regular, but I acquiesced out of obedience, because I saw the necessity ... I was ill."[56] Rossi asked, "Is it true that, despite the Father Provincial forbidding private conversations in the guest quarters, they went on nonetheless?" Padre Pio insisted that Padre Benedetto had made an exception in his case, telling him, "For now you can continue them."[57]

Padre Romolo, however, said that he had confronted Padre Pio, reminding him of the directive from Rome forbidding priests to meet with women alone, which was "read in front of everybody." Padre Pio seemed hurt and said that it was "an extraordinary case" and that he "didn't do anything without advice." Afterward, he stopped meeting with women alone. Padre Romolo felt that Padre Pio had been, in fact, "acting legitimately, with a sure conscience." When the inquisitor asked how Padre Pio acted toward women, Padre Romolo answered: "He is informal, like a child ... he says whatever he feels. But as far as chastity is concerned, he is extremely delicate. As for this, nobody doubts he is an angel."[58] Everyone seemed to agree that Padre Pio's chastity was beyond dispute. Padre Cherubino said, "Padre Pio treats all women with affability and sweetness, but is always most reserved."[59] Padre Lorenzo affirmed: "His demeanor toward women is proper, religious.... With regard to chastity, I believe him to be angelic."[60] This was the reason why Padre Benedetto, as provincial, had allowed him to have "conversations" with women in the guest room — with Padre Pio, sexual misconduct would have been absolutely out of character.

The Inquisitor's Conclusions

In his report to the Holy Office, Bishop Rossi cited the earlier conclusions by Father Lémius, who put forth four possible hypotheses for Padre Pio's stigmata: (1) They were self-inflicted wounds "through a morbid condition of a pathological nature"; (2) they were self-inflicted wounds made through suggestion or "the voluntary application of artificial means"; (3) they were of divine origin; or (4) they were of diabolical origin.[61]

Rossi quickly ruled out the possibility of diabolical origin. He also dismissed the possibility of a "morbid condition of a pathological nature," declaring that it was incomprehensible that someone with "a neuropathic disorder" could work as hard as Padre Pio did. He also noted that the wounds never became inflamed, as they would have if they had been the result of disease. He also ruled out autosuggestion caused by the direction of Padre Benedetto because, in their collected correspondence, it was clear that it was Padre Pio, not his director, who first brought up the idea of sharing in Christ's suffering and afterward talked the most about it. As for the suggestion that Padre Pio created the wounds with carbolic acid, Rossi asked himself, "Were the stigmata a sham, a vulgar fraud? Did Padre Pio, at the cost of suffering pain, cause them, did he cultivate them, did he make them grow artificially so as to increase the fame of his holiness?" He believed Padre Pio's explanation that he obtained the carbolic acid to disinfect syringes and that the veratridine was for a prank, played, not out of malice, but in a "playful spirit." He admitted that "Padre Pio's 'stigmata' do present the supernatural character of the outpouring blood" and other characteristics of "the true stigmata." "Are we then really before St. Francis of Assisi's marvel, renewed somehow in one of his sons?" the inquisitor asked. "I do not know."[62]

Rossi ended his report, stating, "I am not ... an admirer of the Padre ... I feel complete indifference." However, he made four conclusions. The first was that Padre Pio "is a good religious, exemplary, accomplished in the practice of the virtues, given to piety and probably elevated to a higher degree of prayer than it seems from the outside; he shines especially because of his sincere humility and his remarkable simplicity, which did not fail even in the gravest moments when these virtues were put to the test, a test truly grave and dangerous for him."

Second, the inquisitor addressed the reports of miracles. "Of the 'graces' beseeched, as it is said, many do not hold true, many are only asserted, but lack a legal proof."

Third, "Whatever is extraordinary in what happens to the person of Padre Pio cannot be explained, but it certainly does not happen either by diabolical intervention, or with fraud."

Fourth, "The religious community in which Padre Pio lives is a good community, one that can be trusted."[63]

Then he came to the matter of Padre Pio's transfer. This would be "unthinkable," owing to the "fierce opposition on the part of the people of San Giovanni Rotondo." Therefore, Padre Pio's superiors "must be urged to observe and keep watch — tacitly, not in an obvious way." The "Pious Women" had to be "corrected" and "their visits to the church and convent should be less frequent." He continued: "In all this, Padre Pio should be more assertive; Padre Pio should be charitably counseled to be more cautious in his believing in the spiritual elevation of certain souls. Any form of external publicity that is too evident must be reduced as much as possible. The Holy Office must be kept current in all new facts concerning Padre Pio."

Finally, Rossi was concerned about Padre Benedetto, after reading some of his letters. The inquisitor complained: "He insists that Padre Pio ask him about public flagellations and about the special conditions of Father Benedetto's own soul, and then he must write back and report Heaven's answers, but immediately and thoroughly, by virtue of obedience. How much more reserved with the Lord are the ways of true mystics!" Rossi felt that Padre Benedetto was convinced that he was himself a true mystic and "elevated" himself as a teacher. "Benedetto, for all his science and experience, is too *credulous*, too *enthusiastic* before anything that appears to be extraordinary and supernatural." Rossi, moreover, was convinced that his "'mysticism' *is not prudent*, and therefore is not good mysticism." Therefore, the inquisitor recommended that Benedetto's activities be limited, as his "excessive zeal" could lead to "spiritual confusion."[64]

After his visit of eight days, Monsignor Rossi departed from San Giovanni Rotondo, after making everyone he interviewed swear on the Gospels to maintain silence. It was a vow kept conscientiously. For this reason, this episode was never mentioned during Padre Pio's lifetime and was unknown until the Vatican Archives for the period were opened in the early twenty-first century.

Chapter Seventeen

"A True Satanic War"

The "Massacre of San Giovanni Rotondo"

Padre Pio's mysticism did not isolate him from human affairs. He was always very concerned about what went on in the world. We have seen how he expressed his feelings vehemently about a teachers' strike. He was very much disturbed by the civil unrest that plagued Italy in the aftermath of the Great War, between the socialists on the "left" and the fascists on the "right," who each sought, often violently, to bring about their visions of a just and equitable society.

San Giovanni Rotondo was caught up in partisan violence during the autumn of 1920. The socialists, while not using the label "communist," were nevertheless of the extreme left-wing variety. They promised to bring about a "Soviet regime," which would confiscate and redistribute the estates of the great landowners. They blamed the Church and clergy for the poverty of the area, and sometimes physically attacked members of the clergy. In the province of Foggia (where San Giovanni was), where the majority of legislators were then socialist, there were threats to turn the churches into barns.[1] While many of the landless peasants in the area of San Giovanni Rotondo backed the socialists, the local veterans' association supported the landowners and the fascists, as well as the Church, and on August 15, on the feast of the Assumption, Padre Pio rode in an automobile to the main square of the town, there to bless the veterans and their procession.

In the following weeks, prior to the municipal elections, tension increased. One witness noted, "The population here is bloodthirsty, especially the shepherds and farmhands."[2] The socialists gained slightly more seats in the city council than the fascists, who furiously disputed the election, so that forty *carabinieri* (state troopers) and more than eighty soldiers were called in to preserve order.

In early October, Francesco Morcaldi, the thirty-one-year-old mayor of San Giovanni Rotondo, called on Padre Pio. A short, goggle-eyed man who would hold that office off and on for the next four decades, Morcaldi has been described by some as a kind, quiet, gentle, pious individual; by others, he was accused of sexual and financial misconduct.[3] Morcaldi seems to have been something of a political chameleon, who managed to accommodate himself to whomever happened to be in power. One acquaintance described him, however, as "a fascist if there ever was one." One thing cannot be denied: the mayor was totally loyal to Padre Pio. With trouble brewing, he told the priest that he felt it was his duty to warn him that violence was imminent.

"Mind you, you've got to pacify the people," Padre Pio told the mayor. "Go, approach the leaders [of the two factions] and calm them."[4]

On October 14, all hell broke loose in town when a mob of socialists tried to storm city hall, tear down the flag of Italy, and replace it with the red flag of Marxism. They failed, however, to break through the wall of troops surrounding the building. Hordes of fascists then appeared on the scene, and the two factions went at each other with sticks, stones, and knives. According to some reports, a socialist seized a rifle from a state trooper and killed him with it. Perhaps in panic, perhaps deliberately (according to which faction recounted the incident), the troopers began to fire upon the crowd. Then a couple of homemade bombs exploded. Within minutes, about a dozen people lay dead or dying, and more than eighty were injured.

When the riot was over, in tears, Morcaldi cried, "Padre Pio, what are we going to do?"

"Reconcile, my son," he said.

Within a few days, Padre Pio put together a program of pacification for the mayor, which Morcaldi proclaimed as the expression of the wishes of Padre Pio, who was trusted and revered by most of the fascists and many of the socialists as well.

According to this plan, the inhabitants of San Giovanni Rotondo were to be given a fuller voice in the city government. Moreover, to improve the plight of the rural laborers, a municipal office of labor was to be established. Mobile units from agricultural schools were to be engaged to teach better farming methods. A permanent committee of assistance was recommended to aid the children of soldiers killed in the war. A system of good roads was envisioned for the community and in the countryside. Sanitation was to be improved by the construction of sidewalks and public toilets, and by the removal and replacement of numerous slum dwellings, many of which were built of dried mud. A telephone network was to be implemented. And a city hospital, with an operating room, was to be established to provide free health care for the poor.[5]

The Hospital of St. Francis

Almost immediately, Padre Pio began actively trying to set up a hospital in San Giovanni Rotondo. Medical care there and in other parts of rural southern Italy was abysmal, with some doctors still resorting to arcane treatments such as bleeding patients. The nearest hospital of any kind was twenty-five miles of bad roads away in Foggia, and the victims of medical emergencies often died for lack of adequate treatment. Accident victims sometimes lay bleeding for days. With the approval of his superiors, Padre Pio began to solicit funds. By December 1921, the project was well underway. On December 14, he wrote to his cousin, the Marquess Don Giuseppe Orlando (1877–1958), a priest with some influential contacts:

And now I come to ask you a favor and I wish that, as always, you make me happy. You know well that I desired to purchase a building site for the purpose of good works. Now it seems that my desire has been heard by the Lord. The land is ready to be purchased and it's necessary to be quick in buying it. Fifteen thousand lire were offered to me for this purpose. The benefactress doesn't want her work of beneficence known by any living person and wants me to find a trustworthy person, who would come before everyone as the one who would put down the money to buy it. Then immediately I thought of you. You are the only person I trust and I commit this affair to you and you don't dare refuse. The sacrifice that you have to make is that you must come here as soon as everything is ready; I would wish to spare you a trip in this harsh season, but, my dear Peppino [Joey], I can't, and you must pardon me. Write me at once and tell me that you're going to make me happy.

I suggest that you not make known to a living soul what I told you about, because I want to honor the wishes of the benefactress. When you answer concerning this deal, which you'll do at once, say that you're coming here on your own and that, as a gift, you're putting the 15 thousand lire at my disposal for the purchase. The 15 thousand lire you will find here. See that you don't refuse me, Peppino.

If I chose you for this business I did it because in you I have total trust, and because you are honest and also because I believe that you're good at keeping a secret. I await an immediate response by way of Miss Serritelli, so as to avoid your letter being mixed with others.

I think of you always before Jesus and this night I had a dream so beautiful that I will wait to describe it in person to you when you come here....

Look, Peppino, even the religious know nothing, and by the wish of the lady I mentioned must never know anything. Therefore also in front of them you must appear as the benefactor who is making the purchase.[6]

A property was purchased that had once housed a convent of nuns and — with the help of Dr. Angelo Maria Merla, former mayor and physician to the friars, and several other health professionals — it was turned into the Hospital of St. Francis and opened early in 1925, with two wards, twenty beds, and an operating room. Dr. Merla was on call there every day, and a Dr. Bucci from Foggia agreed to come twice a week to perform surgical operations.

"How Is It Possible to See God Saddened ... and Not Grieve, Too?"

Concerned with souls as well as bodies, Padre Pio agonized over "the failure of people to respond to heavenly favors." In October 1920, he wrote to Padre Bene-detto: "The thought of being unable to bring spiritual relief to those whom Jesus sends me, the thought of so many souls who foolishly want to justify their evil in defiance of their Chief Good afflicts me, tortures me, martyrs me, overcharges my mind, and rends my heart.... Of late I have felt two desires growing gigantically within my spirit ... I want to live, so as to be of use to my brothers in exile, and, on the other hand, I wish to die to be united with my heavenly spouse."[7]

A year later, he wrote his director:

> I am devoured by the love of God and the love of my neighbor. God is always fixed in my mind and stamped in my heart. I never lose sight of him. I can admire his beauty, his smiles, his vexation, his mercy, his vengeance, or rather, the rigors of his justice. How is it possible to see God saddened ... and not to grieve, too? I see God on the verge of hurling his thunderbolts, and it seems that there is no remedy except to raise a hand to stop his arm. And we must wave the other hand frantically to warn our brother to cast the evil out of his life ... since the hand of the judge is about to discharge itself on him! I feel nothing except to have and to will that which God desires. And in him I always feel at peace, at least, within my soul. Externally, sometimes, I am somewhat worried, for the sake of my brothers.[8]

An Archepiscopal Vendetta

In January 1922, Pope Benedict XV, who had been suffering from pneumonia, died at the age of sixty-seven. Elected as his successor was the archbishop of Milan, sixty-five-year-old Achille Ratti, who took the name Pius XI. Short, round-faced, balding, and bespectacled, Pope Pius had nevertheless an awe-inspiring presence. Severe, and so distant that even his closest relatives had to apply like total strangers to the master of the chamber for an audience with him (and then wait for a card of invitation), he radiated an aura of majestic dignity. Even the dread Hermann Göring, second in command in Nazi Germany, would quake before him when he met him in the 1930s, writing to a Romanian official, "You know that I've never in my life lacked courage; but before that little figure robed all in white I felt my heart jump as never before. For the first time in my life I was afraid."[9] Pius did not seem to have the interest in Padre Pio that his predecessor did and relied on the reports about him from those he trusted. One of them was the archbishop of Manfredonia, in whose archdiocese San Giovanni Rotondo was included.

Almost immediately after the accession of Pope Pius, Archbishop Gagliardi went to the Vatican in person and complained about the dreadful friar in San Giovanni, who, with his mercenary cronies, was sowing disorder and confusion. Evidently referring to the occasions when the Capuchin denied absolution to those he was certain were in a state of impenitence, Gagliardi deplored Padre Pio's "horrible manner of hearing confessions" that left souls "in a state of agitation."[10] He lamented to the pontiff, "I think I have to answer to God for having authorized Padre Pio to hear confessions." He insisted that Padre Pio created the stigmata with nitric acid, that the mysterious fragrance was created from little bottles of scent that Padre Pio hid under his bed, and that the miracles and cures either were the product of sick imaginations or deliberately staged tricks. Referring to the lascivious and fraudulent folk healer who was treated as a holy man by the recently murdered empress and emperor of Russia, he denounced Padre Pio as a "country Rasputin" — an "impenitent libertine, a robust and insatiable lover."[11]

He denounced the Capuchin to a woman who inquired about him as "a man possessed by a demon, who practices spiritism." His so-called stigmata were nothing but little pimples, Gagliardi proclaimed; he sprinkled perfume around the penitents; he surrounded himself with women with whom he tarried late in the night in the convent.[12] Before the bishops and archbishops of the Consistorial Congregation, which regulated matters related to the governance of dioceses, Gagliardi made even more sordid accusations: "Padre Pio is demon-possessed. I declare to you that he has a devil and the friars of San Giovanni Rotondo are a band of thieves. With my own eyes I saw Padre Pio perfume himself and put makeup on his face. All this I swear on my pectoral cross!"[13] Another time, the archbishop insisted, "Padre Pio is possessed by the devil and knows how to perform voodoo."[14] "He caused these wounds to himself, and different doctors have asserted this. He is a devil and I will imprison him!"[15]

Gagliardi encouraged his priests to bombard the Holy Office with lurid accusations concerning the ministry and character of the stigmatized priest. Don Giovanni Miscio, a priest and schoolteacher from San Giovanni, wrote to the Holy Office, claiming that Padre Pio suffered from sexually transmitted diseases and had regular sexual intercourse with his spiritual daughters. Many years later, the Capuchin Padre Alberto D'Apolito interviewed Don Domenico Palladino, a priest from San Giovanni who had been one of Padre Pio's "most venomous detractors." Confronting Palladino, who was then in his eighties, he said: "For years, you, together with other priests, denigrated and calumniated Padre Pio on his morality. Were you sure of what you asserted? Didn't you think that you were lying and doing evil?"

"No," replied Palladino. "I was convinced that I was doing good. I thought that Padre Pio was an imposter. At that time I had to obey the one who gave me orders."

When asked who gave him these orders, Palladino replied: "The bishop. I was very young to reflect and think about what I was doing. I knew I had to obey."[16]

Gagliardi made no secret of his belief that "this place won't be calm unless Padre Pio disappears and therefore I must make him disappear."[17]

What sort of man would make such extravagant, lurid, and fantastic charges? What was the reason for his hatred?

Sixty-three years old in 1922, Pasquale Gagliardi appears in his few surviving photographs as a wizened little man with pince-nez spectacles, a sour downturned mouth, and a slightly angry expression. A native of Tricarico — a town of a few thousand souls in the province of Basilicata, in the deep south of Italy — he entered seminary at fourteen, was graduated at nineteen from the Alma Collegio Capranica in Rome, and went on to the Gregorian College, where he earned doctorates in philosophy and theology. After his ordination at twenty-three (in 1882), he taught in his hometown until 1888, when he was summoned to the seminary of Benevento to teach philosophy and dogmatics. At the age of thirty-seven, he was named archbishop of Manfredonia by Pope Leo XIII.

In his thirty-year tenure as archbishop of Manfredonia, Gagliardi tried to assert the authority of the pope in an area where, before the unification of Italy, folk traditions often took precedence over orthodox practices and teachings. Gagliardi tried to emphasize the centrality of Christ to people whose devotion, he was convinced, was infected by superstition. In a pastoral letter in 1911, he complained about the celebration of feast days in honor of the Virgin Mary, in which devotion seemed to consist mainly in "loud noises and the firing of guns" but little "interior disposition or sentiment." He insisted, "The true devotion that we must give to Holy Mary must consist in this: that it … unites us with her together with Jesus Christ."[18] He urged the people, "Separated from all superstition and every profanation, organize and offer your gifts to [Mary] so that you can be reconciled with Jesus Christ if you are far from him and so that you will always be bound to him."[19] The next year he complained to his priests, "Many today no longer go to Mass or only rarely go on feast days; many, even in plain sight, work on those days from morning until night."[20]

Gagliardi, combating superficial devotion and idolatry and trying to foster true devotion to Christ, looked with suspicion at the popular devotion to Padre Pio, considering it the product of the superstition of ignorant and credulous peasants, encouraged by unscrupulous people, both within the friary and without, in hopes of bringing business and money to the impoverished region. In the summer of 1923, the archbishop wrote to Archpriest Prencipe, "If God wants Padre Pio to stay, let him stay, but not to perpetuate the exploitation of the good faith of others and the demoralization of the region."[21] He claimed that the "miracles of Padre Pio" were invented "in order to make money."[22]

In May 1919, in the town of Vieste on the Adriatic coast, about forty miles from

San Giovanni Rotondo, a popular statue of the Virgin Mary that the faithful loved to touch and kiss was moved from the area of the altar in the cathedral and put in a side chapel, and the offerings of gold given by the devout and displayed with the image were placed in a special chest out of the sight of the public. Immediately, word went out that the archbishop had stolen the statue and the gold.

Gagliardi, who was in Vieste to preach, was celebrating Mass in a side chapel on the evening of May 15, when a mob of six hundred men, women, and children burst in on him, pelting him with stones and bricks. They grabbed his missal and paten, threw them at him, and knocked him to the floor, punching and kicking him, until several priests intervened, dragging Gagliardi into another room and locking the door. The police came and escorted the archbishop out of the cathedral, but the crowd poured into the streets, broke through the escort, and knocked Gagliardi to the ground, demanding his castration. The chant went up, "Off with his — !"

A crowd of women brandishing knives and shears broke through the police line and started to rip away the archbishop's clothing. Before they could perform their intended anatomical alterations, a contingent of state troopers arrived to save Gagliardi from mutilation.[23]

There seems to have been more to kindle the people's murderous hatred of the archbishop than his condemnation of superstitious devotion. Emmanuele Brunatto, during the mid-1920s, assembled a considerable dossier on Gagliardi, which contained denunciations by a number of priests and religious in the archdiocese. The members of a particular convent of Poor Clare nuns complained that Gagliardi on occasion entered the cloister to spend the night with a niece of the abbess.[24] A priest insisted that he had surprised the archbishop in bed, naked, with another nun. Moreover, it was widely known that some of the clergy, like Prencipe and Palladino, openly lived with their mistresses with the archbishop's knowledge.

Worse, Gagliardi protected priests who were child molesters. One priest, after serving two years in prison for sodomizing a boy, was rehabilitated by Gagliardi and assigned to a boarding high school, where he "ruined" twelve more boys before being sent to prison for twelve years. Despite complaints, Gagliardi refused to remove the archpriest of the town of Caprino, even though the man had been convicted of pederasty in both the lower and appellate courts — until the offending cleric was finally sent to prison. He appointed another priest to serve in the cathedral of Manfredonia after he had been transferred from another diocese because of "habitual pederasty." When the rector of the seminary at Manfredonia was accused of groping students, Gagliardi made him pastor of a church in another town, where the scandals continued. He appointed as archpriest of the town of Vico a man who had been convicted of sodomy three times. It was rumored that priests could get away with the most reprehensible conduct if they offered the archbishop a bribe.[25]

Of course, this had nothing to do with Padre Pio personally and could scarcely account for Gagliardi's hatred of the Capuchin. The archbishop, however, was known for his hostility toward all Franciscans. In fact, Padre Luigi Festa of Avellino (1884–1959), the provincial secretary and definitor, complained that the archbishop, throughout his episcopate, had "persecuted the sons of St. Francis and all their work."[26] When the Friars Minor in Manfredonia were trying to promote the Third Order (for laypersons), Gagliardi told his underlings, "If you want to live in peace, destroy the Third Order!"[27]

Over the years, many lay people and priests complained to the Vatican about Gagliardi, who evidently insisted that the charges were the libelous invention of people who resented his attempts to discourage superstitious practices and encourage more fervent devotion to the papacy. The archbishop was a close friend of the powerful Cardinal Gaetano DeLai (1853–1928), with whom he frequently vacationed, and the cardinal was said to have used his influence to prevent an investigation, despite signed statements from many priests in the archdiocese attesting to Gagliardi's unholy conduct.[28]

Gagliardi actually had only one conversation with Padre Pio, when, in 1920 or 1921, he visited the friary of Our Lady of Grace. Padre Agostino, who was there, wrote:

> The archbishop arrived at the friary around 10:30 and was greeted by me at the door of the friary. I accompanied him to room number 9. I stopped to talk with him alone, since we had known each other for many years. At 10:34 Padre Pio arrived, and knelt to kiss the ring of the archbishop, who was seated. When the archbishop extended his right hand to Padre Pio, I saw him bend over and kiss Padre Pio's hand, which was covered.... After they had exchanged a few words, Padre Pio asked permission to say Holy Mass. [At that time Padre Pio was scheduled to celebrate at 11.] Then the archbishop said to me, "Let's go hear the Mass." So I accompanied the archbishop to the choir. He took a seat there ... with his breviary in his hand to say his office and watch Padre Pio as he celebrated.... At the end of the Mass Padre Pio did not say the Ave Maria. The archbishop asked me why. I answered that this was the Conventual Mass....
>
> After dinner Padre Pio went to rest and we friars went into the garden ... to take our recreation with the archbishop. After the recreation, around three, the [archbishop] had to go home and wanted to say goodbye to Padre Pio. I went up with the archbishop and we met Padre Pio in the hall. The archbishop went up to Padre Pio to speak to him. I stood somewhat aside, but heard these precise words that the archbishop addressed to Padre Pio in a low voice: "Father, pray hard for a sick little niece of mine." The Padre nodded yes

and knelt to kiss the sacred ring of the archbishop. The Padre accompanied the archbishop to the stairway, along with me and others.[29]

Padre Agostino took great pains to describe this encounter in light of Gagliardi's later claim that he had been alone with Padre Pio in his room and saw him perfume himself. At no time, during his one visit to Our Lady of Grace, was the archbishop in Padre Pio's room, nor was he ever alone with him. Gagliardi's request that Padre Pio pray for his niece would seem to indicate that, at the time of the visit, the archbishop was not entirely negative toward the Capuchin — unless he was pretending and hoping that Padre Pio would make some extravagant promise of a miracle. Some speculated that the archbishop turned against Padre Pio because his niece was not healed. For whatever reason, Padre Agostino noted that, shortly after his visit, Gagliardi "began a sordid war" against Padre Pio, forwarding "countless letters full of accusations, exaggerations, libels — a true satanic war."

On June 12, 1922, Archbishop Gagliardi wrote to the Holy Office, complaining:

> Twice recently the Capuchin Fathers of the monastery of San Giovanni Rotondo were fighting with weapons and fire and struck each other until blood ran, leaving some of them wounded. The marshal of the ... police unit rushed in there condemning all of them, including Padre Pio and the pious women, for exploiting the good faith of their neighbors and people from distant countries. The cause of the quarrel and of the fights among the religious seems to have been the distribution of the huge sums (said to be more than three or four hundred thousand francs) accumulated by Padre Pio and from precious objects given by the pious women who were visitors to the monastery, as well as the fact that the brothers visited the women's homes, even at night, and stayed overnight at times in the countryside.[30]

This led Cardinal Rafael Merry del Val, the secretary of the Holy Office, to write Padre Giuseppe Antonio Bussolari of Persiceto, the minister general of the Capuchins, asking for explanations about this. Horrified, the minister general wrote to Padre Pietro of Ischitella, the provincial responsible for the friary at San Giovanni Rotondo, asking him for an explanation.

Padre Pietro was furious, and wrote back, telling the minister general that the integrity of the friars at San Giovanni was "such as not to leave me a moment's doubt as to even the possibility of a crime of such gravity. The most perfect peace has reigned among them, and the spirit of love renders them incapable of resorting even to an offensive word, let alone the crime of which they are accused, which is as unbelievable as the motive said to cause it is false and stupid.... Is it lawful to defame with impunity people who are far removed from suspicion? I want to know

... the name of the person who with unspeakable cunning and malignity, has the nerve to report ... these deep black lies to vilify my religious! Such information would enable me to force a retraction from this crafty and malevolent liar!"[31]

By this time, Padre Pietro and the Capuchins of San Giovanni had a good idea of the identity of the "crafty and malevolent liar," but knew that they were powerless to force a retraction or to do much of anything about the situation.

Chapter Eighteen

The Transfer That Never Happened

Exit Padre Benedetto

In the meantime, the Holy Office, not quite satisfied with the provincial's refutation of the charges by Archbishop Gagliardi of mismanagement and misconduct, sent Padre Celestino of Desio, superior of the Capuchin missionaries to the Orient, to undertake an investigation of the convent at San Giovanni Rotondo. Padre Celestino agreed with Padre Pietro that the Capuchins there were "purely victims of the envy of certain ill-intentioned people who looked unfavorably on so much good these religious were doing, and to stop their activities these people amused themselves by inventing false things." The friars there, Padre Celestino concluded, were "the cream of the crop of the monastic province of Sant'Angelo." There had been no fighting among them. Padre Celestino even consulted the police, who assured him that they had never been called to break up a disturbance at the monastery. Moreover, no priest had spent the night in a woman's home, as Gagliardi had claimed. Occasionally, a friar had permission to spend the night at the home of another priest or of a family member, but everything was legitimate. When, however, the Holy Office asked Gagliardi to explain his charges, the archbishop insisted that the events happened just as he described them and named Padre Palladino (who later said he had been ordered to lie about Padre Pio) as his source of information.[1]

Meanwhile, Cardinal Merry Del Val, head of the Holy Office, along with his aides, was studying Padre Pio's case. He heard favorable testimony from Cardinal Gasparri, the papal secretary of state, and from Cardinal Silj, the prefect of the Supreme Tribunal of the Holy See. Bishops Costa and Valbonesi also spoke on behalf of the stigmatized Capuchin, while Gagliardi continued to attack him. The Holy Office found no evidence of misconduct on the part of Padre Pio, but they were concerned about the fanatical crowds who mobbed "their" "holy man" and snipped off pieces of his clothing, treating him like a star of the emerging film industry. The Holy Office therefore directed that Padre Pio say his daily Mass, preferably in a private chapel, at different hours which were not to be disclosed in advance to the public. Padre Pio was not to bless the crowds from a window in the monastery, as had become his custom. Not only was he forbidden to show the stigmata to visitors, he was not even to speak of the wounds. Furthermore, the Capuchin was not to answer letters from "devout people seeking counsel, graces, and other things." Although Rossi's warning about the danger of a popular uprising put such plans on hold for the time being, it was suggested that Padre Pio take the initiative to ask for a transfer to another friary.

For Padre Pio, the most devastating provision of the Holy Office in 1922 addressed Bishop Rossi's misgivings about Padre Benedetto. It was agreed that "under the pretense of zeal" Padre Benedetto had been, in fact, sowing "spiritual confusion." From now on, the Holy Office insisted that Padre Pio's spiritual adviser had to be "someone other than Padre Benedetto." The two priests were absolutely forbidden to communicate — and never saw each other again or had contact in any other way until Padre Benedetto's death twenty years later. From then on, Padre Pio would never have another spiritual director.

According to Padre Agostino, Padre Benedetto never uttered a word of complaint. Over the years, he frequently passed through San Giovanni by car or bus (as his home and family were in nearby San Marco in Lamis), and when he did, he greeted Padre Pio mentally, but never tried to see him. Then, when Padre Benedetto was dying, in 1942, at the friary at San Severo, his superior asked if he would like him to send for Padre Pio. "No, it's not necessary," Padre Benedetto insisted. "He is here beside me."[2] Evidently, the Holy Office's prohibition could not exclude appearances through bilocation!

According to Padre Agostino, who was Padre Pio's confessor but never took the place of Padre Benedetto as his spiritual adviser, Padre Pio "submitted to the disposition with holy resignation." However, around this time, Padre Pio wrote to Fra Emmanuele of San Marco la Catola: "I am going through a period of unending trials that are indescribable. I need help. Hold me up in your prayers and tell Jesus to … make me die soon, because I'm now tired of living and fighting."[3]

Was Padre Pio Defying the Holy Office?

In and around San Giovanni Rotondo, people were aware that the Holy Office wanted to take their beloved "saint" away from them. It was like removing a sports superstar from a city that adored him. In fact, it was worse, because Padre Pio's devotees were ready to fight — even to kill — to keep the "holy man" they regarded as their personal property. During the summer of 1922, the mayor presented the superior of the friary a petition with nearly three thousand signatures, opposing Padre Pio's removal. Although certain members of the Holy Office were in favor of proceeding quickly with the transfer, Padre Pio's superiors warned that such a move, far from solving any difficulty, would provoke "dangerous reactions" by the local people, who "always talk about their hatchets," which many of them were brandishing.[4]

In February 1923, the Holy Office dispatched Padre Lorenzo of San Basilio to San Giovanni to make yet another investigation. His report was critical of Padre Pio, who, despite an "explicit and formal and categorical" prohibition, was still answering some letters, and who had not complied with the request of the Holy Office to seek a transfer. Padre Lorenzo, particularly, was incensed at the provincial, Padre Pietro, for encouraging the petition. He complained in his report:

> What wonder is it if the measures of the Holy Office have not had their desired effect, and instead, things at San Giovanni Rotondo have gone from bad to worse? Padre Pio's presence, his uninterrupted letter correspondence, and the petition-protests have increased the enthusiasm of the people and in consequence have created new and more serious obstacles for the Authority.... If you combine the total failure to implement the orders of the Holy Office with the interest of those who are very devoted to Padre Pio and the community of Capuchins at San Giovanni Rotondo, then you have a complete picture of the factors that have made any remedy ineffective up to this point. If the orders already given by the Holy Office had been punctually executed, peace would have returned to San Giovanni Rotondo by this time, Padre Pio would be living quietly in some private monastery, and no one would be taking any interest in him.

Padre Lorenzo of San Basilio urged that the Holy Office issue a reprimand to Padre Pio for continuing his correspondence, and to the superior of the friary, as well as the father provincial, for permitting him to do so. Padre Pio was to stop writing letters "absolutely, wholly, and promptly," and was also to make a formal request for his own transfer.[5]

The Holy Office did not go nearly as far as Padre Lorenzo desired, but the provincial superior, Pietro of Ischitella, was summoned to Rome for questioning under oath. He told Padre Giovanni Lottini, commissioner of the congregation, that Padre Pio had not requested a transfer because he did not know that the Holy Office wanted him to do so. Padre Pietro took responsibility for not informing Padre Pio, because "no one expressed that desire to me" and also because he felt that a transfer was the provincial's decision to make. As for Padre Pio's correspondence, Padre Pietro told the commissioner, "I watched over Padre Pio's correspondence to make sure it happened more rarely; I ordered that all his letters be turned over to the superior and that he limit himself to purely necessary letters and write them in a generic and brief manner." In other words, Padre Pietro thought that, as provincial, he had more discretion in the matter than it turned out that the Holy Office wanted to allow him. At any rate, the result was that the "rebuke" of the Holy Office was directed to the provincial, and not Padre Pio.[6]

The Declaration of the Holy Office

In May 1923, the Holy Office issued a formal declaration, published in *The Acts of the Holy See*, which ordered Padre Pio to celebrate Mass only in private and not to answer letters. Moreover, it asserted, "Now that the Holy See has examined the facts in connection with Padre Pio, the Sacred Congregation ... does not declare a finding that the events mentioned have a supernatural character and thus exhorts the faithful to conform their conduct according to this declaration."[7] The abstruse and nebulous declaration said only that the supernatural nature of the events associated with Padre Pio could not be proven. It did not say that the Holy Office was denying that "the facts in connection with Padre Pio" were genuine, although some people interpreted it that way.

When the Holy Office was convinced that any mystical phenomena it investigated were not authentic, it issued clear and unambiguous declarations to that effect and took drastic actions. For example, just a month before, the Holy Office had passed judgment on another stigmatic, forty-eight-year-old Sister Anna Maria Maddalena, of the Augustinian Oblate Sisters, in the Monastery of Holy Mary of the Seven Sorrows in Rome. It was declared that "there is no aura that is supernatural or divine. The spirit of God does not dwell in them [her stigmata]." A year later the Holy Office announced, "The facts do not demonstrate any supernatural character; that this person should be removed far from Rome and never be received into any monastery, but should be treated and cared for like any other unfortunate sick person."[8] The same year, the Holy Office issued a declaration concerning a twenty-eight-year-old woman named Lina Salvagnini, who also supposedly had the stigmata. After investigating her, the Holy Office declared "that the facts about Salvagnini do not demonstrate any supernatural character [and] deplores that people, including ecclesiastics, should have let themselves be deceived." Salvignini was excommunicated, and the priests who supported her were suspended from their duties.[9] In Padre Pio's case, the Holy Office was not so much concerned about him personally as it was about the unruly and fanatical groupies who created a disorderly atmosphere around him, and the declaration was issued in hopes of restraining them. With regard to the stigmata and the reported mystical phenomena, the Holy Office was unwilling or unable to make a judgment.

The Sangiovannese Hold a Demonstration

Before the declaration was officially proclaimed, Archbishop Gagliardi, returning from Rome, announced its contents publicly, and Padre Pio's supporters formed a People's Association to resist any attempt to transfer him. On the morning of June 25, Padre Ignazio of Jelsi, the father superior, announced that from now on Padre Pio had to celebrate Mass in private. Francesco Morcaldi, the mayor, wrote in his diary:

> Padre Pio did not come to the church. He has received the order to celebrate Holy Mass behind closed doors in the inner chapel of the friary, without anyone assisting him. The faithful, who saw his usual assistant [Emmanuele Brunatto] come into the church alone with his eyes filled with tears, came at once to understand the order of segregation.[10]

Immediately, the People's Association vowed to resist any attempt to transfer him. A crowd of three thousand men and women — some estimated the number at five thousand — gathered in the town square, and, led by Morcaldi, marched up the hill to the friary, where they commanded Padre Ignazio to revoke the dispositions. From the convent, the friars watched in amazement a sea of torches that stretched more than a half mile down the road, accompanied by the municipal band, following the mayor and a group of local officials who pounded on the friary door. Presently, Padre Ignazio appeared, with Padre Pio, "with a waxen face and his eyes lowered and swollen with tears," beside him. Morcaldi demanded that the superior permit Padre Pio once more to celebrate Mass in public. "If you don't," he threatened, "I will resign as mayor and fight as an ordinary citizen in the riot that will ensue."

When the superior failed to give in, the throng returned to town and attacked the homes of Don Palladino and Don Prencipe, who were known to be friends of the archbishop and hostile to Padre Pio. It was only with difficulty that the mayor kept the mob from burning the houses to the ground and lynching the offending priests.

Padre Ignazio then telegraphed the provincial, Padre Pietro: "Today I carried out the order not to let [Padre Pio] celebrate Mass in public. This evening, because of an impressively enormous public demonstration, it has become impossible to comply. Afraid of encountering the fanaticism of an entire citizenry who are disposed to undertake all manner of violent measures, I am forced to suspend the measures again."[11]

The association sent a delegation to the archbishop, who smiled and told them: "I'll do everything possible to prevent the removal of Padre Pio. Since, however, such measures don't come from my initiative, I'll send my secretary to Rome at once to plead the cause of the People's Association to the Minister General of the Capuchins." However, as they were leaving, Gagliardi was heard mumbling to an aide, "The next time these Sangiovannese come here, I'll call the police!"

Gagliardi then wrote an indignant letter to Morcaldi, with a copy sent to Archpriest Don Prencipe. In it, the archbishop said: "Let me repeat, neither I nor the local priests have ever requested the removal of Padre Pio from here. Such an allegation is unfounded. It is slanderous of you to make such an imputation!" Along with the copy to Prencipe, he included a note to the archpriest in which he acknowledged that he knew that Rome was planning to remove Padre Pio, to keep people from being hurt by all the fanatics.[12]

Padre Pio's Supporters Go to Rome

In the meantime, Morcaldi, Brunatto, and Don Giuseppe Orlando headed to Rome. Brunatto sought out Padre Gemelli, taking him to task for telling everyone, including the pope, that he had examined Padre Pio's stigmata, reminding him that he had been present during the visit and could attest to the fact that there had been no examination of the Capuchin's wounds. Gemelli dismissed Brunatto with contempt. "The magnificent rector warned me of the risks to which I was exposing myself in challenging a man of his stature," Brunatto recalled. When Brunatto continued to try to argue with him, Padre Gemelli ordered him to leave, threatening, "I'll have you destroyed!" "Thank you for your Franciscan advice," Brunatto answered, and left.[13]

Morcaldi called on Cardinal Donato Sbarretti (1856–1939), prefect of the Sacred Congregation of the Council, which oversaw, among other things, the discipline of the clergy. The mayor told the cardinal: "If Padre Pio had to leave San Giovanni Rotondo for a just reason, we would accompany him from town with music and banners. But if he must leave as one guilty of a crime, at the instigation of an immoral, belligerent, and dishonest clergy who would continue to corrupt our population after banishing a holy priest with ignominy, then, Your Eminence, I will throw away [the insignia of my office] and, in order to take Padre Pio away, you will have to trample on our dead bodies!"[14] In the face of this emotional appeal, the cardinal was noncommittal.

Morcaldi then obtained an appointment with Cardinal Gasparri. The secretary of state was, as usual, supportive, but said that he was not in a position to be of help, since the restrictions came though the Holy Office, with which he had nothing to do.

Marquess Don Giuseppe Orlando approached Padre Giovanni Lottini (1860–1951), the commissioner of the Holy Office, who impressed him as a rather intimidating presence, with "Napoleonic" eyes. Padre Lottini told him that Gagliardi had written a "detailed report" about Padre Pio, attributing the stigmata to "fakery and fanaticism." The archbishop had gone so far as to declare, "Either Padre Pio goes, or I go!"

The commissioner explained to Orlando that his chief concern was Padre Pio's alleged disobedience. "We sent him the order," Padre Lottini said, "calling him under obedience to be transferred.... Instead of obeying, [he] has, by means of the fanatic women who surround him, fostered demonstrations of such magnitude as to put not only the town, but even the civil and military authorities, into confusion."

Orlando told the commissioner that he would go in person to Padre Pio to verify the truth of these accusations. Padre Lottini agreed. "Go on then," he said. "Swear here upon this missal." Orlando knelt, kissed Padre Lottini's right hand, and swore upon the missal that he would question Padre Pio and accurately report his response.

"If My Superiors Ordered Me to Jump Out of the Window ... "

Back at San Giovanni Rotondo, Orlando told Padre Pio about the conversation with the commissioner. "They are accusing you of all kinds of things," he told the Capuchin, "but, most of all, they say that you are disobedient to the orders of your superiors who have imposed upon you the obedience to leave this place."

Immediately Padre Pio dropped onto one knee, opened his arms, and declared: "Peppino, I swear to you on this crucifix ... that I never received such an order. If my superiors ordered me to jump out of the window, I would not argue, I would jump!" Orlando at once conveyed this singular response to Padre Lottini.[15] In the meantime, the townspeople were maintaining a round-the-clock guard at the friary in case someone should try to steal their holy friar away in secret. All the while, street vendors continued to hawk "relics" and crudely painted pictures. From his window, Padre Pio could hear someone bellowing, "Padre Pio for two cents! Padre Pio for two cents!" He turned to another friar and remarked, "The guardian might hold me in great esteem, but, instead — look at this! Padre Pio is worth two cents!"[16]

Brunatto, upon his return from Rome, bitterly execrated Padre Gemelli, Gagliardi, and other Church officials, only to have Padre Pio rebuke him: "You did a wicked thing! We must respect the decrees of the Church. We must be silent and suffer."[17] To Morcaldi, who also angrily reviled the Church, Padre Pio said: "We must beware of putting ourselves against our Mother.... Sweet is the hand of the Church, even when it batters us."[18]

Late in July 1923, the minister general, Padre Giuseppe Antonio, summoned the definitor of the province, Padre Luigi, telling him that he had at last made a firm decision to transfer Padre Pio to the province of Ancona, about two hundred miles north, up the eastern coast of Italy. The provincial there was considering placing Padre Pio in a monastery in the town of Cingoli. Padre Giuseppe Antonio wanted Padre Luigi to go to Padre Pio to "receive his obedience" to go wherever he might be sent.

On August 7, Padre Luigi arrived at San Giovanni. Although it was midnight, he went into Padre Pio's room and read him the order from the minister general. Padre Pio bowed his head, crossed his arms on his chest, and replied: "I'm at your disposal. Let's depart at once. When I am with my superior, I am with God."

"You mean you want to come with me at once? Now?" asked Padre Luigi, incredulous. "Why, it's the middle of the night! Where would we go?"

"I don't know," responded Padre Pio. "I only know that I am going with you, when and where you wish."

"All I have is the order to communicate the obedience to you," said the startled Padre Luigi. "It will be carried out when I receive further instructions from Rome."[19]

Threats of Bloodshed

Meanwhile, the minister general was having second thoughts about sending Padre Pio to the province of Ancona. The minister provincial there had informed him, "Ancona is not a place suitable for saints." Giuseppe Antonio began weighing the possibility of sending Padre Pio to Spain, or even America. Before he had a chance to make a final decision, however, the minister general received a report from Dr. Carmelo Camilleri, whom he had sent to San Giovanni to discuss the possibility of moving Padre Pio with the police commissioner there. Camilleri had been told that the only people in the area of San Giovanni who were really opposed to Padre Pio were Gagliardi, the secular clergy, and the Franciscan Observants of the friary of San Matteo in San Marco in Lamis. Moreover, the police commissioner warned Camilleri that Padre Pio could be taken away only by force, with the certainty of a bloodbath.[20]

This became all too evident on August 10, during Vespers. Padre Pio was about to bless the faithful from the altar during Benediction. As the priest was about to place a Host in the monstrance, a man, identified only as "Donato," a bricklayer, lunged forward and, brandishing a pistol, leveled it at Padre Pio's head. "Either dead or alive," he shouted, "you're going to stay with us in this town!"[21] The would-be-assassin was quickly wrestled to the ground by the policemen who were standing close at hand before he could discharge his weapon, but the incident underscored the explosive nature of the situation.

Expecting to be killed, Padre Pio wrote a memorandum that night: "Lord, what do these people want of me? ... Tomorrow may bring I don't know what.... After this, I have good reason to expect a fatal outcome, knowing the intentions of these dear and beloved people of San Giovanni Rotondo to have me with them, if not alive, at least dead." Even so, he wanted his assassins pardoned. "I don't want a hair touched on my behalf ... no matter whose ... I have always loved everyone. I have always pardoned, and I do not wish to descend to my grave without having pardoned whoever wants to end my days."[22]

On August 12, Padre Pio wrote Morcaldi:

The events that have happened in recent days have profoundly disturbed me and worried me immensely, because they make me afraid that I could be the unwilling cause of disastrous developments for this dear town of mine. I pray that God will prevent such a misfortune.... But if, as I have been informed, my transfer has been decided upon, I beg you use every means to ensure compliance with the will of the superiors, which is the will of God, and to which I will blindly obey.

I will always remember these kind people in my poor prayers, asking for peace and prosperity for them, and, as a sign of my love, since I am not able to do anything else, I express the wish that, if my superiors do not oppose it, my bones might rest in a tranquil corner of this land.[23]

On August 27, Padre Pio wrote a long letter to the provincial secretary and definitor, Padre Luigi, in which he explained:

I think that there is no need to tell you how, I, thank God, am disposed to obey whatever order of which I am informed by my superiors. Their voice is for me that of God, to whom I wish to keep faith unto death, and, with his help, obey whatsoever command, however painful, that might add to my misery.

But, if by order of the superior I have to leave this convent, I predict with complete certainty that, if God does not intervene, directly and miraculously, terrible things are going to happen to the priests, my brothers, and the churches, as now these people, excited, menacing, and prepared, are not heeding my words nor those of my confreres.

Furthermore, my life is in serious danger, and these are not vain threats. My fear is all too well-founded by the events of two weeks ago, well known to you, when, right in church, somebody (and he wasn't even from San Giovanni but from San Marco) pulled out a gun and pointed it at me while I was making the novena of Our Lady of Grace in front of the exposition of the Most Holy Sacrament, yelling, "Better dead among us than alive with others!" And this was because the rumor had spread that I wanted to leave. Please, therefore, consider this precedent that clearly shows that this is not a matter of idle fears, but of very serious threats that, except for a miracle, will certainly be carried out. I offered my life to the Lord a long time ago, and I don't care. In fact, my desire would be to go at once to God. I cannot wish, however, to present my spirit at his judgment seat to answer for the blood of others.

The clergy here, at least on the surface, aren't taking any responsibility whatsoever, nor do the other authorities (which confirms what everybody around here predicts concerning the calamities that are going to happen). And I alone, the principal actor, of this drama even though I am passive, have to bear such responsibility on my part and for the people. What might result from my silence? This would be interpreted as a sign that I know nothing of the seriousness of the threats, or else it would indicate that I give it no credence, dismissing it as a case of the exaggeration of excited minds.

I don't know what measures could be taken to ensure public safety, because nothing bad has happened. But the moment it does happen, it would be vain to hope [that anything could then be done]. It is certain to me and to whoever knows this area, [intervention by force] wouldn't be sufficient — not even a state of prolonged siege — to prevent terrible, bloody retaliation. You better than I know the religious passions of this people. Who could be persuaded that these are just idle threats, from these people, whose instincts are both passionate and primitive?

I have laid bare the state of my soul in this my dark, clouded hours. I have always, thank God, obeyed, and I want always to obey, but I have the duty of conscience to ask you to put me in a situation where my soul is not burdened with the responsibility for the bloodshed that would occur because of my obedience, and of the judicial and criminal responsibility.[24]

Pope Pius XI had asked the minister general of the Capuchins to ask help from the civil authorities to carry out the transfer. However, the prefect of Foggia warned the minister general that because of the people who "venerate Padre Pio to the point of fanaticism," "drastic measures" would have to be taken to keep public order to carry out the transfer, and for that reason was unwilling to intervene.[25] The minister general approached the minister of the interior, but also without success. Then, on July 4, the Holy Office decided to postpone the transfer of Padre Pio.

There is an apocryphal story, circulated in the 1940s by Countess Virginia Silj-Salviucci, sister of Cardinal Silj, that the pope was about to suspend Padre Pio from all his priestly functions when the Capuchin appeared to him in bilocation, but there is no contemporary record of this. It seems clear that it was because of concerns about violence that Padre Pio was allowed, at least for the time being, to remain in San Giovanni Rotondo.

Pope Pius XI, however, was annoyed at Archbishop Gagliardi for hurting the chances for a peaceful transfer of Padre Pio, and directed the Holy Office to warn him: "Having come to the notice of the Sacred Congregation that in his return from Rome [Gagliardi] had revealed to some people that the Holy See issued measures against Padre Pio, and that news, when brought to San Giovanni Rotondo, agitated Padre Pio's proponents, if this is true, as it seems, then this Holy Office exhorts him to be more cautious in talking about Padre Pio, so as not to meddle in the work of the Holy See in regard to the aforementioned priest."

The archbishop admitted that he was wrong and promised to be more cautious in the future.[26]

Chapter Nineteen

Remarkable Providences

Eyes of a Beauty That Dazzled

Padre Pio was shaken and dismayed by all the unrest that swirled around him, from the hostility of the archbishop and the local priests to the violent fanaticism of many of his followers. He had written to Bishop Costa, "At present I'm passing through a period of continuous mortification.... Pray to the Lord that ... he may free me immediately from this harsh prison and from this body of death, calling me to himself. I definitely can't stand this any longer!"[1]

In his mid-thirties, Padre Pio had lost the sickly, emaciated appearance of his early years at San Giovanni Rotondo and his frame began to take on a more robust appearance. A newspaper reporter remarked during this period that there was a dissimilarity between his actual appearance and the unflattering portraits of him that were being sold all over the south of Italy. Padre Pio, the reporter wrote, was "a beautiful young man" with dark blond hair and beard, now liberally shot with grey. He wore a "meek and serene" expression and spoke in a voice of unusual sweetness, "which implants itself in the soul as soon as it is heard, and is never forgotten."[2] Other visitors noted his pale, rosy-hued complexion, his bright, penetrating eyes, and his radiant smile. A priest who knew him well wrote that he did not like to look into Padre Pio's eyes, because "his eyes were too beautiful — of a beauty that dazzled."[3] Emmanuele Brunatto, however, observed Padre Pio in a way that would have surprised those who thought of him as a severe, otherworldly ascetic with little interest in earthly affairs: playing the game of *bocce* with his fellow friars, during recreation in the monastery courtyard, yelling if he missed a shot and cheering if he won, picking up "those wooden balls soiled with dirt in hands covered by fingerless gloves, under which the wounds of Christ are bleeding."[4]

The Healing of a South American Nun

There were a number of remarkable cures attributed to Padre Pio's prayers. Sister

Teresa Salvadores, superior of the Escuela Taller Medalla Milagrosa in Reducto, a suburb of Montevideo, Uruguay, was bedridden at age fifty-eight in 1921. According to her physician, Juan Morelli, she suffered from gastric disorders, characterized by heartburn and pain, and pains in the region of the heart, accompanied by a sense of distress, oppression, and imminent death. She had a large lump in her side. X-rays failed to find the cause of her abdominal problems, although one of her physicians, Dr. Canzani, suspected cancer. Tests did reveal a definite abnormality in Sister Teresa's aorta, called "Coeur en Sabot."[5] The nun was put on a diet of milk and vegetables, given medicine, and told to rest. Her condition, however, continued to deteriorate. Suffering from extreme pain, weakness, and vertigo, she was unable to leave her bed after October 1921. She later wrote:

> The month of November 1921 arrived. My sisters, distressed as never before, having heard people talk about Padre Pio and the miraculous things that happened through him, told me that they were recommending me to him and would write him, asking for my cure. I consented. On December 24 I declared that now my last hour had come and I did not want any more injections. I begged them to leave me in peace and not to torment me any more (according to calculations this was the very time that Padre Pio received the letter written by my sisters). December 31, 1921, came. Among those who came to see me that morning was Signora Estela Martinez, of the family of Monsignor Damiani, Vicar of the Diocese of Salto. She told me that her relative, Monsignor Damiani, had recently arrived from Italy and carried with him a glove used by Padre Pio, and, if I consented, they would be able to apply it to the parts of my body that hurt. The glove was applied to my side where I had a large swelling, the size of a fist, and to my throat, where I felt a sense of suffocation. At last, moved to tears … I fell asleep, and in a dream I saw Padre Pio, who touched my side in the place where it hurt and blew into my mouth and spoke to me of such things that were not of this earth.[6]

According to her physician, Dr. Morelli, Sister Teresa did not recognize the man in her dream as Padre Pio at first. She identified him simply as a Capuchin with a reddish-brown beard and a very sweet expression, noting, "At that time she still would not yet have seen any print or picture whatsoever of Padre Pio. After she became better, she saw a drawing of a picture of Padre Pio and she said it was the same one she saw in her dream."[7]

When Sister Teresa awoke after three hours, she called out, "What time is it?"

"It is seven o'clock, Sister," replied the nun who was watching her.

"Look for my habit," Sister Teresa said.

"What are you going to do?"

"I'm going to get dressed and visit the college."

The other sister thought she was delirious and tried to calm her, but Teresa insisted that she was cured and wanted to go to the chapel in the college to thank God — and she did. At noon, she went into the dining hall and asked, "What's to eat? I'm very hungry," and sat down and ate more than anyone else.[8]

She went to Dr. Morelli, exclaiming that she had experienced a "miracle." He ran another series of tests and found that the abnormality in her aorta, which had been the cause of her pain, weakness, and shortness of breath, was still there, unchanged. Yet, three years later, Sister Teresa was still in excellent health, able to work long hours "without a sign of fatigue." She had no pain, was able to climb tall flights of stairs (now in her early sixties) without shortness of breath, run her school, visit the poor, and attend to "hundreds" of other duties.[9]

Writing in January 1925, Morelli noted: "Because of the persistence of the lesion, I would refuse to issue a certificate asserting that the cure of the Sister was supernatural." However, he admitted that "the rapid disappearance of the sufferings that were in logical relation to the cardio aortic lesion seems to me a very interesting fact." He went on to say that "even though the ... lesion persists, the sudden disappearance of the grim effects connected with the symptoms of steno cardiac problems that had already for so long held the poor sick woman in the grip of mortal agony" was something that "deserves study and consideration.... This sudden and lasting disappearance, in evident contrast with the persistence of the lesions which caused the symptoms" [was] "inexplicable."[10] He said nothing about the lump in Teresa's side. (No record has come to light as to how and when she eventually died.)

The healing of Sister Teresa Salvadores is typical of many cures wrought through the prayers of Padre Pio, in which the sufferer was relieved, for long periods of time, from the pain and incapacity of a disease that *clinically* remained unchanged.

The Healing of Maria Giuliani Cozzi

Maria Giuliani Cozzi worked as a maid in Florence. In early 1919, when she was fifty-six, her tongue began to hurt. In August, her employer, whose name was Boldrini, took a look and found it "horribly covered with a fungus." Cozzi was in great pain and could not chew. Hospitalized there in Florence, she was examined by several doctors who determined that she had cancer of the tongue, and that she needed surgery to remove part of it. Although Cozzi was told that she would be cured by "a simple cut," the surgeons told her employer that they had little hope of stopping the spread of the cancer. Nevertheless, the surgery was set for August 21, 1919, at the Hospital of Santa Maria Novella, and Boldrini gave Cozzi a picture of Padre Pio and urged her to pray to God "to obtain the grace through the merits of this religious famed for his holy stigmata."

Before the surgeons could operate, several teeth had to be extracted. However, when the dental surgeon examined the patient's mouth, he was surprised, because "the tongue was perfectly healthy." When the surgeon who was to do the operation looked at her mouth, he saw no evidence of cancer or any other disease. He canceled the surgery and discharged Cozzi.

A year later, Cozzi, who had been in perfect health, gave her picture of Padre Pio (which she said gave forth "a very sweet odor") to a sick friend, and then felt that the cancer was returning, and asked for it back and felt well again.

Three years later, Boldrini (the employer) wrote to Santa Maria Novella for Cozzi's medical records, but was refused on grounds that the hospital was not obliged to release them. He contacted one of the doctors in her case, who insisted, "It's not a miracle. It's not rare for apparent cancers to disappear all of a sudden." Boldrini retorted, "I don't know anything about medicine, but I know that even a boil could not pass instantly from a tumescent state into a perfect scar."[11] Reportedly, Cozzi was alive and well more than ten years after her cure. It will be recalled that her cure was noted by Rossi in his report in 1921.

One could argue that Cozzi's problem was that of a fungus, as first suspected, and not a cancer. What seems miraculous is that an observable mass, whether fungus, boil, or cancer, instantly, or within a very short period of time, vanished, to be replaced by a perfectly healed scar.

The Healing of Paolina Preziosi

Paolina Preziosi, who apparently lived in or near San Giovanni Rotondo, was a young married woman with five young children who was a very devout member of the Franciscan Third Order (for laity). In early 1925, she developed a severe case of pneumonia, and all treatment proved unsuccessful. When relatives went to Padre Pio to ask him to intercede with God for Preziosi's life, it was Good Friday. "Tell her to have no fear," he told them, "since she will be resurrected with Our Lord."

That night Preziosi was praying to God to heal her for the sake of her little children when suddenly she looked up, and there was Padre Pio. "Have no fear," he told her. "Tomorrow, when the bells ring, you will be cured." Immediately, Preziosi fell into a coma. Her family, giving up hope, spent the next day making preparations for the funeral, preparing the Franciscan habit in which Franciscan tertiaries were often buried. Then, at the very stroke of midnight, as the bells of Easter began to ring out, proclaiming the resurrection of Christ, Preziosi suddenly opened her eyes and jumped out of bed "as if she had been pushed by a superhuman force." From that moment, she was perfectly well.[12] Even before antibiotics, which weren't available until the 1940s, people often recovered from pneumonia. What seems "miraculous" in this case, however, was the fact that it did so suddenly and precisely when Padre Pio said it was going to; and, of course, the fact the patient saw Padre Pio, even though he had not left his monastery.

Exorcism of Demons

Although the demonic attacks Padre Pio experienced in the early years of his priesthood had not occurred in more than five years, according to his testimony to Bishop Rossi in 1921 and also according to Padre Agostino's observations in his diary, he still had to confront the powers of hell in persons who showed signs of demon possession.

Monsignor George Pogany (1912–1993), a native of Hungary, who lived in San Giovanni Rotondo from 1940 to 1957 and assisted Padre Pio with his correspondence, recalled in 1989: "This is what I heard from Padre Pio's own mouth. He was hearing confessions in the sacristy, shortly after he received the stigmata. There was at that time a swinging door. It was noon and the people went home to dinner and the friars closed the church. Still there remained one woman. Padre Pio heard the confession of the woman in the sacristy. He told me, 'I gave her advice and I was about to give the absolution, but when I went to say the first words, *Ego te*, the woman sprang up, gave a cavernous cry, and disappeared. I was frightened. I went to the door. It was swinging." Padre Pio continued: "Padre Ignazio [the superior] was there and I asked, 'Did you see someone go out from the church?' Padre Ignazio answered, 'No, nobody.' I don't know what that woman was. Maybe it was the devil, trying to play a trick on me." Monsignor Pogany declared, "He himself told me this."[13]

Pogany recalled that "many crazy people" would come to San Giovanni Rotondo, and many were disruptive. Father John Schug (1928–2002), when he interviewed the older friars at San Giovanni a few years after Pio's death, was told of one woman who seemed more than just mentally disturbed. Her face was so hideously contorted, and she had such an uncanny light in her eyes, that people began to flee in terror. "I'm the owner of this church!" she screamed. "I'm the only person who gives orders here!" Approaching a picture of Saint Michael the Archangel, who cast Satan from heaven, she began to rave, "You didn't win! I won!"

Padre Pio was in the sacristy, hearing the confessions of men, when he heard the commotion and went into the church. The sacristan urged him not to, saying: "Don't go! There's a possessed woman out there!"

"Don't be afraid," Padre Pio answered. "Since when were we afraid of the devil?"

Walking up to the raving woman, who was "crouching like a tigress" beside one of the women's confessionals, Padre Pio ordered her, "Get away from there!"

The "tigress," seemingly transformed into a kitten, began to plead, "Please don't send me away! Please don't send me away!"

"All right, go away till I finish hearing confessions. Then come back."

When he finished the men's confessions, Padre Pio went back into the church and found the woman sitting quietly. He led her to one of the confessional booths. When she left, "her face was like that of an angel."[14]

Padre Alberto D'Apolito, as an altar boy at fourteen, witnessed an exorcism conducted by Padre Pio on a Sunday afternoon in May 1922:

> After Vespers and Benediction … we returned to the sacristy, where we found a possessed woman, who, upon seeing Padre Pio, began to scream and curse. Padre Pio, impassive and serene, took the book in his hands and began the exorcisms amidst the screams, the curses, and the foul words of the possessed woman. Suddenly she gave forth a very loud scream, and, by an invisible force, was raised in the air to the height of three feet. At that moment, everyone began to run with fear. Padre Pio, without getting upset, continued the exorcisms with faith and energy, in a ruthless struggle with the devil, who, finally vanquished, freed the woman.[15]

"I Know You Inside and Out … Like You Know Yourself"

Far more than for the frequent accounts of physical healings and occasional exorcisms, Padre Pio, by the early 1920s, was renowned for the healing of souls and the conquest of psychological and spiritual demons through the Sacrament of Penance. For most people, he was simply a wise confessor, but then there were those cases in which he claimed to receive supernatural enlightenment, as in the case when he told one penitent, "I know you inside and out, like you know yourself."[16]

It would be interesting to know the percentage of his confessions in which he was "illuminated," but it was probably comparatively small. Even so, it would have involved, over a period of years, hundreds of people. According to some, when Padre Pio was not enlightened, his confessions could be extremely brief — only two or three minutes. However, when he was "illuminated," he seems to have devoted a great deal of time to the penitent concerned, and, consequently, his time in the confessional during the course of a day, in his younger years, could very well have been at times twelve hours or more. Sometimes he would meet with men in his living quarters, and frequently he would speak to women seated in a little room adjoining the parlor or guest room of the friary, speaking to the penitent through a window that connected the two rooms. (This would later cause problems.) Day after day, week after week, month after month, year after year, according to Eusebio: "The rhythm of Padre Pio's day flowed with an obsessive monotony: always the same things at the same hour, in the same way. Never an exception, never a vacation."[17]

Padre Eusebio wrote: "Absolution depended on the recognition of being wrong, having transgressed the commandments of the Lord, and repentance, not just out of fear of hell, but for having offended an infinitely good Father who had sent Jesus to die for us." If the person did not display true penitence, Padre Pio might refuse absolution, insisting, "My son [or my daughter], convert yourself. If only you knew how much blood you cost me."[18]

Padre Pio became notorious for his "gruffness" in the confessional — not surprising considering the hours he spent daily hearing confessions. Reports of harsh remarks and occasional refusals to grant absolution gave Archbishop Gagliardi an excuse for denouncing the Capuchin's "horrible way of hearing confessions." It seems clear that at times Padre Pio did, in fact, lose his temper. In June 1920, he had written to Padre Benedetto: "My only regret is that, involuntarily and unwittingly, I sometimes raise my voice when correcting people. I realize that this is a shameful weakness, but how can I prevent it, if it happens without my being aware of it? Although I pray and groan and complain to Our Lord about it, he has not yet heard me fully. Moreover, in spite of all my watchfulness, I sometimes do what I really detest and want to avoid."[19] Padre Benedetto had told him not to worry about the outbursts. "If the Lord doesn't give you the grace of inexhaustible and continual gentleness, it is in order to leave you a means to practice holy humility."[20] On another occasion, Padre Pio blamed his "fits of temper" in the confessional on overwork and the sight of so many hardened and unrepentant sinners. He thought, at least at times, however, that his own anger might have been a reflection of God's indignation.[21]

Indeed, when Padre Pio denied absolution, he always insisted that the person return when he or she was ready to make a sincere effort to express remorse for sin. Father Schug was told: "So many people would come here for confession and Padre Pio would send them away. But he would torment them with remorse and he would follow them with his prayers and sufferings. Ultimately, they would return, fully penitent.... That's why he minced no words. There was no halfway measure with him."[22]

Apparently, the vast majority of people rebuked and dismissed by Padre Pio returned to him sufficiently penitent and received absolution. There were, however, exceptions. They were apparently very rare, but they happened. One lady told of an uncle, incurably ill, who tried to make his confession to Padre Pio, only to be sent away, he claimed, without any explanation. He went home in a rage and died embittered a year later. The lady conceded, however, that her uncle was never a sincere believer, had little interest in making a sincere confession, but had gone to Padre Pio only to seek a cure.

The Mass

What most impressed the multitudes who visited San Giovanni was Padre Pio's celebration of the Mass. "You truly saw that God was there," recalled an individual who worshiped at many Masses at which Padre Pio was the celebrant.

John McCaffery, a Scots businessman based in Milan, made many trips to see Padre Pio and described his celebration of the Mass in this way:

> For more than an hour one is held spellbound by the deep intensity with which it is said; not a physical intensity, for his movements are slow and deliberate, his voice full and low-pitched, but an intensity of the spirit wherein we now glimpse a Padre Pio obviously inhabiting a world other than the material world around him; at times in apparent mental converse, through all and above all his evident tremendous consciousness of the significance of his words and actions, and there, clearly revealed, the bleeding perforations in his hands. In a way, when you have seen his Mass, you have seen everything, or at least you fully understand and accept everything.[23]

Andre Mandato recalled: "At the beginning of the Mass, his face was really pale, just as if he were carrying our suffering, our pain, and our sin. After the consecration, his face underwent an amazing change. It seemed to be transfigured with radiant light. From the very first time I went to Padre Pio's Mass, I realized that the Spirit of God was there." During the course of the Mass, Mandato and others sometimes heard Padre Pio speak as if he were addressing invisible beings. "Go away! Go away!" he was heard to say, as if evil spirits were trying to interfere.[24]

Although Padre Pio's Mass often lasted nearly two hours, many commented that when it was concluded, it seemed as if scarcely a half hour had passed.

While many of the reports of Padre Pio's supernatural activity are anecdotal, they are too numerous to be dismissed lightly. There may have been something, in some cases, to Padre Gemelli's speculation that people reported miracles because they were expecting them to happen. Certainly, there must have been exaggeration in some of the stories. However the accounts of healings and exorcisms and supersensible knowledge are explained, it cannot be denied that the effect of these was a significant increase in the faith, hope, and love of those who claimed to experience these graces.

Chapter Twenty

Friends, Family, and American Benefactors

Padre Agostino Comes to San Giovanni

Padre Pietro, the provincial, transferred Padre Agostino to the monastery at San Giovanni Rotondo in 1923, to teach Latin and Greek at the "Seraphic College" and also to compensate Padre Pio for the loss of Padre Benedetto. Writing in his diary, the older priest declared, "It is needless to speak of Padre Pio's joy and mine in our living together."[1] Padre Agostino remained there for two years.

Both men soon discovered, however, that deep as their friendship was, there was no way to replace Padre Benedetto, especially in his capacity as spiritual director. Because of the trauma to which he was subjected, through the investigations and attempts to transfer him and the angry reactions of the populace, Padre Pio found it difficult to talk about his spiritual state, even to Padre Agostino. Although Padre Agostino obtained permission from the provincial for Padre Pio to put down his spiritual reflections in writing, Padre Pio confided to Padre Agostino: "All that remains for me is the sole comfort of at least seeing you and talking to you. If tomorrow someone were to learn that I am writing to you, even with the permission of the provincial, it could happen that they might prohibit even you from coming here, and what a grief that would be for both of us!"[2]

Padre Agostino was aware of Padre Pio's ongoing inability to discern his own spiritual state. Padre Pio often asked, "Father, pray and beg for my conversion," as if he were uncertain of his own salvation. He explained, "In other souls, through the grace of God, I see clearly, but in my own I see nothing but darkness."[3] Only Padre Agostino's assurances, which he made Padre Pio receive under "holy obedience," had a calming effect. Sometimes, Padre Agostino noted, Padre Pio experienced the humiliating ordeal of uttering aloud "something which he neither wants to say nor realizes he is saying."[4] Just what Padre Pio said, Padre Agostino did not record.

Family Affairs

Padre Pio's parents were still living in the old home place in Pietrelcina and working their farm outside town. Michele, upon his return from America, went back to
farming. Padre Pio said of his brother, whom most people now called "Zi' Michele"
— Uncle Michael — "He has hard hands but a tender heart."[5] Relatives remembered
him as "a good man, a beautiful man, a happy man," and "a very holy man, warm,
loving and cheerful." Joseph Peterson, who knew him in later years, recalled, "a
very spiritual man, but a great practical joker. You always had to be on guard when
you were near Michael Forgione." He recalled that Michele was fond — perhaps
to excess — of a drink called *birra pirone* and was a heavy smoker of American
cigarettes. A man who grew up on a farm that adjoined Zi' Michele's recalled: "He
was a nice man, a good man, but once, when I was a boy, I was playing with some
of my friends in the field and trampled some of his wheat, ruining it. He saw us
and ran after us, cursing. He wasn't a saint, because he used to curse and swear
when he was upset!"[6]

Michele's wife, Giuseppa Cardone, had conceived six times, but all her pregnan-
cies but one had ended in miscarriages or with infants who were stillborn or died
shortly after birth. Their only living child, Francesco, or Franceschino, was eleven
years old when he went to bed on the morning of November 9, 1920, with a headache and fever. Michele telegraphed Padre Pio, asking him to pray, only to receive
a response telling him to prepare for the child's death.[7] Before sundown that very
day, little Franceschino was dead from meningitis. The parents and grandparents
were devastated. A month later, at Christmas time, Padre Pio wrote Orazio and
Giuseppa: "What can I say to you on the Feast of the Holy Nativity when every
word I feel dies in me and strangles in my throat? I pray Jesus to comfort you and
give you holy resignation, comforting you with the sweet thought that Franceschino
and the people dear to us who have gone before are in heaven, praying for us and
waiting for us up there. Then, take courage and bless the Lord in sorrow."[8]

Pio assured Franceschino's parents that they would have a child who would
survive. The next year Giuseppa gave birth to another son — but he, alas, was
stillborn. Then, on New Year's Day 1924, Michele and Giuseppa, now in their early
forties, became the parents of a healthy daughter they named Pia — who would
survive them and live to the age of ninety.

Padre Pio, evidently, did not see much of his relatives in person. One time
Brunatto drove to Pietrelcina and brought Giuseppa back to San Giovanni to see her
son, but she was upset because she had no more than five minutes of conversation
with him at a time. "I can't even get to say a word to him," she complained. After
another visit, she declared: "I was there for twenty days and still was not able to
have a single word with Padre Pio. Holy Mary, why does he act that way? He doesn't
even let me kiss his hand."[9] It was the custom in southern Italy for people to kiss

the hands of a priest — even if he was their son. Padre Pio, however, insisted that it was the duty of the son, whatever his position in life, to kiss the hand of the parent.

It is not clear why Padre Pio failed to spend much time with his mother, whom he deeply loved — especially when he regularly spoke at length to his spiritual daughters. Perhaps the reason was that he did not feel that God had enlightened him about his mother's soul, and that, therefore, people about whom he was illuminated had a priority over even his blood relatives. Padre Pio, in fact, seems almost never to have experienced divine illumination concerning his family members.

Friedrich Abresch

During the 1920s, many people from outside southern Italy began to visit San Giovanni Rotondo, many from other countries. Some of them were so drawn to Padre Pio that they moved there permanently to be near him.

One such person was Friedrich Abresch, a native of Germany, who came to see Padre Pio in 1925 out of pure curiosity at the age of twenty-eight. A nominal Lutheran in his youth, he became a Catholic when he married an Italian, but he did not practice his religion. He studied theosophy and said he believed in reincarnation. "I had no faith," he later admitted to Father Carty, who wrote down his testimony.

Abresch made his confession to Padre Pio, who dealt with him kindly but informed him that he had omitted certain mortal sins in his previous confessions. When he asked if his previous confessions had been in good faith, Abresch replied, "I consider confession a good institution, socially and educationally, but I don't believe at all in the divinity of the sacrament." Somehow, there and then, Abresch's outlook changed abruptly. "Now I do believe," he said.

Padre Pio did not give Abresch absolution. After explaining to him, convincingly, the errors of theosophy and reincarnation, he told Abresch to go off by himself and try to recall when he had last made a sincere confession and then come back to him later that day.

"Moved and shaken," Abresch did not know where to begin, as he could not remember ever making a really sincere confession. When he returned to Padre Pio, he decided to begin with the sins of his childhood and said, "Father, I happen to be …," when Padre Pio interrupted him and said, "You made a good confession when you were returning from your wedding trip. Leave out the rest and begin from there."

Dumbfounded, Abresch was now certain that he had "come in contact with the supernatural." He recalled: "The day after we returned from the wedding trip, my wife said that she would like both of us to go to the Sacraments, and I complied with her wish. I went to confession to the same priest who brought me into the Catholic Church. He knew I was a novice, little accustomed to such things. That is why I made a good confession. But now, I asked myself, 'Who could have had any knowledge of these thoughts ...?'"

And so, the confession continued. Padre Pio did the talking. Abresch recalled: "He concealed his knowledge of my entire past under the form of questions. He enumerated with precision and clarity all of my faults, even mentioning the number of times that I had missed Mass. I was completely bowled over at hearing things that I had forgotten, and I was able to reconstruct that past by remembering in detail all the particulars that Padre Pio had described with such precision."[10]

The next year Abresch's wife, Amalia, began to hemorrhage, and doctors diagnosed a tumor in her womb. After two years, it had grown so alarmingly that she was advised by several doctors to undergo an immediate hysterectomy. The Abresches had been hoping to have children, so Amalia went to Padre Pio. He told her to have the operation, but when she told him how desperate she was to have a child, Padre Pio then told her not to have the hysterectomy after all. After that, she had no more hemorrhages, and though the tumor remained, she conceived, and gave birth to a son whom she named Pio. (He later became a priest.)

Friedrich, who became "Federico," opened a photography studio. Most of the photographs that were taken of Padre Pio over the years were his work and, later, that of his assistant, Elia Stelluto.

The Pyle Family

In October 1923, a woman arrived at San Giovanni Rotondo who would become one of Padre Pio's most colorful spiritual children. For more than four decades, Adelia Maria McAlpin Pyle would be a fixture at San Giovanni and a "strong right arm" of the Padre. She was a full-figured lady, who, according to her passport applications, stood five feet five inches tall, and had a high forehead, gray eyes, cleft chin, light hair, and a fair complexion.[11]

Adelia Pyle was born in New York City[12] on April 17, 1888, the third of six children of James Tolman and Frances Adelaide McAlpin Pyle, all of whom were given the middle name "McAlpin." She was baptized on September 15, 1888, at the Church of the Covenant, a Presbyterian church where her mother was a member.

Adelia's paternal grandfather was a highly successful manufacturer of granulated soap and, with his two sons, owned a large factory in Shadyside, near Hackensack, New Jersey, that produced "Pyle's Pearline." Adelia's maternal grandfather, David Hunter McAlpin, made a fortune in New York manufacturing "Virgin Leaf" tobacco, and he owned the McAlpin Hotel. One of his sons married Emma Rockefeller, a niece of the billionaire founder of Standard Oil.

Adelia and her parents and siblings, along with eight servants, divided their time between Manhattan, where they owned a large home on the corner of Fifth Avenue and 53rd Street, and their thirty-room summer cottage, Hurstmont, on twenty acres near Morristown. James Pyle was remembered by his descendants as a kind, easygoing man who was fond of horses and "high living," and who spent his money as fast as he made it.[13] Adelaide was a woman of disturbing contrasts. A small, sedate woman, five feet two inches tall (according to her passport application), with penetrating blue eyes, Adelaide loved the "grand style" and aspired to the lifestyle of the "Gilded Age," making many trips to Europe, accompanied by her beribboned lapdogs. The Pyles were wealthy, to be sure, but never reached the top tier of the rising American plutocracy. When Adelaide died, probate records described her estate as "less than" a million dollars, but her wealth, which she expertly managed after her husband's early death, was considerable.

Adelaide Pyle was a brilliant linguist who spoke several languages and strove to promote the teaching of foreign languages in the public schools. She was also interested in early childhood education, and, although she considered it beneath the dignity of a woman of her station actually to teach in a classroom, she is believed to have founded the first nursery school in the United States.

Adelaide had a darker side. One grandchild characterized her as an "irate ... old biddy" who tended to fly into a rage at anyone who dared to cross her. Although her daughters, Adelia and Sara, were warm and sensitive, Adelaide was bossy, domineering, and "hard as nails." She had a tendency to turn on anyone who did not do things her way. Another grandchild described a woman who seemed to be "manic-depressive," given to "experimental religion," whose aggressive and dominating personality could suddenly give way to sullen withdrawal. "She was not normal or well-balanced," the grandchild declared. She would frequently "pull her children out of school according to her whims." On more than one occasion, she decided to leave her husband, ordered her servants to pack her trunks, and took her favorite daughter, Sara, with her to Europe, leaving Adelia and her brothers home with their father.

Although all six Pyle children were highly intelligent and extraordinarily talented, only David Hunter McAlpin Pyle (1886–1944) fulfilled his mother's social, financial, political, and religious expectations as the only "normal" Pyle. After attending Princeton and Oxford universities and Harvard Law School, David became a distinguished attorney and philanthropist who served as president of the United Hospital Fund of New York. He was described by a relative as a cold, stuffy, self-centered man. The eldest son, James McAlpin Pyle (1884–1954), characterized as a sensitive and "delightful" man who wanted to be an architect but was forced by his mother to become a lawyer, suffered a mental breakdown and led a troubled life. Sara (1891–1978), warm and sensitive, yet a "powerful woman," was an accomplished painter and violinist. First and foremost an educator, she founded and operated the Daycroft Schools in Connecticut. Charles, or "Charley," Pyle (1893–1966), the third son, also brilliant and talented, was described by a nephew as "troubled" and "tragic," a man who "had a good mind, but didn't know how to use it." The youngest child, Gordon (1901–1943), described as "a great guy" by his nephew, infuriated his mother by dropping out of Princeton, becoming a musician and composer, and marrying a woman of Irish descent.

Adelia's Search for God

Adelaide did not think a university education appropriate for the society lady she hoped to make Adelia, so, after an elementary education by tutors — including foreign-language instructors who lived with the family and forbade their student to speak any language other than the one she was learning — the young girl was sent to two finishing schools, where she studied music, singing, and dancing.

Adelia's father apparently came from an Episcopalian family but seems not to have gone to church regularly. Her mother, Adelaide, however, was a Presbyterian who had Adelia and most of her siblings baptized in the Church of the Covenant, which was absorbed, in 1894, into the fashionable Brick Presbyterian Church, whose congregation included members of the Carnegie family and whose pastor was Dr. Henry Van Dyke (1852–1933), famous for writing the words to the hymn "Joyful, Joyful, We Adore Thee" and the short story "The Other Wise Man." He left to teach at Princeton University when Adelia was eleven, but she must have maintained a close relationship with him because, when she applied for a passport in 1918, she listed him as one of her contacts.

Van Dyke's successor at the Brick Church, Maltbie Davenport Babcock, author of the hymn "This is My Father's World" and the poem "Be Strong," suffering from depression as well as physical illness, committed suicide in 1901 after a pastorate of only one year. How this event affected Adelia is unknown. Babcock was succeeded by William Rogers Richards (1853–1910). According to a cursory reading of some of his sermons, he seems to have been a middle-of-the-road Presbyterian of his time, who, in sermons still interesting and readable a century after they were written, tried to reconcile orthodox Protestant doctrine with "modernism" and "liberalism." Adelia, who from her early childhood was searching for God, later said that she found his teaching "shallow," and, as she grew older, professed to feel a profound emptiness. At ten, she started attending a Catholic church with an Irish maid of the family, but her mother found out and put a stop to it.[14]

In May 1903, at fifteen, Adelia was confirmed and received her First Communion. At the time, she declared, "The blood of Jesus is in my veins! It runs through my arms!"[15] This was not likely something that she learned at Brick Church, as Presbyterian churches typically taught that Christ was present in the Lord's Supper spiritually but not physically, as Catholics teach. Perhaps Adelia learned of the "Real Presence" from the maid, or perhaps she was convinced through her own reading and reflection. She kept insisting to her mother that she wanted to become a Catholic, until Adelaide invited Dr. Richards[16] to have a talk with her willful daughter and convince her of the truth of Presbyterian doctrines. However, when Adelia pressed him, the pastor admitted that he was really not sure that everything in the Westminster Confession of Faith, which sets forth the doctrines Presbyterians are to believe, was true. Adelia retorted, "Why, then, do you want to impose it on me?"[17] She never again wavered in her conviction of the spiritual bankruptcy, not only of liberal Presbyterianism, but of all "Protestantism."

All of Adelia's siblings were repelled, in fact, by the shallowness of modernism, but each chose a different path. Three of her brothers showed no interest whatever in religion. Charley, on the other hand, tried to invent his own religion, which he called "Egoanalysis." He wrote a book called *Your Way to Happiness* and even tried to contact the pope to interest him in his new religion. According to his nephew, Charley Pyle's "Egoanalysis" failed to bring him happiness, and he led a "pathetic" life and died an alcoholic. Sara, who married lawyer, banker, and yachtsman Paul Smart, was, like Adelia, in search of God all her life. She remarked to her mother, "When I find it, that's it!" While Adelia found "it" in Catholicism, Sara found fulfillment in Christian Science, and devoted her long life to the practice of that religion.

Adelia lived, albeit reluctantly, the life of a New York socialite until she was twenty-four. Then one February day, in 1912, her father, age fifty-seven, went to his office at Shadyside and, sitting down at his desk to dictate to a secretary, pitched forward, dead, of a massive heart attack. Adelaide sold the Pyle Company to Proctor and Gamble and put her children's inheritance in trusts. In the meantime, she had become attracted to the educational theories of Italian educator Maria Montessori (1870–1952) and established the Montessori Education Foundation, a New York–based organization set up to found schools in America based on the teaching of the Italian educator. While visiting the United States in 1913, Dr. Montessori called on Adelaide, who was one of her chief promoters, and met Adelia. Impressed with her fluency in Italian, Spanish, and German, Montessori invited the twenty-five-year-old to become her interpreter. Adelaide, however, refused to permit her daughter to go with Montessori, so Adelia waited until her mother went on an extended trip the next year and then wrote her that she was joining Dr. Montessori. By the time Adelaide's letter forbidding her to go reached New York, Adelia was gone.

Adelia became Montessori's secretary, interpreter, confidante, and "intellectual companion." She accompanied the older woman to California, where she established a school in Hollywood. Then, in 1918, the two went to live in Barcelona, Spain. In a letter accompanying Adelia's application for a passport, Montessori wrote: "My work would be greatly impaired without her assistance, and it would be impossible to replace her, [since] she [is] long familiar with my ways and the delicate detail of my work."[18]

While in Barcelona, in 1921, Adelia requested conditional baptism in the Catholic Church, which she received at the hands of a Capuchin priest at the shrine of the Black Madonna at the monastery of Santa Maria of Montserrat, in Catalonia.[19] As was customary, she chose a baptismal name — Maria — and immediately began to answer to it instead of Adelia. According to Montessori's biographer, the educator now considered the American an adopted daughter, to whom she devoted her life.[20] Adelaide was furious, not only because she imagined Montessori had replaced her in the affections of her daughter, but, even more, because of the conversion to Catholicism. She denounced violently both Adelia and Montessori, stopped supporting Montessori's work, renamed the Montessori Education Foundation the Child Education Foundation, and cut off her daughter's allowance, declaring that she never wanted to see her again.

In 1922, Montessori and Pyle moved to Naples, Italy. While there, Pyle read *Abandonment to Divine Providence*, a devotional book written by an eighteenth-century French Jesuit, Jean-Pierre de Caussade. She began to ask herself, "Why can't I have a spiritual director like Father Caussade?" and from that moment she began a search for a holy man to direct her soul.[21] Soon after her arrival in southern Italy, Pyle learned of Padre Pio's existence. In a short memoir she wrote years later: "I did not want to see him out of mere curiosity. I believed in him, and, in my state of lethargy, that seemed to me to be sufficient."[22]

"My Child, Stop Traveling Around"

In early October 1923, Maria Adelia Pyle and a friend, Rina Caterinovich d'Ergiu, left Capri, where they had been with Montessori for the summer and took a boat to Naples, a train to Foggia, and a bus to San Giovanni Rotondo to see Padre Pio. D'Ergiu was a Romanian, the wife of a colonel in the army of the recently murdered tsar of Russia. For many years, she had been disenchanted with Eastern Orthodoxy. She told Padre Pio that she was "without a true sense of mysticism," because "the Orthodox religion keeps dogmas like those which the Catholic religion has, but, in practice, the priests never seem convinced that we receive the living Jesus in Holy Communion." Convinced that confession in the Orthodox church was "nothing but a formality that frees the spirit neither from oppression nor evil," she had experimented in Eastern religions for eighteen years. When she started weeping, Padre Pio asked her the cause of her anguish, and she cried, "Because I'm not Catholic."

"And who's stopping you?" Padre Pio asked. He gave her a little catechism and showed her various prayers that she needed to learn.

"Do I have to prepare myself by taking instructions?" she asked.

"It's necessary to love, love, and nothing more," was Padre Pio's answer.

Both Rina and her husband Nestor were received into the Catholic Church.[23]

As for Pyle, she knew at once that in Padre Pio she had found her long-sought spiritual director. "We just looked at each other at first," she wrote, "then I fell to my knees and said, 'Father.' He placed his wounded hand on my head and said, 'My child, stop traveling around. Stay here.'"[24]

Pyle didn't stay in San Giovanni that time. She returned to Capri, rejoined Montessori, and accompanied her to England and Holland, where she finally mustered the gumption to tell her mother figure, "There is a living saint in this world and it saddens me not to be near him. I want to return there, and it would please me greatly if you would accompany me."[25]

So Pyle returned to San Giovanni with Montessori and introduced her to Padre Pio. Pyle then told him that she was thinking about his request for her to stay there. Padre Pio told her, cryptically, "Obey your mother." Pyle was convinced that Padre Pio was referring to her mother's opposition to her association with Montessori, even though she hadn't mentioned it to him.[26]

Pyle resolved to return to Rome with Montessori, if only to retrieve her belongings, and then return to San Giovanni. However, just as she was about to board the bus to leave with Montessori, Pyle suddenly cried out, "I can't! I can't! I feel paralyzed, as though someone has nailed my feet to the ground!"[27] So Pyle stayed in San Giovanni and Montessori returned to Rome alone and had her former companion's things sent to her. Montessori was extremely unhappy and resented Padre Pio for taking Pyle away from her. The two women never met or spoke again.[28]

Pyle at first wondered whether Padre Pio would direct her to become a nun. However, as she later told a relative, "I didn't want to become a nun. I don't like to take orders from anyone!" Padre Pio agreed that the convent was not for her and suggested that she joined the Third Order of St. Francis. This she did, with great enthusiasm, even obtaining from the Capuchins permission to wear the habit of the order. Selling all her jewelry and using the proceeds for the work of Padre Pio, she even smashed her watch and gave the diamonds in it to Padre Pio.[29] Until she died, she was never again seen in any other attire but the Capuchin habit, with the white cord wrapped around her waist, a rosary hanging at her side, and sandals on her feet.

With savings left from her work with Montessori, Pyle rented a room with a family about two miles from town, joining the ranks of Padre Pio's other spiritual daughters, climbing the hill each morning for Mass. They called her "*L'Americana*," at first suspiciously, then, later, with reverence and affection.

Mother and Daughter Reconciled

Maria had not been long in San Giovanni when her gruff and practical brother David, the successful attorney, learned of her whereabouts and came to see her. He was horrified that she was betraying her social class by living in what he considered unutterable squalor. He begged their mother to reconcile with her eccentric daughter and permit her to have her share in her father's estate. "You just can't let poor Adelia go on living like a peasant!" he insisted.[30]

Before long, Adelaide, lapdog in hand, swept into San Giovanni. She agreed with her daughter to meet Padre Pio as he passed through the sacristy of the church. The little dog, bedecked in ribbons, fretted at his mistress' feet as she stood in the crowd awaiting the Padre. As he approached, the dog ran out, yapping and nipping at him. Instinctively, Padre Pio, to the horror of the Pyles, kicked the pesky creature out of the way, and Adelaide, gathering up the offended canine, stormed out of the sacristy in high dudgeon.[31]

Padre Pio soon met and came to like "A-del-lie-eed," as he called her, and she returned his affection. Through him, mother and daughter were reconciled. In fact, Adelaide claimed that Padre Pio would appear to her in bilocation.[32] She had an apartment in Rome and began to make frequent trips to San Giovanni Rotondo, sometimes traveling from Foggia in a donkey cart. She reinstated Maria Adelia's allowance and began sending her between five thousand and seven thousand dollars a year — a huge sum for that time and place, which enabled Adelia to construct for herself, across from the friary, a two-story house that looked like a pink castle. Adelaide also regularly sent her daughter beautiful dresses, which she refused to wear.

Moreover, after many years of seeking, Adelaide, through Padre Pio, found religious peace. Much to the dismay of her daughter, however, she did not become a Catholic and remained a Presbyterian. Maria Adelia began to pester her mother to convert to the "True Church," but Padre Pio warned her, "Leave her alone. Don't disturb her peace."[33] When the daughter expressed her fear that her mother was in danger of hell, he insisted, "She will be saved because she has faith [in Christ as Savior]."[34]

Maria Adelia quickly became part of the life of San Giovanni Rotondo. She organized a choir of local ladies, which she accompanied on a reed organ as they sang during services of worship at the friary church. She taught local children catechism, made hosts for the Masses, and made calls to the sick and needy, providing them with food and money. Although many of the locals initially were suspicious of the well-heeled foreigner, she quickly endeared herself to most. "Generally, she was happy," recalled a woman who knew her for many years, "with a smile constantly on her lips, having a good word for everyone."[35] Pyle was particularly admired for her regular visits to a woman called Emerenziana, who was so revoltingly disfigured by a facial cancer that few of the locals wanted to be near her. Maria went to see the recluse every week and made it a point to kiss her face. After her first visit, she returned to her pink castle home, literally jumping up and down with joy, telling her friends, "She's so nice, so very nice. She certainly knows how to suffer!"[36]

Pyle soon filled her home with sick and needy women, at times nursing invalids afflicted with cancer and tuberculosis. Eventually, she gathered several women who lived with her in her home, like nuns, dedicated to charitable works. It was soon said around town that no one who knocked on the door of "Maria's House" was ever turned away. Anyone in need who came to her was given assistance. She received her allowance from her mother in monthly installments, and, invariably, she was broke before the month was over, because she had given everything away. Padre Pio and others (including her mother, of course) were concerned about the gullibility of this "guileless soul," who was occasionally victimized by unscrupulous people. Everyone knew that Pyle had a heart of gold. Among the many people interviewed for this book, almost everyone praised her highly. The two exceptions were a niece who said that she had been stricken from her aunt's will after she admitted that she had left the Catholic Church for the Episcopal Church, and an Italian-American teacher who thought that she had some of the affections of an upper-class snob (a fact of which Pyle may not have been aware).

A Friary for Pietrelcina

For many years, Padre Pio had wanted a Capuchin presence in his hometown. In fact, shortly after his ordination in 1910, as he and Don Salvatore Pannullo were returning to town from the cemetery, Padre Pio pointed to an open field and asked the archpriest, "Don't you smell a fragrance of incense? Don't you hear the singing of the angels?" When the older man answered that he did not, Padre Pio confidently informed him, "Someday a friary with a church will be built here. Every day the incense of prayers and singing of praises will be lifted to the Lord."[37]

One day, shortly after she built her house in San Giovanni, Pyle, unbidden, asked Padre Pio, "Can I build a friary at Pietrelcina?" Without batting an eye, the priest said, "Do it at once and let it be dedicated to the Holy Family."[38]

Pyle contacted her mother, who paid for the construction of the friary as well as a boys' boarding school. The construction was directed by the ubiquitous and versatile Emmanuele Brunatto, who took up residence at Pietrelcina in an apartment owned by Padre Pio's parents. He got Pannullo, now seventy-six, severely diabetic, and almost blind, to point out the spot where Padre Pio had indicated that the church would rise. The land was owned by a man named Alessandro Silvestri, who, out of love for Padre Pio, was willing to sell the land to Maria Adelia Pyle for a modest price. Pyle, however, because she was not an Italian citizen, was legally forbidden to purchase the land. She offered the money to the Capuchin province of Foggia, but they refused, as did the office of the minister general of the order in Rome. Finally, Padre Pio's brother, Michele Forgione, agreed to take the money from Pyle and become the titular owner. Construction began in June 1926, under an architect and engineer from Rome named Todini, whom Brunatto had engaged.

On the day when the cornerstone was to be laid, all Pietrelcina gathered before the local church to march, accompanied by the town band, to the spot where the new church and friary were to be built. After speeches by the mayor and other dignitaries (including Brunatto, who embarrassed the Capuchins and local clergy by his vituperative diatribe against the Holy Office), the crowd moved to the nearby Church of Purgatory, which lay in ruins, to fetch stones for the rising edifice. Brunatto was amazed when he saw a sea of stones, some weighing more than a hundred pounds, being carried uphill with perfect equilibrium on the heads of women, who, with no sign of effort, brought them to the construction site and went back for more. By sundown, all the stones from the abandoned church were at the site of the future friary. That night, in the sky over Pietrelcina, a huge cross of light was seen to rise from the construction site, observed for a half hour before it slowly disappeared.[39]

A few days later, Luigi Lavitrano (1874–1950), archbishop of Benevento (and later cardinal-archbishop of Palermo), stopped to see the construction and bless the cornerstone. Thereafter, every week at the same time, the bells of the church in Pietrelcina were rung to call the populace to gather at the creek to pick up stones to carry to the site of construction. Among them was Archpriest Pannullo, tottering and only months away from his death.

Another problem developed. There was no water. When Padre Pio (who never left San Giovanni) was apprised of this, it is said that he described a certain location and told the laborers to dig there. To everyone's amazement, a large spring was found there. Despite the promising beginnings, however, it would be twenty years before the complex constructed through the beneficence of the Pyles would be occupied.

"I Feel Like I'm Halfway in Hell"

New Attempts to Transfer Padre Pio

Archbishop Gagliardi had by no means given up his attempts to discredit Padre Pio. Throughout 1923–1924, he continued to bombard the Holy Office with reports of "suspicious" activities on the part of Padre Pio and his confreres, including hostile letters from Prencipe, Palladino, and Miscio. He complained to his friend Cardinal DeLai, head of the Consistorial Congregation (known today as the Congregation for Bishops), about the large sums of money at the friars' disposal; accused Padre Pio's supporters of involvement in economic speculation; and protested the hostility of the local population toward him, which was, of course, Padre Pio's doing. He concluded his letter, "I add nothing more, praying that God will free me from such afflictions."[1]

It also came to the notice of the Holy Office that despite the declaration to the faithful that the Church was unable to confirm the supernatural character of Padre Pio's ministry, the flood of laity, priests, and even bishops who were traveling to San Giovanni to see him was unabated. And so, on July 23, 1924, the Holy Office, since "the declaration published last year has been forgotten," issued another declaration to the faithful, advising them to refrain from visiting Padre Pio.[2]

The Holy Office and the Capuchin minister general once more tried to formulate plans to transfer Padre Pio. Minister General Padre Giuseppe Antonio asked the Prefect of Foggia to advise how the stigmatic's removal from San Giovanni could be accomplished without violence.

The prefect replied: "The transfer of the friar should happen suddenly, by surprise, after which there should be at least 150 policemen posted for a long time for the effective safeguarding of public order and protection for churches and local clergy." In addition, a guard would have to be stationed around the palace of the archbishop. However, when contacted, the chief of police in San Giovanni refused to assume any responsibility for the violence he expected as a result of the removal of the resident holy man.[3] As a result, the plans of the Holy Office to transfer Padre Pio continued to be stymied.

Padre Pietro of Ischitella, the provincial, died suddenly from a heart attack at the age of forty-four, and was succeeded by Padre Bernardo Mazza of Alpicella (1883–1937). In April 1925, Padre Bernardo put orders from the Holy Office into effect that forbade visitors to congregate in the sacristy, guest room, or corridors to talk to Padre Pio, who was ordered to refrain from speaking to laypeople after Mass and to proceed directly to the choir to make his thanksgiving without allowing his hands to be kissed.

Attempted Blackmail

Toward the end of 1925, Don Giovanni Miscio, one of the priests in San Giovanni who had been bitterly hostile to Padre Pio, wrote a book "against the honor" of the priest and his family. What it contained evidently has been lost to history. It is supposed to have contained lurid allegations and defamations of Padre Pio's character and morals. Since it was said to have dishonored the Forgione family, perhaps it had something to do with embarrassing activities of Pellegrina Forgione, the family "black sheep." Whatever the book contained, Miscio went to Pietrelcina and showed a copy to Michele, who would have had to get somebody else to read it to him, since he was illiterate. Miscio told Padre Pio's brother that he had been given an advance of five thousand lire but would agree to forgo publication if Forgione would pay him the amount of the advance, which would have to be refunded if the book was not published.

Michele told Don Giovanni that he did not have such a sum on hand, but that he was willing to sell some of his land "so that Padre Pio won't have to suffer anymore." Don Giovanni agreed. Michele, however, informed Emmanuele Brunatto, who, with his extensive contacts, now considered himself Padre Pio's faithful watchdog and protector. Brunatto hurried to Rome and informed Cardinal Gasparri, the secretary of state, of the plot. "Have [Miscio] put in jail!" the cardinal shouted. "That will cast a little light into the thicket at San Giovanni Rotondo!"[4]

Meanwhile, so as not to have to sell his land, Michele had convinced Miscio to accept four thousand lire in cash and a promissory note for the rest. He paid Miscio, however, with bills whose serial numbers he had registered with the police, whom he alerted to the scheme. The police caught the extortionist priest red-handed, trying to destroy a threatening note to Michele Forgione, on which he had written, "Your days are numbered!"[5]

Padre Pio, up to then in the dark about Miscio's scheme, almost fainted when he learned what happened. In vain, he tried to persuade Michele not to press charges against the priest. Michele refused to listen, insisting, "It's my duty to defend my brother against calumny." When Padre Pio still insisted that the matter not be taken to court, Michele informed him that the two of them would have no further contact until the case was established against Don Giovanni.

Quickly, Padre Pio sent for his brother's lawyer, whose name was Caprile, who conferred with him for an hour in his room in the monastery. At least one friar heard the two men screaming at each other. When at last Caprile left Padre Pio's room, the friar took the lawyer's hands and pressed them between his own and pleaded, "Promise me that you won't let Don Giovanni be condemned."

Caprile told him, "Padre, you know I can't work against my own client, and your brother is my client."

Padre Pio snapped, "I have spoken! I am sending you to see that the priest is not condemned!"

"Since this is your wish," the lawyer meekly replied, "and since you are commanding me, I will do everything to extenuate the circumstances and save the priest."[6]

Padre Pio made Caprile repeat the promise. After he left, Padre Pio paced around his room, shaking his head, weeping, and sighing, "A priest in jail! A priest *in jail*! And all because of Padre Pio!"[7] The lawyer kept his promise, and even though the judge, in reading Miscio's manuscript, found that it contained "obscene insinuations, especially repugnant in having been devised by a priest," Miscio received a suspended sentence. He had been a public-school teacher and was fired because of his scandalous behavior. Padre Pio pleaded with the school board to reinstate Miscio — and the priest got his job back.

Although Archbishop Gagliardi never disciplined him for his criminal activities, Miscio went to the Forgione brothers to beg their forgiveness, and Padre Pio and Michele, themselves reconciled, embraced Don Giovanni, telling him that all was forgiven. Until his death more than forty years later, Don Giovanni would regularly go to the friary to see Padre Pio and ask for his prayers. In fact, when he was an old man, he asked the superiors at the friary permission to end his days there, near Padre Pio. (Apparently, this was not granted.)

The Archpriest's Mistress

Around the same time as the Miscio affair, Padre Pio aroused the fury of San Giovanni's archpriest, Don Giuseppe Prencipe, by denying absolution to his mistress, Maria DiMaggio. Concubinage, like homosexuality, seems to have been rampant among the clergy in the Manfredonia archdiocese, and Don Giuseppe and DiMaggio had lived together for more than twenty years. When DiMaggio came to him for confession, Padre Pio declared that her relationship with the archpriest was sinful and had to be terminated at once if she wanted absolution from her sins. DiMaggio was incredulous: she explained that Prencipe had told her that the Bible permits all men and women to "satisfy their bodily needs" once a month, and that, when she tried to refuse Prencipe, he attempted to rape her. Unable to comprehend what Padre Pio was telling her, DiMaggio consulted a priest in another town, who told her that the Capuchin was correct. She then wrote or dictated an account describing how Prencipe had deceived her, but then retracted it — because, she later insisted, the archpriest threatened to kill her unless she did. Through it all, Archbishop Gagliardi supported Prencipe and once more denounced Padre Pio for his "horrible means of hearing confessions."[8]

New Accusations

Two days before Christmas, in 1925, Padre Pio wrote to the provincial, Padre Bernardo:

> My spirit has felt alone — totally alone — accompanied by a complete inner conviction, contrary to my will, of being abandoned by everybody. I try in vain to make acts of conformity to God. I call to him in vain. Without exception heaven itself for me has become like bronze. I feel like I'm halfway in hell. I say "halfway" because, in the midst of this torturous agony, I still don't feel completely without hope ... I feel keenly the need for a true, sincere, and intimate conversation with God, and I don't know where and how to begin. Here is what I constantly ask of Jesus: my conversion. If I am in his disfavor, make me understand clearly and not just suppose and guess, because in this way I will never understand a thing and much less resolve to do anything. I want to save myself at all cost in spite of Satan. Also pray for me for this intention and tell Jesus to turn a kindly ear to my groans, to the agonizing sighs of my heart.[9]

In the early months of 1926, Archbishop Gagliardi, Archpriest Prencipe, and Don Domenico Palladino began to bombard the Holy Office anew with denunciations. Palladino complained about San Giovanni's Mayor Morcaldi, blaming him for inciting the populace against the archbishop and local clergy. Morcaldi, Palladino contended, "understands very well (assisted by the Pious Ladies ...) how to intertwine the permanent residence of the 'saint' with the revenue of the monastery." He insisted, "We are now assaulted by insults, snares, and calumny; the 'saint' daily plots against us not only through the villagers but also through parasitic strangers — especially [Emmanuele Brunatto] ... who writes, publishes and gives lectures." Palladino moreover declared that he had heard Padre Pio declare that he refused his consent to be transferred to another monastery.[10]

Gagliardi wrote to the provincial, Padre Bernardo, that Padre Pio was insisting that his spiritual children make confessions too often and was ignoring the orders of the Holy Office by continuing to talk to women in places other than the confessional and allowing them to kiss his hand.

On May 18, 1926, after Padre Bernardo had shared some of these accusations with him, Padre Pio wrote back in anguish:

I feel my very soul ripped up and annihilated, to the point that I can't go on. My Father, what infamy they have written, knowing that they were lying and that they wanted to lie in a slanderous way. This is the thanks I get after I have spent my entire life in my sacred ministry!

The persons you mentioned were never permitted access to my confessional before the [required] eight day [interval] and much less have I conferred with them elsewhere, as they have erroneously stated.

I have spoken to Nina Campanile somewhat more often, and this for reason of pure charity and compassion, because she is ill and almost completely out of her mind…. The poor little woman has become almost completely deaf and consequently there is the need to hear her confession in the sacristy. And what does it matter, given her irrational state, always wandering around? How am I to blame or how is she herself to blame?

As for Professor Emmanuele [Brunatto], you know what treatment he had from me the first time and this second time he didn't have better treatment than the first. I even tried to keep from hearing his confession. I haven't said anything to him, even a word. Putting him out of church, where did that happen? That's not my job, and with what authority could I do that?

As for coming to kiss my hand when I am in the confessional, God knows and those who are found in our church know, too, how many times I yelled at them, and if I didn't succeed, am I at fault? Should I have punched them? If I at least had good hands, perhaps I would have done it. If the people who talk to me have made me say things that I never dreamed of saying, what can we do? Recommend them to God, and may God help us!

You also tell me that the brothers have no peace because of me. Ah, my Father, this crushes and tortures my soul with cruel agony. What peace have I disturbed? My God, cut short my exile, as I can't take it anymore! I am careful not to disturb anyone's peace or make trouble for anyone whomsoever. As far as my own peace is concerned, this is put to a hard test!

But for this I don't blame anyone, except the devil, and I pour out the anguish of my heart to God and force myself to bury everything in my heart.

Now, in the face of so many slanders and infamous accusations presented so crushingly as to create, as you could say, a dome over hell, thinking about this is enough to make me truly lose my peace and my mind, if the Lord did not come to my aid with his vigilant grace.

And now, my Father, pardon me if I have upset you, but that wasn't my intention. After all I can't go on anymore and you are my father and in you I wanted to confide a part of the anguish that lacerates my heart!

Prostrate at your feet, I ask your help, and, kissing your hand, I declare myself all yours in Jesus and in St. Francis.[11]

In August 1926, Padre Bernardo imposed new, more severe restrictions on Padre Pio's activities: he could not in any way show himself to visitors, and if he accidentally encountered them in the sacristy or elsewhere, he was ordered to "simply nod his head and do nothing else." The new provincial, in his instructions, expressed his negative view of "these fanatical San Giovanni people," complaining about "disingenuous devotees who are around him almost all day long, [which] is something that is not in fact acceptable and should absolutely and immediately stop." Padre Bernardo personally commanded Padre Pio: "Either you immediately begin to keep the women at a distance, even with a threat of denying them absolution … or I will not permit you to use the confessional for women."[12]

Complaints Against the Archbishop

More complaints were being voiced against the archbishop, and they came not only from Padre Pio's devotees. Even within the Vatican, there were rumblings. Bishop Valbonesi frequently referred to Gagliardi in his letters as "the vile archbishop." Complaints grew about widespread homosexual activity among the Manfredonia clergy and the archbishop's preference for "ignorant and immoral" priests. Gagliardi seemed to want to avoid visiting many parishes, perhaps out of fear of violent attacks, such as that which had occurred at Vieste. Consequently, it was claimed that, for almost a decade, because the Sacrament of Confirmation was to be performed by a bishop or archbishop, more than a thousand young people had gone without confirmation, as the archbishop had not visited their parishes. The pope received a petition signed by a number of priests in the archdiocese, asking him to turn his attention to the "disorder, immorality, and clerical degeneracy" in the archdiocese. They accused Gagliardi of gross financial mismanagement as well as simony — awarding favorable assignments to priests in return for money or other favors. They pointed out that he had assigned priests convicted in the civil courts of "infamous crimes" to his parishes. Gagliardi was also accused of personal immorality.[13]

Whenever he heard of complaints against him by any of his clergy, Gagliardi retaliated by stripping them of their priestly faculties. "Vipers," he called those who "betrayed" him. In 1926, he suspended two priests for daring to join a delegation to greet Padre Pio on his name day. He was convinced that Padre Pio was to blame for his own growing unpopularity.

Meanwhile, Brunatto wrote a book called *Padre Pio of Pietrelcina*, in which he provided documentation for the charges against not only Gagliardi, but also his canons. These were priests on the staff of the cathedral without assignment to parishes, including Palladino and Miscio. The Holy Office promptly put the book on the Index of Forbidden Books and bought up all the copies. A priest who read the book, however, commented, "Emmanuele Brunatto has caught a fish in his net (Canon Palladino) and now will catch a big one (the archbishop)."[14] Cardinal Gasparri, however, read the book and told Brunatto, "You've achieved your purpose. An apostolic visitation will take place, and you will participate."[15]

A visitation is an official procedure within the Church for investigating a parish, diocese, or religious community to determine whether everything is in order. In March 1927, a visitation was undertaken, not of the archbishop, but of the cathedral chapter, which involved the canons, the archpriest of San Giovanni, Don Giuseppe Prencipe, and his staff. The investigating team consisted of Monsignor Felice Bevilacqua, Padre Alfredo Quattrino, and Brunatto.

When Prencipe and Palladino learned that they were being investigated, they tried to go over the heads of the visitation team by appealing directly to the pope, writing a sanctimonious letter in which they portrayed themselves the innocent victims of Padre Pio, Brunatto, and their friends. They claimed that Padre Pio and his colleagues had maliciously accused them of all manner of evils. At the same time, they insisted that the Capuchins were inventing miracle stories for the purpose of financial gain. They pleaded with the pontiff to intervene directly. Pope Pius XI, however, permitted the visitation to proceed. As a result, a sordid cesspool of scandal was uncovered, which resulted in Monsignor Bevilacqua censuring Prencipe and his associates, both in writing and to their faces, for "outrages against morality."[16] Even so, Prencipe kept his job as archpriest.

Gagliardi still had powerful friends in Rome, notably his friend Cardinal DeLai, who did all that he could to protect and defend him.

An Enemy Recovers His Health After Padre Pio's Blessing

One of Gagliardi's most vociferous defenders was a sixty-seven-year-old physician in San Giovanni named Francesco Ricciardi, who was a personal friend of Archpriest Prencipe. In the fall of 1928, Ricciardi, who was an outspoken atheist, was diagnosed by five doctors with advanced and incurable stomach cancer. By December, he was near death, and Prencipe went to see him, urging him to consent to the administration of the Sacrament of the Anointing of the Sick. Ricciardi mustered the strength to throw a slipper at the archpriest's head and gasp, "Go away. I intend to die as I have lived!"

Angelo Maria Merla, who was one of Ricciardi's doctors, went to the friary and asked Padre Pio to visit the sick man, and Padre Pio agreed to do so. He arrived at

Ricciardi's house along with the superior, who was now Padre Raffaele of Sant'Elia a Pianisi. Padre Pio entered Ricciardi's sick room alone and shut the door behind him. When Ricciardi's family were readmitted to the room, they found the doctor weeping and embracing the priest, to whom he had just confessed and from whom he had received the anointing of the sick. In front of everyone, the professed atheist begged: "Father, bless me one more time. There is no more hope for me, and in a little time I will be dead, and so I want to leave the world with your pardon and another blessing."

Padre Pio smiled and declared: "Your soul is healed and soon your body will be healed as well. You'll go to the friary and repay the visit that I made this evening."[17]

Within three days, Ricciardi was in remission; he lived for another three and a half years. He died a practicing Catholic in June 1932. (The civil records of San Giovanni Rotondo do not give a cause of death.)

Giuseppa's Last Visit

On December 5, Maria Pyle returned from Pietrelcina with Padre Pio's mother, who expressed the desire to spend the holidays with her son. Nearly seventy, she seemed weak and frail, and it crossed the minds of some that she might have wanted to come to San Giovanni to die near her son.

Giuseppa attended Mass every day. Pyle was touched at the sight of the stately, little old lady, after receiving Communion from her son, kissing the very floor on which he had walked. She took an active part in the conversation of the numerous guests and boarders at the Pyle house. Whenever anyone ventured to criticize Gagliardi and his cohorts, she would cut the discussion short: "Who are we to permit criticism of the ministers of God? The Lord said that we ought not judge if we do not wish to be judged ourselves, and this means that we should judge neither the good nor the evil, because we can see only the deeds people do, whilst God alone can see into people's hearts the reason why they do them."[18]

Two days before Christmas, Giuseppa went up to the superior, Padre Raffaele, and told him, "Take care of my son." The next day was snowy and bitterly cold, but she insisted on going to Mass and refused to wear a fur coat that Pyle offered, saying, "Oh, I don't want to look like a great lady, my dear." After Mass, Giuseppa fell to her knees at her son's feet, and, according to Pyle, "held her hands straight down, like Our Lady of the Miraculous Medal, and looked at Padre Pio as a soul must look at Jesus, and he looked at her as Jesus must look upon a soul."

She asked him: "Padre Pio, how can we know if before God we are not great sinners? We confess everything that we can remember or know, but perhaps God sees other things that we cannot recall."

Padre Pio replied, "Mammella, if we put into [our confession] all our good will and we have the intention to confess everything — all that we can know or remember — the mercy of God is so great that he will include and erase even what we cannot remember or know."[19]

The next day Giuseppa was confined to bed, spitting blood, and Pyle summoned a physician who diagnosed pneumonia in both lungs. Her husband and son Michele were summoned, and Padre Pio came down from the friary to be with his failing mother. While some expected him to work a miracle like the one that restored Dr. Ricciardi to health, all Padre Pio would say was, "God's will be done." He was there when the summons came, at four in the morning, January 3, 1929. Francesco Morcaldi was there, too, and wrote: "Her death was truly beautiful. She breathed her last serenely while they were praying. Unaided, she raised the crucifix, pressed it to her lips [and died]."[20]

As soon as his mother was pronounced dead, Padre Pio collapsed. For hours on end, he sobbed, "Mummy! Mummy! My beautiful Mummy! My sweet darling Mummy!" He was unable to attend her funeral or even leave the Pyle house. For days on end, he cried like a baby. When someone reminded him that Christians do not grieve like those without hope, he responded: "These aren't tears of grief. They are tears of love!" Eventually, Padre Bernardo, the provincial, decided that Padre Pio had been away from the friary too long, and despite the pleas of three doctors that he was in no condition to be moved, ordered him to return. Padre Pio obeyed, although he fainted three times going the short distance from the Pyle house to the monastery.

On January 17, Padre Pio wrote Michele, who had gone back to Pietrelcina: "Thanks to God, I feel a little bit better. It's a fact that the passing days, instead of filling the aching void produced in me by the loss of our beloved Mamma, my grief seems to grow ever more profound; but it is a void that tortures, but does not derange me. And all thanks be to God's infinite mercy."

Some people urged Padre Pio's bereaved father to move to San Giovanni Rotondo. Padre Pio, however, not in agreement, wrote to Michele:

Surround him with affection and keep him from being sad, even in the smallest things. I learned that they have made active preparations … sincere and friendly people, to move him here. But, to tell you the truth, I don't see that as a good thing for an infinity of reasons. It's very good that he comes and goes [to and from San Giovanni] as he pleases. But I think it's a bad idea for him to have almost a true home here. It would be less honorable for you who are the only son [in Pietrelcina]; it would be less consoling for me, who can do very little for him, because of my exceptional situation, and, not a little dishonorable, too, for our neighbors to let an old man who is in the last years of his life go wandering, denied a refuge. Such would be the judgment that outsiders would form. Therefore, it's up to you to avoid such a disgrace, surrounding our dear little old man with affection and kindness. If you think [it proper], gently make him understand the reasons I stated. Anyway, I don't want him to be sad in the least. For my part, I'm willing to submit to any humiliation or embarrassment, so as to spare him.[21]

There was soon another break in the family circle. Giuseppina Masone, the sixteen-year-old daughter of Felicita, Padre Pio and Michele's late sister, had spent a month at San Giovanni with her grandmother the summer before the older woman's death. Unhappily, the girl was afflicted with tuberculosis, and Padre Pio begged his brother-in-law Vincenzo Masone to allow her to seek treatment in a hospital in northern Italy. The father did not want to part with his only daughter, but Padre Pio wrote: "This is the sacrifice that, in the name of God and all that is dear to you in heaven and earth, I come to ask also of you today. Let Giuseppina go. Let this poor creature go to breathe a little of the more mild and healthy air this winter in the good hope that she might get at least a little benefit, even if it's minimal. Let's not deprive this poor daughter of one comfort that she asks of you in the midst of her burden of pain and which we can give her."[22] Giuseppina went to the clinic at Arco di Trento — and there she died, at the age of eighteen.

The Resignation of the Archbishop
Shortly before his mother died, another death occurred that affected Padre Pio. It was that of Cardinal DeLai, Gagliardi's friend and protector. After that, the Vatican swiftly moved against the archbishop.

During the night of May 5, 1929, Padre Pio had a dream about the sixteenth-century Pope Pius V. Padre Pio recounted, "I dreamed about St. Pius. He clearly told me that Archbishop Gagliardi will be deposed and Monsignor Cucarollo will come here in his place."[23] Unbeknownst to him and his confreres, Gagliardi was then being investigated by the Vatican for "mismanagement" of his archdiocese. Several members of the College of Cardinals discussed the situation and in July came to a decision: "Leaving aside the major or minor culpability of [Archbishop] Gagliardi, the Cardinal Fathers are in agreement in saying the best decision would be to ask Gagliardi for his resignation." Declaring that he was "obedient and devoted to the Holy See," the archbishop stepped down in October,[24] was named titular "Archbishop of Lemnos" (a defunct see in Greece), and returned to his hometown Tricarico. There he would, according to the Vatican news service, die "piously" on December 12, 1941, at the age of eighty-two. When Padre Pio learned of the death of his old enemy, he told Padre Agostino, "I'll say a Mass for him tomorrow." Never a word of complaint or denunciation. Padre Agostino wrote in his diary, "Speak no ill of the dead. May God receive him in glory."[25]

The second half of the apparent prophecy of Saint Pius was not fulfilled, owing,

Padre Agostino deduced, to "the fault of men." There was indeed a prelate by the name of Sebastiano Cornelio Cuccarollo, a sixty-year-old Capuchin who was currently serving as bishop of Bovino, and had been, over the years, friendly to Padre Pio. When Pope Pius XI decided that Gagliardi needed to retire, he asked Cuccarollo to take the archdiocese of Manfredonia. Much to the disgust of Padre Agostino and Padre Pio, he declined, holding out for a more lucrative assignment, which he obtained. "The devil has worked his wiles at Rome," Padre Agostino wrote. "The Lord has let men do as they please," Padre Pio observed, "but Monsignor Cuccarollo will have to answer before God because he should have obeyed the Pope and submitted to his cross."[26]

Il Duce Intervenes

The Vatican still wanted to transfer Padre Pio to another monastery "where he could live unknown." Around the time that Gagliardi resigned, the Holy Office decided to make another attempt to transfer the controversial friar. Pope Pius XI approved it and told them to order the Capuchin minister general to make the change. Once again, the minister general turned for help to the civil authorities. This time he got Italy's inspector general of public safety to assess the situation in San Giovanni. The inspector general reported that the transfer could be carried out if ordered by the government. However, he urged a delay until there could be a "clearing of the atmosphere." However, the prefect of Foggia, as he had in 1924, warned that an attempt to remove Padre Pio would trigger "a great explosion of popular indignation," and his advice was "leave him alone in his monastery where … he is only doing good through his modesty, good judgment, and much common sense."[27]

It was apparent now to the Holy Office that, if Padre Pio was to be transferred without provoking an insurrection, it needed the help of the highest government authority, and brought the matter to the attention of Benito Mussolini, who had ruled Italy for the past seven years. Although he did not believe in God, *Il Duce* recognized that the overwhelming majority of Italians were Catholics and was aware of Padre Pio's enormous popularity in Italy's southland. When the matter was brought to him, Mussolini's response was brief: "Things are fine. Leave him undisturbed."[28] This ended, for the time being, the plans of the Holy Office to transfer him, but Padre Pio was by no means left undisturbed.

Taken probably in 1911, this is the earliest known photograph of Padre Pio.

Padre Pio in his early thirties. He soon stopped wearing skullcaps because they would be pulled off his head by fanatics in the crowds that surrounded him each day.

Padre Pio as a soldier in the Italian army, about 1916.

Photo credit: Our Lady of Grace Friary, San Giovanni Rotondo, Italy.

Padre Pio poses in 1920 with one of the lambs villagers frequently donated to the Capuchin friars.

Photo credit: Our Lady of Grace Friary, San Giovanni Rotondo, Italy.

Padre Pio, under obedience, shows his stigmata in 1919.

Photo credit: Our Lady of Grace Friary, San Giovanni Rotondo, Italy.

Pietrelcina, in the province of Benevento, the birthplace of Padre Pio.

Photo credit: Public domain.

The Cathedral of Benevento, where Padre Pio was ordained a priest in 1910.

Photo credit: Public domain.

Padre Pio's mother and father, Giuseppa and Orazio, around 1920, probably in their farmhouse at Piana Romana, outside of Pietrelcina.

Photo credit: Our Lady of Grace Friary, San Giovanni Rotondo, Italy.

Suor Pia of Our Lady of Sorrows, Padre Pio's last surviving sister, whose decision to leave the Brigittine order after forty-eight years plunged Padre Pio into a deep depression.

Photo credit: Our Lady of Grace Friary, San Giovanni Rotondo, Italy.

Michele Forgione, Padre Pio's brother, who spent his last years at San Giovanni Rotondo.

Photo credit: Our Lady of Grace Friary, San Giovanni Rotondo, Italy.

Padre Pio and his brother Michele, probably in the friary garden.

Padre Pio, around 1950, seemingly indifferent to the affectionate gesture of a young friar.

Padre Agostino Daniele of San Marco in Lamis and Padre Pio applaud a skit performed by some of the friary's benefactors. Agostino was Pio's longtime confessor and probably his best friend.

Padre Pio's stigmata is visible during Mass in an undated photo.

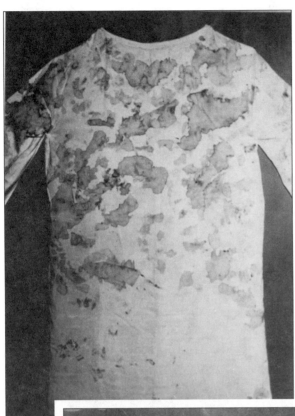

Padre Pio's wounds normally oozed slowly, but on occasion, especially during Holy Week, they bled copiously, as is evident from these photographs of his nightshirt and socks.

Photo credit: Our Lady of Grace Friary, San Giovanni Rotondo, Italy.

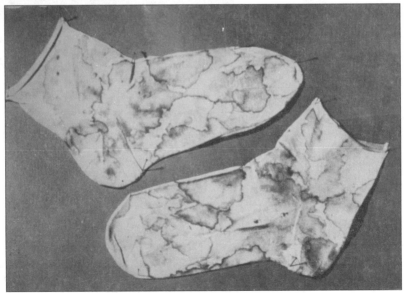

Padre Pio celebrates Mass, assisted by Padre Onorato Marcucci. Note the lesion on Pio's hand. Undated photo.

In 1960, Padre Pio's room was bugged by hostile friars, who even sneaked in at night when he was sound asleep to try to perform exorcisms.

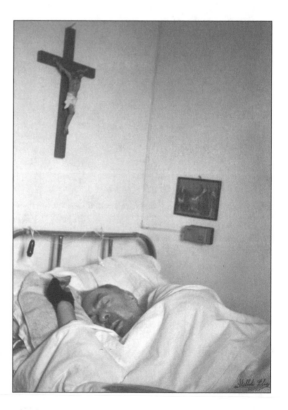

Padre Pio called the Rosary his "weapon" against the forces of hell.

Altar of the Sanctuary of Santa Maria delle Grazie, in San Giovanni Rotondo, where Padre Pio celebrated his last Mass.

Photo credit: Public domain.

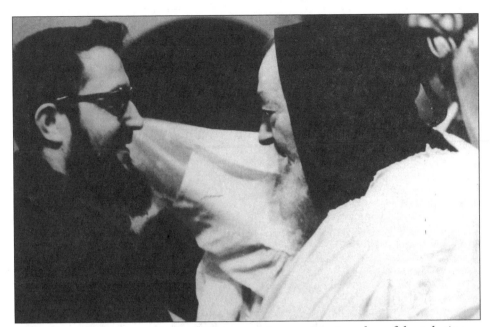

Padre Eusebio Notte was Padre Pio's companion, assistant, and confidant during the early 1960s and helped lift the older man's spirits when he was stressed by hostile Vatican officials.

Padre Pio partakes of a meager supper in his room with two confreres.

Padre Pio in his armchair.

A young altar server holds Padre Pio's scarf as he seems to be getting his hair trimmed.

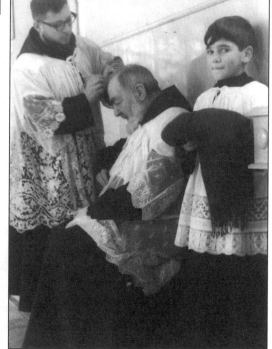

A 1953 postcard depicting a crowd of people visiting the Church of Our Lady of Grace to witness Padre Pio.

Photo credit: Public domain.

Church of Our Lady of Grace, where Padre Pio is buried, today.

Photo credit: Public domain.

Padre Pio in his coffin. As in the case of many, if not most, saints whose remains are put on display after exhumation, the head is covered with a wax mask.

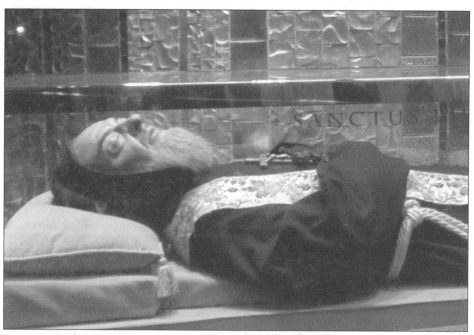

Imprisonment

Monsignor Macchi

Upon Pasquale Gagliardi's resignation as archbishop, the Vatican appointed Alessandro Macchi (1878–1947), the bishop of Andria, as temporary administrator of the see of Manfredonia. Macchi, who was then in his early fifties, seems to have been as hostile to Padre Pio as his predecessor, declaring, "Padre Pio was made into a saint, but actually he's a deluded man, lacking in humility, who uses cologne that the *bizzochi* [using a disparaging term for country women] give him." He threatened to throw Padre Pio into a car in the dead of night and send him to Rome "just like he was a sack of straw."[1] Determined to remove one whom he considered to be a phony saint from San Giovanni Rotondo and the gaggle of superstitious yokels that surrounded him, he proposed to the Holy Office: "How do we succeed in moving Padre Pio elsewhere? ... By sending the Vicar General of the Capuchins, Padre Gregorio of Bruno, who knows the southern area well, from Rome with the mandate to go to Foggia by car and then go to the monastery and invite Padre Pio to leave with him. From there to Foggia, to Milan, and Switzerland. Find a way to get a passport without that being leaked out. Everything will be done with a clean break."[2] The Holy Office, as well as Pope Pius XI, however, were more cautious and decided that it was best to take no action at the time.

In January 1931, Padre Bernardo, Padre Pio's provincial, suggested to the pope that if Padre Pio were to be transferred, it would be best to remove the monastery in San Giovanni from his jurisdiction and place it under the direct supervision of the minister general, who would appoint a religious from outside the province, preferably from northern Italy, to carry out the transfer. The minister general demurred, however, insisting, "Without the cooperation of the public, we will be forced to wait for a change in the attitude of San Giovanni's inhabitants to effect that transfer without encountering very serious drawbacks that would arise from it."[3]

The Holy Office, now headed by Cardinal Donato Sbarretti, after the death of Cardinal Merry Del Val, had given up for the time being on moving Padre Pio. Instead, they decided to separate him from his fanatical followers by forbidding him all contact with the public. In March, the Holy Office directed the Capuchin minister general to choose a new superior for the San Giovanni friary and to forbid Padre Pio celebrating Mass "except in the inner oratory of the monastery" and not to hear confessions "under penalty of suspension [from his priestly faculties] if he does not obey." Pope Pius XI, however, preferred to wait until the new superior was chosen.[4]

On March 31, Padre Raffaele was summoned to Foggia to meet with Padre Bernardo, who informed him that he was going to be shortly replaced with a new superior from the province of Milan. Although this knowledge was strictly confidential, by the time Padre Raffaele returned to San Giovanni, everybody there knew it.

"They're Taking Padre Pio Away!"

Apparently Emmanuele Brunatto had his "spies" in the Vatican — influential clergy, like Cardinal Gasparri, the recently retired papal secretary of state, who were loyal to him and to Padre Pio, who sent word to him and to Morcaldi. Now the town was in an uproar, not only by the news that a new superior was coming from the "foreign" territory of northern Italy, but with the mistaken expectation that he was coming to take Padre Pio away. In short order, the friary was surrounded day and night by citizens armed to the teeth, guarding it in shifts to make sure that Padre Pio stayed in San Giovanni Rotondo. Barricades were thrown up in the streets so that no vehicular traffic could get to or from the monastery.

In the midst of this threatening situation, on the evening of April 7, a traveler arrived at Our Lady of Grace. He was Padre Eugenio Tignola, a member of the Franciscan Observants, who was returning to Naples from a preaching assignment. He arrived in San Giovanni by bus and walked up to the friary, hoping to talk to Padre Pio about a personal problem.

Unfortunately, on the same bus from Foggia was Francesco Morcaldi, who was convinced that Padre Eugenio was the sinister new superior from northern Italy. Within minutes of the arrival of the bus, the news was all over town that the new "foreign" superior had arrived and was about to spirit Padre Pio away. Soon cries were heard all over the town and countryside: "They're taking Padre Pio away! Hurry, hurry to the monastery! They're taking Padre Pio away!" Around 10:00 p.m., a furious mob descended upon the friary and took up the menacing chant: "To the pillory with him! To the pillory with the stranger! Tear him to pieces! Tear him to pieces!"[5]

When Padre Raffaele refused to hand "the stranger" over, the mob uprooted a light pole in the courtyard and used it as a battering ram to smash the wooden door of the friary. Padre Raffaele met them as they poured into the monastery, blocking the way to the stairway with his body. In an "authoritarian voice," he ordered everyone to leave. "It was a dangerous thing to do," the superior wrote in his diary, "because everyone was armed." He was able to persuade the crowd to leave only when he promised that Padre Pio would speak to them.

Padre Raffaele then went to Padre Pio's room and ordered him to go to the choir window, which overlooked the courtyard, to calm the crowd. At the sight of his face, the crowd burst into wild cheers. "My blessed children," Padre Pio began, "you have always been good. You have always conformed diligently to the grace of God.... Now I implore you to listen to me, as you always do, and return to your homes without harming anyone. The guest who is here with me is not the man you think he is. He is a friar who has come here for purely spiritual reasons."

Cries of "It's not true!" pierced the night. The crowd was convinced that Padre Pio was being told what to say by his superiors. "What I just told you is true!" Padre Pio shouted back, but, when the mob persisted in its refusal to listen to him, he closed the window and returned to his room.

At this point, Morcaldi arrived on the scene and was admitted to the monastery. After conferring with Padre Raffaele, he was convinced that "the stranger" was, in fact, a harmless guest. He then went out and told the crowd to disperse. They refused and continued to demand "the stranger's" blood.

"Do you love Padre Pio?" Morcaldi called out.

Cries of "Yes! Yes!" burst from the darkness.

"Then do what he says! Do what I told you! Obey him! Go back to your homes! The guest will leave for Foggia at five this very morning!" Morcaldi promised.[6]

And so, around 2:30 a.m., on April 8, the crowd finally began to disperse, and at five, poor Padre Eugenio, frightened nearly out of his wits, set out by bus to Foggia.

"This Trial of Fire"

Learning of the incident, and after the local law-enforcement authorities once again insisted that the transfer of Padre Pio was impossible, Macchi asked the Holy Office: (1) to withdraw permission for Padre Pio to hear women's confessions; (2) to prohibit him from talking to them in the guest room; (3) to forbid priests and brothers from going to him; and (4) (because he was certain that people were sending Padre Pio money orders) to keep him from receiving all mail. "In this way, Padre Pio can be forgotten by everybody," he reasoned.[7]

When Macchi's letter reached the Holy Office, the "inquisitors general" were in favor of suspending all Padre Pio's priestly faculties except that of celebrating Mass in private. Raffaello Rossi, who had conducted the 1921 investigation by the Holy Office, was now a cardinal and insisted, "Either Padre Pio goes or the religious go." If Padre Pio was allowed to stay, Rossi wanted all the priests and brothers in the monastery gradually transferred away. The final decision was made by the pope: "Padre Pio is to be stripped of all the faculties of his priestly ministry except the faculty to celebrate the Holy Mass, which he may continue to do, provided that it is done in private, within the walls of the friary, in the inner chapel, and not publicly in church."[8]

On June 11, 1931, after Vespers, Padre Raffaele summoned Padre Pio to the guest room of the friary and, without comment, read him the decree. "God's will be done," was Padre Pio's response. Then, covering his eyes with his hands and lowering his head, he murmured, "The will of the superiors is the will of God."[9]

When Padre Agostino came to see him on July 1, Padre Pio was not as stoical. As soon as his old friend entered his room, Padre Pio burst into tears, sobbing, "I never thought this would happen!"

"But it has," answered Padre Agostino. "Jesus wants it this way. Let his will be done. You must remain hanging on the cross. Men will continue to nail you to it, but, in the end, everything will work out for the glory of God and the good of souls."[10]

Thus began two years that Padre Pio called his "imprisonment," a trial he offered as a sacrifice to God for the salvation of the lost.

During this period, he began his day with the rest of the community. After saying the Office with his confreres in the choir, he prepared for Mass, which he celebrated, not in the church, but in a small chapel inside the friary, in the company of one server. Now, at least, he was free to spend as much time as he wished in mystic communion with God. Because there was no congregation, no limit was set on the length of his Mass, which, at times, lasted as long as four hours, although ninety minutes was usual. What protracted Padre Pio's celebration of the Mass to such lengths, Padre Agostino observed, were the Remembrance of the Living and the Remembrance of the Dead. Padre Pio claimed that, while celebrating Mass, he saw all the souls whom God was entrusting to him, and now he had unlimited time to spend in intercession for them.

The rest of Padre Pio's day was spent in study and prayer. He studied the Bible and went through volume after volume of Church history as well as the writings of the Church Fathers. The Capuchin lifestyle had relaxed somewhat from the days when Padre Pio was a very young man, and the friars no longer had as many restrictions on fellowship. Once, when Padre Agostino asked him how he passed his time, Padre Pio replied, "I pray and I study as much as I can, then I annoy my Brothers."

"How is it possible for you to annoy them?" Padre Agostino asked.

"I joke the way I always joke with them, but my jokes are worse than before."[11]

At midnight, when it was time for Matins, Padre Pio would pound on his table to waken his confreres. After going to the choir to recite the Office of Matins with the rest of the community, he finally went to bed.

Frequently alone with his thoughts, Padre Pio was troubled more than ever by his habitual uncertainty as to whether he was pleasing God. He told Padre Agostino, "I would prefer a thousand crosses … to this ordeal of never feeling certain as to whether I'm pleasing the Lord in what I'm doing."[12]

Sometimes all celestial comforts seemed withdrawn. When Padre Agostino visited him in November 1931, Padre Pio confided, "Jesus is silent," leading his friend to believe that now "those visions that once brought so much comfort to his spirit have vanished." Despite being "a bit depressed," Padre Pio insisted that he was ready to submit to the will of God.[13] However, when Padre Agostino returned to San Giovanni on the second day of 1932 to hear Padre Pio's confession, he observed that "often Jesus makes himself felt, speaking to his soul and granting him intellectual visions." Padre Pio also reported experiencing the presence of Mary and of his guardian angel.[14]

Although he was not permitted to see them or write to them, some of Padre Pio's spiritual children claimed that he visited them in bilocation. Padre Agostino was told of such an experience by Suor Beniamina of Florence, who told him that one morning, after she had received Communion, Padre Pio appeared to her, comforted her, and blessed her. With this in mind, Padre Agostino asked Padre Pio, "Do you often make little trips — like, to Florence?" When Padre Pio ignored him, Padre Agostino added, "A nun told me this. Is it true?" Padre Pio answered, "Yes," and that was the end of the matter.[15]

San Giovanni seemed deserted most of the time. Many spiritual children who had taken up residence there to be near Padre Pio left after they were told that the Vatican's decree was irrevocable and that their beloved spiritual father would never again be permitted to have contact with the public. Even so, many busloads of pilgrims continued to come to San Giovanni to pray for his liberation and recite the Rosary in unison in front of the friary. In the next few months, there were frequent peaceful demonstrations. Petitions for the "liberation" of the beloved priest, signed by thousands of people from every strata of society, reached the pope — who did not respond to them.

A group of Padre Pio's spiritual daughters would gather in church around ten each morning to pray for his liberation. One of them later wrote, "The Padre at that hour was in the choir; but we never had even the feeble consolation of seeing him enter or leave. They prohibited him from getting near the railing. One spiritual son, who succeeded in going upstairs, said that the saintly prisoner stayed in a corner of the choir, praying, and that often he wiped away tears." Francesco Morcaldi somehow got a note from Padre Pio, smuggled out of the monastery, in which he wrote: "You must know that the Lord chooses the priest for the altar and confessional. I suffer not for myself, but for the souls. But may God's will be done. To Jesus I say, 'What shall I offer you for this trial of fire?'" His message for his spiritual children was: "Pray always. I bless you with abundant holy affection."[16]

"False and Unworthy Propaganda"

Dr. Giorgio Festa, who had examined Padre Pio's wounds more than a decade before, at this time wrote *The Mysteries of Science in Light of Faith*, a scholarly book favorable to the Capuchin, but it could not be published because the Holy Office had banned all publications on Padre Pio. Morcaldi, however, got the manuscript into the hands of Cardinal Gasparri, who convinced the Holy Office not to place it on the Index of Forbidden Books. The book was published and read by several cardinals, who seemed to be favorably impressed.

Then there came a second publication that set back Padre Pio's cause. Early in 1932, Alberto Del Fante and Carolina Giovannini published *Padre Pio of Pietrelcina: Messenger of the Lord*. In their insistence that Padre Pio was "a messenger of the Lord," the authors were contradicting the Holy Office, which had stated that the supernatural character of his ministry could not be confirmed. The book was put on the Index. When the "Seraphic College" was removed from San Giovanni Rotondo shortly afterward, many felt that this book was to blame. Morcaldi complained bitterly that the Holy Office considered Padre Pio "a noxious Socrates, capable of perverting the fragile lives and souls of boys."[17]

Some of Padre Pio's friends were furious with Del Fante and Giovannini. Padre Agostino described Giovannini as "a truly fanatical, hysterical woman used by Satan to muddy the waters."[18] He accused Maria Pyle — whom he characterized in his diary as a convert from "Lutheranism" (a common catchword in southern Italy for all Christians who were not Catholic) — of giving information to the authors. Even though her guilt in this matter was never established, "the American" was shunned for months by the Sangiovannese. People refused to speak to her, they withdrew from the Communion rail when she went forward to receive the Host, and some women even recited prayers of exorcism against her.

In the meantime, Monsignor Macchi, who had administered the diocese for two years, was appointed bishop of Como, and Monsignor Andrea Cesarano (1880–1969), a gaunt, hawk-nosed man with a flowing beard, was consecrated as archbishop of Manfredonia during the summer of 1931. On April 2 of the following year, Padre Pio wrote to him, defending himself against complicity with the authors of the Del Fante-Giovannini book as well as other friends who had been attacking the Holy Office and the Church itself:

> From the profound silence of my little cell I hear the echo of the sinister voices that surround my poor person. Everything is false. Therefore I want to report to your most illustrious and most reverend excellency that I am completely innocent of all that was said and is said, affirmed, or printed concerning me. I must repeat that I am very disgusted by the unworthy behavior of certain false prophets who speak in my behalf, because, time and time again … I have

let them know that all they do and say is a wound that immeasurably tears my heart, that goes against the truth, and that they should stop this false and unworthy propaganda, but meanwhile they have followed in their morbid fanaticism, not caring about the supreme authority of the church.

I also warned Mrs. Carolina Giovannini, Del Fante, the author of two books about me, Tonelli, the author of the article against the Holy Office, his brother-in-law, the photographer Abresch and Mr. Luigi Dorigo, to stop their false enthusiasm and recalled them to the observation of the dispositions of the Holy Office, and meanwhile I have had no result; rather, it had the opposite effect.

I must add that many times I have appealed directly to [them] ... to stop their rebellious attitude towards the rulings of the Church, but with no result.

I turn, therefore, as a son most humble and completely obedient to the Catholic Church, to your most reverend excellency, that you may wish to intervene with your authority to disperse these bleak clouds and shadows that envelope my poor person and grieve my poor mother province that has suffered silently for so many years, as well as the devoted people of San Giovanni.

With profound humility I kiss your sacred ring and profess myself to your excellency your most humble and obedient son.

P. Pio of Pietrelcina, Capuchin[19]

In October 1932, Morcaldi wrote to the new papal secretary of state, Cardinal Eugenio Pacelli, who had been apostolic nuncio to Germany and was acquainted with the Bavarian mystic and stigmatic Therese Neumann. He told the cardinal about "the seraphic little friar," the fame of whose "heroic virtue ... has burst the confines of the little town hidden in the mountains" where he lived, and how "a humanity laden with sufferings, ... bewildered and perplexed" saw in him a "ray of light to guide it."[20]

Brunatto now announced, however, that he was going to blackmail the Vatican by publishing a book detailing and documenting financial malfeasance and homosexual conduct in the highest ranks of the Church. Morcaldi, who previously had worked with him, was horrified. He called Brunatto a "second Luther ... trying to dismantle the Church of Christ." Brunatto said he had no fear of excommunication and predicted that the faithful would rise up en masse once he brought the "irrefutable documents to light." He planned to publish *The Anti-Christs in the Church of Christ* in French. Cardinal Rossi read a draft of the book and was alarmed. He sent Bishop Luca Ermenegildo Pasetto and Monsignor Felice Bevilacqua to San Giovanni to ask Padre Pio to write to Brunatto and make him desist.

Pasetto and Bevilacqua passed through the armed guard of citizens who guarded the friary and found Padre Pio in the chapel, celebrating Mass, which had begun at

6:00 a.m. They went in to join him, but the Mass dragged on so long they became tired and left. Padre Pio didn't conclude until 10:00 a.m. After that, he joined his guests in the parlor, dined with them, and talked most of the afternoon. Pasetto and Bevilacqua later said that they were impressed with Padre Pio's humility and docility and found a man of prayer who was humorous as well. They expressed their concern, however, to both Padre Pio and his superior Padre Raffaele, about Brunatto's intended publication. Bevilacqua warned Pio of the terrible damage to the reputation of the Church that would be occasioned if Brunatto went through with his threat to publish.

"But the Church has a formidable weapon to neutralize scandal," Padre Pio offered. "Refute the episodes alleged in the book that could create a scandal."

There was silence. Bevilacqua, his eyes brimming with tears, shook his head and admitted, "Unfortunately, those allegations are true."[21]

Padre Pio took two days to draft a letter he sent to Brunatto on March 15, 1933:

I write this to express my surprise and my pain in hearing that you want to put in print what not only absolutely should not be printed, but what no human being ought to know. And my pain is augmented when I think that you're threatening to do this if the undersigned isn't immediately rehabilitated. But I absolutely do not wish to obtain my liberation or rehabilitation by means of actions that are repugnant, that would make the most vulgar criminal blush.

Emmanuele, do you truly wish me well? Then you must, at least for love of me, desist from such an intention and never think of it anymore. Rather, I pray you and implore you to destroy all this horrible stuff, and give up at once the documents you have. You know that I've been good to you and in light of this good I'm sure you won't tell me no. Jesus will take account of this good deed of yours and by means of it will more readily pardon others that sadden his divine heart. No, you can't deny me what I beg you in the name of God. If, in spite of this prayer of mine, made with absolute fervor by one who loves and who suffers everything, you still wish to be obstinate in your intentions, which are unworthy of a good Christian, understand that never more will my hand be raised over you in blessing.

And now I have to tell you in conscience that I absolutely cannot permit you to defend me or try to liberate me by throwing mud and dirt in the face of persons that I, you, and everybody have a sacred duty to respect. Your defense of me is a true dishonor, and I do not wish, I repeat, even if it were possible, to obtain my liberation and the faculties they took away from me, by such means. By the injudicious publication of that book, on top of all evil you'll cause, you'll make things worse for all those you want to defend. And then you say you wish to do good for those you think are oppressed. Think seriously, Emmanuele, and don't make me die of grief before my time.

But, forget my destruction. You remember perhaps that I still have my old father, almost eighty, whom you would cause to die of a broken heart. He's already sick with grief over my situation. Just a little bit more would be enough to give him the coup de grâce. Oh, if you could know how my poor heart bleeds from such pain at the thought of so many worries. So therefore don't you add sorrow to sorrow. Listen to me, Emmanuele, at least do it for my poor daddy who has always loved you like a son. Jesus alone knows the prayers that I've lifted up to the Divine Heart. Therefore, for the sake of the prayers and for the good that I have wished you and wish you still, do not wish to deny this thing which I am asking of you. Yes, burn [the manuscript] and hand over everything that you want to print to the proper authorities as soon as possible.

In the hope that you want to listen to me, I bless you with all the effusion of my heart.[22]

Brunatto, however, suspected that Padre Pio had written through holy obedience to his superiors and wrote back that he was going ahead with publication, promising, "Before Easter ... you will be restored to full priestly exercise" or else "a storm will be unleashed like an earthquake shock that will shake the world."[23]

Padre Pio wrote the minister general of the Capuchins, Padre Vigilio of Valstagna, saying that he had tried to get Brunatto to desist, but, although "he takes time to make a decision, once he's made it, nothing can make him desist, neither fear nor caress nor even the dread of death." He confessed that there seemed to be nothing that anyone could do to stop his determined defender. "May the Holy Spirit and Immaculate Virgin illuminate who they have to illuminate and contain the flood that is about to overflow everything."[24] He told Padre Vigilio, "I am humiliated and terrorized at the thought of the pandemonium that will be created. ... May the Lord intervene directly and save our holy Mother Church from such a disaster."[25]

Once again Padre Pio tried to plead with Brunatto, writing on April 12:

Dearest Emmanuele,

My son ... submit yourself in humility and penitence, and with a contrite heart, resolve to return to the way of the Lord who does not wish his beloved daughter, the Church, to be humiliated and mortified.

Would you dare to pierce the heart of a mother and humiliate her before the entire world!

If you were here, I would press you to my heart, I would throw myself at your feet to implore you and say to you: Let the Lord pass judgment on human wretchedness, not you. Let me do the will of the Lord, to which I am fully committed. All that could cause sadness and harm, leave at the feet of

Holy Mother Church. And the peace of the Lord and his blessings will descend on you and your work.

I bless you with all the effusion of my soul.

P. Pio, Capuchin[26]

A few days later, he wrote Brunatto again, "If … you [still] wish to remain deaf, which I still don't want to believe, to my repeated pleas, I forbid you in any way to involve my name in any publication of such a nature that ought to make you blush for shame and tremble with fear. Moreover, I have the right to make a public warning concerning the publication and make clear that I did this to stop it. May the Lord have mercy on you and may you desire to see the light and return to the right path."[27]

"Don't Weep Anymore. Thank the Lord"

On July 12, 1933, the Holy Office relented. Padre Pio was allowed once more to celebrate Mass in public and to hear confessions, but only of the clergy. Pope Pius XI directed the minister general to "take the necessary precautions to avoid both false interpretations and unsuitable public demonstrations inside and outside the church."[28] According to the Holy Office, this reprieve was given because of "good conduct during these last years."

Cardinal Sbarretti, the secretary, had been impressed by the reports submitted every two months by Padre Raffaele of Sant'Elia a Pianisi, Padre Pio's superior. The father guardian had written that after Mass Padre Pio remained in the chapel "for an hour of thanksgiving, and, after spending another hour of community prayer, he goes to the library where he reads books about ascetics and the Church Fathers. He does the same in the afternoon after Vespers: an hour of prayer and then reading until the evening. He does not eat much food: he never has supper, just as he never has coffee or anything else in the morning. At night he goes to the chapel for more than two hours of contemplative prayer, going to bed at a very late hour. One can say without exaggeration that during the day he prays continuously, because, when he walks the halls, we see his lips moving and he is fingering his rosary beads."[29]

Moreover, the new archbishop of Manfredonia, Andrea Cesarano, who had visited Padre Pio earlier that year and found him cheerful, submissive, and devout, seems to have put in a good word for the Capuchin to the Vatican. Furthermore, on July 7, the Capuchin minister general, Padre Vigilio of Vastagna, had met with Cardinal Sbarretti and asked him to restore to Padre Pio the faculty to celebrate Mass publicly.

Many people were convinced that the real reason for Padre Pio's liberation was Brunatto's threat to air the Vatican's dirty laundry. Others were convinced that the most important factors were the reports documenting Padre Pio's good conduct, the request of the Capuchin minister general, and the support of the new archbishop of Manfredonia.

Padre Pio learned of his liberation on July 15, when the minister provincial, Padre Bernardo, arrived at the monastery. The community was in the refectory for supper, while Padre Pio was in the choir, praying. Padre Raffaele, the father guardian, sent a friar to call Padre Pio "for an important message from the provincial." As soon as Padre Pio was seated at his place in the dining room, Padre Bernardo announced, "It is the will of the Holy Father that you may celebrate Holy Mass in public, starting tomorrow." Padre Raffaele noted in his diary, there was "a clapping of hands and cheers for the Pope and for Padre Pio, who, touched and with tearful eyes, rose and kissed the Provincial's hand, and, with a voice trembling with emotion, asked him to convey his thanks to His Holiness."[30]

The next day, Padre Bernardo announced to the people who happened to be in church that Padre Pio was once more permitted to celebrate Mass in public. The news spread like wildfire, and soon the Church of Our Lady of Grace was packed with worshipers weeping with emotion. One of his spiritual daughters recalled that the beloved priest approached the altar with eyes lowered, obviously in tears. As he distributed Communion, from time to time he whispered, "Don't weep anymore. Thank the Lord."[31]

Padre Pio was still not allowed to hear confessions; but on March 14, 1934, after a request by the minister general, the Holy Office requested and obtained from Pope Pius XI permission to Padre Pio to hear the confessions of men. Authorization to administer the Sacrament of Penance to women was given in May — so long as no disturbances resulted, in which case the superior was to withdraw that permission. Padre Pio was, however, required to return to the part of the friary that was off-limits to the public without engaging in any conversations for any reason. As time went on, this restriction was relaxed. At some point, the "Seraphic College" was returned to San Giovanni Rotondo as well.

As for Brunatto, he was now a *persona non grata* with the Capuchins, who made it clear that he was no longer welcome anywhere around the friary. Although Padre Pio would have no contact with him for years, Brunatto would, nevertheless, play a large and continuing role in the life and ministry of the Capuchin with the stigmata.

"What a Fearsome Thing a Saint Is!"

Padre Pio was forty-seven years old on May 25, 1934. His friends thought that he had aged perceptibly during his "incarceration." His beard was grayer, although his hair, thinning slightly, retained its auburn hue. He was stouter, despite Padre Agostino's observation that his food intake was "not sufficient for anyone who works as he does."[1] Although he generally slept five hours or fewer in twenty-four (two during the afternoon siesta and two or three at night), Padre Agostino said Padre Pio never seemed tired, but always "quick, jovial, and friendly." A visiting journalist thought that he combined the manners of a sheep farmer and a shepherd of souls.

By now, Pio was being accorded an increasing respect by the Church hierarchy, as many Vatican luminaries were now convinced that he really was a saint. Now that Cesarano was archbishop of Manfredonia, the complaints of hostile clergy no longer found a willing ear. For many years, it was assumed that, at least at first, Pope Pius XI held an unfavorable opinion of Padre Pio, but documents that have come to light in recent years reveal that his chief concern was with the disorder and confusion surrounding the stigmatized priest. It seems that by the time he urged Gagliardi to retire, the pope realized that he had been badly misinformed about Padre Pio.

"Who Am I? … Am I Deluded?"

Even though it seemed to others that he was in direct communion with the Divine, somehow Padre Pio did not feel a sense of intimacy with God. All his life, he feared that God would find him guilty of some unconfessed sin. He told Padre Giovanni of Baggio, a priest from northern Italy, "I leave the confessional troubled as to whether I've done good or done wrong. I can't find anything that would either accuse me or excuse me…. Doubt never leaves me. It torments me day and night and I ask myself: 'Who am I? I don't know. Am I deluded? I don't know.'" He wondered whether his visions and illuminations were "diabolical illusions" or "the effects of nature."

After joyous mystical experiences, he often experienced "the continuous torment" of the fear that he was deluded. He told Padre Giovanni that he felt unworthy to administer the sacraments and sighed, "If as a student I had known what I do now, I would have retired to a desert and I would not have been ordained a priest."[2]

Padre Agostino, who regularly heard Padre Pio's confessions, wrote in his diary, "The [trial] continues fixed in his soul without letup. Although it does not drive him to absolute despair, it always keeps him uncertain of whether or not he is doing good or evil and whether he is pleasing or displeasing God." In October 1934, Padre Pio told Padre Agostino of his fears about not being in a state of grace. "I'm thankful to God that he doesn't give me the time to think about this matter for long," he said, "since I have so many other things to think about. But if I did think about this terrible trial, I would surely lose my mind!"[3] In January 1937, he described himself to Padre Agostino as living in "pitch darkness." "I don't know how to go on anymore," he told his confessor. "Even the memory of your assurances ... does not bring me comfort. It is an unspeakable torment. I do not despair, but I don't understand any of this."[4]

It was during this period that Padre Pio composed his meditation on the agony of Jesus in the Garden of Gethsemane, in which he argued that the children of God must suffer Christ's grief and pain for the sake of their own salvation and that of others. He maintained that Christ's "desolate heart has need of comfort" and that it is the duty of Christians to share Christ's pain and mortal anguish.

"The Sainted Padre Pio"

It was also during the late 1930s that the Capuchin minister general, Padre Vigilio of Valstagna, accorded Padre Pio permission to preach *honoris causa*, despite having never taken the examination for a preaching license. During the following years, Padre Pio preached no more than several times a year. A priest who heard his sermons described him as just "an ordinary preacher." Apparently, he preached without notes, as only a handful of his homilies have been preserved.

Padre Bernardo of Alpicilla died of malaria at fifty-four, on the last day of 1937, and was replaced as minister provincial by Padre Agostino. That same year, Padre Vigilio's term as minister general ended, and Father Donatus Wynant of Welle, a Belgian, was elected to take his place.

Father Donatus had heard a great deal about Padre Pio and was eager to meet him, and so, on August 7, 1938, accompanied by Padre Agostino, he appeared at San Giovanni. Father Donatus, who wanted to make a close study of everything concerning the stigmatic and his environment, wrote:

> I examined the stigmata and spoke frequently with Padre Pio on every kind of question. In this first encounter I wanted to inquire concerning ... the

natural humanity of the priest. Was he perhaps neurotic? hysterical? docile? violent? a dreamer? stupid? sad? fanatical? After repeated inquiries, I was able to conclude that in every sense Padre Pio was absolutely sound spiritually, and I was left with the certainty of a sincerity and a simplicity incapable … of saying yes when no was appropriate.

The minister general continued:

I can and must affirm that in all the contacts I had with Padre Pio, I was deeply moved by his practice of virtue, his serenity, his humility … his attitude of forgiveness that never allowed him to say a word against those who had offended him … his habitual recollection … his true affection towards his superiors … his perfect obedience to all ecclesiastical authorities, his sane piety, and his modesty. Personally, I have to add that I consider Padre Pio a great saint.[5]

Father Donatus was not the only one to hold such an opinion. When eighty-one-year-old Pope Pius XI died in February 1939, Cardinal Pacelli was elected to succeed him, taking the name Pius XII. The new Pope Pius held the Capuchin stigmatist in great esteem. From the first, the pope encouraged the faithful to visit him. "Go ahead, it might do you some good," he often told people at audiences who, in light of the decrees of the Holy Office a decade or so earlier, asked him whether a visit to Padre Pio had papal approval. He seemed, from the start, completely convinced of Padre Pio's holiness.

More and more people climbed the rocky hill each year to the monastery of Our Lady of Grace, much to Padre Pio's dismay. "I disapprove of people making pilgrimages to me," he complained to Padre Agostino. "I wish that they would discourage people from coming in groups like this. It keeps me from hearing confessions as I ought."[6] The friary groaned under a deluge of letters from all over the world. One day Padre Pio showed another priest a letter addressed to him and read the salutation aloud: "To the sainted Padre Pio … *Sainted!* … How *beautiful!* … To the *sainted* Padre Pio!"

"You're not getting proud, are you?" asked the other priest.

Spreading his arms and lowering them to imitate someone boasting, Padre Pio quipped, "Oh, yes, friend, I'm getting quite proud of it now!" and burst out laughing.[7] For him, being considered a saint was a joke.

The Pious Women

Fanaticism on the part of the locals remained a problem. The bane of Padre Pio's ministry was the gaggle of enthusiastic women (*Le Pie Donne* — "The Pious Ladies") who haunted the church. They literally fought each other for the best seats when

Padre Pio celebrated Mass and for the opportunity to go to confession with him at the most convenient times, frequently directing their ire, through means of fingernails, hairpins, and even knives, toward outsiders who dared to take up the time of "their" Padre Pio.

One of the first problems at San Giovanni that Padre Agostino had to investigate as provincial was the claim of a certain unnamed "holy woman" who swore that Padre Pio was admitting women into the friary at night, obviously for immoral purposes. The woman told Padre Agostino that at the stroke of eleven that very night a certain woman would be admitted to the church. Sure enough, at eleven, a woman was seen approaching the friary from the courtyard. She stopped behind a stone cross, slipped behind an elm tree, then made a run for the church. A friar was sent to make a thorough search of the church, but found no evidence that anyone had gotten in. At last it was discovered that the woman who had accused Padre Pio of admitting women to the monastery was the very person who had been seen that night: instead of entering the church, she had hidden herself in some building materials outside the line of vision of those who observed her approaching the premises. When she was caught emerging from her hiding place, she admitted that she was angry because Padre Pio was giving too much of his time to a woman she despised. Therefore, she had decided to take revenge on him by carrying out her silly plot. "You can't put anything past a jealous woman, even if she is devout," Padre Agostino noted in his diary.[8]

To keep the "Pious Ladies" in order, Padre Pio would shout at them, even using the cord around his waist as a weapon, swinging and twirling it to keep people from tearing his habit off his body. One day, one of the friars let him know that one of the women was outraged that the saintly priest had lost his temper. "I'm glad I made her think so," he laughed.

Padre Alberto D'Apolito wrote: "The fanatics … were young, single, old maids, widows, dedicated to a life of piety, who regularly frequented the churches, always looking for confessors. Morbidly jealous, they blindly obeyed their spiritual directors, as they would their own husbands, prone always to sentimental effusions and even to things more intimate. Some fanatics, full of scruples, tormented by doubt about their sinfulness, to make themselves feel better, went to other places to make their confessions and went to whatever strange priest would put up with them." After he came to San Giovanni Rotondo, Alberto explained, Padre Pio "attracted about him a huge gathering of souls desirous of spiritual direction.… After the phenomenon of the stigmata, the number of spiritual daughters grew by the day. The fanatics, not satisfied with their [original] confessors, began to abandon them, to put themselves under the guidance of Padre Pio." In fact, "many young women, seeing the dream of matrimony vanish, hurried to the convent of Padre Pio, for a new experience." Alberto (and many others) characterized "most of them" as "gossips … air-headed and jealous," who, hovering around the confessional, noted the time Padre Pio took with each of his penitents, often flying into rages at women with whom he spent more time. Padre Alberto opined, "The poor little women didn't understand that Padre Pio used different methods in direction, according to the state of each soul and her needs. With some he was brief, with others he talked a little longer. This difference in treatment was the reason for unseemly rancor and jealousy that often exploded in blasphemous quarrels."[9]

Among the "Pious Ladies" were two embittered old maids, Angela (1886–1976) and Elvira (1890–1964) Serritelli. Padre Alberto (who was born in 1905) had both of them as elementary-school teachers. At the time, "both were engaged and I still remember the young lovers, who often came into the school classrooms and engaged in intimate conversation, while we students raised Cain. Both of them failed to get married."[10]

Another of the "Pious Ladies" was Countess Rina Telfner, who came to San Giovanni Rotondo in 1936 with her husband from the northern city of Perugia. The countess defended her demand for special privileges because she said they gave up a life of luxury to dwell in a southern backwater town. "I gave up my life to stay near the Padre," she was often heard to say.[11]

Preeminent among the "Pious Ladies," in the estimation of most, was Cleonice Morcaldi, who, like the Serritellis, was an old-maid schoolteacher. She lost her father in early childhood and was extremely attached to her mother, whose death in 1937 devastated her. Three weeks later, Padre Pio comforted her, saying, "Hey, listen! This morning, during Mass, your mother flew to Paradise!"[12] A few weeks later, he wrote to her: "I understand well the mission given to me by Providence. If in the past I made up for your lack of a daddy, from this moment I feel moved to the depth of my heart also to assume the other role of mamma."

Morcaldi was then in her thirties, but Padre Pio treated her as if she were a little girl in desperate need of parental affection. She wrote down everything he told her in the confessional and gave him notes on which he was supposed to write his response. He often addressed her in saccharine language. In one exchange, he scribbled:

Little daughter most beloved in the heart of Mummy: Jesus be the center of all our aspirations and our sustenance and comfort in all our tribulations. Your mummy … wants you to know that she is all yours and her affection is unchangeable for you and will never be less. That which the Lord is pleased to unite with his divine love will never be diminished through all eternity. Live in peace and all in Jesus and for Jesus and in your Mummy and don't fear the tempests that the devil and his apostates stir up. What Jesus has joined no one will ever be able to separate. Mummy sends you a flood of blessings every moment of your life as well as kisses in the sweet Lord. I bless you with paternal and always growing affection.[13]

Cleonice seems always to have been distraught and in need of comfort, and Padre Pio would write on the notes she passed to him: "Little girl, believe that your daddy is burning with the desire of seeing you"; "Mummy sends you a million kisses. I bless you continually with all the effusion of my heart"; "Mummy ... lives for his little daughter and for God. Therefore calm yourself and live serenely."[14]

Out of their context, these notes seem very strange, and a couple decades later they would cause much heartache for Padre Pio, who was convinced that he was treating Cleonice as God directed him.

"Who Said Your Mother Could Not Be Saved?"

Maria Pyle, after Padre Pio's "liberation," was generally back in the good graces of the Sangiovannese, including those of the "Pious Ladies." Likely because she was a foreigner, she was never considered one of them, although she had a similar fervent, even fanatical, loyalty to the Padre. "Neither in heaven nor on earth do I wish to remain without Padre Pio," she insisted. "I should be happy to be the nail of Padre Pio's little finger."[15] She never displayed, evidently, the jealousy and aggression of some of the other followers of the stigmatized priest, and she continually used her considerable financial resources for the benefit of the community.

Adelaide Pyle made annual visits to San Giovanni, and Maria was always trying to convert her to Catholicism. In the summer of 1936, when Adelaide left San Giovanni Rotondo to go home, Padre Pio pointed heavenward, saying, "I hope we will see each other again soon, but if we don't see each other here, we will see each other up there." The next year Mrs. Pyle was too sick to go to San Giovanni and asked Maria to visit her in London, where she had been staying. Maria told Padre Pio that she had no desire to go, but he told her, "For all you know, this could be the last time you see your mother." So Maria went. Adelaide returned to the States, arriving in New York on September 6,[16] and died in her home in Noroton, Connecticut, on September 23, at the age of seventy-seven. Her funeral was conducted at the Brick Presbyterian Church. Because her mother was not a Catholic, Maria worried about her salvation, telling Padre Pio that she had dreamed that her mother was standing outside the door of St. Peter's Basilica. He chided her, "And who said your mother could not be saved?"[17]

Adelaide evidently did not trust her six children to make proper use of her money, so she set up equal trust funds for all of them. She died in possession of property valued at $50,000 and left her summer house in Maine, "The Anchorage," to all her children — except Maria.[18] Pyle had, however, enough money coming from her mother's estate to continue her generous charities for the rest of her life.

The Death of a King

Reports of paranormal experiences continued. For example, on the evening of

January 20, 1936, three laymen were visiting Padre Pio in his room when suddenly the priest knelt down on the floor and asked them to pray "for a soul that is soon to appear before the tribunal of God." They all knelt and joined him in prayer. When they arose, Padre Pio asked, "Do you know who you just prayed for?" They said they did not. He replied, "It was for the king of England."

Padre Pio's companions pointed out that there had been nothing in the papers to indicate that the king's life was in danger. It was reported only that the monarch had a touch of the flu. "It is as I say," insisted Padre Pio.

Around midnight, Padre Pio knocked on the door of Padre Aurelio of Sant'Elia a Pianisi. When Aurelio opened, Padre Pio, without entering, told him, "Let us pray for a soul which at this moment is to appear before the tribunal of God — the king of England." The two priests prayed, and then Padre Pio returned to his room.

The next morning, the Italian newspapers announced the death of King George V of the United Kingdom.

As far as is known, Padre Pio had no contact with any member of the British royal family. It is not known why he should have had such concern for King George. The monarch, a member of the Church of England, of which he was the nominal head, was a moderately religious man who read a chapter of the Bible each day of his adult life, but professed not to understand all of it, frequently remarking, "There are some very queer things in it." When he ascended the throne in 1910, George refused to abide by a two-hundred-year-old tradition whereby a British sovereign, upon addressing Parliament for the first time, declared the invocation of the Virgin Mary as well as the Sacrifice of the Mass as "superstitious and idolatrous."[19] At any rate, at 11:55 on the night of January 20, about the same time that Padre Pio appeared at Padre Aurelio's door, the king, who suffered from emphysema, was euthanized by his physician by means of a lethal dose of morphine and cocaine. As the archbishop of Canterbury rendered the prayer that begins, "Go forth, Christian soul," the king looked at his doctor, muttered, "God damn you!" and died.[20]

A Dream or a Visitor from the Great Beyond?

Another apparently supernatural occurrence, at the end of the same year, was recorded in the diary of Padre Agostino. On December 29, 1936, Padre Giacinto of Sant'Elia a Pianisi, who lived at the Friary of St. Anne in Foggia, came to Padre Pio on behalf of a member of his community, Giuseppe Antonio of San Marco in Lamis, a fifty-five-year-old priest critically ill with Bright's disease (kidney failure). That night Padre Pio went to bed around one in the morning. Sometime before three, he opened his eyes and saw Padre Giuseppe Antonio standing in his cell.

"Why Padre Giuseppe Antonio!" he exclaimed. "What are you doing here? They told me that you were so very ill, but now I have the pleasure of seeing you well!"

"Well, all my pains are over now," said Giuseppe Antonio, and vanished into thin air.[21]

Only a dream, it seemed to be. However, the next day the community at San Giovanni was notified that Padre Giuseppe Antonio had died the previous night, just before three.

A "Two-Year Reprieve"

Sometime in 1939, the celebrated Italian playwright Luigi Antonelli came from his home in Pescara to visit Padre Pio. The sixty-two-year-old author told the priest that he was suffering from cancer, evidently of the head and neck. His doctor wanted to operate, but, even with the surgery, predicted that he could not survive more than six months. After attending Mass, Antonelli went to confession with Padre Pio. "I cannot repeat what he said to me," he later recounted, "because, while he was speaking to me I seemed to be living in a supernatural world." A few months later Antonelli insisted that he noticed an improvement at once: "I don't know whether the word 'miracle' is exact from the theological point of view, but ... we'll not split hairs upon words ... I am now writing ... an article every Sunday for the *Giornale D'Italia*. I go hunting. For the past month I have been working on a comedy which will be produced at the Manzoni Theatre in Milan. I don't know what the doctors may think about it, I don't know what X-rays and histological examination may reveal ... but today I feel that I am miraculously cured."[22]

Without surgery, Antonelli's doctors warned him that he would be dead in three months, but he lived three years, apparently working and active for most of that time.[23] It seems to have been a case of one of the "two-year reprieves" that became associated with Padre Pio's prayers.

The Conversion of a "Materialist"

Before he died, Antonelli told his experience to another noted author, Dino Segre, who wrote under the pen name of Pitigrilli, and whose 1921 novel *Cocaine* had been placed on the Index of Forbidden Books. By his own admission, the forty-six-year-old writer, the child of a Jewish father and a Catholic mother, was a "materialist," although "a seeker of truth." Running into Antonelli in Foggia, Segre learned about the dramatic improvement in the playwright's health, which he attributed to Padre Pio's prayers, and, at Antonelli's suggestion, he went to San Giovanni Rotondo.

Segre attended a Mass Padre Pio celebrated, sitting far back in the church. As far as he could tell, he was unknown and unrecognized, but when the time came for the congregation to pray for various intentions, Padre Pio declared, "Pray, brethren, pray fervently for someone who is here among you today, someone who is in great need of prayer. One day he will approach the Eucharistic Table and will bring many with him who have been in error like himself." Segre was convinced that Padre Pio was talking about him, and he broke down in tears. He went to confession with Padre Pio, who told him: "What does it profit a man to gain the whole world and lose his soul? Truly, God has been good to you." Segre underwent a deep and lasting conversion and even asked his publisher to withdraw from publication certain books that he felt were not consistent with his Christian faith.[24]

Bilocation in Uruguay

Fernando Damiani, vicar general of Salto, Uruguay, had been devoted to Padre Pio for many years. It was he who brought home the glove of Padre Pio that was applied to the body of Sister Teresa Salvadores in 1921. According to Father Hugo Caballero, one of the few people who still remembered Damiani in 1981, the vicar general was "an honest, kindly man who was in love with the liturgy and the beautiful and fascinating ceremonies of that period. He was not a man given to mystical experiences, but was a practical man, but very pious."[25] Born in Uruguay in 1877, of Italian descent, Damiani had been a college chaplain in Salto before going to Chile early in his career to join a contemplative community. After a time, he returned to Uruguay, where he founded a number of agricultural unions and workingmen's savings banks in the rural parish of Rosario, where he was known as a champion of the poor and dispossessed. Eventually, he was appointed general director of all the Church's social works in Uruguay.

Damiani made numerous trips to see Padre Pio. In 1929, he was diagnosed with cancer of the rectum, but, after prayer by Padre Pio, all signs of the malignancy disappeared, so that specialists in both Rome and the parish of Rosario refused to believe that he had ever had cancer, until Damiani showed them X-rays taken in Uruguay.[26]

When Damiani visited San Giovanni Rotondo in 1937, he was then suffering from severe coronary artery disease and in great pain. The sixty-two-year-old asked for no cure but said that he had come to San Giovanni to die close to Padre Pio. In fact, while staying at the friary, he had a major heart attack and for hours it seemed as if he was going to expire any minute. He asked for Padre Pio, who delayed coming until after he finished hearing confessions. "Why didn't you come earlier? I could have died already!" Damiani complained.

"I knew that you wouldn't die," answered Padre Pio, "and so I continued to hear confessions." He went on to tell Damiani that he would die in Uruguay, but "when your hour does come, I promise to see to it that you are well assisted spiritually."

Four years later Damiani was presiding over a congress on vocations in Salto. The episcopal mansion where the vicar general lived was filled with visiting clergy, including Antonio Maria Barbieri (1892–1979), archbishop of Montevideo. Damiani stayed up until 11:00 p.m., talking in his room with Archbishop Barbieri. A little past midnight Barbieri, who had retired to his room, was awakened by a knock at his door. He opened it. The room and the corridor were both dark, but he thought he could make out the form of a man in a Capuchin habit who said, "Go to assist Monsignor Damiani. He's dying." The knocking on the archbishop's door was overheard by a priest named Francisco Navarro, who had been praying in a chapel on the same floor.

In the meantime, Barbieri hurried to Damiani's room. The door was unlocked, and when he got no response to his rapping, he went inside and found Damiani, apparently dying but lucid, requesting Barbieri to administer the last rites. Going to fetch what he needed to administer the sacrament, Barbieri told Navarro to go to Damiani's room at once and hear his confession and alerted everyone else who was staying in the house. Before Barbieri returned, the dean of the cathedral had anointed the dying man. Medical assistance arrived, but around 12:30 in the morning of September 12, 1941, Monsignor Damiani died, surrounded by four bishops and six priests. As Padre Pio had promised, Damiani died well assisted.[27] (Some accounts say that Damiani had scribbled a note, "Padre Pio came," but that story may be apocryphal.)

A few years later Archbishop Barbieri, on a visit to San Giovanni, was alone with Padre Pio and asked him if he had been the Capuchin who had come to his door, asking him to assist the dying Monsignor Damiani. Padre Pio gave an evasive answer, and Barbieri pressed him, getting a similar response. Then the Archbishop laughed and said, "I understand." Padre Pio nodded and said, "Yes, you understand."

"Will you assist *me* on *my* deathbed?" Barbieri asked.

"No, I will die before you, but I'll assist you from heaven," Padre Pio answered.[28]

Archbishop Barbieri, who lived to be eighty-seven, survived Padre Pio by eleven years. The details of his last hours are not known.

"I Have No Miracles"

It would be a serious mistake to assume that life with Padre Pio was a continual experience of the supernatural and paranormal. Many of those who lived with him never saw or experienced anything unusual. The priests and brothers who knew him well knew him as a normal human being whose distinguishing characteristics were kindness, joy, serenity, and humility. Padre Innocenzo Cinicola Santoro of Campobasso recalled: "Padre Pio was a child, with two great virtues: humility and simplicity. Sometimes he revealed marvelous things with great simplicity, but as soon as he saw morbid curiosity around him, he quickly closed up. Gifted with great humanity, he never refused anyone anything. All one had to do was ask. Then if one said, 'Father, could you do me a favor' ... he felt [compelled] to oblige."[29]

Padre Marcellino Iasenzaniro wrote: "The Padre was severe and sharp only in two cases: in the confessional, when striking and denouncing sin as evil, the real evil that harms man; and when one showed excessive veneration for him as a cult figure.... In all other circumstances ... he was the most humble, exquisite, gentle, kind, caring, and affectionate person I have ever met."[30]

When speaking of the Del Fante book, which was a succession of one miracle story after another, a friend of Padre Pio observed, "If anybody reads that book he'd think that every twenty-four hours you make twenty-five miracles."[31] Padre Pio agreed. He told an American Red Cross official, "People think I have miracles. I have no miracles." When people thanked him for a supernatural favor, he usually told them, "If you think you have received a grace, go to Our Lord and thank him, not me."[32]

"The Work"

Padre Pio was not satisfied with the St. Francis Hospital that he had established a decade before, which he found completely inadequate for the care of the San Giovanni area as well as for the increasing numbers of sick people who came to the monastery in search of relief. When the hospital closed in 1938 as a result of the Depression and an earthquake the previous year, he was determined to build a large, modern hospital near the friary.

Late in 1939, he spoke of his dream to his friends Mario Sanvico, Guglielmo "Willi" Sanguinetti, and Pietro Cugino. Sanvico, from Perugia, forty years old, was a veterinarian who also ran his own brewery, which he sold when he took up residence in San Giovanni. Sanguinetti was a short, stocky, egg-bald man of forty-five, from Ronta di Borgo San Lorenzo, outside of Mugello, near Florence. He had been an atheist as a young man, before he was persuaded by his wife, Emilia Spillman, to visit Padre Pio, as a result of which he had become a fervent Christian and a devoted spiritual son of the Padre. Cugino, known as "Blind Pietruccio," then twenty-seven years old, brought the mail from the post office to the friary. He was the only child of a miner who had gone blind from unknown causes. When he was twelve, Pietro came home from play one day, saying that he saw a red veil over everything. Padre Pio sent him to a local doctor, who could not figure out what was wrong, so the priest arranged for the boy to visit a specialist in Bari, who likewise had no idea what was wrong with his eyes. Within five years, Pietro was completely blind, an example of why the area was in dire need of first-class health care. After both of Cugino's parents died shortly afterward, Padre Pio arranged for him to have a room in the friary and treated him like an adopted son.

Back in 1935, Padre Pio had informed Sanguinetti, "You're the man who will come here and build my hospital." When the physician protested that he could not afford to give up his practice, Padre Pio insisted, "The Lord will provide." Returning to Mugello, Sanguinetti learned that he had won a large sum of money in a lottery, enough to buy a farm to provide him rental income, with enough left over to combine with his friends, the Sanvicos, to purchase a cottage in San Giovanni, which they named "Here Is My Calm." For the next few years, Sanguinetti divided his time between San Giovanni and Mugello, and Sanvico divided his between San Giovanni and Perugia.

On the afternoon of January 9, 1940, Mario and Maria Antonietta Sanvico called a meeting of persons interested in setting up a committee to make Padre Pio's dream of a hospital a reality. The Sanguinettis seem not to have been there, but joining the Sanvicos were Carlo and Mary Kiswarday and a lady by the name of Ida Seitz. Dr. Kiswarday, a pharmacist from Yugoslavia, had been startled some years earlier when he visited San Giovanni Rotondo and Padre Pio told him, "I want you to make your home here."[33] He did.

A committee was set up with Sanvico as secretary, Sanguinetti as medical director, and Seitz as director of internal organization. Although Padre Pio had earlier refused to serve on the committee in a formal capacity, everyone agreed that "anything that has to be done must first be put to Padre Pio and must have his approval."[34]

That evening the male members of the group met with Padre Pio in his cell. The priest was delighted, declaring, "This evening my earthly work has begun. I bless you and all those who will contribute to this work, which will become bigger and more beautiful."[35] Padre Pio wanted to make the first offering and produced a gold coin that he had received that very day from a destitute old woman. At first, the priest had refused to accept it, insisting, "I won't take it. You can't afford it and I don't expect it of you." The woman declared that she could do without buying matches and rely on her neighbors for help in lighting her stove and lamps. When Pio still refused to take her money, the woman sighed, "Well, Padre, I guess it's too small." Thereupon Padre Pio gave in, saying, "Give it to me. This is the handsomest donation I could ever hope to receive!"[36] The coin of the poor lady was quickly joined that night by donations of various sizes from Seitz, Kiswarday, Sanvico, Cugino, Pio's nephew Ettore Masone, and four other people.

Next, the committee had to decide what to name the hospital. When Sanvico asked Padre Pio what he wanted to call it, the Padre told him that he would need a few days to think it over. Five evenings later, Padre Pio told Sanvico that the hospital would be called *La Casa Sollievo della Sofferenza* — The House for the Relief of Suffering. Padre Pio explained that the terms "hospital" and "clinic" had negative connotations for him. What he had in mind was a place where science combined with religion to work together for the welfare of the soul as well as the body. The aim of the *Casa*, as he later put it in a letter to the pope, was "to introduce to the care of the sick a concept more profoundly humane and more supernatural, that places the sick in ideal conditions, both from a material and spiritual point of view, to the end that the patient may be led to recognize those working for his cure as God's helpers, engaged in preparing the way for the intervention of grace."[37]

The committee quickly prepared a brochure explaining in several languages the aims of what was thereafter called "The Work." Carlo and Maria Kiswarday set up an office in their home, which was on the road between the town and the friary. Within a short time, the committee had raised one and a half million lire, but "The Work" came to a standstill in the spring of 1940, when Italy became engulfed in the horrors of the Second World War.

A Prophet in Time of War

"We Won't Win!"

"At the beginning, Padre Pio seemed happy with Fascism," Pietro Cugino reflected, many years later. "Then he changed."[1] Increasingly, he was repelled by the coercive tactics eventually adopted by Benito Mussolini to force his countrymen to join his party. Padre Pio told an American official later on, "It reached the point that you couldn't get sugar, flour, or oil without a Fascist [membership] card. It was blackmail. Even the children's books were full of propaganda."[2] What soured Padre Pio most of all against Mussolini was his October 1936 alliance with Germany. Padre Pio feared and despised Adolf Hitler because of his "religion of blood," and because of his virulent hatred of Christianity. During the war, Padre Pio remarked to another priest, "Do you know what I would do with Hitler if I could get my hands on him? I would put him in a cage and take that cage everywhere throughout the world so that Hitler would know what people were saying about him."[3] When another priest spoke of praying for the conversion of Mussolini, Hitler, and Stalin, Padre Pio answered: "Mussolini, down deep, is a good man and has done some good, and therefore, I pray that he might convert. But Hitler and Stalin are two devils and their public conversion, after so much evil, after committing so many massacres, would be a scandal. Compared with them Nero was a little sinner!"[4]

With Europe and much of the world swept up into the firestorm of war, Padre Pio was very disheartened. "Don't you remember, along about 1920 or 1921," he reminded Padre Agostino, "I predicted that the League of Nations wouldn't last? I told you, 'These nations are going to tear each other to pieces.' Well, look, it's happening."[5]

As German troops rampaged through Europe in 1940 and 1941, with Mussolini at Hitler's coattails, many Italians — including some of the Capuchins of San Giovanni — were optimistic that soon Italy would assume a proud place in the new world order. For practical as well as theological reasons, Padre Pio vigorously disagreed. When Germany invaded the Soviet Union in 1941, Padre Pio (like many others as well) was convinced that eventual defeat was a certainty for the Axis. To confreres still sanguine about eventual victory, Padre Pio declared, "Don't you realize how big Russia is? Can a fly swallow an elephant?"

One day, after dinner, when the friars were discussing the situation in North Africa, where Italian and German troops were battling the Allies, Padre Pio commented, "We lack the [military] means to win, and also the help of God, because Mussolini and, especially, Hitler, are too evil."[6] He told another priest, deploring Italy's alliance with Germany: "A people chosen of God uniting with the enemy of God — this is something that will lead to punishment! ... We will retreat to Bengazi and then into the desert, then to Tripoli and then into Sicily and then into Italy." When the priest said that he hoped that this would not happen, Padre Pio answered, "Desire is one thing, facts are another. I speak of facts and the facts are these."[7] His prediction was proven correct.

He furthermore maintained that the Lord would never allow a man as diabolical as Hitler to win. This was the subject of an argument he had with a Capuchin bishop who insisted that the Axis deserved to win and would. "No! We won't win!" Padre Pio said authoritatively. "I don't see how we could possibly achieve victory when [Hitler] goes against the Pope and publicly blasphemes the Madonna! ... Excellency, we won't win! And if we were to win, victory would be given to us as a punishment!"[8] Padre Pio told an official with the Red Cross, "To win the war would not mean that we won it, but that Germany won it. Then we would fall under Nazi slavery, which is the most diabolical slavery that one can imagine."[9]

After America entered the war in December 1941, Maria Pyle, who was still a U.S. citizen, was arrested. For a time, it seemed that she was to be sent to a concentration camp, but the Capuchins interceded with the minister of internal affairs in Rome, who was a devout Catholic and permitted the American to be "interned" in Pietrelcina, at the home of Padre Pio's father, where she would help care for the aging man.[10]

When the Allies invaded Italy in 1943, a desperate Mussolini sent messengers to Padre Pio, requesting his prayers for Italy. "So, *now* you come to me, after you have destroyed Italy!" he fumed. "You can tell Mussolini that nothing can save Italy now! Nothing! You have destroyed her!"[11]

Foggia was savagely bombed by the British and Americans on nine occasions between May and September 1943, because the Allies feared that the airfields and railroad lines would be used by the Germans. Most of the 20,000 people killed there, however, were civilians. The Capuchin friary there was heavily damaged, and, although there seem to have been no casualties among the friars, Padre Agostino as provincial was forced to move the headquarters of the province to San Giovanni Rotondo.

When Mussolini was driven from power in the summer of 1943 and Italy surrendered to the Allies, many Italians hoped that the worst was over, but Padre Pio continued in his role as prophet of doom: "We are still at the beginning. The war will last very long. You will see it pass from town to town, like a river in flood, spreading destruction, blood, and death! God, help us!"[12] His words proved true, as the Germans refused to relinquish Italy without a furious fight, and much of the peninsula was subjected to dreadful carnage for months to come.

In September 1943, a report, later proved false, reached San Giovanni that Hitler had kidnapped Pope Pius XII. Padre Pio took to his bed with a high fever, murmuring dire imprecations on the *Führer* and his "Thousand-Year Reich." "Germany will be destroyed, because she is cursed by God!" he stormed.[13] When people asked him when the war would end, Padre Pio shook his head and said darkly, "People are hardened. They do not turn to God and the Lord is not moved to compassion."[14] In the meantime, in order to show solidarity with the millions who were starving, Padre Pio further reduced his meager diet, vowing not to eat bread during the course of the war, offering his abstinence to God as a sacrifice so that others could eat.[15]

The "Flying Monk"

As for San Giovanni Rotondo, Padre Pio predicted that it would be untouched by the fighting. "The Lord, through his infinite goodness, will spare this blessed place," he predicted.[16] He was proved correct. Although the Gargano peninsula was captured by the American Eighth Army, and Foggia, just twenty-five miles away, was virtually obliterated by Allied bombs, San Giovanni suffered no damage whatever. Moreover, there were numerous reports that Padre Pio intervened, supernaturally, to keep San Giovanni from the depredations of war.

In May 1949 — four years after the war — Father Dominic Meyer (1892–1966), an American Capuchin priest, was serving as Padre Pio's secretary for English and German correspondence. In a circular letter to family and friends in the States, he related what he had been told by Dr. Sanguinetti:

> During the war the Americans had an air base at Bari, about 75 miles from here. There were still Germans in the neighborhood and the American officer in charge at Bari heard they had a munitions dump in or near San Giovanni Rotondo. So he called his officers, planned a raid, and said he would lead in the first plane. He was a Protestant. When they neared San Giovanni Rotondo he saw high in the air, ahead of the plane, a monk with arms outstretched as if to ward off his coming. The General was stupefied. He ordered the formation to return to base and drop the bombs in an open field where they would do no harm. When he returned to base and was asked how things had gone, he

related what he had seen. An Italian officer present told him that there was a monk at San Giovanni Rotondo whom the people consider a saint. Probably he was the one the General saw in the heavens. The General determined to find out. He and another came here and together they went to the sacristy with other laymen to watch as the fathers came down for Mass. He immediately recognized Padre Pio as the one he had seen high in the air in front of the plane.[17]

This is perhaps the earliest recorded account of the appearance of Padre Pio appearing in the sky, in bilocation, to thwart the aerial bombardment of San Giovanni Rotondo or Pietrelcina. Father Dominic was a man with a reputation for impeccable objectivity, frequently expressing irritation in the various letters to family and friends, at some of the extravagant stories told about Padre Pio. Yet he did not doubt the account related to him by Dr. Sanguinetti.

Father Charles Mortimer Carty related the same story, which he probably learned from Father Dominic, in his popular English biography of Padre Pio, which first appeared in 1952. John McCaffery, an Englishman who lived for many years in Italy, gave essentially the same account in his memoirs, which appeared some thirty years after the events he described. He gave his source, however, as one Douglas Woodruff, who, in turn, was informed by one Lord Eldon, who claimed to have met the general and his wife on a train in Italy shortly after the war. Like Father Dominic, McCaffery failed to give the general's name.

There are different versions of the story. The Capuchin Padre Fernando of Riese Pio X insisted that there were *many* sightings of the "flying monk," which were "confirmed by a number of pilots in the Anglo-American air forces, of various nationalities (English, American, Polish, Palestinians) and of various religions and denominations (Catholic, Orthodox, Muslim, Protestant, Jewish)."[18]

Dante Alimenti, an Italian journalist writing nearly forty years after the war, maintained that the pilots were based in North Africa. This would date the "flying monk" appearances to November 1943, when the Fifteenth Air Force was based in Tunis before it moved its headquarters to Bari in December. Alimenti attributed the account of the "flying monk" to an unnamed pilot, who, after reporting his experience, was hospitalized for "battle fatigue" (post-traumatic stress disorder). In this account, Padre Pio thwarted, not an attack on San Giovanni, but a tenth bombing of Foggia.[19]

Alberto Cardone, a resident of Pietrelcina, recounted another incident to the author in March 1990:

They told me about Padre Pio appearing in the air. One day Padre Pio appeared right in front of the plane. And he was holding the plane and guiding it to another area — into a field, where it could [drop] all the bombs where nobody could get hurt. It was after May 1944. The Germans, retreating, were destroying bridges in Benevento. Then [the Allies] were bombing the German soldiers. They went all the way to Pietrelcina to bomb the German cannon. They inflicted no damage at Pietrelcina. They were trying to bomb Benevento when Padre Pio went right in front of that plane and guided the plane. Nobody was killed in Benevento that day, although a few days earlier a thousand people had been killed in the station. The Allies thought there were still a lot of Germans there. I learned about the apparition at the time it happened.[20]

Like Foggia, Benevento was bombed repeatedly and viciously during the war. Evidently, the plane Cardone described was headed for Pietrelcina, either on purpose or accidentally.

Colonel Loyal B. Curry (1924–2011), a native of Ohio and a Presbyterian, served in the 464th Bomb Group of the Fifteenth Air Force, under General Nathan F. Twining, from December 1944 until he was shot down and imprisoned by the Germans a month later. At the base in Spinazola, between Naples and Foggia, Curry heard about the apparition. "Everybody was talking about it, both the American servicemen as well as the Italians who took care of the quarters."[21]

In 1971, Father John Schug, while preparing his biography of Padre Pio, interviewed Alfonso D'Artega (1907–1998), a Mexican-born U.S. composer, conductor, and songwriter, who had served in the Army Air Force in 1944 and 1945. D'Artega told Schug a story about an evening at the air base in Amendola:

One of the pilots said, "I saw that phantom fly again." We were having drinks and at first I didn't know what they were talking about. Then another man made pertinent remarks about the phantom flyer, but I didn't know that they meant Padre Pio. I thought that maybe they had had too many drinks, until about a week later. One chap (not a pilot but a member of the crew) was perfectly sober. He said that there was a photographer taking pictures of the planes as they landed from their missions. One of the planes was badly [damaged], and the men were dazed. They had landed their planes still with their bombs — they had not been jettisoned. They should have dropped the bombs somewhere on the way in the Adriatic. This chap explained that he had been flying, when, all of a sudden in front of him there was a figure of a monk, flying as fast as the plane, waving his arms. The copilot also saw it. So they didn't drop the bombs on the way back, because they were afraid. They sort of froze when they saw this figure. Naturally, in the briefing, when they made their report, they were bawled out for not having dropped the bombs, endangering the rest of the crew.

The only name D'Artega remembered was that of a fighter pilot named Pope, who, even though the plane he was flying carried no bombs, claimed to have seen "the flying monk." According to D'Artega, Pope was killed during the war. D'Artega also spoke of an unidentified pilot who was a Protestant but became a Catholic, and, eventually, a priest, when he learned that the "phantom" was Padre Pio.[22]

The only account of any of these incidents that gives a precise date was written by Padre Bonaventura Massa in 1975. He gives as his source "Graziella Siena and many others." On July 26, 1943, "big bombers were circling the skies of San Giovanni Rotondo," attempting to bomb the public school, where the commanders believed a cache of German munitions was hidden. "The fliers tried twice to release the bombs, but the apparatus would not function.... As they continued flying they saw in the sky ... a cloud containing three people: a bearded friar, a woman with a child in her arms, and a young man with his sword unsheathed" — evidently Padre Pio, the Virgin Mary with the Christ Child, and the Archangel Michael. The planes returned to base without bombing the school or anything else.[23]

If the Massa account is true, the U.S. Army Air Force involved would have been either the Ninth or the Twelfth, which were active in the area of Foggia on July 26, according to the records in the Department of History of the U.S. Air Force at Bolling Air Force Base in Washington, D.C. The commander of each mission was supposed to write a report, but not all records have survived. No mission reports for the Ninth and Twelfth Air Forces between July 19 and August 6, 1943 exist.

Colonel Curry, when he heard the account by Father Dominic, insisted that the incident could never have happened the way it was described. A general could not simply decide on his own to bomb a site and gather a group of pilots to do the job — as if he were getting together players for a pickup game of softball. Decisions of that sort were undertaken through an elaborate chain of command and not on the spur of the moment. Father John D. Saint John (1908–1992), a chaplain with the Fifteenth Air Force, was skeptical of the entire story: "I never heard the story at the time, and I don't believe it. No one would give orders like that. I went to the briefings of the pilots and navigators and bombardiers. The command would say: 'Your target today is ...' Historical targets and churches were circled in red and were not to be bombed. Anyone who disobeyed the order was court-martialed. There was nothing in San Giovanni Rotondo at the time. There would be no point bombing it. There was no military objective. No one would have ordered the bombing of San Giovanni Rotondo. Somebody must have been drunk and made up the story and said it off the cuff. The story is impossible!"[24] Despite Saint John's insistence to the contrary, it is beyond dispute that historical buildings and churches were bombed — frequently — if there was concern that they could be used by the German armed forces.

What, then, is to be made of the story or stories of the "flying monk"? Clearly, they came from different sources and seem to refer to more than one incident in which Padre Pio, in bilocation, supposedly kept bombers from attacking San Giovanni Rotondo and Pietrelcina. These stories were being recounted during the war, very close to the time they supposedly happened. There are no accounts of Padre Pio being questioned about them, although they were believed by some of his close associates. Perhaps the most accurate statement that can be made about the "flying monk" stories is that they were widely believed by many of Padre Pio's contemporaries, including fellow religious and American service people.

"Padre Pio, Save Us!"

There are accounts of people in other parts of Italy who credited their survival to Padre Pio's intervention. A number of people asked Padre Pio whether their town or dwelling would be spared, and sometimes he seemed to know. When a man from Genoa asked if his city would be spared, the Padre began to weep, and groaned, "Genoa will be bombed. Oh, how they will bomb that poor city! So many homes, buildings, and churches will crumble! But, be calm. Your house will not be touched." When, in June 1944, the Allies bombed Genoa to rubble, the only house left standing untouched within a huge area of charred ruin was that of the man to whom Padre Pio had prophesied.[25]

There is an account that describes how several persons were huddled, during an air raid on the city of Pescara, in a room on the ground floor of a four-story apartment. They were clutching a picture of Padre Pio, sobbing, "Padre Pio, save us! Padre Pio, help us!" The building took a direct hit, and a bomb crashed through the upper three stories, tore through the ceiling into the room where the occupants were invoking Padre Pio, and fell to the floor with a terrific thud — but failed to explode.[26]

These reports and others like them are impossible to verify, but also impossible to disprove.

The Man in the Black Suit

One of the most extraordinary war stories was told to the author by Alberto Cardone, who, at eighteen, traveled from his home in Pietrelcina to San Giovanni with several friends in late May 1943 to visit Padre Pio. Despite the ravages of war, large numbers of people still somehow found their way to San Giovanni. After staying for three days in town, Cardone and his friends went to say good-bye to Padre Pio, since they planned to return home the following day. "Why do you want to go home?" Padre Pio asked. "Don't you like it here? Maybe we don't treat you right?"

"No," the men said, "we must go home because our families are expecting us. Second, we haven't enough food to stay longer." (Not only were telephone and telegraph services inoperable, it was impossible to buy food.)

"Hey, you're always thinking about eating," Padre Pio chided. "You're not going to die for one day's lack of eating. You'll last *several* days before you die. You think about food all the time." He then suggested that the five men combine all their food. "Eat together like one family. Don't eat on your own, and there will be enough food for you all."

Cardone and his friends followed Padre Pio's suggestion, and they had enough food not only for the night but for an additional day as well.

The next morning the men went to Mass, after which Padre Pio withdrew to pray, as he customarily did. He usually reappeared by 9:30, but on this morning he did not. When Cardone and one of his friends asked some friars where Padre Pio was, they directed him to the garden, where he was pacing about disconsolately. When he saw Cardone and his friend, Padre Pio called out, "Children, come, let's pray."

Cardone recalled:

He said, "Poor Foggia today." We didn't know what he meant. A few minutes later … planes were coming from all over the place and were going down to Foggia where they started to throw down their bombs.… Padre Pio hadn't been in the friary since Mass, so how did he know they were going to bomb Foggia? … Padre Pio told me and my friend Bernardo, "Look for the others now and tell them I want to talk to them, because tomorrow you've got to go home. Those American planes were trying to destroy the station, which is, I'm sure, destroyed, but the train will travel. It won't be at the station, though. When you get to Foggia, you've got to ask somebody how to get to the train." He didn't have a radio and had no way of knowing the station was destroyed. While we were praying we saw the planes throwing down bombs on Foggia. They unloaded the bombs and then they came up and away from Foggia, making a turn, as if they were going to come over us. Padre Pio told us, "Don't be afraid. They're not going to touch us, but — poor Foggia!" He was crying. These planes made the run three times over Foggia, throwing a lot of bombs. Then they went away. Then Bernardo and I went to look for the other guys. Padre Pio warned us not to try to see him the next morning, for the bus left at seven and if we went to Mass, we might miss the bus.

When Cardone and his companions reached Foggia, they saw mangled corpses and shattered buildings everywhere. Survivors were screaming and crying. The station was destroyed, and in its ruins was a charred and twisted mass of debris — which had been the train on which the men had planned to travel the day before. Cardone recalled, "If Padre Pio hadn't stopped us the day before, we would have been on that train and would have been burned up."

Cardone and his friends now had to find their train. While they debated what to do, a man in a black suit approached them. "Do you need any help?" he asked.

"We need to get to the train to Benevento, and we don't know where to go, because the station is destroyed," Cardone explained.

The man replied, "The train is about to leave. You'd better hurry up. Follow me. We've got to run, not walk."

Cardone recalled:

> After a while we saw the train. It had already started to move. The conductor saw us and shouted, "Run! Run!" We made it. We ran over there, with the man in the black suit in front of us. We reached the last door of the car. We jumped up into it. Now we were in an open field. We wanted to say good-bye to the man who had led us to the train. But there was nothing at all but the open field. The man had disappeared. The man had not [boarded] the train, he had stepped aside to let us in, and then he wasn't there anymore.... Then we started to cry.[27]

"What Do You Think I Am, a Fortune-teller?"

Anguished people were constantly asking Padre Pio for news of loved ones missing in action or after a bombing. Most of the time Padre Pio could give no satisfaction, but occasionally he seemed to have supernatural insight. There was a soldier's mother who asked about her boy, who was missing in action. Padre Pio, who had prayed for the son, told the mother, "He must be alive, for I cannot find him in the other world." Eventually, the son returned.[28] On another occasion, a Franciscan tertiary from Morcone named Giuseppina Gagliardi inquired about her missing son, only to have Padre Pio tell her, "Poor son, he suffered so much! ... He suffers no longer. We must resign ourselves to the will of God." Later, through the Red Cross, Gagliardi learned that her son Italo was among the slain.[29]

When Cardone was in San Giovanni with his friends, he asked Padre Pio about various relatives. He told the priest, "It's a long time since we've heard from my father." He was in America, but Cardone never mentioned this to Padre Pio, who nonetheless told him, "Oh, your father's in America. He's better [off] than you or I. What are you worrying about? He's okay." Cardone asked about his uncle Francesco, who was with the Italian army in Libya. "All of a sudden we stopped hearing from him," he explained. Padre Pio replied, "It could be he's a prisoner. When you get home, maybe you'll hear some good news." Cardone then asked about a second uncle, Nicola, who had been sent to fight in Russia. "We received only one letter, and then we heard nothing more." Padre Pio got up and said, "What do you think I am, a fortune-teller? Let's pray. When you get home, tell his wife and your mother to pray." Then he walked away.

When Cardone returned home, he found a letter from his uncle Francesco, saying that he was a prisoner in England and was working as a cook. Eventually, he returned home in excellent health and spirits. Shortly afterward, Cardone met an American soldier who was stationed in the friary in Pietrelcina, which the Pyles had caused to be built several years before but was being used as a barrack. The soldier was from New York, and it turned out that he knew Cardone's father. "Write him a letter, give the letter to me, and I'll put it in my letter and send it to him," said the soldier. As for the uncle who had been sent to Russia, Cardone said, "Up to today, we've never heard another word."[30]

"I Have Prayed … I Have Suffered"

In January 1944, Padre Pio's sister-in-law Giuseppa Cardone, wife of his brother Michele, died in Pietrelcina, in her early sixties. Reportedly, he had appeared to her in bilocation. Then, on February 19, his troubled sister Pellegrina died at fifty-one. According to her death certificate, which does not give a cause of death, she expired in Chieti, a city about a hundred miles north of San Giovanni. She was a patient in the Hospital of St. Camillo de Lellis. There is an air of mystery about her death. Padre Pio's niece Pia Forgione said that her Aunt Pellegrina "died in the bombing of Naples." Chieti is over one hundred miles northeast of Naples, on the opposite side of the Italian boot. It was never bombed. A friend of the family refused to discuss the circumstances of her death but would say only that Pellegrina was a cause of immense grief and embarrassment to her brother. Father Joseph Pius Martin, who came to San Giovanni long after Pellegrina's death, said that he had heard that she made one trip to see her brother and so scandalized and humiliated him that he slapped her in the face! He refused to elaborate. Pietro Cugino would say only that Padre Pio commented, when she died, "I have prayed. I have made offering. I have suffered."[31] The implication is that his prayers, oblations, and sufferings came to naught, and that Pellegrina apparently died unconverted. A month after her death, Padre Pio wrote his brother: "Let's piously resign ourselves … seeing that other brothers suffer and have suffered more than we. Let's climb, if not cheerfully, at least with resignation and love of God, the Calvary that Providence offers us to purify our spirit."[32]

Soldati Americani

A Peaceful Military Invasion

For Padre Pio, World War II was the cause of greater exposure than ever to the outside world, because of the many foreign military personnel who came to San Giovanni Rotondo during the final three years of the war.

The chronicle kept by the friary first noted the presence of visiting military on September 2, 1942, observing that "there are always officers and soldiers," without indicating their nationality. At Christmas, there was "a great crowd of people ... not lacking officers and soldiers."

In July 1943, the American songwriter Irving Berlin (1888–1989) came to bomb-ravaged Foggia to perform in "This Is the Army," a stage show that he prepared and put on for Allied troops throughout Europe. He made a trip to San Giovanni Rotondo to visit Countess Telfner, who was related to his wife, and she persuaded him to meet Padre Pio. The meeting between the priest and the songwriter seems to have consisted of a perfunctory exchange of pleasantries, and Padre Pio presented the agnostic Jewish composer with a gift of a rosary for his Catholic wife.[1]

After Italy signed an armistice with the Allies in September 1943, the influx of soldiers into San Giovanni accelerated tremendously, first with bands of Italian soldiers who had been forced to surrender their weapons to the Germans pouring into northern Italy to fight the Allies for control of the entire peninsula. After making confessions to Padre Pio and receiving Communion, "They sleep under the porch of the Third Order for Women and then continue on," the chronicle noted.[2] On November 7, "an English military chaplain came from Lucera with twenty Canadian soldiers. All heard Padre Pio's Mass with much devotion."[3] A week later another English chaplain came from San Severo with twelve soldiers, who also made their confession to Padre Pio and took Communion.

American troops began to appear after the U.S. Eighth Army conquered the Gargano peninsula. The first mention of American soldiers in the chronicle is November 21, 1943, but their presence and that of English troops was at first sporadic. On December 12, "several" English soldiers went to Padre Pio's Mass, and in the afternoon some Americans came. At Christmas, the church was crowded, but the congregation included only "several" Americans.[4] That day Padre Agostino noted in his diary, however, "Every Sunday American soldiers come to hear Padre Pio's Mass. All of them are amazed and contrite — even the Protestants."[5]

The beginning of 1944 saw increasing numbers of American visitors from the several camps in Apulia (the heel of the Italian "boot"). On January 16, the chronicle noted, "They come very often to Padre Pio: officers, soldiers, and, from time to time, Red Cross personnel from the American Army. And they are all filled with admiration and enthusiasm for Padre Pio."[6] Throughout the year, "there were many soldiers at Padre Pio's Mass, especially the Americans," and "the composure and recollection with which they hear Padre Pio's Mass and take Holy Communion is wonderful. Protestants are not lacking and even they behave with exemplary deportment at Padre Pio's Mass."[7]

On January 22, 1945, the chronicle noted, "In the evening, at a late hour, there came from Taranto two English chaplains with several English, Irish, and Indian soldiers — all Catholic. There were also two Red Cross Indians — fervent Catholics. Notwithstanding the severe temperature and the snow lasting all month, the American soldiers and officers came here in their usual numbers."[8] Sometimes there were two hundred military visitors a day.[9] This continued until after the Allied victory in Europe was secured in May 1945.

In a 1967 interview, Maria Pyle recalled that between 1943 and 1945, her home was full of American soldiers whom she entertained, serving refreshments and talking about Padre Pio. Sometimes every available space in her large house was crowded, including the windowsills.

A Friend from the Red Cross

One reason for the increasing numbers of American visitors was the efforts of the field director of the American Red Cross in Italy, William Maurice Carrigan (1902–2000), a small, extremely slender Iowa native with dark hair and a ruddy complexion[10] who had taught psychology at The Catholic University of America, in Washington, D.C., until he began his work with the Red Cross at the time of America's entry into the war. Traveling with the Fifteenth Army Air Force, Carrigan reached Naples in late 1943, in the midst of a terrible thunderstorm. The retreating Germans had ruined the water supply, with the result that there were queues blocks long in front of every spring and fountain in and about the city. People waited all night long to obtain a little water. There was no power and little food. Many of the churches, seized by the Germans for the quartering of troops, were left stripped and vandalized.

The next day Carrigan left for Foggia in a convoy. "The very life had been bombed out of Foggia," he recalled. About a third of the population had been killed, and most of the survivors had fled. The few who remained rummaged amidst the rubble for scraps of food.

Shortly after he arrived in Foggia, Carrigan began to hear reports from the soldiers about a man up in the mountains who had the wounds of Christ. Some American soldiers, searching for eggs, he learned, had found themselves at San Giovanni Rotondo, where they had met an American expatriate — Maria Pyle — who welcomed them into her pink castle, fed them, and regaled them with stories about Padre Pio. When the soldiers returned to their base and told their comrades about "the man in the mountains," a number of them wanted to visit the holy man. Because the Army had no available transportation for pleasure trips, several of the soldiers came to Carrigan, whom they knew was a devout Catholic, and he agreed to take them, using Red Cross vehicles.

On a cold winter's day, with eight inches of snow on the ground, Carrigan and twenty American soldiers made the trek to San Giovanni Rotondo. Padre Pio was well into his Mass when the men entered the church. There was no heat, and though the Americans wore heavy overcoats, they were chilled to the bone. But, Carrigan recounted, "It wasn't very long before I experienced a physical warmth. Quickly I realized that [Padre Pio] was very unique."

There was indeed something very unusual going on. Carrigan noticed a transformation in Padre Pio during the consecration: he seemed to "take on physical sufferings." Although he knew nothing at the time about Padre Pio's stigmata, Carrigan noticed that the priest leaned on the altar, first on one elbow and then on the other, as if he were trying to relieve pain in his feet. At the words of the consecration, he seemed to have great difficulty in speaking the words, "*Hoc est enim corpus meum*" ("This is my body"). Carrigan noted that Padre Pio shouted the words, hesitating and biting them off "as if he were in physical pain." When he reached for the chalice, he jerked his hand back violently, "as if the pain were so great he could not grasp it." His facial muscles were twitching and tears were rolling down his cheeks. Occasionally, "he jerked his head to one side or the other, as if he were suffering blows to the head and neck." After the consecration, it seemed as if Padre Pio's suffering had subsided, and he appeared exhausted, leaning forward as if in deep meditation.

Because the war had diminished (but by no means cut off) the number of civilian visitors, the American soldiers had easy access to Padre Pio, who received them after Mass in the sacristy. Carrigan described Padre Pio as a stoutish man of average height who walked slowly but seemed vital, lively, and cheerful. As Carrigan started to kneel, Padre Pio held him up by the elbows and asked, "*Americano?*"

"Si! Si, Padre."

Through an interpreter, Padre Pio told Carrigan that he and his group were the first American military personnel that he had met during the war, indicating that he was delighted to see them. After that, Carrigan recalled that the priest allowed him to kiss his ungloved hand (which if this is true, he wasn't supposed to). Carrigan felt "the rough scales of the blood crystals" and experienced a pleasant aroma, which he thought must have been associated with some sort of medication. Then Padre Pio greeted each of the soldiers and, with his gloves on, allowed all of them to kiss his hand (the normal way of greeting a priest in southern Italy). Carrigan was so moved by the experience that more than three decades later he could say, "Since I met Padre Pio … I can truthfully say that I have had no doubts … regarding Christ's being … the Savior of the world."

At once, Carrigan decided that he would make it possible for all soldiers in need of spiritual guidance to go to Padre Pio. Pio was enthusiastic about the idea and at once contacted Archbishop Cesarano, requesting permission to arrange for a Midnight Mass on New Year's Eve for the Americans. Pio had not sung a High Mass since his confinement in 1931, but was given authorization to do so for the Americans. Unfortunately, it snowed so heavily that night that few were able to get to the church.[11]

According to Carrigan, Padre Pio seemed to know exactly one English word: "Okay" (actually, he knew a few more), but some of the troops were first generation Italian-Americans, who had little difficulty understanding him. The majority of the troops, however, were not Italian speakers, but there were several people around who were happy to interpret. Not only was there Maria Pyle, the professional linguist, but also Don Giorgio Pogany, a Hungarian-Jewish priest, who spoke good English. Less fluent, but still eager to help was Padre Agostino, who, with his massive frame and gigantic white beard, reminded the soldiers of Santa Claus. Padre Pio's father, who now lived in town, was delighted to see the *Americani*, because it gave him a chance to speak English, which, according to most of those who spoke with him, he did rather badly. Despite the language barrier, Carrigan knew personally of hundreds of men who received "reconfirmation of their faith" through their encounters with Padre Pio. Others underwent outright conversions.

Padre Pio talked enthusiastically about the hospital he was planning and encouraged the Americans he met to contribute something to *La Sollievo della Sofferenza*, declaring, "This is a work of God. When you return to the States, tell people about it." He also encouraged the American servicemen to contribute to the poor and urged each unit to adopt a needy family.

Carrigan recalled a soldier who was a discipline problem and had reached the point where he was refusing commands. Carrigan convinced the man, who spoke Italian fluently, to talk with Padre Pio. After fifteen minutes of conversation, the soldier's attitude changed radically, and there were no more problems. In fact, that very afternoon, walking through the ravaged streets of Foggia, he came upon some children kicking a ball made out of string and cloth. More than eight thousand children were living in the streets, and, with the schools destroyed, many of the boys spent their time robbing soldiers or inviting them, for a fee, to their sisters' beds. The soldier, who had been employed as a civilian at a recreation center in Chicago, persuaded his unit that very evening to organize a recreational program for the children. Because of his connection with the center in Chicago, he was able to obtain a supply of sports equipment for the children.

Allowed to stay at the friary, Carrigan slept in a room across from Padre Pio, ate with the friars, and was impressed by their brotherly love and deep spirituality. Padre Agostino, as minister provincial, was "kind and gentle" but nonetheless maintained strict discipline. Carrigan got the impression, however, that Padre Pio was the unofficial leader of the community, the "magnet." On at least one occasion the Padre invited Carrigan to pray with him in the choir, escorting him to his stall and locking his arm around the American's as they knelt in prayer. Padre Pio, according to Carrigan, was not the stereotype of the mystic, but rather the sort of man "you could have gone fishing with." Carrigan maintained that he saw no evidence whatsoever of mystical charisms. Although Padre Pio spoke very little English, he nevertheless seemed to understand the Americans when they spoke to him.

Padre Pio told Carrigan (evidently through an interpreter), "I need very little of the world's goods: a cover for my body, enough food to survive, and a little rest, and that's enough." Carrigan saw for himself that the Padre's physical needs were indeed minimal. At the midday meal the friar never ate a complete serving of food. In the evening, in his room, he sipped wine and fruit juice (he especially loved pineapple juice), but took no solid food. Moreover, he seldom seemed to remain in bed longer than four hours a night.

Carrigan noted some unusual occurrences. We will recall Amalia Abresch, who bore a son despite a dangerous tumor. One day Pio sent for Carrigan and told him that she was deathly ill: "She's going to die unless she gets to the hospital at Ancona." The Red Cross director protested that there was still fighting around that city and that many of the roads had been destroyed. Pio, adamant, ordered him, "Get an army ambulance and take her there!"

"Padre, you know I can't do that!" Carrigan objected. "You know as well as I do that the U.S. Army does not permit its vehicles to be requisitioned for civilian use."

"You must take her to Ancona, or else she will die," the priest insisted.

"I don't think I can help you," answered Carrigan. However, he agreed to explain the situation to the colonel in charge of the military hospital on his base, and did so the next morning. To his amazement, Carrigan was told that he could use the ambulance. He went to San Giovanni at once and picked up Amalia Abresch, who, though deathly ill, was smiling all the way to Ancona, where she was successfully treated.

Joe Peterson

Many of the soldiers who made their way to San Giovanni to meet Padre Pio were stationed at Foggia or in Cerignola, where Padre Paolino was the superior of the friary. Padre Paolino was fluent in English and French, and he befriended many of the military people who attended Mass at his church, telling them about Padre Pio and inviting them to go with him to visit the stigmatized priest. Several Catholic chaplains, including Fathers John Saint John and John Duggan, encouraged their troops to visit Padre Pio.

Joseph Francis Peterson (1923–1992), a member of the ground crew of the Fifteenth Air Force's base at Bari, some seventy miles distant, had heard of Padre Pio from a friend in an adjoining tent who showed him an article that his mother had sent him from Wilkes-Barre, Pennsylvania. The article, written by an American pilot, amazed Peterson, who had grown up in a Capuchin parish in Yonkers, New York, but had never heard of Padre Pio. At once, he went to his chaplain, who tried to discourage him from visiting San Giovanni Rotondo. "He lives a long way from here," he told Peterson. "You have the Blessed Sacrament and you don't have to believe in private revelations, like Lourdes and Fátima — or Padre Pio." But every day Peterson went to the chaplain, begging him at least to give him directions to Padre Pio. Finally, he was given the address of Father Saint John in Foggia, who, in his reply to Peterson's letter, invited him to come and bring as many friends as he could. Peterson and three others hitched a ride on a British truck and arrived at San Giovanni just after noon. Little Fra Gerardo, the diminutive doorkeeper, took the soldiers up to Padre Pio's room and knocked on the door, eliciting a grunt, "Eh?"

"*Soldati americani!*" shouted the little brother.

Within a few minutes Padre Pio appeared and exchanged pleasantries with the four men, with the help of one of Father Saint John's assistants who served as interpreter. Although his talk with Padre Pio lasted but a few minutes, Joe Peterson was so convinced of the Capuchin's sanctity that, following his return to the States, where he went to work for the Post Office, he began to spend all his vacations at the friary.[12]

"He Couldn't Get Enough of Everybody"

Padre Pio loved the Americans. Like Carrigan, several of them, at various times, were allowed to eat with him at the friary. One of them was Joseph R. Peluso (1917–1999), who recalled a time when Pio excused himself from the table and beckoned the American to come with him, explaining, "There is a group of American soldiers waiting outside to see me." Peluso recalled, "I went out and there were three truckloads of GIs getting ready to leave, and I called them back and they all met him. He met everybody like this. He couldn't get enough of everybody."

Peluso recalled Padre Pio as "always laughing, always jovial. At the dinner table, he had the priests cracking up. They were going bananas. They cracked up so bad that they had to excuse themselves and leave the dining room to recompose themselves." Joe smelled the famous aroma "very often," but experienced nothing else of a supernatural nature. He made his confession to Padre Pio and commented, "It was so easy. I wish I could go to confession here [in America] and get off that easy."

Peluso spoke little Italian and Padre Pio little English, and "there was no gift of tongues," but "it didn't take words to understand one another." Peluso heard people talking of the cure of a woman who had been deaf for twenty years, but he did not witness it or the exorcism that "happened just before I got there." He said, "Mary [Pyle] found a lady stomping her head on the floor … [Padre Pio] exorcised her right there in just a matter of a few minutes. It was a very brutal thing."[13]

"The Only Piece of Heaven on Earth That I Ever Knew"

Mario Avignone (1918–2011), who in peacetime worked for the Sherwin-Williams Paint Company in Illinois, was assigned to the headquarters squadron of the 304th Bomb Wing of the Fifteenth Air Force in Cerignola. The superior of the friary there was Padre Paolino, until the fall of 1944, when he was elected minister provincial. Avignone recalled Padre Paolino as a heavyset man, about five feet five inches tall, with a short beard, "beautiful, sparkling Italian eyes," and a personality "friendly and full of fun." Avignone and his friends Joseph Asterita (1913–1967) and Leo Fanning (1922–2008) met Padre Paolino when they became regular worshipers at the Benediction service at the Capuchin church in Cerignola. Padre Paolino invited them to dinner one evening and told them about Padre Pio, asking them if they would like to go with him to San Giovanni Rotondo to meet him. Avignone and Asterita signed for a jeep and, along with Padre Paolino, at 3:30 one morning made the drive to San Giovanni Rotondo.

Avignone's response was similar to Carrigan's:

The Mass lasted almost two hours. It was a Mass that I could not describe. It was so beautiful. The room was filled with a perfume that came from Padre Pio's wounds. As I knelt next to the altar, I could clearly see the suffering Padre Pio was going through from the pain in his wounds. His feet and hands would jerk as if great pain was shooting through his body. He made painful expressions all during the Mass, never noticing anyone in the church. I had the sense that he was physically here but spiritually … with Christ at the foot of the cross. At times he wept with tears running down his face, as if he were watching Christ being nailed to the cross. He was actually living the Passion of Our Lord. When he raised his hands I could clearly see the painful-looking wounds on his hands.... The only words that came forth from my mouth as I knelt watching a living saint celebrate the Holy Mass were, "My Lord and my God."

The two soldiers were treated by the friars to a breakfast that consisted of bread and "a liquid that tasted like coffee." It was not until the noon meal that they met Padre Pio, who entered the dining room last of all. "Everyone stood up as a sign of respect for him as he limped slowly to the place where Padre Damaso, the guardian, and Padre Agostino, the provincial, sat." Padre Pio knelt and kissed their sandals before rising to go to his table, where he merely pushed the food around on his plate as he talked to his American visitors (who spoke Italian). Although Padre Pio's conversation consisted of jokes and small talk, the soldiers were deeply impressed. After the friars went to take their siesta, Avignone and Asterita went to see Maria Pyle, who served them American coffee and introduced them to Padre Pio's father. When they returned to the friary that evening to bid farewell to the Padre before returning to Cerignola with Padre Paolino, Avignone again smelled the "heavenly and indescribable" fragrance. He left convinced that Padre Pio was a living saint and that the friary was "the only piece of heaven on earth that I ever knew."[14]

Perscrutatio Cordium

Father John D. Saint John (1908–1992) was a Jesuit, serving as chaplain in the Fifteenth Army Air Force. At the suggestion of his assistant, Joseph Asterita, Saint John accompanied him on a visit to Padre Pio. On January 3, 1944, he met the celebrated priest in the sacristy of the church in San Giovanni.

Speaking in Latin, Saint John asked, "How is it, Father, that you do not follow the order of the day? You spend all night in the choir chapel in prayer." Courteously, Padre Pio answered him, "I have the permission of the superior." The Jesuit put a second question to the Capuchin: "Why do you have the stigmata?" To which the friar replied, "My superiors have forbidden me to reveal why I have the stigmata." Despite the brash questions of the thirty-five-year-old chaplain, Padre Pio did not become upset, and his responses convinced Father Saint John that he was at least a good religious, obedient to his superiors.

Father Saint John noted that during the Mass Padre Pio "seemed to be in ecstasy. At the consecration, holding the host up, he seemed to be out of this world. He seemed not to know where he was. His eyes were aglow." But the length of the Mass led him to ask Padre Pio, "Since the rule is that the Mass last no longer than an hour, how can you say a two-hour Mass?" Once again, Padre Pio replied, "I have permission."

Father Saint John made nine trips to San Giovanni during the next year and a half, sometimes alone, but usually with between fifty to one hundred men, who came in trucks. The chaplain would advertise in the daily bulletin: "Those interested in going to visit Padre Pio should see Father Saint John." The men would go to Mass and sometimes speak with the Padre in the sacristy. Some of the soldiers who spoke Italian began to go regularly to Padre Pio for spiritual direction.

Father Saint John's recollections of Padre Pio were of "a happy man." "He had a nice chuckle. He was a holy, prayerful man, who spent much of his time in the confessional. He had bright eyes and a nice smile. He was a gentle person. He never raised his voice and had mild, controlled gestures. He spoke a few English words. He walked normally. He did not limp. He had a very dignified walk ... I smelled the perfume when I kissed the wounds. It was very mild. It was a pleasant odor. It was no big deal. It could have been shaving lotion. That's what it smelled like. I once asked him how long the war would go on, and he replied that he didn't know how long it would go on."

In his diary, Father Saint John noted two extraordinary experiences.

One day Padre Pio asked him if he knew a certain sergeant. "I don't know him," the Jesuit replied.

"Well, he's in the Second Bomb Group," Padre Pio said.

"I don't know him," the chaplain repeated.

Nevertheless, Padre Pio said, "You tell him that the baby was born yesterday and the wife and baby are doing fine."

Without inquiring how Padre Pio knew, Saint John drove to the squadron indicated and found the sergeant. Introducing himself, the chaplain asked if he had ever heard of Padre Pio. The sergeant was a Catholic, but admitted, "No, I've never heard of him." After explaining that Padre Pio was a Capuchin priest who had the five wounds of Christ, Saint John told the sergeant, "However, that isn't the reason I'm talking to you. He told me to tell you that your baby was born yesterday."

The sergeant turned pale. His wife was, in fact, expecting a baby, but he had not known that she had given birth. In fact, it was not until two days later that he was notified by the Red Cross that his child had been born. "I'm not saying this was a miracle," Saint John said, "but it was very remarkable to me."

Another time Saint John was describing his visits to Padre Pio to a group of soldiers in a squadron mess hall at the base in Foggia. Several of them said with contempt, "We don't believe in that kind of stuff!" Nevertheless, two soldiers took up the chaplain's invitation to visit Padre Pio and, along with an army nurse, went with him to San Giovanni the next day. Saint John recalled:

I made no appointment with Padre Pio. He didn't know who the people I brought with me were. I met the little brother [Fra Gerardo] at the door who looked like one of Snow White's Seven Dwarfs and asked for Padre Pio, who came down in a few minutes and gave me the ... Roman embrace, kissing both my cheeks. When he was introduced to the people I brought, he became very cold. He had nothing to say to them. He was normally very effusive, especially with the GIs, but all he said when he shook each hand was, "*Buon giorno.*" I talked for a few minutes with Padre Pio, then told the group of people to wait outside. I asked, "*Che passa, Padre?*" He replied, "Those people are *cattivi e peccaminosi*" — bad and sinful. He knew nothing about their background, but I knew that what he said was true, as I knew some of the sinful events in their lives. I don't want to go into too much detail, but one was a drunk and the other was sleeping with the nurse, whom he had the effrontery to bring with him.

On the way back, I asked the driver, with whom I was sitting in the front of the jeep, "What do you think?" He replied, "Father, that man has done something to me. I can't explain it." There was deathly silence all the way back to the base. I suppose some psychologist would explain it by some sort of ESP, but I don't think it was. I think it was supernatural."

Father Saint John was convinced, from the two episodes, that Padre Pio was gifted with what he called *perscrutatio cordium*, or the ability to read hearts.[15]

"The Conversion of the United States Will Be Slow, but Sure"

Another chaplain who regularly brought his men to see Padre Pio was Father John P. Duggan (1908–1996) of the 304th Wing of the Fifteenth Air Force, headquartered in Cerignola. Duggan was "very impressed by this holy man and found him a man of wisdom, piety, and not afraid to spend hours daily in the confessional." On the other hand, Padre Pio was "very friendly and jovial" and liked to play ball with little kids. The chaplain witnessed no extraordinary events, but recalled, "I thought I smelled an aroma. I never advertised that fact. There was a slight odor of perfume. At the time I thought it was a fancy soap." Duggan asked about the future of the United States and the Soviet Union, prompting Padre Pio to declare: "The Russian people will be converted. Their total conversion will happen very fast. The conversion of the United States will be slow, but sure."[16] Perhaps Padre Pio was referring to the sudden collapse of communism in the U.S.S.R., but his prophecy about America, if reported accurately, seems to correspond to nothing that occurred in the ensuing seven decades.

"Your Name Is Not Just Leone. Someday It Will Be *Father* Leone"

Leo Fanning, from Cornwall-on-the-Hudson in New York, was a close friend of Joe Asterita and Mario Avignone. He wanted to be a priest but had been drafted before he had a chance to enter seminary. Asterita urged him to go with him to see Padre Pio.

When they arrived at San Giovanni and told little Fra Gerardo that they wanted to see Padre Pio, the dwarfish brother laughed and, in Italian, which Asterita translated for Fanning, said, "Are you kidding?" and pointed to a huge line of people waiting to make their confession to Padre Pio. The Americans were told to return between noon and 12:30 p.m., when the Padre was expected to finish hearing confessions. So they went to visit with Maria Pyle until then.

When they met Padre Pio in the sacristy, he recognized Asterita, who, in turn, introduced Leone Fanning. In Italian, Padre Pio said, "Your name is not just Leone. Someday it will be *Father* Leone." (Asterita translated this for his friend.) Padre Pio had never been told that Leo Fanning aspired to the priesthood.

The next time Fanning visited Padre Pio, it was late in 1944, after Padre Paolino had been elected minister provincial. Padre Paolino wanted to confer with his predecessor Padre Agostino at San Giovanni. So Padre Paolino, Asterita, and Fanning left Cerignola in a jeep at 3:00 a.m. When they arrived at San Giovanni, Padre Paolino entered the friary. Minutes later he came out and opened the gate to let the jeep through. He said to the Americans, "Come on in. You're expected."

"What do you mean?" Fanning asked.

Padre Paolino replied, "I met Padre Pio in the sacristy and he said to me, 'Good morning, Padre Provincial. You have arrived with my two soldier friends, Leone and Giuseppe.'"

The Americans attended the Mass, after which they met Padre Agostino, who informed them, "A couple of days ago I remarked, 'I wish I could see the Provincial,' and Padre Pio told me, 'Don't worry. He'll be here this week, along with my two soldier friends, Giuseppe and Leone.'"

After Mass, Joe Asterita went to make his confession. When he returned, Fanning recalled, "his eyes were big as saucers" as he declared, "I hardly had a chance to open my mouth and Padre Pio said, 'Giusep, you did this and this and this' — right down to the letter of what I did that was wrong!"

The young Americans became friends with Pasquale Tortora, the organist at the cathedral in Cerignola, who had lived in America and spoke English. One of his daughters, Angelina, an unmarried schoolteacher, was very religious and frequently visited Padre Pio. One evening she told Asterita and Fanning about Padre Pio's "perfume" and how she smelled it one day in her classroom. On their way back to their base, Fanning said to Asterita, "Angelina is a nice person, but she's a religious fanatic. That story she told about the perfume tonight is ridiculous. She was sixty miles away from Padre Pio, and she could detect that perfume! All I can say is, that's some B.O.!"

A few months later, Fanning was sitting in his office in the Battle Casualties Department, when around ten in the morning, he recalled, "All of a sudden this perfume came up to my nostrils. Up till then Padre Pio hadn't been on my mind.

[The fragrance] might have lasted a minute or so. I looked to see if there was a wind that might have been blowing in some scent. There wasn't a leaf stirring. It was a very warm day. I tried to deny it."

He tried to forget about the aroma but could not, and, after an hour, decided to see Father Duggan and ask if he could give some sort of explanation. Duggan was not in his office, but Joe Asterita was there. "Joe wasn't saying too much," Fanning recounted. "Finally, he says to me, 'I'm going to tell you something. Remember the story Angelina told about Padre Pio and the perfume in her classroom? Well, it happened to me about an hour ago.' So, having a sense of humor, I kidded him a bit. Finally, I said, 'Joe, this is the very reason why I'm up here — because I had that same experience about the same time. I came up to ask Chum [Father Duggan] if he could explain anything to me."

One day Padre Pio insisted that Joe Asterita take five visitors back to their home in Foggia. Even though Joe explained that U.S. Army regulations forbade the transportation of civilians, Padre Pio persisted. Asterita at first agreed, but, after thinking it over, once more explained, "I can't take the people home," again citing the regulations. Speaking deliberately, emphasizing each word, Padre Pio shook his finger in Asterita's face, declaring, "Giusep, you made me a promise and I expect you to keep it. But, remember this: any time I tell you to do something, have no fear!" So Asterita loaded the five Italians (two men, two women, and a little boy) into the jeep and set out for Foggia. Since there was no room in the jeep for anyone else, Fanning remained in San Giovanni. When Joe returned, he reported to Leo: "Have I got a story for you! We got down off the mountain and were on the Manfredonia Road to Foggia, and who's coming in my direction? Not one MP, but two! They looked, but went right on by, and at that moment, the perfume was there. It was with us all the way to Foggia. We passed one MP after another. We were never stopped. I got those people home. It was only after those people got out of the car that the perfume left."

Leo Fanning recalled that he and Joe Asterita "used to act as messengers for Padre Pio. He used to call Joe and me his postmen. People brought letters to the Tortora family in Cerignola to give us to pass on to Padre Pio. We would sit on a bench with Padre Pio before lunch in the monastery and he would read the letters. Sometimes he said, 'Tell them, "I will pray for your intention."'"

Fanning remembered Padre Pio as a "rather robust" man with fair skin and a "nicely trimmed beard." Like most everyone else who met him, Fanning found that Padre Pio's most striking physical characteristic was his "penetrating eyes," which "looked as if he were reading you." But "he could laugh. He had a nice smile. He had a sense of humor. For example, Angelina Tortora once said to us, 'Bring me back something from Padre Pio.' When the request was made, Padre Pio was in the refectory and reached into a cereal box and took out one rice crispy and said, 'Give her this,' and laughed. And Angelina was very happy with the rice crispy."

At table, Fanning recalled that Padre Pio "ate what he was served, but very little." Yet the thing that most impressed the American was the fact that the Capuchin was "always in the presence of God, one way or another. He was aware of God's presence in an extraordinary way."

Like Father Duggan, Fanning asked Padre Pio about the conversion of Russia and received the reply, "Yes, Russia will be converted, as the Blessed Virgin said she would be. However, Russia will teach the United States a lesson in conversion."

Like Mario Avignone, Leo Fanning found San Giovanni "a little paradise," not only because of Padre Pio but because of the "lesser stars in that constellation of sanctity and love." There was Maria Pyle, the "beautiful soul," and Padre Paolino, who was also "very holy," affable, and jolly as well. Then there was Padre Agostino. Fanning and his friends were struck by the superior's magnificent beard. "Do you sleep with your beard outside the covers or inside?" they asked him. Agostino simply laughed. For all his affability, however, as superior he ran a tight ship at San Giovanni. Whereas Padre Paolino, when he was superior at Cerignola, allowed the soldiers to give cigarettes to the friars, Padre Agostino, when in charge at San Giovanni, permitted nothing of the sort. As Fanning recalled:

> We used to take things to give to the monks, such as beer (especially for Padre Pio), candy, and we used to take up cigarettes. We put everything there on a bench. Now the Capuchins had a rule that allowed them to smoke only if the superior permitted. One day Padre Agostino came along. He went to the bench and asked what we had brought. "What is this? And what is this? And what is this?" When we came to the cigarettes, Joe said, "Those are cigarettes for the Fathers."
>
> Father Agostino's blue eyes sparkled and danced as he slowly asked, "For the *Fathers*?" We nodded. "For my friends, yes! But, for my Fathers, no!" And he took the cigarettes. He must have detected smoke and wondered about the source.[17]

Matchmaker

Frequently, Padre Pio's young visitors inquired about their future. Father Duggan brought not only soldiers but also seminarians from Rome. One of them, named Mark, had an interview with Padre Pio, who advised him to leave the seminary, which he did. Duggan asked the Capuchin seer about several devout female army personnel who were thinking about becoming nuns when they left the service. "Let them get married," Padre Pio insisted. They did.[18]

Although he encouraged Leo Fanning to study for the priesthood, when Joe Asterita told Padre Pio that he wanted to become a priest too, he was told, "No, no! When the war is over, go home and marry a nice Italian girl and raise little citizens for heaven." When Asterita objected that he didn't know any girls and added, "What girl would want to marry me, a short little Italian?" Padre Pio looked into his eyes and said, "Giuseppe, if you can't find a nice girl to marry, then I will have to find you a wife myself." Asterita asked how this was possible, since Padre Pio was in Italy and he lived in New York. Padre Pio answered, "Leave it to me. I will find you a nice Italian wife." Less than a year later, Asterita, now an employee of the Internal Revenue Service, met and married an Italian-American lady.[19]

Non-Catholics

Not all the people in the service who came to see Padre Pio were Catholics. Some Sangiovannese were horrified when they learned that some of the soldiers who attended Mass and made holy hours were actually Protestants. Nonetheless, Joe Peluso recalled, "He'd welcome everybody with open arms." Father Duggan recalled that there were many Episcopalians and Presbyterians who attended Mass celebrated by Padre Pio, including at least one chaplain. A concerned Duggan asked Padre Pio, "Is there any chance of their becoming Catholic?" The priest seemed untroubled and said, "If they intend to convert, the Lord will show a way."[20] Giorgio Pogany recalled that Padre Pio "was friendly with all of them" and never pressed anyone to convert.

Many soldiers from the army of the British Empire also visited. Some of them were not even Christian but showed a great reverence for Padre Pio. Joe Peterson told of a soldier from India who fell at Padre Pio's feet, pressing his fingers into his feet, unaware of the stigmata there. Padre Pio shouted in pain and, instinctively, slapped the man in the face! Later, when it was explained that the painful gesture was actually a token of deep respect in Hinduism, he broke down and wept.

On September 14, 1945, Padre Agostino noted that Padre Pio was visited by an Indian captain who said that he believed in Buddha, Confucius, and Jesus Christ. The captain, whom Padre Agostino regarded as a "pagan," went to Mass and received Communion from Padre Pio's hand. Padre Agostino didn't question Padre Pio but reasoned that he must have given the "pagan" Communion so as not to raise a fuss, but noted in his diary, "I'm sure that Our Lord was received by that pagan. Who could deny that one day he will come to know the true faith and become a Christian?"[21]

After the war finally came to an end and the soldiers returned to their homes, San Giovanni Rotondo was never the same. These men and women made Padre Pio known throughout the United States and the British Empire, and, as soon as passenger service was reestablished in the sea and air lanes of the world, a growing flood of pilgrims from every corner of the earth poured into what had been an isolated mountain outpost, for Padre Pio now had a mission to the whole world.

Seer on the Mountaintop

By the postwar years, Padre Pio was venerated as a holy man and prophet by thousands throughout Italy and many in other parts of the world. Pilgrims from all walks of life ascended the rocky mountaintop to consult him and participate in the Masses he celebrated, and mountains of mail — not just from Italy, but from America, the British Empire, Germany, and even remote parts of the globe — increasingly swamped the friars, who tried to deal with it. Moreover, politicians increasingly sought his advice, and voters were often swayed by his opinions when they went to the polls.

Life and Death in the Forgione Family

Padre Pio's immediate family were now all living at San Giovanni. His father had been for some time one of several boarders in the Pyle house, where he is said to have inspired the other people who lived and visited there with his joy, serenity, and fervent piety. Orazio insisted that everybody in the house eat on their knees during Lent and exercise other severe penitential practices that were a part of his life. He loved to regale visitors with anecdotes from the boyhood of his famous son, to whom he was deeply devoted. Whenever people complimented him on being the father of Padre Pio, tears welled up in the old man's eyes as he insisted, "I didn't make him. Jesus Christ did."[1] So great was his veneration for his son that, when he conversed with him, Orazio refused to make use of the familiar second person singular form of address (*tu*) that was normal between family members, but instead used the more formal *voi*.[2] Like his late wife, he insisted on kissing his son's hand, announcing, "I'm not kissing your hand, I'm kissing the wounds of Jesus Christ."[3]

After the death of his wife, Michele Forgione and his daughter Pia joined Orazio in San Giovanni, living in a house near that of Maria Pyle. Of Orazio's fourteen grandchildren (Padre Pio's nieces and nephews), only two survived: Pia and Ettoruccio Masone, Felicita's son. The former was married by her uncle in May 1945 to Mario Pennelli, a teacher. Whenever he performed a wedding, Padre Pio was wont to wish the couple eight children — his idea of an ideal family. In this case, his wish was fulfilled: Pia and Mario were to have eight offspring.

Ettoruccio, the nephew, also lived in San Giovanni for several years, but, after the war, he went to Pietrelcina and opened a movie theater. Uncle Pio warned him, however, to be careful about the films he showed: "You don't want to contribute to the propagation of evil."[4]

Shortly afterward, Ettoruccio, who was an epileptic, suffered a severe seizure, which was followed by pneumonia, then pleurisy. Maria Pyle went to Pietrelcina to look after him and informed Padre Pio that the doctors wanted to operate. He said that they should proceed, if they thought it necessary. After the surgery, however, Ettoruccio, who was only about thirty, grew worse. Resigned to death, he asked for prayers, not for his recovery, but for his soul. Then he fell into a coma. It seemed as if poor Orazio Forgione would soon be bereft of the next to the last of his grandchildren. Ettoruccio then found himself at the gates of heaven, where his long-departed sister Giuseppina was standing, and beside her was Padre Pio. Both of them refused to allow him to enter heaven. Meanwhile, family and friends in the sickroom heard the comatose man cry, over and over, "Uncle Pio! Uncle Pio! Uncle Pio!" The older ones among them recalled how Ettoruccio's mother cried out that she saw Padre Pio, amidst her dead babies, just before she died. It was decided to call the undertaker to make arrangements. No sooner had that been done, however, when Ettoruccio awoke and shouted, "I'm not dying anymore!" His recovery was instantaneous.[5]

With his grandson now returned to the land of the living, it was Orazio Forgione's time to depart the earth. In the spring of 1946, he became ill with an unspecified illness that confined him to bed. On October 3, it was clear that the end was near, and Padre Pio came down from the monastery to stay at Maria Pyle's house to help her and his brother Michele care for the old man, who would eat only when spoon-fed by his favorite child. On October 7, at the age of nearly eighty-six, he entered into his rest. According to Pia, he cried out, "All of you have to get out of the way, because I'm going to call the angels and tell them to take me to heaven because I can say, 'I'm Padre Pio's father!'"[6]

While Pyle and Michele made the funeral arrangements, Padre Pio collapsed, sobbing onto the bed where his father had died. Don Giorgio Pogany recalled that he "cried out his very heart." He wrote a tribute to his father, which was placed on a prayer card given out at the funeral, in which he praised the simplicity of Orazio's "beautiful soul," his winning smiles, his goodness, and intelligence. "On your bed of pain you became a little child again, and so presented yourself before the Friend of little children. Now your children, your grandchildren, the souls who assisted you, and all those who knew and loved you, remember you and beseech you to remember us before God."[7] After the funeral, Padre Pio returned to the friary, but it was a week before he could resume his normal activities. After celebrating Mass, he would go to bed and remain there for the rest of the day.

Christian Democrat

After the war, Padre Pio became involved in politics more than at any other time in his life. The Italian monarchy had been discredited, in the eyes of most Italians, by its cooperation with Mussolini, and a referendum was held to determine the fate of King Umberto II, whose wife, Marie José, had once paid a visit to Padre Pio. Huge crowds converged around the cortege of cars that brought Padre Pio to the polls at San Giovanni, and reporters and photographers fought to get to him, while police cleared a path through screaming, groaning crowds so that the priest could vote. As he was driven back to the monastery, the car had to stop every few yards because of the mobs of people demanding the opportunity to kiss the Padre's gloved hand. The monarchy was abolished. Apparently, Padre Pio was pleased. Why he was opposed to the monarchy is not clear. Pogany believed that Padre Pio thought that the members of the royal family were lacking in religious faith. However, although some of their predecessors were decidedly anti-clerical, Umberto and Marie José seemed to be devout Catholics.

When the time came for the election of delegates to the Italian assembly, Padre Pio urged people to vote for the Christian Democrats, who won an absolute majority over the Communists, many of whom blamed the priest for their defeat, claiming that his "very presence" had taken votes from them. Two years later, there was again danger that the Communists would prove victorious in the elections, and Padre Pio wrote to Premier Alcide De Gasperi to express his support for the Christian Democrats. With the elections a few weeks away, Padre Agostino noted in his diary that Padre Pio was "lining up victory on the side of law and order," by urging everybody who visited him to vote Christian Democrat.

The Communists, of course, took a dim view of such priestly interference in the political arena. A few days before the elections, a Communist from San Marco in Lamis was campaigning from the back of a truck. As he passed near the friary, he shouted, "Down with Padre Pio!" His truck proceeded down the hill toward the town center, where, suddenly, he was stricken with violent pains. Taken to the hospital (which would have been in Foggia), he was found to be incurably ill.[8] The pious attributed his condition to divine retribution.

There was the usual pandemonium as Padre Pio arrived at the polls on April 18, 1948. As he was emerging from the car, a woman who supported the Communists ran into the street, shrieking obscene imprecations at him, then stumbled and fell, and was taken away to a hospital with a broken leg, without having a chance to vote for the Communists. In this, too, the faithful saw divine intervention.[9] The

Christian Democrats were once again victorious, and in southern Italy, where Padre Pio was easily the region's best-known personality, he was widely hailed as instrumental in keeping Italy from going Communist.

The Friary in Pietrelcina

At the same time, Padre Pio was concerned with the future of the Holy Family monastery in Pietrelcina, which had been built through the largesse of Adelaide and Maria Pyle. It had never been occupied by the Capuchins as intended because the archbishop of Benevento refused to grant the necessary authorization. During the war, the building had been requisitioned for the billeting first of Italian, then of German, and, finally, of Allied soldiers. It was now a wreck, its walls covered with obscene graffiti in Italian, German, English, and Polish.

Even after the war, Archbishop Agostino Mancinelli (1882–1962) continued to oppose the establishment of a Capuchin friary at Pietrelcina. Padre Pio was so disgusted with the prelate that in July 1946 he had sent word to him that "Benevento was bombed and lost the cathedral and episcopal residence as a punishment for the Archbishop. My heart bleeds to say this, but it's true…. Worse, not even after this punishment from God is the Archbishop willing to understand his responsibility. He is truly hard of heart. Souls are being lost and the enemies of God are wreaking havoc, all because the Archbishop sleeps and does not want the friars at Pietrelcina."[10]

The "enemies of God" were not Communists, but Jehovah's Witnesses, organized in Pietrelcina by Michele Cavaluzzo (1880–1946), who had been converted while living in Buffalo, New York. The community was thriving in Padre Pio's hometown, holding meetings, distributing literature, and even handing out money to the peasants. A number of Pietrelcinese had been baptized by them in a nearby stream. The Witnesses now wanted to buy the vacant friary and turn it into a "Kingdom Hall." After he was approached by the group, the alarmed mayor informed Padre Pio. Although the Padre's attitude to non-Catholic Christian groups was quite tolerant for a man of his time and place, he evidently felt that the Jehovah's Witnesses, who deny that Jesus is God, were not Christian. Convinced that a Capuchin presence in Pietrelcina was necessary to combat what he seemed to consider a pestiferous sect, he dispatched his friend Don Giuseppe Orlando to see if he could find out the reason for the archbishop's opposition.

After some time, Orlando managed to arrange a meeting with Mancinelli, in which the archbishop frankly stated the reason for his opposition: "The Capuchins cannot come to Pietrelcina because it would raise the question of their interests against those of the parish clergy…. Everyone would give their … offerings to the Capuchins because they are Padre Pio's monks, and [would] no longer [contribute] to the secular clergy, and I have to defend the secular clergy because they are my dependents."[11] The archbishop conceded, however, that if a means were found to compensate the clergy who stood to lose the most by the Capuchin presence, he might be disposed to change his mind.

Orlando also learned that the Observant Franciscans from the municipality of Paduli, six miles away, were lobbying the Vatican to thwart the establishment of a Capuchin friary in Pietrelcina because Pietrelcina was too close to Paduli, and the Capuchins would infringe upon the right of the Observants to solicit funds in that region. "Only we may solicit in that area!" insisted the Observant provincial, causing Orlando to shake his head and sigh, "Monks against monks!"[12]

Orlando then went to Rome and, after several serendipitous meetings with prominent officials, was able to meet with Cardinal Luigi Lavitrano, head of the Sacred Congregation for Religious, who had headed the archdiocese of Benevento for four years during the 1920s. The cardinal persuaded Mancinelli to drop his objection, and the Congregation for Religious approved the opening of the friary in Pietrelcina.

Padre Pio was sick in bed one January day in 1947 when he was awakened by the sound of applause in the corridor. Orlando then told him that the Pietrelcina friary was going to be a reality. Embracing his friend, kissing him, and blessing him, weeping with joy, Pio cried, "See, Peppino, God chose you to accomplish this work!" Orlando told him about all the "fortuitous meetings" in which he just happened to make the right contacts. "Were they a matter of coincidence?" he asked Padre Pio. "Yes," the Capuchin replied, "but there is Somebody up there who arranged those coincidences."[13]

The first Capuchin friars arrived in Pietrelcina in April 1947. Many Pietrelcinese hoped that Padre Pio would be transferred to his hometown. Although this was out of the question, Padre Pio hoped to return home for the formal consecration of the monastery in May 1951. When word of this reached San Giovanni, however, many of the residents became convinced that if "their saint" were allowed to return to Pietrelcina, if for only a day, the Pietrelcinese would never allow him to return. So townspeople formed a guard around Padre Pio's friary, threatening to riot if he left, forcing him to cancel his plans.[14] He was truly a prisoner of his famed sanctity.

Father Dominic

William Carrigan, upon his return to America, had written an article about Padre Pio, describing his wartime experiences and the huge numbers of American soldiers who had visited the stigmatized priest, many of whose lives had been dramatically changed. Carrigan later recalled that within months practically every Catholic periodical in the United States carried the story. This helped to increase the volume of mail Padre Pio received from the United States.

Maria Pyle also did her part to make Padre Pio known in America when she returned to the States in 1948 to settle the estate of an aunt and solicit funds for the

Casa Sollievo della Sofferenza. After traveling around giving talks about Padre Pio, Pyle found herself without money. When she went to her lawyer to ask for help to get back to Italy, he promptly gave her a check for twenty thousand dollars — a sum of money her mother had withheld from her regular trust fund payments over the years. Adelaide had long ago feared that her daughter, who had demonstrated little skill in managing money, would find herself without funds, and had therefore made provision for that possibility.[15]

Pyle, who was fluent in several languages, had been handling Padre Pio's foreign correspondence. By 1947, he was receiving over two hundred letters a day. Within a few years, every two months, ten thousand letters were arriving, many from English-speaking countries. By the mid-1950s, the number would double. In many of these letters, people would write their confessions and request absolution. Pyle, with several volunteers, would sort the letters into bushel baskets according to language, and then she would answer them, often without consulting Padre Pio, because she thought she knew his thoughts. She wrote to a correspondent, "Those who receive letters signed by Mary Pyle can rest assured that, while they are receiving the words of Mary Pyle, they are at the same time receiving the thoughts of Padre Pio."[16] When Father Clement Neubauer from Milwaukee (1891–1969) became minister general of the Capuchin order, he made a trip to San Giovanni Rotondo, and, after taking note of the situation, appointed a longtime friend, Father Dominic Meyer, to be Padre Pio's secretary, in charge of handling English and German correspondence.

Fifty-six years old when he arrived in San Giovanni in November 1948, Dominic, whose birth name was Aloysius, came from a large, pious German family in Belleville, Illinois. By his own admission a "wild guy," Meyer never thought about the priesthood until he was a senior in a high school run by the Capuchin order, and he was jolted to his senses when a priest complimented him on the role of a bandit he played in a school play because he thought it was a perfect fit with the boy's personality. Joining the order, Meyer was ordained at thirty and earned a doctorate in sacred theology at the Gregorian University in Rome. He taught dogmatic theology for many years until problems with his voice made it difficult for him to give lectures, and he then became confessor of novices at the friary of St. Felix in Huntington, Indiana.

Father Dominic has been described as a grim, humorless man with an air of austerity. According to Father John Schug, who knew him well, Dominic was "completely unconcerned about his physical appearance," completely without self-consciousness, and reserved to the point of seldom showing even the slightest sign of emotion. Nearly six feet tall, he was gaunt and wasted, with, nevertheless, a large belly. He had dark, sunken eyes, sunken cheeks, bushy eyebrows, and a long, dirty-gray beard. He was even more abstemious in food and drink than Padre Pio, who would urge him to eat more, only to be told, "I have a smaller stomach."[17] Many of his American confreres regarded him as fussy and irascible, and, when he was appointed secretary to Padre Pio, one of them remarked, "Well, if Padre Pio isn't a saint already, he will be!"

Dominic wrote to his cousin Albert (then bishop of Superior, Wisconsin) that he arose at quarter past three in the morning, prayed the Office and said Mass, and began answering letters at seven. He also met with English- and German-speaking pilgrims and arranged brief meetings with Padre Pio for them. "Most of them came out of devotion," he noted, but "some came out of mere curiosity, not so many."[18]

Of the hundreds of letters he handled each week, there were usually only about a dozen that Father Dominic selected as meriting Padre Pio's attention. About once a week, Padre Pio came to Dominic's room to ask him about the prayer requests in the letters. Dominic would read questions from the letters. Sometimes Padre Pio would say, "Tell them to be resigned and trust to the mercy of God." To others he would reply, "There is no answer to that question." Dominic wrote, "Many continue to ask whether their boy or husband, missing in action, is still alive or not. Sometimes he answers definitely, 'He is dead,' but more often he merely gives an evasive answer to show that God did not reveal this to him."[19]

The Italian correspondence was handled by a Padre Ermingildo, and, eventually, an English priest, Father Eustace, took over the English correspondence, leaving Father Dominic with only the German. Pyle continued to answer some letters, since she was fluent in French and Spanish. Padre Agostino began the practice, continued to the end of Padre Pio's life, of having all correspondence, no matter who the author was, signed "Father Superior."

Celebrity Encounters

The prominent as well as the humble came to see Padre Pio. Father Dominic wrote to his cousin Albert Meyer, in October 1950: "During the last three weeks there were seven Bishops here from Brazil, Venezuela, Colombia, India, Bluefields [Nicaragua], Iceland, and Switzerland. The Indian bishop … is a convert…. Then the other day there was an Abyssinian [that is, Ethiopian] Cistercian here, a negro about 6 ft 2 in, dark as the ace of spades, who celebrated in the Coptic Rite. The Bishop of India was of the Syro-Antiochean Rite. There were plenty of priests here from the U.S., England, Austria, Switzerland, Ireland, Australia, etc."[20]

In 1949, the Uruguayan operatic baritone Victor Damiani (1893–1962) and the soprano Mafalda Rinaldi gave a concert of operatic arias for the friars. Padre Agostino did not allow the performance to interfere with the liturgical life of the friars, so when the bell rang for the Angelus, he interrupted the concert, calling out, "Everybody get up!" Everyone, including the performers, rose, prayed the Angelus, and sat down again to enjoy the rest of the performance.

Two years later Beniamino Gigli (1890–1957), considered by many the foremost operatic tenor of his time, came to San Giovanni. Gigli was notoriously arrogant, known to be an inveterate womanizer, but he was also very religious, and was a significant contributor to the *Casa Sollievo della Sofferenza*. When Father Dominic met him in the friary garden with Padre Pio and other members of the community, the *primo tenore* seemed shy, "with no arrogance about him." Dominic said that Gigli "told us a number of humorous incidents of the operatic stage which didn't get out into the public." Then, with Dr. Sanguinetti holding up the microphone of a recorder, the tenor sang the popular Neapolitan song "Mamma." Afterward, Gigli talked alone with Padre Pio. He later remarked, "I've met thousands of people on my concert tours, but no one has ever impressed me as Padre Pio has!"[21] Gigli returned to San Giovanni Rotondo several times in the six years that remained to him and contributed generously to the *Casa* and other charities of Padre Pio.

It was around this time that the Italian-American composer Gian Carlo Menotti (1911–2007) called on the Padre. After attending his Mass, the composer met with Padre Pio for a few minutes.

"Do you believe in the Church?" asked the priest.

"No, I'm afraid I don't believe in the Church," replied the musician.

Padre Pio asked, "But who do you think gave you this great gift and talent that you have?"

"I did not say I don't believe in God," Menotti answered. "I only said I did not believe in the Church."

Rather at a loss for words, the Padre looked at him for a time and asked, "Why do you come to see me then? I believe in the Church."

Recalling his encounter with Padre Pio many years later, Menotti observed, "Somehow I wanted him to tell me why I came to him. At any rate, Padre Pio failed me. I think if he had simply taken me in his arms, I would immediately have gone back into the arms of the Church." Nonetheless, the composer conceded, "Still, it was quite an experience — one I shall never forget. I did have the feeling I had met a saint."[22] Some of Menotti's friends believed that his encounter with Padre Pio inspired him to write the opera *The Saint of Bleecker Street* — about a young woman who has the stigmata.

Francisco Franco (1892–1975), who had seized power in Spain in the 1930s, in a bloody civil war, and ruled his country with an iron fist, sent a message to Padre Pio, asking, "How shall I handle the people?" According to Don Giorgio Pogany, the priest sent word to *El Caudillo*, "Concern yourself more with morality and spirituality than with physical things."

Earthquake

In the summer of 1948, San Giovanni Rotondo was shaken by a series of earthquakes, prompting some local women to complain that "Padre Pio didn't do anything" to prevent them. Evidently, there was not much damage and no fatalities, but many people were frightened enough to sleep outdoors for several days. Among them was Padre Pio, who, along with other friars, camped out in the monastery garden. While other friars slept under trees, Padre Pio wandered around for almost the entire night, a rosary in his hand and a blanket under his arm. He was not immune to fear and made it clear that although all his life he welcomed the opportunity to become a martyr, he did not want to die ignominiously under a pile of rubble.[23]

Padre Agostino Retires

In June 1952, seventy-two-year-old Padre Agostino finished his term as father guardian at San Giovanni Rotondo. As a former superior, he had the right to choose the friary where he would spend his retirement, and, to no one's surprise, he elected to stay near Padre Pio. *Tatone* — Big Daddy, as he was called behind his back — was in deteriorating health. Padre Alessio Parente recalled, "He could hardly walk, he was so fat and heavy." His limited mobility was not, however, the result of his weight, but of painful leg ulcers, from which he had suffered for years. Joe Peterson, the American veteran who now spent his summer vacations in San Giovanni, remembered seeing him in his room with newspapers covering his legs, obviously suffering greatly. Padre Agostino never complained, and it was understood that he had offered his life to God as a victim soul and that his affliction was his cross.[24]

During the years following the war, the most significant development at San Giovanni was not the number of celebrities who visited, nor the change in superiors, nor the increase in mail, nor Padre Pio's occasional involvement in politics, but the construction of the *Casa Sollievo della Sofferenza.*

Chapter Twenty-Seven

"A Magnificent Work of Charity"

"A Hospital on a Mountain! They're Crazy!"

Work on *La Casa Sollievo della Sofferenza* began in earnest immediately after the war. On October 5, 1946, the hospital was incorporated as a shareholding company with a capital of one million lire and a thousand shares of one thousand lire each, to be divided among the shareholders, each of whom signed a document renouncing any profit. The first members of the company were Dr. Sanguinetti, Dr. Kiswarday, Don Giuseppe Orlando, Dr. Eleonora Figna (an engineer from Florence), Dr. Guglielmo Pancali (an agricultural scientist), and Pasquale De Meis (a wealthy landowner).[1]

During the next few days, other friends of Padre Pio joined the company, among them Dr. Sanvico, Angela Serritelli, Count Telfner, Marquess Gianbattista Sachetti, and Marquess Bernardo Patrizi (a Roman aristocrat and great-grandnephew of General Robert E. Lee). Three days after the *Casa* was incorporated, land was donated for the building by Maria Basilio, a wealthy woman from Turin, who owned land adjacent to the friary. A day later, Angela Serritelli donated a parcel of land that she owned that adjoined the Basilio tract.[2]

The next spring Padre Pio appointed Don Giuseppe Orlando as director and urged him to commence construction. "He always took it out on me," Orlando recalled. "Each evening he used to elbow me in the sides, to the extent that I avoided sitting beside him."

"Do you understand that you must start the work?" Padre Pio nagged.

"But, Piuccio, why do I have to make them laugh behind my back and yours? Start work for a big clinic without a drawing, without a design, without an engineer?"

"You must start the work," Padre Pio nonetheless insisted.[3]

And so, in the spring of 1947, Padre Pio blessed the first stone, and on May 19, 1947, ground was broken for a road leading to the site of the hospital by twenty workmen hired by Orlando. When he learned of the project, a prominent physician in Foggia said publicly, "A hospital on a mountain! They're crazy!" Other prominent members of the medical profession throughout Italy decried the folly of the impossible project.[4]

"You Will Be My Architect"

Orlando still needed to find an architect and engineer, and he solicited proposals and building plans submitted by a number of architects and engineers, some of them prominent and highly respected. Padre Pio insisted on examining all the blueprints, and he finally approved a design submitted by a man named Candeloro, who claimed to be an engineer from Pescara. "Candeloro," however, turned out to be Angelo Lupi (1906–1969), an eccentric genius from Abruzzi, who had only five years of elementary schooling. A large man who typically dressed in a sweater, knickers, and big boots, over the years he had worked as a surveyor, photographer, carpenter, interior decorator, machinist, and set designer, but never as an architect or engineer![5] Nevertheless, Padre Pio assured him, "You will be my architect."[6] When his lack of credentials were called into question, and he was accused of practicing the profession of architect illegally, Padre Pio reassured him, "The man who has denounced you received his degree from man. You instead have received it from God."[7] Lupi's personality was just as his name sounds in English. Some people described him as manic-depressive. It was said of him: "He was either in the stars or in the doldrums. He could be as soft as a baby or wild as a beast." He flew into towering rages when limits were placed on his creativity or when he felt hamstrung by red tape. Sanguinetti frequently had to soothe Lupi's volatile feelings to keep the project running smoothly.[8]

Financing the Construction of the Hospital

How was the construction to be financed? Padre Pio refused to seek loans from banks or elsewhere and relied on private donations. "This is the house of Providence," he insisted. "When Providence doesn't have any funds available, let work be stopped."[9]

Once again Emmanuele Brunatto came to Padre Pio's aid. Even though, in his words, he had been "kicked out" of San Giovanni and had not seen Padre Pio in years, like a fairy godfather he stepped in to help. During the war, he had been living in Paris, stocking warehouses full of canned meat, soap, sugar, coffee, condensed milk, mints, liquor, and chocolates which he sold on the black market to both the French and the occupying Germans.[10] After the war, as an offering of "reparation" for his sins, Brunatto donated 3.5 million francs to the *Casa*.

In the summer of 1948, British economist Barbara Ward (1914–1981) came to Italy to write a report on the postwar reconstruction of that country for her magazine, *The Economist*. Her fiancé, Sir Robert Gillman Allen Jackson (1911–1991), was deputy director in charge of field operations of the United Nations Relief and Rehabilitation Administration (UNRRA). Ward, a devout Catholic, learned of Padre Pio and his work from her friend the Marquess Patrizi. Writing in 1980, Ward recounted that the Marquess urged her to stop at Foggia on her way to Taranto "and allow him to take me up to San Giovanni Rotondo to encounter the saintly Padre Pio, who, with his stigmata, his endless hours in the confessional, and his reputation for healing the sick, was already the drawing power for immense pilgrimages from Italy and … other lands." Ward set out with the Marquess and Marchioness Patrizi, "passing through the baking heat of Foggia into the cooler air of the Gargano hills." Arriving at San Giovanni Rotondo, they stayed with the Sanguinettis, "a charming, intelligent, and devoted pair."

The next day, Ward attended a Mass celebrated by Padre Pio and was deeply impressed. Afterward, she and the Marquess had a long talk with Sanguinetti, who explained how, since he had come to San Giovanni, the responsibility for caring for sick and dying pilgrims had largely fallen on his shoulders. He spoke of how "the problem of caring for the deeply sick was nearly defeating him, despite the neighborly cooperation of the whole village." Then he told her about the *Casa*. "Subscriptions are coming in," Sanguinetti told Ward, "and I have no doubt that they will continue to do so, but they just aren't enough. Signor Lupi, the architect, and I have dedicated ourselves to the preparation of plans and estimates. We are confronted, however, with the stark fact that we haven't enough money to carry through a hospital project of this size."

Ward and Sanguinetti began to wonder whether the *Casa* might qualify for aid from UNRRA, which had as its priority the restoration of health services in areas ravaged by the war. Even before the war, hospitals and medical services were desperately scarce in southern Italy, and during the fighting many hospitals had been destroyed and the area was swept by epidemics of typhoid and malaria. Foggia had been virtually obliterated by bombing, and Sanguinetti argued that "a well-conceived and well-run hospital would serve the health of the whole region, and by its elevation in the hills of the Gargano, it would be more suitably sited than out in the burning summer plains."[11]

Ward explained the situation to Jackson, suggesting that UNRRA could provide funds for the *Casa* as part of the rehabilitation of the Foggia region. On June 21, 1948, UNRRA approved a grant of 400 million lire for that purpose. The money was awarded to the Italian Administration for International Aid, which, in turn, was to provide funding for the project. Padre Pio was furious when the government passed on only 250 million lire for the hospital and called the failure of the AAI to provide the totality of the UNRRA grant an act of thievery.[12] The grant stated that the hospital be named "The Fiorello Henry LaGuardia Hospital," in memory of the recently deceased general director of UNRRA and three-term mayor of New York City, whose father was a native of Cerignola. In a ceremony attended by Archbishop Cesarano, Padre Pio blessed the plaque naming the hospital for LaGuardia, but insisted on ignoring it and calling "The Work" *La Casa Sollievo della Sofferenza,* the name he had chosen years before.

Work Begins on the Hospital

Work now proceeded rapidly. Lupi maintained a payroll of 350 workers. He built a lime kiln behind the construction site and set up a workshop to prepare artificial marble. Previously unskilled farm laborers were trained to be carpenters, blacksmiths, bricklayers, woodworkers, decorators, and painters, trades which they were able to put to use after the hospital was completed.

Soon tons of mountainside were blasted away, and, even before the UNRRA grant was received, the foundations were finished and the first walls erected. To raise money, Padre Pio authorized lotteries, raffles, theatrical shows, artistic evenings, and even the showing of carefully screened movies. Many of these performances were put together by Cleonice Morcaldi. Padre Pio would collect money from pilgrims, place it in a handkerchief, and hand it over to the managers of the building site. Local shopkeepers put collection boxes in their establishments. Large individual contributions began to come in from individuals all over the world, especially the United States and Switzerland. Beniamino Gigli is said to have donated a percentage of his earnings to the *Casa.* In 1949, the magazine *La Casa Sollievo della Sofferenza* was begun by Dr. Sanguinetti, with editorial duties assumed later on by Carlo Trabucco, a journalist from Rome, who served without salary.

Dr. Kiswarday managed the finances of "The Work," paying the workers their wages from his office in a green shack that served as the accounting department. Sanguinetti served as jack-of-all-trades, driving trucks, supervising workers, locating technical experts, and selecting materials. One of his greatest accomplishments was the planting of thousands of seedlings on the barren and rocky hillsides that rose above the friary and rising hospital. Most of the young evergreens he planted himself, setting off charges of dynamite to blast out holes large enough to accommodate the carloads of soil that he hauled up the slopes by mule, since the incline was too steep for trucks.[13]

The "Prayer Army"

Padre Pio had been organizing informal prayer groups since the time he was in Foggia. In 1947, he announced, "It is time to unite both intentions and actions, to offer Our Lord collective prayers imploring his mercy for a humanity that appears to have forgotten him."[14] Sanguinetti functioned as Padre Pio's right arm in coordinating the establishment of formal groups in twenty-three Italian cities, in which the faithful met monthly, with the consent of the local bishop, to pray for the pope, for Padre Pio's ministries, for world peace, and for their own intentions. Aware of the possibility of fanaticism, Padre Pio insisted that each of the Prayer Groups be under the guidance of a priest, "because only a priest can guarantee union with the Church."[15] He envisioned the Prayer Groups as "a tremendous chorus, linking heaven to earth and men to God." His chief purpose in organizing the groups was "to bring souls to the Lord, to encourage them to pray ... together ... with Jesus," insisting that "this certainly displeases Satan."[16] By the time Padre Pio died two decades later, his "Prayer Army" numbered seven hundred groups in fourteen countries, with a membership of more than seventy thousand.

Changes in Leadership

On July 26, 1954, the outpatient clinic of the *Casa* was blessed by Padre Pio and opened. But, as "The Work" neared completion, some of Padre Pio's friends became concerned because the directors could bequeath their shares to whomever they chose. "They are honest people," fretted Padre Paolino, "but what will happen when they die?" Giuseppe Orlando, himself a director, raised the concern: "Tomorrow the heirs of the founders might be Protestants, Communists, Jews, or atheists! And then what?"[17] Padre Pio expressed interest in having the *Casa* run directly either by the Vatican or the Capuchin order, but neither was willing to take on that responsibility. In August 1954, therefore, the *Casa* was reorganized so as to be administered by a board of fifty who would constitute a special Congregation of the Franciscan Third Order.

Padre Pio considered Dr. Sanguinetti indispensable in making the *Casa* a reality. He was a man described as "without haughtiness or inhibitions, selfless and generous."[18] Tirelessly, he supervised "The Work," mollifying the temperamental Lupi, as well as directing the Prayer Groups. Then, without any warning, on September 9, 1954, the doctor was stricken at home with a massive heart attack and died almost instantly at the age of sixty. Padre Pio was shattered by the death of his friend. For days, other than celebrating Mass, he could do nothing, seemingly paralyzed by bitter grief. He seemed completely unnerved. At the mere mention of his friend's name, he burst into bitter weeping. When friends tried to comfort him by reminding him that the good doctor had gone to his reward and that he should not mourn like one without hope, Padre Pio replied, "You know, not just the mind, but the human heart claims its share."[19] Padre Pio, in fact, seemed angry with God. He was overheard complaining to his heavenly Father: "You took him without first telling me! If you had told me that you were going to take him, I wouldn't have given him to you! I would have snatched him out of your hands!"[20]

"We all have to die," a friend said, but Padre Pio replied, "We all have to die, it's true, but the Lord should have spared him to me for just a little longer."[21]

Then, in April 1955, the second director to die prematurely in a space of seven months, Mario Sanvico, succumbed to cancer in Perugia at the age of fifty-five. In the meantime, Lupi's attitude was proving intolerable. He instantly took a dislike to Alberto Galletti of Milan, who succeeded Sanguinetti as the director of the *Casa*, and made life so unbearable for him that the new administrator resigned after three months. The council of the *Casa* then chose Luigi Ghisleri, a tough, no-nonsense modern business manager. When Lupi continued to throw hissy fits, Ghisleri fired him. Lupi then barricaded himself in his office and challenged his dismissal in the courts. When the case was decided against him, Lupi left in violent rage, taking all his architectural plans with him.[22]

Ghisleri approached "The Work" in a way that was quite different from the approach of the pious Sanguinetti, who had intended to hire only doctors who were Padre Pio's spiritual children. Instead, Ghisleri announced a policy of hiring top-notch physicians and specialists from all over the world, on the basis of their professional qualifications alone. Sanguinetti had expected doctors and staff to serve without salary, "driven by a mission of fraternal charity and Christian love," but his successor found this idea visionary and impractical, and provided for the payment of competitive salaries.[23] The nurses, however, were all to be nuns — from the zealous Missionaries of the Sacred Heart of Jesus.

"A Magnificent Success"

Finally, the great day arrived on May 5, 1956. A crowd of more than fifteen thousand was present for the inauguration of the *Casa*. The assembled throngs beheld a platform full of dignitaries from church, state, and university, including the president of the Italian senate, the minister of state, and the archbishop of Bologna, Cardinal Giacomo Lercaro (1891–1976), who spoke first, insisting that "here is a clear, precise address where God can be found ... where charity and love are, where [God] passes, where he touches ... where he is allowed to enter, where he is permitted to come. He brings this mark, this unmistakable seal of charity and love. Have you remarked this fact at San Giovanni Rotondo? Yes, everyone has remarked it. God is here. Obviously charity and love are also here."

Padre Pio then rose to address the crowd, thanking his benefactors throughout the world. "This is what Providence created with your help," he said, and added:

> Admire it and bless it together in the name of God. A seed has been placed in the earth which he will warm with his rays of love. A new army formed through sacrifice and love is about to rise up to the glory of God, and to comfort sick souls and bodies. Do not deprive us of your help. Collaborate with this apostolate for the relief of human suffering, and the Divine Charity, which knows no bounds and which is the very light of God and the eternal

life, will accumulate for each one of you a treasure of graces, to which Jesus, on the cross, made us inheritors. This work which you see today is only starting out on its life, but this creation, to grow and become adult, needs and asks for your generosity so that it does not perish from inanition, and so that it may become a hospital city, technically adapted to the most demanding needs and also to the disciplined order demanded by militant Franciscanism, a place of prayer and science, where human beings can be united in Christ Crucified, as a single flock with a single shepherd.[24]

After the ribbon was cut jointly by Padre Pio and Cardinal Lercaro, the *Casa* was opened to host an international symposium on cardiac surgery, presided over by Professor Pietro Valdoni. Eminent heart surgeons from all over the world admired the institution, which Dr. Gustav Nylin of Sweden, president of the European Society of Cardiology, called "a magnificent work of charity."[25] Padre Pio charged the doctors, "Bring God to the sick. It will be more valuable than any other treatment.... You have the mission of curing the sick, but, if at the patient's bedside you do not bring the warmth of loving care, I fear that medicine will not be of much use."[26]

Pope Pius XII lauded the *Casa* as "a magnificent success"[27] and gave Padre Pio the absolute right of administration, which meant that the friar was released from his vow of poverty to the extent that he was able to hold the title deed to the institution and make all decisions regarding its operation. He could hire and fire administrators and doctors; he could order the construction of additions; he could determine the kinds of services offered to the public. In practice, however, Padre Pio left such decisions in the hands of his directors.

Indeed, the *Casa* was (and remains) one of the best equipped hospitals in all of Italy. When it opened, it boasted two operating rooms; departments of general surgery, urology, cardiology, orthopedics, traumatology, pediatrics, obstetrics, radiology, and physical therapy; as well as laboratories for clinical research and an outpatient clinic. The *New York Times* described the *Casa* as "one of the most beautiful as well as one of the most modern and fully-equipped hospitals in the world. It even has a helicopter landing place on the roof for emergency patients.... Its different shades of lovely green marble, its fine tile-work, its bright, pleasant rooms ... its ultra-modern operating rooms, laboratories, and kitchen, its little chapel with its precious stained glass windows, its staff of top-flight surgeons and specialists — every detail — makes it as beautiful and up-to-date a place to take away suffering as one can hope to find."[28] The building was even air-conditioned — a rarity in Italy in the 1950s. Padre Pio was, in fact, criticized by some for allowing too much to be spent on luxuries. He answered such objections by saying, "Nothing is too good or too beautiful for the sick and suffering!"

Although nearly all Italian citizens treated at the hospital were covered under the national health plan, Padre Pio insisted that those who were not covered must still be treated, if not for free, at least for a manageable fee. Shortly after Padre Pio's death, the typical daily rate for an uninsured patient was the equivalent of $14.75. A fund maintained by contributions from all over the world provided for uninsured patients and procedures.[29]

Padre Pio emphasized that the hospital was created not only for the relief of sick bodies but for the benefit of the whole person. "The suffering patient," he insisted, "must have in himself the love of God by a wise acceptance of his pains and a serene meditation on his destiny before God. Here the love of God must be strengthened in the spirit of every patient through his love of Jesus Crucified. Here patients, physicians, and priests shall be reservoirs of love which will communicate itself to others in proportion to the extent that it is found in them."[30] He sometimes referred to the *Casa* as a "Clinic for Souls," contending that "the goal of the Work is ... to care for the bodies to [assist] the souls."[31]

On May 10, 1956, the first patient was admitted. By the end of the month, however, there were only twenty-five patients in a hospital with three hundred beds. It was whispered that Padre Pio's hospital was proving to be a white elephant after all. Then, in June, on the feast of Corpus Christi, Padre Pio carried the Blessed Sacrament in procession throughout the entire building. Almost immediately the *Casa* began to fill with patients.[32]

On the first anniversary of the opening of the hospital, Padre Pio announced plans for a medical and religious center that included nursing homes for both men and women, "where tired and exhausted bodies and souls can be with the Lord and obtain succor from him" and an "intercontinental study center" to "stimulate medical people to perfection in their professional culture and Christian studies." Padre Pio also wanted a center for the Prayer Groups and retreats for priests and also for laity, where "men and women will ... be able to care for their spiritual development and their ascent to God."[33] Later he expanded his vision to include Christian day-care centers as well as institutions to train handicapped and intellectually disabled children. "These are not simply my works," Padre Pio declared, "They are God's works, just as he shows me."[34]

Giuseppe Gusso, a physician on the staff of the *Casa*, said that he believed that the creation of the hospital was the greatest miracle associated with Padre Pio. He was certain that the way the hospital came about was a sure indication of the active hand of Providence.

During the next few years, Padre Pio visited the *Casa* many times, walking through the halls and visiting the bedsides of the sick. Occasionally, he presided at Benediction in the chapel and carried the Blessed Sacrament in procession through the wards. Several times he went there to preside over meetings of the Franciscan Third Order and bless additions to the building.

A New Church

There were now so many pilgrims at San Giovanni Rotondo that the little church of Our Lady of Grace was entirely inadequate. Therefore, plans were drawn up to build a larger church next door. Padre Pio actively involved himself in the plans. In March 1956, he wrote to the current minister general, Padre Benigno of Sant'Ilario Milanese, informing him that "the little old existing church will remain *intact* in its entirety, including the nave and the altars of St. Francis, St. Felix, along with [those of] the Madonna and St. Anthony." He insisted that, considering the rapidly increasing number of visitors, "the new church can't be smaller or even just a little bigger than the existing one, which would make the work useless." Padre Pio was impatient with those who complained that the architectural style of the church would clash with that of the area, because in and around San Giovanni "a unique and uniform building style does not exist." There were concerns that the plans drawn up by the architect were too grand, but Padre Pio insisted that if there should be "a significant reduction of the actual dimensions of the project Gentile [the architect] approved, it would be better not to do the church."[35] The new church, which seated 500, was opened in 1959.

"The Padre's Life Is Always the Same"

Padre Pio was now an international celebrity. He was even offered the chance to have a weekly radio program, but he declined, saying, "I always pray for the sick. Rather than talk to them [on the radio], I prefer to speak a prayer to God on their behalf."[36]

Despite his worldly engagements, "The Padre's life is always the same," Padre Agostino wrote in his diary, "notwithstanding the continuous crush of his sacred ministry. His interior life is always caught up in contemplation of God and union with him. His mystical union with God is habitual and definitely real. His outward deportment is a source of admiration and joy to anyone who approaches him or speaks with him."[37]

During the 1950s, many political leaders came to consult Padre Pio, including Aldo Moro, Antonio Segni, Mariano Rumor, and Giovanni Leone, all of whom, at one time or other, headed the Italian government. People from all over the world, moreover, were coming to settle permanently at San Giovanni, to be near "the man of God." One lady, a former devotee of Eastern religions, settling near the friary in what she called a "Christian ashram," declared, "There is no place on earth where you get so much light for the interior life as at San Giovanni Rotondo."[38]

The Twenty-Hour Day

"Hale and Hearty Looking"

Padre Alessio Parente described Padre Pio in his prime as "a stout, strong man." At five feet five-and-a-half inches tall, he was just slightly shorter than a typical southern Italian man of his generation. A reporter from the *New York Times* described Padre Pio in his sixth decade as "hale and hearty looking, with a clear skin, a bushy beard and head of hair, a tendency to corpulence, a pleasant smile, [and] twinkling brown eyes." As always, his eyes were the most striking characteristic. Nearly everyone who met him was struck by Padre Pio's "beautiful," "luminous," and "bright" eyes, which seemed to penetrate the very depths of the soul. Those meeting him for the first time, expecting a pale, emaciated man, stern and severe, were surprised by his substantial frame, ruddy complexion, deep booming voice and hearty laugh, and his extroverted character.

All those who knew him unanimously agreed that Padre Pio ate very little: no breakfast, occasionally a cup of coffee in the morning, and very little in the evening: perhaps a few cookies and a glass or two of beer or fruit juice. His only real meal was the midday dinner he took with his confreres in the refectory. In response to an article which claimed that Padre Pio consumed nothing but a few mouthfuls of vegetables each day and a few sips of lemon juice, Father Dominic, who sat next to him at table, wrote, "He eats also macaroni, cheese, peas, beans, fruit, liver, etc., and, as all good Italians, he drinks a glass of wine."[1] He also enjoyed fried sausage and dried ham, but everything in very small quantities. He routinely forked over much of the content of his plate to those sitting near him. When he tried to share his food with the equally abstemious Dominic, and the American priest protested, Padre Pio would smile and exhort, "Courage (*Coraggio*)!"[2]

Even though Padre Pio got very little exercise, every doctor who had anything to do with him insisted that his food intake was quite insufficient to support his weight, which was usually around 170 pounds. Moreover, there were several occasions when, ill with a stomach virus, Padre Pio ingested nothing but sips of water for several days, but nevertheless gained weight. On one such occasion, Dr. Sanguinetti noted, with amazement, that his patient gained six pounds after an eight-day siege of illness during which he could hold down only a small amount of water. He asked Padre Pio how he could possibly gain weight when fasting. "Assimilation," was his answer. "Everything depends on assimilation."

"But there's nothing to assimilate if you don't eat," objected the physician.

"Well, every morning I take Communion."

"No, you're not convincing me," Sanguinetti responded. Knowing that Padre Pio liked to joke, he suggested, "You must be hiding food somewhere, so as to trick me."

"I haven't eaten anything, just as you have seen," the Padre insisted. "But we must think of the parable in the Bible about the sower. The grain fell on good ground and produced a hundredfold. You see that my soil is good and I have produced much."

"These are spiritual things," answered the physician. "What does the spirit have to do with the body?"

Padre Pio went on to say that he was nourished solely by the Eucharist: "It is the Lord who does this and not I. It is the Lord who is working in me."[3]

According to all the priests who lived with him, Padre Pio had need of less sleep than the average man and often slept for as little as three or four hours in twenty-four.

In his fifties and sixties, Padre Pio's health was generally good. Father Dominic, in his letters to relatives, usually described him as being in "excellent health." He was still subject to occasional respiratory complaints as well as high fevers. Although Dr. Sala, who became Padre Pio's doctor in 1956, recalled only "normal rises" in temperature when the priest was ill, Father Dominic, in September 1949, described a bout with "Sister Fever" in which Padre Pio's temperature was measured, with a special thermometer used by Sanguinetti, as 114 degrees Fahrenheit.[4]

"A Hushed and Awed Silence"

Padre Pio's day usually began at 3:30 a.m., when his alarm clock sounded, and he rose to prepare for Mass by means of nearly two hours of meditation and prayer. Because of their unique mission, the community at San Giovanni had dispensed with the midnight office of Matins observed in most Capuchin monasteries. By the side of his bed, he kept three pictures: Saint Michael on the left, the Virgin Mary in the middle, and the pope on the right. He adjusted his window shade so that the first light of day — still several hours off — would fall on the likeness of the Holy Father.

Father Dominic had already been up for fifteen minutes, and, outside the church, a huge crowd of people had been queuing up for hours, waiting for the doors to open at 4:30 a.m. The crowd was made up both of pilgrims from all parts of the world as well as locals, including the infamous "Pious Ladies," who often appeared a few minutes before the church opened, taking what one writer likened to a "flank position" near the head of "the enemy column." The moment the doors were opened they would "charge the enemy ranks" and — armed with hat pins, pocketbooks, and fingernails — jab, kick, and even bite their way to the front, often literally trampling their victims.

These women dismayed Padre Pio and everyone around him. Padre Agostino would frequently post himself in the choir overlooking the church and roar: "You uneducated ignoramuses! Don't you know that you are in the House of the Lord?"[5] It was all to no avail. The "Pious Ladies" forced their way into the seats in the front of the church, and the rest of the throng had to pack in behind them.

As soon as Padre Pio appeared, a hush came over the crowd. Barbara Ward wrote:

> The profound hush of expectancy, hope, and anguish fell on that vast congregation … I cannot remember, in all those hours, any sound above the whimper of sick children and the whispered words of comfort of their mothers. Whoever they were — the healthy, the young, the curious, the penitent, the hopelessly crippled, and above all, sick children and their parents longing for a miracle — the hushed and awed silence covered everyone. It was almost as though, without signs or cures, one were living through a minor miracle. Never have I heard a silence so full of prayer and anguish and hope.[6]

"A Supernatural Mass"

When Padre Pio celebrated Mass, the crowds were deeply aware that it was "a supernatural Mass," according to Padre Gerardo Di Flumeri.[7] A Salesian priest observed that when Padre Pio celebrated, "The most intimate fibers of my being vibrated with feelings of emotion and sweetness which I had never before experienced."[8] Another witness reported that it seemed as if Padre Pio, in celebrating Mass, "came from another humanity superior to ours, speaking … through an atmosphere beyond this life."[9]

Padre Pio described the Mass as "a sacred fix with the Passion of Jesus," in which "all Calvary" was presented again, extended into the present.[10] Apart from any merit on his own part, he believed that he was allowed to relive Jesus' passion in a direct way. "All that Jesus has suffered in his Passion, inadequately I also suffer, as far as is possible for a human being. And all this against my unworthiness, and thanks only to his goodness."[11]

Writing to his cousin, Bishop (later Cardinal) Albert Meyer, Father Dominic cautiously conceded that Padre Pio's Mass was different because of "the intense fervor of the celebrant."[12] Paolo Carta (1907–1996), bishop of Foggia in the 1950s and, after 1962, archbishop of Sassari, explained: "At the altar Padre Pio was transfigured. His face was deathly pale, radiant, and sometimes bathed in tears. There was an intensity in his fervor; there were painful contractions of his body.... Great silent sobs shook him from time to time. Everything about him told us how intensely he was living the Passion of Christ. One had the impression that space and time had been cancelled between that altar and the hill of Calvary."[13]

Padre Giovanni of Baggio observed: "He seemed to be meditating on every word, and to be carried out of himself by every action of the rite. He read with emotion, in a low and almost weary voice, unhurriedly, pronouncing each word distinctly. Certain nervous twitchings of his face, certain glances upward, certain movements of his head as if he were chasing away something vexatious, suggested deep suffering and great efforts to keep himself from being caught up into ecstasy" — the sort of ecstasy that, if unchecked, could cause his Mass to go on for hours.[14]

Padre Marcellino Iasenzaniro wrote: "One can only say that it was clearly perceivable that [Padre Pio] was in agony and had difficulty celebrating that sacred rite, after stopping for a long time at the consecration formula: 'This is my body ... This is my blood.' It was the moment in which he joined in the offering of the divine victim, the Son of God who gives his life for mankind.... He stayed completely still in ecstasy from this meeting with Christ." As he prayed "Lamb of God," he would weep. "People assisted dumbfounded, amazed, and moved."[15]

Father Clement Naef noted that Padre Pio seemed to spend ten to fifteen minutes adoring the consecrated bread and wine. As he did so, his head jerked sharply from time to time, "as though he had been struck on the face."[16] Padre Francesco Savino, who was a teenager when he saw Padre Pio celebrate Mass, noted: "It seemed as if his eyes wanted to leave their orbits, so great was the intensity with which he contemplated [the Host]."[17] Padre Alessio noted that when Padre Pio received Communion, his face, which had been pale and taut, was "transformed and became beautifully radiant." It was then that Padre Pio claimed that he felt all over his being "the kiss of Jesus — all one mercy, all one embrace."[18]

Joe Peterson, who frequently served Mass for Padre Pio during his visits from New York in the 1950s and '60s, recounted: "During Mass you would see his eyes, very large, fixed on a particular spot. He would speak, although you couldn't hear him. You would see his lips moving. Those weren't the prescribed prayers of the Mass. Everyone who was there thought he saw Jesus and was pleading with Him for the sins of mankind. He would go into ecstasy without moving. He seemed to be in conversation with invisible beings."[19]

Cleonice Morcaldi, one of the "Pious Ladies," wrote: "Padre Pio fixed his eyes for a long time on the Host with such love and quiet trembling, struck his chest hard, while two big tears coursed down his face. When united with Jesus, as if taken by a profound sleep of love, he rested his arm on the altar, held the chalice with his right hand, and slumbered like a baby on his mother's bosom. When [after ten minutes] he awoke from that blessed sleep, he took his hand from the chalice, joined his hands and continued to pray, before blessing the chalice."[20]

Padre Pio paused for about five minutes during the Commemoration of the Living (when the priest offers up prayers for the intentions of the congregation and others), during which many were convinced that he saw, as in a mirror, all his spiritual children. When he paused for a similar length of time during the Commemoration of the Dead, it was believed that he could see souls in the other world (as when he told a woman, "I can't find [your son] in the other world").

Although Padre Pio's celebration of the Mass lasted longer than an hour, and he seldom distributed Communion, many people who experienced it insisted that it seemed to last only a few minutes and that they never experienced boredom or distraction.

"This Is Paganism! This Is Fanaticism!"

The silence ended with the Mass. As Padre Pio made his way toward the sacristy, the "Pious Ladies" surged toward him. Some of them, standing on the pews, held out babies or religious objects to be blessed. Others grabbed at his robe or the cord around his waist, while others incessantly screamed: "Bless me!" "Help me!" "Touch me!" "Grant me a favor!" Father Dominic wrote his family, "The crowd would steal his handkerchief, cut pieces from his habit and cut off his cord. He would not even notice it with all the people pushing and pulling." In January 1953, the American priest wrote his cousin Bishop Meyer: "During the cold weather we all wear our skull cap, except Padre Pio. I wondered whether he WOULD wear one. I had an extra one ... and I offered it to him. He just smiled and said, 'No, they would steal it anyhow.' Fr. Bernardo ... told me afterwards that he had given P. Pio six or more skull caps and all were stolen by the 'Pious' faithful." In his old age, Dominic insisted that the sight of the fanatical women "crawling all over him" was his most painful memory of San Giovanni, a memory so unpleasant that he found it difficult to think about.

Sometimes Padre Pio reacted in good humor. Once, when a woman grabbed his arm and refused to release it, he said, "All right, take it! You can have it! But let me go!"[21] Another time, when a group of adoring nuns screamed, "Padre, give us a relic!" he shouted back, "Sisters, go back to your convent and make your own relics!"[22]

On other occasions, he was not so accommodating. Carrigan recalled an instance when a woman literally flung herself into Padre Pio's path and lay, screaming and moaning, clutching his habit. Seeming furious, he bellowed, "Get up from there!" Frightened, the groupie withdrew. Once in the sacristy, Padre Pio insisted that he was not really angry, but, "You've got to be sharp with these people! It's the only thing they understand." Joe Peterson recalled, when women grabbed at him, Padre Pio often shouted, "Oh, get away! Get away! (*Ah, via! Via!*)" and took his cord and twirled it at them menacingly. Sometimes he roared, "This is paganism! This is fanaticism!"[23] Leo Fanning declared, "If he lost his temper, I would not blame him for one minute. If you could have been there and seen how those people would act, the pushing and the shoving, how they'd try to poke him with their hands!"

Padre Pio's reactions were sometimes so extreme as to provoke a reprimand from his superior. Nevertheless, he justified his outbursts, insisting, "If we do not behave so, the people will eat us.... They squeeze my hand in a vise, they pull my arms, they press me on every side. I feel lost. I am forced to be rude. I'm sorry, but if I don't act this way, they'll kill me!"[24] He more than once remarked in frustration, "There should be a big fence around this area with the sign, 'Lunatic Asylum.'"[25]

Reporters and photographers were unwelcome. "Throw them out! Call the police!" Padre Pio was known to shout if they pressed in on him. Padre Agostino, when he was father guardian, had a standing policy of noncooperation with reporters. One had only to identify himself as a journalist for "Big Daddy" to lay a hand on his shoulder and politely inform him that it was not his custom to speak to reporters or to permit his friars to do so. And then he showed him the door.

At last, Padre Pio reached the sacristy. Most of the time, he was allowed to receive people there. Even here, he was sometimes the victim of the disorderly adulation of the faithful. From the sacristy, Padre Pio proceeded to the choir on the balcony above the little church, there to make his prayers of thanksgiving. After that he was ready to hear confessions.

Tickets to Confession

From about 1923, Padre Pio's superiors limited him to no more than eight hours each day of hearing confessions. He heard the confessions of about fifty women in the morning in a confessional booth. Men he heard face-to-face in the afternoon in the sacristy. Sometimes men were allowed to make their confessions to him in his room, and certain spiritual daughters were allowed to confess to him in the friary guest room, speaking to him through a window in a wall behind which he sat in a small, closetlike space.

Because of the huge number of people who wanted Padre Pio to hear their confession, after World War II a chaotic situation developed. Long lines of women waiting to make their confessions would form in the wee hours of the morning. Often they had to stand all morning, until the time Padre Pio finished hearing confessions, without having a chance to meet with him. The next day their place in line would be determined by the order in which they arrived, not where they had been standing when the confessions ended the day before. A woman who had been first in line at the time Padre Pio heard his last confession Monday might find herself last in place if she were late getting up on Tuesday. Moreover, if she did manage to get to the head of the queue, she risked being attacked by the "Pious Ladies" and pushed out of line. Sometimes women from out of town were kicked, punched, and even dragged out of place by their hair. Some "Pious Ladies" were more civil: they would offer to keep places in line for pilgrims who did not care to fight for their position in the wee hours of the morning — for an exorbitant fee, of course! Men had an easier time, since they were much less numerous.

Things reached an ugly pass in 1950, when a woman from Sicily attained first place in line after a week of being pushed out of place by the "Pious Ladies," only to be attacked by several women who punched her and shoved her out of line again. In desperation, she pulled out a knife and threatened her attackers. Immediately the "Pious Ladies" began to scream that the Sicilian was about to kill them. Padre Pio, irate, left the confessional, demanding to know what was going on. Before the Sicilian pilgrim could say a word, the "Pious Ladies" told him their side of the story, with the result that the indignant priest (not favored in this case with divine enlightenment) turned on the hapless woman, and, without hearing her story or confession, ordered her to go back to Sicily.

The aggrieved woman reported this incident to the provincial, who was then Padre Paolino, who, in turn, asked Father Clement Neubauer, the minister general, for permission to issue tickets for confession. At first, Father Clement said that this idea was more appropriate for the theater than for the church but was persuaded that the violence around Padre Pio's confessional made this a necessity. He required that everyone wishing to confess to Padre Pio had to register in person. People from out of town were given tickets of a different color from those issued to locals. Two lines were formed, one for locals, the other for pilgrims. To guard against the black market, each ticket had to be signed in person in front of a priest by the person to whom it was issued. The priest who issued the ticket had to sign and date it.[26] It was common for women to have to wait for weeks to confess. For men, the interval was shorter. Sometimes people would make arrangement for the hotel or boarding house, where they booked lodgings in advance, to notify them when it appeared that their few minutes with Padre Pio were just days away, and they would then be assigned a room for that period of time.

A Gift of Tongues?

Normally, Padre Pio heard confessions only in Italian. Although, like all priests of his time were supposed to be, he was reasonably fluent in Latin, he disliked hearing confessions in that language, often telling those intent on speaking it that they needed to find a "more learned confessor." He did not like to hear the confessions of other Capuchins, who had regularly assigned confessors. However, there were exceptions.

Don Giorgio Pogany recalled that when foreigners confessed to Padre Pio, "he sometimes spoke with them one or two phrases in their own language." Padre Agostino noted that Padre Pio told a Swiss priest, who had confessed in Latin, with regard to a woman for whom he requested prayer, *"Ich werde sie an die göttliche Barmherzigkeit empfehlen"* (I must commend her to the divine compassion).[27] There was not necessarily anything supernatural about this. Over the years, he could easily have picked up words and phrases of commonly used languages.

However, there were occasions when Padre Pio agreed to hear the confessions of people who spoke a language other than Italian or Latin, when the other person would confess in her own language and Padre Pio would talk to her in Italian, and they nevertheless understood each other just as if they had been conversing in a common language. For example, during the late 1920s, Maria Pyle urged her sister-in-law Zene to make her confession to Padre Pio. "Now, Adelia," Zene protested, "you know I don't speak Italian." Adelia told her not to worry, and Zene went to confession. "I spoke in English and he spoke in Italian and we understood each other perfectly. I came out looking rather dazed," Zene recounted.[28]

"As Though He Was Reading from a Book"

Although most of his confessions were "as normal as apple pie," as Carrigan described his own confessions with Padre Pio, accounts of confessions when Padre Pio was "enlightened" about the souls of penitents and displayed supersensible knowledge are too numerous to be lightly dismissed. Clarice Bruno, an Italian American, spent less than two minutes in the confessional booth. The moment she entered, the Padre announced, "I will do the talking." With that, he began "reciting" her sins to her, pausing between each one only long enough for her to confirm it by saying, *"Si, Padre."* At one point he said, "You have been impatient and lost your temper … but you immediately repented." Bruno remembered how she had lost her temper the previous day with a restaurant waiter, and murmured, "I hope I repented." "I *said* that you repented right away," Padre Pio affirmed sternly. "He was not asking — he was telling me," Bruno recounted. Then, "suddenly, in the middle of the confession, contrary to custom, and before I had, therefore, the occasion to formulate my question, he gave me the advice that I, in that moment, particularly needed." He absolved her and closed the little door between them and turned to the next penitent. The confession over, Bruno left the church feeling "lighter" and "at peace with God."[29]

Umberto Antonelli of Marcianise, in a memoir written in May 1993, said that in 1954 or 1955 he made his confession to Padre Pio. When he was finished, Padre Pio asked, "Is there anything else?" and he replied, "No." Padre Pio asked a second and then a third time. Then "He, with a voice that was not his, but that of the Holy Spirit, shouted, 'Get out, get out, because you are still not sorry for your sins!'"

"I remained petrified, also because I felt ashamed in front of so many people.

I tried to say something but he pressed on, 'Be quiet, you chatterbox, you've said enough. Now I wish to speak. Isn't it true that you go to dance halls?'"

Antonelli answered that he did, and Padre Pio said, "And don't you know that dancing is an invitation to sin?" Padre Pio then gave Antonelli absolution.[30]

Eolo Soldaini of Taranto wrote on May 31, 1999, that when he was a naval officer in 1956–1957 he went to confession with Padre Pio. After confessing the first sin, his memory went blank and he couldn't remember anything, but Padre Pio went on to recall for him the four sins he had committed since his last confession, after which Soldaini claimed that he experienced an "inner illumination of both mind and heart" and a distancing from earthly things. Then he felt a mysterious voice from within which clearly said, "You must not go to Australia [he was considering a position there], because serious family problems would drive you to desperation; you would have to throw yourself in the sea." He resolved to stay in Italy. A few months later "serious problems" did in fact occur in his family, which he could not have solved had he been away. "In those few minutes near to the Padre I had three miracles," Soldaini wrote, "Padre Pio read my heart, he illuminated me with regards to spiritual life, and he gave me the answer to my future."[31]

Francesco Messina (1900–1995), a noted sculptor, described going to confession with Padre Pio, feeling unprepared psychologically. "But he told me in a voice that left no room for a reply: 'Don't say anything to me. Just answer.' Then he began to list my sins with incredible precision. It was as though he could read my soul."[32]

When Graziella Mandato made her first confession, she recalled, "I was too scared to talk, but Padre Pio told me everything I did wrong."[33]

Luisa Vario, on making her confession to Padre Pio, explained: "I don't know what to say."

"Then I will speak," said he.

"Then he proceeded to tell me my whole life's story as though he was reading from a book. At the end, he asked me if I had something to add. There was still one sin that he hadn't mentioned. I felt very ashamed. I couldn't decide whether I should say something. Yet, if I kept silent, my confession wouldn't be valid. I said to my myself, 'Why should I confess something that he didn't mention after having told me everything?' Padre Pio was waiting in silence for me to answer. Finally, I found the strength to confess even that sin. 'That's the one I was waiting for,' he said. 'You've won the victory. Don't get discouraged.'"[34]

Sister Pura Pagani, who died in the province of Verona in 2001, declared on May 10, 1997: "I went to Padre Pio's confessional well prepared after a careful examination of my conscience, but the Padre, after making the Sign of the Cross, with which he began the sacramental conversation, anticipated my sins as if he could read them in my heart. He also assured me that I would receive graces which afterwards I really have obtained."[35]

Pina Patti, of San Giovanni Rotondo, testified on May 6, 1995: "Padre Pio's way of confessing was always new and very particular. When he saw commitment and effort he encouraged. For some persistent faults he said: 'Thank the Lord that he keeps you in humbleness.' Or, 'There are certain faults that we will take to heaven.' When we were deeply sorry for our mistakes he treated us with motherly kindness; [on the other hand], if he thought we were stuck to sin, he treated us badly."[36]

Father Pio Mandato, an American priest who was born in Pietrelcina, was visiting his native town in 1989 when he was approached by "an older man" who related a story to him. Although most people in town held Padre Pio in great reverence, this man, for many years, did not; instead, he considered him a charlatan. However, eventually a brother-in-law persuaded him — even though he declared that he didn't believe that Padre Pio was a man of God — to accompany him to San Giovanni Rotondo. After attending Mass, the skeptic decided that he wanted to see Padre Pio "out of curiosity" and forced himself through the crowds and into the sacristy, where Padre Pio was seated, his face covered by his hands, deep in prayer. He stood silently behind the priest for several moments before declaring, "Padre, I'm here. I've come to see you." Without turning around, Padre Pio called him by name and said, "I've been waiting for you. So, you don't believe I'm a man of God, huh?" Even though the visitor, now convinced that Padre Pio knew his thoughts, had no ticket, the Padre heard his confession.[37]

Alberto Cardone described the experience of a neighbor whose name he would not disclose. She told him that when she went to make her confession to Padre Pio in the mid-1940s, he told her that before she could receive absolution, she needed to "try to remember the other sin."

"Padre, I think I gave you all the sins I know and I think this is it."

The priest responded, "Then, for your penance, go to the cross to say fifteen Ave Marias and fifteen Our Fathers."

Cardone explained, "Now the cross was at the top of the mountain. The penance was not the Aves or the Our Fathers, it was the journey to get there, as it was a very bad road.… So she did that and said the prayers and went back to Padre Pio for a second confession and Padre Pio asked, 'Do you remember all your sins?'"

She replied, "Padre Pio, I've confessed everything."

"No, you still don't remember all. You've got to go to the cross at the top of the mountain again."

When she returned and still did not remember "the other sin," he sent her to the mountain for a third time. "So, do you remember everything now?" he asked. When she insisted that she had nothing more to confess, he said "in a loud voice," "What do you mean, you don't remember anything? Don't you know he could have been a good priest, a bishop, even a cardinal?"

According to Cardone, the woman "started to think and then began to cry." "Padre, I never knew that abortion was a sin," she said.

"What do you mean," Padre Pio answered, "you didn't know this was a sin? That's killing."

"Nobody knows about this, only me and my mother," the lady exclaimed. "How could you say it could have been a priest or a cardinal?"

Padre Pio simply responded by saying, "But it's a sin, a great sin."[38]

"To Rouse Certain Souls You Need Cannon Balls!"

Padre Pio often refused to hear the confessions of people whom he considered inappropriately attired. Bare legs were anathema to him — even on little children. He was known to remark, "Bare skins will burn."[39] Women with uncovered heads, with plunging necklines, with see-through sleeves, with skirts that did not extend at least to mid-calf or whose sleeves did not cover at least three quarters of their arms were liable to be told, "Go back and get dressed." This was not much of a problem in the early days, but as the world became more casual about dress, Padre Pio most emphatically did not. Nor could he abide women who smelled of cigarettes. "Women who smoke are disgusting!" he told a kindergarten teacher named Nerina Noe, who immediately gave up her habit.[40]

He complained about lipstick: "Giving out Communion, you dirty your fingers and then you dirty the lips of those who come next." When another priest pointed out, "All women wear lipstick nowadays," Padre Pio objected to his justifying it, warning, "By reasoning that way, you're ruining the Church." When the priest asked, "What should we do, send them away?" Padre Pio answered, "Yes, sometimes.... Better to have a few convinced than a lot of people without faith."[41]

Most often a man or woman would be refused absolution by Padre Pio for insufficient contrition. He complained that many people made appointments, not because they wanted to be freed of their sins, but because they wanted favors or supernatural answers to their questions. He would explain that he was not a fortune-teller and dismiss them. He was particularly annoyed by people who came simply out of curiosity.

Padre Pio was most gravely offended, however, by people who tried to justify serious sin. In such cases, he was not above calling people rude names, such as "filthy creature," to a man who saw nothing wrong with shacking up with his girlfriend.

A married man who was unfaithful to his wife went to Padre Pio, confessing "a spiritual crisis." Padre Pio sprang to his feet, shouting, "What spiritual crisis? You're a vile pig and God is angry with you! Go away!"[42] He horrified twelve-year-old Mariella Lotti from Cosenza, declaring, "Go away, I can't hear your confession. You hardly ever go to Mass on Sundays and disregard the catechism because your parents take you elsewhere. If I hear your confession and listen to your usual trifles, while you continue fearless in neglecting the essential things, we would get nowhere."[43] At no point had the girl described the situation which Padre Pio delineated to her.

Father Dominic recalled three young men, waiting in the sacristy to make their confession on January 4, 1949. Padre Pio entered and told them, "Go home. Prepare better. Make an act of contrition, then come again." Dominic mused, "I wonder what I would have done if a confessor had told me that before I even had a chance to open my mouth!"[44]

Many were troubled by Padre Pio's occasional curtness and his refusals to grant absolution. He told a fellow priest, however: "I use this system with certain souls … to shake them, because, especially for some kind of sins, it is easy to go from Confession to the sin and from the sin back to the Confession. One sins, confesses, and is absolved; then one sins again, confesses, and is absolved. It becomes a routine, a custom … I ask myself if it is [better] to make the penitents used to sin and to a confession that would actually be sacrilegious, either for lack of purpose or repentance, or to make them aware that they are in God's disgrace. I prefer the latter."[45] "I don't give sweets to someone who needs a purge," Padre Pio was known to say.[46] When Padre Carmelo of Sessano, who was father guardian in the 1950s, questioned Padre Pio, he said, "To rouse certain souls you need cannon balls. Treating them with gentleness is a waste of time. They need to feel God's anger when the strength of his mercy is not enough."[47]

Years before, Padre Benedetto explained Padre Pio's strictness in the confessional in light of his awareness of the horrors of hell and his sense of urgency in trying to prevent people from ending up there. In his unpublished "Notes on Padre Pio," Benedetto wrote, "Padre Pio has experienced the torments of hell in seeing the damned suffer. About two years ago [this would have been 1919] every ten or fifteen days he underwent this agony. He felt the pains of the senses and of damnation, finding himself in body and soul amongst the damned and the demons, in order to save others and himself from that place where they were destined if grace had not helped them."[48] For this reason, Padre Pio said, "Remember that it is better to be reprimanded by a man in this world than by God in the next."[49]

Most people who were denied absolution by Padre Pio returned to him in a spirit of godly contrition. A man whom Padre Pio had dismissed three times without absolution later explained, "Now I understand the gravity of my failings. Up to then no one had really shaken me, so that I easily justified my errors to myself. Now I understand and thank the Good God that he used the firm … paternal force of Padre Pio."[50] Another person with a similar experience declared, "He made me aware that when you commit a mortal sin, that's a grievous offense against God."[51]

Stories of Padre Pio's harsh comments and refusals of absolution created, for some, the impression that the stigmatized priest was a harsh, ill-tempered man. The vast majority of those who made their confessions to him, however, found him kind and gentle. Because of the horror stories, many approached his confessional with fear and trembling. Often, he would reassure trembling penitents, "Calm yourself. Calm down." Joe Peterson recounted how Padre Pio would often put his arms around terrified male penitents as he heard their confessions.

Padre Pio's Attitude Toward Other Faiths

In early 2017, an article appeared in *The Voice of Padre Pio* which claimed that, in the early 1950s, Padre Pio heard a report that one hundred people in the area were going over to the evangelical faith each day. Deeply troubled, he asked his superior, Padre Carmelo, "What's going on? … Have you heard that the Protestants have opened a kindergarten and that the children are going about blaspheming Our Lady? Something has to be done!"[52] Determined to rescue "those poor innocent souls" from "the Protestant propaganda," he persuaded Archbishop Cesarano to authorize the creation of a Catholic kindergarten next door to the Protestant one. It proved so successful that after only a few months, the evangelical kindergarten closed.[53]

Through email and a translator, the author of this book contacted Luigi Bocci, the pastor of the evangelical church in San Giovanni Rotondo. He denied that the event ever happened. (The author also reached out for comment to the author of the article, but received no reply.) The school was organized only after Padre Pio's death. Pastor Bocci insisted that Padre Pio never had any contact with the evangelical congregation — none whatsoever. He explained that in Padre Pio's day, especially after the Lateran Pacts of 1929, which made Catholicism the sole approved religion of the Italian people, hostility toward Protestants was intense, and it was actually "dangerous" for people to meet as a "non-Catholic church." Evangelicals were considered heretics, and priests were actually not permitted to engage in any formal dialogue with Protestant ministers. "No Catholic could meet with heretics except to communicate [a pronouncement of] excommunication and the consequences thereof." Pastor Bocci explained that, in terms of their attitude toward non-Catholic Christians, most Catholic priests in Padre Pio's day fell into two categories. The first were characterized by "condemnation," "persecution," and "implacable repression," while the second were "supporters of tolerance, charity, mildness." He concluded, "We think that Padre Pio was more oriented to the second behavior."[54] There remains no record of what Padre Pio thought of the evangelical church in San Giovanni Rotondo — if, in fact, he thought of it at all.

In the 1920s, an Eastern Orthodox friend of Maria Pyle asked Padre Pio to hear her confession, and he refused.[55] However, several years later, when Maria related to him that her Presbyterian mother Adelaide had said, "How I should like to kneel in that confessional! But I don't know how to speak Italian," Padre Pio responded, "Oh, if she had only done it! As for the language, I would have taken care of that."[56] Padre Pio, as we have seen, after seeing evidence that she was a committed Christian, did not try to convert Adelaide Pyle. Her son Gordon, a musician and composer who professed to have no religion at all, sometimes visited Maria at San Giovanni, and, according to his widow, Zene, Padre Pio never proselytized him.

Nearly everyone who remembered the visits of British and American soldiers recalled that, from time to time, there were some Protestants among them, and that Padre Pio treated them kindly and respectfully. Padre Pio also had Jewish friends, some of whom converted to Christianity, and some of whom did not. Giorgio Pogany (a convert from Judaism) recalled Padre Pio commenting wistfully about a friend: "Too bad he's a Jew." In October 1967, a Jewish convert to Christianity asked Padre Pio whether her father, who had lived and died a practicing Jew, was saved. He replied, "Julius Fine is saved, but it is necessary to pray much for him."[57] Padre Pio always recommended prayer for the departed, so his insistence that Fine needed prayer should not be necessarily understood as a denigration of the man's religion.

"I Believe That Not a Great Number of Souls Go to Hell"

Despite the occasions when Padre Pio told penitents that they were going to hell unless they mended their ways, he told a British friend: "I believe that not a great number of souls go to hell. God loves us so much. He formed us in his image. God the Son Incarnate died to redeem us. He loves us beyond understanding. And it is my belief that even when we have passed from the consciousness of the world, when we appear to be dead, God, before he judges us, will give us a chance to see and understand what sin really is. And if we understand it properly, how could we fail to repent?"[58] On another occasion, he was heard to remark, "It is difficult for a soul not persistently evil to be damned, because God, at the moment of death, appears to the soul and says, 'Do you want me?' Those who want to go to hell go there."[59]

On Purgatory

When Dr. Sanguinetti died and someone asked Padre Pio if he were in heaven, he answered, "There are some souls destined to attain a high level of glory, and if they haven't attained it on earth, they attain it after a stay in purgatory."[60] Cleonice Morcaldi, one of the "Pious Ladies," reported that he told her that in purgatory, at least for some people, "You suffer without reward and without knowing when you will leave. You suffer the fire as if you had a body."[61] Yet he wrote to Padre Bernardo of Pietrelcina, who had lost his mother: "I hasten to assure you about the eternal well-being of your dear mother. Brother, be of good cheer concerning your mother's salvation.... Be calm and despise every thought to the contrary as a true temptation [from the evil one]. I do not cease to raise my poor prayers to Jesus in behalf of that holy soul, so that, purged of the stains of which no one is exempt, she might go to enjoy Jesus in glory."[62]

Padre Pio believed that people could avoid a painful purification after death "by accepting everything from God's hands, by offering everything up to him with love and thanksgiving so as to enable us to pass from our deathbed to paradise."[63] He urged Cleonice Morcaldi "to do [purgatory] here, accepting from the hand of the Lord all that he sends us, offering it to him, united with the merits and sufferings of the Madonna. Every day let us ask him forgiveness from the punishment we deserve for our sins."[64]

"It's Up to the Lord to Give Us Our Cross"

Although Padre Pio embraced a ministry of suffering, he usually discouraged people from seeking suffering beyond that which they experienced in the course of life. It was enough to endure that in patience and good cheer. Once a woman came to him, saying, "Father, I want to help. Give me some suffering."

"My dear," he replied, "you already have a lot of trouble, and yet you want to help me in suffering? Think about your present troubles and don't court additional ones!"[65]

When another woman, in order to do penance for her sins, ate poisonous weeds, Padre Pio sternly rebuked her, "I won't permit any more of this madness! There are many ways to do penance, such as offering to the Lord whatever trouble comes to us day by day. It's up to the Lord to give us our cross. If he hasn't sent you one, it's because he's not sure that you could bear it."[66] There were a very few individuals whom Padre Pio encouraged to offer themselves to God as "victim souls."

Raconteur

After the midday dinner, which was around 1:00 p.m., Padre Pio went into the garden for about a half hour of "recreation," one of two periods in the day free for unrestricted socializing. He and his confreres were often joined by laymen, who stood around and chatted. It was during these times that Padre Pio was liable to regale his friends with funny stories. Although he could, at times, be earthy, he was never coarse. When anyone told a dirty joke, he would either ask them to leave or excuse himself.

Nearly all the stories he told had some religious moral; many of them concerned saints or biblical figures. For instance, he told a story about a tailor who died and went to heaven:

Now this tailor, who used to curse and swear, was a crude, drunken lout, and when he died, he found himself a beggar before St. Peter. St. Peter took the Book of Life and read it and decided to throw the tailor out. When he learned what St. Peter was about to do, the tailor screamed and hollered until St. Joseph, who happened to be nearby, came running and asked St. Peter what the matter was. When the tailor saw St. Joseph, he threw himself on his knees and besought him, saying, "Dear St. Joseph, you remember that I always prayed to you. I was a pig, yes, even a hog, it's true, but every day I thought about you because you were always one of my favorite saints, because you were a working man." St. Joseph was moved and, seeing the tailor tearing out his hair, he told St. Peter to let him enter the pearly gates. St. Peter, however, refused. Thereupon St. Joseph went to the Madonna and said, "Listen, Mary, I don't count for anything around here anymore in this heaven. I ask a favor of St. Peter, and he won't let a fellow in. My recommendations count for very little. Let's leave." The Madonna answered, "You're right! I'm sure that Peter was misbehaving, and, besides, I'm your wife and the wife must follow the husband. Therefore, I'm going with you. But let's not leave Our Lord here, because he's our son. Let's go and take Our Lord with us." Then the Holy Spirit saw the Madonna, Jesus, and St. Joseph leaving, and decided to go along with them. God the Father followed them, as well as the other saints. Then St. Peter opened the gate of heaven and let the tailor in.[67]

One of Padre Pio's jokes concerned St. Eligius (Eligo) (588–660), patron saint of horses and metalworkers, who lived in what is now France:

St. Eligio was a formidable blacksmith, who called himself the "master of masters." One day Jesus himself came down to earth and, dressed in the rough clothing of a poor laborer, went into the countryside, begging for work. At once they said, "Go to Master Eligio and you will find work for sure."

Jesus … at once appeared at Eligio's. Greeting him with great deference, he said, "Good day, Master. Is there work for me?"

"No!" he replied unceremoniously. Jesus, mortified, returned to the one who directed him to Eligio. "He told me bluntly that he had no work for me."

"But what did you say to him?"

"Good day, Master. Is there work for me?"

"You should not say it like that, but, 'Good day, Master of all Masters, is there work for me?' Go back and you'll see that he'll accept you."

Jesus went back and said, "Good day, Master of all masters. Is there work for me?"

"Come on in. Here there is work for all." Eligio at once put his new apprentice to the test and tried to teach him to shoe a horse. With unique craftsmanship and in very little time, with a hammer and appropriate nails, Eligio shoed the hoof. Yet he observed, "In my country, it's not done that way."

Somewhat annoyed, Eligio said, "Oh, yeah? And how is it done?"

Jesus took the horseshoe, and with a little saliva made it adhere solidly to the hoof in no time. Eligio barely managed to hold back a cry of wonder and, to divert the attention of the other workers, said, "Let's go to the second lesson. I'll show you how to forge a drill."

With pliers he took a piece of raw iron and, after heating it red hot on the furnace, calling attention to his movement, with a heavy hammer produced a fine specimen of a drill. Again, this time Jesus observed, "In my country it's not done like that."

Annoyed as before, Eligio replied, "Oh, yeah? And how is it done?"

Jesus, without the help of pliers, grabbed the piece of iron, heated it without burning himself, and with one blow of the hammer forged a splendid drill. Eligio this time couldn't suppress an "Oh!" of wonderment, and falling on his knees, said, "I see that I still have a lot to learn!" The apprentice disappeared from his sight. Eligio learned very quickly that he wasn't the "master of masters," but he had to learn to be the "servant of servants for everybody."[68]

St. Peter was frequently the subject of Padre Pio's jokes, like the following:

Jesus hadn't made an inspection of heaven for a long time, and one day he wanted to verify the efficiency of his faithful key-keeper, Peter. At first all seemed to be in order, and Jesus was very pleased at seeing all his servants who had passed through the "great tribulation" rejoicing and enjoying the eternal rest they had earned. Little by little, however, as he proceeded in the inspection, he began to notice suspicious activity and disreputable faces, whom he would never have admitted into his holy kingdom. Immediately, he called his key-keeper to account: "Peter," he asked, excited, "why are these forbidden people in my paradise?"

"Master, I'm very sorry, but I don't recognize these faces. Truly I don't know."

"No? And who ought to know if not my faithful gatekeeper? Be attentive in the future, otherwise you'll be surely fired!"

Poor Peter, embarrassed and much perplexed about those who entered from who knows where, returned to his usual work, doubling his vigilance.

This time he was more strict than usual in checking the documents and credentials of the new arrivals who sought admission to the kingdom. Nevertheless, in his inspection Jesus found many other "irregulars." The poor key-keeper tried very hard to convince Jesus to give him one last chance. This time, besides watching the gate of entry, he looked out of the window and ... discovered something truly irregular, but was unable to speak. The next day, Jesus, seeing the influx of "irregulars" was not ceasing, after giving a stern lecture to his Vicar, gave him his notice of dismissal. Peter, very sorry, accepted it but finally blurted out, "All right, and then fire your Mother, too, because I close the door and she opens the window!"[69]

———

Padre Pio told another joke about two men from the backwoods who had never ridden a train before. "Where do you want to go?" asked the ticket seller.

"What business is it of yours?" said the bumpkins. Once on board, they were terrified when the train puffed into a tunnel.

"Where are we going?" asked the one.

"I think we're going into hell!" screamed the other.

"Don't worry," reassured the first. "We have round-trip tickets!"[70]

———

Not all of Padre Pio's jokes had a direct theological reference. Sometimes he would imitate the unsteady gait of a drunkard. Slurring his speech to mimic an inebriate who saw a centipede crawling up the wall, he said, "Why, O Lord, did you give this critter a hundred legs and me, who can't stand up straight, only two?"[71]

———

Joe Peterson recalled a time when he, Pietro Cugino, and a physician were sitting in the garden with Padre Pio, who asked Peterson to do his chicken imitation: "*Giuseppe — galina!*" So Joe did his chicken imitation. Then the doctor said, "Padre, Giuseppe's from New York. They don't have any chickens there — only skyscrapers. But you're a farm boy. Let's hear your chicken!" Padre Pio made a feeble imitation. "What's the matter with your chicken?" asked the doctor. The priest replied, "Giuseppe does a chicken who is well. My chicken is convalescing after paying the doctor bills."[72]

———

Peterson also recalled that once the friars gave him a birthday dinner during one of his annual vacations in San Giovanni. After eating a piece of cake baked in Peterson's honor by Maria Pyle, Padre Pio stepped into the center of the dining room and summoned Joe: "*Giuseppe, vieni qui.*" He put his arms around Joe's neck as if he were wrestling him, and the American, who stood a full foot taller than Pio, cried, "*Aiutemi!*" (Help me!), as the friar wrestled him to the floor. Padre Pellegrino Funicelli came running over and held up Padre Pio's arms, saying, "*Padre Pio — il campione del mondo! Giuseppe, il bambino americano, requiescat in pace!*" (Padre Pio, the champion of the world! Joe, the little American boy, rest in peace!).[73]

Padre Pio liked to play jokes on his fellow friars. In November 1945, there was a cholera scare and everyone in the monastery went to get immunized. Padre Pio was the first to get his shot. Afterward, he said to one of the other religious, "In a little while, Padre Bernardo will be coming. Let's play a joke on him and pretend the vaccination is really painful — then we can have a good laugh."

As soon as he saw Padre Bernardo coming, Padre Pio pretended to be talking to the doctor. Standing in the doorway, he said loudly, "But, Doctor, this vaccination is really painful!" The physician agreed but insisted that it was necessary to protect against cholera.

Padre Bernardo turned white as a sheet when he heard the conversation and protested, "Piuccio, I'm not going to be vaccinated." Padre Pio answered, "Samson died with all the Philistines. I have been vaccinated and everyone else must be as well." He grabbed another friar and said, "Let's start with him." Nudging him in the ribs, he whispered in his ear, "Yell! Give a loud yell!" The friar made such a blood-curdling shriek that another priest, waiting his turn and unaware of the joke, actually fainted.

Padre Bernardo protested, "Piuccio, I'm afraid. I'm old and I've fought in the [First World] War. I'm not going to be vaccinated!" Assuming a severe countenance, Padre Pio repeated, "I said, Samson died with all the Philistines. I had it done and everyone else must."

Finally, Padre Bernardo, with his eyes raised to heaven, walked toward the doctor and got the injection. "But, Piuccio, I didn't feel anything!" he said. "Of course," replied Padre Pio, "the vaccination saw that you were afraid and was afraid to hurt you."[74]

Padre Pio was much more likely to joke with penitents and counselees than he was to snap at them. Don Giorgio Pogany recalled, "Once, while making her confession to Padre Pio, a nervous woman broke wind loudly, then began to shuffle her feet. Padre Pio said tenderly to her, "Don't do that, my dear. You won't succeed in covering up what you did."[75]

One afternoon, after dinner, Padre Pio was on his way from the refectory to the sacristy when he realized that he still had a sugarcoated almond in his mouth.

He halted before the sacristy door, telling the priest who was about to open it for him, "Wait, let me finish this candy. Otherwise people will say, 'What kind of saint is this? He even eats sweets.'"[76]

———

One day Padre Pio was hosting some Pietrelcinese, for whom he arranged a table to be set in the guest room of the friary. While the adults were at table, engrossed in their food and conversation, Padre Pio noticed a six-year-old boy who looked bored. Leaving unobserved through the main doorway, he went around to the little service window (from which he sometimes heard confessions) and, from the other side, attracted the child's attention. Holding a finger to his lips as a signal for him to keep silent, Padre Pio beckoned the boy to climb through the little window. Taking the child into his arms, Padre Pio carried him upstairs to his room, where he treated him to two chocolate bars. After a few minutes, he brought the boy downstairs and slipped him through the window again, instructing him to take his place once more at table. The adults, busy talking and eating, had not noticed his absence.

Still standing at the service window, Padre Pio began to bang on the wall, shouting, "What's the matter? Is everyone asleep?" When the diners looked up, Padre Pio announced, "I've been standing here for one hour, calling you, and you haven't heard. Were you perhaps in ecstasy?"

"But, Padre Pio, that's just what they say about you," announced a bewildered guest.

"Then what's the matter? I've been standing here for an hour and you haven't heard," continued the Padre, with a poker face. "Well, if you don't believe me, ask the boy. Ettoruccio, what did we do?"

"He took me and carried me to his room," said the boy.

The adults laughed, thinking that the child was just agreeing with whatever Padre Pio said — until the boy produced the chocolates.[77]

———

One day an Austrian psychiatrist came to San Giovanni, hoping to examine Padre Pio to determine whether a case could be made for a neurotic origin of the stigmata. Father Dominic, in one of his letters to his family, related that the superior told the psychiatrist that the exam was out of the question but invited him to observe Padre Pio during recreation. After watching the Padre for a half hour and witnessing his jovial conversation, the psychiatrist told the superior, "Well, he certainly is not hysterical. Hysterical people have no sense of humor."

"I Am Always in Our Lady's Arms"

After the afternoon recreation ended, the friars retired to their rooms for their siesta. Padre Pio would often use part of the time to sleep, but he spent much of that period of leisure praying the Rosary, usually sitting in a wicker chair in the veranda next to his room. In fact, throughout the day, whenever he had a spare moment — in the hallway, on the stairs, even going to and from the confessional — Padre Pio could be seen fingering his beads. For him, the Rosary was his "habitual prayer" and his "weapon" against the powers of hell. "Let's love the Madonna," he would say. "Let's make her loved and let's pray the Rosary that she taught us."[78]

It was from Mary that Padre Pio said he derived his strength. "I feel like a sailing ship," he declared, "pushed by our heavenly Mother's breath. Even if I am lost on the high seas, I am not worried … I never feel uncertain, because I am spiritually directed by her…. She accompanies me in the confessional, to let me aid my brothers and sisters, and she shows me, already covered by the veil of her pity, the numberless souls waiting for an absolution which will destroy all evil…. I always pray her to come close to me and let me know what I must say and pray that she suggest to my spiritual children that which they must tell me. I am sure that she listens to me."[79]

Asked if he actually saw Our Lady, Padre Pio told a man named Enzo Bertani, "Yes, during Holy Mass. Every morning she is at the altar with Jesus."[80] When a priest asked Padre Pio if the Virgin Mary ever came to him in his cell, he replied, "You should rather ask me if she ever leaves my cell."[81] "The Holy Virgin is the perfect example of God's mercy on earth," he maintained. "She acts as his double."[82] "Her motherly smile encourages me to remain always serving in this world, from which I would like to leave," the Padre insisted. "I am always in Our Lady's arms and she gazes on me sweetly!"[83]

For some, Padre Pio's devotion to Mary seemed excessive. A younger priest, Padre Pellegrino Funicello (1927–1988) challenged him, saying that his admiration for Mary was "exaggerated and even seems heretical." Padre Pio replied, "I will not hit you in the face, because, interposed between me and you I see Holy Mary…. My dear defender of the faith … I always remain within orthodoxy."[84]

Padre Pio and the Birds

Like Saint Francis, Padre Pio had a remarkable affinity for nature. Dr. Nicola Centra, a radiologist, recalled that one day, in 1956, while Padre Pio was talking to his friends, a flock of birds "began to settle all around, as if they were obeying a summons." Within a few minutes, "the entire garden vibrated from a symphony of blackbirds, sparrows, goldfinches, and other birds who all chirped, whistled, and trilled, accompanied by the sounds of crickets and cicadas." The noise from his feathered visitors was so great that it drowned out human conversation. So Padre Pio looked up at the trees, put a finger on his lips, and said, "That's enough."

According to Centra, "The effect was like pouring water on a fire, with not a sound heard; a silence such as found in a cathedral descended upon them."[85]

Father Joseph Pius Martin recalled a meeting of the Franciscan Third Order when Padre Pio was trying to give a talk in a private home in town and a canary was making so much noise that his audience had a hard time hearing him. Padre Pio turned to the bird and insisted, "Now I have to praise God!" To everyone's amazement, the canary went to the bottom of the cage and remained silent until the lecture was over.

An Evening Ritual

Padre Pio seldom joined his community for supper in the refectory, but spent the time reading or praying in his room, partaking of a couple of cookies or crackers and a glass or two of beer or fruit juice. At sundown, a crowd of townspeople would gather beneath his window, calling, "Padre Pio! Padre Pio!" As he appeared at the window, they would stand, cheering, waving handkerchiefs, blowing kisses, and serenading him with hymns until he blessed them and shouted, "*Buona notte, bella gente!*" (Good night, good people!), and they would shout back, "*Buona notte, Padre Pio!*" It was an evening ritual.

Evening was spent in various pursuits. Sometimes it was hospital business. For many years, Padre Pio was a member of the friary council, which voted on matters that pertained to the life of the community. In this capacity, he had to review, periodically, the registers and accounts of the friary. Occasionally, he would leave the friary to deliver an informal lecture nearby to members of the Third Order. He also held spiritual conferences with other priests at night, counseling them on personal problems. Sometimes Father Dominic would confer with him again, putting questions to him asked by various correspondents.

Things the Padre Disliked

By the mid-1950s, the friary had its television room, but no one ever remembered Padre Pio darkening the door, except for an event such as the funeral of Pope Pius XII, and then only for a few minutes. Padre Pio, in fact, believed television a pernicious invention that corrupted morals and destroyed family life, and he strongly discouraged people from acquiring televisions. He told Joe Peterson, "The man who invented refrigeration went to heaven, but the man who invented television...." He pointed downward. He considered reading newspapers a waste of time.

Smoking was another thing that met Padre Pio's intense disapproval. In October 1936, he wrote to one Mario Melchioni to give up smoking, "because it is deadly for you. Give up that blessed smoking from now on, for love of God, and then in consideration of us who wish you well.... Listen to us, dear Mario, and don't make us live in fear."[86] One English visitor recalled that, during a conference with some cancer researchers, Padre Pio asked one of them, "Do you smoke?" When the doctor replied that he did, the priest pointed his finger censoriously and muttered, "Very bad!" Then, with almost the same breath, he asked another doctor, "Have you got any snuff?" While he was opposed to the use of cigarettes, cigars, and pipes, Padre Pio, like many of his fellow friars, kept snuff in a little pocket of the sleeve. In his youth, doctors actually recommended sniffing it to keep the sinuses clear, and he evidently saw no harm in smokeless tobacco.

"Good night, Padre Berna"

Late in the evening, Padre Pio joined the community for Compline, the night office. After that, the friars retired to bed. Before going to his room, Padre Pio always went to his superior, joined his hands, bowed, and asked for a blessing. Then he would usually stop to chat a few minutes with Padre Agostino, and the two would embrace. Sometimes he stopped at the room of another old friend, Padre Bernardo of Pietrelcina (1882–1974). He would call out, "Padre Berna, good night!" If he got no answer, he typically raised his voice and repeated, "Good night, Padre Berna." Padre Bernardo, lying in bed, would keep quiet, hoping Padre Pio would leave him alone. But his friend kept up, "Padre Berna,' good night. Good night, Padre Berna.'" Finally, the sleepy priest would reply in a weak voice, "Piuccio, let me sleep," but Padre Pio continued until the superior growled, "Go to sleep! The bell for silence has already rung!"[87]

During most of his time at Our Lady of Grace monastery, Padre Pio resided in Room Number 5, an eight- by ten-foot bedroom and study typical of the friary. It was not particularly austere. It had an excellent view of what was then a breathtaking expanse of countryside. In the room, he had a desk, a nightstand, a washbasin, and an armchair. The communal bathroom was down the hall. For years, Padre Pio insisted on sleeping on a hard, rough pallet, characteristic of Capuchin austerity in the days when he was a young priest. Dr. Sanguinetti had bought Padre Pio a modern, comfortable bed, and the superiors ordered him to use it. Later someone bought him an air conditioner, but he refused it. The Franciscan way was that the members of a community would share everything in common, and unless the donor could furnish all the friars with air conditioners, Padre Pio wouldn't use one.

Before going to sleep, Padre Pio would pray and read Scripture, sometimes until one in the morning or later, when his nearly twenty-hour day would finally end.

Asked how he managed to do so many things in the end, Padre Pio once replied, "They say that Napoleon could do four things at once. I'm not Napoleon, but three I can pull off."[88]

Signs and Wonders

"I Never, Never Observed Anything Miraculous"

Reports of miracles attributed to Padre Pio proliferated after the Second World War. With increasing frequency, Italian newspapers carried headlines such as these:

- PRODIGIOUS CURE ATTRIBUTED TO PADRE PIO
- PARALYTIC WALKS THROUGH INTERCESSION OF PADRE PIO
- MIRACULOUS CURE OF A WOMAN SICK WITH CANCER
- AFTER SIX YEARS OF TORTURE, LITTLE OLD LADY IS HEALED
- CURE OF A NUN AT BOLOGNA AFTER THIRTY YEARS OF SUFFERING

Many came to think of Padre Pio as a kind of magical man — one who worked twenty-five miracles every twenty-four hours, a fairy godfather who knew everything and could do anything. It was assumed that the friars who lived with him were constantly awed by stupendous displays of prophecy, supernatural knowledge, and miraculous healing. Such was not the case, however. To most of those who knew Padre Pio and lived with him, he was a kind, gentle, devout, and holy man, but an ordinary one. When asked, late in life, "Weren't you thrilled to be living with Padre Pio?" Father Dominic replied, "The thrill left me after two or three days. Not because I was disappointed, but because Padre Pio, as saintly as he is, was just as human as anyone else."[1]

Father Joseph Pius Martin, who lived with Padre Pio for three years, remembered him as "a nice old guy in golfing gloves," who, after meeting a long-haired pilgrim in the mid-1960s, remarked, "Did you get a load of that fellow's hair?" and who, after celebrating a wedding, commented on the bride's fingernails: "She could really scratch your eyes out with those!"[2]

Padre Gerardo Di Flumeri, who lived with Padre Pio for two years, observed,

"He had human emotions. He was not an angel. He was a human being. He got angry for the same reasons that other people get angry. He was a normal man, sometimes sad, sometimes very happy, sometimes a little angry." What impressed Gerardo the most about Padre Pio was his character: "Yes, I believe that on occasion he did have supernatural gifts. I've seen it in books, and sometimes he surely had these gifts. But when you spoke to Padre Pio, he was natural. You were impressed by his spirituality, by his obedience, by his charity, but nothing else."[3]

William Carrigan expressed extreme skepticism about Padre Pio's reputation as a wonder-worker. "In all my experience with Padre Pio, I never, *never* observed anything miraculous." He had been given several boxes of written accounts of miraculous events but refused to allow the author to see them because he considered the stories "just too far out to be true."[4]

"They Can't All Be Tall Tales"

Yet, there is incontrovertible evidence that Padre Pio was sometimes gifted by supernatural charisms. Dr. Giuseppe Gusso of *La Casa Sollievo della Sofferenza*, who himself observed almost no supernatural activity associated with Padre Pio, said to the author concerning the miracle stories: "They can't all be tall tales."[5]

Maria Pyle kept two notebooks, written in English and French, in which she recounted the various graces that people obtained through Padre Pio's intercession, as they were told to her. These notebooks, which are lost,[6] became the source of many of the miracle stories about Padre Pio that were published in English. Carrigan's contention that Pyle lacked objectivity was shared by others who knew her. One of these wrote that, although she was sincere and loving, Pyle "was not an exacting historian dedicated to analyzing what she heard, to reviewing and weeding out, to ascertaining the details of the story. She believed everything that everybody told her."[7]

Even so, there were many careful and objective persons who left contemporary accounts of occurrences that seemed to be supernatural. Among them were Padre Agostino, Padre Paolino, and Father Dominic. Dr. Sanguinetti is said to have been the source of several miracle stories, which he related orally to others, but he was evidently too busy in his work of establishing the hospital to write anything down.

Miracles

Before we discuss any "miracles" related to Padre Pio, it is necessary to establish just what is meant by the term. A miracle is generally perceived as a direct intervention by God in the natural world, an intervention which involves the apparent suspension of the laws of nature. *The New Catholic Encyclopedia* notes three characteristics: A "miracle" must be an "extraordinary" event; it must be perceptible to the senses; and it must be produced by God in a religious context as an evidence of his presence.

For example, a rebellion against Moses is recounted in Numbers 16. The Lord caused the earth to open, to swallow the opponents of the prophet whom the Lord had set over Israel. This was certainly extraordinary. It was evident to the senses of everyone present. It was wrought by God as a demonstration of his power, his approval of Moses, and his wrath toward those who resisted divine authority.

Similarly, miracles recorded in the New Testament are extraordinary perceptible signs of God's activity and, in particular, of the divinity of Jesus. For instance, Jesus healed a paralytic as a sign that "the Son of Man has authority on earth to forgive sins" (Mk 2:10). The Gospel of Mark later recounts how Jesus stilled the sea, prompting his disciples to remark, "Who then is this, that even wind and sea obey him?" (Mk 4:41). In John 9, there is a description of Jesus' healing of a man born blind, asserting that the affliction was not the result of sin, either of the blind man or his parents, but so that "the works of God might be made manifest in him" (Jn 9:3). In other words, the man was born without sight, in part to occasion the opportunity for Jesus to demonstrate his divinity.

Also in the New Testament, after Pentecost, the Twelve Apostles performed many miracles. The writings of the early Church Fathers indicate that in the four or five centuries that followed the time of the apostles, abundant miracles continued to occur. While the Egyptian scholar Origen (c. 185–254) believed that only "traces" of the signs and wonders worked by Christ were visible in the Church of his day, Saint Irenaeus (c. 130–202), who was bishop of what is now Lyon, France, wrote that miracles were taking place on a regular basis among his flock — miracles that included even the raising of the dead. Saint Augustine (354–430), bishop of Hippo (in what is now Tunisia), maintained that miracles are only apparent violations of the laws of nature, as God does not contradict himself.[8] Moreover, he insisted that miracles are invitations to faith that call attention to God's greatness: "witnesses to that faith which proclaims the supreme miracle of the Resurrection of the flesh into life everlasting."[9]

Throughout the centuries, miraculous occurrences were associated with the ministry of certain holy men and women. Although all candidates for sainthood in the Catholic Church are required to have interceded in the working of least two miracles after death, very few performed miracles while they were living. Among those who were reputed to work miracles in their lifetime were Saint Jean-Marie-Baptiste Vianney, the Curé of Ars (1786–1859), and Padre Pio's older contemporary Saint André Bessette (1845–1937). Padre Pio's fellow Capuchins, Padre Raffaele of Sant'Elia a Pianisi (1816–1901) and the American Blessed Solanus Casey (1870–1957), were also noted for ministries tinged with the miraculous.

Padre Pio's reputation as a wonder-worker was very much in keeping with the tradition of his Church and the Christian faith in general, although the great number of alleged miracles and wide variety of mystical gifts attributed to him are extraordinary. Some of these phenomena, such as his conversations with other-worldly beings, were not usually perceptible to anyone's senses but his own. Some might be called coincidences, although Padre Pio often remarked, "Who makes things happen?" But others, however, seem miraculous in the fullest sense, in that they were not only extraordinary and visible, but also tended to reveal the glory of God and convince skeptics of the Lord's power and goodness and love.

Baptism in the Holy Spirit

Although it is internal and subjective and therefore does not meet all the criteria of the miraculous, one of the supernatural gifts or charisms experienced by some in the Christian life is what is called the "Baptism of (or in) the Holy Spirit," an experience in which a person receives greater spiritual power and boldness, often accompanied by various "spiritual gifts," one of which is the gift of "tongues." Until the "Charismatic Movement" of the 1970s, this was not a gift spoken about much by Catholics.

Padre Pio probably never heard the term "Baptism of the Holy Spirit," but he seems to have had a similar experience when he was confirmed, which caused him to feel God's "fullness and perfection." He told Padre Agostino that he "wept with consolation" whenever he thought of the day of his confirmation, because "I remember what the Most Holy Spirit caused me to feel that day ... a day unique and unforgettable all my life! What sweet raptures the Comforter made me feel that day! At the thought of that day, I feel aflame from head to toe with a brilliant flame that burns, consumes, but gives no pain."[10]

Conversation with the Angels

This brings us to a charism that many find difficult to accept — Padre Pio's apparent ability to converse with the angels, Mary, and various otherworldly beings. When Father Dominic was first assigned to San Giovanni, he was amused when he read a letter from a woman in America which contained the question, "Dear Padre, when I send my guardian angel, does the angel come to you with the message?" When he went to Padre Pio with the letters that he thought worth his attention, Dominic included this one, just for the sake of amusement. "Padre Pio, wait till you hear this," Dominic said. "A woman from America wants to know, when she sends her angel from America, do you see or hear the angel with the message?" Padre Pio looked sternly at his secretary, and, pointing his index finger in front of Dominic's face and moving closer and closer, declared, "Domenico, tell that woman that her angel is not like her. Her angel is obedient. And, Domenico, when she sends her guardian angel," he said slowly, emphasizing each word, "I ... see ... that ... angel ... just ... like ... I ... see ... you!"[11]

If they were in trouble, Padre Pio urged his spiritual children to send their guardian angels to him. A spiritual son from England, Cecil Humphrey-Smith, was injured in a car crash in Italy, and a friend decided to telegraph Padre Pio, requesting his prayers. When he presented the message to the telegraph desk of his hotel, he was dumbfounded when the clerk handed him a telegram from Padre Pio that assured him of his prayers for the recovery of his friend. When Humphrey-Smith recovered, he went to San Giovanni and asked Padre Pio to explain how he came to telegraph his promise of prayer even before anyone notified him of the accident. Padre Pio simply smiled and asked, "Do you think the angels go as slowly as the planes?"[12]

Back in July 1915, Padre Pio had written to his spiritual daughter Anita Rodote about the guardian angel whom God assigns to each individual:

> Have great devotion … to this good angel. How consoling it is to know that near us is a spirit who, from cradle to the tomb, does not leave us even for an instant, not even when we dare to sin. And this heavenly spirit guides us and protects us as a friend, a brother. But it is extremely consoling to know that this angel prays without ceasing for us; offers to God all our good actions, our thoughts, our desires, if they are pure. Do not forget this invisible companion, always present, always ready to listen to us and even more, ready to console us.… Always keep him present to your mind's eye. Often remember the presence of this angel. Thank him, pray to him, keep him good company. Open yourself up to him and confide your suffering to him. Have a constant fear of offending the purity of his gaze.… Turn to him in times of supreme anxiety and you will experience beneficial help. Never say that you are alone in sustaining the battle against our enemies. Never say you have nobody to whom you can open up and confide. You would do this heavenly messenger a grave wrong.[13]

Several of the friars at San Giovanni believed that they had, at one time or another, encountered Padre Pio's guardian angel. Don Giorgio Pogany said, "Once, at Solemn High Mass, they wanted me to assist. I think it was a Sunday morning. In the morning, when I was supposed to be there, I fell asleep in my room in town. I felt somebody wake me up. I felt four fingers on my shoulder. I thought it was Padre Pio, saying, 'Come, you have to assist me now.' There was nobody there in the room. I really felt four fingers … on my shoulder."

Almost the same thing happened to Padre Alessio in the mid-1960s, when Padre Pio was old and feeble. Alessio recalled, "As I was with him most of the day and most of the night, I really didn't get too much sleep. I used to take him to the altar or confessional box and then go to my room to have a little rest. Sometimes I slept over and when this happened, I always heard someone knocking on my

door or calling me in my deep sleep, and I would go downstairs to find Padre
Pio towards the end of his Mass or confession. One day I missed picking him
up from the confessional box and when I approached him to ask forgiveness
for not being on time, he looked at me and pointed his finger at me and said,
'Do you think I will continue to send my guardian angel to you every morning
to wake you up?'"

A car dealer from Florence named Piergiorgio Biavati recounted to Padre Alessio an incident that took place in 1960 or 1961. En route to San Giovanni Rotondo,
he ran into heavy traffic on the "Highway of the Sun" and lost time. He had expected
to be at San Giovanni by sunset, but nightfall found him only as far as Naples,
still three hours from his destination. After stopping at a rest area for coffee, he
continued his journey. Biavati explained, "I remember only one thing: I started the
engine, put my hands on the wheel, and, after that, I have no recollection whatsoever.
I don't remember any second of the three hours' drive. Not only that, but when I
reached the square in front of the friary, someone shook me by the shoulder and
said, 'Come on now, take over.'"

Biavati told Padre Pio, "I drove here from Naples, but I don't remember driving
my car at all." Smiling, Padre Pio answered, "You were right. You were sleeping all
the way and my guardian angel was driving for you."

Padre Alessio believed that Padre Pio communicated not only with his own
guardian angel but with those of his spiritual children while he prayed the Rosary
each afternoon. Sometimes, when the younger priest tried to get his attention,
Padre Pio responded, "Come on, my son, leave me alone. Don't you see that I'm
very busy? Don't you see all those guardian angels going backwards and forwards
from my spiritual children, bringing messages from them?" When he prayed the
Rosary at night, Padre Alessio heard him murmur, "Tell her I will pray for her" or
"Tell him that I will knock at the heart of Jesus for this grace" or "Tell her that Our
Lady will not refuse her this grace."

Moreover, Padre Alessio recalled a time when "voices singing in beautiful har-
mony" were heard in the friary and nobody was able to determine the source.
Someone decided to ask Padre Pio about the singing. Absorbed in prayer at the
time of the interruption, he started, as if aroused from sleep, responding, "Why
are you so surprised? They are the voices of the angels, who are taking souls from
purgatory into paradise."[14]

Padre Pio was reluctant to speak about supernatural phenomena, but in his
correspondence with his spiritual directors in his youth he described almost continuous contact with his guardian angel, who not only protected him from enemies, both human and supernatural, but also performed such tasks as occasionally
translating parts of letters written in foreign languages. However the skeptic may be
inclined to explain the phenomena which Padre Pio attributed to angelic activity,

it is beyond question that he was convinced of the physical and literal intervention of angels — as well as the Madonna — in his life.

Seeing Into the Other World

It was also said that Padre Pio saw the souls of those, both living and dead, for whom he prayed, "as in a mirror." "Whether Padre Pio *always* sees the souls for whom he prays is a mere conjecture," Father Dominic wrote. "That this happens sometimes is quite possible, from some of his remarks, but Padre Pio does not speak of these things expressly. One need not make conjectures about Padre Pio. 'Truth is stranger than fiction' is verified in him also. Some things are far more strange than the imagination of magazine writers."[15]

In the summer of 1949, Dominic went to Padre Pio after night prayers and asked, "Tomorrow I have a Mass for my Mamma…. Will you exchange intentions with me? You say the Mass for my Mamma and I shall take your intention." Padre Pio, pressing Dominic's hand, gladly consented. Dominic actually wanted to see whether Padre Pio, during the Mass, would see his mother, Catherine, who had died three years before at the age of seventy-nine.

The next day, after both priests had celebrated their Masses, Dominic encountered Padre Pio standing at the door to his room, talking to another priest. Writing to his father, Dominic recounted: "He looked at me with a big smile and my first thought was, 'Can he tell me about Ma?' He seemed so happy, came to me, embraced me and, pressing both cheeks to mine, said something. All I understood was '*Mamma in Paradiso.*' I then asked him whether Ma was in heaven and he answered, 'As far as I can tell, yes.' I asked him again, 'Then you believe she is in heaven?' Still smiling happily, he said, firmly and definitely, '*Si!*' I kissed his hand, thanked him, and went to the choir to make my thanksgiving."[16] (Of course, Padre Pio was not saying that he knew for sure that Catherine Meyer was in heaven — only that he believed she was, which would not necessarily require supersensible knowledge.)

Father Joseph Pius was present when a woman inquired about the soul of her husband, who had committed suicide. Padre Pio seemed to gaze into the other world, as if focusing on it. "There's very little hope," he said at first. Then his face darkened and he sadly said, "There's no hope." He allegedly said to the widow of another suicide, "He's saved. Between the bridge and the river he repented."

Often this information on the eternal state of the departed totally was unsolicited. Father Dominic met a man in the summer of 1949 who was stunned when Padre Pio told him, out of the blue, "They are saved." Only then did the man reveal that for several years he had been burdened with concern about some relatives who had been killed in a bombing raid during World War II. He did not mention them nor his concern about their eternal destiny to Padre Pio, but nevertheless, the Padre seemed to know, not only what was on the mind of his visitor, but the situation in the other world of his deceased family members.[17]

Seeing into the Future

At times Padre Pio seemed to be able to foretell future events. He was convinced that the future was not always predetermined. For instance, there was a professor named Filippo De Capua, who was told by specialists both in Foggia and Naples that his pregnant wife would either lose her child or she herself would perish in childbirth. Padre Pio told him, "Neither the mother nor child will die." When De Capua continued to fret, Padre Pio declared, "It is not yet written in the decrees of God, but, if anything happens, it will be because of your lack of faith."[18]

In 1945, Father Duggan, the chaplain, was transferred to Bari and requested Leo Fanning's superiors to send him as his assistant. "I didn't want to go, because of Padre Pio," Fanning recalled. "I didn't have the guts to tell Father Duggan, for fear of hurting him. Finally, one day in San Giovanni, I said to Padre Pio, 'Father Duggan wants me to go down to Bari, where he is.'" Padre Pio replied authoritatively, "You are not going anywhere." Then Fanning learned that his captain refused Father Duggan's request for the transfer.[19]

Soon after that, now that the war was over, the time drew near for the Americans to leave Italy. Mario Avignone recounted:

> The top brass in Washington decided that members of the armed forces would be discharged and sent home by … the Accumulated Service Record Point System. The ones with the highest points would be discharged first. You were given points for each year in the war, overseas service, if married, how many children, etc. Joe [Asterita], Leo [Fanning], and I were in different classes. Joe, having served overseas the longest, had more than enough points to get him out of uniform immediately; myself, I had not quite the number of points to go home yet, so I was to go to the Army of Occupation somewhere in Europe; and poor Leo, he had the least amount of points and he was told that he would go to Japan for the Army of Occupation [there]. It looked as if we were going to part as army buddies. We decided that we must go to see Padre Pio.

On their way to San Giovanni in a jeep, the three soldiers smelled the "aroma of paradise." "There was no doubt about this," Avignone wrote, "We three all smelled the perfume and felt [Padre Pio's] presence."

When they arrived at the friary, Asterita explained the point system and where each man was going to be assigned. Avignone wrote, "Padre Pio just smiled and said, 'Points, points, I don't know what you mean by points. I tell you that you three will go home together.'" When the soldiers returned to their barracks at Cerignola, they learned that their orders had been changed and that they were all to be discharged within a few weeks' time."[20]

People had the understandable tendency to ask Padre Pio when they would die. According to Father Joseph Pius, one day Padre Pio was together with Maria Pyle and three priests when someone asked him the order in which they would die. He obliged, and time proved correct the order in which he predicted their deaths. When the two were in their thirties, Padre Pio had told Padre Romolo that "it has been determined that you will die an old man," and, in fact, he lived to be ninety-five. Maria Pyle asked Padre Pio, "What am I going to do when God calls you?" Padre Pio responded, "You're going to greet me."[21] She died a few months before he did.

Not all of these apparent prophecies proved true. One day Padre Alessio and a Padre Vito asked Padre Pio how long they would live. Padre Pio told the latter, who was suffering from cancer, that he would live five years, and told Padre Alessio that he would live sixty years. Padre Vito lived five *months*, not years. This led Padre Alessio to speculate that he had sixty months (five years) rather than sixty more years to live. When five years passed, Alessio concluded that Padre Pio had been joking.[22] However, Padre Alessio, when he died, was in his mid-sixties, so perhaps Padre Pio had meant that his lifespan would encompass approximately sixty years, not that he would live sixty years after the day he made the prediction.

He Did Not Know Everything

It is certain that Padre Pio did not always see into the heart, into the next world, or into the future. Consider how he believed the lies of the "Pious Women" concerning the Sicilian woman who had threatened them with a knife in self-defense. Or recall how he was angry at God for taking Dr. Sanguinetti without warning. Elia Stelluto, a photographer who grew up in San Giovanni Rotondo, recalled a woman who, just after the end of the First World War, was wed long-distance to a mail-order husband whom she had never met, after he sent her a photograph of himself. The picture had been taken, however, before the war, and when the husband arrived in person, the bride, to her horror, saw that he had been gruesomely disfigured, with half of his face destroyed. She hurried to Padre Pio, informing him of her plight. The priest explained to her that the mail-order marriage was valid and that she would have to live with her maimed groom. "Besides, he can't be as horrible to look at as _____."

"But, Padre Pio," cried the woman, "my husband *is* _____!"

Padre Pio had no supernatural insight there, but the woman consented to live with the wounded veteran, and they had several children and a successful marriage, although the unfortunate man's appearance was so appalling that people averted their eyes when he approached them on the street.[23]

One day Padre Pio gave his nephew Ettore Masone an unjustified rebuke. Ettore had been dismissed from college because of his epilepsy and the unwillingness of the administration to take responsibility for him. When Pio heard that his nephew was no longer in school, he assumed, incorrectly, that he dropped out voluntarily or had been dismissed for poor scholarship.

"Get away from me, you bum!" Padre Pio shouted at Ettore, who had come to his uncle for comfort and counsel. "You have a lot of gall just to come into my sight!"

"Why are you talking to me this way, Uncle?"

"Because you dropped out of college. Go away!"

"Uncle, read this letter."

When Padre Pio read the letter and learned the reason why Ettore could not continue in college, he laid his head on his desk and began to sob.[24]

The source of Padre Pio's supersensible wisdom was not some psychic power over which he had any control. As he said, "If nobody up there says something, what answers can I give?" When not enlightened by Christ, Mary, or his guardian angel, Padre Pio was simply a good and holy priest and wise counselor.

"Padre Pio Grabbed Me with the Claws of a Lion and Turned Me to God"

Another charism attributed to Padre Pio was the grace to effect "illumination" in the souls of his spiritual children. A striking example of this is the testimony of Padre Antonio Savino, who, as a young man, sought Padre Pio's blessing before setting out by sea for a job in Australia. He recounted: "On the thirty-second day of the voyage I lay ill in the ship's infirmary with pharyngitis, running a high fever. I was too weak to get out of bed. Suddenly I was overwhelmed with a brilliant light. The room was pitch black, but I was filled with an intense inner light. It was the light of God. At that moment all things became clear. I understood everything. When I awoke I was completely healed." He insisted that through this experience, "Padre Pio grabbed me with the claws of a lion and turned me to God." This experience was reported, from time to time, by other spiritual children of Padre Pio, who reported that their lives were suddenly and dramatically changed through the Capuchin's prayers — sometimes in confession, sometimes at Mass, sometimes, as in the case of Padre Antonio, from afar.

The Shining Countenance

Like Moses, whose face glowed so brilliantly after communicating directly with God that he had to wear a veil to keep from dazzling the children of Israel, Padre Pio reportedly, at prayer, was sometimes seen to glow with supernal light. A friar who lived with him recalled that on one occasion he observed Padre Pio's face "shining with a rosy flame of light such as I had never seen before and shall, I think, never see again."[25]

The Aroma of Paradise

The paranormal attribute associated with Padre Pio most frequently was the "aroma of paradise." People could live around Padre Pio for years without ever experiencing him prophesying or reading the heart or witnessing a physical healing. However, many people who lived with him, on many occasions, experienced a delectable fragrance that some associated with the blood which issued from the stigmata. Some claimed that it emanated from his entire body. Others, meeting Padre Pio, assumed that he used cologne (which he didn't). However, many people insisted that they scented the aroma when separated from Padre Pio by hundreds of miles, and, in later years, by physical death.

What did Padre Pio's aroma smell like? Carmela Marocchino, who lived for many years with Maria Pyle, claimed to have experienced it often over a period of many years — and even after Padre Pio's death. She said it was like the scent of roses and violets. Padre Rosario of Aliminusa, father guardian at San Giovanni in the early 1960s, smelled it every day for nearly three continuous months during Vespers. He described it as "a strong and pleasant odor, whose characteristics I cannot describe."[26] Padre Gerardo Di Flumeri recalled, "I experienced the perfume twice.... I don't know how to describe it: very beautiful and very nice, but you can't describe it."[27] Dr. Giuseppe Gusso was one of five people standing at Padre Pio's door one evening when all of them "got a perfume." "It wasn't the same perfume for everyone present. When Padre Pio opened the door and they went into his cell there was no perfume at all. I was with Padre Pio every day. There was never any perfume on him, so this was supernatural."[28]

Amanzio Duodo, a physician, testified that on February 15, 1950, he was talking with friends when "suddenly and unexpectedly an intense perfume of violets enveloped us all. It lasted about a half hour, although the doors and windows were open. Later on, a pungent and strong odor of perfume assaulted us." Eduardo Bianco, another doctor who was present in the room likened the aroma to roses, violets, and carnations and declared that it eluded "all scientific explanation."[29]

Maria Pyle explained: "We once gave a very simple American — and many Americans are very simple — something that had something of Padre Pio's in it. We didn't smell the perfume any longer, but he did and he went to the telephone and held it to the telephone and phoned New York and asked his wife, 'What do you smell on the other side?' and she replied, 'I smell a strong smell of incense.'"[30]

What was the purpose, the meaning, of the aroma? Pyle said, "When they smell incense, it means that [Padre Pio] wants prayer." Bishop Antonio D'Erchia (1911–1997) of Monopoli described the aroma as "almost always a premonition of happy events or favors or as a reward for generous efforts to perform virtuous acts."[31] Yet Padre Pio himself told Joe Peterson that the aroma was merely "sweets for the children."[32]

"I'm Afraid Because of All That the Lord Has Given Me"

Padre Pio did not like to discuss his charisms. He said, "God made all things. His creation includes the stars and the humblest domestic utensils. I belong to the second category.... I realize to the full the greatness of the gifts that God has bestowed upon me. But that terrifies me because I know only too well what miserable use I have made of them. If he had given them to the lowest scoundrel in the world, he would have employed them better. I dread the thought of death and having to answer for it."[33] He told his nephew Ettore Masone, "I'm afraid because of all that the Lord has given me, since the more we are given, the more we are responsible before him. I'm fearful because of all the goodness and mercy that he has shown me."[34]

Chapter Thirty

Bilocation

The Difficulty of Confirmation

Perhaps the most curious charism of Padre Pio, and the one least capable of normal explanation, is the phenomenon of bilocation, or astral projection, as the phenomenon is sometimes called, through which Padre Pio, while remaining in San Giovanni Rotondo — often in full view of others — was nonetheless seen, heard, and even touched in other parts of Italy, Europe, and the world.

We will recall the incident in 1905 in which the seventeen-year-old Fra Pio found himself, through bilocation, at the birth of Giovanna Rizzani in northern Italy. We will also recall how he was questioned about reports of bilocation by an inquisitor in 1921 and how in 1941 an archbishop in Uruguay was convinced that Padre Pio knocked on his door and told him to go to the assistance of a colleague who was on the point of death. Throughout the years, there were "sightings" of Padre Pio from Hawaii to South Africa. It is alleged that he was seen at the canonization of Saint Thérèse of Lisieux in the Vatican in 1925. Many of these stories are doubtless the product of hearsay or fertile imaginations; many probably were reported by people seeing what they wanted to see or hearing what they wanted to hear. Any unexpected encounter with an unknown bearded man dressed in monastic attire would be, for many of the pious, an instance of Padre Pio in bilocation. Padre Lino Barbati, who served as vice postulator for the cause of canonization for Padre Pio, was of the opinion that credible bilocation accounts are the rarest of Padre Pio stories and the most difficult to confirm.

The Account of an Old Nun

When Padre Lino was taking testimonies in America in 1978 and 1979, he visited "an old nun" in a nursing home in Montauk, Long Island. She had been a devotee of Padre Pio and talked about him to the children at the grammar school where she taught. In 1953 or 1954, she became ill with stomach cancer and was admitted to a hospital run by the Poor Clares, who urged her to pray to Padre Pio. The nun, who had been told that her condition was terminal, was resigned to death. One night she was startled to see a bearded priest in her room. (Even though she was devoted to Padre Pio, she had never seen a picture of him.) Though he spoke in a language she didn't understand, she understood that he was telling her, "Don't worry. You're not going to die." He touched her hand, and she turned her head away and he was gone. The whole incident lasted three minutes. When she was next examined, all traces of the cancer were gone. At the same time, she was shown a picture of Padre Pio, whom she identified as the man who had come to see her. Unfortunately, the story is thirdhand. The nun told the story to Padre Lino, who told it to Andre and Graziella Mandato, who told it to the author. The name of the nun was not recorded, nor was the nursing home where she was interviewed, and Padre Lino's actual notes (although they may exist somewhere) were not accessible to the author.

Padre Carmelo's Account

But not all accounts of bilocation stand on such shaky historical ground. Padre Carmelo Durante of Sessano (1916–2000), who was father guardian at San Giovanni between 1953 and 1959, whom William Carrigan considered "one of the smartest monks I've ever met," described an incident which took place in 1953 at a concert in a building that then adjoined the friary (and which was demolished when the new church was built). Padre Pio was in attendance and seemed interested and enthusiastic during the first part of the production. During the intermission, he put his arms on the back of the chair in front of him and rested his head on them, silent and motionless. Those around him thought he was sleeping. When the concert resumed five minutes later, he sat up and paid attention to the end, and no one thought anything more about it until the next day, when a sick man in town whom Padre Carmelo was visiting thanked him for allowing Padre Pio to call on him the previous evening. Padre Carmelo knew that Padre Pio had spent the evening at the concert and then gone straight back to the friary. He hadn't been out of his sight. Yet the sick man and his family insisted that Padre Pio had been in their house. When Carmelo asked the time, the family indicated the very time of the intermission in the concert, when Padre Pio seemed to be dozing.[1]

Padre Alessio's Account

Padre Alessio entered Padre Pio's room one night and found him shivering, even though it was a warm evening, and Padre Pio was generally more sensitive to heat than cold. He seemed to be in a trance. Padre Alessio piled blanket after blanket on Padre Pio, but he was still shivering. Later he learned that at that very hour a man who was dying high in the Alps insisted that Padre Pio was present there with him.[2]

Pia Forgione's Account

Pia Forgione, Padre Pio's niece, recounted:

> I was sick at home with three children and a fever in 1948. My mother-in-law was also ill. Uncle Pio felt that he should visit her in her home. I thought to myself, "Certainly, he'll stop and say hello to me, since he's passing right in front of my house." He didn't stop. I was at the window with the baby as he passed in the car and he didn't even so much as look at me. I got angry and slammed the window. When my husband and father came back, I threw a tantrum. Finally Mario [her husband] told me, "Calm down. That's enough." I refused to go to the friary. My fever got worse and I went to bed. I was waiting for Mario to come home when I heard a key turn in the door and heard Uncle Pio walk into my bedroom. He stood so close that I could feel the sheets being pulled tight by the pressure of his body. I closed my eyes. He slapped me on the face and said, "You haven't offended your uncle. You've offended the Holy One." Then he vanished. When Mario came in, I told him. I went to the friary when I recovered and knelt down before Uncle Pio's confessional. I asked, "Was it real?" and he said, "You're still doubting it was me. Remember, you didn't offend your uncle. You offended the Holy One."[3]

It was established that Padre Pio had returned directly to the friary after visiting the sick woman and was there at the time Pia saw him. Moreover, nobody had informed him of her fit of temper.

Padre Alberto's Account

It will be recalled how Padre Pio was forced to cancel his plans to attend the consecration of the friary at Pietrelcina in 1951. Yet, he told Padre Agostino, "I will be present in Pietrelcina and at the same time I will be in the confessional at San Giovanni Rotondo." After the ceremony, Padre Alberto D'Apolito attempted to describe the church at Pietrelcina. "I know it better than you do," insisted Padre Pio. "I was there. I can describe to you the most minute details and even the number of steps on the stairway in the entrance, which you don't know."[4] This is one of the few accounts which describes Padre Pio raising the subject of bilocation. One has to wonder whether, on this occasion, he was joking, or whether he had seen a picture of the church, or, as Alberto was convinced, he had really bilocated to Pietrelcina.

Father Dominic's Letters

Father Dominic recounted several instances of bilocation in his correspondence with his cousin Albert Meyer. On February 15, 1953, he wrote: "A lady in Chicago had written several times asking [prayer] for her sick son who was married and had two children. In her last letter she wrote that her son had died a peaceful death. The Drs. had feared a violent struggle. Five days before the young man's death the mother visited him in the hospital. He told her: 'This morning Fr. Pio stood right there,' pointing to where the mother stood."

Father Dominic wrote of a Viennese woman, Anny Seidl, who lived at San Giovanni Rotondo. In 1943, she was incapacitated by a sore and swollen arm. Padre Pio appeared to her in a dream and pressed both hands on her arm. When Seidl awoke, she was cured completely. Several months later she mustered the courage to ask Padre Pio if he had in fact appeared to her and cured her. He replied, "*Si.*" Then, on June 29, 1948, she was sleepless one morning at 4:00 a.m., depressed and weeping over conditions in her war-ravaged homeland, when "Fr. Pio appeared at the side of her bed with a large cross which she later recognized as the one we have in our choir. Fr. Pio blessed her with it and she immediately felt consoled and at peace. On her name day, August 26 … she asked Fr. Pio in the confessional whether it was he who had appeared to her. He said: 'To dispel the evil spirits.'"[5]

Father Dominic wrote to his cousin Albert on October 31, 1952:

One of our lay brothers, Fra Daniele, formerly cook in Foggia, is staying here at present … for recuperation from a severe illness. Last summer he took very sick and the Dr. advised he be sent to Rome to a cancer hospital. He was at the Regina Elena Hospital and was operated. The Drs. and nurses did not give him a chance. The evening of the operation Fr. Pio appeared beside his bed, laid his hand on the forehead of Fra Daniele and said: "Non avere paura. Tutto andrà bene." [Have no fear. All will go well.] Brother was not cured miraculously, but it was a real bilocation … and Fr. promised his eventual recovery. Br. also kissed Fr. Pio's hand as he left. He appeared another time, but did not speak … Br., who told me himself, said he is positive he was fully awake both times.

Father Dominic was convinced that Padre Pio had appeared in bilocation to his own dying father in America. John Joseph Meyer had written his son, asking him to request Padre Pio to assist him at his death. When Dominic relayed the message to Pio, the latter smiled and said, "I'll do what I can." A year later, on June 25, 1950, Meyer, eighty-one and suffering from a severe heart condition, was sitting on his front porch while a daughter and son-in-law were preparing his lunch. Another son was also there at the house. When the daughter went to call the father to lunch, she found him collapsed on the sofa, and, seconds later, he died. "They could not understand how he got in without [their] hearing anything," Father Dominic wrote family members a few days later. "The screen door screeched so you could hear it all over the house, Dad usually let the door slam as old people do, he shuffled his feet — but they heard nothing." Immediately it occurred to the son-in-law that maybe Padre Pio had been there, and he asked Father Dominic to inquire. When he asked, "Did you assist my Dad in his final moments?" Padre Pio smiled and answered, "Yes." When Father Dominic asked, "Is he in heaven?" Padre Pio replied, "If he's not in heaven, he's at the gate, ready to enter." A year later, when Father Dominic asked again, he received the reply, "He's in heaven long already."[6]

The Case of Padre Placido

In July 1957, Padre Placido Bux of San Marco in Lamis (who had taken the earliest photographs of Padre Pio's stigmata) was hospitalized in San Severo with cirrhosis of the liver, and his condition was deteriorating. One night Padre Pio appeared to him, assuring him that he would recover, and placed his hand on the glass of the window of the hospital room before vanishing into thin air. Padre Placido assumed that it was all a dream until the next morning, when he saw the imprint of a hand on the window. When he told his story, nobody believed him. Padre Alberto D'Apolito, who had visited Padre Placido, wrote:

> I was also skeptical. I thought that some male nurse could have placed his hand on the glass, leaving the imprint. Padre Placido told me exactly what had happened during the night. As I did not want to believe, he begged me to go to San Giovanni Rotondo and ask Padre Pio himself. At San Giovanni Rotondo I met Padre Pio in the hallway of the friary, and before I could open my mouth, he asked me: "How is Padre Placido?" I replied that he was getting better; then I added: "Spiritual Father ... Padre Placido states that you came to visit him during the night and that, before leaving, you left an imprint of your hand on the window pane.... Is it true? Was it a dream or a fantasy of Padre Placido, or did you really go to see him?" Padre Pio answered, "Is there any doubt about it? ... Yes, I went, but do not say this to anyone."

Padre Placido lived another eleven years. Then, in October 1968, now in his eighties, he insisted that Padre Pio (who had died the month before) had appeared to him in a dream and told him, "You will join me very soon.... You will not see the end of this year." Padre Placido died in San Severo that Christmas.[7]

"I Only Know That It Is God Who Sends Me"

Most of the bilocation stories are subjective and circumstantial. Many have the characteristic of dreams. However, they usually relate to a concrete reality — to a healing or a prediction of events that actually transpired. In some of these occurrences, Padre Pio was seen to be present only spiritually. A woman who claimed to be seeing Padre Pio in bilocation was asked if he was there physically. She replied,

"Of course not," and jabbed at the spot where she saw him. But in other instances, it was claimed that he could be touched (or that he left a handprint).

There is no question that Padre Pio believed that he visited people through bilocation. He had admitted that to Monsignor Rossi of the Holy Office in 1921. Padre Eusebio Notte questioned him about it in the 1960s. Speaking of a mutual acquaintance, he asked, "Padre Pio, you know that man's house in Rome, don't you?"

Padre Pio responded, "Me? How could I know it when I haven't been away from the friary for ever so many years?"

Padre Eusebio persisted: "But, Padre, that man says you went to his house and that he saw you."

Padre Pio then answered: "Ah, that's a different matter. When these things occur … the Lord only permits the person concerned to be seen, not the surroundings."[8]

Asked whether people experiencing bilocation know where they are going and what they are doing, Padre Pio replied, "Certainly they know. Perhaps they don't know whether it is the body or the soul that moves, but they are fully conscious of what is happening and they know where they are going."[9] Another time he described bilocation as an "extension of body and soul" and that he sometimes went "with body and soul," but, on other occasions, his angel assumed his bodily form and voice.[10] He told Padre Alessio: "I know only that it is God who sends me. I do not know whether I am there with my soul or body, or both of them."[11]

Padre Pio evidently was not interested in analyzing the phenomenon. He was interested only in doing God's will. "Whether it's true or not that I am found in various places by bilocation, trilocation, or whatever," he told another priest, "you must ask God and not me. All I can tell you is that I always try to remain attached to the thread of his will. For this reason, I am always where I am."[12]

There was one question about bilocation that Padre Pio could and would answer clearly and directly. When asked what language he employed in his "travels," he replied: "Italian. And how many miracles would you want the Lord to perform?"[13]

"I Only Pray ... God Heals"

The Man of Miracles

Next to his stigmata, Padre Pio is perhaps most famous as a healer. Few people who lived around Padre Pio ever witnessed miracles of physical healing, but nearly everyone remembered *hearing* about them. Padre Pio, unlike many people renowned for "healing ministries," did not usually touch or lay hands on the sick. In fact, he would never have said that he had a "healing ministry." He simply responded to requests to pray for the sick — and in response to his prayers there are several fairly well-documented instances of remarkable recoveries from illnesses or accidents that are hard to explain naturally.

At times, though, Padre Pio discouraged people who came to him seeking the miraculous. Cardinal Clemente Micara (1879–1965), vicar general of Rome, seeking relief for pains in his legs that made walking difficult, asked Padre Pio for a pair of his shoes in hopes that he would be cured by wearing or touching them. The "man of miracles" replied, "I have pain in my legs and feet, too, but my shoes, which I wear all the time, haven't yet cured me. When they cure me, I'll send them to His Eminence, but I have little confidence that they will bring about this miracle."[1]

Savino's Eye

There were, however, some undeniably striking cures that were attributed to Padre Pio's prayers. One of the most famous was the case of Giovanni Savino. A day laborer who lived in San Giovanni with his wife and children, he was devoutly religious — so much so that Padre Pio would tease him, saying, "For just a bit you missed a vocation. If only you'd started coming to me before you were married!"

In February 1949, Savino, who was then thirty-five, was working on the construction of an addition to the friary. Every morning he would attend Mass celebrated by Padre Pio at five, before going to work. On the twelfth, after Mass, he went into the sacristy and knelt with a number of other men to receive Padre Pio's blessing. Savino was startled when Padre Pio, ignoring the other men, went to him, raised him to his feet, and whispered, "Courage, Giovannino [Johnny], I'm praying to the Lord that you might not be killed."

"Padre Pio, what's going to happen to me?" the laborer asked. But the priest was silent.

The next day Padre Pio said the same thing, without any further comment, as he did also on the third day. When he repeated his disturbing remarks for the fourth time on February 15, Savino murmured to one of the other friars, "I'm afraid something wrong is going to happen today," and suggested to the other members of his crew, "Let's not work today," telling them about Padre Pio's remarks. The crew, however, proceeded in their plans to blast away a huge boulder from the place where the annex to the friary was to be built.

At 2:00 p.m., Savino and another worker placed a charge of dynamite under a boulder. Savino set the charge and lit the fuse. It failed to detonate. After a few minutes, he went over to check the charge. Just as he got to the spot, the dynamite blew up and a violent explosion of rock fragments struck him in the face and hurled him into the air. Dr. Sanguinetti, along with Padre Raffaele and Father Dominic, were at the side of the injured man within minutes. They carried Savino to Sanguinetti's car and the doctor drove him to the Hospital of St. John of God in Foggia (this was several years before the opening of Padre Pio's hospital), where he was admitted for surgery.

According to Savino's son Francesco, writing many years later, "In truth, the eyes weren't there anymore. The right eye was nothing but a mush and there was nothing left of the other."

Sanguinetti drove back to San Giovanni, where he told Savino's wife, Rosa Di Cosimo, who was then in an advanced stage of pregnancy, "Your husband's eyes are both destroyed," and warned her not to try to visit him. He then went to Padre Pio, who asked him how Giovannino was.

"He's been blinded. He's lost his eyesight."

"Don't you know that this isn't certain yet?" Padre Pio replied.

"Well, if you say that and you and Our Lady of Grace assist him, anything is possible, but, as of now, Giovanni has lost his eyesight."

"It's not certain yet," Padre Pio repeated.

It was three days before Savino regained consciousness. His head and face were bandaged like a mummy, and he was in atrocious pain. Padre Pio begged everyone he knew to pray for Savino for three days. He exposed the Blessed Sacrament on behalf of the blinded man. He was heard to pray, "Lord, I offer you one of my eyes for Giovanni, because he's the father of a family."

In an interview with Father John Schug on July 17, 1971, Savino recounted:

"After three days I heard the doctor enter my room. I told him, 'Doctor, I don't want to make Padre Pio seem strange, but I smelled his tobacco as I lay in bed. I was saying to Padre Pio: "Send me a little tobacco," and I smelled his aroma.'" He continued, "Ten days after I entered the hospital, I woke up at 12:30 or 1:00 o'clock in the morning. I could hear the breathing of the two or three men sleeping next to me. I felt someone give me a light slap on the right side of my face, the right side where the eye was completely gone. I asked, 'Who touched me?' There was nobody. Again I smelled the aroma of Padre Pio. It was beautiful."

Later that morning the ophthalmologist came to remove the bandages from Savino's face and eyes. Francesco Savino wrote that as soon as he did, his father exclaimed, "Doctor, I see you!" The physician thought he was hallucinating. When Savino again cried, "Doctor, I can see you," the doctor told him, "Giovanni, stay calm. The medication is very powerful. It's not possible that you're seeing."

"Even so, doctor, I see you," the patient insisted. "Your black hair, your mask, the nurse ... I also see the crucifix on the wall."

According to Savino's son, the doctor examined Savino again, and examined the left eye, which was "crushed but not completely compromised." Savino could see nothing from that eye. Where the right eye had been there remained "a profound cavity," yet Savino "saw very clearly, distinguishing even the tiniest letters."

Savino himself, when interviewed by Father Schug, affirmed that "my right eye had been blown out of its socket. My right eye was gone entirely. The socket was completely empty.... There was not much hope of saving my left eye. They thought they could save it by an operation." When the ophthalmologist came in to examine him he asked Savino, "Turn to the right so you can see me with your left eye." Savino, however, insisted, "No, I see you with my right eye. I don't see anything out of my left eye."

"Are you crazy?" said the doctor. "I am telling you that your right eye isn't there anymore. I'm treating only your left eye."

"Doctor, I'm not crazy. The right eye is the one I see out of it, not the left."

Savino recounted: "[The doctor] was an atheist and didn't believe anything. He didn't understand anything. He covered my left eye and asked me: 'How many fingers am I holding up?' 'Five,' I answered. 'That's how many!' He was astonished. He asked: 'Who is your protector?' I told him, 'Padre Pio.' He looked at me and saw that my right eye was in its socket. He could see it. He said: 'Now I believe, too, because of what my own hands have touched.'" Savino affirmed to Father Schug, "Now, I can't see out of my left eye. I can see only with my eye which was miraculously healed."

In April, Savino was still in the hospital, being treated for his other injuries, and Rosa was due to deliver her child any day. On the seventh of the month, she told Padre Pio that she was going to Foggia to visit Giovanni the next day. "Oh, no you're not!" he told her. "You're staying at home." The next day, at 8:00 p.m., the baby came suddenly (named Francesco, after Padre Pio). "If I had gone to see Giovanni, I would have been on the bus at 8:00 p.m.," Rosa recalled. "Imagine what would have happened!"

That summer, after Savino's discharge, Padre Raffale wanted to send him to the Polyclinic Hospital in Rome for further treatment, apparently for the left eye. Padre Pio, however, was not in favor of that, telling Savino, "No, you have already received the grace we prayed for. Even though you go to Rome, your sight won't improve any more than it is now."

It was widely believed that a miracle had occurred. Five months after the accident, Father Dominic, writing to his relatives in a circular letter, recounted that Padre Raffaele, who examined Savino immediately after the explosion, declared, "The right eye is gone entirely. The socket is simply empty." Giorgio Pogany, then a monsignor in New Jersey, told the author in 1989 that he remembered the incident and how "a man saw with his ruined eyes."

Savino became a receptionist at the *Casa Sollievo della Sofferenza* when it opened a few years later, and he possessed good eyesight until he died, in his early sixties, of nonalcoholic cirrhosis, in 1974.

The records from Foggia's Ospedali Riuniti (which the author obtained in 1989), without recording his condition at the time of his discharge, stated that Savino had been admitted with injuries that consisted of one eye blown out ("emoptalmo") and the other with the cornea pierced with "numerous foreign objects." Could it be possible that the other parts of the left eye remained intact? Corneal transplants could be done in 1949, and perhaps this is the reason why it was suggested that Savino go to the hospital in Rome. It might be conjectured that Savino was actually seeing through the eye that had been merely damaged. However, both Savino and his son and his wife, as well as Father Dominic and others, insisted that this was not the case, that he saw out of the eye that had been completely destroyed.

In the summer of 1989, when I was in San Giovanni Rotondo, I asked Father Joseph Pius to take me to see Savino's widow, Rosa Di Cosimo. She said "a small amount of bloody flesh" remained in the socket and that "it was always with his own eye that he saw. It was a mess, but he could see perfectly out of it."

In July 2017, in response to my question, Giovanni Savino's son Francesco, a Capuchin priest, declared: "After the accident, my father's eyes were destroyed, especially one of them where a deep crater was created. Padre Pio offered himself to God and also offered one of his eyes, so that my father was given his sight back. Miraculously, my father's more damaged eye healed completely and recovered its sight, whilst the less damaged one healed but remained sightless.... My father did not wear a prosthetic eye.... His eyes were normal and completely healthy."

Francesco had been in his mother's womb at the time of the accident, but would certainly have seen his father's eyes in later life, and would have known how well he could see. This seems to conflict with his mother's statement that the eye was "a mess." Perhaps it was that way at first, but somehow grew into a normal eye. There are several photographs of Savino in later life, and in them both eyes look normal.

It is hard to dispute the miraculous — or at least inexplicable — nature of this occurrence without calling into question the good faith or good sense (or both) of a number of people, including Savino, his wife, his son, and Father Dominic, all of whom insisted that he was able to see out of an eye that had been obliterated.[2]

When, after his release from the hospital, Savino went to Padre Pio to thank him, he was told, "If you only knew what this cost me!" What did he mean? Francesco Savino recounts that Padre Pio offered God one of his own eyes. According to Pietro Cugino, around the time of Savino's cure (he wasn't positive about the date), he was in the friary garden with Padre Pio, when, suddenly, Pio cried, "I'm blind! I can't see a thing!" After twenty minutes, his sight returned. Cugino (who, it will be recalled, was himself blind), believed that Padre Pio's episode of blindness came as a result of the offering he had made for the healing of Cugino. (On another occasion, however, Cugino insisted that this happened sometime between 1919 and 1925, and that Padre Pio was blind "for many days.")

More Graces in the Savino Family

Savino's widow, Rosa, declared decades later, "I don't know why Padre Pio treated us so well. I'm old now and I forget a lot of things, but I shall never forget what he did for my husband and children." In addition to her husband, two of her children also received remarkable graces of healing.

In 1951, two years after Giovanni's cure, he was taking his little daughter Maddalena, called "Lena," to a friend's birthday party. As he was holding her hand, she was hit by a drunken motorcyclist who came roaring recklessly down the street. Taken to a first aid station in town, Lena was in a coma, hemorrhaging severely in her abdominal cavity, and seemed to have suffered a serious head injury. The nearest hospital was twenty-five miles away in Foggia, and Lena was in no condition to endure the trip there, so there was nothing to be done but wait. Giovanni and Rosa hurried to the friary and told Padre Pio. Rosa recalled that he "looked into heaven like he saw another reality," and said, "Let's pray and we'll leave everything in Our Lord's hands." Three days later Lena opened her eyes and cried, "Papa! Papa!" She recovered quickly and completely.

A few years later Giuseppe, another one of the Savino children, was hit by a motorcycle on his birthday, outside the family home. By now, the *Casa* was open, and the boy was rushed to the emergency room, in a coma with a head injury. As in the case of his sister, when Padre Pio prayed for him, Giuseppe regained consciousness and recovered quickly.

The Healing of a Crippled Man

In 1997, Pietro Cugino recalled an apparent miracle that occurred in front of many witnesses in San Giovanni. "One day a crippled peasant implored [Padre Pio's] help to be healed. The friar ordered him, 'Throw away your crutches.' He threw them away. He felt a tingle through his entire body, especially in the legs. Then he began to walk without the sticks. Then he walked around the convent. Finally, he returned in tears to thank the friar."[3] Unfortunately, Cugino did not give the man's name nor the date of the incident, nor any details.

Gemma Di Giorgi

In the spring of 1946, a nun from Ribera, Sicily, wrote to Padre Pio about Gemma Di Giorgi, a seven-year-old girl from her town, who, she said, had been born without pupils in her eyes and was totally blind. Shortly afterward, the child's grandmother brought her to Padre Pio. When they arrived, the grandmother claimed that Gemma began to see while they were on the train. Padre Pio heard Gemma's first confession, administered her first Communion, and made the Sign of the Cross over her eyes.

Di Giorgi told Father John Schug in July 1971: "I had no pupils in my eyes. I had no sight at all. When I was three months old, my mother took me to a very famous oculist in Palermo. He told her that, without pupils, I would never be able to see."[4] Father Schug noted: "She looks like a blind person. Her eyes are sallow and lusterless. But there is no doubt that she can see. I saw her reach for a phone book, check a number, and dial the number without groping.... Questioned by a Sicilian Capuchin ... she described the progress in construction of a building fifteen yards away and mentioned the color of the various sections of the building."[5]

However, the question remains as to what exactly was the matter with Di Giorgi's eyes. When he learned of the cure, Padre Agostino spent two full years trying to obtain documentation. Finally, in February 1948, he received an affidavit from a Dr. Contino, who had examined Gemma when she was three and who had not seen her again until after her reputed cure. Saying nothing about a lack of pupils, Contino maintained that "she was not born blind, but that her ability to see was uncertain."[6] He stated that he examined the child again in December 1947 and found that it was now clear that the child could see, for she could count his fingers at a distance of sixteen feet. Dr. Sanguinetti, who was trained in ophthalmology, studied Dr. Contino's affidavit and told Padre Agostino that he did not think that the cure exceeded "natural powers." When someone praised Padre Pio for obtaining the cure of the blind girl, the priest sternly asked, "Did you witness it? I said, Did you witness it? Did you witness it?"

Father Joseph Pius Martin, in a letter to the author in August 1979, wrote, "Gemma has pupils. As a matter of fact, the entire eye is one very large pupil." It would seem that Di Giorgi was born with a condition known as "aniridia," in which her eyes lack irises. In some people with this condition, the visual defect is only slight, but in others, it is severe. Gemma, if not completely blind, had a severe visual defect which dramatically improved after Padre Pio's prayers were enlisted — even though the physical structure and appearance of her eyes remained completely unchanged. In fact, she remained classified as legally blind. One characteristic of aniridia is a severe sensitivity to light, and Di Giorgi always wore dark glasses — but otherwise she had no difficulty in seeing. "I see with the eyes of God, not the eyes of my body," Di Giorgi told an audience in the Philippines in March 2003.

A Throat Tumor Healed

A man named Danilo Gonin testified on March 6, 1996, that in the 1950s he was told by his doctor that he had an incurable "throat tumor" and was going to die. His wife suggested that they visit Padre Pio. He had been living in Canada and returned to Italy to die. When he went to confession, Padre Pio, who apparently had no earthly way of knowing anything about him, said, "Eh, Canadian!" Gonin was so upset that Padre Pio told him to calm down and come back. He returned the following day and confessed. After absolving him, without Gonin giving "a single hint about his problem," Padre Pio asked, "So what do the doctors say about your illness?"

Gonin said that the doctor had given him three months at the most to live. Padre Pio touched Gonin's "swollen throat" and said, "Have faith. Jesus is doctor and medicine."

While returning by car to Vicenza in northeastern Italy, Gonin realized he was breathing without any difficulty, and when he arrived home he went to his doctors, who examined him and found no trace of illness.[7]

Healings Noted by Padre Agostino

Padre Agostino noted several other apparent miracles in his diary. On June 10, 1945, Signora Massari, a native of San Marco la Catola and a resident of the town of Volturara Appula, came to San Giovanni. Soon she was telling everyone that for twenty years she had been totally deaf, and then "asked the Lord [for a cure] through the intercession of Padre Pio." While at Mass, she claimed, she suddenly began to hear the priest chanting. As she left the church, she heard the bells ringing and the conversation of the people.

Hearing of the alleged cure, Padre Agostino insisted on seeing her, and ascertained that, in fact, she could hear perfectly. Her traveling companion insisted that Massari had in fact been stone deaf for years — until that very day.[8]

In November 1947, Padre Agostino noted that he had received a medical certificate documenting the almost instantaneous cure of a uterine disease, incurable except through surgery. It took place immediately after Padre Pio prayed for the patient. He did not record the name of the patient nor the exact name of the condition from which she suffered.[9]

Padre Agostino obtained a medical certificate from Dr. Antonio Buda of Laureano, Calabria, stating that a medical examination of Maria Rosa De Angelis on March 25, 1947, revealed "an aneurysm of the ascending aorta." When the doctor examined her on July 24, 1948, after she sought the prayers of Padre Pio, he found "a noticeable improvement … with a marked reduction of the aortic swelling." He declared that "the reason for the verified improvement cannot be attributed to the usual medical treatments."[10]

In early 1949, Carla Minola from Milan was suffering from "acute ascending myelitis," an inflammation of the spinal cord, sometimes fatal. With it, paralysis begins in the lower extremities and ascends to the arms, chest, and throat. Minola was in "great agony" when, suddenly, she declared that Padre Pio's prayers had cured her. Her doctor, Professor Grossoni, while he admitted the "instantaneous cure" and expressed "amazement" to his colleagues, attributed his patient's recovery to "special radiotherapy." Padre Agostino considered the physician unreasonably skeptical and seemed personally convinced of the miraculous nature of Minola's recovery.[11]

Healings Noted by Father Dominic

In his letters to his family in America, Father Dominic Meyer recounted several remarkable graces of healing. In a circular letter in March 1950, he wrote of a cure that had taken place a month earlier, confirmed and corroborated by Dr. Sanguinetti, Dr. Sanvico, and Count Telfner. The son of Leonello Marinelli, superintendent of public works in the town of Montignana di Corelano, near Perugia in northern Italy, had suffered for five years with a "functional disorder of the heart" which had rendered him completely incapacitated. Two physicians, Dr. Tommaso Schicollini and Professor Calabro, the latter a heart specialist, confirmed that the boy (whose Christian name was not mentioned by Father Dominic) was beyond medical help. Marinelli had a frank talk with his son, telling him of the gravity of his condition. The boy asked his father to go at once to San Giovanni to beg Padre Pio to pray for his cure. Leaving by train for Foggia that very evening, Marinelli was met by his friend Dr. Sanvico, who took him to the friary. Before Marinelli had a chance to open his mouth, Padre Pio said calmly, "I know why you came. The boy is better and gradually will be cured." He invited Marinelli to stay overnight and make his confession the next day. Twice more, during confession and just before Marinelli left for home, Padre Pio assured him that within two months his son would be completely cured.

When he returned home, Marinelli found that his son was indeed improved. The boy told him that he had seen Padre Pio in a dream. After examining the boy, his doctors affirmed that the heart disorder had disappeared and declared that there was no way that this could have occurred naturally. A month after Padre Pio had predicted his cure, the young Marinelli was completely well and able to go with his father to visit Padre Pio.[12]

On February 29, 1952, Frances Pasqualini of 527 Kansas Street, San Francisco, California, wrote a letter in English to Padre Pio. She recounted how her six-year-old daughter was suddenly stricken with violent coughing, repeated vomiting, and high fever. While they were waiting for their doctor to make a house call, the parents prayed to the Blessed Mother and Padre Pio. No sooner had they finished their prayers than the little girl opened her eyes and said to her mother that she could smell something sweet, "like the incense they have in church." By the time the doctor arrived, the girl was completely well. Mrs. Pasqualini attributed this remarkable providence to Padre Pio.

Mrs. Pasqualini also recounted how, in December 1951, her husband's brother, aged twenty-nine, was suffering with "a rare illness of the nervous system" (which she did not name), which left him paralyzed from the neck down. The doctors "gave him no hope for his life." She and her family wrote to Padre Pio for his prayers. Two months later the brother was "back home with his wife and children, eating by himself, learning to walk without the use of even a cane, and showing signs of a thorough and complete recovery."[13]

On March 12, 1953, Father Dominic wrote to his cousin Bishop Albert Meyer:

> A few weeks ago a lady wrote from California that her husband had been cured of cancer. He had been dismissed from the hospital as incurable…. He was told to return in three weeks for X-rays and a checkup. It was then, the lady wrote, the man began to improve. When he went for X-rays they found no sign of the tumor (in the colon …) nor of the cancerous cyst. He then asked the man to come to the office. The Dr. placed a tube into the colon — absolutely no sign of the tumor. He told the man: "This is a miracle. As you had a tumor and now there is nothing there." The name of the man is Fred Baliardi and he lives at Waukegan (?) California."

(Waukegan is in Illinois, not California, and the author has found no record of anyone with that name in the U.S. Census or any other public record. Father Dominic apparently got the names of the man and his town wrong or misspelled them.)

Father Dominic also noted the case of Lucia Bellodi, which involved not only a physical cure, but a bilocation as well. It took place on June 12, 1952, the feast of Corpus Christi. Father Dominic's account is corroborated by a deposition by Bellodi herself, made on June 4, 1955.

Bellodi was twenty-one in 1952. Ever since she was fourteen, she had suffered from a severe case of diabetes insipidus, the result of an earlier attack of encephalitis. (Not to be confused with diabetes mellitus, or sugar diabetes, diabetes insipidus is a chronic metabolic disorder, frequently associated with damage to the pituitary gland, characterized by a failure of the body to maintain its water content through the limitation of the formation of urine. Those afflicted with this condition excrete enormous quantities of urine — often nearly ten gallons a day. To compensate for the loss of fluid, they are compelled to drink a similar quantity of liquids.)

Bellodi, a farm girl from near Modena in northern Italy, was totally incapacitated. "The doctor who treated me during this period made use of every modern treatment," she wrote, "but I grew worse rather than better. My disease … was resistant to every therapy." She was treated first at a hospital at Mirandola, then at a sanatorium at Gaiata, then at a hospital at Sondrio, and then at one in Modena. Finally, at twenty, declared incurable, she was placed in a nursing home in the same city.

Her condition was indeed deplorable. She was forced to drink up to twelve gallons of water a day. When she went to sleep, nurses had to insert into her mouth a rubber hose attached to a jar holding six gallons of water, since she had to drink even while she slept. If she did not, she would hemorrhage from her mouth and her tongue would swell to the point that she could not close her mouth. Because she was constantly urinating, her bed linen had to be changed several times a day. Almost every two weeks she had epileptic seizures, along with high fevers and violent headaches.

The nursing sisters who ran the facility encouraged Bellodi to "pray to" Padre Pio. "I often prayed to him," wrote Bellodi, "but never asked the grace of a cure. Rather, I asked him to give me resignation to my affliction or else free me through death."

On the feast of Corpus Christi in 1952, Bellodi had a seizure, and, after regaining consciousness, she asked to go to Mass in the chapel of the nursing home. She made her confession, but then collapsed and was put to bed again. She remained semiconscious until two in the afternoon, drinking more than ever. The nurses were sure that she was about to die. Just then, recounted Bellodi, "I smelled all around me a fragrant perfume of violets and asked where it came from." Then she fell asleep and felt an invisible presence who told her, "Get up, Lucia, because you will be cured this evening or tomorrow. Come here to see me at San Giovanni Rotondo." After a half hour, a nurse nudged Bellodi awake, concerned that she was not drinking and fearing that she would hemorrhage. But Bellodi announced that she was cured and wanted to get up. After she told of her experience, they allowed her to go to the chapel to thank the Lord. She ascended the stairs with "firm and lively step," and said she felt wonderful, as if she had never been sick for seven years.

The doctors who examined her immediately declared that Bellodi's cure was the result of "divine intervention," but were unwilling to release her for another month. When she was finally discharged, she went to Padre Pio, who greeted her warmly, saying, "I've been waiting for you. I recognize you before the Lord."

Pronounced completely well by her physicians, Bellodi returned home to a strenuous life as a farmer. In 1961, at the age of thirty, she married and, several years later, she disproved her doctor's prediction that her long sickness had made her incapable of becoming a mother.[14]

The Exorcism of Carboni

Father Dominic described the exorcism of Maria Palma Carboni. A native of the town of Confiento in northern Italy, Carboni was a servant in the home of a wealthy Tuscan family. In April 1952, she was diagnosed as suffering from a "nervous crisis" and was taken to a local hospital. There she grew progressively worse. Doctors were baffled by her condition. Some specialists thought she had a mental illness, others suspected a brain tumor.

Carboni returned to her family home, where her relatives became convinced that she was possessed by demons. "Her condition," Father Dominic wrote to his family, "was such to terrify everyone, not only by its violence, but by its strangeness. During the day, she was normal. But as soon as night came, she became violent, beat herself, and began 'to speak with the devil.' She knew beforehand just how long the conversation would last and she told the bystanders it would last 35 or 47 minutes, etc."

Carboni claimed that she could see the devil. Others in the room felt "a sinister presence" when she claimed to be speaking to Satan. Windows rattled, and there was loud rapping on the door. People came from surrounding villages to watch Carboni shrieking, gibbering, and writhing in unspeakable agony.

The local priest, Don Deglesposito, was at first skeptical and thought that Carboni was mentally ill, not possessed. As the days went by, he changed his mind. "For three nights," he wrote Father Dominic, "the girl had such severe attacks that four persons could hardly keep her in bed. Her eyes were closed. She screamed that the devil wanted to enter by the window. At the same time (there were ten people in the room), we heard the windows rattle, doors slam, and felt the small house tremble." The unfortunate woman "recited poems she never heard before, from classical authors." Deglesposito sprinkled Carboni and the room with holy water, but to no avail. At that point, the priest decided to take Carboni to San Giovanni

Rotondo and hired a taxi, setting out with the sick woman, another priest, and two of Carboni's relatives. En route to San Giovanni they had "dozens of accidents," including two collisions with trucks. Carboni had thirty-three violent seizures during the journey.

Somehow, on June 20, 1952, the frazzled party in their battered car arrived at San Giovanni Rotondo. Carboni was carried to a bench in the church and lay there, apparently unconscious, until Padre Pio appeared and blessed her. "Poor little thing," he said. "Who knows what she has suffered! Let's hope that she will get better." Then he walked away. From that moment, Carboni was perfectly normal. She returned home, and the friars at San Giovanni Rotondo kept in touch with her for some time. One of Carboni's relatives, a communist and atheist, was so impressed by the cure that he became a Christian.[15]

Giuseppe Canaponi

Giuseppe Canaponi (c. 1913–1983) was an electrician who worked for the railroad and lived in Sarteano, in the province of Siena. On May 21, 1948, on his way to work on a motorcycle, he was hit by a truck. He was left badly crippled and in pain, with an ulcerated leg and a knee that could not be bent. He was later issued a statement, signed by a Dr. Giuntini, from the *Ospedali Riuniti di Santa Maria della Scala*, which read, "This is to certify that Giuseppe Canaponi was treated in this clinic in 1948 for a stiffening of the left knee as a result of a fracture to his femur. Since medical and physical therapy proved unsuccessful, an attempt was made to move the rigid joint by force under general anesthesia. This procedure was of no avail, and a fracture of the femur occurred once again. Therefore he was released with his knee as rigid as it was after his recovery."

Canaponi was not a believer, but friends suggested that he and his wife and son visit Padre Pio, and so they went to San Giovanni Rotondo on Christmas Eve 1948. He wrote: "I had never seen a photograph of Padre Pio, so I didn't know how I would recognize him. There were several Capuchin monks in church. One was near me hearing the women's confessions. The curtain that was used to hide the priest who was hearing confessions was partly opened. The eyes of the monk who was sitting there were cast down, and his hands were hidden in his tunic. When he raised his right hand to give absolution, I realized he was wearing half gloves. 'It's him,' I said to myself. At that very moment, Padre Pio raised his eyes and stared at me for a couple of seconds. My body began to shake when he looked at me, as though I had been struck by a powerful bolt of electricity."

Canaponi made his confession to Padre Pio. "I tried to say something, but he didn't give me a chance. He started talking, painting a perfect portrait of my life, my personality, and my behavior. It seemed as though he had always lived with me. He spoke in a soft voice, and didn't scold me in the least.... I was completely enthralled with his words and wasn't even thinking about my leg.... When Padre Pio raised his hand to give me absolution, once again I experienced my body shaking like it had earlier that morning. Without noticing it, I knelt down and made the sign of the cross." He had no pain and was able to flex his leg. "I took my pants off and looked at my leg. The wounds, which had been very painful and bleeding, had healed over ... 'I've really been healed,' I cried out to my wife, and broke down in tears.'"

Canaponi thanked Padre Pio, who said, "I didn't do the miracle. I only prayed for you. The Lord healed you."

When Canaponi returned to the Orthopedic Clinic in Siena, the doctors were amazed, first of all, because he had full and painless use of his leg, but also because the X-rays showed no change. Canaponi said, "The fibrous ankylosis of the left knee was still there, and there was no way in which I should have been able to walk." When, a few months before his death at seventy, a journalist interviewed him, Canaponi, with only a barely detectable limp, was able to walk long distances with a "quick and vigorous" stride.[16]

"Let's Pray to God"

Padre Alessio believed that there had been at least a thousand claims, during Padre Pio's lifetime, that people had been healed through the prayers of the stigmatized priest. Giuseppe Sala, who was Padre Pio's physician during the last decade and a half of his life, insisted, "Certainly, there were healings and miracles." The doctor himself experienced a remarkable grace in 1955. His young son Paolo had been stricken with spinal meningitis and was in critical condition. There was fear that he would be left with severe brain damage. Sala telegraphed Padre Pio, requesting his prayer. He answered, "On the third day he will have no more fever and he will turn out to be the most intelligent of your children." The prophecy proved true.[17]

Most of the healings took place away from the Padre's physical presence. Padre Alessio recalled, "I don't remember any healings here at San Giovanni, but I heard people thanking him for being cured. The healings happened, not here, but away."[18] When people asked him to pray for them, Padre Pio would attempt to draw attention away from himself. Often he said, "I will bless you," and made the Sign of the Cross, very quickly and perfunctorily. Often he said, "Let's pray to God." Father Joseph Pius recalled only one instance in which Padre Pio laid hands on the sick. That was when a man and wife from California brought a little boy suffering from bone cancer. Padre Pio did not promise a cure, and the boy eventually died of his illness.

"I knew from experience," Padre Alessio recalled, "that when Padre Pio said to the sick person, 'I will pray for you' or 'Let's pray to God,' the sick person was going to be healed. On the other hand, if he said, 'Let's resign ourselves to the will of God' or said nothing at all, the grace of healing was not to be."

People unable to approach Padre Pio in person were often granted a cure through contact with some object that had been touched or used by him. When Sister Teresa Salvadores was ill in 1921, one of Padre Pio's gloves was applied to her body. This is not a superstitious practice; in Scripture it is written, "And God did extraordinary miracles by the hands of Paul, so that handkerchiefs or aprons were carried away from his body to the sick, and diseases left them and the evil spirits came out of them" (Acts 19:11–12). Most often, however, cures took place after Padre Pio simply exhorted the pilgrim or correspondent to pray to God. As we have seen, they sometimes took place after a spiritual child invoked his guardian angel to go to Padre Pio, or called upon him mentally.

Those around Padre Pio believed that sometimes he seemed to obtain permission from God to take on himself the person's physical sufferings so that the patient, while not cured, experienced a respite from the symptoms. For example, Padre Eusebio, who assisted Padre Pio in the early 1960s, recalled that every day, during that period, he would visit Padre Agostino, who, by that time, was an invalid. One day Padre Agostino said: "My Piuccio, last night I didn't close my eyes because of the pain in my knees. This pain makes me sees stars.... Do something for me!"

Padre Pio answered, "Courage! Courage, Father Lector. We'll see what happens."

Padre Pio, who had been walking normally before, began to hobble painfully after leaving the room, and had to lean heavily on the younger priest. When Padre Eusebio got Padre Pio into his own room, he asked him what happened, and got the answer: "And did you see that poor old man, how he was crying out in pain! It made me so sorry."

Leaving Padre Pio seated, Padre Eusebio decided to return to Padre Agostino's room and found the aged priest pain-free. "Padre Eusebio, you wouldn't believe it," he said. "The pain has completely disappeared."

Padre Eusebio was convinced that Padre Pio had taken Padre Agostino's pain, but, when he questioned him, Padre Pio replied, "Well, it doesn't matter. Let's thank the Lord and the Madonna."[19]

Padre Alessio recalled several instances in which people whom he knew, in the last stages of cancer, asked Padre Pio to pray for their healing, only to be told that it was not God's will. However, in these causes, the patient was relieved of pain and other distressing symptoms, even though the illness persisted and ultimately proved fatal. Padre Alessio believed that this was because Padre Pio had taken on their sufferings.

Two-Year Reprieves

Just as interesting are anecdotal accounts of what some people call the "two-year reprieves," in which a grave physical illness disappeared, but only temporarily, often for a period of two or three years, sometimes for a longer interval. The case of Dr.

Francesco Ricciardi, whose cancer suddenly went into remission for several years, is one, and that of playwright Luigi Antonelli, who apparently obtained relief for three years, is another. Then there was the case of Giuseppe Scatigna, from Palermo, Sicily, who was interviewed by Father Schug in 1971. Early in 1968 Scatigna was diagnosed with malignant melanoma, with metastases widespread throughout his body. When admitted to the *Casa* later that year, his condition had deteriorated to the point that his doctors were convinced that it was unlikely that he could survive for more than forty-eight hours. Padre Pio himself was then dying, but Scatigna's wife begged a piece of Padre Pio's clothing from the friars. She applied the cloth to her husband's wasted and jaundiced form, while the two of them prayed that he might have five more years of life so that he could see their adopted daughter reach her teen years. Immediately, he felt better. A few days later X-rays revealed no trace of cancer in his body. He went back to Sicily, where he enjoyed almost a decade of good health before his remission ended and he died at the age of fifty-five. Before he died, he remarked to his wife, "I wanted five years so that our daughter could grow up. Padre Pio obtained nine, so I'm grateful." According to his wife, Scatigna died "a beautiful and happy death."[20]

Tony Lilley, of the Padre Pio Information Centre in Kent, England, recalled three similar cases of "two-year reprieves" when the author spoke to him by telephone on July 6, 1990. One concerned a sixteen-year-old girl named Therese Sexton, who had a history of failed kidney transplants. After the fifth transplant failed, physicians told her family that Therese was only hours away from death. The young girl was virtually comatose when several friends prayed for her. One man, who himself had been healed through Padre Pio's prayers of an unspecified illness, stayed up all night, praying. The next morning, Therese was out of bed, skipping down the hospital corridor after visiting the beauty parlor. For two years, to the amazement of her doctors, she lived a normal life, during which Tony Lilley and his wife, Stella, who were family friends, arranged "every kind of treat that she'd ever wanted in her life.... She did everything she always wanted to do and went everywhere she wanted to go." Then, cheerfully, "accepting everything as the will of God," she passed into eternity at the age of eighteen.

Lilley recounted the case of John and Ellen Lynch, a couple in their early sixties who lived in Canterbury. In 1981, John was terminally ill with congestive heart failure and Ellen with pancreatic cancer. Death was expected for both within a matter of days. But then Padre Pio (by then dead thirteen years) appeared to John — as well as (so it seemed) his dog! — and immediately both husband and wife recovered almost instantaneously. Doctors could find no evidence of John's heart disease or Ellen's cancer. They continued so well that the physicians began to doubt their original diagnoses, although these had been confirmed by the usual tests and, in Ellen's case, exploratory surgery. For two years the Lynches continued well, and during that time Ellen, who had not been religious, entered the Catholic Church, and their son and his wife resolved their marital problems. Then, first John and then Ellen suffered recurrences of their original distempers and died, convinced that Padre Pio obtained time for them to sort out their lives.

Of course, it is not uncommon for seriously ill people to have good days, but extremely uncommon for good days to stretch into years. Sometimes some illnesses go into spontaneous remission, but one wonders how frequently patients, as gravely ill as Lilley's friends were supposed to be, rise literally from their deathbeds to full health — immediately after (in the case of Therese) fervent prayers are offered up for their recovery, or (in the case of John and Ellen) after a vision. Some would say that these cases were mere coincidences, but, in such matters, Padre Pio would often say, "But who makes things happen?"

Padre Pio's Attitude Toward Medical Science

As is evident by his founding his hospital, Padre Pio was by no means averse to the ministrations of medical doctors. Throughout his long life, he submitted to them, undergoing surgery on several occasions. "It's our duty to do all we can [through natural means] to achieve healing," he insisted. "God wants us to help ourselves in seeking healing, and we have the duty to submit ... to medicines and other treatment."[21]

Father Joseph Pius recounted that he once had a boil "in a very upsetting location." He went to Padre Pio, begging him, "Make it go away"; but Padre Pio said nothing, and the younger man had to submit to a painful surgical procedure. Later, while talking to a group of friars, as well as Father Joseph Pius, without making any specific reference to anybody, Padre Pio explained, "Now, for instance, if you have a boil, you've got to follow the doctor's advice and medicate and clean it, and perhaps even submit to surgery. Miracles occur only when human intervention cannot achieve the purpose."

At times, Padre Pio seemed to know when medical treatment would be useless or counterproductive. He was known, sometimes, to advise against operations that doctors had recommended. The friars often referred to him as "The Doctor," and many would not undergo any major medical treatment without first consulting him. For example, Padre Costantino Capobianco was supposed to have surgery on his sinuses. When he showed Padre Pio his X-rays, "The Doctor" declared authoritatively, "What are these things? They're all wrong!" Padre Costantino told him that they had been studied by three ear, nose, and throat specialists, all of whom recommended surgery. Padre Pio insisted that Padre Costantino go to a fourth specialist, and, when he did, the fourth doctor told him that the X-rays had been misread and that there was no need for an operation. The condition cleared up without the need for surgical intervention.[22]

Some years later Padre Costantino was advised to go under the knife for an intestinal problem. He told his surgeon that, before he signed the papers authorizing the surgery, he wanted to telephone Padre Pio. The surgeon encouraged him, "Go to Padre Pio, because, when I am faced with a difficult case, I go to him, too!" Padre Pio told Padre Costantino to go ahead with the operation. He did, and it was successful.[23]

Father Joseph Pius told about a plastic surgeon named Piero Mellilo, who was one of Padre Pio's spiritual sons. Mellilo had a brain hemorrhage, which was determined to be the result of an aneurysm in one of the major blood vessels in his brain. In order to prevent a devastating stroke, which could occur any minute, his doctors insisted on surgery. Mellilo was not even allowed out of bed, for fear that the slightest movement could precipitate the rupture of the aneurysm. Mellilo, before allowing the doctors to open his head, phoned the friary, hoping to speak to Padre Pio. It so happened that the phone rang just as Padre Pio was walking by, and he picked it up. When Mellilo explained the situation, Padre Pio snapped, "No, don't have the operation! Tell those confounded doctors to operate on themselves! You get out of there!"

When Mellilo told the brain surgeons that he was refusing the surgery, they warned him that if he got out of bed to leave the hospital, the aneurysm would rupture and he would drop dead on the floor before he ever had a chance to get out the hospital door. As Mellilo dressed and signed out and headed for the exit, doctors and nurses followed him, expecting him to keel over any moment. Mellilo resumed his practice and, without any treatment of the aneurysm, was perfectly well.

"Prepare for Death"

On the other hand, Padre Pio seemed to know when death was near, even in the case of an apparently healthy person. For example, in May 1962, Padre Teofilo of Pozzo della Chiana, a former minister provincial from Florence, visited San Giovanni Rotondo in the midst of a preaching mission. Padre Pio warned him about overtaxing his strength. An active, dynamic man, Padre Teofilo assured him that he was in the peak of health and had no trouble maintaining his busy schedule. Before he left, Padre Teofilo and Padre Pio embraced. Padre Teofilo asked prayers for a sick woman and Padre Pio replied, "That's enough. Instead, think about your life. It's hanging by a thread of parsley." Padre Teofilo thought that Padre Pio was joking, but, four months later, he became ill and was taken to a hospital in Florence, where it was determined that he had cancer of the stomach. Days later, he was dead at the age of fifty-two.[24]

In the 1960s, Fra Dionisio of Cervinara was very ill with kidney disease, and expected to die, but Padre Pio prophesied that he would live to be ordained. He did, and came to San Giovanni to celebrate his first Mass. After several days, he was about to return to Venice for further studies. Padre Eusebio and Padre Michele Placentino were accompanying Padre Pio to his room, when Padre Dionisio came up and said, "Spiritual Father, I came to greet you, because tomorrow I'm leaving."

"And where do you have to go?" asked Padre Pio.

"I'm going to Venice, to continue my studies."

Padre Pio shocked everybody by saying, "Rather than Venice and studies, prepare for death, so that when it comes ... "

Padre Eusebio interrupted: "Spiritual Father, is this the way you talk to people who are leaving?"

Padre Pio shrugged and said sadly, "There's nothing I can do."

Padre Dionisio, who seemed well, kissed Padre Pio's hand. The very next day he was taken to the hospital with signs of acute kidney failure. After a couple of weeks, however, he seemed on the mend and was scheduled to be released the next day. Padre Eusebio told Padre Pio, "Spiritual Father, thank goodness you were mistaken. Sometimes even the saints make mistakes." Padre Pio, however, repeated his prophecy of doom. The next day, Padre Dionisio, aged twenty-six, was found dead in bed.[25]

Sometimes, when crowds were especially large, the superiors at the monastery requested *carabinieri* — the state police — to keep order. Renzo Allegri, a journalist who authored dozens of books, including several on Padre Pio, claimed that on one such occasion, while removing his vestments after saying Mass, Padre Pio turned, smiling, to one of the state troopers and said, "After I've made my thanksgiving, come to my room. I need to speak to you." When the officer went to Padre Pio's room, he was horrified when the priest told him, "Listen, son, in eight days, at the most, you will die and go to the Eternal Home."

"But, Father, I am well."

"Don't worry about it," assured Padre Pio. "In eight days you will be better than you are now. What is this life? Son, we're on a train. Take a leave of absence and go and take care of everything at home."

"May I tell others what you told me?"

"For now, no. Speak of it only when you go home."

Eight days later, the officer was dead.[26]

Allegri, however, provides neither his source, the name of the officer, the date of the incident, nor, most important, the cause of his death.

"For the Good of My Soul"

Padre Pio did not believe that the relief of suffering was always God's will. He did not agree with those who insist that God desires all Christians to have health, material prosperity, or even spiritual consolation at all times. Although he founded a hospital "for the relief of suffering" and prayed for and obtained material — and even financial — blessings, he did not believe that people had a right to health and prosperity or that the absence of these blessings was a result of their lack of faith or God's chastisement. Stressing the value of redemptive suffering, Padre Pio often told people to accept their pain and sorrow and offer their trouble to God so that it could be joined to the sufferings of Christ for the redemption of souls.

Andre and Graziella Mandato had a friend, Salvatore Sciogliuzzi, from northern Italy, who lost his sight in middle age. He had been a government employee but could no longer work at his job. With a wife and several children to support, he was in dire financial circumstances. The disability pension for which he had applied had not yet been approved. Depressed about both his disability and his financial state, he went to Padre Pio, who told him, "Trust in God, and in a little while, everything will work out."

Sciogliuzzi left San Giovanni in good spirits. Although he did not regain his vision, he soon obtained his pension and was situated comfortably. Every year after that he went back to San Giovanni Rotondo and never embarked on any major undertaking without asking Padre Pio's counsel.

One day Sciogliuzzi's youngest son asked, "Why don't you ask Padre Pio to give you your sight?"

"Why don't you ask him?" suggested the father.

When, on their next trip to San Giovanni, the son asked Padre Pio, the priest told him, "Ask your father."

In confusion, the boy returned to his father, who kissed him and said, "Padre Pio told me when I first came to him that any time I want to ask for the grace, the grace is there. But, when I thought of how much Jesus suffered for us, I said to Jesus, 'I give up my sight for your glory.'"

Sciogliuzzi came to experience a remarkable providence one day at San Giovanni. Going to the hotel room of his friend Andre Mandato, he asked, "What does Padre Pio look like? Is he a big, heavy man with a gray beard?" Mandato said that he was. Sciogliuzzi became quite agitated and told his friend that, earlier that day, he had been in the group awaiting Padre Pio's appearance in the sacristy. He heard slow, heavy steps, and then he saw clearly "this monk with a gray beard, a stout, heavy man, and he smiled at me, and then I became blind again."[27]

In 1997, in an interview with a reporter from an Italian magazine, Pietro Cugino spoke about a conversation he had with Padre Pio sometime between 1931 and 1933 (when Padre Pio was forbidden contact with the public). Padre Pio remarked to Cugino, who lived in the monastery, "How can you say that you are content?" When Cugino assured him that he was happy, Padre Pio responded, "You're content even in this condition?" When Cugino said he was, Padre Pio asked if he wanted his sight back. It was then that the blind man replied, "If to see is useful for the good of my soul, then may the Lord restore my sight. But if it is harmful to my spiritual salvation, then I prefer to remain blind." Padre Pio was astounded and remarked to a doctor friend, "Pietruccio prefers not to see. I truly cannot conceive of a blind person being contented." Cugino commented to the interviewer, "From then on, speaking with his devotees, he did not fail to comment how marvelous was the fact that I had refused to have my sight restored."[28]

One wonders whether Cugino or Sciogliuzzi could really have gotten eyesight had they told Padre Pio that they wanted it. Perhaps Padre Pio was able to interpret God's purpose in their affliction so effectively that each willingly embraced his handicap when he became convinced that it was necessary in God's redemptive plan.

Thousands of people sought healing from Padre Pio. Some were healed, but most were not, at least physically. However, many whose physical condition remained unchanged experienced an inward healing. An embittered paralytic went to Padre Pio and left, commenting, "It does not matter that Padre Pio has not willed to … cure me.… Something was changing in me and I felt [an urge] to come back to God and [receive] Holy Communion."[29]

"Don't Thank Me, Thank God"

Padre Eusebio asked Padre Pio one day, "Have you ever worked a miracle?"

"Well, I think so," he replied, and told about visiting a sick woman who begged him to bring her something "that had been on my table." While putting his utensils away after dinner, Padre Pio noticed a hard, dried biscuit at the bottom of the drawer. He put it in his pocket and took it to the woman. "When I went to see her the next time, I found her up, and she thanked me because she was cured after having eaten the biscuit!"[30] This was the only miracle he was willing to admit to performing, and, of course, it was with tongue-in-cheek.

Although some people assumed that Padre Pio could obtain favors from heaven without limit and at will, like everybody else, he frequently did not get what he prayed for. The heavens were often silent. He liked to tell the story of a priest "who was asked by a farmer to say Mass for the recovery of a sick cow. Raising his voice at the Memento, he said, 'Lord, let that good man's cow die.' At the end of the Mass the farmer went into the sacristy to complain, but the priest said, 'I know what you are going to say, but don't worry, because, in reality, I prayed for your cow, but … the Lord always does the opposite of what I ask of him!'"[31]

To those who hailed him as a miracle worker, Padre Pio answered that he was just a poor sinner who prayed and encouraged others to do likewise, pointing out that healing comes from God and God alone. When thanked for healing a sick person, he would say, "Don't thank me, thank God."

"Those Dreadful Women"

"Do Not Say No to the Sick!"

On May 19, 1957, Father Dominic Meyer wrote to his cousin Albert, by then archbishop of Milwaukee: "Fr. Pio is busy as ever. He will be seventy on May 25 and he is slowing up a bit in comparison with eight years ago when I first came. He is also human — as some of his visitors don't seem, or *want*, to realize. He does not distribute Holy Communion on Sundays and Feast Days anymore. It used to take an hour and a quarter to an hour and a half. He can't stand on his wounded feet as long anymore. But otherwise his health is fine. His beard is white."[1]

The friary of Our Lady of Grace was no longer in the middle of a barren wilderness, accessible by a donkey path. The monastery and old church were now dwarfed by the new house of worship being constructed beside it and, even more, by the hospital, which towered above them across the street. Thanks to the efforts of the late, lamented Dr. Sanguinetti, the hills around were no longer bare, but covered by a handsome growth of young evergreens. The donkey path was now a paved road, lined with houses and shops. Many of the townspeople now worked at the hospital and in businesses catering to the ever-growing multitude of visitors. Those who still worked the earth were frequently doing so with tractors rather than draft animals. Buses were bringing pilgrims, no longer over bumpy and rutted dirt roads, but over modern highways.

There were twenty-five friars living at the convent. There were many younger priests and brothers, many of whom venerated the aging priest, now in his early seventies, who had borne the stigmata for as long as they could remember. There were others, though, who seemed to resent his celebrity.

Just two years after its opening, the *Casa* was already overcrowded. From the first, Padre Pio had insisted that no one was to be turned away, and when told that the number of beds was inadequate for the number of patients, he urged the administrators, "Add extra beds. Even sacrifice the offices and the library, but do not say no to the sick."[2] When those steps were taken and there was still insufficient room, he insisted, "Nothing can ever be denied the sick. We cannot close the doors in their faces. What will you tell St. Peter: 'I have a good degree in medicine, but I closed the doors of the hospital in the faces of the sick'? ... Enlarge the hospital."[3] And so, on May 5, 1958, Padre Pio, from the office of the hospital chaplain, detonated, by remote control, the charge that commenced the work on the addition, and two months later he blessed the cornerstone of the new wing that would not only contain more beds, but also house a nursing school and provide a residence for the nursing sisters.

"Let Them Put the Madonna on Trial. It Was She Who Healed Me"

Although Padre Pio's health was good at the time of his seventieth birthday, it didn't remain that way long. He was admitted to his hospital shortly afterward for the treatment of painful kidney stones. He also suffered increasingly from "chronic rhinitis" (runny nose, itching, sneezing) and ear infections. Earlier motion pictures showed him, despite the stigmata, walking normally and, entering the dining hall, kneeling and rising smoothly and strongly. His increasing inability to stand for long periods of time seems to have been the result of the arthritis that progressively crippled him after he entered his seventies. More ominously, he began to complain of "general exhaustion," episodes of lightheadedness, and a sensation of pressure in his chest that forced him to stop walking or whatever he was doing.[4] Apparently, he was told that this was a result, not of a heart condition, but of "asthma."

Then, in April 1959, Padre Pio took to his bed with what his doctors diagnosed as bronchial pneumonia. A month later he was still bedridden, unable to celebrate Mass or hear confessions, and now the physicians decided that he had pleurisy. Three times during May, they extracted more than a quart of bloody serum from his pleural cavity without obtaining relief. The father guardian, Padre Carmelo, summoned a team of specialists, who diagnosed a "pleural neoplasm with bloody exudations" and recommended chemotherapy. However, when they told him that he had cancer, Padre Pio burst out laughing and told them that they didn't know what they were talking about. Giuseppe Sala, his regular physician, agreed with him, and insisted that the patient had, not a cancer, but "a pleural inflammation superimposed on a chronic bronchial catarrh," and rejected chemotherapy.

Padre Pio continued to be deathly ill. Every day, by means of a speaker installed in his room, he listened to Mass and spoke a few words to the faithful through a microphone.

On July 1, the new church was consecrated. Informed by his doctors that he could resume some of his activities, Padre Pio dragged himself to the chapel of the *Casa* to celebrate Mass for the patients there. When he finished, he was so weak and in such pain that he had to be admitted to the hospital, where more fluid was removed from his chest. Two days later, he insisted on returning to the friary, declaring that he wanted to die there, and Dr. Sala and the superiors at the convent arranged for the ailing priest to go home on a stretcher.

Another month passed, and on August 5, what is known as the International Pilgrim Statue of Our Lady of Fátima was brought by helicopter to San Giovanni. It had been brought to Italy on tour from its home in Fátima, Portugal, commemorating the celebrated apparition of the Blessed Virgin to three local children in 1917. For a day, the faithful in San Giovanni gathered before it in prayer and devotion. On the afternoon of the sixth, before being taken through the wards of the hospital, the statue was placed in the sacristy of the old church. Carried down to see it on a chair, his eyes filled with tears, Padre Pio leaned forward and kissed the statue, draping a golden rosary around it. Then, breathless and in pain, he was carried back to bed.

The helicopter bearing the statue lifted off from the heliport at the *Casa*, as the crowds yelled, *"Viva! Viva!"* and circled the friary three times in a gesture of farewell to Padre Pio. Seeing the statue airborne, he prayed aloud, "Dear Mother, ever since you came to Italy, I have been laid low with sickness. Now that you're leaving, aren't you going to say even one word to me?"

In the twinkling of an eye, it was reported that Padre Pio felt a "mysterious force" surge through his body. Those with him saw him shudder from head to toe. Then he leaped from his chair, shouting, "I'm healed!" Within two weeks, he had resumed all his duties and did not hesitate to declare that he had been miraculously delivered by the mercy of the Blessed Virgin. When a doctor claimed that the pleurisy had already cleared up and that he was well on his way to recovery at the time, Padre Pio replied, "I know that I was still sick and that I felt extremely bad. I prayed to the Madonna and the Madonna healed me. If people don't want to believe this, then let them put the Madonna on trial. It was she who healed me."[5]

"Padre Pio Is My Dear Patron Saint!"

As he grew older, Padre Pio seemed increasingly dependent on his female disciples, who constantly surrounded him. For decades, probably the most respected was Maria Pyle, who many Sangiovannese now called "Mamma." With the women who lived with her in her pink castle across from the friary, she cut, sewed, and embroidered clothing and vestments, either to send directly to missionaries or to sell to raise funds for them. When asked if she wanted ever to return to America, she responded, "What? Go back to my *Protestant* relations? Never!" A niece recalled her:

She was an immense woman — huge! She had a round, jolly face and lovely hands. My most distinct memory of her is when she lectured me for not eating. She actually accused me of vanity. "You just don't want to get *fat!*" she said. "You know, vanity is a sin!" She served and ate lots of pasta, ricotta, and manicotti. It was a very Italian diet, quite different from anything she'd been used to in America. She believed it was a self-effacement to eat what she did. Was she a saint? I've often thought about it. Her life-style was saintly. She ran a peasant boarding house for women.... I often wondered why she didn't go stir-crazy, around all those peasants! ... Aunt Adelia could be naughty and mischievous. She used to make caustic remarks about people, with a sense of humor, but she was incredibly sweet and generous.[6]

Pyle liked to show visitors pictures of Padre Pio as a young man, and, clasping them to her bosom, exclaim, "And, just think, I knew Padre Pio when he looked like *this!*" She would gush, "How can anyone keep quiet about Padre Pio? I feel as if I am going to burst! I want to shout and tell everyone who this man is!"[7] At times, her enthusiasm seemed a bit excessive. One American visitor was put off by the way she clasped Padre Pio's picture and cried with almost childish glee, "Padre Pio is my dear patron saint!"[8] Perhaps, in reaction to her excess of enthusiasm, her "patron saint" seemed cold and curt to her at times, but he kept her picture in his room, along with those of his parents. Pyle was, after all, and had been for years, his generous benefactor, and she was universally considered a kind, unselfish, and well-meaning woman.

"An Uncomfortable and Embarrassing Situation"

This was not the case with some other female disciples. Padre Amedeo Fabrocini (1907–1985), who became provincial after Padre Agostino, expressed a concern felt by many of Padre Pio's friends and associates: "There were many spiritual daughters who Padre Pio directed. The greater part put his teachings into practice with a more perfect life. One group created an uncomfortable and embarrassing situation with their overbearing and domineering behavior. There were three women in particular in this group: Cleonice Morcaldi, Countess Telfner, and Elvira Serritelli. Each of them insisted that she was the best loved and therefore they became officious and insolent."[9]

He explained: "They even had their designated places in church and they were bullies because they wanted to command. They were deaf to the recommendations of [Padre Pio] to be calm and respectful. They were hostile to the friars and in particular to the Provincial." Some of them seemed to have connections with important people in the Vatican, leading Padre Amedeo to insist, "These three women were mysteriously powerful. As enforcement agents, they succeeded in causing friars to be transferred, if they weren't to their liking."[10] Padre Amedeo furthermore claimed, "There was the conviction that this was a situation that had to be accepted and that perhaps no one would be capable of undoing. If you wanted to be on the good side of Padre Pio, you couldn't complain to him about the privileges he gave to [Morcaldi], and consequently to the group who followed her and served her. Those who believed in Padre Pio had to admit that this was the will of God."[11]

"A Dear Little Soul and Little Daughter"
Cleonice Morcaldi (1904–1987) was a short, round-faced, rather nondescript, unmarried schoolteacher. In addition to laundering Padre Pio's linen, she solicited financial contributions for the hospital and even staged plays and entertainments to raise money. She also kept two dozen notebooks, which she gave to the friars after Padre Pio's death, containing brief replies the priest gave — some verbally, some in writing — on scraps of papers, used envelopes, and holy cards, in response to her questions of all kinds, over a period of many years, on all subjects, including the most personal.

"If Adam had not sinned, would he have gone to paradise?" Morcaldi asked. "Certainly, and without dying," Padre Pio answered. "He would have been transported in body and soul to the paradise of God."[12]

"Was [the Garden of Eden] on earth? And, when Adam fell, where did he go?" she asked. Padre Pio replied: "He remained where he was, but the earth of delights turned into thorns and thistles. While, at first, all creation bowed to him, after sin, it rebelled against him just like he had rebelled against God."[13]

Cleonice: "Why did Jesus say to Mary Magdalen [after his resurrection], 'Don't touch me'?"

Pio: "To make her live by faith."[14]

Cleonice: "When they told me that there's life on other planets, my faith was shaken."

Pio: "So what? Don't you want there to be other beings? Do you think that the omnipotence of God is limited to this little planet?"[15]

Cleonice: "How do I pray for a good death?"

Pio: "'Lord, may I finish my life in a perfect act of love and with sorrow for having offended you.'"[16]

Cleonice: "What is my mother doing in heaven?"

Pio: "Loving, and enjoying herself."[17]

Cleonice: "In heaven, I fear, because of all the angels and saints, I won't be allowed to be alone with Jesus and you in paradise."

Pio: "Up there we will be alone, even in company. No one can impede our communicating with those we desire."[18]

Cleonice: "So many impure thoughts come to me. I fear offending Jesus."

Pio: "Stop these useless fears. Remember that it's not the thought that constitutes the sin, but the consent to such thoughts. Only the free will is capable of good and evil. But when the will groans under the weight of temptation and doesn't desire that which is presented to it, not only is it not sin for you, it is a virtue. Offer this to Jesus.... Don't make me say this anymore. Therefore, stop if you don't want to make me angry, which would be really bad. Live in peace and don't deceive yourself."[19]

Cleonice: "What must I do when I'm sad?"

Pio: "Offer everything to Jesus in Gethsemane."[20]

Morcaldi often called Padre Pio "Mummy" and "Rachelina." She would ask: "Rachelina, how much do you love me?" and Padre Pio would answer: "Without limit."

Cleonice: "Does it displease the Lord if I say that I want to love you like the Heavenly Mamma loves Jesus?"

Pio: "I don't think so."

Cleonice: "What comfort would you prefer: that of an angel or that of a daughter?"

Pio: "I wouldn't know how to choose, but if I chose, I guess I'd prefer [the comfort] of one of my peers."

Cleonice: "When I feel myself full of love for you, is it then that you are with me?"

Pio: "But I am always there."

Cleonice: "When I tell you certain things, I feel these words: 'You are impudent.' Is it you telling me that?"

Pio: "No, little daughter. I think it's the enemy of souls. So, scorn him."

Cleonice: "My heart is full of desires. Must I reveal them all to you?"

Pio: "It's not necessary."[21]

Cleonice: "Is it as a punishment that Jesus continually makes me feel the hee-bie-jeebies?"

Pio: "No, but it is a most loving trial."[22]

Morcaldi continually begged Padre Pio to be with her at night. She had such a fear of ogres and witches that she was afraid to go from one room to another in her own home in the dark. "Tell me, even at night, are you near me?" she asked. He answered, "Always, without interruption." "But why don't I feel your presence?" "Because you were sleeping," he responded.[23]

Cleonice wrote: "Must I fear thieves this evening?"

Padre Pio scribbled back: "Stop it. Be calm. Mummy is always with you. Warmest kisses."[24]

Cleonice: "For about 15 days I've been hearing loud sounds in my stove. Could it be a spirit?"

Pio: "Nonsense."[25]

———

Morcaldi claimed that Padre Pio was God's elect, the "new [John the] Baptist."[26] She gushed, "Could it truly be ... that Jesus himself came to earth, dressed as a Franciscan?" Even the saints "didn't communicate this joy, this fire, and this happiness" that she experienced from the person and presence of Padre Pio. She would look in the direction of the convent and sigh, "Oh, I'd like to live forever beside the Padre [who is] Jesus visible!"[27] She proclaimed, "Only you, besides God, can I call my father; only you, besides the Virgin, can I call my mummy! ... After nineteen centuries, the earth feels once more the odor of Christ ... and says, 'Jesus has returned among us.'"[28]

Constantly craving Padre Pio's assurance that he loved her better than anybody else, Morcaldi asked, "Does Rachelina love me like he loved ... that soul in Foggia to whom he wrote all those letters?" Padre Pio responded, "More, more."[29] He often called her "Little daughter, most beloved in the heart of Mummy." She seemed perpetually distraught, and Padre Pio often used saccharine language to calm her, as if she were a little child. "Mummy ... lives for his little daughter and for God," he assured her. "Therefore calm yourself and live serenely.... She ... sends you a torrent of hugs and ardent kisses in the sweet Lord."[30] On the scraps of paper she gave him, he wrote, from time to time, such things as "Your mummy ... wants you to know that she is all yours and her affection is unchangeable for you and will never be less."[31] Cleonice claimed that he called her "my goddess, my little queen, my delight."[32]

Nevertheless, in one of her letters, Morcaldi wrote: "Rachelina sends me kisses in writing, but never one in reality." "You're bad!"[33] was his response to the troubled woman he called "a dear little soul and little daughter."[34]

"Capable of Almost any Insane Act"

While Cleonice Morcaldi and her close friends, Countess Telfner and Tina Belloni, who claimed for themselves the right to sit on the first row in church when Padre Pio was celebrating Mass, could be pathologically possessive of Padre Pio, the Serritelli sisters, Elvira and Angela, could be furiously aggressive. "Bitter and venomous," "aggressive, overbearing, and dangerous," and "hysterical, deranged, mentally ill" were adjectives frequently used to describe these unmarried schoolteachers. Elvira Serritelli (1890–1964), who was in charge of preparing fresh flowers to decorate the church, was the more obnoxious of the two. Padre Alberto D'Apolito described how she would loiter around the confessionals, timing how long Padre Pio took with each penitent. Insisting that he spent more time with Morcaldi, Nina Campanile, the Countess, and Belloni than he did with her, "she began a war of insults and aggression" against them. Cleonice was so afraid of Elvira and Angela that, when they swept into church, she would hide in a corner.[35] Padre Alberto recalled a time when he sat beside Padre Pio, while he was praying in the choir, overlooking the altar area. "Elvira, down there, on the steps of the altar, with a vase of flowers in her hands, raised her gaze towards Padre Pio" who, "from time to time, in the fervor of prayer, opened his eyes to gaze at the tabernacle." She imagined that he was gazing at the cleaning ladies, rather than at her. Imagining that Padre Pio preferred the cleaning ladies to her, Elvira "became unnerved, shaking and trembling with rage. At that moment she would have been capable of almost any insane act."

Maria Pennini, another schoolteacher, described Elvira Serritelli as "a very terrible, vindictive woman" who "went into rages and couldn't bear for anyone else to speak with Padre Pio." Pennini recalled a tantrum Elvira threw in Maria Pyle's home because Padre Pio had spoken to Pennini's sister Marietta. "She went on a rampage, not listening to the words of those who ... wanted to calm her." Pyle snapped, "You and your sister are crazy!" To calm Elvira, Padre Pio permitted her to patch the elbow of his habit in front of everybody.[36]

Pio's Greatest Cross

As he aged, Padre Pio lacked the energy to repel the aggressions of the "Pious Women." The other friars were appalled as these women strong-armed their way into Padre Pio's presence, demanding various blessings and favors, and insisted on long audiences in the guest room, where they drove Padre Pio almost to tears with their mindless and petty chatter. "These women had absolutely nothing important to say," Father Joseph Pius recalled. "There was nothing spiritual, just tiresome, silly things." When asked why he allowed these strident groupies to monopolize so much of his time, Padre Pio replied to the effect that they would give him no peace unless he gave in. However, Padre Pio also believed that they were among those whom God had entrusted him to direct.

Joan Milazzo, an American, fled in horror and disgust after seeing Padre Pio interrupted by the petty importunities of the "Pious Women," even while he was hearing confession. She encountered Padre Pio's brother Michele on the plaza in front of the church. He told her, "Do you know what my brother's greatest cross is? Do you think it's the stigmata? It's not. It's those dreadful women!"[37]

Joseph Peterson had a differing view of the "Pious Women." "As for the 'Holy Women,'" he said shortly before his death, "I've always had a soft spot in my heart for them. They were right from the town. They knew Padre Pio as young girls. They confessed every ten days. They felt that pilgrims were keeping them from their priest. They especially resented people who came only for the day or just stayed overnight. Once you were there a few days, it was different. They invited you into their homes. They did a lot of good for those who were sick and alone.... They were bossy, but they were good women."

Not everyone agreed, however. There were concerns that the women were badgering Padre Pio to request transfer to the *Casa*, where he would set up a new "religious family."[38] There was also concern about the mail, which was coming in ever-increasing volume and for which lay help was required. As a result, some of the "Pious Women" — Morcaldi in particular — were handling the mail, opening letters addressed to Padre Pio, which often contained money or intimate personal information. Sometimes confidential matters were leaked to the media. Padre Carmelo, whose tenure as father superior at San Giovanni ended in 1959, warned Padre Pio that throughout the region people were saying that he allowed himself to be bossed by the "Pious Women," only to have Padre Pio object: "These are people who have been around me for forty years, and therefore I try to please them, but it's not at all true that I let them boss me around!"[39] Some of the friars appealed to Padre Pio's best friend and mentor, Padre Agostino, asking him to warn about the dangers these women posed by their presence and by the importance he gave them. Agostino replied, "From the beginning I made him aware of this, but I saw his great resistance and I gave up, saying to myself, 'The right time will come.'"[40]

The Affair of the Tapes

The Kiss

On May 2, 1960, Padre Amedeo, the provincial, was visiting his family in San Giovanni Rotondo when Padre Emilio D'Amato, the superior of the convent, and Padre Giustino Gaballo appeared, insisting that they had urgent need for a meeting with him. When the three men retired to a room to confer in private, Padre Giustino, who had been appointed a personal assistant to Padre Pio since his illness the year before and lived in the room adjoining his, revealed that he had recorded a conversation between Padre Pio and one of the "Pious Women" in the friary guest room, and, in the words of Padre Amedeo, "with sorrowful surprise, learned of serious matters." He had come to ask Padre Amedeo to authorize him to make further tapes.

When Padre Amedeo asked what precisely the tape had revealed, Padres Emilio and Giustino were silent. "For love of God, tell me! I have a right to know! Why, then, did you come to me?"

"It's the matter of a kiss," replied Padre Emilio.

"A kiss!" exclaimed the provincial. "But of what kind?"

The father guardian merely shrugged his shoulders, and Padre Giustino declared, "We repeat that we came for you to authorize us to continue to tape the confidential conversations of Padre Pio. It's absolutely necessary."

When Padre Amedeo demurred, Padre Giustino grandiosely pontificated, "Then, know for certain that, because Padre Pio's name is renowned everywhere, extremely gave consequences will come from your failure to give your authorization, and you will bear tremendous responsibility before the Order, the Church, and the world."[1]

When those who had known Padre Pio were interviewed during the process for his beatification, Padre Giustino Gaballo of Lecce (1919–2003), a late vocation and a former teacher, was just about the only one who spoke of him in a negative way. He was, it turned out, in the habit of going into Padre Pio's room, when he wasn't there, and rifling through his trash basket to retrieve Cleonice Morcaldi's notes, which were so cloying and worshipful that they read like love letters. These led him to suspect the worst. When, however, in the 1970s, he was asked why he had decided to spy on him, Padre Giustino gave this reason: "Padre Pio was plotting in his house against the brothers of the convent and they defended themselves with the recordings."[2] Padre Giustino was convinced that Padre Pio wielded power within the Capuchin order, and, at the bidding of the women by whom he was controlled, was about to get Padre Emilio removed as superior of the San Giovanni convent and Padre Amedeo as provincial, and other friars whom he disliked transferred to other friaries. It is not clear what grievance Padre Pio supposedly had against these people. Padres Amedeo and Emilio were both relatively new to their positions and had replaced old friends. Perhaps there had been some sort of disagreement or misunderstanding.

Padre Eusebio wrote in his memoirs that, because of the influence of the "Pious Women," some of the friars were referring to Padre Pio as "Rasputin."[3] Padre Giustino claimed that the women were boasting, "The atomic bomb is going to fall on the convent of San Giovanni Rotondo," and "The broom will sweep away all friars of the convent."[4] Something had to be done, he was convinced, to show the extent of Padre Pio's "diabolical possession" by the "Pious Women."[5] Padre Giustino maintained that some of the women even went to a witch, seeking power to control Padre Pio: "On one occasion one of these women confided to me that she had gone to the witch to bind Padre Pio to herself and asked me how to make reparation for the evil she had done."[6]

Padre Giustino made regular trips, after dinner, to confer with a nearby seer named Sister Lucina, whom he considered a saint. She claimed to have revelations that Padre Pio was "in constant peril of damnation" because he was having sex with women. Convinced that Padre Pio was a fraud and a sinful man, Padre Giustino believed that the revered priest was actually "possessed by the devil."[7]

Padre Giustino seems to have been, at the very least, a peculiar man. A fellow priest described him as "very serious and rigorous, but sick on the subject of sex."[8] He saw "shadows and deficiencies wherever he looked." Moreover, he would "single out and accuse his companions of consenting to impure thoughts and having committed acts against purity."[9] It was said that he used to prowl around the friary at night, convinced that he would discover friars engaged in unholy activity. One night, in 1960, Fra Celestino Di Muro passed Padre Pio's room, and, to his amazement, saw that Padre Giustino and a Fra Masseo had sneaked in while the stigmatized priest lay sound asleep. With "a little book" and Signs of the Cross, the two were trying to perform an exorcism on Padre Pio.[10]

After he made his tape, Padre Giustino invited Padre Crispino Di Flumeri, assistant to the minister provincial, to listen. Crispino later recalled that the tape was supposed to record a conversation between Padre Pio and Cleonice Morcaldi — and perhaps other women — "that, in the opinion of Padre Giustino gravely compromised the moral character of Padre Pio of Pietrelcina." However, "In truth the recording was unclear and perhaps a copy, and even if the voice of Padre Pio could be made out, the phrases and sounds were scarcely intelligible, and, to be able to understand them, the interpretation of Padre Giustino was necessary, who identified and explained phrases and sounds of 'grave immoral actions' such as kisses, and phrases like this: 'Here is my pleasure,' expressed almost in dialect. For me the entire tape was almost indecipherable. Listening to the tape didn't convince me at all of the theory supported by Padre Giustino. Rather, I was horrified at the unthinkable and unacceptable reality that I was facing: the voice of Padre Pio had been recorded to catch him doing wrong."[11]

Padre Giustino was determined to inform the pope: "When I listened to the first recording, it seemed alarming to me because of what it indicated about Padre Pio and the preeminent woman [Morcaldi]…. I made known to the Pope through Don Terenzi that I possessed a document that would throw a little light on the whole plot."[12] Don Umberto Terenzi (1900–1974), an influential priest who ran the Sanctuary of Divine Love in Rome and was a friend of Padre Giustino, took the recording to the Vatican a few days later.

"Look What My Brothers Are Doing!"

A few weeks after his meeting with Fathers Giustino and Emilio, Padre Amedeo was summoned to Rome for an urgent meeting with the minister general of the Capuchins, Father Clement Neubauer of Milwaukee. The minister general, without providing details, informed Padre Amedeo that he was hereby being placed under the authority of Don Terenzi and was consequently to report to him.

Terenzi, who was highly respected by the Vatican for his work with the poor and disadvantaged, was a small man with a round face, dark hair, and heavy eyebrows. Evidently, he was no fan of Padre Pio. It was alleged that, sometime earlier, heavily in debt, Terenzi had asked Padre Pio for aid for his sanctuary. Ever since the Vatican had allowed him control over the *Casa*, people and institutions had been asking Padre Pio for financial assistance: so much money was pouring in from everywhere for the hospital that, surely, they thought, it should have posed no hardship for Padre Pio to give or lend some to worthy causes. Even some officials of the Capuchin order, which had lost money through bad investments, asked him for money. The bishop of Padua, who was a Capuchin, reportedly asked Padre Pio to help him build an orphanage, but he refused to give money specifically designated for the *Casa* for other purposes, however worthy, because he believed that this would be a breach of the donor's trust — that it would be unethical to take funds donated for the hospital and divert them elsewhere.

Terenzi, however, later insisted that his negative attitude toward Padre Pio was the result of the tape which Padre Giustino sent him. When Padre Amedeo came to see him, Terenzi asked him to listen with him to the "scandalous tape." "Holding my ear very close to the device, I heard almost nothing of the conversations of Padre Pio with the Pious Women," Padre Amedeo recounted. "The recorded voice was so faint that I could pick up only certain words, never a complete sentence. There was a certain point when Don Terenzi … said, 'Pay attention! Here you will hear the sound of a kiss.' But I didn't hear this kiss at all. I don't know how Monsignor Terenzi was able to affirm that, at that point in the tape, a kiss was being heard."[13]

Terenzi played back the tape several times, but Padre Amedeo still could not make out a kiss, or anything else. Nevertheless, Terenzi declared, "Grave things, dear Father, sad things….A thorn for the Church! What delusion and what scandal for countless souls, and even for me, who had affection for him. But it's necessary to face this ugly business at once, with severe, effective sanction." Speaking of Padre Raffaele D'Addario, who, because of Padre Agostino's ill health, was frequently hearing Padre Pio's confessions, Terenzi threatened, "He'll get what he deserves. He'll be exiled to Africa!"[14]

Terenzi, disclosing that he was expressing the decision of the Holy Office, told Padre Amedeo, "Do not prohibit Padre Giustino and his collaborators from recording the private conversations of Padre Pio." He had a trusted associate who would collect the tapes; if he was not available, Padre Giustino would take the tapes to Rome himself. In his absence, Padre Amedeo would have to do this.[15] The entire business was to be secret. Padre Amedeo was not to inform even his superior, the minister general, Father Clement. In fact, shortly afterward, Padre Amedeo had to meet with Clement, who noticed that he was deeply distraught. When the minister general asked what was wrong, Padre Amedeo had to tell him that he was forbidden by a higher authority to tell him. Shortly afterward, Terenzi informed Clement about the tapes.

Two microphones were planted, one in Padre Pio's cell, the other in the guest room, where he sometimes had conferences with the "Pious Women." Don Attilio Negriscolo, a diocesan priest from Padua, insisted that there was a third recorder, in the confessional, but Padre Amedeo denied this. (Had this been true, it would have been a case of sacrilege.) Between October 29, 1960, and March 19, 1961, twenty-three tapes were made, recording Padre Pio's conversations, not only with the "Pious Women," but with the administrator of the *Casa*.

Although the Holy Office and its representatives insisted on secrecy, several friars discovered what was happening. One day Padre Pellegrino was taken by another priest to a room adjoining the visitor's parlor, where Padre Pio would sit as he talked to visitors. Pellegrino was shown a crack in the top part of the wall. "Look, here's a microphone," the other priest indicated. Pellegrino recalled, "Without hesitation, I struck my fist against the wall, found it empty, and finally told them that the recorder was certainly in a little compartment in the wall, situated under the little window."[16]

Padre Eusebio went to see Padre Pio one day in his room. "Look here, son," Padre Pio said, raising the pillow of his bed and showing him a piece of wire. It came through the wall that separated his room from Padre Giustino's. "They put a microphone to spy on me and I cut it myself with this knife," he said, showing Padre Eusebio a ball-bearing knife, with the main blade blackened by smoke and teeth dented by contact with the electrical wire. Padre Pio said that he discovered that the wire was connected to a recorder that turned on automatically whenever the light switch was flipped on. He had also discovered that the guest room was similarly bugged. When his friend Don Giuseppe Orlando came to see him, Padre Pio showed him the recorder and lamented, "Look what my brothers are doing!" When Orlando answered lamely, with Christ's words on the cross, "They do not know what they do," Padre Pio retorted, "They know what they're doing!"[17]

Most of the tapes were apparently inaudible; the ones that were audible recorded mundane and innocuous business. (In one of them, Padre Pio made some unflattering remarks about a particular cardinal.) Those who examined them have claimed that no sacramental confessions were recorded. Padre Giustino and Don Terenzi were, however, able to convince some Vatican officials that the recordings picked up what sounded like loud kisses.

Most of those who knew Padre Pio laughed at the suggestion that he was having an affair with Cleonice Morcaldi in the guest room, where the priest conversed with visitors from the secular world through a window while seated in a closetlike space behind a wall. The thought of either one, both stout, aging, and out of shape, wriggling through the narrow window for an amorous assignation was hilarious. Moreover, the sound of kissing could be readily and innocently explained. Padre Eusebio wrote, "If perhaps the listeners could have remotely imagined that those intimate conversations between Padre Pio and the Pious Women took place at a distance, separated by a wall almost like the Berlin Wall — a meter thick! — and the part of the body incriminated was the wound on the hands, then the judges and interpreters would certainly have been more benevolent. It was well known that kissing Padre Pio's hand was the order of the day and under the eyes of everyone and on the part of everyone."[18]

The Pope Is Informed of the Tapes

The tapes were passed on to Monsignor Pietro Parente (1891–1986), the former archbishop of Perugia and one of Italy's most respected theologians, whom Pope

John XXIII recently had appointed to the Holy Office. Parente, while admitting that the tapes were poorly recorded and hard to decipher, commented that "these conversations show that Padre Pio loses precious time listening to and participating in banal chatter while people wait [to make their confessions]." Worse, despite the faintness of the recordings, he heard Morcaldi say, "I feel all hot" and Padre Pio say, "Here is my glove." Although he had no proof of any real wrongdoing, he observed, "One has the sensation of being confronted with verbal relations and actions that are a scandal to every honest soul."[19]

On June 25, 1960, Pope John XXIII wrote in his journal:

> Extremely serious information about Padre Pio and San Giovanni Rotondo from Monsignor Parente this morning. Thanks to the Lord's grace I feel calm and almost indifferent, in dealing with a troubling religious mania that is, however, nearing a providential resolution. I am sorry about Padre Pio, who does have a soul to save, and for whom I pray intensely.... The discovery by means of tapes, if what they imply is true, of his intimate and improper relations with the women who make up the impenetrable praetorian guard around his person, point to a terrible calamity of souls, a calamity diabolically capable of discrediting the Holy Church in the world, and here in Italy especially.[20]

Padre Pio had been plunged into "terrible grief" on the death of "the beautiful little" Pope Pius XII in October 1958, but was comforted when he had a vision of him in his heavenly home.[21] He had been pleased, however, when the Patriarch of Venice Angelo Roncalli had been elected as John XXIII. The new pope knew about Padre Pio, and, up to that time, his impression had been favorable. He first had learned about Padre Pio while he was serving as apostolic nuncio to France in the 1940s, from none other than Emmanuele Brunatto (who seemed to know everybody). Having heard his enthusiastic descriptions of the Capuchin's sanctity, in February 1947, the future pope wrote to his friend Andrea Cesarano, archbishop of Manfredonia, "I'd be pleased to hear what his bishop thinks of him," and Cesarano replied:

> I know Padre Pio well. He's a Capuchin who resides in the Convent of San Giovanni Rotondo, in this archdiocese. Before I came to Manfredonia, popular fanaticism was so extreme as to provoke severe measures on the part of the Holy Office. It was necessary.
>
> I saw him for the first time in 1933 and he lived in his convent as a true recluse. He was prohibited every contact, even by letter, with the outside world. My impression was very good. I found him calm, serene, cheerful, fully

submissive to the orders he received. He was even prohibited from celebrating Mass in church, but only in the private oratory of the convent.

They say that he has the stigmata, and in fact always wears gloves. It's not for me to make a judgment on his sanctity, miracles, prophecies, etc. However, I can't deny that he is a man of prayer, of profound piety and solid virtue.... Since my first report in 1933, Padre Pio was again authorized to confess, first men, then women, only in the morning and to celebrate [Mass] in church. I am certain, even now, that he is regarded by everyone as a saint, and the spiritual good that proceeds from him is immense. Obstinate sinners are converted, prominent personalities return edified and moved, all leave him comforted and reconciled to the Lord. For this there are eyewitnesses, and through my continuing contacts in that Convent, I can attest, aside from all the supernatural attributes, that he is a man of exceptional virtue, and that his hidden apostolate is a veritable source of fruitful spiritual life for souls. What is important is that everything now proceed there with order, regularity, and edification for the many faithful, without fanaticism and without exaggeration.[22]

Pope John never met Padre Pio. At the time he learned of the tapes, he wrote, "I avoided going [to San Giovanni Rotondo] twice on the occasion of my two visits to Manfredonia, so that I never knew or was in any way in personal contact with Padre Pio, nor do I remember having taken the occasion to speak or express interest in him with anyone [except Cesarano], while always deploring the mythomania created around his name."[23]

Pope John had always taken a dim view of the popular religion of southern Italy, deploring "the cheap altars where male and female saints are worshiped" and where "the ignorant devotion of the faithful is stirred up to exploit their faith and their money."[24] He worried about the mixture of superstition with true piety at San Giovanni, which was a "benefit for many naive people," but also "terribly complicated by commercialism ... at the expense of true charity ... by the Capuchin Fathers of that place who own nothing but possess everything."[25]

When an Italian magazine ran an article claiming that Padre Pio had prophesied to Cardinal Roncalli that he would become pope, and that the pope had sent him his blessing, Pope John angrily dispatched a message to Archbishop Cesarano: "What was reported is completely invented. I never had any relations with Padre Pio, nor have I ever seen him or written him, nor has it ever passed through my mind to send benedictions nor has anyone asked me to do so, either directly or indirectly, either before or after the conclave, nor ever." Cesarano assured the pope that Padre Pio was "a religious of great virtue and great wisdom, a priest tireless in doing good," and would never have made such claims.[26]

Concerns About Financial Mismanagement

Cesarano, however, was not without his concerns, not about Padre Pio, but about the people around him: "Who are the people who get this money? Where does it go? How is it spent? How is it used?"[27] Padre Bonaventura of Pavullo, the assistant to the Capuchin minister general, believed that Padre Pio was "upright, simple, and soft," but that there were "certain lay people" who were "interfering unduly" in his life and "in the affairs of the convent," and that Padre Pio naively "supported and defended … those who were for him only affectionate children and faithful collaborators."[28]

There was concern about mismanagement at the *Casa*. Padre Raffaele D'Addario, in a memorandum written "for the sake of history," recounted that Carlo Kiswarday, the last of the original hospital directors, had, shortly before his death, confided to him that things were not going well at the *Casa* and that he was aware of certain "irregularities." Padre Raffaele wrote that, after the deaths of Sanguinetti and Sanvico, the "relationship of mutual trust" between the friary and the hospital administrators had degenerated into an atmosphere of suspicion and distrust. Cleonice Morcaldi, who had been for years a tireless fundraiser for the *Casa* and had produced plays and pageants to raise money, was in charge of handling donations to the hospital that were sent by mail. Some of the Capuchins complained that contrary to the intentions of the donors some of the offerings intended for the friary were instead diverted to the hospital. On the other hand, hospital administrators charged that funds intended for the *Casa*, in care of Padre Pio, did not reach their intended destinations.

Indigestible Sweetmeats

There were prominent church leaders in Italy who disapproved, not so much of Padre Pio himself, but what they perceived to be a cult that was springing up around him. Bishop Girolamo Bortignan (1905–1992) of Padua wanted an investigation of the activities around Padre Pio. Although he insisted that he "had nothing against Padre Pio personally," his grievance concerned the "irregularities" in his own diocese relating to Padre Pio's spiritual children and prayer groups.[29] For example, there were several fanatical priests who allegedly placed Padre Pio's photograph in front of the tabernacle where the Sacred Host was reserved — as if he were Christ.

Albino Luciani (1912–1978), later Pope John Paul I, then bishop of Vittorio Veneto, in his diocesan bulletin of February 4, 1960, wrote that Padre Pio's ministry was like "an indigestible dessert" and was concerned that the stigmatized priest appealed to people with an "exaggerated craving for the supernatural and unusual." He went on to say that "the faithful need solid bread (the Mass, catechism, the Holy Sacraments) to nourish them, not chocolates, pastries, and sweetmeats that fill them up [and fail to nourish them]."[30] Among the "indigestible sweetmeats" were pilgrimages and organized bus tours, and Luciani forbade his priests to lead or participate in pilgrimages to San Giovanni. The existing prayer groups in his diocese were allowed to continue, but no new ones were to be created.

"God's Banker"

Another problem related to what was called "The Giuffrè Scandal." A former bank clerk in northern Italy, Giovan Battista Giuffrè, known as "God's Banker," starting in the early 1950s, encouraged people and institutions to invest in his bank, promising interest between 70 and 100 percent. He was able to make payments for a while, not from returns from the investment of the monies received, but from the funds of new investors. Giuffrè invited Padre Pio to invest hospital funds in his bank, promising 90 percent interest. But, without need of supernatural illumination, Padre Pio commented, "Ninety percent interest! There's something fishy here!" He refused to allow any of the money of the *Casa* to go to "God's Banker." The Capuchin order, however, was not so prudent and invested heavily in Giuffrè's bank; and when, inevitably, it collapsed in the summer of 1958, the order was left deeply in debt. It was noised about that the Capuchin minister general, Father Clement Neubauer, was angry because Padre Pio refused to use money donated to the hospital to bail out their order.

It was said that Father Clement denounced Padre Pio to the pope as "a poor administrator ... immoral ... disobedient ... rebellious." This rumor, however, was completely untrue. Many Italian religious distrusted the cold, phlegmatic, undemonstrative American minister general, whom they nicknamed "Padre Vedremo," because of his tendency to mull over issues rather than take forceful stands, stroking his long white beard and muttering, "We'll see" (*Vedremo*). In fact, according to Father Adrian Holzmeister, a classmate and lifelong friend, Father Clement "completely believed in Padre Pio."[31]

"A Dangerous Situation Emerging"

Father Clement, in fact, asked the pope for an apostolic visit "as soon as possible," to "prevent a big scandal." He was concerned about "a dangerous situation emerging in San Giovanni Rotondo around the venerated person of Padre Pio, and, often in his name." Clement entertained no doubts concerning Padre Pio's character and integrity but was alarmed by the activities of some of the people around him. If he had any misgivings about the priest with the stigmata, they concerned his naive trust in some of those he considered his friends. Among the minister general's concerns were:

- There was no responsible director or manager for the *Casa*. "The lay people" — that is, Morcaldi, the Serritellis, Belloni, and the Countess — refused to allow "any role in the administration of the *Casa* to the religious sisters who were *supposed* to be in charge."

- "The board of administrators is seldom assembled," Clement wrote, "and everything is decided arbitrarily by a certain element [the 'Pious Women,' that is] that profits from the trust of Padre Pio, who cannot actively take charge of the financial or technical aspect of running the hospital."

- The "Pious Women" "receive, open, and answer correspondence directed to Padre Pio, which contains many delicate cases of conscience."

- Offerings were misdirected and not used for their intended purposes, and there was no accounting for the use and distribution of monetary contributions.

- The superiors of the friary were "unable to address issues of discipline, ethics, and finance" because of the interference and opposition of the "Pious Women."

- The "Pious Women" meddled "even in spiritual affairs," such as the prayer groups, and tried to silence or force to leave San Giovanni anyone "who tries to control their way of operation," even opposing and fighting civil and Church authorities.

- It was feared that the "Pious Women" were trying to "take Padre Pio out of the convent and set him up him in the *Casa*."

- The "Pious Women" were creating "an ambience of false mysticism" and "fanaticism," combined with "cleverly disguised commercialism."[32]

In addition, Father Clement wanted to dispel the rumors that the Capuchin order was trying to seize control of money donated to Padre Pio and the hospital in order to pay the debts incurred through the Giuffrè affair.

Consequently, in July 1960, Monsignor Carlo Maccari (1913–1997), a priest who was secretary general of the Diocese of Rome, was sent by the Holy Office as apostolic visitor, "to regulate several aspects of the function of the convent of the Friars Minor Capuchin of Santa Maria delle Grazie in San Giovanni Rotondo and of the *Casa Sollievo della Sofferenza*, as well as all the associations and works dependent on the two above named entities." It was also to "address the person of Padre Pio, his spiritual and moral life, in order to clarify doubts, misunderstandings, and weaknesses."[33]

The Maccari Investigation

The Apostolic Visitor

Monsignor Carlo Maccari, the apostolic visitor, was a native of Parrano, a small town in the northern Italian region of Umbria. Though some described the forty-seven-year-old priest as mild-mannered and soft-spoken, others found him hard, authoritarian, and unyielding.[1] Arriving at San Giovanni on July 30 with his assistant, a priest named Giovanni Barberini, Maccari, "haughty and frowning," complained that he had been met neither by the superior of the convent nor any other priest, but a mere servant, and that he had been forced to wait ten minutes before he saw the provincial.[2] When Padre Amedeo finally appeared, Maccari ordered him to gather the entire community, including Padre Pio. Maccari addressed the community to inform them of the purpose of his visit, after which the provincial began to speak, but Maccari cut him short, snapping, "Remember that it is I who am to be the last to speak — not you!"[3]

Not everyone in the Capuchin community was unhappy to learn of Maccari's arrival. Padre Agostino, appalled by the pandemonium at church, indications of a "diabolical conspiracy" at the *Casa*, and the interference of the "Pious Women" in Padre Pio's ministry, wrote in his diary, "Let's hope that Satan will come away with broken horns and thus the adorable omnipotence of God will be glorified."[4] On the other hand, Padre Raffaele D'Addario felt that Maccari came to San Giovanni Rotondo "totally prejudiced against Padre Pio and the Capuchin priests of San Giovanni."[5]

Maccari stayed at the *Casa* and kept notes for the Holy Office in what he titled "My encounters with X [that is, Padre Pio]." He announced that he would be interviewing every member of the community. Padre Raffaele wrote, however, "He called a pair of religious, and no more. The others waited in vain." Maccari did confer with Don Michele De Nittis, archpriest of San Giovanni Rotondo, who had succeeded Prencipe, and shared some of his predecessor's hostility toward Padre Pio. In fact,

Maccari summoned all the surviving members of the faction that had attempted to undermine Padre Pio more than three decades before. De Nittis was overheard remarking to Don Domenico Palladino, who had been one of Padre Pio's most unyielding detractors, "Well, Dumi, the hour of revenge has come!"[6]

"Running, Trampling, Screaming, Yelling"

Maccari noted that people started gathering in front of the church before two in the morning, waiting for the doors to open at 4:30. When the church opened, crowds of women "burst with savage violence … into the church: running, trampling, screaming, yelling, so as to be able to occupy the first pews on the sides of the high altar so as to be near the Padre, watching over him while he celebrated, and perhaps to be seen with him."[7] There were dozens of local groupies, but he noted three who appeared to dominate the others. Among them, there appeared to be a hierarchy of sorts. At the top was Cleonice Morcaldi, who seemed to consider herself a religious authority, and conducted herself, Maccari thought, as if she were an abbess. He understood that she had control of the distribution of donations between the *Casa* and the friary. Second in command was Tina Belloni, whom Maccari found "unbalanced and hysterical." Third was Countess Telfner, whom he characterized as "pitiful."

Morcaldi, Belloni, and the Countess would force their way through the pandemonium to the front of the church, armed with umbrellas and folding chairs. "During the attack, their prayers, at the top of their voices, intermingled with angry blows, shoves, [and even] laughter.… They sat on the first row and didn't allow anyone else — even priests — to sit there. If outsiders sat there, the women would attack them violently, using hairpins, pinches, and jabs with their elbows. Occasionally, people were shoved to the ground, punched on the side or in the head, grabbed by the arms or legs, and badly bruised." "The Three" and their friends acted as if Padre Pio were Elvis, leaping at him after Mass, kissing his wounded hands and side, and squeezing and caressing him.[8] One of the first things Maccari did was to forbid the three women from claiming the front seats as their exclusive possession. This order proved to have limited effect, because on those occasions when a stranger had the temerity to sit on the front row with "The Three" and their friends, the women would take a seat on either side of the intruder and press against her so closely and make her so uncomfortable that she would leave. One woman whom the "Pious Women" considered an outsider complained to Maccari that one of "The Three" struck her on the head with her pocketbook, telling her to lower her head because she was obstructing the view of Padre Pio.[9]

Moreover, one of the friars pointed out to Maccari that Padre Pio, who, because of his difficulty in breathing in the closed space of the confessional, was allowed to hear confessions without a curtain and with the door open, was often interrupted by women who kissed his hand and even tried to talk with him while people were making their confessions to him. To make things even worse, "The Three" and their friends would hover around the confessional, insisting that they were guarding Padre Pio. It was also clear that they were listening to the confessions and noting the instances when he refused absolution.[10]

In addition, Maccari was appalled at the vendors who peddled crudely painted likenesses of Padre Pio along with fake relics. "This is superstition!" he complained. Padre Raffaele, however, reminded him that this kind of commerce was a problem in sites of religious devotion throughout the world, even in Rome, "under the very eye of the Vatican." Padre Raffaele added that, at San Giovanni, there were also "souls who have renounced the world and who live a true Christian life!"[11]

Maccari noted: "Today there is a real industry that lives and prospers with propaganda about the 'sanctity' of 'the first stigmatized priest.'" He continued: "A clever and unscrupulous propaganda, based on rampant religious ignorance, … knows how to exploit the easy enthusiasm and naive credulity for what it understands to be miraculous," and so, gradually, the "myth of the wonder-working saint" is created, a saint "untouchable, called by God to an 'extraordinary and mysterious mission' … a perfect 'reincarnation of Christ,' admired as 'the sweetest, purest, humblest of human beings.'" Once people start to believe this, "it is inevitable that in the name of the celebrated Capuchin, religious ideas should arise there and spread that [give birth] to superstition and magic, the idolatrous cult of an individual, and certain attitudes that can lead to heretical aberrations."[12]

"His Authority Over Me Is Zero!"

Shortly after Maccari's arrival, he summoned Padre Pio. To his annoyance, the Capuchin replied brusquely, "I don't have time to waste."

Padre Pellegrino, who had overheard the exchange, when the two were alone, warned Padre Pio, "That wasn't right to give an answer like that to an envoy from the pope, to whom you owe allegiance."

Padre Pio shot back, "But I haven't acknowledged him [as such], and therefore, I'm not obligated to speak to him out of obedience, because his authority over me is zero!"[13]

And so, relations between Padre Pio and Maccari got off to a decidedly rocky start. Clearly, neither man liked the other. Padre Pio remarked to a friend, "We've got to be a little wary of this monsignor. He's sick with 'cardinalitis' [that is, he wants to make a name for himself and become a cardinal] and wants to crucify me. Nevertheless, I want him with me in paradise."[14] Even though Padre Pio desired his salvation, he didn't like or trust Maccari. And the distrust was mutual.

"Puppets of Satan"

When he was interviewed by Maccari, Padre Raffaele was alarmed by Maccari's attitude. "From the way he talked, he seemed to want to let me understand that he thought that everything connected with Padre Pio was a show and foolery."[15] Padre Raffaele wrote that Maccari's secretary, Barberini, acted "more like a police detective than a priest," visiting restaurants, bars, and shops, trying, far into the night, to learn what people thought of Padre Pio. Padre Raffaele related that Padre Pio was repelled by Barberini (who later left the priesthood and married) and tried to avoid him whenever possible. In fact, Padre Pio's face seemed to "show signs of nausea."[16] On the other hand, Padre Gerardo Di Flumeri told the author that Padre Pio actually was fond of Barberini and liked to joke with him.

Barberini, however, started going through the correspondence that came to the friary, opening all letters, even confidential ones, checking the offerings to see if the Capuchins were really passing on to the *Casa* those which were so designated. He even followed the mailman as he handed over his sack of letters to the receptionist, and shadowed the receptionist as he distributed the mail. "He thought he would find millions of *Lire* [the Italian currency at the time] and uncover who knows what scandal!" Padre Raffaele wrote. After helping Barberini go through the mail on two mornings, he refused to continue, insisting, "We are religious, not thieves!"[17]

Cleonice Morcaldi was summoned twice by Maccari, made to swear on the Gospel to tell the truth, and interrogated for two hours. When asked if she were aware that Padre Pio had sometimes rebelled against the Holy Mother Church, Cleonice shot back: "The Padre is immolated on the altar. He lives, he prays, he suffers for the Church of God, for the pope, for souls, and the Church perhaps has never had a son more holy and more obedient than Padre Pio!"[18] Her answers were recorded by Barberini, whom she called "the big ape." "Puppets of Satan," she called Maccari and his secretary.

"They forbade us to kiss the hand of the Padre," Morcaldi wrote, and "to get near the confessional, to sit in the first seats, to congregate in the space in front of the convent, to go in the sacristy and on the altar." Barberini, "finely dressed and perfumed, an ape in a priest's clothing, … passed up and down in front of the Padre's confessional while he was hearing confessions; he measured the length of the Mass, often gazing at his elegant watch. Then he went to the Casa Sollievo to fool around with the young women."[19] Every evening, Morcaldi claimed, Padre Pio sent her a little note. In one of them he urged, "My little daughter, keep up your spirit…. There is One who takes care of me. Stay calm … Mummy is always with you."[20]

The third time she was summoned, Morcaldi refused to go. "By now I understood what they wanted me to confess … I refused to go along with them."[21]

Sex Twice a Week!

What Maccari evidently wanted Morcaldi to confess was that she was Padre Pio's mistress! Soon, the visitor confronted Padre Pio with this bombshell of an accusation. Elvira Serritelli, the woman who exploded with rage whenever she thought Padre Pio was paying more attention to someone other than herself, who was so hostile to Cleonice Morcaldi that the latter would run and hide when she approached, had made a deposition to Maccari in which she swore that she had been Padre Pio's lover until the priest forsook her for Cleonice, with whom he now had sex twice a week in the guest room![22] Maccari evidently took the accusation seriously, although Padre Pio vehemently protested that he had been chaste all his life.

Maccari told Padre Pellegrino, when he interviewed him, "Padre Pio was observed with reddened cheeks after he had been with the usual women in the guest room." He observed that "it could be concluded" that this was from the kisses he received. Pellegrino, insisting that Padre Pio's conduct was "honest and pure," explained that his cheeks were red because, while listening, he would rest his elbows on a table with the palms of his hands on his cheeks.[23] It is not certain that Maccari believed this.

The apostolic visitor began asking the people he interviewed explicit questions about the rumored sexual activity of Padre Pio. One of the local women, horrified, complained to Padre Raffaele, "Only a devil from hell would ask the questions that he did!"[24] When questioned about Padre Pio's chastity, Padre Raffaele cut Maccari short, asserting, "All I can say is that if all priests, both secular and religious, prelates included, had the baptismal purity and innocence of Padre Pio, the Church would be truly holy in all her members! I have nothing more to say."[25]

Maccari confronted Padre Pio with Cleonice's "love letters" which Padre Giustino had given him. For certain, she frequently expressed herself in the words and phrases of romantic love, and Padre Pio often assured her of his affection in effusive and cloying language — but more like a parent to an insecure child than a lover. Maccari apparently failed to see things that way and wrote: "The conversation ... was, by far, extremely disconcerting and revealed a moral character that, at least now, had fallen to a very low level." He went on to aver, "Almost never was I able to see on his face an expression of sincere grief and humiliation about the things with which he was charged.... Reticence, mental reservations, lies: these were his weapons to evade my questions.... Often he acknowledged serious observations with a smile, not really arrogant, but as if he wished to say [concerning his correspondence with Cleonice].... And what can I do? What evil is there in it?"

Maccari maintained: "His defense, when confronted with the letters of Cleonice, was wretched. He heard the letters [read] and, when asked if he'd already read them, he answered yes or no, according to whether they pertained to matters that were useless and of little value or whether to matters that were serious and offensive to the Visitor. If a letter contained compromising material, [he would say that] he had read only the first page of that letter and ignored the rest.... General impression: pathetic!"[26]

"What Have I Done?"

Next, Maccari announced to Padre Pio that he had proposed to the Holy See to limit the local women to making their confessions to Padre Pio once a month, instead of every ten or fifteen days, "so as to accommodate a greater number of people who come from afar, so that they can make their confessions more easily." Padre Pio protested, however, declaring, "Don't do this! You can't do it! Why deprive these poor souls of a spiritual guide?" When Maccari went on to tell him that he himself needed a new spiritual guide and confessor — someone other than Padre Agostino — Padre Pio insisted that he had known Padre Agostino "since boyhood" and had confessed to him all his life, even when he was provincial and superior of the monastery."[27]

Like a schoolmaster to a wayward pupil, Maccari lectured Padre Pio: "I am not here to condemn nor to judge severely, but to convey the maternal concern of the Church and its most amiable head [that is, the pope] for a person and a work ... I am here to help you find, with greater clarity, serenity and peace of spirit, so that you can continue to do good to many souls. Speak to me with complete freedom, with absolute confidence, certain that you will find me an attentive, understanding, and fraternal listener."

Padre Pio was distraught and looked as if he were about to burst into tears. "I'm watched constantly, like somebody who has committed who knows how many crimes!" he complained. "Is it possible, under these conditions, to work serenely for the many souls who come in search of light and comfort?" The persecution to which he was subjected, he said, "doesn't stay within the walls of the convent, but, instead, spills out and compromises my spiritual work.... It's whispered — even said openly — that I'm the victim of a spell! They have isolated and prohibited those poor creatures, who are so good and generous, from having contact with me! What have I done, what have they done, to deserve this?" He insisted, "These poor creatures have sacrificed so much to help me in my charitable work, without asking anything." He even maintained that he found nothing wrong with them occupying the front-row seats in church. "They get up early to have this right."[28]

Maccari found Padre Pio unyielding in his defense of the "Pious Women": "He defended them from every accusation and described them as generous souls, completely dedicated to doing good." The visitor concluded, "The fruit of this encounter was ... almost resentful and angry."[29]

When Maccari met with Padre Pio again the next day, he described the atmosphere as "more relaxed, but I wouldn't say cordial." The visitor complained about the inefficiency of the hospital administration. When he criticized the administrator Angelo Battisti, Padre Pio defended him with what Maccari described as "surly rudeness," shouting, "I wouldn't trust anybody like I trust him!"[30] Maccari went on to criticize Padre Pio for building his hospital in a one-horse town like San Giovanni Rotondo, instead of in Rome or in some other large urban center. "A month after you're dead, your hospital will have to close its doors!"[31]

A few days later, Maccari met with Padre Pio again and asked him if there was anything that he would like him to tell the Holy Father. "Say that I would like to be able to perform my ministry in behalf of souls with the necessary liberty," the Capuchin replied. Maccari agreed but said that he wanted to convince him that "certain problems" concerning the altar and confessional were actually an obstacle to his liberty of ministry. On this occasion, he thought Padre Pio seemed less "combative" about the rights of his female disciples and more willing to work things out, as well as agreeable to a reorganization of the legal structure of the hospital. The interview that day ended with both men embracing.[32]

"Even Crazy People Can Have Need of Our Care"

In early September, Maccari conceded in his notes "the immense good that radiates, or seems to radiate from the person of the Padre and his work," although he believed that the reports of miracles mostly resulted from people's expectations that extraordinary things were going to happen. He acknowledged that his conversations with Padre Pio had become "a true torment" for both of them, and was convinced that "he didn't trust me and hid the truth from me."[33]

The first week of the month Maccari interviewed Padre Pio once more, and questioned him about the way in which he guided souls. "My system," Padre Pio explained, "is to take souls as the Lord sends them.... Some have more need for a piece of sweet candy and to be treated with gentleness, to wean them gradually from worldly things." Padre Pio's insistence that God assigned certain souls to his care went over like a lead balloon with Maccari, who skeptically observed that Padre Pio thought he had a "mandate" known only to God and himself that "conferred on him a kind of power so vast as to be on a par with that of the pope."[34]

When Maccari demanded to know why he wasted so much time with "crazy people," Padre Pio answered, "And if they're crazy, is it my fault?"

"But why waste time, so much precious time, with people who are so little deserving of your attention and spiritual concern?"

With "his usual good-natured smile," Padre Pio replied, "Even crazy people can have need of our care to be able to go to paradise."[35]

Maccari then pointed out that some of his female followers had the temerity to "declare themselves enemies of the representative of the pope." By supporting them, Padre Pio was making himself complicit in this revolt against the Holy See. This Padre Pio vehemently denied. "But for love of God, Monsignor," he cried, "if it were my father or my mother, I would condemn them if they did such a wicked thing!"

"I, Too, Have Need of Some People to Love Me"

Maccari then demanded to know why, after he had forbidden him to do so, Padre Pio continued to have contact with "The Three." He denied he had, but Maccari insisted that "the young blind man" — Cugino — was bringing him notes from Morcaldi three times a day.

Maccari said, "You're hiding something. I have documentary proof of this. Tell me, for love of God, tell all to one who comes to save you from a most dark and grievous matter that is a stumbling block to the salvation of who knows how many souls!"

Padre Pio mumbled to himself, "Lord, call me [home] to yourself!"

Maccari pressed on: "I ask you plainly: during my visit, have you ever received letters from Cleonice?"

When Padre Pio denied this, Maccari snapped: "Father, at least spare me and spare yourself the disgrace of lying! I have the original of more than one letter addressed to you from Cleonice, in which she used vulgar expressions and hurled curses at the Visitor and his secretary."

Padre Pio explained that the letters were written during the first days of the visit, before he had been forbidden to correspond with the women. If Maccari had received any since then, they were forgeries, "because there are people so evil as to even forge letters to harm these creatures."

Maccari apparently did not believe him.

A few days later he suggested to Padre Pio that he write "a filial letter" to Pope John, "renewing to him your attitude of absolute obedience and your devout love." According to Maccari, Padre Pio answered, "You put me into a state of agitation and I can't do more.... Write to the pope ... I'm not able." "My hand shakes," he said.

By now, with his chastity, honesty, and integrity under attack, Padre Pio was close to a breakdown. "I can't go on!" he cried out in front of Maccari. "I hardly sleep anymore! I have little appetite! I can hardly eat anything! I feel weak, sad, and alone." Crazy though they might have been, Cleonice and her friends were like children to him. "You've given my heart a wound that's too painful," Padre Pio protested. "I, too, have need of some people who love me — a relative, a sincere friend, with whom I can spend a few minutes, like family.... I don't ask any more.... I fervently pray to the Lord to call me to himself. My spirit is willing, but my flesh, dear Father, is weak.... I'm an old man and I suffer too much!"[36]

"Such a Deficient Instrument"

Maccari wrote, "How is it that a man who has no exceptional natural qualities and who is anything but free of shadows and defects has been able to build a popularity that has few equals in the religious history of our times? How does one explain the irresistible fascination exerted by this man of faith with a weary air about him, with rough manners and a disagreeable voice? [Others described Padre Pio's voice as melodious.] How do we adequately account for the growing fanaticism around his person, the blind faith of the humble and great in his powers, considered almost superhuman?" He could not deny that for years Padre Pio had been an "instrument of mercy, pardon and peace." He could not understand why God would give such a mission to such a "small and petty person.[37]

With the disdain many northern Italians had for those from the south, he described Padre Pio as poorly educated and theologically unsound, due to his "southern origins." He wondered, "If this man does not live inwardly the life of sanctity that the multitude of his 'devoted' attribute to him, why does the loving providence of God permit such deception and concede to such a deficient instrument the ability to accomplish so vast and great a work of good?" He suspected that Padre Pio had "a double personality," playing the role of a saint to the throngs of the credulous faithful, while living the life of a profligate in private. Convinced that his investigation was effectively discrediting Padre Pio with his followers, Maccari reflected, "People very close to Padre Pio and very connected to his work and priestly ministry today feel a wavering of their faith in the sanctity of the Capuchin. It is a revelation immensely painful for them, as if for each of them a pillar of their spiritual life is torn down and the light of an ideal is suddenly destroyed."[38]

Maccari observed, "All this atmosphere of false supernaturalism is none other than the fruit of a colossal and extensive organization controlled by a few spiritual daughters, aided and blindly supported by other men and women," and that the real person of Padre Pio was "completely obscured by a machine that becomes increasingly mastodonic and spreads the fame of his 'sanctity' and 'miracles' throughout all the world."[39] Maccari concluded, "The visit confirmed certain painful doubts about Padre Pio's spirit and conduct, especially in terms of obedience to the monastic rules, his ascetic behavior, and his reserve in relations with women."[40]

On November 5, 1960, Maccari submitted a 208-page official report to Cardinal Alfredo Ottaviani, secretary of the Holy Office. This report, which as of this writing (2018) has remained off-limits to the public, was said, by the few privileged to read it, to be quite negative, and for years many feared it would prove an unsurmountable obstacle to Padre Pio's eventual canonization. Some years later, in a letter to the Holy Office, Maccari wrote, "I realize — at a distance of years and with an experience I hope more mature, of men and things — that my attitude towards Padre Pio may have played a part in the way I proceeded," and he conceded that he might have been "too frank and harsh."[41] By the time Maccari died in 1997, the cause for Padre Pio's canonization was moving rapidly, and, according to some reports, the aged prelate, who had become archbishop of Ancona, had joined the bandwagon and was referring to Padre Pio as a "saint." But he certainly did not feel that way in

1960, when he seemed to believe that there were credible grounds to assume that the Capuchin was leading an immoral life.

Although deeply hurt and shattered emotionally, Padre Pio told Cleonice Morcaldi, when she ranted about his enemies, "I don't have enemies. Haven't I always told you that truth can be attacked, but not destroyed? Let's pray for those who persecute us, that they may mend their ways and repent of the evil that they have done."[42]

"An Idol of Straw"

Early in August 1960, Padre Pio celebrated the fiftieth anniversary of his ordination. The ongoing investigation and the accusations dampened considerably what should have been a joyous occasion for Padre Pio and his friends and confreres. Even so, three bishops were present, including one from Uruguay, and messages were read from Cardinals Giacomo Lercaro of Bologna, Giovanni Battista Montini of Milan, and Albert Meyer (Father Dominic's cousin) of Chicago, and seventy-eight other archbishops and bishops.

During this time, Maccari was in Rome, conferring with the Holy Office. As unfavorable reports reached the Vatican, Pope John wrote in his journal, "What to think of this religious [that is, Padre Pio], who certainly does good, yet one can't succeed in dissipating shadows and doubts concerning his alleged sanctity? Lately, the shadows are growing and the doubts are becoming more grave."[43] After meeting with Maccari on September 9, Pope John wrote: "Unfortunately ... Padre Pio is revealed as an idol of straw. Spare us, Lord. Spare your people."[44]

Many years later, Cardinal Loris Francesco Capovilla (1915-2016), who was secretary to Pope John, asserted, "On the part of John XXIII there was no prejudice. They were giving unfavorable information on what was happening at San Giovanni Rotondo and the Pope could not but take notice."[45]

The Most Colossal Fraud in the History of the Church

Maccari's report was so negative that in February 1961 the Holy Office sent Paul-Pierre Philippe (1905–1984), a French Dominican priest (and future cardinal), who was secretary of the Congregation of the Affairs of Religious, to visit Padre Pio, to warn him that his situation was such as "to put his soul in peril." Philippe confronted Padre Pio with the charges of immorality which he said had been related by Maccari. "It's absolutely false!" Padre Pio protested. When the Dominican accused him of kissing women, Padre Pio raised his hand to heaven and declared, "I never kissed any woman, Father. Moreover, I say before the Lord, I didn't even want to kiss my Mamma. I made her weep because I didn't return her kisses, but I always thought I did wrong."

Philippe then criticized his manner of hearing confessions — his occasional harsh words and refusal to grant absolution to some penitents. "I do this in conscience," said the Capuchin, "when I see souls who don't come to make their confessions, but to talk to me about a lot of other things."

Claiming that the pope was worried about Padre Pio's soul, Philippe told the Capuchin, "The Church fears and trembles for you. The Holy Father wants you to be sure that you think about the salvation of your own soul! I can't return to Rome without your promise to do everything to put in order not only your soul, but also your priestly ministry, especially concerning your favored women, consecrating yourself from now on to one and all without distinction and energetically preventing every form of cult of your person."

Padre Pio answered, "Thank the Holy Father for his interest in my soul, but also ask him to allow me to exercise my ministry freely, especially concerning the women of town. Let me have my freedom!"[46]

In the report he subsequently composed, Philippe viciously excoriated the revered priest: "Padre Pio appears to me to be a man of limited intelligence, but very astute and obstinate, a clever peasant who does what he wants without clashing with his superiors, but hasn't any desire to change. He is not nor can be a saint.... He is not even a worthy priest." He went on to make the accusation that "Padre Pio passed indifferently from minor expressions of affection to acts even more serious to the carnal act. And then, after so many years of sacrilegious life, perhaps he is not aware of the gravity of evil. This is the story of all the false mystics who have fallen into sexual immorality. From this it is obvious that the stigmata were not the work of God." He denounced Padre Pio as passing for a saint before millions of the faithful while leading "a life of total immorality," giving souls "a direction that is completely false." He concluded that "Padre Pio is not only a false mystic, who knows that his stigmata are not from God, who nevertheless allows all his fame of sanctity to be built around him," but is actually "a wretched priest, who profits from his reputation to deceive his victims.... The case of Padre Pio is the most colossal fraud that can be discovered in the history of the Church." He urged that Padre Pio be forbidden from hearing any confessions, kept from saying Mass, and be removed from San Giovanni as soon as possible and sent to a convent far away.[47]

This devastating report notwithstanding, Pope John was not entirely convinced that Padre Pio was an Italian Catholic Rasputin. The stigmatized Capuchin had a number of supporters among the Church's hierarchy. Among them was Cardinal Giuseppe Siri (1906–1989), archbishop of Genoa, who later said: "For months I defended Padre Pio to Pope John XXIII. We spoke about him at every meeting we had. I had many responsibilities at the time, and I would often meet with the pope. Each time we met we ended up talking about Padre Pio. The pope was a very good man, a true saint. But he was worried and confused by what was reported to him." Siri pointed out to the pontiff that Padre Pio was the victim of slander.[48] Pope John turned to his old friend, Archbishop Cesarano of Manfredonia, and asked him about Padre Pio when the prelate came to Rome. He told the pope, "Padre Pio is always the man of God whom I have known since the beginning of my [tenure as archbishop in] Manfredonia. He is an apostle who does immense good for souls." When the pope brought up the evil reports, Cesarano objected, "It's all slander. I've known Padre Pio since 1933 and I assure you that he always was a man of God."

"Then … those women, those recordings," the pope went on. "They even recorded kisses."

"For charity's sake," insisted Cesarano, "it's not the case of sinful kisses." He explained how women continually grabbed Padre Pio's hand and kissed it, despite his complaints that this hurt his stigmata. Cesarano even observed his own sister kissing Padre Pio's hand over and over again.[49]

The archbishop was shown photographs of Padre Pio in compromising positions with women. Cesarano convinced the pope that they had been doctored. What about Elvira Serritelli's deposition that she was Padre Pio's mistress? The archbishop told the pope that it was well known that she was mentally unstable and not a trustworthy witness.[50] This — and the defense of Padre Pio from other churchmen that he respected — seemed to implant some distrust of Maccari's report in the mind of the pope. He did not follow through with Philippe's devastating recommendations to ban Padre Pio from saying Mass and hearing confessions — or banish him from San Giovanni Rotondo.

Directives from the Holy Office

Nevertheless, Cardinal Ottaviani, head of the Holy Office, on the last day of January 1961, sent a memorandum to the superior at San Giovanni Rotondo. It stated that the Maccari investigation had uncovered "not a few violations of the religious Rule," and in order to "stop the repetitions of acts that have the character of a cult directed towards the person of Padre Pio," the following directives were to be carried out: first, priests and bishops were henceforth forbidden to serve at Mass celebrated by Padre Pio; second, the time he celebrated Mass was to be varied from day to day; third, the faithful were strictly forbidden to congregate around the confessional or to try to talk to Padre Pio as he entered or left; fourth, no one was to be admitted to the church without a ticket during the hours when the Padre was hearing confession; fifth, Padre Pio was prohibited from receiving women alone in the guest room or anywhere else; sixth, the faithful were forbidden to congregate in the sacristy or friary garden; and, seventh, railings were to be erected around the women's confessionals so that the penitents waiting in line could not eavesdrop or pester the priest.[51]

Moreover, certain changes were made in the friary personnel. Even before Maccari concluded his visitation, Padre Emilio was removed as superior and replaced by Padre Rosario Pasquale of Aliminusa (1914–1983), from the province of Palermo, Sicily. Padre Amedeo was removed as provincial. Although Padre Pio was allowed to stay in San Giovanni, Cardinal Ottaviani ordered the transfer of a number of friars from the convent, among whom were some of Padre Pio's longtime friends, and their "substitution" with "fathers with a spirit perfectly conformed to the [Capuchin] Rule and proven zeal in the exercise of sacred ministry."[52] Pietro Cugino, who had lived in the friary for more than thirty years, was now forced to leave. Stricken by the loss of his friends, Padre Pio broke down in tears. There was, however, one man whose departure surely did not grieve him. Padre Giustino, who helped to bring on the apostolic visitation through his fear of being transferred from San Giovanni, had, with his intrusive self-righteousness, made himself offensive even to those who were no friends of Padre Pio. He was sent to the island of Malta to work as a teacher.

The directives of the Holy Office were bitterly resented by the "Pious Women." They denounced Padre Rosario as "The Rosary of the Devil." Actually, the round-faced priest, whose thick round spectacles gave him an owl-like look, had, according to Padre Alessio Parente, "a great love for Padre Pio." Every evening throughout his life Padre Pio would kneel down in front of his superior — whoever he was — to request his blessing. When Padre Rosario took charge, he announced that it was inappropriate for a man of Padre Pio's age to kneel down to kiss his hand and insisted that, instead, each night, the two would embrace and kiss each other. Anyway, the "Pious Women" tried to convince Padre Pio that they had an order from the Vatican that overruled his superior, an order that transferred him to the *Casa*. Padre Rosario thought the threat was serious and, for a time, locked Padre Pio in his cell every night.[53] Padre Alessio said this measure was necessary, because "Padre Pio was like putty in the hands of these women." When this became known, Padre Rosario was roundly denounced as "The Jailer," not only by the "Pious Women," but by the former mayor Francesco Morcaldi. Maria Pyle wrote to American friends that "we can only approach Padre Pio when we go every ten days to confession,"[54] and insisted that Rome, by restricting Padre Pio, was "trying to bring Mont Blanc down to the level of the sea," but that the mountain "continues to tower high above all other mountains and … with all the restrictions, bars, and barriers, seems ever greater, ever more saintly, ever more similar to our crucified Lord."[55]

The next year the Capuchin minister general, Father Clement, came in person to San Giovanni, along with the new provincial, Padre Torquato Cavateri of Lecore (1910–1995), to ask Padre Pio to sign over the title deeds of the *Casa* to the Vatican. This Padre Pio did without protest. The hospital would henceforth be the property of the Holy See, managed by "The Foundation of Religion and Worship of the Casa Sollievo della Sofferenza, the Work of Padre Pio." (In 1980, the *Casa* was recognized by the Italian government as a general regional hospital, and thus entitled to government funding.)

"You Can't Love the Son by Mortifying the Mother"

Emmanuele Brunatto, now living in Paris, became involved in Padre Pio's life once more, after the priest was forced to relinquish his control of the *Casa*. It was claimed by some that Padre Pio actually sent word to him, asking him to return to Italy.[56] In 1962, Brunatto traveled to Rome and met with Cardinal Ottaviani, head of the Holy Office, who told him, "We acted in Padre Pio's best interest, so that the Capuchin Order could not touch Padre Pio's work."[57] The Holy Office was apparently concerned that the Capuchins had been exerting pressure on Padre Pio to divert monies intended for the hospital to pay the debts of the order. Brunatto was not mollified and drew up a brief, which he sent to the United Nations, claiming that Padre Pio was subject to inhuman persecution in violation of the United Nations Declaration of Human Rights of 1950. He argued that since the money for the *Casa* was donated exclusively for Padre Pio, it was illegal for the Vatican to force him to give up control of the hospital. Maintaining that it was impossible for Padre Pio to obtain justice from Italian and Vatican officials, Brunatto urged the United Nations to take up Padre Pio's case. He prepared a "White Paper," which he threatened to send to all U.N. delegates and, reportedly, to the governors of all fifty American states. It was said to contain the same sort of explosive material that he had threatened to publish a quarter century earlier when Padre Pio had been held incommunicado. Once again, Padre Pio begged Brunatto to desist. Early in 1963, he wrote:

> My dear little son Emmanuele,
>
> In the most holy name of Jesus, I ask of you a great proof of filial love; and I don't doubt that you will do it for me even if it costs you much sacrifice.
>
> If truly you love me as a father, don't continue doing what they say that you are doing for me and for that which concerns me, because it will mortify people in the Holy Mother Church and the Capuchin Order, of which I am a humble devoted son. You can't love the son by mortifying the mother. Likewise entrust yourself with faith into the hands of God, and leave everything in the loving hands of Providence.
>
> Thus your love will be pleasing and meritorious because it is free of human passion.
>
> May Jesus bless you,
>
> P. Pio of Pietrelcina[58]

Brunatto evidently heeded Padre Pio's plea, and no more was heard about the "White Paper."

"An Act of Perfect Love Cancels All Sins"

Although he constantly and invariably insisted that his supporters "turn the other cheek" to his persecutors, Padre Pio was deeply hurt by the Maccari investigation and its aftermath, and especially by the accusations of unchastity. Some of the younger friars were hostile to Padre Pio and acted as if they believed the charges that he had been in a carnal relationship with some of the "Pious Women" might have been true. One of them even called him "Rasputin" to his face.[59] A young seminarian had the gall to ask him directly, "Is it true that you had affairs with women?"

"Listen, son," Padre Pio patiently replied. "I never did these things even when I was young. Now, even if I wished to do them ... I'm an old man." Then, according to the young friar, he made a "crude" gesture, holding the thumb and forefinger of each hand together, and, with arms extended, he rotated his wrists, as if to suggest a limp rope, cloth — or something else.[60]

Elvira Serritelli, after blackening Padre Pio's name, remained in San Giovanni Rotondo. A few years later, she became gravely ill. Dying in the *Casa* in February 1964, she confessed her sins and received Communion. Then she expressed a desire to make her confession again, which she did the following day. Shortly after, she fell into a coma and died. A few days later, when a woman asked him if Serritelli was saved, Padre Pio answered, "An act of perfect love cancels all sins." Ten days later, he told the same lady that his slanderer had gone to paradise. When Serritelli's family asked Padre Pio for a message to put on her funeral prayer card, he wrote: "In life she constantly aspired toward heaven, and death found her prepared for her encounter with Jesus. Now from on high she watches over those she left to mourn her on earth."[61]

"I Cannot Bear My Cross Anymore!"

Padre Eusebio

The ordeal of the Maccari investigation had taken a grievous toll on the health of Padre Pio, now in his early seventies. His heart was failing, he was frequently short of breath, and his lower extremities were swollen so badly that his feet looked like melons to some observers. Because of this, the stigmata on his feet, and the arthritis, walking was painful and difficult. It was the custom in the order for younger friars to be assigned as caretakers to those who were old and infirm. Padre Giustino had been assigned to be Padre Pio's companion and assistant — with tragic results. He was replaced by Padre Eusebio Notte of Castelpetroso (1932–2018), a cheerful, lively twenty-seven-year-old. Because he had studied in Ireland and was fluent in English, he was also given the task of handling letters written to Padre Pio in that language.

Padre Eusebio wrote, "The Padre lost his smile, which from that time on became very rare. He very rarely spoke, and he was lonely and immensely sad." His old friends were transferred away, and even the students from the "Seraphic College" were sent to another province. He would sob, "My poor children ... how much they have to suffer — because of me!" Unable to sleep, he sat for hours at night in front of the Blessed Sacrament.[1]

Padre Pio was deeply depressed, but Padre Eusebio was one of the few people capable of lifting his spirits. For instance, one day, in August 1962, the young priest found him sitting at his desk with his head between his hands. Agitated and in a state of desperation, Padre Pio called out, "Help me, son! I can't deal with it anymore! I'm losing my faith!"

Padre Eusebio assured him, "The devil is coming to torment you with these doubts, but don't give them a thought. Be calm. Soon we'll go to say Mass and he will be defeated."

"Then, give me a blessing, son," he said. Padre Eusebio blessed him, and Padre Pio seemed to calm down.[2]

When Padre Agostino became incapacitated by age and illness, Padre Raffaele, who had heard Padre Pio's confessions at times in the past, became his regular confessor. However, one day he wasn't available, so Padre Pio asked Eusebio to administer the Sacrament of Penance. Throughout his confession, Padre Pio was sobbing. Although he was not at liberty to recount what sins Padre Pio confessed, Padre Eusebio, in his memoirs, implied that they were inconsequential. He told Padre Pio that he saw no connection between the sins he had confessed and his disconsolate weeping. "Son, you think sin is the breaking of law," Padre Pio responded. "No, son, sin is the betrayal of love. What has the Lord done for me and what have I done for him?"[3] He was convinced that he had not adequately responded to God's goodness to him.

Padre Eusebio slept in the adjoining room, and Padre Pio kept a little bell that he could ring to call him. Padre Pio wanted Padre Eusebio with him all the time, so much so that he became upset when the younger man wanted to visit his family for a few days. "Don't leave me!" he often pleaded.

Padre Eusebio held Padre Pio's hand when he underwent an operation, without anesthesia, for a cancerous tumor on his left ear. As a dermatologist from Rome cut into his flesh, Padre Eusebio comforted him as he moaned, "My Jesus! My Jesus!" (The doctor was confident that there would be no recurrence, and there wasn't.)[4]

Padre Eusebio helped Padre Pio in and out of bed, but he didn't bathe him. Padre Pio did not want people to see his stigmata. Padre Eusebio saw the hand wounds when Padre Pio was celebrating Mass, but Padre Pio continued to clean and wrap the lesions in his hands and sides and put socks over his feet. Only one time was Padre Eusebio able to get a reasonably good look at one bare foot, on which he saw a "black spot." Padre Pio was, in fact, so modest that he resisted Padre Eusebio's suggestion to pull up his sleeves and open his undershirt just a little on a stifling hot evening. "You must know that I've never sinned against modesty," he protested. "And you want to make me sin in my old age?"[5]

The young priest was moved by Padre Pio's love of the Virgin Mary, a devotion, Padre Eusebio wrote, that was expressed through "continuous prayer, of groans, sighs, acts of love, even in a loud voice."[6] Padre Pio was constantly praying — even on the toilet. When Padre Eusebio asked him, "Doesn't this show a lack of respect to the Madonna?" Padre Pio asked, "But, on the toilet, is it possible to sin?" When Padre Eusebio agreed that it was, Padre Pio replied, "Then you can also pray."[7]

"Where Did You Find This Funeral Dirge?"

The Midnight Mass on Christmas Eve was always one of Padre Pio's favorite celebrations of the year. It was the tradition at the friary church for him to sing the last lesson, which described the birth of Christ. Then he would carry a statue of the Infant Jesus in his arms and place it on the high altar. Next, according to Padre Eusebio, he would sing the *Te Deum* in a "merry baritone" to a "peasant tune," while everyone else followed in chorus. However, the year after the investigation, orders were received that Gregorian chant would now be used, and that Padre Eusebio would chant the *Te Deum* instead of Padre Pio. As the procession began, since hardly anyone was familiar with plainsong, only Padre Eusebio was singing. Eventually, Padre Pio went up to him and said, "Son, where did you find this funeral dirge?" Then he began to chant the *Te Deum* in the old way, and everyone joined in. Padre Eusebio said that Padre Pio's "powerful voice ... seemed to rival the voices of the angels who sang that first Christmas night," and when he gazed at the statue of the Christ Child, he "broke into a broad grin that reflected the joy of a vision of which we were spectators without seeing anything."

"I'm Praying That She Might Get a Brain"

Padre Eusebio went through about a thousand letters a week. To people who simply asked for prayers, he sent a little printed card assuring the writer that Padre Pio would pray and send a blessing. He wrote thank-you notes to people who sent money. Often Padre Eusebio would answer people's questions himself when he thought it appropriate. He troubled Padre Pio only with "very challenging" matters. After hearing some letters, Padre Pio would direct Padre Eusebio to write, "Let's pray together that the Lord enlighten you to make the right decision."

Sometimes, when Padre Eusebio would start to read a letter, Padre Pio would say impatiently, "I understand ... I understand," and, even without a translation, he "gave an exact answer, not an approximate one."[8]

One girl sent a letter plastered with clippings. "I am a girl, unfortunately not pretty enough," she wrote to Padre Pio, "and I come to ask your prayers to help me." She informed him that she wanted a nose like that of a particular actress, enclosing a picture of the woman she wanted to resemble. She went on to say she wanted lips like another actress and the eyes and ears of a certain model, and enclosed likenesses of both. After Padre Eusebio translated the letter for him, Padre Pio asked, "Did she say anything about a brain?"

"No, Padre, she didn't say anything."

"Then answer that I'm praying that she might get a brain."[9]

In 1962, a woman wrote from London: "Padre, I'm a prostitute. Every evening, at nine, I'm dragged out onto the street. I am ashamed. I'm writing to you so that you might help me overcome this shame." She didn't ask to be freed from her "protector," or her profession, only from her shame. Padre Eusebio, who expected Padre Pio to give a severe warning to repent from her sin, was astounded when he said, "Answer that I will pray for her with all my heart." After a while the woman wrote back, "Dear Padre, thanks to God after receiving your letter, nine o'clock comes, but I no longer go down on the street. I succeeded in ridding myself of the one who dragged me there."

"*Deo gratias*," he responded.[10]

Freedom

Padre Pio bore no ill will toward Pope John XXIII. When people complained about the way the pope treated him, he would say, "The Papa has nothing to do with it. He judges on the basis of what they tell him."[11] When the pope died on June 3, 1963, Padre Pio, after remembering him in his Mass, declared that the pope had gone straight to heaven. Now the friars in his monastery were pressing him to reveal who was going to be the next pope. Padre Eusebio was unusually persistent, and finally Padre Pio told him, "It's going to be Montini. Now, will you be quiet?"[12] Shortly afterward, the archbishop of Milan, Cardinal Giovanni Battista Montini, was elected, taking the name Paul VI. Padre Pio's prediction, by itself, would not have been remarkable, since many people were predicting Montini's election, except for the fact that, five years earlier, through Alberto Galletti — a former administrator of the hospital — Padre Pio had sent a message to Montini: "Tell the Archbishop that he will one day be Pope, and to be prepared. Mind you, tell him this." When Galletti relayed the message to Montini, the archbishop laughed and said, "Oh, these saints get some strange ideas!"[13]

Pope Paul, entirely convinced of Padre Pio's sanctity, decided to relax the restrictions placed on him by his predecessor, which were keeping the Capuchin, in the new pope's words, confined "like a criminal." Not long after his coronation, Pope Paul placed Padre Clemente Vincentino of Santa Maria in Punta (1904–1986) over the Capuchin province of Foggia as apostolic administrator, and told him, "Liberate him from those restrictions. Make the work of Padre Pio easy so that he can fulfill his apostolate."[14] Therefore, on January 30, 1964, Cardinal Ottaviani, secretary of the Holy Office, announced, "It is the will of the Holy Father that Padre Pio exercise his ministry in full liberty."[15]

Padre Clemente later wrote, "Pope Paul VI was aware of the crisis in the friary. All their students and novices had been sent to another province. The definitors and provincial had been dismissed. Therefore, my work was twofold: to release Padre Pio from his restrictions and to restore normalcy to the province."[16] He rescinded the order that forced Padre Pio to say Mass at irregular hours and allowed him once again to talk to people after he had heard confessions. Once more, lay people were allowed to gather in the sacristy to converse with him, and the faithful Pietro Cugino was once more allowed to live at the friary.

In the Sacristy

Padre Eusebio was Padre Pio's constant companion. Every morning he accompanied him as he celebrated Mass. After Mass, Padre Pio entered the empty sacristy and prayed for ten minutes, his head covered with his hood, his eyes filled with tears, taking no notice of the men who were admitted to the room. Gradually, Padre Pio came to himself and greeted and blessed his visitors. Then, leaning on Padre Eusebio, he made his way through the sacristy through the lines of men. Occasionally, he would place his hand on a head or let someone kiss it, sometimes giving a quick response to a request. When he reached the second floor, he blessed people who were peering in through the windows. When he reached his room, he drank two or three sips from a thermos of coffee and gave the rest to Padre Eusebio. Then he lay down in bed. He seemed to be "talking to God" aloud, but Padre Eusebio never tried to make out what he was saying.[17]

When it was time to hear confessions, Padre Pio would stop at a statue of Mary, fingering his beads and murmuring prayers. First, he went to the sacristy to hear the confessions of the men who had appointments on that given day. After an hour, he went to the old church to hear the confessions of the women.

He returned once more to the sacristy, surrounded by crowds of importunate people. Padre Eusebio sometimes noted conversations. One particular day, Padre Pio was accosted by a woman who said, "Padre, I have to go in the hospital to have an operation. Can I go there with your blessing?" He answered, "Go, daughter. I'll accompany you with prayer."

But when a second woman announced, "Padre, I have to have an operation," he responded, "Eh! If you want to get yourself killed!"

"Then, I shouldn't have the operation?"

"I told you — if you want to get yourself killed!"

A third woman told him, "Padre, I feel terrible, but the doctors don't understand anything. Help me!"

"I'll pray for you, daughter."

When she asked why he couldn't give her a more precise answer, Padre Pio pointed to heaven and said, "If nobody tells me anything, what can I say?"

When a man asked, "Padre, what should I say to my wife, Rose?" he quipped, "Tell her to be a carnation."[18]

Padre Pio, when they were alone, once remarked to his young companion, "Son, you've seen everybody asking Padre Pio to help them with this and that. I wish somebody would say, 'Padre Pio, pray that the Lord might help me to bear the cross.'"[19]

The Possessed

Some of the most unsettling and frightening occasions for the friars at San Giovanni Rotondo happened when people brought relatives or friends who they believed to be possessed by demons, in hopes that Padre Pio would perform an exorcism. The old priest realized, however, that he no longer possessed the stamina to perform the rite, which can prove time-consuming and extremely draining, physically and psychologically. When people were brought to him who seemed to be possessed, he simply blessed them, and sometimes that seemed to be enough.

William "Bill" Martin, from Brooklyn, New York, first met Padre Pio in 1959, when he was twenty-one. When he returned five years later, Padre Pio invited him to stay, and he did. Martin, who later became Father Joseph Pius, first lived in the friary as a lay member of the Franciscan Third Order, helping with the English correspondence and with visitors. He personally observed two cases of possession.

One day he entered the church to find a priest sprinkling holy water on a woman in her thirties. "She exhibited a strength that you would have to say was supernatural. Two men could not hold her in the chair. Her head and scarf were all disheveled, her clothes were pulled apart, her shoes were off. She would rise up out of the chair and throw the men back. They would grab her again and push her down, but she would throw them back again. Her strength! It was … animal power," the friar recounted. Yet, the moment Padre Pio entered, "It was as if she were dead. There was no movement, there was no sound, there was nothing. He blessed her and went on. Then it started in a way that actually scared me to see her, because you saw something that wasn't human. It was frightening, because I had not seen anything like it in my life. The minute he left her, she went back to … hooting and howling and showing her supernatural force." Father Joseph Pius seemed not to know whether the woman was delivered.

On the second occasion, another woman was brought into church so that Padre Pio could bless her. She was "twisting like a snake in agony. It was the most fantastic thing to see. She could not have been an actress, because she could not have kept up the motion uninterruptedly for so long. Padre Carmelo [the superior] told everyone to leave." As in the first case, Father Joseph Pius never learned what happened.[20]

On July 5, 1964, a twenty-year-old woman was brought to San Giovanni Rotondo from Brescia because, in the words of Padre Eusebio, "she showed signs of being possessed by the devil." She was taken inside the cloister, apart from the gaze of the crowds, so that Padre Pio could bless her as he passed by. As soon as he approached, accompanied by Padre Eusebio, the woman leaped at him, screaming incomprehensible words in a deep, hoarse voice. She tried to scratch his face, but both he and Padre Eusebio were able to keep their distance. "I was terrified," Padre Eusebio wrote, "but Padre Pio less so."

"In the Name of God, go away!" Padre Pio yelled, moving past the madwoman, who didn't follow, but kept screaming, "I'll make you pay! I'll make you pay!"

When they were back in Padre Pio's room, Eusebio asked, "What's going on?"

Padre Pio answered calmly, "It's what you saw."

Later that day, the woman was taken to a room in the friary, where, in the presence of a crowd of people "laughing and joking" and "enjoying the spectacle,"

Padre Placido Bux of San Marco in Lamis tried to conduct an exorcism, "throwing buckets of holy water on her," with no effect.[21]

A little after ten o'clock that night, the friars on the floor where Padre Pio lived heard "a frightful thud." Padre Eusebio wrote that it was "an incredible noise, as if the big door of the church was being slammed." Then they heard Padre Pio crying, "Brothers! Brothers!"

Padre Carmelo Di Donato of San Giovanni in Galdo (1927–1971), who had replaced Padre Rosario as superior in January 1964, and several other friars hurried to the room. Padre Pio was lying on the floor in the center of the room, his arms extended, his head in the direction of the bed, and his feet toward the door. "With one hand he had managed to pull a cushion from the kneeler and place it under his face, which was bleeding heavily," Padre Eusebio noted. Padre Pio was raised from the floor and helped into bed, and Padre Eusebio tried to stanch the blood with a towel. Minutes later Dr. Sala arrived and sewed up the wound. Padre Pio, his head supported by Padre Eusebio, didn't cry out at all, but his lips moved as if he were forgiving someone. Shortly afterward, he ordered everyone out of the room, except for Padre Eusebio; he wanted him to stay to help him change his undershirt, which was soaked in blood. He handed his helper a handkerchief and told him to drape it over the table light and turn off the main light in the room. In the dim light, Padre Eusebio, for the first and only time, saw Padre Pio's naked upper body. Although Padre Pio tried to hide it with his arm, Padre Eusebio could see the wound in the side. "It was an open wound, vivid, in the form of a cross," he wrote. "The vertical part, about seven centimeters long, was crooked, and ran from the right side to the left. The transverse wound was not less than three centimeters. There were neither scars nor crusts, but, from the lower end of the vertical part, blood flowed slowly." Padre Eusebio helped Padre Pio put on a new jersey and helped him get back in bed.

The next morning, when Padre Eusebio came to accompany him to the church, Padre Pio told him, "I can't celebrate Mass this morning. Bring me Communion." His face was bruised and his eyes were black. "He looked like a prize fighter," Padre Eusebio thought.

Meanwhile, in the crowd waiting outside for the church doors to open was the madwoman, sniggling, and boasting loudly, "Ah, I got my vengeance on that miserable old man!" Moreover, she kept shouting, "Ah, that cushion! That cushion!" When the doors were opened, it was announced that the superior would celebrate the Mass, as Padre Pio was "indisposed."

Nevertheless, at 9:30 a.m., Padre Pio told Padre Eusebio that he was going down to hear the confessions of the women. One of the first was a woman from Naples named Giuseppina Bove, who afterward went to Padre Eusebio and reported that she had asked Padre Pio for a special blessing, explaining to him: "Everything's been going extremely badly. Everything's going wrong, just as if the devil were causing it ... except I don't believe in the devil."

At this, Padre Pio cried: "You don't believe in the devil! Can't you see the marks he put on my face?"

Later that day, Padre Eusebio remarked to Padre Pio, "When you were young, you fought with the devil.... One time he won, and one time you won."

Padre Pio immediately shot back, "No, I *always* won! ... But, now, I've gotten old.... See how diminished I am! ... So be it! ... And that girl yesterday night ... I feel so sorry for her."[22]

Meanwhile, word spread around San Giovanni Rotondo that the devil had attacked Padre Pio. Maria Pyle insisted that the demon possessing the woman had shrieked at Padre Pio, "Pio, I've known you since you were small!" and that when the priest who had been trying to exorcize her the day before began once more, the woman shrieked, "Where were you last night? I was upstairs to see the old man I hate so much because he is a source of faith. I would have done more, only the White Lady stopped me."[23] It was said that the cushion found under Padre Pio's head was put there by the Virgin Mary.

The exorcism of the apparently possessed woman could not continue because of numerous threats the local people made against her, and she was forced to flee from the town. However, some time later, a letter came to Padre Pio from Brescia. It was from the woman, thanking him for doing battle with Satan in her behalf. She claimed that she was "liberated" and "the most happy woman in the world."[24]

"It's Impossible to Refuse This Man"

In the meantime, the Second Vatican Council had been opened in Rome, in 1962, by Pope John, and, after his death, continued by Pope Paul. One of the ecclesiastical officials attending the council was the administrator of the archdiocese of Kraków, Poland, Bishop Karol Wojtyła. He had visited Padre Pio in person in 1947, a year after his own ordination to the priesthood; and when, in 1978, he became Pope John Paul II, rumors spread that on that visit, Padre Pio had prophesied that he would become pope. Actually, he had not. However, Wojtyła held Padre Pio in tremendous esteem, and on November 18, 1962, wrote him a letter in Latin, saying: "Venerable Father, I ask that you pray for a forty-year-old mother of four little girls in Kraków, Poland (who during the last war spent five years in a concentration camp), who is now in very grave danger related to her health and possibly may die because of cancer: that God may extend his mercy to this woman and her family in the presence of the Most Blessed Virgin. Most obligated in Christ, Karol Wojtyła."[25]

Padre Pio allegedly told the man who hand-delivered the letter to him, "It's impossible to refuse this man." Naturally, years later, many assumed that he said it was impossible to refuse Wojtyła because he knew Wojtyła would one day be pope.

The object of the future pope's concern was Wanda Półtawska, a psychiatrist, born in Lublin, Poland, in November 1921, who had been imprisoned by the Nazis at Ravensbrück. A few days earlier, in November 1962, she had written to Wojtyła:

> I can tell you that my suspicions were confirmed. I am amazed not so much for the diagnosis of cancer, but for my tranquility. The source of pain is a hard round cystic ulcer of 13 cm. When I left the doctor's office I went in Planty Park and walked for an hour. The last golden leaves. Suddenly everything has a different meaning and at the same time everything has become meaningless. What do I do now? How to live these two or maybe three years? I realized that the twins are only five years old. I decided to immediately stop work and spend the rest of my life with them so that they have something to remember of their mother.... The doctor is my friend; he has agreed to operate on me. He kissed my hand twice and swore, "This world is shit."

The doctor told Półtawska that surgery might possibly extend her life two or three years; otherwise she would die in eighteen months. Wojtyła encouraged her to have the surgery, so she went under the knife. When the bishop telephoned Półtawska's husband to learn the results of the operation, he was told, "The doctors found that there was nothing that could be done." Wojtyła, naturally, assumed that the cancer was inoperable and said, "Oh, my God, it's awful for you, Andrzej!"

"Oh, no, you don't understand," replied Półtawska. "The doctors are confronted with a mystery.... They couldn't find anything."

The lesion in Wanda's intestine had disappeared.

On November 29, Wojtyła wrote Padre Pio: "Venerable Father, the woman living in Kraków, Poland, mother of four young girls, on November 21, just before a surgical operation, suddenly recovered her health. Thanks be to God. Also to you, Venerable Father, I give the greatest thanks in the name of the husband and all the family. In Christ, Karol Wojtyła."

Dr. Półtawska later wrote: "At the last moment they found that the tumor had disappeared. Without giving it much thought, I assumed my case fell into that five percent category." For her it was "too difficult to assume a supernatural intervention." She believed that it was the case of an inflammation that healed on its own, and not a cancer after all. "Only later," she wrote, "when I returned home from the hospital, did I find out about those letters to Padre Pio.... Was my recovery a miracle? Frankly, I didn't know what to make of it, and I tried to put the whole thing out of my mind."

In May 1967, Półtawska went to San Giovanni and knelt in the sacristy, awaiting Padre Pio. Evidently, she had not notified him that she was coming, but, when he appeared, he immediately recognized her and asked, "Now, are you all right?" That went a long way toward convincing her that her recovery was the result of divine intervention through the Padre's prayers.

In 1988 she wrote, "Today I realize that the Lord is so gentle and delicate that he does not want to force gratitude upon us, or force our faith in things so difficult to believe."[26]

The Second Vatican Council

There is no record of Padre Pio's feelings about the opening of the Second Vatican Council. He may have been in favor of some reforms. Years before, a journalist had reported, "According to Padre Pio, the Pope will pay a price for his attachment to worldly things, for the opulence he displays as an Earthly Power. He will have to return to the spirit of Christ and be no more than His representative on earth, with humility." The pope "will have to live in just two rooms, remain far from politics, and be open to all.... An aristocratic pope, far from the crowds, whom no one may approach, is not the pope of Christ, and the treasures he possesses, he should not possess; he should distribute them to the poor."[27] If he was being quoted accurately, the context in which he was speaking is not clear. Padre Pio's attitude toward the papacy was generally one of reverent awe and virtually uncritical submission.

In early 1965, Padre Carmelo, the superior at San Giovanni, requested and received permission from Cardinal Ottaviani of the Holy Office for Padre Pio to continue to celebrate the Tridentine Mass (in Latin), on account of his advanced age, ill health, and poor eyesight. This was evidently a dispensation that was granted to many elderly priests, and Pio asked permission not because he was in opposition to what became known as the "Novus Ordo" Mass, but because he feared that he could not read the words. He did, in fact, adopt the modern practice of saying Mass facing the congregation. From time to time, he attended the "New Mass," celebrated in Italian by other priests, but nobody remembered him making any comment, one way or other.

However, many changes taking place in the Church filled the aging priest with dismay. For instance, when told that the Rosary was no longer in fashion, he responded, "Let us do as we have always done, what our ancestors did. And let's pray. He who prays much is saved. He who prays little damns himself. Let's love the Madonna and make her loved and let's recite the Holy Rosary that she herself has taught us."[28] He was almost embittered by the protests and criticism leveled at the pope and at the Church by radical priests, religious, and laity. The decline in vocations, especially in the Capuchin order, distressed him. More than once he remarked, on learning of some depressing development, "Thank God I am old and near death!"[29]

There were some "progressives" in the Capuchin order who toyed with the idea of replacing the traditional habit with jeans, so as to be more in spirit with the times. To tease him one day, one of the friars, during recreation, brought out a tape measure and told Padre Pio, "I have to take measurements."

"Whose?"

"Yours."

"Mine? Do you want to make me another habit?"

"No, I have to take measurements for trousers. One never knows. Don't you know that the Special General Chapter is in session? Maybe they will order us to wear civilian dress. So we'd better be ready."

The humor was lost on Padre Pio, who started to weep bitterly. "Have you lost your senses?" he cried. "I have lived and I will die with this blessed habit on! Do you understand?"[30]

Although there were some high-ranking Church officials who evidently despised Padre Pio, like Maccari, Philippe, and Gemelli (who died in 1959), many others, like Wojtyła and Pope Paul, considered him a saint and prophet. Maria Pyle wrote to a friend, "So many bishops from the ecumenical council come up to see Padre Pio that sometimes it seems that the Council is at San Giovanni Rotondo."[31] That was, of course, an exaggeration, but from time to time distinguished Church leaders attending the council came to visit him.

One of them was Cardinal Antonio Bacci (1885–1971), a vigorous opponent of the conciliar liturgical reforms, who came in the summer of 1965. When he left, Padre Eusebio asked what the visit was all about. "The pope sent him," explained Padre Pio. "He wanted to know what I think of the Council. I said, 'Tell the pope: what he had to do, he has done. Close it.'"[32] This is evidently the extent to which he expressed his sentiments about the council: there were certain changes necessary, but things were getting out of hand. When the Second Vatican Council closed that December, Padre Eusebio and others wondered whether Padre Pio's message had anything to do with it.

"Don't You See That the World Is Catching on Fire?"

Although he apparently made few, if any, recorded political comments during the 1960s, leading Italian politicians continued to visit Padre Pio, presumably to confer with him on spiritual matters. How much he kept up with world affairs is unclear, as he seldom (if ever) read newspapers, much less listened to the radio or watched television. He was apparently upset over the assassination of U.S. President John Kennedy in 1963. One of the priests who lived with him, Padre Aurelio, insisted that Padre Pio announced that President Kennedy was in heaven — a reaction similar to one made on the death of Franklin Roosevelt in 1945. It is unknown whether these statements were the result of a revelation or simply his own opinion, based simply on the information available to him at the time.

Padre Pio was convinced that society was in rapid decline. "My daughter, don't you see that the world and the human race are going to rack and ruin?" he said to Morcaldi.[33] "Don't you see that the world is catching on fire?" he exclaimed to Bill Martin. He hated to see women in short skirts and often refused to hear their confessions until they went back and "got dressed." "Why, you can see all the way up to her bottom," he commented to Martin about a woman who had the temerity to enter church in a miniskirt.

Padre Pio warned that television was destroying family life. Instead of talking to one another, he pointed out, family members spent their evenings staring at the set. He strongly advised people not watch television. And he was similarly negative about movies, commenting that "the devil is in the cinema."[34] "I don't condemn dancing as such," Padre Pio remarked, "but there's always the danger of sin and the Holy Spirit says in Sirach 3:27: 'He who puts himself in danger perishes in it.'"[35]

Divorce, he said, is "a passport to hell."[36] God did not intend for everyone to get married. "You've got to get it into your head," he would tell people looking for a mate, "that the Lord loves you more than you love yourself. If he wants you to get married, he knows where you live, and he will come and look for you."[37] But, of course, the single state was not an excuse for immorality.

Abortion, according to Padre Pio, was "not only homicide, but suicide" — leading to a world "populated only by old people and depopulated of children — burnt, like a desert."[38]

People interested in the occult asked Padre Pio his opinion. With regard to séances, he advised, "I can't say that these things that take place are all foolishness or that they are true. No, however, don't go anymore. This isn't the way Jesus taught.… The devil could play an evil trick on you."[39]

Rumors circulated that Padre Pio was predicting the imminent end of the world. Maria Pyle is said to have quoted Padre Pio as saying that millions of people would die in a cosmic catastrophe, but by no means was everyone convinced of the accuracy of some of the things that she said and claimed. It was also said that Padre Pio confirmed somebody's prediction of three days of darkness near the end of the world. Actually, he did not. However, it was a fact that in his old age, Padre Pio frequently urged people: "Pray that Christ comes soon!"[40]

In the early 1960s, several girls in Garabandal, a small town in northern Spain, reported apparitions of the Blessed Virgin Mary. Some claimed that unsigned letters affirming the authenticity of the visions, written in Italian with no return address, were written by Padre Pio. The only proof of this claim is the insistence of one of the visionaries that the Virgin Mary had told her this. Padre Pellegrino Funicelli, who was frequently with Padre Pio during this time, described in his memoirs a visit by one of the visionaries — Conchita González — to San Giovanni Rotondo early in 1967. González was accompanied by three or four people, including a Spanish princess and a Professor Medi.

Medi asked Padre Pio: "Padre, will you say yes or no to Garabandal?"

"I cannot answer that," the priest replied.

When Medi persisted, Padre Pio was silent. Afterward, when Padre Pellegrino asked him why he failed to give the professor any response, Padre Pio answered, "Because there are some little fanatics among my spiritual children who could go against the authority if my reply did not coincide with the opinion of authority."[41]

The position of the Church was (and, as of this writing in 2018, still is) that the supernatural origin of the events in Garabandal could not be confirmed. Padre Pio, always careful not to contradict "Holy Mother Church," repeatedly insisted that he was not at liberty to express an opinion (if, in fact, he had one) concerning the apparitions.

Losses

On May 14, 1963, Padre Pio's dearest and oldest friend, Padre Agostino, died at the age of eighty-three. "The Lector" had been in decline for several years. Visitors to San Giovanni in the 1960s mostly remembered him as a cranky old man who would stand in the choir of the old church overlooking the nave and shout at the disorderly crowds, "You ignoramuses!" until someone led him away. Eventually, he declined into total invalidism, according to Padre Alessio, "half out of his mind." Padre Rosario, while superior, served him as his assistant and nurse, even "cleaning up his messes." Although it was said that he had a vision of his friend in his heavenly home, Padre Pio, for months, was unable to pass the room of his old confessor without bursting into tears.

Indeed, the mid-1960s were a time of loss. Father Dominic died several years after returning to America, at Crown Point, Indiana, in August 1966, at the age of seventy-four. His last words: "Jesus … Mary …"

The next year Padre Paolino concluded his earthly pilgrimage of seventy-eight years at the *Casa*. Then, in February 1965, word came that Emmanuele Brunatto had been found dead in his apartment in Rome. The coroner declared that he had succumbed to a sudden heart attack, though some of his friends suspected foul play. When he learned of the passing of his longtime defender, it was said Padre Pio showed no surprise, as if he already knew.

Michele Forgione, now in his early eighties, was declining into dementia and was virtually bedridden.

Padre Pio's eyesight was poor, and he seldom read anymore. He had a pair of reading glasses, but seldom used them. He sometimes expressed a fear of going deaf; but his greatest fear, according to the friars who took care of him, was losing his mind, like his brother.

Another terrible blow was the loss of Padre Eusebio, the man who was able to lift his spirits the most. He didn't die, but was transferred after a disagreement with the superior.

The superior and provincial made little effort to soften the blow. They came to Padre Pio when he was in bed and said bluntly, "Now, Padre Pio, we have decided to send Padre Eusebio to rest abroad, because he's tired." (Padre Eusebio had never complained of fatigue.)

"No, don't take that boy away," the old man pleaded. "I need him too much, especially now!"

"Oh, Father, don't worry," said the superior. "You won't be lacking in assistance."

"For charity's sake, don't take him away!" Padre Pio pleaded.

The superiors walked out.

Padre Pio begged Padre Eusebio pitifully, "My son, don't leave me! Don't leave me! I need you."

Padre Eusebio, who was also deeply hurt, asked Padre Pio to pray to change the minds of the superiors, but he said, "I can't, because I made a vow to the Lord never to pray for myself, never to ask for anything, but to pray only for others." The night before Padre Eusebio left in May 1965, Padre Pio spent the night in great agitation, and in the morning, told him, "Son, I offer this Mass this morning to the Lord for you and for me — that I might die … rather than see you part."[42]

One reason why Padre Pio needed Padre Eusebio more than ever was that, two months earlier, he had suffered what some felt was the most devastating tragedy of his life.

The Last Trial

One day in March 1965, a tall, lean, gray-haired woman of seventy, dressed in a dark business suit, appeared at the friary. For nearly fifty years, until shortly before, she had been a Brigittine sister, in Rome, known as Suor Pia. Her secular name was Graziella Forgione. She was Padre Pio's surviving sister.

Some people claimed that Suor Pia was herself a saint, and some of Padre Pio's followers traveled to seek the counsel of his sister, in the motherhouse of her order in Rome. Some reported "an aroma of flowers" and claimed that Pia had the invisible stigmata. When questioned about this, her niece, Pia Forgione remarked, "Yes, yes, I've always believed this." A member of her order, however, commented, "Her religious life was ordinary, without any special sign of divine intimacy." Another sister, who, like the first, declined to be identified, insisted that Suor Pia was a woman of deep holiness and spirituality who was not appreciated by her order. Pia Forgione characterized her aunt as "very strong willed, except in front of her brother, and then she became a little lamb." It is not clear what Padre Pio thought of his sister. A man who had just visited Pia in Rome reportedly praised her to her brother as "so good and holy," only to have him shoot back, "Don't come talking this rubbish," adding, "Listen, *I* am the best one in my family. Only one surpassed me, but she [Felicita] is no more."[43]

Anyway, according to Padre Eusebio: "In the house where the sister of Padre Pio lived piously and drew people who came to recommend themselves to her prayers there were people who didn't live at all with the same strictness of life. There were blatant abuses. At night, a certain monsignor came to recite the rosary … with a certain young nun. Suor Pia was aware of it, because the shady business went on for some time. She was the vice-superior of the monastery and complained to those in authority, without result." Eventually, she and another sister left and "found themselves out on the street, not knowing where to go."[44] According to Padre Alessio, the two women found an apartment in Rome, and when their niece Pia found out about it, she brought her aunt to San Giovanni.

The younger Pia wanted to take her aunt to see Padre Pio. According to Padre Eusebio, Padre Pio was resentful toward his sister and didn't even want to speak to her. "He couldn't understand why she would do something like that." Eventually, he was persuaded to meet with his sister "so she could clarify the situation."

It was Padre Alessio who accompanied Suor Pia to meet with her brother. Looking at her civilian dress, he remarked rather disdainfully, "Just look at what you've become!" According to Padre Eusebio, she "screamed in his face: 'And you … what would *you* do?'" She explained the reasons why she left the convent, but Padre Pio insisted that nothing — absolutely nothing — could justify her breaking her vows. "They are wrong and you are right, but still you must obey. You must return." When Pia refused, Padre Pio told Padre Alessio, "Take me back to my room," and turned his back on his sister, weeping uncontrollably.

Later, brother and sister were persuaded to meet again, this time in Padre Pio's room. No one knows what was said, but when the niece entered the room, she found her aunt collapsed in a chair on one side of the room and her uncle collapsed in a chair on the other side. Both were completely exhausted. Brother and sister never spoke again.

Exactly what Pia did after that is hard to determine. One friar at San Giovanni said that she became a member of a particular order. However, upon inquiry, it was discovered that this was not true. In 1989, when interviewed, the niece Pia said her aunt joined a religious community in Rome that was "not very strict," called *Le Figlie Misericordiae*, but those sisters have no record of her. Later, a longtime associate of Padre Pio stated that Suor Pia never joined another religious order. He would not elaborate further, however, saying that it was all so shameful that he would never want to talk about it and that the greatest cross in Padre Pio's life was his two sisters, Pellegrina and Pia.

Many of the defectors from religious life were leaving because they considered their communities too strict, but Suor Pia was leaving, apparently, because hers was too permissive. That made no difference. For Padre Pio it was a sin and a terrible disgrace for a religious, for any reason whatsoever, to turn her back on her vocation after making her vows. Continually, he prayed that his sister would come to her senses and return to religious life, even if she had to find another order. He sought to understand, through prayer, why his sister turned her back on her vocation, and no answer came. He was heard to pray: "Lord, you *have* to give me this grace! Lord, why don't you give me this grace?" Padre Eusebio observed that, while Padre Pio was often illuminated about other people, concerning himself and his family "he was able to do absolutely nothing."[45]

Evidently, Pia was supported by friends of her brother. At one time, she was living in a retirement home called Mater Misericordiae. By 1968, Pia, wearing a nun's habit, was working as an assistant in managing a community shelter in the town of Buggiano, about two hundred miles from Rome.[46] The next spring she died in an apartment in Rome, and her remains were taken by her niece to San Giovanni Rotondo for burial.

Padre Alessio, who replaced Padre Eusebio as Padre Pio's assistant, heard him frequently complain, "The Lord doesn't listen to my prayers anymore!" Padre Alessio, in fact, considered the defection of his sister Padre Pio's "last trial." After Pia's withdrawal from religious life and the loss of Padre Eusebio's companionship, Padre Pio's depression grew profound. "He hardly ever talked after that," Padre Alessio recalled. "He might as well have been called 'The Silent Friar.'" Frequently, the friars heard him pray, "Lord, I cannot bear my cross anymore!"

The Great Passage

"Never in My Life Have I Suffered So!"

After the rancorous meeting with his sister Pia, in the spring of 1965, Padre Pio's health declined precipitously. One of the physicians who treated him noted that he suffered hemorrhages in the bladder, renal colic, an "irreducible hernia," gastric ulcers, and migraines.[1] He complained of terrible pains in his ears and in his teeth and gums. He could hobble about on arthritic knees only if he leaned on the arm of a helper. So great was the pain of his arthritis that he was heard to remark, "Never in my life have I suffered so!" Even with assistance, he often fell. "I feel completely paralyzed from the head to the feet, and I fall," he told a friend.[2]

Padre Alessio, who replaced Padre Eusebio as Padre Pio's companion and slept in the adjoining room, recounted, "Physically, he was prostrated, weak in the legs and arms. He walked slowly and painfully, supported by the arm. It was a very painful life. He was very discouraged and depressed.... Every time he would go out of his room to hear confessions or say Mass, he would, *'in dubitas libertas'* (in doubt, liberty).... He doubted whether he was solving the problems the right way.... He could not talk. He wasn't able to hold a conversation. He preferred to remain silent. His breathing was heavy because of asthma and bronchitis and he coughed all the time, like a horse. At night he would be more tired than if he'd been working all day, because of the coughing."[3]

During the sleepless nights, Padre Alessio heard Padre Pio murmuring continually, "My Jesus, my mother Mary, I offer up to you the groaning of my poor soul!" During the day, he would moan, "Jesus, call me!" and "I can't carry on anymore." Every night he would beg Padre Carmelo, the superior, "Give me the obedience to die."[4]

"For two or three months, he was hardly sleeping at all," Padre Alessio recounted. "He would sleep ten minutes, then he was up two or three hours, then he would sleep ten minutes more. You could hear him moving, turning, praying. He could no longer read. I gave him two books on Our Lady. He managed to read two or three pages. He could hear when he wanted to hear.... He was irritable sometimes for no reason.... But he was never irritable with me. In fact, he asked forgiveness for the trouble he was causing. He used to cry because he was a burden to me and to the community."[5]

Late in the spring, Padre Pio seemed very low, and Padre Alessio was convinced that much of his lethargy and confusion, as well as his frequent falls, were due to the Valium his doctors were prescribing in an attempt to get him to relax at night. "One at a time I took him off [the Valium pills] and gave him only vitamins," Padre Alessio recalled. "Little by little I would give him the drink *caramela*, an herbal tranquillizer." By summer, Padre Pio was sleeping better and was more active and alert.[6]

Nevertheless, Padre Pio continued to be silent and withdrawn. He fell more than once during Mass. Since late 1965, he had celebrated Mass seated, facing the congregation, and eventually he needed to be pushed in a wheelchair much of the time. In September 1966, Padre Carmelo, the guardian, wrote: "He has lost almost all his vivacity and high spirits. He speaks very little. He is completely withdrawn into himself. He very rarely behaves as he once did: telling stories, jokes, and using witticisms and lively words from which he opened up [conversations] on spiritual matters."[7]

"The Devils Won't Leave Me Alone for One Minute"

As he weakened, both physically, mentally, and emotionally, Padre Pio seemed to be oppressed more than ever by diabolical phenomenon. Bill Martin would sit with him sometimes in the evening. As he prayed in his armchair, Martin noted, Padre Pio would "look around in a semicircle, watching something that would rotate around him. It would make you feel eerie, because you knew he was seeing something." One time he startled Padre Raffaele, who had just heard his confession, by shouting, "Turn around!" He told him that a devil had just "gone at him," and he wanted to see if it was clutching the back of Raffaele's habit.[8]

Padre Alessio recalled, "He was afraid of devils.... One night he called me so many times that I got mad. 'Why don't you let me sleep at least a half-hour?' I asked him, and he said, 'Stay with me! The devils won't leave me alone for one minute!' So I stayed in his room all night. Devils appeared to him or threatened him. Once I would be there, he wouldn't be scared."[9] Padre Mariano remembered Padre Pio's face turn pale with terror. When asked what he saw, Padre Pio gasped, "I see a face."[10] Father John Schug was told by an unidentified friar that Padre Pio, in his last years, "had fear even of a mouse, because the devil would start out as a mouse and turn into a claw and go for his eyes."[11]

There were also heavenly manifestations. Padre Alessio recalled: "I saw Padre

Pio in ecstasy, completely absorbed. He was in a different world. His face was beautiful. Many times in the afternoon I would go into his room, open the door, and find him beautiful like this ... I would say, 'Father, it's time to go down for your confessions,' and he would become normal."[12]

"We're Leaving the Earth and Heading Toward Heaven"

On December 26, 1966, the city council proclaimed a day of celebration to mark Padre Pio's fifty years in San Giovanni Rotondo. Padre Pio was presented with a medallion, and a memorial tablet was unveiled in front of the old church. But any joy the aging priest might have felt was tempered by a series of newspaper articles which quoted extensively from his correspondence with Padres Benedetto and Agostino. "I beg you to see that my writings which I sent to my spiritual father and priests who have guided me spiritually are not published," Padre Pio wrote to his superior Padre Carmelo. "I kiss your hand and beg your holy blessing."[13] Knowing that they would not be sued, the editors ignored the request and continued the series.

Padre Pio's health continued to disintegrate, and eventually he needed to be pushed in a wheelchair much of the time. Some nights he was unable to rest at all because of a pain he compared to "an internal sword ... moving up and down my left side."[14] Awake most of the night, he would nod off during the day. His chest pains were worse, and he was now diagnosed with cardiac arrhythmia. His shortness of breath was so bad that at times he could hardly speak, and he now needed assistance in dressing, bathing, and other necessities. "I'm reduced to a state of helplessness," he lamented. "May the Lord call me now because I'm no longer permitted to be of any use to my brethren." He would pray, "Lord, what more can I do on this earth? Come and take me."[15] "One day, after he heard confessions, he began to cry like a baby," Padre Raffaele recounted. "He was mortified that he could not even get out of bed by himself and he was very much humiliated in front of those priests assigned to stay at his side day and night."[16] Nevertheless, Padre Pio managed to celebrate every day, although his Mass now lasted forty minutes or less. He still heard about fifty confessions a day, and each evening he was helped to his window to wave his handkerchief to the faithful assembled to wish him good night.

On April 26, 1968, he was told that eighty-year-old Maria Pyle had been taken to the *Casa* after suffering the latest in a series of strokes. When asked if he wanted to visit her, Padre Pio shook his head and said, "No, I'm going to pray to the Lord to take her home to be with the angels." When informed that she was gone, he remarked, "Now, at long last, she'll be able to listen to the celestial harmonies without having to accompany them."[17] He was too weak to attend her funeral in the crowded church or accompany the cortege that, to the tolling of the bells in the friary, conveyed her mortal remains to the mausoleum in the city cemetery that contained the bones of Padre Agostino, Pio's parents, and his brother Michele, who had finally succumbed at the age of nearly eighty-five, in May 1967.

Although most of those whom Padre Pio had loved best now slept in the cemetery, he knew that he was not destined to rest beside them. A tomb was being prepared in the crypt under the new church to receive his body. He predicted that as soon as the tomb was complete, he would die.

By July, he was in bed much of the time and frequently in great pain, and often now he was unable to celebrate Mass. He coughed constantly and had violent fits of suffocation, relieved only when he was "able to emit an abundant, viscous expectoration."[18] A spittoon was kept by his side at all times. Padre Alberto D'Apolito, notified by one of the doctors that Padre Pio was dying, sought and received a transfer to San Giovanni so as to be near him. Padre Pio told him, "I can't take it anymore! Lord, what am I doing here on earth now? Come and take me!" He would murmur, "They have all betrayed me." Nobody was quite sure what he meant.[19]

Cleonice Morcaldi described him as a "grieving phantom." "My Father, I'm tired to seeing you suffer and suffer," she cried. "At least tell me if this is the last station of your way of the cross."

"Yes, it's the last," replied the Padre. "But remember that it's the longest, most painful and torturous. It's agonizing."[20]

Often, when asked how he felt, Padre Pio would answer, "I am as God wills."[21] Other times, he would say, "Bad! Bad! Bad!"[22] He told Cleonice, "I'm dying! I'm dying! I'm preparing myself for the great passage."[23] "We're leaving the earth and heading toward heaven."[24]

Despite the obvious, many could not or would not believe that Padre Pio was dying. Some believed what a local prophet predicted: that Padre Pio would live to the age of ninety-nine. His niece Pia was incredulous when she asked him about a particular problem and he told her that it would be resolved in two years' time, but, by then, he would be gone.

By now, the stigmata were disappearing. For more than a year they had been gone from the feet, although they still hurt. The wound in the side no longer bled, and, by the spring of 1968, the hand wounds were vanishing. By summer, there were now only scabs, with just a touch of redness. Padre Onorato Marcucci, who, now that Padre Alessio was studying in Ireland, helped care for Padre Pio. He commented, "The ministry was finished, so the signs were finished."[25]

At times, Padre Pio seemed to doubt that he was in a state of grace. "You have respect for me, because you do not know me," he told a friend. "I am the greatest sinner on this earth."[26] His "every good intention was marred with vanity and pride," he insisted.[27] It was deeply disturbing to hear him lament, "I am not good! I don't know why this habit of St. Francis, which I wear so unworthily, does not jump off of me. The greatest criminal in the world is nothing compared to me. Compared to me, he is a gentleman. Pray for me, that I might become good."[28] Begging his fellow friars to pray for "final perseverance," he declared, "I'm afraid to meet Christ. I haven't corresponded to his love and to his infinite graces."[29]

A Letter to the Pope

In September, Padre Pio stopped eating almost entirely. Sometimes he could be coaxed to put a slice of fruit in his mouth, but he would vomit almost immediately. He said that he tried to eat, but nothing would stay down. Nevertheless, he mustered his last ounce of strength on September 12 to dictate a letter to Pope Paul VI, who had issued the encyclical *Humanae Vitae* on July 29, which reaffirmed traditional Church moral teaching, reiterating opposition to all forms of artificial birth control and immediately igniting an explosion of condemnation. With Pope Paul assailed by criticism of many laity and even some prominent figures in the Church, the dying priest was determined to express his support to the pontiff:

> I know that your heart is suffering much these days in the interest of Christ, for the peace of the world, for the innumerable necessities of the people of the world, but, above all, for the lack of obedience of some, even Catholics, to the high teachings that you, assisted by the Holy Spirit and in the Name of God, are giving us. I offer you my prayers and my daily sufferings as a small but sincere contribution on the part of the least of your sons in order that God may give you comfort with his grace to follow the straight and painful way in the defense of eternal truth, which never changes with the passing of the years. Also, in the name of my spiritual children and the Prayer Groups, I thank you for your clear and decisive words that you pronounced, especially in the last encyclical, *Humanae Vitae*, and I reaffirm my faith, my unconditional obedience, to your illuminated direction. May God grant victory to the truth, peace to his church, tranquility to the world, health and prosperity to Your Holiness, so that, once these fleeting clouds are dissipated, the Kingdom of God may triumph in all hearts, guided by your apostolic work as supreme pastor of all Christendom.[30]

"Jesus … Mary … "

September 20, 1968, was the fiftieth anniversary of Padre Pio's visible stigmatization, and San Giovanni Rotondo was packed with crowds of people, including delegates from the prayer groups, for the celebration on Sunday the twenty-second. Padre Pio, who had been murmuring, "Only the cemetery remains," celebrated Mass at five in the morning and then heard confessions. Later that day, he attended the public recitation of the Rosary and the Benediction. That evening a huge crowd, led by the mayor and city council, carrying torches and shouting, "*Viva Padre Pio,*" marched to the friary and gathered in the square in front of the church. They were disappointed that the Padre did not appear at the window. He was asleep and had no idea that the procession had taken place until he was told about it in the morning. When another priest wished him another fifty years, he responded, "What harm have I ever done you?"[31]

He was suffering terrible pains in the chest, palpitations, and breathlessness, and was unable to say Mass. Squeezing the hand of the superior, Padre Carmelo, he gasped, "It's over! It's over!"[32] By afternoon, he had rallied enough to be wheeled into church to attend the Benediction service, and that evening he was able to bless the huge throng that had assembled beneath his window. He seemed bewildered by all the acclamation, saying, "I'm so confused I could run away and hide."[33]

That evening, when Pietro Cugino went into his room, Padre Pio told him, "Good night, Pietru. I'm sorry, but I have to leave you." When Cugino answered, "Padre, let's hope that the Lord ..." Padre Pio interrupted, "Hey, I have to leave you."[34]

Sunday, September 22, marked the convocation of the First International Convention of Prayer Groups, and every hotel, inn, and boarding house in the city was packed. The *Casa* was resplendent with lights and flags, and a platform had been erected on the square in front of the church for the speakers of the day.

Padre Pio wanted to say the usual spoken "Low Mass" that morning, but the superior insisted that he sing High Mass for that festive occasion. The crowd broke into a cheer as he was wheeled in and helped to the altar — "almost dragged," Cleonice Morcaldi thought — by three friars. A hush fell on the congregation as, falteringly, his rheumy eyes seemingly fixed on another world, he began the Mass. He appeared "dazzled by the lights and lamps, defeated by the organ and the singing," and tears were rolling down his cheeks. Morcaldi noted that he seemed "absent." "He wasn't with us. We didn't feel his presence or his love.... He didn't seem to be aware that he was on the altar."[35]

Uncharacteristically, the dying friar made no attempt to hide his hands at any point during the Mass. Morcaldi observed that his hands were "beautiful, white, chubby, like those of a healthy child. His skin was clear like white marble."[36] And no wounds were visible.

The congregation had to strain to hear Padre Pio's weak, quavering voice. He needed prompting by the priests assisting him to get through the Mass. When he finished, cheers and cries of "*Viva Padre Pio*" went up. As he was being helped down and into his wheelchair, his legs gave out entirely, and only the efforts of Bill Martin and the other assisting friars kept Padre Pio from falling onto the floor. As he was wheeled into the sacristy, he held out his wasted arms and called weakly, "My children! My children!" After that, he was taken into the elevator and up to his room.

Shortly afterward he received his nephew Ettoruccio and his five-year-old son

Pio. When the nephew asked if, on the night of the candlelight procession, he had been in ecstasy, he answered, "You want to know too much. Kiss my hand and go about your business. Leave me alone, for I'm weary, very weary." He turned, however, to the little grandnephew and bade him, "You carry my name. I want you to live up to it. Understand?"[37]

The crypt was blessed in the morning, and in the afternoon the first stone was laid for the Way of the Cross that was being erected on the hillside above the church. Unexpectedly, around ten o'clock, supported by two friars, Padre Pio appeared in the window of the old choir and blessed the throng in the plaza below, who, in turn, responded by waving their handkerchiefs and crying, "*Viva! Viva! Viva!*"

After that, he was wheeled back to his room, where lunch was brought to him. He was able to eat a bit of pasta and spinach rings and seemed to enjoy it. Then he went to bed, with Padre Onorato and Bill Martin taking turns watching him.

At six, Padre Pio asked to be taken to the balcony overlooking the big church, where Mass was being celebrated. At its conclusion, he tried to rise to bless the congregation, but doubled up, unable to move. Finally, he succeeded in lifting his right arm to bless the people. Later he was able to appear at the window of his room to wave his handkerchief to the immense crowd who stood with torches and candles.

"I belong more to the other world than to this one," he told his old friend Padre Raffaele. "Pray to the Lord for me to die." Distressed at seeing him in such terrible pain, Padre Raffaele summoned a Dr. Bruno Pavoni from the hospital, and asked him why Padre Pio had been given no painkiller. "He doesn't want it," the doctor told him. As Padre Raffaele left, he bent over and kissed Padre Pio on the forehead. Padre Pio embraced him, kissed him, and said, "Thanks for everything. May the Lord reward you for your love."[38]

Padre Pellegrino came on duty at 9:00 p.m. and stayed in the adjoining room. During the next three hours, Padre Pio called him five or six times. His eyes were wet with weeping. He seemed to be under diabolic assault. Padre Pellegrino was reminded of a frightened child as the old man wrung his hand and pleaded, "Stay with me, my boy, stay with me." Again and again he asked the time and inquired, "Have you said Mass yet, son?" When Pellegrino replied that it was still too early, Padre Pio told him, "This morning you'll say Mass for me."

Padre Pio then received the Sacrament of Reconciliation. He told Padre Pellegrino, "Son, if the Lord calls me tonight, ask all my brothers to forgive me for all the trouble that I've caused them, and ask all our fellow priests and my spiritual children to say a prayer for my soul." When Padre Pellegrino asked a last blessing for all fellow priests, spiritual children, and for all the sick, Padre Pio whispered, "Of course. I bless them all. Ask the guardian to give them all this last blessing from me."[39]

Having renewed his vows of poverty, chastity, and obedience, Padre Pio expressed a desire to get out of bed. It was 1:30 in the morning of the twenty-third. Pellegrino helped him rise, and Padre Pio walked with surprising vigor into the adjoining veranda, where he turned on the light and sat down. Five minutes later, however, he asked Pellegrino to help him back into his room. He was now unable to walk, and Padre Pellegrino fetched the wheelchair. When he reached his room, Padre Pio collapsed into his armchair, looked up, and whispered, "I see two mothers."[40] He seemed to mean his own mother and the Virgin Mary. His lips were turning blue.

"I'm going to call a doctor," Padre Pellegrino said, but Padre Pio objected, "Don't disturb anyone." After a few minutes, Padre Pellegrino insisted that he was calling for medical assistance. When Padre Pio once more objected, Padre Pellegrino asserted, "Spiritual Father, leave this to me."

Padre Pellegrino ran down the corridor to phone Dr. Sala, alerting the other friars as he passed their rooms. Martin entered the room and, finding Padre Pio slumped in his chair, dripping wet, took a towel and tried to dry him. "Don't worry.... You'll come out of it," he told him. Padre Pio's only response was to murmur: "Jesus ... Mary ..." Padre Pellegrino came back into the room, along with other friars. Soon Dr. Sala and Dr. Gusso arrived and started to administer oxygen. Since she was a woman, Pio's niece Pia was not allowed to enter the enclosure, but when she was notified that her uncle was dying, her husband, Mario Pennelli, hastened to the friary. Two more doctors arrived.

Sala began to administer injections to stimulate Padre Pio's failing heart. Padre Carmelo administered the Sacrament of the Sick. Padre Pio continued to whisper "Jesus ... Mary ... Jesus ... Mary."[41]

At 2:30 a.m., weeping, Dr. Sala cried, "Padre! Padre!" Padre Pio opened his eyes, looked at him, and closed them again, turned his head to the right, gave a little cough, and, as the group standing around the armchair offered the prayers for the dying, stopped breathing. Sala administered mouth-to-mouth resuscitation and pounded on the chest of the moribund man. The heart started again, and there followed the sound of a few more breaths — and then, silence. Sala noted that the face of Padre Pio was "pale, distended, and bloodless," and the lips "slightly parted, like a little bird's."[42] Gusso observed "the clinical signs of death, the most peaceful and sweet I have ever seen."[43] So peaceful had been his transition that most of the friars in the room failed to realize that Padre Pio was gone.

Soon the corridors rang with the cries of weeping women. Cleonice Morcaldi and a friend, observing the doctors rushing toward the friary, followed one of them unobserved and sneaked into the room where Padre Pio's body lay, and, wailing, started embracing and kissing his lifeless form until the superior discovered them and ordered them, "Get out! Get out!"[44] Meanwhile, the usual crowd had been gathering outside the church, waiting for Padre Pio to celebrate Mass and unaware of his passing. When they were informed that their beloved priest was dead, in the words of Morcaldi, "They bellowed like wounded bulls."[45]

"No Traces of Wounds"

Ten minutes after Padre Pio's death, in the presence of four other friars, Padre Giacomo Piccirillo photographed the hands, feet, and thorax of the dead priest. The wounds on the feet had disappeared around 1966, and the wound in the side stopped bleeding and healed the next year. From Easter 1968, the wounds on the backs of the hands began to go and were gone by mid-summer. Likewise, the wounds on the palms began to heal, and the last crust had fallen off at the moment of death.[46] Dr. Sala, who supervised, noted:

> The hands, feet, and trunk and every other part of the body showed no traces of wounds, nor were there scars present on hand or foot, neither on the front or back, nor on the heel, nor on the side, where in life there had been visible and well-demarcated wounds. The skin in those places was the same as that in every other part of the body, and the pressure of the finger showed no evidence of a depression in the skin or subcutaneous tissue nor a displacement of the bones or recession of either. The appearance, the color, the consistency revealed nothing in particular nor the presence of signs of previous incisions, lacerations, cuts, wounds, or inflammatory reactions.

The skin of the hands, feet, and trunk was "normal, intact, and of uniform color, the same as the rest of the corpse."[47] Those who had examined the stigmata over the years had disagreed about the depth of the wound. However, with the exception of Monsignor Rossi, the inquisitor, who was not a doctor, they all agreed that the wounds, whatever their origin or explanation, were sufficiently deep to have left a scar when they healed. Now there was no sign that they had ever existed. The body was placed in a wooden coffin, a stole around the shoulder, a rosary, crucifix, and Franciscan Rule in the hands, which, even without the wounds, were covered with gloves.

"A Marvelous Spectacle"

Almost immediately, word of Padre Pio's passing spread throughout Europe and the rest of the world. "An immense sea of people" congregated outside the friary, and the *carabinieri* were called to keep order. They nailed pews together to form a barrier and placed the coffin at the foot of the altar. When the troopers were at their places all over the church, the doors were opened between 8:00 and 8:30 a.m., and hundreds of people, "shouting, praying, and crying,"[48] surged forward to view the mortal remains of "The Wise Man of the Gargano."

All day long the faithful moved past the coffin. At nightfall, in order to relieve the troopers and police, the friars closed the church, but the crowds went berserk and forced them to reopen after a few minutes. During this interval, the body was injected with formalin (a preservative) to slow the process of decomposition and was placed in a closed steel casket with a glass top, to prevent fanatics from dismembering it to obtain relics. For another sixty hours, the faithful, pouring in from all parts of the world, filed by the casket, until noon on September 26. Among those present was Padre Pio's estranged sister, seven months away from her own death. Also there was Padre Giustino. A Venetian priest who had been a friend of the deceased reproached him, saying, "You made Padre Pio die before his time!" only to have Padre Giustino refuse to apologize, insisting, "What I did I would do again!"[49]

That afternoon the casket was placed on an open hearse and driven through the streets of the city. An observer wrote:

> Along the road, in front of doors, on the footpaths, balconies, at the windows, everywhere, were people who cried, prayed, and invoked Padre Pio, who passed among his spiritual children for the last time. It was a marvelous spectacle; those who did not see it could neither believe it nor imagine it.... Helicopters [dropped] flowers and leaflets on the crowd which followed the sad cortege in an orderly and devout manner. Many people, furthermore, preferred to remain on the piazza in front of the church and clinic, fearing that they would not find a place when the cortege re-entered the church. From the microphone on the platform, the Honorable Enrico Medi engaged all those people in prayer, reciting the Rosary and commenting on the various mysteries with touching, uplifting, and devout references to Padre Pio.[50]

It was estimated that more than one hundred thousand people attended the funeral.

It was dark when the body was brought back to the church, where, at 7:00 p.m., the Requiem Mass was celebrated by Father Johannes Franciscus Maria Schutijser, minister general of the Capuchin order, assisted by more than twenty other priests. The eulogy was given by Padre Clemente of Santa Maria in Punta, now definitor general, who read a message from Pope Paul, conferring an apostolic blessing on the religious community, the staff of the hospital, and the entire population of San Giovanni Rotondo. At 10:00 p.m., the coffin was lowered into its niche in the crypt and enclosed in a sarcophagus of blue Labrador granite. Padre Pio's earthly pilgrimage was finally at an end.

"Padre Pio Lives!"
Miracles of Intercession

Six Million Visitors a Year

With Padre Pio gone, some newspapers predicted that San Giovanni Rotondo would soon be a ghost town, dried up like an uprooted plant. Visitors to the city did decline somewhat for a while, then picked back up and generally increased every year. As of this writing, with approximately six million visitors a year, San Giovanni Rotondo draws more pilgrims than any other religious shrine in the world, except Guadalupe in Mexico (ten million), St. Peter's Basilica in Rome and Lourdes (seven million each), and Jerusalem (six million). Moreover, in 2017, the *Casa*, with 1,200 beds and a full waiting list, was considered one of the best hospitals in Europe. In addition, an outpatient hospital facility called Poliambulatorio Giovanni Paolo II is now in operation, as well as a retirement home and a center for scientific research.

On the fifteenth anniversary of Padre Pio's death, Pope John Paul II visited San Giovanni Rotondo, and, speaking to a crowd of 18,000, praised the Capuchin "who for almost fifty years lived out and realized his religious consecration to God almost exclusively in continuous, persistent, and fervent prayer, and in the ministry of reconciliation, guiding and directing thousands of the faithful who were seeking the authentic way of perfection and of Christian holiness."[1] The pope returned there in 1987, on the hundredth anniversary of Padre Pio's birth, to address a massive crowd at a park constructed specially for the occasion, and prayed at the tomb of the stigmatized friar. The same year saw a visit by Mother Teresa of Calcutta, who also prayed before Padre Pio's sarcophagus.

"Send That Friar Away!"

In the years following his death, there have been reports of people who insist that they have encountered Padre Pio in visions and through the "aroma of paradise."

For example, Padre Alberto D'Apolito interviewed a woman who, in 1972, asked Padre Pio to intercede for her husband, who was suffering miserably with terminal cancer. Shortly afterward, lying in bed at home with several family members around him, the invalid began to shout, "Send that friar away! Get him away from here! He's telling me to go with him! I don't want to go!" When assured that there was no friar in the house, the man shouted, "Don't you see him? There he is at the foot of the bed! He's insisting that I go with him. Send him away. He's a Capuchin friar and has a white beard. Now he's leaving. He told me that he will come for me on the fifth of February."

It was then November. Immediately, the man began to improve until he seemed to be almost well. When shown a photograph of Padre Pio, he quickly identified him as the friar he had seen at the foot of his bed. For more than two months, this unnamed man was well and went to church every day and received the Blessed Sacrament. Late in January 1973, however, he relapsed. His wife told Padre Alberto: "This time he was serene. He prayed almost without ceasing. Every day he received Holy Communion.... On the fifth of February 1973, Padre Pio kept his promise and returned for him. My husband died serenely, with the name of Jesus on his lips."[2]

"Nothing Will Be Done Without My Hand"

Father John Schug, in 1971, interviewed a twenty-four-year-old German-Swiss woman named Agnese Stump, who lived in Voghera, in northern Italy. Four years earlier, she had developed occasional pains in her left knee, which her family physician attributed to arthritis. When the pains grew worse, X-rays revealed a "neoplasm of the tibia in the left knee."

Afraid of surgery, Stump asked her parents to go to San Giovanni, to consult Padre Pio. On December 27, 1967, he said to tell her to "go ahead and have the operation. Don't be afraid. Nothing will be done without my hand. I will assist Agnese in my prayers and guide the hand that operates on her."

In January 1968, the tumor was removed, and Stump returned home with her leg in a cast. In October (a month after Padre Pio's death), the pains returned, and this time a biopsy revealed osteosarcoma (bone cancer), which had already spread to her bone marrow and bloodstream. One doctor was in favor of amputation, but all others felt that the cancer was too advanced and her case was terminal.

On December 20, 1968, Stump went to San Giovanni and prayed at Padre Pio's tomb. Later, she dreamt that Padre Pio told her to discard her crutches. When she awoke, she was able to walk with only a cane. After several months, she was completely well. Her doctors were impressed, even more than by the disappearance of the cancer, by the replacement by healthy bone of the large portion of her tibia that had been destroyed. She reported that the surgeon who had operated on her wept when he saw the X-rays, declaring, "It is a miracle," and called all his doctor friends into his office to "look at the miracle woman." When Father John Schug interviewed her at her home two years after her cure, she showed him "before and after" X-rays, and he, though untrained in medicine, was able to detect a striking difference in the two sets.[3]

Not a Ghost

Father Joseph Pius related an account of a woman from Palermo, Sicily, who was in Padua in June 1976 for surgery for a perforated ulcer, while the prayer group in her home city interceded for her. Shortly before she was to have part of her stomach removed, she saw Padre Pio "in broad daylight," beside her bed. He was not a ghost, because he touched her physically, placing his hands on her stomach. Instantly, she felt a change, and the doctors, upon examining her, found that the ulcer had vanished. She left the hospital without surgery or medication.

A Hip Restored

While he was on earth, Padre Pio's family were seldom, if ever, recipients of healing graces. Almost all of his nieces and nephews died young. However, the son of Padre Pio's niece Pia Forgione received a grace. Michele Pennelli, at twenty-three, was suffering from aseptic necrosis at the head of the femur (thigh). Caused by poor blood supply, this condition leads to the decay of the bone. Pennelli could not walk without excruciating pain. Hoping for a hip replacement, he traveled to the Gemelli Clinic of Rome — named for an archenemy of his granduncle, but one of the best hospitals in Italy. There he was told that the operation might not be successful and that he might be confined for life to a wheelchair. Nevertheless, he decided to have the operation and returned home to San Giovanni Rotondo to attend to some matters before returning to Rome for surgery. Then, suddenly, without any supernatural manifestations — no visions, no aromas — he was healed. When he went back to the Gemelli Clinic, the doctors there said that the signs of bone damage had vanished and there was no need for a prosthetic hip. After several years, he was still free of pain and disability.

"Isn't that Uncle Charley?"

On December 2, 1983, Paul Walsh of Ridley Park, Pennsylvania, then a seventeen-year-old senior at St. James High School in Chester, Pennsylvania, lost control of his car on an icy road at 10:30 at night and crashed at high speed into a telephone pole. Taken by ambulance to Taylor Hospital in Ridley Park, it was determined that he had sustained serious head injuries and multiple facial bone fractures, including severe damage to his "middle face," nose, and jaw, as well as deep facial lacerations. Because of the severity of his injuries, Paul was transferred to Crozer-Chester Medical Center. After ten hours of surgery, he seemed to improve. He regained consciousness, and his recovery seemed to be proceeding well until December 26, when he became delirious, and it was discovered that cerebral-spinal fluid was leaking from the broken bones on the floor of his shattered skull. His doctors tried unsuccessfully to seal off the leaks by means of daily spinal taps, and finally, in order to drain off the fluid, a shunt, or drainage tube, was implanted in the brain. Even so, Paul continued to suffer from hydrocephalus, which is an accumulation of fluid in the ventricles of the brain. He also developed spinal meningitis. As a result of damage to the pituitary gland, he developed diabetes insipidus. In this disorder, the body is unable to conserve water, and the patient excretes huge amounts of urine and suffers from extreme thirst. Intravenous injections were used to control the condition. The physicians told Paul's parents that the diabetes insipidus would persist for whatever remained of his life — which did not appear to be long, as the meningitis and hydrocephalus refused to clear up, and the patient remained comatose and feverish, his breathing and heartbeat irregular.

The Walsh parents, who were devout Catholics, as well as their nine other children, offered a nightly Rosary for Paul. "We called on all the saints that we could think of to pray with us for Paul," recalled his mother, Betty. "I blessed him with relics of St. Pius X and St. John Neumann, a small statue of St. Anthony, holy oil, and holy water from Lourdes and Fátima." When Paul still showed no sign of improvement, his father inquired among his friends whether there was "someone who was being considered for sainthood who needs a miracle credited to his or her intercession." Someone suggested Padre Pio, and so the Walshes began to ask for his intercession as well. As soon as they did this, Paul's mother noticed that the patient, while still otherwise unconscious, nevertheless crossed himself whenever the name of Padre Pio was invoked.

The Walshes then found some prayer leaflets with the name of Vera Calandra (1934–2004), director of the National Centre for Padre Pio, which was then in Norristown, Pennsylvania. They phoned her, and she sent her husband, Harry, to Crozer-Chester the very next day with one of Padre Pio's gloves. When Calandra blessed Walsh with the glove, nothing seemed to happen, but a few days later his mother noticed that some of the intravenous medications had been removed. She was told that on the very day that he had been blessed, the diabetes insipidus (which was supposed to have been permanent) suddenly disappeared.

Nevertheless, Paul's condition continued to worsen. The first shunt was not working, and on March 21 another was inserted. This, too, did not work. At this point, the physicians informed the parents that their son had suffered "permanent, irreversible" brain damage. The frontal lobe of the brain had collapsed due to the hydrocephalus. The most that the Walshes could hope for was Paul's survival in a persistent vegetative state, in a nursing home that would provide lifetime care.

Then, one night, Betty Walsh smelled a beautiful aroma in Paul's hospital room.

"It was if I had walked into a flower garden," she wrote. Shortly afterward, while she and her mother stood at his bedside, Paul suffered a seizure, stopped breathing, and was put on a respirator. They were sure that the end had come for the unfortunate boy, but, after four days, Paul began to breathe on his own.

On April 6, Harry Calandra returned to Crozer-Chester, after a trip to San Giovanni Rotondo, during which he and Vera had touched Padre Pio's tomb with a picture of Paul. Once again he blessed Paul with Padre Pio's glove. Suddenly, Paul opened his eyes, but closed them again. However, the next day, when his parents came to see him, Paul was fully alert and talking coherently, and from then on, he began to improve.

When his parents visited on April 22, which was Easter Sunday, Paul insisted that his uncle Charley had been in to see him early that morning. By this time, Paul was no longer in intensive care and was in a semiprivate room. The boy who shared the room confirmed that a man had indeed come to visit that morning. When Paul's mother asked, "What did he look like?" Paul related, "He was fat and had a beard." The mother responded, "That does sound like Uncle Charley, but it couldn't have been him, since he lives out of state and I know he wasn't here." The roommate said that the bearded fat man seemed to be a priest dressed in a brown robe. "When I woke up early Sunday morning I saw this man standing at the foot of Paul's bed, staring at him and smiling." Paul continued to insist that the visitor was his uncle, while his mother was mystified, since Charley most definitely was not in town, and she didn't know of any priest who wore a brown robe.

In the meantime, a niece of Betty Walsh had seen a leaflet of Padre Pio on her mother's coffee table, and, picking it up, said, "Uncle Charley!" When the girl's mother heard what she had seen, she called her sister Betty to ask, "Do you think it was possible that Padre Pio came to Paul on Easter Sunday and Paul thought it was Uncle Charley?"

Paul's mother then took the leaflet with Padre Pio's picture on it and folded it so that Paul could see only the face. Showing it to him, she asked, "Is this who visited you on Easter Sunday?"

"Yes," replied Paul. "Isn't that Uncle Charley?"

Unfolding the picture, the mother answered, "No, it's Padre Pio."

Paul objected, "You think Padre Pio came to visit me? But, he's dead! That's who visited me, but I thought it was Uncle Charley." When asked what the visitor had said, Paul could recall only that he stood at the foot of the bed, smiling, and saying, "You're looking well!"

Was Paul Walsh's recovery a miracle? The physicians Ravreby and Nelson, who wrote the "Summary on Discharge" of Paul's case history at Crozer-Chester Medical Center, refused to sign a statement certifying to the miraculous nature of his recovery. However, in a letter dated June 19, 1985, one of the doctors on the case,

Michael Ryan, an oral and maxillofacial surgeon, wrote, "It was my feeling, based on previous experience, that he would not survive. The fact that he did survive and survive with almost total normal return to his cerebral functions is unexplained to me on a purely medical and scientific basis. It is my feeling that without the help of a supernatural influence, Paul would today be dead or continue to be in a comatose state." That same year, three physicians who examined Paul's cortical-tissue (CT) scans and the records of his case — but who had not actually treated him during his hospitalization — affirmed that the young man's recovery "without any neuro-logical deficit" is "without logical medical explanation."[4]

"When I Reach Heaven, I Will Ask Someone to Help My Girl"

Another instance of a dramatic recovery attributed to the intercession of Padre Pio is the case of Mrs. Alice Jones of St. Helen's, Merseyside, England, who suffered a disabling injury while working as a teacher at St. James Infant School when she was forty-one years old. She wrote:

On the afternoon of March 27th 1973, I was injured whilst stacking tables in the Parish Room of St. James [Anglican] Church in Haydock. The room was being used as a temporary classroom during re-decoration of the Infant School. As I lifted one of the tables, a small boy ran towards me, and I twisted my body and fell onto a radiator.... At first, my lower back and legs felt numb, but gradually, as sensation returned, I became aware of severe pain. My doctor ordered complete bedrest for 3 weeks, then I was referred to an orthopaedic consultant, who issued me with a corset, and advised more rest. During the next twelve months, the pain intensified, and I was advised to have an operation.

Mr. Heron carried out the operation at Broadgreen Hospital in Liverpool. He found that the nerve leaving the spinal cord had been trapped in such a way that it had ballooned, causing a neurofibroma. This tumour could not be removed, so part of the bone structure of the spine was hollowed out, so that the nerve could pass through an opening. I made good progress after this surgery, but my left foot and leg remained numb. Mr. Herron was never fully satisfied with the result, and decided to review me again in January, 1975. Unfortunately, Mr. Heron died just days before I was due to see him.

Arrangements were made for me to be placed under the care of Mr. Jackson, a young man with new ideas. He carried out several manipulations and injections, but I still had severe pain and I began to fall. After a lengthy consultation, I agreed to undergo further surgery, to stabilise my weak spine. In November, 1976, I had an operation to fuse my lower back, and, after this, I lay for 14 weeks totally encased in plaster of Paris, being turned every four hours by a crane. Fortunately, my husband was an orthopaedic nurse and was able to assist with the procedure. Bone had been taken from my right hip to "make" a new spine. The operation was a complete failure. I suffered more intense pain, and more potent drugs were prescribed to combat the painful spasms of the muscles. Within 12 months I was back in hospital for further surgery, when my hip became infected in the donor site. By this time I could hardly walk at all, even with the aid of elbow crutches and calliper. I became very despondent. After each visit to the consultant I came away without any hope.

My family doctor referred me to a neurosurgeon in Liverpool, who looked at the X-rays and decided that I had had too much unsuccessful surgery. He was very unwilling to advise any further treatment. I became completely disabled, unable to look after myself or my family. I found it very difficult to talk about it, [and] my faith in God began to fail.

On April 1st 1979 my daughter Alison brought my mother to our house; it was her usual Sunday visit. Mother sat in the chair. I was lying on a sheep-skin rug on the floor, and she began to talk about her death. My daughter became very angry and accused my mother of being morbid. (My disablement had had a disastrous effect on Alison.) With tears in her eyes my mother said, "When I reach Heaven, I will ask someone to help my girl." The following Friday, April 6th [my husband] Frank found my mother dead in bed at her flat. To me, this was the final straw. I could not come to terms with the manner of her death and I began to rely more and more on the drugs to ease both the pain and the bitterness I felt within me.

At the beginning of 1980, St. James Church was planning a celebration to mark the Centenary of the Liverpool Diocese. It was decided that there would be a Mission in May of that year, conducted by the [Anglican] Community of the Resurrection at Mirfield. There would be 2 visiting priests, Fr. Gabriel and Fr. Eric Fisher, who was reputed to be a healer. Fr. Fisher's parish was St. Mary's in Buxton, Derbyshire, where he held regular healing services.

I cannot honestly say that I was enthusiastic about the Mission, and when Canon Wilson telephoned Frank on May 18th and told him that Fr. Fisher would visit me the following morning, I was extremely reluctant to see him. I had spent so much money, almost all our savings, seeking medical opinions, that I did not believe that a healer could help me.

The following morning, Lesley, my daughter, arrived with Andrew, my grandson, who was 6 months old. Then, at 11 o'clock, Fr. Fisher arrived on my doorstep. I told him that his visit was a waste of time, but he sat down and talked to me for quite some time. I found I was able to unburden myself to him, and, before leaving, he suggested that he put his hand on my back. I felt a great surge of heat, even though I was wearing a steel corset. He went out, and I thought that was the end of it. Lesley commented on the smell of "aftershave," and I thought perhaps he carried herbs. I was always aware of the smell of the discharge from the ulcer under my left heel, which was dressed every morning. It looked like a small "cauliflower," but was very deep at the core. It would not heal, due to the poor nerve conduction in my left leg. I joked to Lesley that someone had obviously warned Fr. Fisher about my foot.

The following morning, I was very surprised to find Fr. Fisher on my doorstep again. Lesley and Andrew were also there, and my son-in-law Stephen came in. Fr. Fisher said that he had held an intercession for the sick during the night, and he had been "told" to come back to me. He knelt down, and began to remove the calliper from my leg, although I protested, being afraid of bringing my back into a painful spasm. Once the calliper had been removed, he put his hands onto my leg and began to pray. I could not tell what he was saying, because I began to feel pain in my leg, which became so severe that I cried out for him to stop. As I looked down at him, he seemed changed. I saw an older face, a man with a beard. I looked away, it was an hallucination, but when I turned back the older man was standing by my side. I thought it must be Fr. Gabriel. I was aware of two men in my home. Fr. Fisher was kneeling at my side; the older man was dressed in a monk's habit, standing at my side. They were entirely different people. The older man seemed to take over. Although I could hear Fr. Fisher's voice, I also heard the older man speaking to me in a foreign language. Neither my daughter nor Fr. Fisher saw anyone else, although my daughter smelled perfume. The older man blessed me twice, making the sign of the Cross, saying, "Gesu, Maria, Gesu, Maria." There was a great feeling of love and warmth, and he took my arm, saying, "In the name of Jesus, get up and walk." With his help I got out of the chair and walked across the living room, half way. I knew that he had released my arm, and when I turned at the door, only Fr. Fisher remained kneeling. I had no pain, and my leg had filled out and my tilted pelvis had straightened. I looked at my daughter, who was in tears, and then at Fr. Fisher. We were all in quite an emotional state, and Lesley commented again on the smell of perfume. Fr. Fisher left us, to take in what had happened, and I promised to attend the Healing Service that evening in Church. Frank telephoned at lunch to see whether I needed anything, and I shouted down the phone that I could walk. My main concern was shoes; the shoe attached to the calliper had a foot support which I no longer needed, so the shoe was useless. Lesley helped me out of my spinal support, and we searched the wardrobe for shoes. We found a pair of high heels, very outdated, but I put them on and managed to walk around the room. Frank came home early and I ran down the drive to meet him. We hugged each other, weeping tears of joy.

That night we went as a family to give thanks in Church. Fr. Fisher called me out to speak to the large crowd. I met Fr. Gabriel and realized that he was not the stranger I had seen in my living room earlier in the day. After the service we went home and I became emotional and told Frank that I had seen "Moses." Frank thought I was overwrought and suggested that I go to bed. I did not need any tablets or sleeping pills. I slept all night, but Frank kept a "vigil" by the bed. He was afraid it was all a dream. He woke me the next morning to do the dressing on my foot, but the ulcer had gone. We found the dressing rolled up in the bed. Frank wept, and said it was a miracle.

I decided to go to Holy Communion and give thanks to God through the Sacrament. I find it very difficult to describe, but it was as though I saw everything with new eyes. The words of the Liturgy became very real and in some way I felt an actual participant in the Lord's Supper. As I left Church, Fr. Fisher stood in the doorway. He handed me a prayer card and I looked down at the face of Padre Pio, the friend who had been in my home the previous day. I experienced a sense of relief, at least he was real and not imaginary, but, on reaching home, I was very shocked to find that he had died in 1968. I returned to Church to find Fr. Fisher, but he had gone back to Buxton. I tried to explain my feelings to Canon Wilson, and he gently told me that I had had a vision. I had never heard of Padre Pio, but he seemed to dog my footsteps. I was anxious to discover more about him, and despite numerous enquiries, I could find no explanation.

We went to the Commemoration Day at Mirfield in July and there in the book shop was a poster advertising a book, "Who is Padre Pio?" I went to Frank, "That is for me," and I bought the book, then went in search of Fr. Fisher. I discussed the matter with him. I had begun to think I was going insane. He suggested I go to San Giovanni Rotondo, with all my medical records, but I told him that this was financially impossible. He then invited Frank and I to a Healing Service in Buxton the following Wednesday.

We went to St. Anne's Church, and in the pew were two envelopes, one with the air tickets to Naples and the other containing forms to hire a car. We were due to go in late October, accompanied by Fr. Fisher and Betty Packham, who planned to go into the Church as a deaconess. Both Frank and I were absolutely overwhelmed by this gift....

As the time drew near for the pilgrimage, I began to experience strange dreams. It was as though I was being shown pictures which meant nothing to me. I did not see any real detail of the pictures, but the frames were a peculiar bell-shape. I jumped out of bed in the early hours one morning to draw the shape of the picture frame. I saw a door which I felt I wanted to go through, but none of this made any sense....

It was agreed that I would go into the Providence Hospital for X-rays and tests. The physical examination showed a straight spine within normal limits, but the X-rays showed a badly deformed spinal column. Dr. Mooney [a pathologist] was so puzzled that he asked a Dr. McCarthy to examine me and re-X-ray the spine. The results were the same, so the two doctors wrote, "There must be a supernatural intervention in the disease, otherwise this patient would not be able to walk unaided." Both doctors signed the statement.

At the end of October, 1980, we all left England for Italy.... We arrived in San Giovanni Rotondo late in the evening and stayed at a Convent near the Church of Our Lady of Grace. The following morning we went to the church to pray.... In the small church I noticed my pictures on the walls. They were Stations of the Cross, with the same peculiar bell-shaped frames I had seen in my dreams. I found the door at the side of the Altar, and Frank tried to pull me back, but Fr. Fisher said, "Let her go." I found the staircase which brought me right to the foot of the cross where Padre Pio had received the Stigmata. Fr. Fisher said, "Look where he has brought you; now you can only go forward from here...."

During the next three days I was questioned by Fr. Alessio, Fr. Gerardo, and Fr. Joseph Pius, an American.... On the third day, Fr. Joseph took us to Padre Pio's cell, where all the items were sealed in glass. I approached a chair and as I touched it I felt compelled to say, "Gesu, Maria." Fr. Joseph asked me why I had used those words, and I explained that Padre Pio had greeted me in that way. He told me that the Padre had died in that chair, repeated, "Gesu, Maria," over and over again until his last breath. I began to see once again his face and I described a mark which I particularly remembered. Fr. Joseph ... embraced me, saying, "Go in peace, you have seen him...."

I have often wondered why Padre Pio appeared to me, an Anglican, but in his own words he answers, "I belong to everyone, everyone will say Padre Pio is mine. I can refuse no one, since the Good Lord has never refused my humble requests."[5]

For many, Padre Pio, long after his physical death, lives indeed, fulfilling a promise he allegedly made, that he would be able to do more for his children after death than in life. Although some will try to explain away some or all of the testimonies, as Dr. Giuseppe Gusso of the *Casa*, one of Padre Pio's doctors, told the author, "They can't *all* be tall tales."

Saint Pio

Beatification

After Padre Pio's death, many of his devotees expected his rapid elevation to the altar, but for a decade and a half his cause virtually stood still. Kenneth L. Woodward wrote in *Making Saints*, in 1990, that the Capuchin order began informally to gather information on behalf of Padre Pio almost as soon as he died, but then "something mysterious happened: someone in Rome, surely with the authority of Pope Paul VI, decreed that the local process on Padre Pio could not be opened."[1] Not a few people felt that the Maccari report was proving an insuperable obstacle.

Whatever the cause for the delay, it ended in 1983. Some have speculated that Pope John Paul II, because of his own devotion to Padre Pio, broke the impasse. The diocesan process for the cause of Padre Pio's canonization — supported by "postulatory letters" by eight cardinals, thirty-one archbishops, and seventy-two bishops[2] — opened at San Giovanni Rotondo with a service attended by twenty thousand worshipers on March 20 of that year.

The diocesan process took six years. It consisted of studies by an ecclesiastical tribunal composed of five members, which was authorized to collect evidence from witnesses, and a historical commission, which consisted of five experts whose task was to collect and examine the published and unpublished writings of Padre Pio, as well as any other documents relevant to the cause. The ecclesiastical tribunal interviewed seventy-three persons (starting with Padre Onorato Marcucci, on April 7, 1984), in no less than one hundred eighty-two sessions. The historical commission amassed ten thousand pages of writings by and about Padre Pio, divided into twenty volumes![3]

On January 21, 1990, thousands jammed into the friary church at San Giovanni Rotondo to celebrate the completion of the diocesan process. Then, on February 12, the volumes of documentation were presented to Monsignor Antonio Casieri, chancellor of the Congregation for the Causes of Saints, by Monsignor Valentino Vailati, archbishop of Manfredonia, Padre Paolino Rossi, postulator of the cause, and Padre Gerardo Di Flumeri, the vice-postulator.

It took seven years for the Congregation for the Causes of Saints to study the massive documentation. Then, on June 13, 1997, the theologians of the congregation voted that Padre Pio had in fact practiced the theological and cardinal virtues to a heroic degree. On October 21, the cardinals and bishops of the congregation concurred and informed the pope, who accepted and approved the verdict of the congregation and ordered the preparation of a decree on the heroic virtues of the Servant of God. A year later, on December 18, Pope John Paul II declared: "I verify that the Servant of God Padre Pio of Pietrelcina, in the world Francesco Forgione, a professed priest of the Order of the Capuchin Friars Minor, practiced to a heroic degree the theological virtues of faith, hope, and charity, towards God and his neighbor, as well as the cardinal virtues of prudence, justice, fortitude, and temperance, and those virtues related, to the ends and effects that they regard."[4]

Now, all that was necessary for Padre Pio's beatification was a canonical miracle, and one was ready for approval. It had occurred three years earlier. Consiglia De Martino, wife of Antonio Rinaldi, was taken to the Riuniti Hospital in Salerno on November 1, 1995, where it was determined that a thoracic duct in her neck had ruptured, with the result that a huge lump containing two liters of lymphatic fluid had formed in her neck. This was confirmed by two CT scans performed that day. De Martino was informed that it was necessary for her to undergo a "difficult and complicated" operation "as soon as possible." Surgery was scheduled for November 3.[5] In the meantime, De Martino, a longtime devotee of Padre Pio, who had been invoking his intercession ever since she arrived at the hospital, telephoned Fra Modestino at San Giovanni Rotondo, asking him for prayer. Modestino later reported, "I went immediately to the tomb of Padre Pio and addressed my prayer to him for the cure of Mrs. De Martino."[6] In the hospital, De Martino claimed to have experienced "extraordinary manifestations of Padre Pio through a typical and intense perfume."[7] On November 2, she felt better, and on the day of the scheduled surgery her physicians were amazed that the lymphatic fluid had all been reabsorbed. She left Riuniti Hospital on November 6 without ever having surgery or medication.[8]

De Martino was an ideal candidate for certification as a canonical miracle. Her illness had been serious, incurable without surgery, and disappeared very rapidly without any medical intervention.

On July 15, 1996, Postulator General Paolino Rossi requested the archbishop of Salerno-Campagna-Acerno to open the "process" for the apparent miracle with which De Martino was favored. A special "tribunal" met on July 24 in the presence of Archbishop Gerardo Pierro. De Martino and fourteen other witnesses, including doctors and others connected with the cure, were examined under oath. A year later, the investigating committee concluded its work and sent its documentation to the Congregation for the Causes of Saints, where five medical experts went over De Martino's records. On April 30, 1998, the experts unanimously agreed that the prognosis was serious, that there was no medical or surgical therapy carried out, and that the cure was very rapid, complete, lasting, and scientifically incapable of explanation. Only theologians officially authorized by the Church can declare a healing, however extraordinary and inexplicable, to be a "miracle." So, the documentation was studied by seven theological consultants, who unanimously concluded that the healing of Consiglia De Martino in fact met the conditions of a canonical miracle.

Thus, on December 21, 1998, three days after declaring that Padre Pio practiced the theological and cardinal virtues to a heroic degree, Pope John Paul declared, "I verify the miracle worked by God through the intercession of the Venerable Servant of God, Padre Pio of Pietrelcina ... namely the cure of Mrs. Consiglia De Martino, to be very rapid, complete, and lasting from the effusion of a liquid in the upper-clavicular region ... from a rupture of the thoracic duct."[9]

September 23, the anniversary of Padre Pio's death, was set aside as his feast day. A special prayer was composed for the Liturgy of the Hours and Mass celebrating Blessed Pio: "O God, may Blessed Pio, to whom you donated the grace to participate in a wonderful way in the Passion of your Son, concede to us, through his intercession, to conform ourselves to the death of Jesus, to attain then to the glory of the resurrection."[10]

On May 2, the day of Padre Pio's beatification, more than a thousand tour buses began to unload pilgrims at the crack of day near the Vatican. A massive crowd of more than two hundred thousand crowded St. Peter's Square for the three-hour service, while another one hundred thousand watched the proceedings on a giant television screen outside the Basilica of St. John Lateran, two and a half miles away.

John Paul II declared: "With our apostolic authority we concede that the Venerable Servant of God Pio of Pietrelcina will from now on be called Blessed and that his feast can be celebrated in the places established, but always within the golden rule of respect and moderation."[11]

After Mass, the pope gave a sermon in which he declared:

Those who went to San Giovanni Rotondo to attend his Mass, to seek his counsel, or confess to him saw in him a living image of Christ suffering and risen. The face of Padre Pio reflected the light of the Resurrection. His body, marked by the stigmata, showed forth the intimate bond between death and resurrection which characterized the Paschal mystery. Blessed Pio of Pietrelcina shared in the Passion with a special intensity: the unique gifts which were given to him, and the interior and mystical sufferings which accompanied them, allowed him constantly to participate in the Lord's agonies, never wavering in his sense that Calvary is the hill of the saints.[12]

Pope John Paul also mentioned the *Casa*, declaring: "His charity was poured out like balm on the weaknesses and sufferings of his brothers and sisters. Padre Pio thus united zeal for souls with a concern for human suffering, working to build at San Giovanni Rotondo a hospital complex." Concluding, the pontiff prayed: "Blessed Padre Pio, … Come to the help of everyone; give peace and consolation to every heart."[13]

Canonization

One additional miracle — occurring after beatification — was necessary for Blessed Pio to become a saint, and on December 20, 2001, the pope cited the cure of eight-year-old Matteo Pio Colello, whose recovery from meningitis, after state-of-the-art medical treatment proved unsuccessful, was ruled by the medical council of the Congregation for the Causes of Saints as "quick, complete, and lasting, without consequences and scientifically inexplicable."

Matteo was the younger of two children of Antonio Colello, a physician in San Giovanni Rotondo, and his wife, Maria Lucia Ippolito. Both parents were deeply devoted to Padre Pio, to the extent that they displayed his likeness in every room of their home. The year before their son's illness, the mother had a dream in which Padre Pio came to her and gently asked, "Why are you crying?" When she replied that she did not know, he stroked her cheek with his mitten and said — in the dream — "What are you afraid of? I am with you. I will always be near you."

Six or seven months later, Maria Lucia dreamt that she was in a strange cemetery, "shaking with fear," when Padre Pio again appeared and asked, "What are you doing here?" When she said she did not know why, he told her, "Come on, get a move on. Leave this place. It is not for you."

When Maria Lucia awoke, she smelled, in her bedroom, "an unusual perfume, very sweet and cheerful, of mixed flowers, roses, and violets." Looking around, she failed to find anything responsible for the fragrance. She went to the balcony, thinking that perhaps there was something within or outside giving off the perfume, but there was nothing. Calling to her husband, she asked him if he smelled anything. He told her that he smelled flowers, but shrugged and said, "So what?"[14]

On the morning of January 20, 2000, Matteo began to experience high fever, shaking, weakness, headache, vomiting, and mental disorientation. His physician father at first thought the boy had the flu, but, by evening, it was clear that it was something worse. Purple spots were spreading all over the boy's body, so Matteo was taken at once to the *Casa*, where he was diagnosed with acute meningitis.

Despite the intense ministrations of the staff there, Matteo was soon in a state of septic shock, breathing with difficulty, his pulse irregular. He was placed on a respirator. His heart stopped and had to be restarted. The physicians then told the parents that none of the treatments were having any effect and that their prognosis was that the comatose boy "would die soon."[15]

The next day the mother went across the street to the friary and asked for permission to pray in Padre Pio's room and at the tomb. She recounted: "Padre Rinaldo opened them both, and I had the privilege to kneel and beg in front of Padre Pio's bed and on the block of granite that covers his body ... I asked him not to destroy [our family] and to carry our miserable prayers to Our Lord with our tears and not to take my angel away." That night she said the Rosary at the tomb with the friars, and "while praying with my face on the cold granite, I saw with closed eyes, in black and white, a friar with a beard who advanced resolutely to a bed and picked up with both hands the small rigid body of a child and put him on his feet."[16]

On the fourth day of Matteo's illness, Fra Modestino told the boy's parents, "Have faith, have faith. Do not rebel against the will of God, but pray. And say simply to God, 'You gave him to us and you must give him back to us.' Do not rebel against God's will. Pray: 'I offer my life to God for Matteo; I offer my life and my sufferings.'" He took a crucifix that Padre Pio had given him and urged the parents to kiss it. He blessed them and repeated, "Have faith, have faith. Do not rebel against God's will. I said to Padre Pio: 'Pray for Matteo. Let this be the miracle for your canonization. You need a miracle to become a saint. Help Matteo. Be raised to the altar with him.'"

"I am sure this will happen," Modestino said to the Colellos. "Matteo will be cured and raise Padre Pio to the altar."[17]

Three days later, after praying at the tomb, Maria Lucia was "assailed" by a "very strong smell of flowers, a penetrating and most pleasant perfume," by which she understood "that the Padre was certainly there, telling me he is near me and that something good was about to happen to Matteo."[18]

Five days later, Matteo began to emerge from his coma. He opened his eyes, but could not speak. The next day, February 1, he was able to open and close his right hand and say, "I want Padre Pio. I want Padre Pio."

A day or two later, when he was fully conscious, when questioned by his mother if he had dreamt anything in his "deep sleep," Matteo said, "Yes, I saw myself while I was sleeping from a distance, all alone on the bed."

"All alone?" asked his mother. "Were there no doctors, nurses, Daddy, or me?"

He seemed to concentrate, and then he said, "No, Mummy, I was not alone.... There was an old, old man with a white beard.... He had a long brown habit.... He gave me his right hand and said, 'Matteo, don't worry, you will get well quickly.'" When the mother showed him a picture of Padre Pio, the boy identified him as the old man in the dream. In addition, he later said, there were some "big angels," one white with yellow wings, the other red with white wings. "I couldn't see [their faces] because they were too bright."[19]

Matteo recovered quickly. The curia of Manfredonia began the diocesan inquiry and submitted the records to the Congregation for the Causes of Saints, whose medical council recognized it on November 22, 2001, as "quick, complete, and lasting, without consequences, and scientifically inexplicable." On December 11, the Congress of Theological Consultants was held, and four days later the Ordinary Session of Cardinals and Bishops convened, to discuss whether the miracle was the result of divine intervention. They concluded that, in fact, it was. The cardinal prefect then made a detailed report to the pope, who confirmed the votes of the Congregation for the Causes of Saints.[20]

On June 16, 2002, a crowd of more than three hundred thousand packed St. Peter's Square, sweltering in the sultry heat beneath a cloudless blue sky to hear the aged Pope John Paul II, now stooped and palsied, read:

> In honor of the most Holy Trinity, for the exaltation of the Christian faith, with the authority of our Lord Jesus Christ, the holy Apostles Peter and Paul, and ours, after long consideration, having invoked often divine assistance and having listened to the opinion of many of our brothers in the episcopate, we declare and define Blessed Padre Pio of Pietrelcina a saint.[21]

Two friars then placed relics of Saint Pio near the altar: a silver sculpture of Saint Francis and Saint Clare, which contained a cloth soaked in the blood of the new saint, along with some scabs from his stigmata. Up to that time, the body had been left undisturbed. Several years later, when a cavernous church holding 6,500, built in a style of avant-garde modernity, was opened nearby, Padre Pio's remains were, despite the strenuous objections of his niece and her family, exhumed, and transferred there. (Pronounced in "fair condition," the head, as in the case of most saints put on display — for example, Saint Bernadette — is covered with a lifelike mask.)

Meanwhile, at San Giovanni Rotondo, Bishop Luigi Moretti celebrated Mass with fifty priests at the foot of the Way of the Cross, and more than 40,000 pilgrims watched the launching of 12,327 blue and yellow balloons, to commemorate the days between Saint Pio's death and his canonization, while the bands of the State Police and Military Marines accompanied the crowds in singing the Italian national anthem.

At the Vatican, the pope read a short sermon in which he quoted the words of Christ from the eleventh chapter of Saint Matthew: "My yoke is easy and my burden is light." The image of the "yoke," the pontiff pointed out, "recalls the many trials that the humble Capuchin of San Giovanni Rotondo had to face. Today we contemplate in him how gentle the 'yoke' of Christ is, and how truly light is his burden when it is borne with faithful love. The life and mission of Padre Pio prove that difficulties and sorrows, if accepted out of love, are transformed into a privileged way of holiness, which opens onto the horizons of a greater good, known only to the Lord."

He went on to quote Saint Paul (Gal 6:14): "But may I never boast except in the cross of our Lord Jesus Christ," recalling how Saint Pio, throughout his life, sought to be conformed to his crucified Lord, "since he was called to collaborate in a special way in the work of redemption."

The pope spoke of the new saint in his role of confessor: "I also had the privilege, during my young years, of benefiting from his availability for penitents." Saint Pio's example, he continued, should serve as an inspiration to "encourage priests to carry out with joy and zeal this ministry which is so important today."

The "ultimate reason" for the effectiveness of Padre Pio's ministry, John Paul said, "can be found in that intimate and constant union with God, attested to by his long hours spent in prayer and in the confessional." His spirituality continues in the Prayer Groups, "which offer to the Church and to society the wonderful contribution of incessant and confident prayer," to which Saint Pio joined "an intense charitable activity, of which the 'Home for the Relief of Suffering' is an extraordinary expression. Prayer and charity, this is the most concrete synthesis of Padre Pio's teachings which today is offered to everyone."

John Paul concluded by quoting the words of Christ: "I bless you, Father, Lord of heaven and earth, because … these things … you have revealed to little ones" (Mt 11:25). "How appropriate are these words of Jesus," he said, "when we think of them as applied to you, humble and beloved Padre Pio." Then, addressing the saint, he prayed:

Teach us … humility of heart, so we may be counted among the little ones of the Gospel, to whom the Father promised to reveal the mysteries of his kingdom. Help us to pray without ceasing, certain that God knows what we need even before we ask him. Obtain for us the eyes of faith that will be able to recognize right away, in the face of the poor and suffering, the face of Jesus. Sustain us in the hour of the combat and of the trial, and, if we fall, make us experience the joy of the sacrament of forgiveness. Grant us your tender devotion to Mary, the Mother of Jesus and our Mother. Accompany us on our earthly pilgrimage toward the blessed homeland, where we hope to arrive in order to contemplate forever the glory of the Father and the Son and the Holy Spirit.[22]

After celebrating Mass, the pope announced that Padre Pio's feast day, September 23, would be inserted in the liturgical calendar as an "obligatory memorial." The festivities of the day at St. Peter's Basilica concluded with a spectacle of fireworks and the rendition of Beethoven's "Hymn to Joy."

"He Made God Real"

Padre Pio has his detractors. Shortly after his canonization, the author of this book was interviewed (at three o'clock in the morning!) by phone on an Irish radio station, along with Richard Dawkins, the well-known atheist writer, who argued that Padre Pio was surely a fraud who faked his wounds.

In 2008, Sergio Luzzatto, a professor of history at the University of Turin, published *Padre Pio: Miracles and Politics in a Secular Age*, which was soon translated from Italian into English and became, for a time, a selection of the History Book Club. Luzzatto focused on the charges made by skeptics of Padre Pio: that he faked his wounds by using acid; that he was perhaps mentally unbalanced; that he had unseemly relations with his female followers.

A careful study of Padre Pio's life and scrutiny of his letters and those written to him will almost certainly lead to the conclusion that it is highly unlikely that the friar was a deliberate fraud. Whatever one believes about the alleged supernatural attributes and charisms, it is overwhelmingly clear that Padre Pio was a sincere, conscientious man who was reluctant to call attention to himself. Although he was glad for the opportunity to share in Christ's sufferings by means of stigmata, he was always reluctant to show his wounds to others, even before the order came from the Vatican to keep them covered except during Mass. He would have preferred for the wounds to have remained invisible, as they had been in the early days of his priesthood. The idea that his modesty was only a pretense and that he wounded himself, day after day, week after week, for nearly fifty years — and with no one noticing it — until he was too weak and addled to do it anymore is scarcely believable, in light of everything that is known about him.

Unlike most psychics and faith healers, Padre Pio never claimed that he had in himself any ability to heal sickness, to prophesy, to read minds or souls. Often, when asked to make some revelation about something or other, he would say,

"Unless someone up there tells me something, I can't give you an answer." When he directed an individual as a result of what he believed to be divine illumination, what he said accorded with reality. One wonders if there were times when Padre Pio made a prophecy that did not come true or directed someone in a way that turned out to be disastrous; however, there are no credible accounts of this happening. In the 1970s, I encountered a husband and wife who were Protestant missionaries in Milan, Italy. They told me of a man who joined their church who was enraged at Padre Pio for prophesying his recovery from an illness that nevertheless persisted. After he left the Catholic Church and "gave his life to Christ," his illness vanished, but he continued to disparage Padre Pio — even though the prophecy came true. That story is, of course, like so many concerning Padre Pio, anecdotal and incapable of confirmation. (I wrote the couple for written confirmation of what they had earlier recounted in conversation but received no answer.)

Clearly, there was something very unusual going on with Padre Pio. I have often wondered whether a small percentage of humanity have what some call a "sixth sense," by which they can perceive and connect with the nonmaterial world. If this is the case, Padre Pio had this gift to a remarkable degree and used it as such to further the cause of Christ. However, this was not something Padre Pio had all the time or could turn on or off. It was something that he was given from "up there" on special occasions. He was known to remark that if the biggest wretch in the world had been given the gifts he had been given, that wretch would have made better use of them than he.

It must be understood, however, that Padre Pio gained a reputation for holiness and was finally made a saint, not because he had mystical gifts, but because he led a godly life. People who knew him well were impressed by his faith, his hope, and his love, as well as his prudence, justice, temperance, and courage, even if they never experienced any of his mystical gifts. Padre Alessio declared, "The greatest thing about Padre Pio was his humility. He never took credit. He considered himself the last one of the people of the world." Padre Aurelio DiIorio, who lived with him for many years, was most impressed by the warmth of his humanity. Nearly everyone who had anything to do with him described Padre Pio as a sincere, kind, and loving human being. Carmela Marocchino, who lived with Maria Pyle for many years, explained, "He was such a good man.... In everything and with everybody he was a *good man*. That was the greatest thing about Padre Pio!"[1] Everyone who knew him well, with the exception of a handful of people widely considered disgruntled or unbalanced, knew him as a man of impeccable chastity.

Padre Pio is arguably one of the most remarkable personages in the twentieth century. He did a great deal of material good, most notably establishing a first-rate medical center in what was then a remote, impoverished area of Italy, and set up institutions for the aged and handicapped. Although many people have involved themselves in social works that improved the life of humanity, Padre Pio, more than almost anyone else in a time of materialism and religious skepticism, fulfilled the role of an Old Testament prophet and a New Testament apostle. Like Moses, he seemed to talk directly to God, as well as Mary and the angels, just like most people talk to their friends. He relayed messages to human beings from the unseen world. Like the apostles, his ministry was accompanied by "signs and wonders" which led people to Christ. He bore "the wounds of Christ," the stigmata, on his body. Seeing these signs enabled many people not only to believe in God and in the Bible, but also to identify more fully with Jesus' suffering and to participate more vitally and fully in the Sacrament of the Altar, so that they understood in their mind and experienced in their very soul the eternal sacrifice Christ made at Calvary, in which a window opens in time and space so that the faithful may be united in body, blood, soul, and divinity with their Savior and God. In the Sacrament of Penance, Padre Pio enabled people to understand the gravity of their sins and the mercy of the God who died to annihilate those sins. The "Wise Man of the Gargano" was often given the gift to reveal God's will to individual men and women. Countless people thought so and testified to their experience. Theologian Monika Hellwig said, Padre Pio had an almost unique gift by which he was able to "mediate the presence of God."

Padre Alberto D'Apolito likened Padre Pio to an apostle "sent by God to stem the evil of people and to lead souls along their way to Christ."[2] Padre Eusebio explained, "He was a man who put the theology of the cross in a special way: why you have to suffer to *help God*, because God wants you to help him brings souls to him. Not to go against God because you suffer. You must accept [suffering] because God is a Father who sees value in your suffering."[3] Sister Pia of Jesus Crucified, a Carmelite nun from Philadelphia, declared, "With Padre Pio, God seems to be making another little breakthrough in our time, giving a reminder to everyone that Christ really lived and died on this earth for us."[4] Padre Gerardo Di Flumeri, who was the vice-postulator of Padre Pio's cause for canonization insisted, "Padre Pio is the testimony of the Passion of Christ in the twentieth century of materialism and technological progress. Padre Pio is the heart of the gospel suffering and resurrection."[5]

Even the most superficial reading of Sacred Scripture will reveal that the sanctity to which all Christians are called is surrender of the self to God in Jesus Christ. Padre Pio lived this commitment totally, absolutely, unconditionally. Padre Pellegrino opined, "He loved the Lord in a violent way."[6] He gave himself over entirely to his Lord and to the service of humanity. The thing he cared most about was saving souls. To him, every soul was the object of a concern so powerful that he was willing to immolate himself on its behalf.

Padre Pio was a man who, like all human beings, was influenced by his family, by his environment, by his education. He was a man who, like all men but One, made mistakes and had human flaws and failings. He was, unlike most people, an individual who surrendered himself *totally* to God, who strove from childhood to his last breath to be an imitator of Christ. No suffering — physical, spiritual, emotional — was so great as to hinder him in this mission.

He accomplished much in his long life. Of all his many achievements, however, perhaps the greatest is that, for immense numbers of humanity, he made God real.

NOTES

Prologue: The Wise Man of the Gargano

1. Alberto Bobbio, "I piu amati dagli italiani: I santi nella storia," *Famiglia Cristiana* 76, no. 45 (November 2005), pp. 66–69.
2. *National Review*, October 22, 1968, pp. 1050–1051.
3. Eusebio Notte, *Padre Pio e Padre Eusebio: Briciole di storia)* (Foggia: n.p., 2008), p. 413 (hereafter, Eusebio).
4. *The Voice of Padre Pio,* Vol. III, No. 1, 1973, p. 6 (hereafter, *Voice*).
5. Ibid., Vol. I., No. 3, 1971, p. 3.
6. Interview with Andre Mandato, North Plainfield, New Jersey, November 19, 1978.
7. Interview with Monika Hellwig, Washington, D.C., 1978.
8. Rudolf Bultmann, *Kergyma and Myth* (New York: Harper & Row, 1961), p. 5.
9. Marco Tosatti, *Quando la Chiesa perseguitava Padre Pio* (Casale Monferrato: Piemme, 2005), 17 (hereafter, Tosatti).
10. Sergio Luzzatto, *Padre Pio: Miracles and Politics in a Secular Age*, trans. Frederika Randall (New York: Henry Holt, 2007), p. 276 (hereafter, Luzzatto).

Chapter One: The Roots of a Saint

1. Dennis Mack Smith, *Italy: A Modern History* (Ann Arbor: University of Michigan Press, 1959), 150 (hereafter, Smith).
2. Ibid.
3. Dante Alimenti, *Padre Pio* (Editrice Velar: Bergamo, 1984), 11 (hereafter, Alimenti).
4. ibid., p. 38.
5. Ibid. p. 15.
6. Gherardo Leone, *Padre Pio: Infanzia e prima giovanezza* (1887–1910) (San Giovanni Rotondo, [hereafter SGR], 1973), p. 35 (hereafter, Leone).
7. *Voice,* Vol. VII, No. 2, 1977, p. 5.
8. Ibid.
9. Michael Anthony Di Giovine, *Making Saints, (Re)-Making Lives: Pilgrimage and Revitalization in the Land of St. Padre Pio of Pietrelcina* (Chicago: University of Chicago, 2012), p. 104 (hereafter, Di Giovine).
10. Ibid.
11. Ibid.
12. Di Giovine, op.cit. p. 425.
13. Leone, p. 14.
14. Lino da Prata and Alessandro da Ripabottoni, *Beata te, Pietrelcina,* (SGR, 1976), p. 112 (hereafter, *Beata Te*).
15. *Voice,* Vol. VII, No. 2, 1977, p. 5.
16. Maria Adelia Pyle, unpublished manuscript, in Rev. John Schug's possession, 1990 (hereafter Pyle manuscript).
17. Ibid.
18. Giuseppe Pagnossin, ed., *Il Calvario di Padre Pio,* Vol. 1 (Padova: Pagnossin, 1978), p. 349 (hereafter, *Il Calvario*).
19. Augustine McGregor, *Padre Pio: His Early Years* (SGR, 1985), p. 30 (hereafter, McGregor).
20. He would be confirmed at the age of twelve, on September 27, 1899, by Monsignor Donato Maria Dell'Olio, archbishop of Benevento, at St. Anna's.
21. *Beata Te*, p. 206.
22. Leone, p. 31.
23. Alberto D'Apolito, *Padre Pio of Pietrelcina: Memories, Experiences, Testimonials* (SGR), p. 179 (hereafter, Alberto-Eng).

Chapter Two: A Boy Who Talked to the Angels

1. Leone, p. 28.
2. Alessandro da Ripabottoni, *Pio of Pietrelcina: Infancy and Adolescence* (SGR, 1969), p. 100 (hereafter, *Infancy and Adolescence*).
3. Ibid.
4. Cleonice Morcaldi, *La mia vita vicino a Padre Pio. Diario intimo spirituale* (SGR, 2013), p. 233 (hereafter, Morcaldi).
5. *Voice*, Vol. IV, No. 3, 1974, p. 1.
6. Morcaldi, op.cit., p. 232.
7. Leone, p. 28.
8. Ibid., pp. 73–74.
9. Interview with Pia Forgione, San Giovanni Rotondo, June 30, 1989.
10. Leone, p. 76.
11. Alessandro da Ripabottoni, *Padre Pio da Pietrelcina: Un cireneo per tutti* (SGR, 1974), p. 43 (hereafter, *Cireneo*).
12. McGregor, p. 72.
13. Leone, p. 89.
14. Interview with Riparta Masone De Prospero, New Castle, PA, June 20, 1985.
15. *Beata Te*, p. 128.
16. Pia Forgione interview.
17. DeProspero interview.
18. *Beata Te*, p. 239.
19. Ibid., p. 207.
20. Alessio Parente, *The Holy Souls* (SGR, 1988), pp. 68–69 (hereafter, *Holy Souls*).
21. Ibid., p. 81.
22. Leone, pp. 41–42.
23. Agostino of San Marco in Lamis, *Diario* (SGR, 1975), p. 58 (hereafter, *Diario*).
24. *Beata Te*, p. 113.
25. *Holy Souls*, p. 67.
26. *Beata Te*, p. 186.
27. Ibid., p. 185.
28. DeProspero interview.
29. *La Casa della Sofferenza*, English edition, November–December 1978, p. 23 (hereafter, *La Casa*.)
30. Ibid.
31. "Don" was an honorific title generally accorded to priests, teachers, physicians, and other professionals.
32. Andre Mandato interview.
33. *Beata Te*, pp. 134–135.
34. Ibid., pp. 386–387.
35. Padre Pio of Pietrelcina, *Letters, Vol. II, Correspondence with Raffaelina Cerase, Noblewoman (1914–1915)* (SGR, 1987), p. 154 (hereafter, *Letters, Vol. II*).
36. Padre Pio of Pietrelcina, *Epistolario IV* (SGR, 2012), pp. 687–688 (hereafter, *Epistolario IV*).
37. Emmanuele Brunatto, *Padre Pio da Pietrelcina* (Rome: n.p., 1926), p. 9.
38. *Cireneo*, p. 62.
39. Interview with Monsignor George Pogany, Irvington, NJ, July 29, 1989.
40. *Voice*, Vol. XX, No. 1, 1990, p. 14.
41. *Padre Pio of Pietrelcina, Epistolario I: Corrispondenza con le direttori spirituali (1910–1922)* (SGR, 1973), pp. 1281–1282 (hereafter, *Epistolario I*).
42. Ibid., p. 1283.
43. Ibid., p. 1284.
44. *Voice*, Vol. XLII, No. 1, January/February 2012, p. 13.

Chapter Three: Fra Pio

1. Marion A. Habig, ed., *St. Francis of Assisi: Writings and Early Biographies* (Chicago: Franciscan Herald Press, 1973), p. 57 (hereafter, Habig).
2. Smith, op. cit., p. 89.
3. Ibid.
4. Ibid.
5. Ibid., p. 91.
6. Leone, p. 14.
7. *Epistolario I*, p. 807.
8. Gerardo di Flumeri, ed., *Acts of the First Congress of Studies on Padre Pio's Spirituality* (SGR, 1978), p. 155 (hereafter, *First Congress.*)
9. *Voice*, Vol. XIX, No. 12, 1989, p. 15.
10. *Voice*, Vol. XLII, No. 2, March/April 2012, p. 14.
11. Leone, pp. 120–123.
12. Eusebio, p. 85.
13. Leone, p. 123.
14. *Voice*, Vol. XLII, No. 2, March/April 2012, p. 13.
15. *Voice*, Vol. XIX, No. 12, 1989, p. 6.
16. McGregor, p. 109.
17. Ibid., pp. 102–103.
18. *Voice*, Vol. XIX, No. 10, 1989, p. 6.

19. *Beata Te*, p. 224.
20. *Cireneo*, p. 25.
21. Alessandro da Ripabottoni and Orazio and Carmela Micheli, *L'Umanità di Padre Pio* (SGR, 1975), pp. 158–159 (hereafter, *L'Umanità*).
22. Ibid.
23. Capuchin Constitutions, Capuchin College Library, Washington, D.C.
24. *Voice*, Vol. XLVI, No. 3, May/June, 2016, p. 6.
25. *Diario*, p. 80.
26. *Voice*, Vol. XLVI, No. 3, May/June 2016, p. 7.
27. *Epistolario IV*, p. 938.
28. Ibid., pp. 935–936.
29. New York Passenger Arrival Lists (1892–1924), Ellis Island.
30. *Voice*, Vol. II, No. 4, 1972, p. 16.
31. Ibid.
32. Ibid., p. 33.
33. *Diario*, p. 186.
34. A critical biographer would later make much of the fact that Padre Pio, in his correspondence with his directors, often quoted St. Gemma word for word without citation, suggesting that he was guilty of plagiarism. In his letters, Pio often failed to indicate that he was quoting someone else. He evidently saw no need, since he was not preparing a thesis or writing a theological treatise, but rather expressing his feelings or conveying advice.
35. Gerard Greene, *All on Fire: A Story of St. Gemma Galgani* (Notre Dame, IN: Dujarie Press, 1953), pp. 68–69.
36. *Epistolario* I, p. 267.
37. *Diario*, pp. 40–41.

Chapter Four: Encounters with the Invisible World

1. Interview with Joseph Peterson, April 1989.
2. Evelyn Underhill, *Mysticism: A Study in the Nature and Development of Man's Spiritual Consciousness* (New York: n.p., 1961), p. 282.
3. *Epistolario I*, pp. 373–375
4. Ibid.
5. Ibid.
6. Ibid.
7. Ibid. p. 56.

8. Ibid., p. 259.
9. Alberto D'Aplito, *Padre Pio da Pietrelcina: Ricordi, Esperienze, Testimonianze* (SGR, 1978), pp. 251–252 (hereafter, Alberto-It).
10. Ibid., pp. 253–262.
11. Gerardo DiFlumeri, *La permanenza di Padre Pio a Venafro* (SGR, 1977), p. 80 (hereafter, Venafro).
12. *Cireneo*, p. 29.
13. Ibid.

Chapter Five: "A Holy Priest, a Perfect Victim"

1. *Voice*, Vol. XLVI, No. 3, May/June, 2016, p. 8.
2. *Epistolario I*, p. 179.
3. Ibid., p. 180.
4. Ibid., p. 185.
5. Ibid., p. 188.
6. Ibid., p. 182.
7. Ibid., p. 192.
8. Gerardo di Flumeri, *The Mystery of the Cross in Padre Pio of Pietrelcina* (SGR, 1977), p. 22.
9. McGregor, pp. 133–134.
10. *Epistolario I*, p. 229.
11. Pia Forgione Interview.
12. *Epistolario I*, p. 219.
13. Ibid., p. 224.
14. *Diario*, p. 131.
15. *Epistolario I*, p. 194.
16. Ibid. 199.
17. Ibid., pp. 200–201.
18. Ibid., p. 204.
19. Ibid., 210.
20. Ibid., pp. 217, 385, 386.
21. Interview with Pietro Cugino, San Giovanni Rotondo, July 1, 1989.
22. *Epistolario I*, p. 229.
23. Ibid., p. 231.
24. Ibid., p. 206.
25. Ibid., pp. 207–208.
26. Ibid., p. 304.
27. Ibid., p. 127.
28. *Beata Te*, p. 209.
29. *Epistolario I*, p. 234.
30. *Il Calvario*, Vol. II, p. 358.

Chapter Six: Illness and Ecstasies

1. *Venafro*, pp. 67–68.
2. Ibid.
3. *Epistolario I*, p. 234.

4. Ibid., pp. 237–238.
5. Ibid., pp. 239–240.
6. Ibid., pp. 240–241.
7. *Diario*, pp. 268–269.
8. Ibid., p. 266.
9. *Venafro*, p. 84.
10. *Diario*, p. 269.
11. Ibid., pp. 35–36.
12. Ibid., p. 37.
13. Ibid., pp. 37–40.
14. Ibid., pp. 40–44.
15. Ibid., p. 47.
16. Ibid.
17. Ibid., p. 48.
18. Ibid.
19. Ibid., p. 49.
20. Ibid.
21. Ibid. pp. 66–67.
22. Ibid. pp. 55–56.
23. *Epistolario I*, pp. 442–443.
24. *Venafro*, p, 77.
25. Ibid. pp. 76–77.
26. Ibid., pp. 70–71.
27. Ibid. p.72.
28. *Diario*, p. 255.

Chapter Seven: The Double Exile

1. Dominic Meyer, circular letter, April 1949, from Provincial Archives, Province of St. Joseph of the Capuchin Order, Detroit (hereafter, Detroit).
2. Pia Forgione interview.
3. *Beata Te*, p. 205.
4. *Epistolario I*, p. 363.
5. Ibid., p. 256, 387.
6. Ibid., p. 363.
7. *Beata Te*, 94.
8. Ibid., pp. 133–134.
9. Ibid., pp. 193–195.
10. *Epistolario I*, p. 300.
11. Ibid., pp. 442–443.
12. *Beata Te*, p. 203.
13. Ibid.
14. *Epistolario I*, p. 302.
15. Ibid., p. 315.
16. *Beata Te*, pp. 205–206.
17. *Epistolario I*, p. 330.
18. Ibid., pp. 338–339.

Chapter Eight: "Supernatural Graces"

1. *Epistolario I*, p. 420.
2. Ibid., pp. 420–421.
3. Ibid., p. 461.
4. Ibid., p. 304.
5. Ibid. p. 308.
6. Ibid., p. 424.
7. Ibid. p. 462.
8. Ibid., pp. 264–265.
9. Ibid., p. 273.
10. Ibid., p. 382.
11. Ibid., p. 297.
12. Ibid., pp. 327–328.
13. Ibid., p. 682.
14. Ibid., p. 476.
15. Ibid., pp. 640–641.
16. Ibid., p. 466.
17. Ibid.
18. Padre Pio of Pietrelcina, *Epistolario III: Corrispondenza con le figlie spirituali (1915-1925)* (SGR, 1977), pp. 164–165 (hereafter, *Epistolario III*).
19. Ibid., p. 194.
20. Ibid., p. 196.
21. *Epistolario I*, pp. 614–619.
22. Ibid., p. 619.
23. Ibid., pp. 311–313.
24. Ibid., pp. 341–342.
25. Ibid., pp. 677–678.
26. First Congress, p. 253.

Chapter Nine: Return to the Friary

1. Francesco Castelli, *Padre Pio under Investigation: The Secret Vatican Files*, trans. by Lee and Giulietta Bocham (San Francisco, 2011), p. 152 (hereafter, *Investigation*).
2. *Epistolario I*, p. 473.
3. Ibid., p. 779.
4. Ibid., pp. 375–376.
5. *Eusebio*, p. 78.
6. *Letters, Vol. II*, p. 92.
7. Ibid., p. 452.
8. Ibid.
9. Ibid., p. 229.
10. Ibid., p. 176.
11. Ibid., p. 369.
12. Ibid., p. 164.
13. Ibid., p. 64.
14. Ibid., p. 266.
15. Ibid., pp. 415, 390.

16. Ibid.
17. Ibid.
18. Ibid.
19. Ibid.
20. Ibid.
21. Ibid.
22. Ibid.
23. Ibid.
24. Ibid.
25. *Epistolario I*, p. 439.
26. Ibid., p. 479.
27. *Letters, Vol. II*, p. 122.
28. *Epistolario I*, p. 537.
29. Ibid., p. 496.
30. Ibid., p. 500.
31. Ibid., p. 519.
32. Ibid., p. 468.
33. Ibid., p. 554.
34. *Letters, Vol. II*, p. 446.
35. Ibid., pp. 457–458.
36. *Epistolario I*, p. 579.
37. Ibid., p. 582.
38. Ibid., pp. 587–588.
39. Ibid., pp. 67, 68, 97, 251, 204, 470, 311, 313–314, 391.
40. DiGiovane, p. 154.
41. *Epistolario I*, p. 704.
42. Ibid., pp. 727–728.
43. *Letters, Vol. II*, p. 493.
44. Ibid.
45. Ibid., pp. 511–512.
46. Ibid., p. 525.
47. Ibid., p. 529.
48. Ibid., p. 545.
49. *Diario*, p. 258.
50. *Epistolario I*, p. 730.
51. *Diario*, p. 261.

Chapter Ten: San Giovanni Rotondo
1. *Diario*, pp. 260–261.
2. *Epistolario I*, p. 769.
3. *Diario*, p. 261.
4. Ibid.
5. *Epistolario I*, p. 773.
6. *Diario*, pp. 261–262.
7. Paolino of Casacalenda, *Le mie memorie intorno a Padre Pio* (SGR, 1975), pp. 57–59 (hereafter, Paolino).
8. Ibid., pp. 62–68.
9. Ibid.

10. *Epistolario I*, p. 792.
11. Ibid., p. 821.
12. Paolino, p. 236.
13. *Investigation*, p, 84.
14. Alberto-Eng, pp. 47–48.
15. Ibid., p. 55.
16. Luzzatto, p. 13.
17. Francesco Savino, *Padre Pio: L'Astro del Gargano: testimonianza di una famiglia* (SGR, 2014), pp. 19–20 (hereafter, Savino).
18. Luzzatto, p. 170.
19. *Voice*, Vol. XVIII, No. 3, 1988, p. 4
20. Marcellino Iasenzaniro, *The "Padre": Saint Pio of Pietrelcina: Testimonies* (SRG, 2006), 3, p. 434 (hereafter, Marcellino).
21. Alberto-Eng, p. 54.
22. Interview with William Carrigan, c. 1978.
23. *Voice*, Vol. XLIII, No. 3, May/June 2013, pp. 15–17.
24. These and other recollections of Padre Aurelio come from a taped interview by Father John, July 19, 1971.
25. Alberto-Eng, pp. 57–58.
26. *Epistolario III*, p. 266.
27. Pia Forgione interview.
28. *Epistolario I*, p. 896.
29. Archival material furnished by Padre Alessio Parente, O.F.M., Cap.
30. *Epistolario I*, p. 978, 393.
31. Ibid., p. 980.
32. De Prospero interview.

Chapter Eleven: The Stigmata
1. *Voice*, Vol. XIX, No. 3, 1989, pp. 6–7.
2. Alberto-Eng, pp. 85–86.
3. *Holy Souls*.
4. In July 2017, the author obtained a death certificate for "Precoco," which states only that Pietro "De Mauro," born in San Giovanni Rotondo on May 26, 1831, died there on September 8, 1908 (ten days earlier than the date given by Padre Paolino). The place and cause of death are not given. There is probably more information contained in the actual record that the bureaucracy does not release to the public, but which Padre Pio and Padre Paolino, because they were priests, may have been allowed to see.

5. Alberto-Eng, pp. 87–88.
6. Paolino, pp. 95–100.
7. Ibid., pp. 102–104.
8. *Epistolario I*, p. 767.
9. Ibid., p. 803.
10. Ibid., p. 1063.
11. *Epistolario IV*, p. 586.
12. Tosatti, p. 45.
13. *Epistolario I*, p. 1063, 38, 394.
14. Ibid., pp. 1067–1068.
15. Ibid., pp.1068–1069.
16. Paolino, p. 114.
17. Gerardo DiFlumeri, ed., *Le Stigmata di Padre Pio da Pietrelcina* (SGR, 1985), pp. 143–145 (hereafter, *Le Stigmate*).
18. Paolino, p. 114.
19. *Epistolario I*, p. 1090.
20. Ibid., p. 1091.
21. Ibid.
22. Ibid.
23. *Investigation*, p. 202.
24. *Il Calvario*, Vol. II, p. 355.
25. Ibid., p. 357.
26. *Le Stigmate*, p. 141.
27. *Epistolario I*, p. 1095.
28. Ibid.
29. *Diario*, p. 262, 395.
30. Saverio Gaeta and Andrea Tornielli, *Padre Pio: L'ultimo sospetto: La verita sul frate delle stimmata* (Casale Monferrato, 2008), p. 21 (hereafter, Gaeta and Tornielli).
31. Ibid., pp. 23–24.
32. *La Casa*, September, 1973, p. 20.
33. *Beata Te*, p. 230
34. *Epistolario I*, p. 1098.
35. Ibid., pp. 1115.
36. Paolino, p. 117.

Chapter Twelve: "Holy Man"

1. *Epistolario I*, p. 1129.
2. *Voice*, Vol. XVIII, No. 11, 1988, p. 4.
3. Paolino, p. 128–129
4. *Il Calvario*, Vol. I., p. 3.
5. *Voice*, Vol. LXIII, No. 2, January/February 2013, pp. 9–11.
6. Paolino, pp. 143–144.
7. *Epistolario I*, p. 1145.
8. Paolino, pp. 160–161.
9. *Investigation*, p. 143.
10. Paolino, pp. 160–161.

11. Ibid., p. 192.
12. Ibid., pp. 142–143.
13. Ibid., p. 238.
14. Ibid., p. 239.
15. *Voice*, Vol. VIII, No. 1, 1978, pp. 11–12.
16. *Il Calvario*, Vol. I, p. 29.
17. Ibid., p. 3.
18. Ibid., pp. 4–7.
19. Ibid., pp. 24–25.
20. Gaeta and Tornielli, pp. 185–186.

Chapter Thirteen: Holiness or Hysteria?

1. *Le Stigmate*, p. 75.
2. Interviews, Padre Alessio Parente, O.F.M. Cap., San Giovanni Rotondo, September 1–5, 1978, Alexandria, VA; January 4, 1979, Washington, D.C.; San Giovanni Rotondo, June 30–July 2, 1989.
3. *First Congress*, p. 124.
4. Ibid.
5. *Le Stigmate*, pp. 302–303, 398.
6. Interview by telephone, Giuseppe Sala, M.D., July 2, 1989.
7. *Le Stigmate*, p. 9.
8. Ibid., pp. 312–313.
9. *Voice*, Vol. XIX, No. 3, 1989, p. 29.
10. Ibid.
11. *Le Stigmata*, p. 9.
12. Ibid., p. 314.
13. *First Congress*, p. 134.
14. *Le Stigmate*, p. 9.
15. Gaeta and Tornielli, p. 44.
16. *First Congress*, pp. 132–133.
17. *Voice*, Vol. XVIII, No. 9, 1989, p. 7.
18. *Le Stigmate*, p. 12.
19. Ibid., p. 171.
20. *First Congress*, p. 130.
21. Ibid., p. 132.
22. Dominic Meyer to Edmund Kramer, letter, April 10, 1949, Capuchin Archives, Detroit.
23. Ibid.
24. Angelo Maria Mischitelli, *Padre Pio Un Uomo Un Santo* (Rome: n.p., 2015), p. 559 (hereafter, Mischitelli).
25. Diary of the Rev. John D. Saint John, S.J. (He read from this diary when visited by the author.)
26. *Le Stigmate*, pp. 208–209.
27. *First Congress*, p. 129, 399.

28. *Voice*, Vol. XLII, No. 6, November/December 2012, p. 20.
29. Ibid., pp. 21–22.
30. Interview with Joseph Peterson, Cromwell, CT, December 9–10, 1988, and Reston, VA, April 1–3, 1989.
31. Padre Alessio interviews.

Chapter Fourteen: The Spiritual Director
1. *Epistolario III*, p. 185.
2. Ibid., p. 238.
3. Marcellino 3, p. 676.
4. *Epistolario III*, pp. 48–49.
5. *Epistolario IV*, p. 562.
6. Ibid., pp. 587–588.
7. Ibid., p. 443.
8. Ibid., pp. 444–445.
9. Ibid., p. 451.
10. Marcellino, Vol. I., p. 198.
11. Ibid., pp. 469–470.
12. Ibid., p. 470.
13. Ibid., pp. 479–480.
14. Ibid., p. 488.
15. Ibid., p. 480.
16. Ibid., pp. 490–491.
17. *Il Calvario*, Vol. I, p. 40.
18. *Letters, Vol. II*, p. 158.
19. Morcaldi, p. 27.
20. *Il Calvario*, Vol. I., p. 41.
21. *Epistolario III*, p. 59.
22. Ibid., pp. 250–251.
23. Ibid., p. 251.
24. *Letters, Vol. II*, pp. 291–292.
25. Ibid., p. 292.
26. *Il Calvario*, Vol I, p. 41.
27. Ibid.
28. Ibid.
29. Marcellino, Vol. III, p. 563.
30. *Epistolario IV*, p. 653.
31. Ibid., p. 656.
32. *Epistolario III*, p. 251.
33. Ibid., p. 425.
34. *Il Calvario*, Vol. I., p. 41.
35. *Epistolario III*, pp. 666–667.
36. *Voice*, Vol. XVII, No. 11, 1987, p. 48.
37. Ibid., p. 47.
38. *Letters, Vol. II*, p. 426.
39. *Holy Souls*, 103.
40. Morcaldi, p. 47.
41. *Epistolario III*, p.48.

42. *Epistolario IV*, p. 1041.
43. *Epistolario III*, p. 55.
44. Interview with Pietro Cugino, July 1, 1989.
45. *Letters, Vol. II*, p. 259.
46. Ibid., pp. 190–191.
47. Cugino interview.
48. *Letters , Vol. II*, p. 179.
49. *Holy Souls*, p. 104.
50. Ibid., pp. 178–179.
51. *Epistolario III*, p. 300.
52. Morcaldi, p. 210.
53. *Epistolario III*, p. 831.
54. Giovanni Gigliozzi, *The Spouse's Jewels* (Subiaco: n.p., 1958), p. 106.
55. *Epistolario IV*, p. 504.
56. Ibid.
57. *Il Calvario*, Vol. I., p. 41.
58. *Epistolario IV*, p. 488.
59. *Epistolario I*, p. 1260.
60. *Epistolario IV*, p. 1040.
61. Ibid., p. 1041.
62. *Epistolario III*, p. 800.
63. Ibid., p. 809.
64. Pia Forgione interview.
65. Cugino interview.
66. *Letters, Vol. II*, p. 490.
67. Morcaldi, p. 208.
68. Marcellino, Vol. 3, p. 689.
69. Ibid., p. 662.
70. Ibid., p. 691.
71. Ibid., p. 680.
72. *Letters, Vol. II*, p. 490.
73. *Epistolario IV*, p. 1039.
74. Ibid.
75. Dominic Meyer to Cyprian Abler, letter, June 2, 1951, Capuchin Archives, Detroit.
76. Ibid.
77. Cugino interview.
78. Dominic Meyer, circular letter, July 1949 Capuchin Archives, Detroit.
79. Ibid.
80. Cugino interview.

Chapter Fifteen: Skeptics and Detractors
1. *Epistolario IV*, p. 208.
2. *Il Calvario*, Vol. I, p. 42.
3. Ibid.
4. Francesco Castelli, *Padre Pio e il Sant' Uffizio (1918–1939), Fatti, protagonisti, documenti inediti*, (Rome: Studium,

2011), pp. 48–49 (hereafter, *Padre Pio e il Sant'Uffizio*).

5. Ibid., p. 49.
6. *Il Calvario*, Vol. I, p. 128.
7. Ibid. p. 170.
8. Ibid.
9. Ibid.
10. Luzzatto, p. 52.
11. Ibid.
12. *Investigation*, p. 57.
13. Ibid., p. 58.
14. *Il Calvario*, Vol. I, p. 139.
15. *Investigation*, p. 58.
16. Ibid., p. 59
17. *Il Calvario*, Vol. I, pp. 139–144
18. *Investigation*, p. 59
19. Ibid., p. 60.
20. Gaeta and Tornielli, *Padre Pio*, pp. 135–136.
21. *Investigation*, p. 62.
22. *Il Calvario*, Vol. I, p. 147.
23. *Investigation*, pp. 64–65.
24. Ibid., pp. 66–67.
25. Ibid., p. 68.

Chapter Sixteen: The Friar and the Inquisitor

1. *Investigation*, p. 220.
2. Ibid., p. 93.
3. Ibid., p. 94.
4. Ibid., p. 95.
5. Ibid., p. 224.
6. Ibid., p. 115.
7. Ibid., p. 90.
8. Ibid., p. 161.
9. Ibid., p. 191.
10. Ibid., p. 187.
11. Ibid., p. 188.
12. Ibid., p. 175.
13. Ibid., pp. 191–192.
14. Ibid., p. 135.
15. Ibid., p. 138.
16. Ibid., p. 140.
17. Ibid., pp. 149–150.
18. Ibid., p. 206.
19. Ibid., p. 222.
20. Ibid.
21. Ibid., p. 204.
22. Ibid., pp. 215–219.
23. Ibid., p. 225.

24. Ibid., p. 231.
25. Ibid., p. 117.
26. Ibid., pp. 200–201.
27. Ibid., p. 213.
28. Ibid., p. 221.
29. Ibid., p. 213.
30. Ibid., p. 221.
31. Ibid., p. 191.
32. Ibid., p. 201.
33. Ibid., p. 207.
34. Ibid., pp. 124–126.
35. Ibid., pp. 172–173.
36. Ibid., p. 153.
37. Ibid., p. 127.
38. Ibid., p. 26.
39. Ibid., p. 89.
40. Ibid., pp. 88 and 182.
41. Ibid., p. 157.
42. Ibid., p. 175.
43. Ibid., pp. 103–104.
44. Ibid., p. 229.
45. Ibid., pp. 105–106.
46. Ibid., p. 208.
47. Ibid.
48. Ibid.
49. Ibid., p. 222.
50. Ibid., pp. 227–228.
51. Ibid., p. 102.
52. Ibid., pp. 180–181.
53. Ibid., p. 163.
54. Ibid., pp. 177–178.
55. Ibid., p. 193.
56. Ibid., p. 212.
57. Ibid., p. 225.
58. Ibid., p. 185.
59. Ibid., p. 98.
60. Ibid.
61. Ibid., p. 23.
62. Ibid., pp. 24–25.
63. Ibid., pp. 27–28.
64. Ibid., pp. 239–240.

Chapter Seventeen: "A True Satanic War"

1. Luzzatto, p. 70.
2. Ibid., 76.
3. Mischitelli, p. 495n.
4. Gaeta and Torniello, p. 171.
5. *Il Calvario*, Vol. I, pp. 128–129.
6. *Epistolario IV*, pp. 639–641.
7. *Epistolario I*, p. 1181.

8. Ibid., pp. 1247–1248.
9. Carlo Falconi, *Popes in the Twentieth Century, from Pius X to John XXIII* (Boston: Little, Brown & Co., 1967), p. 217.
10. *Il Calvario*, Vol. I., p. 153.
11. Gaeta and Tornielli, pp. 113–114.
12. Ibid., p. 117.
13. *Il Calvario*, Vol I., p. 168.
14. Angelo Guiseppe Dibisceglia, *L'arcidiocesi di Manfredonia e l'episcopato di Pasquale Gagliardi Relazione al Convegno di Studi La Capitanata nel decennio della stimmatizzazione di Padre Pio (1910-1920)*, San Severo-Sala "Mario Fanelli" del Convento dei Cappuccini, February 6, 2010 ("The Archdiocese of Manfredonia and the Bishopric of Pasquale Gagliardi") (hereafter, Dibisceglia), p. 8.
15. Ibid.
16. Gaeta and Tornielli, p. 115.
17. Ibid., p. 117.
18. "Perchè picchiammo il vescovo Gagliardi," *C'era una volta Vieste* blog, May 22, 2016, https://ceraunavoltavieste.wordpress.com/category/accadde-a-vieste/.
19. Dibisceglia, p. 3.
20. Ibid.
21. Ibid., p. 6.
22. Ibid.
23. *Il Calvario*, Vol. I, pp. 517–518.
24. Gaeta and Tornielli, p. 117.
25. Francesco Chiocchi, *I nemici di Padre Pio* (Rome: n.p., 1968), pp. 43–46.
26. Gaeta and Tornielli, p. 116.
27. Ibid., p. 118.
28. Renzo Allegri, *Padre Pio: Man of Hope*, (Cincinnati: Charis Books, 2000), p. 121 (hereafter, Allegri).
29. *Diario*, pp. 265–266.
30. *Padre Pio e il Sant'Uffizio*, pp. 116–117.
31. *Il Calvario*, Vol. I., p. 128.

Chapter Eighteen: The Transfer That Never Happened

1. *Padre Pio e il Sant'Uffizio*, pp. 118–119.
2. *Voice*, Vol. VII, no. 4, 1977, p. 13.
3. *Epistolario IV*, p. 510.
4. *Padre Pio e il Sant'Uffizio*, p. 120.
5. Ibid., pp. 122–123.
6. Ibid., pp, 125–126.

7. Ibid., p. 128.
8. Ibid., p. 137.
9. Ibid., pp. 134–135.
10. *Il Calvario*, Vol. I., pp. 175–176.
11. Ibid., p. 182.
12. Ibid., p. 189.
13. Ibid., p. 208.
14. Ibid., p. 260.
15. Ibid., pp. 232–233.
16. Costantino Capobianco, *Detti e anedotti di Padre Pio* (SGR, 1973), p. 61 (hereafter, Capobianco).
17. *Il Calvario*, Vol. I., p. 252.
18. Ibid., p. 260.
19. Ibid., p. 225.
20. Ibid.
21. *Voice*, Vol. I., No. 3, 1971, p. 13.
22. *Epistolario IV*, p. 988.
23. Ibid., p. 734.
24. Ibid., pp. 397–400.
25. *Padre Pio e il Sant'Uffizio*, pp. 145–146.
26. Ibid., p. 144.

Chapter Nineteen: Remarkable Providences

1. Padre Pio to Alberto Costa, letter, December 10, 1922 (provided by Giuseppe Pagnossin).
2. *L'Umanità*, p. 430.
3. Eusebio, p. 168.
4. Luzzatto, p. 158.
5. *Le Stigmate*, pp. 285–286.
6. Ibid., p. 283.
7. Ibid., p. 288.
8. Ibid.
9. Ibid., pp. 288–289.
10. Ibid., p. 290.
11. Ibid., pp. 295–297.
12. Charles Mortimer Carty, *Padre Pio, the Stigmatist* (Rockford, IL: TAN Books, 1963), pp. 162–163 (hereafter, Carty).
13. Interview with George Pogany, Irvington, NJ, July 29, 1989.
14. John A. Schug, *Padre Pio: He Bore the Stigmata* (Huntington, IN, 1976), pp. 51–52 (hereafter, Schug).
15. Alberto-Eng, p. 74.
16. Schug, p. 51.
17. Ibid. p. 168.
18. Ibid., pp. 156–157.

19. *Epistolario I*, p. 1170.
20. Ibid., p. 1172.
21. Ibid., pp. 1246–1247.
22. Schug, p. 51.
23. John McCaffery, *Tales of Padre Pio, the Friar of San Giovanni Rotondo* (Kansas City, MO: Darton, Longman & Todd, 1978), pp. 133–134 (hereafter, McCaffery).
24. Andre Mandato interview.

Chapter Twenty: Friends, Family, and American Benefactors

1. *Diario*, p. 62.
2. Ibid., pp. 65–66.
3. Ibid., p. 62.
4. Ibid., p. 65.
5. *Beata Te*, pp. 224–225.
6. Interview with Alberto Cardone, New York City, c. 1989.
7. DeProspero Interview.
8. *Epistolario IV*, p. 942.
9. *Il Calvario*, Vol. I, p. 547.
10. Carty, pp. 104–109.
11. "U.S. Passport Applications, 1795–1924," Ancestry.com (database on line).
12. Many sources claim that Pyle was born in Morristown, New Jersey, but, according to the U.S. Census of 1910 and her applications for passports, she was born in New York City.
13. Information on the Pyle family was provided through phone conversations on August 4, 1990, and January 4, 1991, with Hilary H. Smart (1925–2000), who was Adelia Pyle's nephew; on January 19, 1991, with James Tolman Pyle (1913–1993), a nephew; on August 20, 1990 with Anne Pyle Dennis (1915–2011), a niece; October 21, 1990 with Zene Montgomery Pyle (1906–1993), sister-in-law; and March 24, 1990 with Diana Pyle Rowan, a great-niece.
14. Joseph Peterson interviews.
15. Bonaventura Massa, *Mary Pyle: She Lived Doing Good to All* (SGR, 1986), p. 94 (hereafter, Massa).
16. Massa simply states that it was her "pastor," and Richards would have been Pyle's pastor at the time. However, given the apparent close relationship with Van Dyke,

it is quite possible that it was he that Adelaide summoned.
17. Ibid.
18. "U.S. Passport Applications, 1795–1924," Ancestry.com (database on line).
19. Joseph Peterson interviews.
20. Ruth Kramer, *Maria Montessori* (New York: Diversion Books, 1976), p. 220.
21. Massa, p. 18.
22. Ibid., p. 20.
23. Carmelo Camilleri, *Padre Pio da Pietrelcina* (Castello: PG, 1952), pp. 114–121.
24. Ibid., p. 21.
25. Ibid., pp. 21–22.
26. Ibid.
27. Dorothy M. Gaudiose, *Mary's House* (South Williamsport, PA: Hilsher Graphics, 1986), p. 50.
28. Massa, p. 22.
29. Ibid., p. 28.
30. Pyle family interviews.
31. Massa, p. 185.
32. Ibid., pp. 228–229.
33. Massa, p. 108.
34. Ibid., p. 116.
35. Ibid., p. 124.
36. Ibid., p. 171.
37. *Beata Te*, p. 73.
38. Ibid., p. 50.
39. Ibid., pp. 50–52.

Chapter Twenty-One: "I feel like I'm Halfway in Hell"

1. *Padre Pio e il Sant'Uffizio*, p. 146.
2. Ibid., p. 149.
3. Ibid., p. 150.
4. *Il Calvario*, Vol. I, p. 272.
5. Ibid., p. 276.
6. Ibid., p. 286.
7. Ibid., p. 283.
8. Ibid.
9. *Epistolario IV*, pp. 92–93.
10. *Padre Pio e il Sant'Uffizio*, p. 154.
11. *Epistolario IV*, pp. 95–97.
12. Ibid.
13. *Il Calvario*, Vol. I, pp. 284–292.
14. *Padre Pio e il Sant'Uffizio*, p. 155.
15. *Il Calvario*, Vol. I, Ibid., pp. 284–292.
16. Ibid.

17. Ibid., pp. 401–402.
18. Pyle manuscript.
19. Ibid.
20. *Il Calvario*, Vol. I., p. 537.
21. *Epistolario IV*, pp. 955–956.
22. Ibid., p. 974.
23. *Il Calvario*, Vol. I, p. 537
24. Dibisceglia, p. 7.
25. *Diario*, p. 267.
26. *Il Calvario*, Vol. I., p. 543.
27. *Padre Pio e il Sant'Uffizio*, p. 157.
28. Ibid., p. 158.

Chapter Twenty-Two: Imprisonment
1. Gaeta and Torniello, p. 198
2. *Padre Pio e il Sant'Uffizio*, p. 159.
3. Ibid., p. 161.
4. Ibid.
5. *Il Calvario*, Vol. I, pp. 580–582.
6. Ibid. p. 583.
7. *Padre Pio e il Sant'Uffizio*, p. 167.
8. *Il Calvario*, Vol. I, p. 573.
9. Ibid., p. 605.
10. *Diario*, p. 79.
11. Ibid.
12. Ibid., pp. 93–94.
13. Ibid., p. 81.
14. Ibid.
15. Ibid., p. 82.
16. Morcaldi, p. 100.
17. *Il Calvario*, Vol. I., p. 376
18. *Diario*, p. 84.
19. *Epistolario IV*, pp. 48–50.
20. *Diario*, p. 84.
21. *Il Calvario*, Vol. I., p. 667.
22. *Epistolario IV*, pp. 740–742.
23. *Padre Pio e il Sant'Uffizio*, p. 172.
24. *Epistolario IV*, p. 67.
25. Ibid., pp. 67–68.
26. Ibid., pp. 742–743.
27. Ibid., pp. 744–745.
28. *Padre Pio e il Sant'Uffizio*, p. 75.
29. Ibid., p. 176.
30. *Il Calvario*, Vol. I, p. 689.
31. Morcaldi, p. 105.

Chapter Twenty-Three: "What a Fearsome Thing a Saint Is!"
1. *Diario*, p. 102.
2. Mischitelli, p. 602.

3. *Diario*, p. 96.
4. Ibid., pp. 113–114.
5. *Il Calvario*, Vol. II, p. 24.
6. *Diario*, p. 124.
7. Ibid., p. 66.
8. Ibid., pp. 140–141.
9. Tosatti, pp. 36–37.
10. Ibid.
11. Marcellino, Vol. 3, p. 551.
12. Morcaldi, p. 126.
13. Ibid., p. 129.
14. Ibid., p. 132.
15. Alberto-Eng, p. 59.
16. "New York, Passenger Lists, 1820–1957," Ancestry.com (database online).
17. Alberto-Eng, p. 108.
18. Adelaide McAlpin Pyle, will, Clerk of Probate Court, Morris County, NJ.
19. Kenneth Rose, *King George V* (New York: Knopf, 1984), pp. 363–365.
20. *History Today*, December 1986, pp. 21–30
21. *Diario*, p. 115.
22. Carty, pp. 113–114.
23. Pescara, *Il Giornale D'Italia* (Rome), November 22, 1942.
24. Carty, pp. 116–118.
25. Emilio Ghidotti to Bernard Ruffin, letter, June 23, 1981.
26. Dominic Meyer to Albert Gregory Meyer, letter, May 8, 1949.
27. *Diario*, pp. 198–199.
28. Dominic Meyer to Albert Gregory Meyer, letter, May 8, 1949.
29. Marcellino, Vol. 3, p. 605.
30. Ibid., p. 544.
31. Pogany interview.
32. Interview with William Carrigan, Kensington, MD, November 29, 1979, and January 21, 1980.
33. Gherardo Leone, *Padre Pio and His Work* (SGR, 1986), p. 24. (hereafter, *Padre Pio and His Work*).
34. Ibid.
35. Ibid.
36. McCaffery, p. 21.
37. Francobaldo Chiocci and Luciano Cirri, *Padre Pio: Storia d'una vittima*, Vol. I. (Rome: I Libri del No, 1968), p. 255 (hereafter, Chiocci and Cirri).

Chapter Twenty-Four: A Prophet in Time of War

1. Cugino interview.
2. Carrigan interview.
3. Pogany interview.
4. Mischitelli, p. 593.
5. *Diario*, p. 115.
6. Mischitelli, p. 593.
7. Ibid., p. 594.
8. Capobianco, pp. 18–19.
9. Carrigan interview.
10. Massa, pp. 33–36.
11. Carrigan interview.
12. Alberto-Eng, p. 107.
13. *Diario*, p.163
14. Ibid., p. 162.
15. Cugino interview.
16. Alberto-Eng, p. 75.
17. Dominic Meyer, circular letter, May 1949, Capuchin Archives, Detroit.
18. *Voice*, Vol. XIX, No. 3, 1989, p. 7.
19. Alimenti, pp. 128–129.
20. Interview with Alberto Cardone, March 24, 1990.
21. Interviews by phone with Colonel Loyal Bob Curry, October 1989 and July 1990.
22. Transcript of an interview kept by John A. Schug and shared with the author.
23. Massa, p. 195.
24. Interview with John D. Saint John, S.J., Dorchester, MA, August 17, 1989.
25. Schug, pp. 155–156.
26. Capobianco, pp. 9–10.
27. Cardone interview.
28. Carrigan interview.
29. Alberto-Eng, pp. 107–108.
30. Cardone interview.
31. Cugino interview .
32. *Epistolario IV*, p. 960.

Chapter Twenty-Five: *Soldati Americani*

1. *Voice*, Vol. XX, summer 1990, p. 36.
2. Chronicle of the Friary at San Giovanni Rotondo (hereafter Friary Chronicle), Provincial Library of San Severo (Italy), p. 186.
3. Ibid., p. 189.
4. Ibid., p. 191.
5. *Diario*, p. 163.
6. Ibid., pp. 191–192.
7. Ibid., p. 196.

8. Ibid., p. 200.
9. Ibid., p. 201.
10. "U.S. WW II Draft Cards Young Men, 1940–1947," Ancestry.com (database online).
11. Friary Chronicle, p. 191.
12. Peterson interview.
13. Interview with Joseph R. Peluso, conducted by Rev. John Schug, c. 1990.
14. Mario Avignone, *My Friend and Spiritual Father* (unpublished).
15. Saint John interview.
16. John P. Duggan to Bernard Ruffin, letter, October 10, 1989; telephone interview with Duggan, October 15, 1989.
17. Interview with Leo Fanning, Dover, NJ, July 29, 1989.
18. Duggan interview and letter.
19. Avignone.
20. Duggan interview.
21. *Diario*, p. 171.

Chapter Twenty-Six: Seer on the Mountaintop

1. Interview with Carmela Marocchino, San Giovanni Rotondo, June 30, 1989.
2. Pogany interview.
3. *Voice*, Vol. XIX, No. 7, 1989, p. 20.
4. *La Casa*, December 1973, pp. 20–21.
5. Ibid.
6. Forgione interview.
7. Funeral memorial card in possession of Mario Avignone.
8. *Diario*, p. 87.
9. Ibid.
10. *Il Calvario*, Vol. I., p. 95.
11. Ibid., p. 92.
12. Ibid., p. 93.
13. Ibid., p. 94.
14. Dominic Meyer, circular letter, May 1951.
15. Telephone interview with Diane Pyle Rowan, March 24, 1990.
16. Massa, pp. 9–12.
17. Dominic Meyer to Albert Gregory Meyer, letter, January 26, 1949.
18. Ibid.
19. Dominic Meyer to Albert Gregory Meyer, letter, January 26, 1949.
20. Ibid.
21. Dominic Meyer, circular letter, July 1951.
22. John Ardoin, "Gian Carlo Menotti's Faith

and Doubt," *The Washington Opera*, Issue 53, December 1990, pp. 24–25.

23. Mischitelli, pp. 635–636.
24. Interview, Joseph Peterson.

Chapter Twenty-Seven: "A Magnificent Work of Charity"

1. *Padre Pio and His Work*, p. 29.
2. Ibid.
3. Ibid., p. 34.
4. Ibid., p. 36.
5. Allegri, p. 196.
6. *Voice*, Vol. XLIV, No. 3, May/June, 2014, p. 15.
7. Ibid., p. 16.
8. *Padre Pio and His Work*, p. 56.
9. Allegri, p. 197.
10. Luzzatto, pp, 205–208.
11. Barbara Ward to Bernard Ruffin, letter, February 16, 1980.
12. *Padre Pio and His Work*, p. 38.
13. Francesco Napolitano, *Padre Pio of Pietrelcina: Brief Biography* (SGR, 1978), pp. 150–152.
14. Ibid., p. 153.
15. Alberto-Eng, p. 214.
16. Ibid., p. 213.
17. *Il Calvario*, Vol. I, p. 195.
18. *Padre Pio and His Work*, p. 52.
19. McCaffery, p. 66.
20. Alberto d'Apolito, *Padre Pio da Pietrelcina: Ricordi, Esperienze, Testimonianze* (SGR, 1978), p. 98.
21. Ibid.
22. *Padre Pio and His Work*, p. 60.
23. Ibid.
24. Ibid., p. 67.
25. Schug, p. 223.
26. Ibid., p. 222.
27. *Padre Pio and His Work*, p. 69.
28. *New York Times Magazine*, July 29, 1956.
29. Interview with Father Joseph Pius Martin, June 1978.
30. *Voice*, Vol. VIII, No. 3, 1978, p. 14.
31. *Padre Pio and His Work*, p. 72.
32. Ibid., p. 74.
33. Ibid., p. 81.
34. Schug, p. 226.
35. *Epistolario IV*, pp. 77–79.
36. *Voice*, Vol. VIII, No. 3, 1978, p. 15.
37. *Diario*, p. 219.
38. *Voice*, Vol. VIII, No. 4, 1978, p. 15.

Chapter Twenty-Eight: The Twenty-Hour Day

1. Father Dominic Meyer, book review, Capuchin Archives, Detroit.
2. Dominic Meyer to Albert Gregory Meyer, letter, May 19, 1957.
3. *La Casa*, March 1974, p. 20.
4. Dominic Meyer, circular letter, October 1949.
5. Paolino, p. 203.
6. Barbara Ward to Bernard Ruffin, letter, February 16, 1980.
7. Interview with Gerardo Di Flumeri, San Giovanni Rotondo, July 1, 1989.
8. *Voice*, Vol. XX, No.1, 1990, p. 6.
9. Ibid.
10. Tarcisio of Cervinara, *Padre Pio's Mass* (SGR, 1975), p, 20 (hereafter, Tarcisio).
11. Ibid.
12. Dominic Meyer to Albert Gregory Meyer, letter, July 24, 1956 Archives of Chicago Archdiocese.
13. Mary Ingoldsby, *Padre Pio: His Life and Mission* (Dublin: Veritas Publications, 1984), 101–102 (hereafter, Ingoldsby).
14. Ibid., p. 103.
15. Marcellino , Vol. 3, p. 491.
16. *Voice*, Vol. XVIII, No. 2, 1988, p. 11.
17. Savino, p. 91.
18. Tarcisio, p. 36.
19. Peterson interviews.
20. Morcaldi, p. 78.
21. Carrigan interview.
22. Peterson interviews.
23. Alberto-Eng, p. 145.
24. Ibid.
25. Ibid.
26. Paolino, pp. 199–208.
27. *Diario*, p. 167.
28. Pyle interview.
29. Clarice Bruno, *Roads to Padre Pio* (Rome: n.p., 1968), pp. 79–80 (hereafter, Bruno).
30. Marcellino, Vol. 1, pp. 45–46.
31. Ibid., pp. 52–53.
32. Allegri, p. 159.
33. Interview with Graziella Mandato, November 1978.
34. Allegri, p. 174.
35. Marcellino, Vol. 1, p. 67.

36. Ibid., p. 54.
37. Interview with Father Pio Mandato, c. 1990.
38. Cardone interview.
39. Marcellino, Vol. 1, p. 150.
40. Bruno, p. 183
41. Marcellino, Vol.1, p. 154
42. *Voice*, Vol. XIX, No. 7, 1989, p. 5.
43. *Voice*, Vol. XIX, No. 10, 1989, pp. 4–5.
44. Ibid., p. 5.
45. Marcellino, Vol. 1, pp. 28–29.
46. *Voice*, Vol. XIX, No. 7, 1989, p. 6.
47. Marcellino, Vol. 1, p. 30.
48. Ibid., p. 32.
49. Ingoldsby, p. 68.
50. Voice, Vol. XIX, No. 10, 1989, p. 5.
51. Interview with informant who wished to remain anonymous, 1989.
52. *Voice*, Vol. XLVII, No. 1, January/February 2017, p. 11.
53. Ibid.
54. Luigi Bocci, interview by Silvia Porcelli, in response to questions of author, August 2017.
55. Mischitelli, p. 447n.
56. Massa, p. 101.
57. *Holy Souls*, pp. 105–106.
58. McCaffery, p. 67.
59. Marcellino, Vol. 1, p. 198.
60. Morcaldi, p. 167.
61. Ibid. p. 138.
62. *Epistolario IV*, pp. 334.
63. *Holy Souls*, pp. 105–106.
64. Morcaldi, p. 128.
65. *La Casa*, November 1973, p. 20.
66. Ibid., p. 21.
67. *L'Umanità*, pp. 168–169.
68. Savino, pp. 115–116.
69. Ibid., p. 117.
70. John A. Schug, *A Padre Pio Profile* (Petersham, MA: Saint Bede's Publications, 1987), p.117.
71. *L'Umanità*, p. 162.
72. Peterson interviews.
73. Ibid.
74. *Voice*, Vol. XIX, No. 2, 1989, pp. 10–11.
75. Pogany interview.
76. *Holy Souls*, p. 41.
77. *La Casa*, September 1973, p. 20.
78. Morcaldi, p. 214.

79. Marcellino, Vol. 3, pp. 691–692.
80. Ibid., p. 665.
81. Ibid., p. 661.
82. Ibid., p. 689.
83. Ibid., p. 694.
84. Ibid., p. 696.
85. *Voice*, Vol. XVII, No. 12, 1987, p. 20.
86. *Epistolario IV*, p. 919.
87. *Voice*, Vol. XVII, No. 12, 1987, p. 20.
88. Capobianco, p. 47.

Chapter Twenty-Nine: Signs and Wonders

1. Dominic Meyer, interview, 1966, Capuchin Archives, Detroit.
2. Interviews with Joseph Pius Martin, San Giovanni Rotondo, September 5, 1978, and June 30–July 3, 1989.
3. Di Flumeri interview.
4. Carrigan interviews.
5. Interview with Giuseppe Gusso, M.D., San Giovanni Rotondo, June 30, 1989.
6. Carrigan insisted that the papers he refused to share with me (or apparently anyone else) were given to him by Pyle.
7. Massa, p. 227.
8. Philip Schaff, ed., *A Select Library of the Nicene and Post-Nicene Fathers of the Christian Church*, Vol. 4 (*St. Augustin's Writings against the Manichaeans and Donatists*) (Buffalo: The Christian Literature Co., 1901), pp. 321-322.
9. Augustine, *The City of God*, trans. Gerald C. Walsh and Daniel J. Horan (New York: n.p., 1954), p. 451.
10. *Epistolario I*, p. 471.
11. Peterson interviews. Unfortunately, this incident is not recounted in any of Father Dominic's surviving correspondence.
12. "A Day with Padre Pio," audiotape, September 23, 1983.
13. Marcellino, Vol. 3, pp. 526–527.
14. Parente interviews.
15. Dominic Meyer, circular letter, April 1949, Capuchin Archives, Detroit.
16. Dominic Meyer to John Joseph Meyer, letter, August 16, 1949, Capuchin Archives, Detroit.
17. Dominic Meyer, circular letter, October 1949, Capuchin Archives, Detroit.
18. Capobianco, pp. 75–76.

19. Fanning interview.
20. Avignone.
21. Joseph Pius Martin interviews.
22. Parente interviews.
23. Elia Stelluto, in conversation with the author, Barto, PA, May 2015.
24. *La Casa*, October 1973, p. 21.
25. Capobianco, p. 77.
26. *Voice*, Vol. XIX, No. 3, 1989, p. 5.
27. Di Flumeri interview.
28. Gusso interview.
29. Schug, p. 211.
30. Maria Pyle, filmed interview, in possession of Mario Bruschi, New York City, 1990.
31. *Voice*, Vol. XIX, No. 3, 1989, p. 6
32. Peterson interviews.
33. McCaffery, pp. 66–67.
34. *La Casa*, November 1973, p. 21.

Chapter Thirty: Bilocation

1. McCaffery, p. 26.
2. Parente interviews.
3. Forgione interview.
4. Alberto-Eng, pp. 116–117.
5. Dominic Meyer, circular letter, May 1950, Capuchin Archives, Detroit.
6. Dominic Meyer to "Brothers, Sisters, Nephews, and Nieces," letter, June 30, 1951, Capuchin Archives, Detroit.
7. Alberto-Eng, pp. 135–138.
8. Ingoldsby, p. 92.
9. *Voice*, Vol. XIX, No. 3, 1989, p. 7.
10. Ingoldsby, p. 92.
11. Parente interviews.
12. *Voice*, Vol. VII, No. 3, 1977, p. 17.
13. *Voice*, Vol. XIX, No. 3, 1989, p. 7.

Chapter Thirty-One: "I Only Pray ... God Heals"

1. Gaeta and Tornielli, p. 69.
2. Schug, *Padre Pio*, pp. 172–175; Savino, pp. 67–70; interview with Rosa Di Cosmo, San Giovanni Rotondo, June 30, 1989; Dominic Meyer, circular letter, July 1949, Capuchin Archives, Detroit; Pogany interview; certificate from Ospedali Riuniti, February 15, 1990.
3. Paolo Scarano, "Per 49 Anni Sono Stato il Segretario di Padre Pio," *Gente*, c. 1997, p. 14.

4. Schug, p. 176.
5. Ibid., p. 180.
6. *Diario*, p. 169.
7. Marcellino, Vol. I, p. 62.
8. *Diario*, p. 169.
9. Ibid., p. 185.
10. Ibid., pp. 192–193.
11. Ibid., p. 194.
12. Dominic Meyer, circular letter, March 1950, Capuchin Archives, Detroit.
13. Frances Pasqualini to Padre Pio, letter, February 29, 1952, Archives of Archdiocese of Chicago.
14. Chiocci and Cirri, pp. 670–672.
15. *Voice*, Vol. VI, No. 3, 1975, pp. 15–16.
16. Allegri, pp. 182–187.
17. Sala interview.
18. Parente interview.
19. Eusebio, pp. 183–184.
20. Schug, pp. 181–185; Joseph Pius Martin interview.
21. *La Casa*, No. 2, 1974, p. 20.
22. Capobianco, pp. 32–34.
23. Ibid.
24. Capobianco, pp. 32–34; Eusebio, pp. 411–412.
25. Eusebio, pp. 222–223.
26. Allegri, pp. 151–152.
27. Andre Mandato interview.
28. Scarano, pp. 124–126.
29. Marco Mottola, *My Diary of Life: Two Mini Stories of Franciscans* (unpublished, 1987), p. 10.
30. *Voice*, Vol. XVII, No. 11, 1987, p. 49.
31. Ibid., p. 48.

Chapter Thirty-Two: "Those Dreadful Women"

1. Dominic Meyer to Albert Gregory Meyer, letter, May 19, 1957, Archives of Chicago archdiocese.
2. Alessandro da Ripabottoni, *Padre Pio of Pietrelcina: Everybody's Cyrenean* (SGR, 1986), p. 188 (hereafter *Cyrenean*).
3. Ibid., pp. 188–189.
4. *Le Stigmate*, pp. 302–303.
5. *Il Calvario*, Vol. II., p. 294.
6. Rowan interview.
7. Massa, p. 181.

8. Interview with Joan Milazzo, Vienna, VA, October 20, 1990.
9. Tosatti, p. 45.
10. Ibid., p. 41.
11. Ibid., p. 45.
12. Morcaldi, p. 49.
13. Ibid., p. 50.
14. Ibid., p. 52.
15. Ibid., p. 85.
16. Ibid., p. 87.
17. Ibid., p. 303.
18. Ibid., p. 75.
19. Ibid., pp. 158–169.
20. Ibid., p. 170.
21. Ibid., pp. 135–136.
22. Tosatti, p. 164.
23. Morcaldi, p. 137.
24. Ibid., p. 135.
25. Ibid., p. 163.
26. Ibid., p. 77.
27. Ibid., p. 55.
28. Ibid., pp. 199, 202.
29. Ibid., p. 160.
30. Ibid., p. 133.
31. Ibid., p. 129.
32. Tosatti, p.147.
33. Morcaldi, p. 162.
34. Ibid., p. 303.
35. Tosatti, pp. 37–39.
36. Ibid., p. 40.
37. Milazzo interview.
38. Stefano Campanella, *Oboedientia et pax: La vera storia di una falsa persecuzione* (SGR, 2011), p. 92 (hereafter, Campanella).
39. Tosatti, p. 94.
40. Ibid., p. 44.

Chapter Thirty-Three: The Affair of the Tapes

1. Tosatti, p. 55.
2. Ibid., p. 75.
3. Eusebio, p. 94.
4. Tosatti, p. 43.
5. Ibid., p. 83.
6. Ibid., pp. 43–44.
7. Ibid., p. 89.
8. Ibid., p. 93.
9. Ibid., p. 92.
10. Ibid.
11. Ibid., pp. 80–81.
12. Ibid., p. 44.
13. Ibid., p. 63.
14. Ibid., p. 57.
15. Ibid., p. 59.
16. Ibid., p. 50.
17. Ibid., p. 77.
18. Ibid., p. 74.
19. Campanella, p. 121.
20. Ibid., pp. 121–122.
21. *Diario*, p. 225.
22. Ibid., pp. 56–57.
23. Gaeta and Tornielli, p. 202.
24. Luzzatto, p. 267.
25. Campanella, p. 123.
26. Ibid., pp. 85–86.
27. Ibid., p. 96.
28. Tosatti, p. 171.
29. Campanella, p. 108.
30. *Il Calvario*, Vol. II, p. 93.
31. John A. Schug to Bernard Ruffin, letter, April 28, 1980.
32. Tosatti, pp. 203–204.
33. Ibid., p. 210.

Chapter Thirty-Four: The Maccari Investigation

1. Gaeta and Tornielli, p. 210.
2. Campanella, p. 134.
3. Ibid., p. 135.
4. *Diario*, p. 245.
5. *Il Calvario*, Vol. II, p. 93.
6. Ibid., p. 99.
7. Tosatti, pp. 100–101.
8. Luzzatto, pp. 274–275.
9. Tosatti, pp. 101–102.
10. Ibid., p. 104.
11. *Il Calvario*, Vol. II, p. 100.
12. Campanella, pp. 152–153.
13. Tosatti, p. 92
14. Ibid., p. 349.
15. *Il Calvario*, Vol. II, p. 100.
16. Ibid.
17. Ibid.
18. Morcaldi, p. 190.
19. Ibid., p. 148.
20. Ibid., p. 191.
21. Ibid., p. 150.
22. Ibid., p. 38.
23. Ibid., pp. 93–94.
24. *Il Calvario*, Vol. II, p. 99.
25. Ibid., p. 100.

26. Tosatti, p. 95.
27. Ibid., p. 96.
28. Ibid., p. 100.
29. Ibid., pp. 97–99.
30. Ibid., p. 99.
31. *Il Calvario*, Vol. II, p. 101.
32. Tosatti , pp. 105–106.
33. Ibid., p. 117.
34. Ibid., pp. 117–118.
35. Ibid., pp. 118–119.
36. Ibid., p. 108.
37. Luzzatto, pp. 276–277.
38. Campanella, p. 154.
39. Ibid., p. 153.
40. Luzzatto, p. 277.
41. Gaeta and Tornielli, p. 212
42. Morcaldi, p. 202.
43. Campanella, p. 126.
44. Ibid., p. 152.
45. Gaeta and Tornielli, p. 200.
46. Campanella, pp. 177–179.
47. Ibid., pp. 179–180.
48. Allegri, Man of Hope, p. 220.
49. Campanella, p. 184.
50. Ibid., p. 186.
51. *Il Calvario*, Vol. II, p. 133.
52. Tosatti, p. 173.
53. Parente interviews.
54. Massa, p. 133.
55. Fernando da Riese Pio X, *Padre Pio da Pietrelcina: Crocifisso Senza Croce* (Rome: n.p., 1975), p. 384.
56. Campanella, p. 226.
57. Ibid., p. 229.
58. *Epistolario IV*, pp. 747–748.
59. Eusebio, p. 94.
60. Ibid., pp. 218–219.
61. Campanella, p. 160.

Chapter Thirty-Five: "I Cannot Bear My Cross Anymore!"
1. Eusebio, p. 241.
2. Eusebio, pp. 267–268.
3. Ibid., p. 255.
4. Ibid., pp. 329–330.
5. Ibid., p. 362.
6. Ibid., p. 236.
7. Ibid., p. 166.
8. Ibid., p. 118.
9. Ibid., pp. 114–115.

10. Ibid., pp. 116–117.
11. Gaeta and Tornielli, p. 200.
12. Joseph Pius Martin interview.
13. *Il Calvario*, Vol. II, p. 26.
14. Ibid.
15. Tosatti, p. 174.
16. *Il Calvario*, Vol. II, p. 26.
17. Ibid., pp. 145–146.
18. Ibid., pp. 160–161.
19. Ibid., p. 322.
20. Schug, p. 73.
21. Eusebio, pp. 196–197.
22. Ibid., pp. 199–202.
23. Ingoldsby, p. 115.
24. Eusebio, p. 203.
25. *La Casa*, May 1988.
26. *30 Giorni* [30 Days], No. 9, March 1989, p. 65.
27. Luzzatto, p. 249.
28. Morcaldi, p. 214.
29. *First Congress*, p. 149.
30. Ibid.
31. *30 Giorni* [30 Days], No. 8, December 1988, p. 75.
32. Eusebio, p. 413.
33. Morcaldi, p. 213.
34. Joseph Peterson interviews.
35. Marcellino, Vol. 1, p. 147.
36. Ibid., p. 139.
37. Ibid., p. 137.
38. Ibid., p. 130.
39. Ibid., p. 178.
40. Morcaldi, p. 221.
41. Pellegrino Funicelli, *Padre Pio: Jack of All Trades* (SGR, 1991), p. 400.
42. Eusebio, pp. 449–458.
43. *La Casa*, No. 2, 1974, p. 21.
44. Eusebio, p. 442.
45. Ibid.
46. Mischitelli, p. 755.

Chapter Thirty-Six: The Great Passage
1. Gaeta and Tornielli, p. 138.
2. Morcaldi, p. 213.
3. Parente interviews.
4. Ibid.
5. Ibid.
6. Ibid.
7. *Cyrenean*, p. 241.

8. Schug, p. 56.
9. Parente interviews.
10. Schug, p. 55.
11. Ibid., pp. 55–56.
12. Parente interviews.
13. *Cyrenean*, p. 241.
14. Morcaldi, p. 214.
15. Alberto-Eng, p. 308.
16. *Il Calvario*, Vol. II, p. 319.
17. Massa, p. 52.
18. Alberto-Eng, p. 320.
19. Ibid.
20. Morcaldi, p. 209.
21. Ibid., p. 230.
22. Ibid., p. 223.
23. Ibid., p. 222.
24. Ibid., p. 215.
25. Schug, p. 241.
26. Alberto-Eng, p. 320.
27. Ibid., p. 223.
28. Ibid., p. 221.
29. Ibid., p. 223.
30. *First Congress*, p. 257.
31. Schug, p. 232.
32. *Cyrenean*, p. 246.
33. Ibid., p. 247.
34. Scarano, p. 56.
35. Morcaldi, pp. 244–245.
36. Ibid., p. 243.
37. *La Casa*, June 1974, p. 21.
38. Raffale D'Addario, interview by John A. Schug, San Giovanni Rotondo, July 19, 1971.
39. Schug, pp. 237–238.
40. *Voice*, Vol. I, No. 1, 1971, p. 11.
41. Martin interviews.
42. Schug, p. 239.
43. Ibid., p. 241.
44. Morcaldi, p. 251.
45. Ibid., p. 253.
46. Gaeta and Tornielli, pp. 155–156.
47. *Le Stigmate*, pp. 309–312.
48. *Cyrenean*, p. 251.
49. Tosatti, p. 75.
50. *Cyrenean*, pp. 252–253.

Chapter Thirty-Seven: "Padre Pio Lives!" Miracles of Intercession

1. *The Evangelist* (Albany Diocese), October 6, 1983.
2. Alberto–Eng, pp. 311–312.
3. Schug, pp. 188–191; Martin interviews.
4. A CT Evaluation of the Hospitalization of Paul Walsh, February 1, 1985, signed by Joseph S. Kenney, D.O., Delaware Valley Medical Center, Langhorne, PA; John A. King, D.O., Department of Medicine, Cuyahoga Falls General Hospital, Cuyahoga Falls, OH; and Raymond J. Salamone, M.D., Department of Radiology, University of Cincinnati Medical Center.
5. Alice Jones to Bernard Ruffin, letter, September 11, 1990.

Chapter Thirty-Eight: Saint Pio

1. Kenneth L. Woodward, *Making Saints: How the Catholic Church Determines Who Becomes a Saint, Who Doesn't, and Why* (New York: Simon & Schuster, 1990), p. 185.
2. Ibid.
3. *Voice*, Vol. XX, No. 5, 1990, p. 23.
4. *Voice*, Vol. XXIX, Nos. 7–9, 1999, p. 11.
5. Ibid., pp. 12–13.
6. Ibid., p. 16.
7. Ibid.
8. Ibid., p. 13.
9. Ibid., p. 24.
10. Ibid., p. 46.
11. Ibid., p. 33.
12. Ibid., p. 40.
13. Ibid., pp. 40–41.
14. *Voice*, Vol. XXXII, No. 2, 2002, p. 20.
15. Ibid., p. 18.
16. Ibid., p. 21.
17. Ibid., p. 23.
18. Ibid., p. 24.
19. Ibid., p. 25.
20. Ibid., p. 18.
21. *Voice*, Vol. XXXIII, No. 4, 2003, p. 6.
22. Ibid., p. 158.

Epilogue: "He Made God Real"

1. Interview with Carmela Marocchino, San Giovanni Rotondo, June 1989.
2. Schug, *A Padre Pio Profile*, p. 49.
3. Ibid., pp. 121–122.
4. Ibid., p. 155.
4. Ibid., p. 158.
6. Tosatti, p. 92.

BIBLIOGRAPHY

Writings of Padre Pio

The Agony of Jesus (St. Paul, MN, 1952).

Epistolario I: Corrispondenza con le direttori spirituali (1910–1922) (San Giovanni Rotondo [SGR], 1973).

Epistolario III, Corrispondenza con le figlie spirituali (1915–1925) (SGR, 1977).

Epistolario IV: Corrispondenza con diverse categorie di persone (SGR, 2012).

Letters, Vol. I: Correspondence with his Spiritual Directors (1910–1922) (SGR, 1980).

Letters, Vol. II: Correspondence with Raffaelina Cerase, Noblewoman (1914–1915) (SGR, 1987).

Meditation Prayer on Mary Immaculate (St. Paul, MN, 1953).

Memoirs, Testimonies, Documents, and Other Sources

Agostino of San Marco in Lamis. *Diario* (SGR, 1975).

Avignone, Mario. *My Friend and Spiritual Father* (unpublished).

Bruno, Clarice. *Roads to Padre Pio*, (Rome, 1966).

Capobianco, Costantino, *Detti e anedotti di Padre Pio.* (SGR, 1973).

D'Apolito, Alberto. *Padre Pio da Pietrelcina: Ricordi, Esperienze, Testimonianze* (SGR, 1978).

———. *Padre Pio of Pietrelcina: Memories, Experiences, Testimonials.* Trans. by Julia Ceravolo (SGR, 1986).

Iasenzaniro, Marcellino. *The "Padre": Saint Pio of Pietrelcina: Testimonies*, 3 vols. (SGR, 2006).

Meyer, Dominic. *Letters* (unpublished) (Archives and Record Center, Archdiocese of Chicago and Provincial Archives, Province of St. Joseph of the Capuchin Order, Detroit).

Morcaldi, Cleonice. *La mia vita vicino a Padre Pio: Diario intimo spirituale* (SGR, 2013).

Mottolo, Marco. *My Diary of Life: Two Mini Stories of Franciscans* (unpublished, 1987).

Notte, Eusebio. *Padre Pio e Padre Eusebio: Briciole di Storia* (Foggia, 2008).

Pagnossin, Giuseppe, ed. *Il Calvario di Padre Pio*, 2 vols. (Padua, 1978).

Paolino of Casacalenda. *Le mie memorie intorna a Padre Pio.* (SGR, 1975).

Pyle, Maria Adelia. Unpublished manuscript, 1990.

Savino, Francesco. *Padre Pio: L'Astro del Gargano: Testimonianza di una famiglia* (SGR, 2011).

Scarano, Paolo. "Per 49 Anni Sono Stato Il Segretario Di Padre Pio," *Gente*, c. 1997 (The memories of Pietro Cugino).

Schug, John A., ed. *A Padre Pio Profile.* (Petersham, MA, 1987).

Walsh, Elizabeth Kindregan. *A Healing from God through Padre Pio* (unpublished).

Secondary Sources

Alimenti, Dante. *Padre Pio* (Bergamo, 1984).

Alessandro da Ripabottoni. *I Cappuccini a San Giovanni Rotondo* (Foggia, 1966).

———. *Dietro le sue orme: guida storico-spirituale al luoghi di Padre Pio* (SGR, 1976).

———. *Padre Pio da Pietrelcina: Il Cireneo di tutti* (SGR, 1978).

Alessandro da Ripabottoni and Grazio and

Carmela Micheli. *L'Umanità di Padre Pio* (SGR, 1975).

Allegri, Renzo. *Padre Pio: Man of Hope* (Cincinnati, 2000).

Augustine. *The City of God*. Trans. by Gerald C. Walsh and Daniel J. Horan (New York, 1950).

Babb, Lawrence. *Redemptive Encounters: Three Modern Styles in Hindu Tradition* (Berkeley, CA, 1985).

Biot, René. *The Enigma of the Stigmata* (New York, 1962).

Bobbio, A. "I piu amati dagli Italiani: I santi nella storia," in *Famiglia cristiana* 76, No. 45 (November 5, 2005).

Boyer, Onesimus. *She Wears a Crown of Thorns* (Mendham, NJ, 1958).

Camilleri, Carmelo. *Padre Pio da Pietrelcina* (Castello, 1952).

Campanella, Stefano. *Oboedientia et pax: La vera storia di una falsa persecuzione* (SGR, 2011).

Capuchin Constitutions, Capuchin College Library, Washington, D.C.

Carty, Charles Mortimer. *Padre Pio, the Stigmatist* (Rockford, IL, 1963).

Castelli, Francesco. *Padre Pio under Investigation: The Secret Vatican Files*. Trans. by Lee and Giulietta Bocham. (San Francisco, 2011).

———. *Padre Pio e il Sant'Uffizio (1918–1939)* Fatti, protagonisti, documenti inediti (Rome, 2011).

Chiocci, Francobaldo. *I nemici di Padre Pio* (Rome, 1968).

———. and Luciano Cirri. *Padre Pio: Storia d'una vittima*, 3 vols. (Rome, 1968).

Chronicle of the Friary at San Giovanni Rotondo, Provincial Library of San Severo (Italy).

Cillis, Anne McGinn. *Brian: The Marvelous Story of Padre Pio and a Little Anglican Boy*. (Ottawa, 1974).

De Liso, Oscar. *Padre Pio: The Life of Padre Pio, the Stigmatized Brother of Pietrelcina* (New York, 1966).

DiFlumeri, Gerardo, ed. *Acts of the First Congress of Studies on Padre Pio's Spirituality* (SGR, 1978).

———. ed. *La Permanenza di Padre Pio a Venafro* (SGR, 1977).

———. *Le Stigmate di Padre Pio da Pietrelcina* (SGR, 1985).

Di Giovine, Michael Anthony. *Making Saints, (Re)-Making Lives: Pilgrimage and Revitalization in the Land of St. Padre Pio of Pietrelcina* (Chicago, 2012).

Fernando da Riese Pio X. *Padre Pio da Pietrelcina: Crocifisso senza croce* (Rome, 1975).

Finney, Charles G. *Memoirs of Rev. Charles G. Finney* (New York, 1876).

Gaeta, Saverio and Andrea Tornielli. *Padre Pio L'Ultimo Sospetto: La verità sul frate delle stimmate* (Casale Monferrato, 2008).

Gallo, Antonio. *Il Nostro Padre Pio* (SGR, 1974).

Gaudiose, Dorothy M. *Prophet of the People: A Biography of Padre Pio* (New York, 1974).

———. *Mary's House* (South Williamsport, PA, 1986).

Gigliozzi, Giovanni. *The Spouse's Jewels* (Subiaco, 1958).

———. *Padre Pio: A Pictorial Biography* (New York, 1965).

Greene, Gerard. *All on Fire: A Story of St. Gemma Galgani* (Notre Dame, 1953).

Guttenberg, Elisabeth von. *Teresa Neumann: A Message from the Beyond* (Chumleigh, Devon, 1978).

Habig, Marion A., ed. *St. Francis of Assisi: Writings and Early Biographies* (Chicago, 1973).

Ingoldsby, *Mary, Padre Pio.* (Dublin, 1984).

John of the Cross. *Counsels of Light and Love.* (New York, 1980).

Kramer, Ruth. *Maria Montessori* (New York, 1978).

Leone, Gherardo. *Padre Pio: Infanzia e prima giovenezza (1887–1910)* (SGR, 1973).

———. *Padre Pio and His Work* (SGR, 1986).

Lercaro, Giacomo. *Don Primo Mazzolari, Padre Pio da Pietrelcina* (Vincenza, 1969).

Lino da Prata and Alessandro da Ripabottoni. *Beata Te, Pietrelcina* (SGR, 1973).

Luna Guerrero. Luis-Jesus. *El Padre Pio: El Tragedia de Fe* (Madrid, 1975).

Luzzatto, Sergio. *Padre Pio: Miracles and Politics in a Secular Age* Trans. by Frederika Randall (New York, 2007).

Massa, Bonaventura. *Mary Pyle: She Lived Doing Good to All* (SGR, 1986).

McCaffery, John. *Tales of Padre Pio, the Friar of San Giovanni Rotondo* (Kansas City, MO, 1978).

McGaw, Francis. *Praying Hyde* (Minneapolis, 1970).

McGregor, Augustine. *Padre Pio: His Early Years* (SGR, 1985).

Monroe, Robert A. *Journeys Out of the Body* (New York, 1971).

Napolitano, Francesco. *Padre Pio of Pietrelcina, Brief Biography* (SGR, 1978).

Parente, Alessio. *The Holy Souls* (SGR, 1988).

———. *Send Me Your Guardian Angel* (SGR, 1987).

Plass, Ewald, ed. *What Luther Says: An Anthology*, 3 vols. (St. Louis, 1959).

Rose, Kenneth. *King George V* (New York, 1984).

Rosewell, Pamela. *The Five Silent Years of Corrie ten Boom* (Grand Rapids, MI, 1986).

Schaff, Philip, ed. *A Select Library of the Nicene and Post-Nicene Fathers of the Christian Church*. Vol. IV, *St. Augustine: The Writings Against the Manichaeans and Against the Donatists* (New York, 1901).

Schug, John A., *Padre Pio: He Bore the Stigmata* (Huntington, IN, 1976).

Smith, Dennis Mack. *Italy: A Modern History* (Ann Arbor, MI, 1959).

St. Albans, Suzanne. *The Magic of a Mystic: Stories of Padre Pio* (New York, 1983).

Tarcisio of Cervinara. *Padre Pio's Mass* (SGR, 1975).

Ten Boom, Corrie. *Tramp for the Lord* (Old Tappan, NJ).

Teresa of Ávila. *The Life of Teresa of Jesus: The Autobiography of St. Teresa of Ávila* (Garden City, NY, 1960)

———. *The Way of Perfection*. (Garden City, NY, 1964).

Thérèse of Lisieux. *The Story of a Soul* (London, 1951).

Thurston, Herbert. *The Physical Phenomena of Mysticism* (London, 1977).

Tosatti, Marco. *Quando la chiesa perseguitava Padre Pio* (Casale Monferrato, 2005).

Trochu, Francis. *The Curé of Ars, St. Jean-Marie-Baptiste Vianney* (Westminster, MD, 1960).

Underhill, Evelyn. *Mysticism: A Study in the Nature and Development of Man's Spiritual Consciousness* (New York, 1961).

Vogl, Adalbert Albert. *Therese Neumann, Mystic and Stigmatist, 1898–1962* (Rockford, IL, 1987).

Ware, Timothy. *The Orthodox Church* (Hammondsworth, UK, 1964).

Warfield, Benjamin. *Miracles: Yesterday and Today, True and False* (Grand Rapids, MI, 1965).

Wesley, John. *Works*, Vol. V (New York, 1856).

Wilson, Ian. *Stigmata* (New York, 1989).

Winowska, Maria. *Il vero volto di Padre Pio* (Paris, 1975).

Woodward, Kenneth L. *Making Saints: How the Catholic Church Determines Who Becomes a Saint, Who Doesn't, and Why* (New York, 1990).

Journals

La Casa Sollievo della Sofferenza. 1973, 1974, 1988.

The Catholic World. July 1987.

Il Giornale d'Italia (Pescara). November 1942.

History Today. December 1986.

The Month. June 1952.

National Review. 1968.

The New York Times Magazine. July 1956 Thirty Days. 1988, 1989 TheVoiceofPadrePio. (1971–2014) Oral History.

Oral History

Cardone, Albert. New York City, March 24, 1990.

Carrigan, William. Kensington, MD, November 29, 1979, and by phone, January 21, 1980, and August 18, 1980.

Cugino, Pietro. San Giovanni Rotondo, July 1, 1989.

D'Addario, Raffaele. Interviewed by John Schug on July 19, 1971.

Dennis, Anne Pyle. By phone, August 20, 1990.

De Prospero, Riparta Masone. New Castle, PA, June 20, 1985.

Di Cosimo, Rosa. San Giovanni Rotondo, June 30, 1989.

Di Flumeri, Gerardo. San Giovanni Rotondo, July 1, 1989.

Di Iorio, Aurelio. Interviewed by John Schug on July 19, 1971.

Duggan, John P. By phone, October 15, 1989.

Fanning, Leo. Dover, NJ, July 29, 1989.

Forgione, Pia. San Giovanni Rotondo, June 30, 1989.

Gusso, Giuseppe. San Giovanni Rotondo, June 30, 1989.

Lilley, Tony. By phone, July 6, 1990.

Mandato, Andre and Grace. North Plainfield, NJ, November 19, 1978.

Marocchino, Carmela. San Giovanni Rotondo, June 30, 1989.

Martin, Joseph Pius. San Giovanni Rotondo, September 5, 1978, and June 30-July 3, 1989.

Milazzo, Joan. By phone October 22, 1990.

Parente, Alessio. San Giovanni Rotondo, September 1-5, 1978; Alexandria, VA, January 4, 1979; and San Giovanni Rotondo, June 30-July 2, 1989.

Peluso, Joseph R. Interviewed by John Schug, c. 1990.

Peterson, Joseph. Cromwell, CT, December 9-10, 1988; Reston, VA, April 1-3, 1989.

Pogany, George Irvington, NJ, July 29, 1989.

Pyle, James Tolman II. By phone January 19, 1991.

Pyle, Zene Montgomery. By phone, October 21, 1989.

Rowan, Diane Pyle. By phone, March 24, 1990.

Saint John, John D. Dorchester, MA, August 17, 1989.

Sala, Giuseppe. By phone, July 2, 1989.

Savino, Antonio. San Giovanni Rotondo, July 3, 1989.

Smart, Hilary. By phone, August 4, 1990.

INDEX

(Members of religious communities will usually be listed by their religious name, rather than their surname; in addition, life dates of religious and others are also included when known.)

About the Author

C. Bernard Ruffin is a native of Washington, D.C., with a degree in history from Bowdoin College and an M.Div. from Yale. He taught history in the Fairfax County high schools for twenty-five years and is the pastor of the Lutheran Church of the Holy Comforter in Washington, D.C. He is the author of several books on Christian history and genealogy and the biographies of Padre Pio, Saint Andre Bessette, and Fanny Crosby.

38 Jurors
2 AA women